1001 Ways to be a Good C

Margaret Paterson was born at Whickham,
County Durham, and was educated at Queen
Margaret's School, Scarborough, and at
Benenden. Between qualifying in Advanced
Cookery (1st Class) in 1938 and teaching cookery
in 1968, she worked during the war years in
YMCA army camps as a canteen organizer and
later spent many years enjoying cooking simply
as a housewife and mother.
1001 Ways to be a Good Cook (first published in
1978 as *The Craft of Cooking* but here revised
and extended) was her first book.
She is now a widow, has two grown-up sons and
lives in Hampshire.

Margaret Paterson

1001 Ways to be a Good Cook

Pan Books London and Sydney

First published 1978 by Macdonald & Jane's Publishers Ltd
as *The Craft of Cooking*
This revised edition published 1986 by Pan Books Ltd,
Cavaye Place, London SW10 9PG
9 8 7 6 5 4 3 2 1
© Margaret Paterson 1978, 1986
Illustrations by Andrew Macdonald
ISBN 0 330 28973 X
Photoset by Parker Typesetting Service, Leicester
Printed in Great Britain by
Richard Clay (The Chaucer Press) Ltd, Bungay, Suffolk

Acknowledgements

My greatest thanks are to Mrs Joyce Westcott (née Arnison) who first taught me to cook, passing on both her knowledge and her infectious enthusiasm. She has given me a lifetime of happiness and interest.

I would also like to thank Mrs Margot Mayes, Mrs Vivienne Hines and Miss Marjorie Stone who taught me in later years, after we moved south to live.

It is difficult to express in words my gratitude for all the help I have received from company chairmen, directors, home economists, dieticians, sales and marketing managers, PR and information officers up and down the country, without whom this book would have been much less informative. (For a list of these companies and organizations, in alphabetical order, see page 347.)

I am also extremely grateful to the librarians at Winchester County Library for their unfailing and willing help, and to Mrs Helen Norris for typing my manuscript and supporting me so professionally in her own field in countless other ways. I cannot, in words, express my thanks to her fully enough.

Contents

Please note that where quantities are given in this book in spoonfuls, I am assuming you'll be using traditional average-sized spoons from your kitchen drawer, not the measuring spoons in a set, which are smaller. (See also Metric quantities and measurements page 75.)

Introduction

As I revise and extend this book now, in 1985, the hints and help I try to give are based on trainings, experience, travel, reading and research over more than 45 years. I would like to think that it may enable others to start where I have left off – but beware! It is not a recipe book, so if that is what you are looking for, this book is not for you. My book aims to be different from all other cookery books – by complementing and helping you to make the best of your *own*. Whether you like or dislike cooking, my hope is that I may be able to help you understand and enjoy it more and, as a result, to eat better.

When I was once bewailing the lack of practical guidance in so many recipe books, a cookery expert commented: 'Cook books can't tell you everything you need to know about a recipe – that's why people should have lessons.' This book aims to fill those gaps, by providing the knowledge which most recipe books must take for granted: it could help anyone who wants to learn more about English and French cooking. If, for instance, you are frightened of using yeast or gelatine, you find some kinds of fish tasteless, your soufflés are a disaster, your meringues 'weep', or your melting chocolate turns to rock, let's hope I can help you to discover why.

Scores of books give recipes for things like pea soup, sausage rolls or fish cakes, but they don't tell you why one type of ingredient may be preferable to a marginally different one; they don't advise a suitable piece of equipment for a particular task, nor give you the ABC of *how* to do it. If I can help you to make all the basic dishes, of which most others are an elaboration, it should be easy to put together the combination of your skills and knowledge to use any reliable recipe book with success.

Wouldn't we enjoy cooking more if we knew *why* we should do things in a particular way? Wouldn't we, for instance, remember to stir boiled rice with a two-pronged fork if we knew it becomes a solid mass when we use a spoon? Wouldn't we cook better and make more of our housekeeping money if we knew *all* the whys and wherefores?

This is a reading and reference book. For good measure, you'll find hundreds of hints, snatches of history, the origin of some familiar names and words, and some ways to help you beat fatigue in the kitchen. Ideally, read from cover to cover and only then use as a reference book: otherwise all sorts of unexpected tips may escape you.

Most of all, I hope you're going to love cooking as I do and enjoy years of good eating.

Margaret Paterson
January 1985

1

The dilemma of kitchen equipment

And dilemma it is, with so much choice. Some things have no equal, some are expensive and impractical, while others are more practical although less expensive. Just as a pretty face may be no criterion of anything but looks, so it may be with kitchen needs, which one should never judge by their outward appearance.

Because the kitchen is no longer the Cinderella of the house, kitchen shops have multiplied to meet demand, selling generally well-designed, well-made and sensibly-priced goods. In such specialist hands, or at catering equipment shops – easily found through the Yellow Pages for your area – there is usually more choice, better designed merchandise and, importantly, better advice than elsewhere: less chance that one of these (as opposed to a general ironmonger) would for instance sell inaccurate measures, impractical rolling pins, dangerous pans or useless pallet knives.

Your needs may not be mine, nor mine yours. Some people like a working kitchen, others a dining-kitchen; some will enjoy making and eating the sort of dishes from which others would shrink. Some can afford the luxuries, others must live to a strict budget, improvising where possible, as I'll try to show how. You will, however, cook better, eat better, save time and enjoy cooking more if you have the right tools for the job, so my aim in writing this chapter is to try and guide your choice by sharing with you some of my own experiences. Having worked in numerous well-equipped colleges over several years, I have had the opportunity to see and use a wide range of kitchen equipment, so the opinions I express, although personal, are broadly based.

Not only do I know better now what is necessary and unnecessary, but I have also learnt from the good, bad and indifferent things I have been fortunate or unfortunate enough to buy myself. If nothing more, I hope that I may spare you repeating my mistakes.

BAGS

Paper icing bags cost nothing to make and eliminate the need for one of those expensive, difficult-to-manipulate and rather useless icing syringes. It's not much trouble to make several bags at a time if you ever have ten minutes to spare, then they're ready for use when you want them. Although not re-useable, they're efficient as well as economical. Cut an accurate 10in/25cm square of greaseproof paper so that you can cut it into two identical triangles and make them, one at a time, into two identical bags:

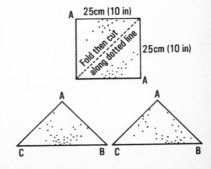

1 Fold square in half and cut along diagonal line, as illustrated.

2 Hold triangle up in front of you with the right-angle A at the top, held between thumb and first finger of left hand.

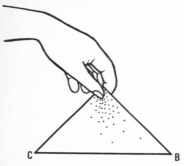

3 Now bring the point B to the point A, turning it so that the *underside* of the paper at point B faces you, giving a single thickness cornet.

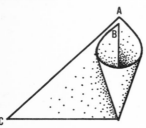

4 Bring point C around in front of the cornet and up around the back to join

points A and B precisely, giving a double thickness cornet. The bottom of the cornet, D, see below, should be a sharp point.

5 Fold down the points A, B and C, to hold them tightly together and to hold cornet in shape.

6 Cut off tiny tip at D if to use for writing (or if without any tubes) or cut off about ¼in/6mm to let point of chosen tube come right through. Drop tube into bag.

7 Make up second bag with the other triangle.

8 Half fill bag with prepared icing, fold front of bag over it, then the back, and press icing down to bottom, see illustrations.

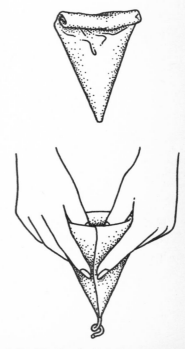

9 Put filled bag inside other (empty) bag and fold *it* down too.

10 Hold and use as illustrated.

Piping bags Made of nylon, these come in graded sizes. If you can rise to only one, choose a medium-sized bag, but for bulky things like meringue mixture or choux pastry, a larger bag (14in/36cm in length) will save time. You may also want a smaller one. Unlike twill bags, you can wash, dry and re-use nylon as soon as you like. See also *paper icing bags,* above.

Polythene bags Much cheaper if you're able to buy them in bulk. You may be lucky enough to live near a shop which sells odd sizes, numbers and thicknesses in 2lb/1kg or 6lb/3kg packs, their surplus from large orders. The bags are perfect, but it's a blind buy so your luck and your selection may be better some times than others. A pack may last you for months, or even years, according to use and care.

■ For the freezer, heavy-weight bags are best, and essential for things like meat, poultry or game, to prevent freezer burn (see page 63) and consequent loss of flavour from the food: remember, the bag is usually the only barrier between food and freezer. Thinner bags will become brittle at freezer temperatures and will eventually split, leaving the food exposed. If the bags are thin, use one inside another, but even then not for poultry, etc. Bags large enough to tie a knot at the neck are easy enough to open blindfold, and eliminate the need for wire ties which often pierce other packs.

■ Three or four really large strong bags will save rummaging and electricity, and prevent your freezer from becoming a jumble: you can then lift out a whole bagful at a time, sorting it at leisure. It's ideal to have coloured bags if you can buy them – red for meats, blue for fish, green for vegetables and another colour for fruits. Freezers with several baskets are naturally easier still, or you can buy baskets individually.

BAIN-MARIE

Sounds slightly daunting but need only be a roasting tin half-filled with hot water, and any small strong pans with lids (or foil) to cover them.

■ The water should be 'shivering' – slightly cooler than simmering – when using the bain-marie as a double saucepan for the thickening of tricky sauces likely to curdle if put over direct heat.

■ It should be even cooler when used to keep this sort of sauce hot, and cooler still for sauces of the Hollandaise family. It's fatal to try and keep these hot either in the oven or in a pan over direct heat, because they'll curdle.

■ Small pans are best because there's room for more of them and because the sauce will be deeper, with a smaller surface over which skin can form. In addition, when a large household strains a small cooker, you can keep three or four pans of food hot over just one burner, in a bain-marie of simmering water.

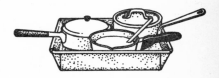

BAKING SHEETS

These should always be sold with a cooker, I think. They must fit because you'll waste oven space if they're too small, and the hot air can't circulate properly if they're too large: you'll probably feel it's your fault when foods burn or cook unevenly.

■ Why, you may ask, should at least two baking sheets be part and parcel of every cooker? Because:

1 They're vital for safety, to lift dishes in and out of the oven and to give protection from burns and scalds.
2 Without them, you can't make such things as pastry, scones, dinner rolls, biscuits, etc. successfully.
3 They save individual handling of dishes and foods, so saving your time and

also cutting down heat loss, which may spoil some dishes and certainly wastes fuel.

4 They save work, by protecting both oven and shelves from spills.

■ To save labour and to make full and proper use of a hot oven when you want to, you need as many baking sheets as you have oven shelves, plus one for the 'floor'. For good measure, if you're bulk baking for the freezer, you'll perhaps even be glad of one or two more than that.

■ Good quality sheets are vital, otherwise foods will burn on the bottom. The heavy aluminium baking sheets are excellent, added to which you can see when they're dirty.

■ There are two main types:

1 Those with four shallow sides – the safest to hold pie-dishes, casseroles, large cakes or puddings, etc, and therefore the best for general use.

2 Those with one end turned up. Pastry and scones slide off easily when you want them to, but so, unhappily, can casseroles or anything else. In addition, spilt liquids are not contained, and some foods spread over the edges as they cook.

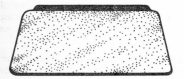

BALLERS

Known also as ball-scoops, these are for making balls of the flesh of fruits or vegetables, often as a garnish, e.g. melon, potato, cucumber. They are made in various sizes from a pea upwards, French ones having a sharper, better cutting edge than British, which are double-ended, and cheaper.

■ It's easy to make half a ball but more difficult to make a complete one: hold your thumb under the back of the scoop as illustrated, press hard into the vegetable or fruit and twist your wrist right round. Use a baller also to hollow out such fruits as apples or small melons, to serve 'stuffed', and to core apples for a flan or tart. With this, you can cut a more even crescent than with an apple corer, making a prettier flan.

BASKETS

Blanching basket For the quick boiling of vegetables before freezing. Shops which fail to stock them or have possibly run short may try to persuade you that a chip basket or salad basket serves the same purpose. Some designs are unsuitable,

however, because small things like peas or sliced beans will fall through the gaps. You'd be better off using a nylon wine-straining bag if you have one, which is quite practical anyway. If you grow and freeze lots of vegetables, you'll save both fuel and labour by buying a large-size basket.

Chip basket See *deep fat pan,* page 35.

Garlic basket May be an extravagance to buy for oneself but is a very welcome present for the friend who enjoys cooking. It stores garlic as it should be stored, so if hung in the right place, where it's airy and convenient, your garlic will keep in good condition. In appearance, it's like a miniature salad basket. Alternatively you can buy special terracotta pots at a kitchen shop.

Salad basket Dries lettuce and other plants efficiently, and without bruising. Dryers which spin the lettuce dry by

centrifugal force don't soak the kitchen, but are pricey and may be space-taking compared with others – fine for anyone without a garden.

■ If short of space, you may like a collapsible basket as below. They're usually more costly, and some designs are more fiddling than a two-sided one.
■ If without, just gather up the lettuce in a clean tea-towel, then swing it to and fro.

BIN

A pedal bin may be impossible to house if your kitchen units form a continuous line and all reach to the floor, otherwise it is ideal. Flies can't dine on your rubbish, pets can't poke about in it and even the strongest smells are contained. For good measure, there's nothing unsightly to look at and, with both hands either sticky or full, you can still open the lid – with your foot.

BLENDER

See *liquidizer,* page 32.

BOARDS

Wooden chopping boards Will warp gradually if too thin or of poor quality, making it impossible to chop herbs, vegetables and so on properly. A once-in-a-lifetime buy, it pays to buy a good, thick one about 14 × 9in/36 × 23cm, say, of sycamore or utile (a hardwood), which can, if necessary, double as breadboard or cheeseboard as well. You can use it for anything and foods don't slip about as they do on melamine.

Melamine chopping boards Both decorative and handy. Herbs don't stain, nor does the smell of onions or garlic penetrate, but it's best to use the 'wrong' side for chopping, to avoid wearing away the design on the colourful side. Knives are blunted more quickly by melamine than by a wooden board.

Wooden pastry board An asset if you can afford and house one. It keeps cooler than a formica table top, and flour dusted over it is distributed more evenly, making it easier to roll pastry well. Often made of sycamore. Though expensive, a slab of marble is cooler still.

■ For a very small household, you *might* manage with a board 18 × 12in/46 × 30cm, otherwise go for one 20 × 14in/51 × 36cm, or better still 24 × 18in/61 × 46cm.

BOWLS

Copper bowl Ideal for whisking egg whites if you're lucky enough to have one. You might find one cheaply, as I did, on a market antique stall. If badly stained, rub with salt and lemon juice. A useful household size is 10in/25cm in diameter. See also *whisking,* page 84.

Mixing bowls Much wider at the top than pudding basins (see illustrations below), to allow room for your hands to move about freely when doing things like rubbing fat into flour, beating a sponge mixture, or whisking egg whites, etc. This means you can incorporate more air in the mixture than you could in a pudding basin so you'll make lighter pastry, sponges, meringues, and so on.

■ They may be old-fashioned but I think it's difficult to beat the thick china bowls illustrated, glazed inside and out: they don't wobble about; you can use any and every utensil in them with ease; they're good for mixing pastry or bread-making; will withstand considerable heat; nest perfectly for easy handling and minimum storage space, and with care will survive years of punishing use (sometimes to be found in junk or charity shops). Pyrex-type bowls would be my second choice; stainless steel, aluminium and plastic bringing up the rear.

■ One needs at *least* three, say 9½, 10½ and 12in (24, 27 and 30cm) in diameter.

■ Aluminium bowls may give a greyish cast to such foods as whisked egg white, royal icing or ice cream.

Plastic washing-up bowls As light as a feather when empty and have a huge capacity, so may sometimes be useful for certain stages of some jam or wine-making. Keep one specially for the purpose, of course.

■ A smallish, smooth-sided, round bowl (kept especially for bread-making) is practical because polythene is less cold than glass or china. (If a dough cools below 80°F/27°C, rising is slowed down.)

Wooden salad bowl Should be large enough to turn the contents over easily in the dressing. Small individual ones look lovely on a table and are perfect to use when you serve a salad with hot food. Look out for them if you're abroad – they're much cheaper.

■ Keep your bowl well clear of a dishwasher, otherwise it will dry out and crack.

BRUSHES, PASTRY

Should be of good quality, otherwise they shed their bristles and can be just as maddening as poor quality paint brushes. You need a small compact one to glaze a narrow strip of pastry without also egging its cut edges, and a bigger one – perhaps even a household paint brush – for brushing fat quickly over large areas of a baking sheet or cake tin, etc.

CAKE TRAY

A tray or rack allows hot cakes and bread, etc. to cool without sweating, and pastry to become crisp as air circulates around. Round ones may be cheaper than, and are just as spacious as, rectangular, especially if the latter has sides, which are a nuisance. You can't do without cake trays if you bake much.

■ You may sometimes need a cake tray for cake icing, or for coating foods such as cold cooked fish with aspic jelly or chaud-froid sauce, with a dish or large bowl underneath to collect the drips.
■ The rack in a grill pan will substitute for very small amounts.

CHERRY STONER

This does a fiddling job quickly and well (it also serves for olives). It's worth having if you use a lot of either fruit. The design illustrated below is easily used.

CLOTHS

Dish cloths Become positively anti-social if they aren't washed, and preferably boiled, too, regularly.

■ On a non-polished work surface or in the sink, a wet dish cloth keeps a mixing bowl steady and cuts down the noise if spread underneath a bowl when beating a

mixture, kneading a dough, etc.

Oven cloths Not nearly as costly as a burn or scald. The type illustrated below is practical, safe and one of the least expensive (but do make sure you buy the top-quality heat-proof make because there are also some dangerously thin ones on the market): it's quick and easy to slip your hands in or out of; long enough to hold a baking sheet or large casserole (even when grabbed in a hurry); both hands are protected from scalds or burns, and it is easily kept clean.

■ It is amazing how some people never think of washing an oven cloth: these, if white, can join the weekly wash, but coloured ones may not be dye-fast.

COCOTTE

French for casserole. Foods cooked and served in them are described as 'en cocotte' or 'en casserole'. Ramekin is the English word for an individual cocotte. Ramekins don't have lids, and are used for such dishes as oeufs en cocotte and individual savoury soufflés. They may be made of ovenproof china or glass, pottery, fine porcelain or sometimes of metal.

COLANDER

One of these is essential, to avoid serving sodden vegetables. If you drain off the water with the pan lid, you're not really giving your vegetables a fair chance. You may need a colander as well to refresh vegetables under a running cold tap (see page 77).

COOKERS

With ever new time-saving, labour-saving and eye-appealing innovations, cookers improve yearly. The most expensive are not by any means necessarily the best, nor the nicest looking necessarily the best designed and most practical, so it's a good idea to be informed and to work out your priorities. Take time, if you're wise, to weigh up the pros and cons of what may seem to be your dream cooker in a shop before reaching any irrevocable decision. With, say, fifteen years ahead of you, blessed (or stuck) with a cooker, this is not the time to make a mistake.

Though I can't know your priorities, I can perhaps bring several thoughts to your notice.

British or otherwise? In principle, all British manufacturers follow the same dial settings, temperatures and physical construction. This is an important reason for Britons buying British, if only because you should then be able to cook anything in your oven from a British recipe without first having either to consult or master a different set of temperatures, or to look up other things in your own cooker's instruction book – which can be time-consuming and frustrating.

Be wary of the cheaper continental cookers. Although the more expensive ones may, they do not have to conform to British standards and are very different from British cookers – partly because the continental housewife's use of a cooker is different. For example, no other European cooks use the oven as frequently as the British, which explains why British ovens are normally larger and better designed to turn out the best of cakes,

pastry and so on. In cheap continental gas ovens, the heat runs along the bottom, so small cakes, for instance, have a dry texture and burn readily on the bottom. You may also find you can only cook things on one shelf, so the rest of the oven space is wasted. Nor will the grill of a gas cooker perform as you might expect: the rating is often only one third of the typical UK rating and hot enough only for surface browning, not for actually cooking dishes. According to Southern Gas, not even for toast do they need to meet the basic UK requirement. Other features which differentiate cheap continental from British cookers are: poor controllability of the hotplates; inadequate pan supports, some of which discolour easily; an absence of storage space due to the location of the oven burners; generally a lack of spark ignition. The last straw is that it may quite soon prove impossible to get spare parts when needed, compared with a ten-year minimum UK guarantee, in practice probably much longer.

■ If you buy a cooker from the gas or electricity board, where there is strict testing, it is much less likely that you will get a faulty cooker than if you buy from a discount house or store where there may not be such quality control. (Although guaranteed, and the guarantee honoured, a faulty cooker can cause a lot of inconvenience and incidental expense.)

■ The price of a cooker increases with the extras for which you may opt: what may be essential to you may be quite unnecessary to someone else, so choose the make and model which best meets your needs and your pocket.

■ If you're blind, you can even buy a braille cooker; if handicapped, one geared in other ways to your needs – just contact your gas or electricity showroom.

Choice of fuel Electricity is more at the mercy of storm and strikes than are gas, Calor gas or solid fuel, so how will you cope in a power cut? You may want something additional for such emergencies. After, when younger, swearing I would never use anything but gas, I now prefer electricity for these main reasons:

a Some modern gas ovens have an 'S' (slow) setting – a most valuable investment – others a special low thermostat setting which is below mark ¼, but on many traditional (zoned-heat) cookers (especially an older, second-hand one you might be tempted to buy) a gas burner will go out if set too low, while electricity can be set and used at the lowest temperatures without any such problems. On many gas hobs, one cannot simmer slowly enough (far less 'shiver' anything) to make a stew without much of the liquor boiling away before the meat itself is cooked.

b Unless you have a fan-assisted oven (see below) the temperature gradient (variation in temperature) between the top and bottom, or between the upper and lower shelves, in a zone-heated (traditional) electric oven is generally less than in most traditional gas ovens, the temperature in such a 'box' being more easily and therefore more accurately controlled. In a gas oven, the variation is greater because of the high ventilation required. That is a drawback for those of us who may want to double up on say a sandwich cake recipe, or make six egg whites into meringues: we want all, not just half of them to cook properly, and with only minimal juggling.

c One cannot forget or fail to ignite an electric oven when one has turned on the source of heat: an important aspect of safety.

Solid fuel ensures a constantly warm kitchen (hot water, too, perhaps), heated ovens and hob, but lacks the immediate temperature control of gas and electricity. Those who have had an Aga (or similar, which could also be oil- or gas-fuelled) never want to be without. Ideally, have an Aga and electricity.

Gas – natural gas (unlike coal gas) makes no more dirt than electricity and, on many modern cookers, there's no need for matches or flame gun. Turn it on and cooking starts at once; off, and the food immediately stops cooking.

Cost Have you a blank cheque book or a limited budget? Whichever it is, buy a reliable make, preferably a tested and approved appliance: BSI (British Standards Institution), BEAB (British Electrotechnical Approvals Board) or whatever.

Space available A split-level cooker or a 'cooking centre' – oven, hob and working surface all incorporated in one unit – may fit in more easily (besides having other advantages) than a traditional cooker.

The oven Probably the most vital part of the most vital piece of equipment in the kitchen. On this, to a much greater degree than you might expect or know, may depend your results.

The thermostat Through inheriting recently (when I moved house) an expensive, modern, well-known make of gas cooker in which I found the thermostat not to be working at all, I have been dismayed to unearth the fact, two thermostats and three months later, that in all British gas and electric cookers, manufacturers are allowed a wide tolerance for the thermostat: an inaccurate thermostat is *allowed!* In gas ovens, the tolerance is ± 18°F/10°C, while in electric cookers, according to the Electricity Council, the accepted tolerance for conventional ovens is ± 27°F/15°C. 'In practice,' they say, 'this is found acceptable bearing in mind that the user/reader is likely to introduce many variations on the recipe selected, e.g. temperature of ingredients, ambient temperature, size of container, material of container, size of eggs.' Man can be sent to the moon, but, as I write this in 1985, it seems that manufacturing accurate, mass-produced thermostats for the ordinary domestic oven at a price we would be prepared to pay defeats us, in Britain anyway. To me, such inaccuracy is *not* acceptable. Of course we make errors and alterations ourselves, but why should we not expect the set heat to be right?

It seems we are expected to get used to a new cooker. In practice, that is probably what most of us do, protest though, at first, we may. Can anyone bring pressure to bear for greater accuracy to be made obligatory?

In practice, what this must mean is that (fanned ovens excepted) the heat at any given setting in one electric oven may be up to 54°F/30°C hotter or cooler than in another – 36°F/20°C maximum difference in a gas oven! Is it surprising that some of us appear not to be good cooks, or perhaps dislike cooking because we are not successful? It means that any oven temperature one is given may be wrong for those of us unfortunate enough to have 'badly-out' thermostats, and seems to explain why, if twelve or even more people make a cake to a set recipe for a competition, no two may be the same.

In a gas cooker, the central oven temperature may be different in each one but, according to Southern Gas, all British models should perform in the same way: they must conform to the British Standard Cooking Test. (The variation of heat in different ovens is caused mainly by their basic shape. Besides varying capacity and flue arrangements, irregularities such as your cooker not standing level or a badly sealed door can also alter performance.)

See also *oven thermometers*, page 46, and point *b* above.

Shelf positions Here again, yet another variable is introduced. Since there are literally scores of different cookers on the market, the difference in distance between, say, the roof of the oven and the first or second shelf, or between the first shelf and the second, may, in different makes or models, be quite wide. This means that other than when using your own cooker's instruction book, somebody else's idea of using 'the second shelf from the top' could easily be the top or the third shelf in your oven: so when 'the top of the oven' or shelf places are given in a recipe, they can only be read as approximate.

Double or single oven Do you need one or two ovens, and should the main one be able to take a medium-sized or a huge

turkey? If you're elderly or crippled, would an oven at waist height be easier? Should the door open sideways or downwards (providing a shelf on which to rest things temporarily) and do you want a see-through glass panel or inner glass door to have a quick peep at what's happening without loss of heat? Is automatic control essential (some are very complicated) and do you want a self-cleaning lining? If a built-in oven, is there a grill? If not, you'll either have to do without (but how?) or buy one as an extra.

Fan-assisted Fanned, or forced air convection ovens have several advantages (though also the odd disadvantage) over traditional zoned-heat ovens, but you must follow a cooker's instruction book because even fanned ovens vary from make to make. For instance, the given cooking temperature for a recipe can usually be reduced by 25°C (because of the constant, even heat in these ovens), but some manufacturers offset the thermostat to account for that. The advantages of a fanned oven are:

a Even heat throughout, making them ideal for large batches of baking etc., but less good to cook things which need slightly different temperatures.

b Economy – besides cooking things at a lower temperature, the oven heats up about 5 minutes faster and cooks about 8 minutes faster in the hour.

c The oven is wider because there are no space-taking elements at each side, so no elements to wear out either, as in time most do.

d Roast meats are said not to spit or shrink so much.

Beware of one possible disadvantage, and a big one: a make with a noisy cooling fan. A friend who has a huge and luxurious kitchen/dining room tells me that if you eat where you cook it's difficult (for up to an hour later) even to think clearly, far less try to chat, the noise is so frustrating. In sheer desperation, she is now resigned to switching the whole cooker off – to continue its row and complete its job when the meal is over.

The hob How easy is cleaning? Little is simpler than the ceramic hob (see below), and nothing worse than a collection of fiddling parts, to be removed and scoured at every splash or spill. Some gas cookers come complete with drop-down lid to hide the hob when not in use, also keeping everything clean and giving extra working surface.

On a gas cooker, do you want individual pan supports where the pan is flat on the easily-washed burner, or would you prefer to be able to slide your pans across the hob on an all-over pan support? For arthritics, for instance, the latter is both safer and easier.

Will the smallest pans stand steadily on the burners, and do you want (for deep fat especially) a thermostatic or 'thermoset' hotplate to maintain a constant check on the contents of a pan, reacting instantly and automatically to a set temperature? Also now standard on many hobs is a special slow-cook facility.

The ceramic hob Very eye-catching, with a neat, clean, flat area which hides all the elements and would dress up even the most dreary kitchen – but there are some drawbacks. I know those who were happier with a conventional hob; others who would never go back to one. Some thoughts are:

a Is the cost justified, and if you can't afford or don't want to insure the ceramic glass, are you prepared for the unlikely risk that the glass can break? Although a hard blow with a sharp object can fracture the surface, ceramic glass is in fact an extremely tough and resilient material, manufacturers having put each piece through a fierce test; in one instance, by dropping a 1lb/500g steel ball four times on to the surface from a height of up to 30in/75cm.

b Are you basically a careful person, with normal hands strong enough to lift pans rather than slide them around on the surface, which can scratch the glass if a pan bottom is at all rough? Will you remember that you can never use an asbestos mat, foil, or any abrasive powder on the surface? (While with careful use the glass is very easily kept clean, it is vital to follow a manufacturer's instructions concerning dos and don'ts.)

c Are you constantly making jams, caramels or confectionery? Boiling syrup will caramelize on the glass if not quickly wiped off when splashed or spilt.

d Might you have to buy new pans, or will your own do? To quote the Electricity Council:

> The best cooking results and the wisest use of electricity are achieved by using good quality ground-based pans with clean, dry outside surfaces but other good quality, really flat-based pans will also give good results, especially those with a matt black enamelled base. If thin, distorted or dented pans or those with uneven bases are used, the cooking will take longer, as there is not a good contact between the pan and hob, with a consequent loss of efficiency. Pans which are approximately the same size as the cooking area should be used where possible.

To minimize spillage from contents boiling over, pans should also be large enough to accommodate such contents.

If you are undeterred by the above, a ceramic hob has lots in its favour. Appearance and easy cleaning; excellent control of heat, the controls themselves also being easy to grip and turn; minimum waste of heat and automatic regulation of it if by mistake one leaves a ring full on, uncovered by a pan; pans remain spotlessly clean on the outside, with the incidence of sticking and burned-on foods considerably reduced.

There is no lateral spread of heat, so only the heated areas on the hob get hot. Be sure you know what sized rings you want. You might prefer to have all four the same; two each of different sizes; one large, two medium-sized and one small or some other combination. There is some choice, just as there is on conventional hobs – gas or electric.

The grill If you want toast made in two minutes, then a gas grill will probably do it. Whether you prefer gas or electricity, however, the best grills cook evenly at any setting along their entire length and breadth. Do you like it at waist or eye level and, if at waist level, enclosed, perhaps, in the smaller of two ovens, may it restrict the use of that oven? Most of today's cookers have pull-out, stay-out grill pans, leaving one's hands free for turning the food. A 'surface combustion grill' (sola) is excellent for those who like grilled food because the heat is absolutely even at all temperatures.

Rôtisserie see page 40.

Plate warming Is there anywhere to heat plates and vegetable dishes without actually cooking them? This need is easily overlooked and not met by having a drawer at the bottom.

Baking sheets Are these included? If not, it means buying them separately, see page 13.

Mobility of cooker Some have castors, or drop-down wheels which are controlled by a concealed lever – saving strain when you want to clean behind.

Hood From my own experience, a charcoal-operated hood is of strictly limited use – not worth the expense and noise. Smells still reached my bedroom, steam still clouded my kitchen windows and I could only trust that the monster filtered out some grease. To get rid of smells and steam, it needs ducting, through an outside wall – which I've now had done. With hindsight, I'd consider more closely having a good extractor instead.

Microwave cooker Probably indispensable now in many households, especially in those where good eating is not a priority, where latecomers need or want a quick meal, or when cooking is nothing but a burden – certainly not a pleasure. This isn't so for all of us, however, so I personally looked to this invention for other benefits: time-saving; lower fuel costs; less washing-up; no oven-cleaning (hated job); rapid defrosting; versatility and portability (quite easy and so useful I had read – especially for hot drinks – to be able to take it into one's bedroom when ill). What I had failed to anticipate however, was the nature (and the importance) of the *dis*advantages. After six disturbing months, the microwave and I parted company: it did not justify its place in my (good-sized) kitchen. This is why:

a Apart from some vegetables, notably peas, nothing tasted better and hardly anything as good as when cooked by conventional methods. Flavour, texture and often the appearance all suffered.

b For accompaniments such as roast potatoes and Yorkshire pudding, the conventional oven must be on as well, so why, I wondered, heat two ovens when the old one will cook everything together, and much better – or does one forego those tasty things?

c Reheating a main course on its plate for the late-home breadwinner sounds so easy as to be positively inviting, but in some extraordinary and inexplicable way both the flavour and the texture seemed each time to change – for the worse.

d My cooker was far from portable. I wonder how many actually are?

e The frustrations: my knowledge of cooking, my skills and my recipes were of only very limited use, the rules and methods for microwave cooking being so different.

f I repeatedly felt cheated. Some examples will show why:

Roast meats These could be better described simply as cooked meats – which may be fine for anyone who doesn't know or mind about the glorious smell, succulence, colour and texture of a real roast.

Jacket potatoes Waxy flesh inside a pale, soft skin: not dry, floury potato inside a deliciously crisp brown skin. Hailed as being 'cooked in five minutes', this seems only to apply to one potato: one must double the time for two, nearly treble it for three. How long for potatoes for a crowd? (I was not eager to experiment.)

Raising a dough Quicker in hot water I found (see page 308) and no electricity then used.

Chocolate melting Hot water again quicker (see page 92).

Defrosting foods A great advantage for small to medium-sized things, but quite the opposite I found for a solid 6lb/3kg mass of minced meat brought to me one day by a harassed neighbour who had forgotten to thaw it and needed it in time to cook for a farmers' lunch – a morning I shall not forget!

If space and money are of no consequence, a microwave oven would have its moments: for that occasional quick meal; when one forgets to defrost something; when friends unexpectedly turn up. If on the other hand good food, space and cost are important to you, think thrice, not just twice, before investing.

■ For further information, there are many books on the subject. Disenchanted as I myself am, my thoughts must end here.

Pressure cooker Something people seem to swear by or swear at. Be quite convinced you need one and will trouble to read all the instructions before you take the plunge and buy. A pressure cooker is designed to harness the steam which in an ordinary saucepan escapes and is wasted. The sealing in of this steam and the consequent build-up of pressure causes a rise in temperature. It is this high heat, coupled with the fact that the pressure generated in the cooker actually drives the heat into and through the food, which explains the rapid cooking action of even normally slow-cooking foods such as tough meat or butter beans.

■ Even if you don't like vegetables or fruit from a pressure cooker, it certainly scores in *some* ways. Here are a few:

1 It can save hours of cooking when using for things like stock, pulses, steamed puddings, marmalade or chutneys. This cuts down on fuel costs, and also on your time.

2 It's a way of saving on the weekly cost of meat because cheaper cuts cook in a shorter time.

3 A meal can be on the table long before it would be cooked in the traditional way.

4 Many frozen foods can be cooked or reheated straight from the freezer, substantially cutting the time otherwise involved.

CUPS

American measuring cups save a lot of calculations and muddles if you ever want to use an American recipe. A nest of four is quite inexpensive, lasts indefinitely with care, and is available in many good kitchen shops. A set consists of:

¼ cup (approx. 2 fluid ozs or 65ml) – 1oz (25g) of flour or 2oz (50g) of butter or sugar

⅓ cup (scant 3 fluid ozs or 85ml) – approx. 1½oz (40g) of flour or 3oz (75g) of butter or sugar

½ cup (approx. 4 fluid ozs or 125ml) – 2oz (50g) of flour or 4oz (100g) of butter or sugar

1 cup (approx. 8 fluid ozs or 250ml) – 4oz (100g) of flour or ½lb (225g) of butter or sugar

CUTTERS

Parsley cutters A Mouli-Parsmint, for instance, is useful if you've no idea how to chop parsley otherwise (see page 56), but for sheer speed, efficiency, results and easy washing-up, you can't easily beat the simplest pair of things, a sharp knife and a chopping board. Why waste money and drawer space on *this* kind of gadget?

Pastry or scone cutters Must have a sharp edge, otherwise they 'drag' pastry edges, and so prevent the pastry from rising properly. Plain cutters are normally used for savoury things, fluted for sweet, then there's no confusion at the table, in larder or freezer.

DISHES

Casserole dishes Exist in so many shapes, sizes, types and materials, and so much depends on your taste that it's impossible to say what's the best choice. You may want a colourful oven-to-table dish, a shallow wide one to fit easily into a smallish oven, or perhaps the earthenware pot-au-feu type with its narrow neck, and from which, consequently, there's less evaporation of liquid? Alternatively there are the lead-weight Le Creuset vitreous-enamelled cast iron casseroles, the pyrex type of dish if you want something really simple, or the sophisticated colourful enamelled steel or cast aluminium dish which you can put on top of the cooker *or* in the oven. You name it, some shops have got it – at a price.

■ Whatever you have, it's easier to keep most of them spick-and-span if you remember to grease them before use. See also *cocotte,* page 17.

Fluted gratin or baking dish Made of ovenproof china, they are perfect for those purposes but not so good for a flan: a metal flan ring (see page 26) produces crisper pastry because it's a better conductor of heat than china. Should your flan pastry have a hole in it, or shrink badly at one side, however, (when liquid could escape) then you're safer with this dish than with a mere flan ring! See also tart tin with removable base, page 47.

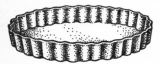

Soufflé dishes They vary enormously. The thin, fluted, white, ovenproof, porcelain French type are the ideal kind for a hot baked soufflé because, *being* so thin, the heat penetrates the mixture almost as soon as you put it in the oven, which helps it to raise well. I prefer the wide shallow shape to the narrower deeper one, because a soufflé firms up better in the middle when the mixture isn't so deep – but you may prefer a soufflé that is slightly moist in the centre.

■ French soufflé dishes come in litre sizes and you'll possibly want at least two: say scant 1¼ pints/750ml and approx. 1 pint 12fl ozs/1 litre for a household of four: scant 1 pint/500ml and scant 1¼ pints/750ml if for only two people. It's a bonus to have some individual ones as well, see *cocotte,* page 17.

■ English fireproof china soufflé dishes are so thick by comparison that, using them, you can't hope to bake an equally good soufflé. If you are without a soufflé dish at all, you can improvise with any ovenproof dish of similar size and depth.
■ For pâtés and terrines, if you haven't got a proper terrine, a *deep* soufflé dish is best, while for cold soufflés a wider shallow one seems to set the sweet off better.

DOUGH HOOK

This attachment, on a mixer, saves a lot of energy and does the job well, but the average domestic machine will only knead smallish quantities of dough. It's of no help when baking a large batch of something for the freezer.

DOYLEYS

These can kill several birds with one stone:

1 They make an attractive background to set off food, like a frame round a picture.
2 They absorb excess fat from fried foods such as croûtons, fried fish, fritters or chipped potatoes.
3 They prevent foods and dishes sliding

about on their serving plate.

■ Fancy doyleys are used for cakes and all sweet dishes, but plain ones for savoury, to indicate the nature of the food, particularly of pastry, scones or sandwiches, etc. Then, of course, there are gold, silver or Christmas doyleys for any special occasion. Many things look less attractive without.

DREDGERS

Flour dredger One of these, or a coarse strainer, is essential if you want to make light pastry or scones. Without, you can't (with your hand) distribute the flour evenly and thinly over the surface of a pastry board: excess flour gets rolled into the dough which, when baked, is spoiled.

■ A flour dredger has larger holes than a sugar dredger or caster, (see below).

Sugar dredger Used to sprinkle either caster or icing sugar over the surface of something like a fruit pie, shortbread or a plain sandwich cake. Improvise with a small fine-mesh strainer if without the real thing.

EGG UTENSILS

Egg coddlers Like deep egg-cups, with a tight-fitting lid. They're easy for those who dislike the messiness of an egg in its shell. See also page 145.

Egg poachers Would be better called 'egg steamers'. Poaching is done *in* water, not over it, and the steamed egg is a tougher and less digestible egg than the poached.

Egg poaching rings Like miniature metal flan rings. Shallower than a scone cutter, so that water can flow over the top, they help to control the antics of the egg white. I have some made of aluminium, others of tin, but the latter tends to stick to the cooked egg. Go for aluminium.

Egg pricker Has a needle on a spring.

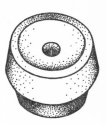

■ Prick egg at the blunt end, where there's air: the shell won't usually crack when boiled because the trapped air now has an escape when, due to the heat of the water, it expands. See also page 142.

Egg separators Come in various designs. They are useful for the handicapped, for those who often buy or use cracked eggs – or for anyone with ten thumbs!

■ The snag about a separator is that when you want to get the clinging bobbles (called the chalazae) off the yolk, you can't. You need the sharp edge of the egg shell for that. (The chalazae are one cause of curdling, see page 143.)

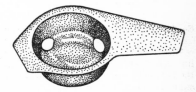

Egg stands One in your kitchen should ensure that at least some eggs are always at room temperature if you want to boil any or make a creamed mixture (see page 143). Eggs keep longer if stored point downwards, see page 142.

FISH SLICES

These should be flexible enough to slide *flat* along the bottom of a small frying pan, and long enough to hold a fillet of fish without breaking it; not stiff, small or square, like so many on the market.

■ One costly model fools the buyer even more – the blade is solid, so you can't drain the food on it. Why can't *all* manufacturers realize it's the functional end of a utensil that matters, not the beautiful handle?

Do buy

Don't buy

FLAN RINGS

Metal rings and frames used in conjunction with a baking sheet make much better flans than a flan-shaped, fluted, ovenproof china gratin dish (see page 24). This is because metal is a better conductor of heat, so the underneath and sides of the pastry bake more crisply. A plain ring is meant for savoury dishes, fluted for sweet, then there's no chance of getting them mixed on the table, in your larder or freezer. I'm a glutton for frames of all shapes and sizes – round, square or rectangular – the big ones are excellent for large numbers.

For 4oz/100g pastry (or for shortbread) you need a 7in/18cm ring.

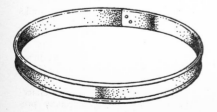

FOIL

One of the most indispensable modern inventions. Unlike polythene, it keeps out light, which makes fatty foods go rancid and hastens the deterioration of many others. This explains why saltless butter and some kinds of margarine and cheese are sold in foil wrappers. The one great snag is that you can't *see* what's in or under foil.

■ Its qualities are extraordinary: it gives food neither smell nor taste; it is waterproof, malleable (marvellous for the freezer the way it fits so closely and tightly to anything wrapped in it), non-absorbent, non-inflammable, non-perishable and impervious to grease. It won't let food smells or flavour out, light or air in. It conducts heat quickly and evenly.

■ As long as you use the heavy-duty quality, and seal foods in it properly (covering them finally with a polythene bag to prevent foil being torn), they will be almost immune to dehydration even after weeks in a freezer.

■ Its uses are legion. Here are just four you may not have thought of:

1 Use a strip to protect the rim of your best ovenware dishes when under a fiercely hot grill.
2 Use instead of greaseproof paper as a 'collar' round the top of a soufflé dish (see page 298).
3 Interleave sliced cold meat, chops, fillets, sandwiches, etc. with a strip of foil before putting in freezer; to simplify taking out a limited quantity later.
4 Cut a good-sized circle of foil – for repeated use – to prevent cakes, flans, etc. overbrowning. In the centre, cut a 50p-sized hole, so that the oven heat can still penetrate the middle of whatever you're cooking (which is the last place to set).

FORK

A two-pronged meat fork, rather like a carving fork, is better for stirring boiled long grain rice than a conventional fork or a spoon, either of which tends to turn the separate grains into a solid mass.

FREEZER

A deep freeze is surely the most revolutionary piece of kitchen equipment of our time. It is quite amazing that for generations we have preserved in sugar, vinegar and salt, by drying, smoking and various other methods, but we failed to think out the simplest and most obvious of them all: preserving foods in their natural state in freezing conditions.

■ A freezer can be as valuable to someone living alone as to a family, to the old as to the young, to townsfolk as to countryfolk and to those who dislike cooking as much as to born cooks. If you can't afford one or lack the space to accommodate it that's final, but those who are unaware of a freezer's boundless help can have no idea of what they're missing in terms of convenience, economy, time saved, increased variety of food, and the new interest and dimension it gives to cooking.
■ Making the best of a freezer doesn't, in my opinion, mean filling it with a carcase, or even a quarter carcase, of meat and commercially prepared, expensive frozen foods, but using it more as an ice-cold larder-cum-store cupboard where the life of everything is extended. A wide range of raw ingredients like meat, fish, poultry, fruit and vegetables, as well as partly prepared foods like pastry, breadcrumbs, fruit rinds and juices, fruit purées, etc. enable one to make all kinds of recipes at almost any time.
■ If you live alone and eat very little bread, for instance, why not freeze half the loaf when you buy it, or freeze half a cake when you've baked it? Whatever the size of your household, you can have ready (or put there as leftovers), prepared foods such as cooked cold meat, cakes, cake fillings, puddings, cold sweets, etc., and the only thing a freezer asks of you is to defrost it occasionally – about twice yearly for a chest type, three or four times for an upright, or when the frost build-up exceeds ³⁄₁₆in/½cm thick. (Some modern freezers are self-defrosting. Not only is the frost melted, drained and evaporated automatically, sparing you the nuisance of defrosting, but also running costs are kept lower because the system never becomes choked with frost.)
■ Choosing a freezer, be it a first or second-time buy, needs more knowledge than most of us have got, so there are advantages in going to a freezer specialist where the selection is wide, the models reliable and the advice professional – rather than to a store or general electric shop where the advice may be as limited as the choice. In a store, for example, one can so easily be lured off course by the cosmetics of a unit-matching, built-in fridge-freezer, some models of which are totally impractical. Unless you are a giraffe, would you, for instance, want to have to get out steps to reach things on the upper shelf (if the freezer is at the top) and, while searching for your goal, where would you put (or throw) the frozen packs it may be necessary to move?
■ Besides these and more obvious considerations like size of family, the amount of entertaining you do, money and space available, and the type you prefer (chest, upright or fridge-freezer), it's worth having a good long think before you buy. The capacity is all-important and will depend on how you want to use a freezer.

1 What basically do you want it for?
 a To save you shopping three weeks out of four, or seven out of eight?
 b For carcase meat, or will you only be buying smallish pieces of meat?
 c To preserve your garden produce? Could you perhaps grow more if you could freeze more?
 d To store bread galore and space-taking packs of commercially pre-

pared foods like ice cream?

e To save you work in the summer? Do you for instance enjoy bottling and making jams, or would you be thankful almost to throw some of your fruit into the freezer?

f To have a constant supply of home-made goodies which you'll be able to bake in bulk?

2 Are you methodical or higgledy-piggledy, thrifty or wasteful? Have you time on your hands, or not, to use it to its greatest advantage, and to pack things neatly in the minimum of space?

3 If making a choice between pull-out drawers or a fixed interior, do you realize the foraging you may have to do in the latter? May you want easy-to-get-at ice trays? If so, some modern models have a special compartment for these.

4 The fuller a freezer, the less its running costs as a rule, but beware of over-filling it. What price your back if you have to lift out heavy baskets? And have you contemplated the problems of an arctic bran-tub?

5 Where are you going to keep the freezer? Though much less convenient in a garage or shed, especially when these are not integral with the house, the motor uses less electricity than when the freezer is in the kitchen. Also, in the event of a power cut, food outside will remain frozen longer in winter than food in a warm kitchen. (In temperatures below freezing, little will go wrong outside; everything could go wrong inside.) At all costs avoid the larder: the warmth from the motor will make other foods go off.

It may be difficult before you have a freezer to understand why a small one won't do. It is just as baffling a year or two later, when you're experienced, to know why you were so short-sighted.

FRUIT DECORATOR

Helps you to cut things like lemons, oranges, cucumber or courgettes attractively. Pare off the peel in strips lengthwise down the fruit, to give a striped appearance, then slice the fruit. Alternatively, you could use a sharp-pronged fork on a cucumber or courgettes.

FUNNELS

Bottle funnel Besides its obvious function of making easy the transfer of a liquid from a wide-necked container to a bottle-necked one, a funnel can save a horrid mess with many types of liquidizer: those without a central cap are the problem. If you're making mayonnaise, for instance, in such a liquidizer, a funnel in place of the lid enables you to pour in the oil without splashing.

Metal jam funnel Useful to fill jars with piping hot jam because one can do so without handling them, as well as without waste or mess. Use also to transfer dry ingredients like coffee, rice or lentils to a storage jar.

Pie funnels Shouldn't be necessary in a fruit pie because the fruit should be deep enough to support the pastry, which will set (and therefore stay put) before the fruit cooks and shrinks. If there isn't enough fruit to do this, it's going to be a somewhat mean and miserable sort of pie.

■ One can't do without a funnel for a meat pie of course (2 for a large pie), because it's this, not the meat, which supports the pastry. Otherwise the pastry will collapse into the middle before it can set.

GARLIC PRESS

Handy if you use much garlic, and will last a lifetime. The garlic, with all its volatile oil released, is more pungent than when crushed with a knife (see page 98).

■ Although quick and easy to use, a press can be bothersome to wash. The model illustrated is more costly, and claims to be self-cleaning: a spiked part is pressed against the similarly shaped holey part, to push out any tiny bits of garlic stuck there. (It's cheaper to buy a toothbrush for the purpose.)

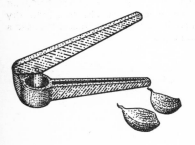

GIRDLES

They are usually made of cast iron or heavy aluminium, and may be square, with a frying pan type of handle, or round with a similar or half-hoop handle spanning the top: these are a curse to store unless the handle drops down. Unlike a frying pan containing fat, a girdle is just greased, so it pays to buy a good one

which will stand up to the heat without burning the food.

■ One can't really make do with a frying pan: many aren't strong enough, and the high sides make it difficult if not impossible to turn some kinds of scone over. A *galettière* (pancake pan), if you have one, is better. Griddle is just another name for a girdle. Some cookers have one built in.

GLOVES, RUBBER

Like a thimble in a way; an item some of us can't do without, some can't do with. Skin and nail savers, once you've discovered their benefits and got used to wearing gloves, they may even go away with you on holiday.

■ *To turn them inside out (or vice versa) quickly:*
1 Turn the cuff over, as far down as possible, then hold the inside of the cuff with one hand and with the other hand pull as much of the glove through as possible.
2 Holding the cuff edges together tightly at each side between your thumb and first finger, glove fingers hanging downwards and the cuff itself taut, swing the glove towards you, up over the held-together edges (perhaps *twice* round) to trap air inside.
3 Grip the bottom of the glove tightly with that hand (to prevent the air escaping again) and with the other hand squash the air up to the thumb and fingers so that one by one you can shoot them out full length, inside out. (It may be necessary to repeat 3 to get all four fingers and thumb through.)

■ If one has weak or arthritic hands, rubber gloves give a better grip for opening jam jars, etc., just as do nut-crackers for unscrewing small bottle tops.

GRATERS

They are of all shapes and sizes, some easy to handle, others not. The coarser ones are for grating carrots, onions and potatoes, etc., rather than for cheese or suet, which would be guaranteed to give indigestion if so roughly prepared. A circular one, or a conical-shaped grater as illustrated below, is practical to use and has several shredding sizes: things like lemon rind or nutmeg on the finest part; cheese or suet on the next; vegetables on the coarsest.

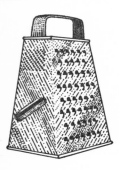

Mouli grater It grates cheese, suet, nuts or chocolate finely, and in a trice – also efficiently and without cut fingers. You only have to put in the food, turn a handle and lo and behold! This is a gadget I wouldn't be without, but beware, the plastic type breaks easily: you need the metal one. See illustration below.

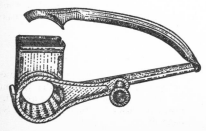

Nutmeg grater Ensures a strong fresh spicy flavour, 100% nutmeg. If spare time is scarce, ready-ground nutmeg is itself spicy and temptingly convenient.

HATPINS

Are just the thing for decorating cakes, sweets and moulds, the bottoms of which are awkward to reach with your fingers! Use one to place the decoration, and a second to slide the decoration off the point. This is an easy way to handle sticky things like glacé cherries or angelica.

■ Use hatpins also to prick bubbles in royal icing before they set; to clear the point of an icing tube if a lump obstructs it while you're icing; to break icing off the tube when doing trellis-work, or to pull the colours together when doing marbled icing.

KETTLES

Electric kettles, which switch off automatically, or others which whistle when they boil, ensure the best cup of tea – because over-boiled water is flat. Although the automatic one may be initially fairly costly, it's a long-term saving on fuel. Alternatively, you may like the more modern type of jug kettle in which you can boil as little as one cupful of water. Compared with a conventional kettle, though, do you realize that these may be too tall for your taps at the sink and, also because of their height, are more easily knocked over and more tricky to pour from into something low like a cup? In addition to these possible drawbacks, the element on some has a lower rating, so takes longer to boil 2pts/ 1.14 litres of water. I'd ask about this when buying.

KNIVES

Knives are an important part of any kitchen's equipment, though I can't cover them all here. Basically, they should be comfortable to hold, easy to use and, when possible, made for the particular job. Above all, a knife which is supposed to be sharp shou!d be sharp, because a blunt one wastes time, bruises vegetables, makes cutting up food hard work and drags pastry edges, which may prevent a pastry from rising properly. If you can't sharpen them yourself on a steel (see page 68), it's worth buying a knife sharpener. Apart from certain specialized knives, high grade stainless steel ones are nowadays extemely good, providing they are properly ground. One leading kitchen shop in London claims they are 'excellent to use, very practical to care for, and keep their cutting edge as well as carbon steel does' – but they tend to be costly.

Bread or slicing knife One of these is basic to the good cutting of bread – unless you have an electric saw-knife.

Filleting knive Makes it much easier to fillet fish well, if you like to do this yourself. It's rather like the cook's knife illustrated below, but the blade – about 7in/18cm is a good size – is thinner and more flexible, so that it will bend enough to take fillets off the bone.

French cook's knife With its handle designed to keep your fingers tucked away, and with its curved steel blade, this knife makes it quick and easy to slice or chop vegetables, or to chop herbs (see page 56) and nuts in the professional way. Use it to cut up meat, chicken or even a delicate cake as well. One with a 7 or 8in/18 or 20cm blade is useful without being cumbersome.

Grapefruit knife Has no substitute, and is essential for preparing the fruit properly and without waste. If left-handed, be sure to buy one serrated down *both* sides.

Pallet (or pallette) knife One of the most necessary of all specialized knives: use it to clean foods off the sides and bottoms of basins and pans (excepting non-stick); for turning and lifting pieces of fried food; for lifting or turning over pancakes or drop scones; for spreading cake mixture in its tin, or for icing work.

■ Because it's often easier to find a bad pallet knife than a good, one can't help wondering if some manufacturers find that an elegant handle is a better selling point than a perfect, forged blade? When pressed on a flat surface, a good pallet knife should bend gradually and evenly towards the handle, like this:

If it bends in only one place, like this:

there's no point in buying it at all. Take professional advice in a professional shop if you're uncertain how to choose.

■ Made in various lengths, a 6½in/16½cm blade is a good all-purpose sized knife.

Saw knife Fine, small, stainless steel, it is especially good for tomatoes or citrus fruits, whether for slicing them finely or just cutting in half. There isn't then the need for a tomato knife, which has little other use.

Vegetable knife One with a 3in/7½cm blade gives you complete control when scraping potatoes or old carrots because the blade becomes like a short extension of your hand.

LARDING NEEDLES

These are of different thicknesses, pronged (or with a clip) at the eye end, for piercing and larding with strips of fat, lean cuts of meat, poultry or game. See page 69.

LIQUIDIZER

Turns tedium into pleasure, effort into relaxation, minutes into seconds, oily liquids into emulsions and, of course, many solids into liquids or purées. It does things you cannot do by hand, and does better many that you *can* do by hand.

■Be careful what you buy. It's no exaggeration to say I've found some makes more trouble than they're worth, while others are too small or too limited by their power to be of real value. Those with a single high-speed motor, for instance, are unsuitable for making mayonnaise, which requires a slowish speed.

■ The big Kenwood liquidizer – adjustable through a range of speeds – is worth its weight in gold and indeed deserves a gold medal for being one of the best ever kitchen gadgets. It is reliable, strong, a good and sensible size, easy to handle and wash up, and 100% efficient with the minimum of human effort. I'd sell almost anything I possess to replace mine if necessary. (I have no shares in Kenwood!)

■ If you're thinking of buying a liquidizer consult consumer magazines first. It's worth remembering, too, that the prices of electrical goods are highly competitive, so it pays to shop around.

MEASURES

Measures ensure accuracy about liquid quantities, which can often make the difference between good and disappointing (or bad) results. This is because the texture of a dish will frequently depend upon the correct consistency of the mixture.

Almost unbelievably, however, many measures are themselves not absolutely accurate, as you may discover about your own if you can test them. As it's a once-and-for-all buy, it must make sense, therefore, to go to a kitchen shop rather than a general ironmonger, and look for one made to BSI (British Standards Institution) or other official standard. I like the stainless steel ones best: they are clearly marked at frequent intervals, will hold boiling liquids, and don't crack or break if knocked or dropped. You may want two: a 1pt/500ml measure marked at 2fl ozs (or 50ml) intervals, and a quart-sized measure marked at ¼pt and/or 100ml intervals. Even smaller quantities can be measured in a medicine glass, obtainable at any chemist's.

Beware when using American recipes because the American pint is only 16fl ozs, whereas the British pint is 20. I once bought an 8-pint plastic measure at a bring-and-buy sale for marmalade and wine-making, and did not realize until long after that it measured American pints. No wonder I had some odd results!

MILLS

Pepper mill A gadget for which there's no real substitute, if you like freshly ground black pepper. As it's in constant use, it is ideal, if you can afford it, to have one mill at the cooker and another for the table. See also *pepper*, page 120.

Vegetable mill Does most things a sieve will do, excluding breadcrumbs – but in a fraction of the time. The Moulin-Légumes illustrated below, particularly the larger size, makes purées in a jiffy – wonderful for such things as potatoes, spinach, apples or blackberries. A bonus, too – it's as quick and easy to wash up as to use.

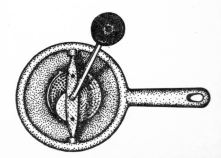

MINCER

One of the old-fashioned types, as illustrated below, is as efficient as they come: there's nothing to go wrong with it, you can't hurt your fingers and it doesn't need power. Beware of one snag though: you must have a good sturdy table or unit with a 'lip' to which you can screw it, otherwise you may not be able to use it.

MIXER

An electric mixer, if you get a really good one, is a sort of mechanical kitchen maid who is always standing by, ready and willing to do the heaviest slogging whenever you ask. It may have its limitations, but who and what hasn't? Choose one with a reliable name, a strong motor with varying speeds, a whisk which is nice and wiry (see page 49), and, very importantly, a wide-topped bowl the sides of which are easily cleaned with a pallet knife (or plastic spatula).

■ Some people scorn mixers, but (given a good make) have you given yours a fair chance? For a creamed mixture, did you really cream the butter and sugar until soft as cream, beat in the whisked eggs gradually and fold in the sieved flour with a tablespoon? Have you cut game chips or marmalade oranges in the slicer, kneaded a dough with the hook, whisked

six egg whites whilst you were getting on with something else? It will do all these things and a whole lot more. With some makes, a liquidizer can be used on the same motor.
■ Being really greedy, one also needs an electric hand-mixer, for jobs the fixed model can't do, like beating egg and other mixtures over hot water.
■ There's a need for both.
See also *processors*, page 37.

MOULDS

Bread moulds See *loaf tins*, page 47.

Brioche moulds Fluted outward-sloping tins (large ones may have a 'chimney') used especially for brioche. Small ones are either round or square.

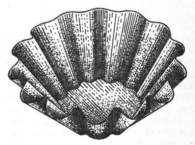

Charlotte moulds Plain, deep, copper or tin moulds with sloping sides. They're used for things like charlotte russe, fruit charlottes, crème caramel or a steamed soufflé. When turned upside down, the wide top makes a wide, firm base, which reduces the risk of the shape (or whatever it is) collapsing.

■ Some have handles and some also have a lid, depending upon purpose: it's better to have a lid for crème caramel for instance, to protect it properly during cooking, but you wouldn't need a lid for charlotte russe.

A 4in/10cm mould holds ¾pt/375ml. A 5½in/14cm mould holds 1¾pts/875ml.

Dariole moulds 'Castle pudding' tins.

Hinged raised pie mould Ideal if you can afford one and enjoy making hot-water-crust-pastry. Alternatively, one can manage with a loose-bottom oval mould or, at no cost at all, make tiny individual ones with cartridge paper or very fine card; use each as if it were a metal flan ring, rolling and moulding the pastry to fit inside. (Remove card when pastry is about half-cooked, glazing it now to make nice and brown.) This is how to make it (use 4ozs/100g pastry for each case and lid):

1 Cut a strip of fine card 14in/36cm long × 1½in/4cm wide.
2 Make it into a flan ring 4in/10cm in diameter and join overlapping ends at top with 2 paper clips.
3 Stand it on a baking sheet before moulding the pastry inside.

Jelly moulds Not as easy to choose as one might expect; it is sometimes difficult to visualize what a shape will look like when turned out. If you select something very plain, don't be surprised if whatever comes out of it looks very plain! If you're lucky enough to have a tin-lined copper mould, that's the one to use. Very easily unmoulded – because copper is such an excellent conductor of heat – there's no other to compare with them for sheer beauty of design. Next to copper, I like

aluminium (also a good conductor of heat) while plastic moulds are quite good too, because flexible and easily unmoulded. China and glass on the other hand are a nightmare because neither conducts heat. To avoid years of irritation and innumerable spoilt sweets, I'd use the former (well-greased) only for a steamed sponge pudding, and I'd smash the latter – I mean that. I'd feel guilty even to put one in a jumble sale. Why any manufacturer makes either, I have yet to learn.

OIL DROPPER

A special one, for making mayonnaise by hand, isn't necessary when you can improvise with any medium-sized bottle and a fitting cork. Simply make a small groove down the opposite sides of the cork, one for air to get in so that the oil will drop out at the other.

OIL WELL

A most useful little invention, for greasing almost anything that needs greasing, such as baking sheets, cake and bread tins, cooking dishes of all kinds, grease-proof paper, etc. A tiny mop inside a well (with a coil spring) which holds oil, ensures quick, easy and mess-free handling. Some chain stores do a much cheaper version of the original, but the spring is different and, I find, can be rather bothersome.

PANS

It's a false economy to buy cheap pans: they have a short life, burn readily (as do foods cooked in them) and, often because of badly fitting lids and handles which get dangerously hot, may be hazardous. No matter how well made or costly, however, the cooking efficiency and lifetime of any pan will depend upon the way it is looked after and used. Here are some tips:

1 Keep handles away from any other burner or hotplate, to avoid charring and blistering.

2 Use an electric hotplate which fits the pan, or adjust a gas flame to cover only the base of the pan. (The handle will deteriorate if it gets greatly overheated where joined to the body – and a loose handle can be dangerous.)

3 Generally speaking, pans should never be heated empty: non-stick coatings deteriorate; the tin lining of a copper pan may blister; a thin-based pan will buckle; long-term, *all* pans will gradually deteriorate.

4 Hot pans should not be plunged straight into cold water: it can cause buckling.

5 There's less wear and tear involved in cleaning a soaked pan than one which isn't soaked and, besides, it is far easier to do. Because hot water glues on some foods, soak pans which have contained eggs, milk or starches (potatoes, floury sauces, etc.) in *cold* water. Hot soapy water and a nylon scourer are harmless even to a non-stick pan, scouring powders are much too abrasive.

Oval baking pans A type of baking tin with lid, made in various metals. Aluminium is good because it's strong, yet light in weight and easy to keep clean.

■ Meat steams rather than roasts in a covered tin so it's more suitable for braising than roasting if you haven't got a real braising pan. It is particularly good for cuts of meat which require longer, slower cooking. You can of course use it without its lid as a roasting tin. See also *roasting*, page 78.

Deep fat pan Should be thick, strong and deep, otherwise the fat is liable to bubble over and catch fire. It should be large enough to meet family needs: this not only saves fuel and time, but ensures things can be served in crisp and perfect condition if you can fry whatever you're cooking in just one, or at the most two, batches.

■ A thermostatically controlled plug-in fryer is the safest if you haven't got a thermostatically controlled hot-plate on your cooker. Just in case you're unaware of it, this is because if fat is greatly overheated, it will burst into flame (see page 67).

■ You can use the same fat repeatedly if it is strained regularly and the pan is kept clean inside and out; you *may* be able to use the fat more than once without straining for something like chips, as long as you leave no floating morsels, but never after anything coated with batter or egg and breadcrumbs, because 'bits' or crumbs fall off and burn.

■ A frying (chip) basket should fit loosely inside the pan: choose one with a fairly close mesh, then you won't waste time fishing for the small things that slip through. (If you *don't* fish for them, they'll burn and make the fat bitter.)

Egg poaching pan See *egg poachers*, page 25.

Frying pans Should be thick, strong and preferably not too heavy because they're more difficult to handle. You need at least two or three, of different sizes – one of which I'd have non-stick, two with lids – then you can use them to sweat vegetables as well as fry and, if deep enough, to complete the cooking of some foods *after* frying. Of all materials used for pans, copper is the best conductor of heat, becoming hot almost instantaneously when in contact with any source of heat. Usually tin-lined, copper is ideal when foods are to be cooked fast as in frying, sautéing or browning, and requires a lower than normal flame.

Some lightweight imported pans are more decorative than practical, while the solid copper pans are excellent – but costly. Avoid overheating a copper pan, especially if empty: the tin lining may begin to melt. If you've abused your pan, consult an expert about retinning.

■ If you do not have a sauté pan, a deep frying pan is useful for poaching eggs, as well as for sautéing.

Omelette pan Possibly an unnecessary expense if you have a good quality non-stick frying pan of the right size and strong enough to withstand the heat required for omelettes: perfect omelettes almost slide out of them, you can rinse them in a second, and the only worry is that it's easy to spoil the pan itself if it's too thin or greatly overheated.

■ Of the true omelette pans, I prefer non-stick or iron to the poor quality aluminium ones which many people buy, because they are apt to become inseparable friends with the omelette inside. To prevent rusting, keep an iron pan covered with a film of oil.

■ It is difficult to recommend a size without knowing your needs, so see page 148.

Preserving pan Really essential if one makes much jam because they're designed especially for their purpose. They allow the fast evaporation of liquid over a large surface so that the jam will reach setting point with the minimum of cooking, to have the best possible flavour and colour.

■ You may envy friends with a copper or brass jam pan but as they weigh a ton empty, what about laden? There's less risk of a slipped disc with a strong aluminium one. The acid in fruits keep it shiny, so it's dead easy to clean.

Sauce pans Needn't break the bank but it does help to have a range of sizes and a range of metals, so that you've got the right one for the job. Some will double as a stewpan; good quality aluminium, for instance, is ideal for caramel or for stewing fruit but a curse to clean after

boiling vegetables or using with a steamer. Top-quality enamel pans are good for lots of things, including vegetables and steaming, but not so good as some other types for a stew or for sauce-making. Non-stick pans are perfect for sauces and green vegetables but are not the kind in which to mash potatoes or make caramel. Stainless steel pans are versatile but expensive: in the early ones, food tended to collect at the bottom of the pan where the heat was also concentrated, but today's top class stainless steel pan has no such imperfections. Unlike copper or aluminium, stainless steel is not a good conductor of heat so it is better to choose a pan with a thick aluminium or copper base, especially if you have an electric cooker. Enamelled pans have the great advantage of being decorative, many of them 'oven-to-table', which saves washing up too. There are others as well, excellent cast aluminium pans, for instance.

■ Lids? By and large you're better to buy pans with them than without. You can always leave a lid off but can you always conjure one up?
■ Handles? These also need thought: some pans, especially the heavier type, have a small 'ear' at each side: it's more difficult to drain water out of these without scalding yourself in the steam, but on the plus side they're compact, and some will go both in the oven and on top.

Sauté pans Have an extra-thick base and straight sides and are deeper than a frying pan: they are used for sautéing small steaks, liver, veal scallops, or foods like chicken that are browned then sometimes covered to finish their cooking there. It's therefore better to have one with a lid than without.

■ A strong frying pan will frequently do instead but there may be some dishes you want to make, and can't.
■ Sauté pans are made in tinned copper, cast aluminium, stainless steel, etc., and in various sizes.

POTATO MASHER

One with a round head is an impractical design because, unlike an oval-headed masher which fits snugly into the contours of a pan, you can't get at the potato round the sides. What about the handle? Some, like the first one illustrated below, are round-ended and comfortable to press on with the palm of your hand, others are painful – they make one wonder if some designers have ever themselves tried mashing a big panful of potatoes?

Don't buy   Do buy

POTATO PEELER

Unless you're a wizard at peeling thinly, a peeler is better than a knife because it removes the minimum of skin (in and close beneath which is much of a potato's goodness). For almost magically quick results, the design of peeler illustrated below has, to my knowledge, no equal. Infinitely easier – whether you are left, right or weak-handed – than the old traditional peeler, it will also slice

potatoes wafer-thin for game chips, or is just as efficient used to peel or slice apples, cucumber or any other fruit and vegetable with a thin firm skin. I prefer the metal type (type A) to the plastic because unbreakable and also more comfortable to hold. The version of peeler also illustrated below (type B) is good but not as quick to use as the above, though excellent for getting the strings off runner beans.

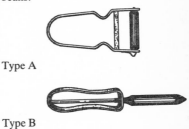

Type A

Type B

PROCESSOR

Has advantages over a food mixer because of its speed and versatility – 1lb/500g dough made in a minute, or the same quantity of vegetables chopped (or cheese grated) in 30 seconds; a cake mixture or pastry made in even less time. Though the capacity isn't large, a food processor seems to become as indispensable to those who have a large household or who entertain a lot, as does a liquidizer or freezer. With optional attachments on certain machines, one can cut chips, squeeze citrus fruits, beat soft ice cream and, depending on the make and model, whisk egg whites and sponge mixtures.

I myself haven't got a food processor because, with a powerful food mixer (which will make 3lbs/1.5kg dough at a time), a Moulinette chopper, and now only a small household, it would be extravagant, but if you're thinking of buying one, you'd be wise (from what I have heard, read, seen and know) to buy a good one: generally speaking, the cheaper makes are less efficient. Given the best, the motor is more powerful, and there is usually a range of speeds, instead of just the one as in the cheaper models. In addition, more attachments are often standard items with the best. It's worth consulting consumer magazines for this sort of thing, if only to highlight the shortcomings or other problems which could affect your choice. Besides cost, quality, size, weight and attachments (either as standard or available extras), it is important also to consider:

1 Whether the machine is easy to operate. If, for instance, you have weak or crippled hands (possibly your reason for buying) avoid a make which needs considerable strength to press down the metal blade.
2 Will the machine stand firmly when operating? Some makes have non-slip feet, others are held down by suction.
3 Are you tall enough to reach the food tube without strain?
4 Are the instructions clear? If complicated, will you be able to make full use of the machine?
5 What, if any, are the cleaning problems? At least one make has its snag, so be sure to ask as well as think and look.

RECIPES

Recipes on filing cards are useful because:

1 You can add to them indefinitely without overflowing from say, *cakes* into *soups*, as one is apt to do in a book.
2 By using dividers, you can have as many sections as you like, in the order you like.
3 You can re-write or tear up any recipe you want to alter or don't want to make again.
4 If you acquire new tips about a recipe, there's usually space to add them.
5 If kept in alphabetical or some kind of order, it is easy to find what you want quickly.
6 There's no book to close up on you just as your fingers are stuck up with dough – or have you got one of those acrylic cookbook holders?

7 A card takes up no space on your table if propped up against the wall, or say, the pepper pot. With three or four plastic covers to keep recipes clean while in use, they won't get splashed either.

■ 6 × 4in/15 × 10cm cards give plenty of room for long or short recipes, unless your writing is giant-sized, and a filing box keeps them clean and orderly. For easy finding, I like to have the name of the dish and any tips on the front, the recipe on the back; that way there's seldom any need to turn a card over once your hands are messy.
■ How do you cope with friends' and magazine recipes without ransacking a drawer to find the one you want? One way is to have a number of large strong envelopes, labelled Soups, Starters, Fish, etc. – and one for Miscellaneous.

REFRIGERATOR

If buying a refrigerator, first be sure (as with a cooker, page 18) to think out your personal needs, otherwise it's all too easy to get carried away by an attractive looking but gimmicky interior – easily-broken, often unnecessary plastic fittings and compartments which take up valuable space. Apart from size, cost and colour, the questions you should perhaps ask yourself are:

1 Will it cope with enough milk and/or wine bottles? Taller than most other bottles, they won't fit in just anywhere.
2 Without removing a shelf (and everything on it), is there somewhere to put a large bowl of soup, a corner of gammon or a good-sized chicken? (Some manufacturers appear to think we only eat bantams and beefburgers.)
3 Is there a salad box and, if so, what size? Will it, if necessary, hold cabbage, carrots and so on as well as salad plants?
4 Is it self-defrosting and easily kept clean?
5 Is the ice compartment big enough to meet ice-cube needs, and to make ice cream if you want to?
6 Do you *need* egg rests? (Eggs are

much better and take up less room if boxed – and boxes will stack.)

A refrigerator is not just for keeping food fresh or cool; it also extends even the best cook's skills. Here's why:

1 Salad foods such as lettuce, watercress or cabbage are crisper and more delicious after being chilled an hour or two. Even slightly limp lettuce may revive.

2 Pastry is easier to manipulate when fat is firmed up between rollings, and will rise better and be lighter because trapped chilled air expands more than warmer air when heated.

3 If chilled, Yorkshire pudding batter, whose raising agent is air, will also rise better when cooked – again because cold air will expand more than warm.

4 One's range of dishes is widened: including making ice cream, masking a mould, setting layers of fruit or fish in a jelly, making dishes containing gelatine on a hot day.

5 Fat-free stock is guaranteed, because most fats will go solid enough by the next day to lift off.

6 There is a constant supply of ice cubes to help cool a mixture quickly if necessary, or to use in iced drinks of all kinds.

7 Nutrients are better retained because enzyme action is slowed down. This is important for something like a green vegetable, which you may occasionally have to prepare in advance of a meal.

■ Some foods keep better in one part of a refrigerator than another, *sometimes* in one particular type of wrapping rather than another: for instance, because the coldest part is nearest the ice box, foods like lettuce which would be affected by frost outdoors are just as likely to suffer if put near the ice box. Some foods are better always stored in the refrigerator, others should be there only temporarily.

■ To prevent solid foods drying out, the evaporation of liquids, and smells passing from one food to another, it is best to keep most things closely covered: foil, film-wrap, a polythene bag, a plastic

(elasticated) pudding basin cover or a container with a lid will meet almost every need. Be sure, though, to leave enough space between foods for the cold air to circulate – it's asking for trouble to pile things up on top of each other.

Here are a few dos and don'ts which may help:

Bacon rashers Keep unwrapped rather than wrapped, in a polythene (or similar) container with lid.

Breadcrumbs, fresh white Will keep for days if not weeks in a polythene bag in the coldest part of the cabinet.

Cheeses Wrapped in foil or polythene, should be taken out of the refrigerator at least an hour or two before serving, otherwise they'll lack flavour. *Soft* cheeses, like Camembert, Brie or Dolcelatte will suffer permanently in texture if refrigerated so are better in a cold larder. (If you must, put them at the very bottom of the cabinet.)

Chives See *herbs,* below.

Cream Keep low down in cabinet, otherwise it may go thick and icy.

Eggs
In shell Those about to be used are usually better in a cold larder than refrigerator, with a few in the kitchen *at room temperature* (see page 143). Refrigerating is the ideal for reserves, or when you go away.
Whole, but mixed up Keep in a small covered container.
Whites Keep in a small polythene container with lid.
Yolks Either mix with 1 tsp. cold water or cover lightly with water if whole. Prevent drying out by covering.

Fats Won't suffer in the coldest part. If short of space, white cooking fats will keep for weeks without refrigerating.

Fish Cover well with foil to prevent smell passing to other foods.

Fruit juices Have more flavour when served chilled.

Herbs Keep well in a salad box or poly-thene bag well away from coldest part of cabinet. They'll keep fresh longer here than in a jug of water in the kitchen.

Leftovers As long as they're covered, will go in almost any part of the cabinet.

Lemons or oranges If refrigerated, retain their natural oils and keep fresher for longer, in a polythene bag away from the coldest part. (Foil is unsuitable as wrap-ping, because acid affects it.) Refrigerated fruits don't produce so much juice: you'll get more out of them if they're at room temperature when squeezed. Surplus juice keeps well in a tiny bottle, or almost indefinitely if you freeze it as ice cubes.

Lettuce and other salad plants Keep best in the compartment or box often pro-vided – otherwise a polythene bag with holes in it, well away from the ice box.

Meat Joints will, if necessary, keep three or four days if covered loosely with foil, and placed low down in the cabinet: remove two hours before roasting, for their best flavour. Cover other cuts of meat with foil or waxed paper.

Milk Should live in the refrigerator unless for drinking: at room temperature it not only has a better flavour but is also more easily and quickly digested, because nearer blood temperature.

Mushrooms Keep well in a heavy-duty (never thin) polythene bag in the least cold part of refrigerator. Wipe with kitchen paper just before using, to remove any grit or sliminess.

Parsley See *Herbs*, above.

Stock Always handy to have, both in liquid form and as ice cubes, if you have a spare ice tray. To store in the freezer, tip out into a thick polythene bag.

Tonic water This and bitter lemon, etc., makes better drinks when served chilled – few people will thank you for a warm gin.

Vegetables Prepared green vegetables (and some others) will keep fresher and longer refrigerated than if exposed to light and air outside it, even if only for half an hour. Wrap in foil or a polythene bag with holes in it and put in lower part of cabinet.

ROLLING PIN

This can affect one's pastry for better or worse. With the 'handle' type, there's a tendency to put too much weight and pressure on the sides of the pastry, not enough in the middle, so the pastry rises unevenly. In addition, because some have as much handle as 'pin', you may only be able to roll a doll-sized piece of pastry.

■ What price the gaily coloured china ones? Being designed to roll (!), they don't even make a practical ornament, never mind a practical rolling pin.
■ A long, no-fuss rolling pin made of beech, as illustrated below, is the least expensive and also the best for the job. Unless you make very large quantities of pastry, a good average size is 16in/40cm long and about 5½ – 6in/14 – 15cm in circumference.

RÔTISSERIE

This, or a spit roaster, as it's alternatively known, is the modern way to cook an old-fashioned roast. The meat is cooked over direct heat, instead of in indirect heat in a closed oven. The great advan-tages of a spit are the flavour, succulence and tenderness of the food, because the initial intense heat seals in the juices – many of which, in oven roasting, escape into the tin. Once the juices are trapped, slower cooking starts because the heat has to penetrate and cook the inside with-out overcooking the outside.

■ Birds need brushing with oil or melted fat first, their fat being under the skin, but there's no need to baste – unless you want additional flavour – because they and meat are self-basting on the rotating spit.

■ 'Accompaniments' are one of the disadvantages of spit-roasting: roast potatoes and Yorkshire pudding, for instance, can't exactly join the beef on the spit so, with an oven on as well, it can be extravagant on fuel.

■ Gravy? If enough fat and juices don't drip into the pan below, you'll have to use another, appropriate, fat to make the roux, then finish with really good stock. Otherwise you could serve a savoury butter (see page 169).

■ Some rôtisseries are fiddling to operate and much more difficult to keep clean than others. This may explain why some people say 'I wouldn't be without a rôtisserie', while others vow 'I'd never have another'. *Caveat emptor!* 'Easy clean' spits are what they claim to be, others may be a curse. If tempted to protect the surrounds with foil, it *could* be dangerous except in the drip pan – better be safe than sorry. If I had a kitchen maid to clear and clean up after me, I'd have a rôtisserie: otherwise not.

SCALES

■ Those which weigh small as well as large quantities accurately are essential for constant success: I fear those who pride themselves in never weighing or measuring anything, can't realize how much *better* they'd cook, and eat, if they did.

■ Balance scales are ideal if you haven't a cash or space problem, when wall scales with a dial may be Hobson's Choice. It pays to know just what you want. What about capacity – 2lbs/1kg, 4lbs/2kg, or larger? Do you like the type with a scoop for easy pouring and frequent washing, or do you prefer weighing ingredients on paper on a *flat* pan?

■ Some of the main advantages of balance scales are:

1 They're accurate enough to weigh ¼oz or 5g precisely.

2 They are generally more spacious than others for weighing bulky ingredients like flour or cornflakes.

3 You can use them almost blindfold: the correct weight is when the two sides are perfectly balanced. (If old scales don't balance precisely when empty, correct by adding the exact weight of plasticine to the 'light' half, then stick the piece underneath).

■ To know more about scales, why not consult a consumer magazine? At least you'll learn the snags of some types and makes, the advantages of others.

SCISSORS

Are as basic as knives and forks. You need a pair strong enough to do the tough jobs, but also pointed enough to do the precise – like taking the core out of a lamb's kidney, or cutting the tightly tied string on a trussed bird. Scissors, dipped in hot water, are good for cutting glacé fruits or marshmallows.

SIEVES

In these days of liquidizers, food processors, choppers and vegetable mills, sieves are not so necessary as in the past, but you may still want:

A wire sieve (about 10 or 12in/25 or 30cm is a good size) to make fresh white breadcrumbs, and for vegetable purées or soup-making, etc.

A nylon or hair sieve to make a seedless fruit purée such as raspberry or blackberry. Unlike a metal sieve, neither of these will discolour or give an unpleasant flavour to the fruit.

SINK

The kitchen sink is a good working height for those of us who are not of the right height to work at standard-height units and tables! I use the sink when:

1 Rubbing fat into flour: you can lift your hands well above the bowl, trapping lots of air.

2 Kneading a bread dough in a mixing

bowl: it is less tiring than at table level.

3 Whipping cream: it is easier, and if you're over-enthusiastic with the whisk, it doesn't matter.

4 Whisking eggs and sugar over near-boiling water. The strain is reduced, and a scald unlikely.

SKEWERS

Skewers' many functions do not include getting knots out of string, which is a good way to lose an eye. Besides using them for meat, game, poultry or even fish, stainless steel skewers can have a varied role. For example:

1 Thread bacon rolls on a skewer for cooking, to serve with game or poultry. It is as easy to handle 12 rolls as one.

2 To use food colouring sparingly, not glaringly, dip skewer in bottle, shaking off a drop or two into whatever you are colouring.

3 Test with a very fine skewer if a fruit cake is cooked.

4 To spike and blanch the leaves of, say, tarragon, if you find it too strong fresh. (You'll need a very short skewer, to fit easily in a small pan.)

5 To garnish, with a straight line of chopped parsley (see page 103).

Brochette The French name for a skewer.

Shish The Turkish name for a skewer – kebab on a skewer. These skewers are flat, long and arrow-headed, to pierce the meat easily. Food doesn't slip about when turned over, as it does on round or butchers' skewers and, because they are so long, they're easier to handle when very hot.

■ The important quality of metal skewers – and the reason why wooden ones are unsuitable – is that they conduct heat through the centre of the meat, cooking it from the inside at the same time as it's being grilled *outside*. If you like kebabs, they're a good investment.

SNIPPIT

One of those really imaginative and excellent gadgets, simple and inexpensive too, to cut open in a second freezer packs made of even the thickest polythene wrap. A clip/handle on one side, a magnet on the other (to attach it to the freezer if one wants to) and a tiny angled razor blade at its head, it does indeed do instantly what it says: snippit.

SPATULAS

Flexible metal spatula Popular with some people for folding whisked egg white into a mixture, or for folding sugar into egg white. I personally prefer a tablespoon.

Plastic or rubber spatulas Marvellous for cleaning out bowls, basins, dishes and pans – even non-stick pans: good if you're slimming as it leaves nothing to lick! Plastic is cheaper than rubber.

Wooden spatulas Sometimes more practical than wooden spoons, particularly for stirring sauces, creaming potato, etc. They are easily scraped off on the edge of a pan as well.

SPIKE-MURPHY

This, of course, takes its name from the slang reference to a potato as a Murphy, because for the Irish the humble spud was at one time their staple diet.

■ This gadget is a pronged stand for baking jacket potatoes: they cook more quickly and evenly than lying on a baking sheet because the metal prongs conduct heat through the centre of each potato. You can buy them for 4 or 6 potatoes. If

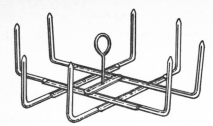

without, spear the potatoes (a gap between each) on to metal skewers.

SPOONS

Measuring spoons Those which come in sets, made according to BSI specifications, must be one of the most controversial subjects in British cookery because they're a different measure from the average-sized spoons most of us have in our kitchen drawer. The standard tablespoon for instance holds 3 teaspoons, whereas your own may hold 4. Many of us don't have a set anyway, and many who do, don't use it.

■ These standard spoons would be incorrect for any recipe book written before 1964 and not revised. Today, most magazine writers and manufacturers – but not all authors – base their recipes on them, but there's no hard and fast rule about it, so how are we to know who uses what unless each author makes it clear, as many of course do?

■ There's also a set of metric spoons but I'm not going to confuse you any more. *Quantities given in this book are based on the assumption that you'll be using traditional spoons from your kitchen drawer.* See also *spoonfuls,* page 82.

Metal tablespoons These are used variously:

1 To fold whisked egg white or sieved flour into a light mixture because a wooden spoon, with its thick edges, would squash out some of the air just beaten in, spoiling the lightness of things like cakes or soufflés.

2 For fried onions and similar pungent foods: a wooden spoon picks up and holds the flavour, passing it afterwards to delicately flavoured foods such as cream.

3 To stir a syrup, because a metal spoon is free of smell and ensures a clear syrup with a pure taste.

4 To turn over grilled meat, because a fork pierces it, delicious juices escape into the grill pan below and, with them, some of the flavour. You'll need *two* spoons for this, or grill tongs if you have them.

■ Table and other metal spoons are *not* used for dishes containing wine or vinegar because of the reaction to the metal and the possibility of spoiling the flavour.

Wooden spoons More practical than metal spoons for many jobs because they are more comfortable to hold and don't transmit heat. Also, being flatter, it is easier to beat thoroughly things like mashed potatoes, or butter and sugar. It pays to buy good quality, because those with a rough unfinished surface absorb flavours from strong foods. A long spoon sticking out over the edge of a small pan can be dangerous; a small spoon will disappear in a large panful of soup, so it is important to have at least three or four of different lengths.

STEAMER

An adaptable one to fit on more than one size of pan, makes it easy to handle steamed foods, and gives you wider scope than steaming direct in a pan. The lid

must fit tightly and the steamer itself must fit the pan snugly, otherwise there won't be enough trapped steam to cook the food properly. I find this more practical than the modern collapsible type, which you may prefer.

STORAGE JARS

These are the best way to keep dry ingredients in good condition. If not in an airtight container, sugars, for instance, will go lumpy, dried fruits will really deserve their name, and nuts will lose their freshness.

■ Glass jars aren't decorative but they're practical; you can *see* when the jar is getting empty and you can see, too, if you've stored sugar in the rice jar!
■ They are less expensive than many and you can name them with labels of your own choice.

STRAINERS

Made in various materials and many different sizes. At least one – say about 5in/12½cm in diameter – is essential and it is better to have more. It depends what you're doing as to which you should use:

1 A tiny fine mesh aluminium one is useful for straining pips out of fruit

juices, or even to strain tea.

2 A medium-sized wire strainer is essential to sieve dry ingredients together and – if this is your only one – for anything that needs straining.

3 A largish-sized wire or nylon strainer is practical for bulky things like boiled rice or pasta.

4 A conical strainer is the ideal type to use for clean pouring into a jug or sauceboat – useful for other liquids too, of course.

TERRINE

Used, of course, to cook terrine or pâté and takes its name from the Latin *terrineus*, 'made of earth', which explains why most of them are made of glazed earthenware. Nowadays they're also made of ovenproof porcelain or vitreous-enamelled cast-iron.

■ Oval, round or rectangular in shape, with a small hole in the lid for steam to escape, all of them are fairly deep but it isn't essential to have one – just a bonus. Providing a dish is deep enough, you can cook pâté in a soufflé dish, casserole, foil freezer dish or even a bread tin, using foil and a lid to cover.
■ To *serve* it direct from the dish, you should have the real thing.

THERMOMETERS

I imagine I am not alone in always having thought that when I bought a thermometer, of all things, it would (unless a rogue) be accurate. How wrong I was! For mass production for the domestic market, even with a top-quality thermometer – and you should buy no other – it appears that some tolerance is allowed. Worse still, it is I'm told always possible that you could buy an instrument which is below even the best normal commercial standards, themselves below what many of us may have assumed they are.

Although your queries or disasters could, therefore, well be caused by your thermometer being inaccurate, they could also equally easily be caused by your incorrect use of it. A possible remedy about the tolerance, say the Electricity Council, is to write to the manufacturer of your thermometer to ascertain the tolerance of their instruments. Thus informed, you could then adapt, by experiment, to the variation of your own instrument. Myself, I find this situation not only difficult to swallow, but also incredible: if nothing more, should not manufacturers be obliged to state on every thermometer package what the tolerance of their particular make is – to protect the good manufacturer as well as you and me? No wonder I threw one sugar-boiling thermometer into my dustbin!

To quote Brannan Thermometers, a leading British manufacturer in this field to whom I wrote:

> There are no standards with regard to quality, design or accuracy of kitchen thermometers. There are, on the other hand, British Standard Specifications applying to, for example, medical thermometers and scientific instruments. There are, however, bodies such as the Design Council who are prepared to give their seal of approval to certain products, and some of our instruments have been designated in this way.

Speaking strictly of their own products, not of other manufacturers or suppliers of imported products, Brannan continued:

> In manufacture, we take considerable precautions to ensure the accuracy of individual instruments, and individual instruments are calibrated at two independent points on the temperature scale to ensure the maximum degree of accuracy in the working range. The degree of accuracy which is applicable to instruments will depend upon the temperature range covered and the length of the measuring scale; generally we would expect an accuracy of between one and two per cent of temperature scale, although at specific points of calibration this accuracy

would be substantially better, and naturally the points selected for calibration tests are relevant to the final use to which the thermometer is to be put . . . There is, however, a more important point . . . We refer to the correct use of the instrument. While an instrument is carefully calibrated and manufactured to assist the purchasers to get the maximum and most satisfactory results, it always assumes that the purchaser follows the instructions given carefully, since the immersion of the thermometer probes, or in the case of the glass thermometers the thermometer stems, to the appropriate height is quite critical to the ultimate result.

Meat thermometer Referring again to the errors we can make, if you have such a thermometer and were to experiment with it, you will find it gives differing results if it is inserted insufficiently into the joint or poultry, or indeed if it is inserted into a part of the poultry which is insufficiently fleshy. The recommendations may be that in the case of a turkey, for example, the probe should be inserted parallel to the thigh bone, or in the case of a chicken it should be inserted through the breast into the stuffed bird. If, however, the bird is not stuffed fully (or at all) the result will be different. All that can be assumed is that if the thermometer is always used in the same way, a constant result will be achieved.

The zones on the dial of the instrument are a guide to assist in determining the degree to which the meat or poultry has been cooked and are not necessarily to everybody's individual taste. There are widely differing views for example as to the exact nature of beef when it is rare – rare to the French may be almost raw to many British – and obviously the cooking temperature has to be taken into account. It may be that you would adopt by choice a position on the dial which is either below or above the indicated temperature on the thermometer.

Oven thermometer It is probably less costly to buy one of these (providing it's accurate) than to pay for even the shortest visit from your gas or electricity company if your thermostat seems out of order or if you want to know the difference in heat between one part of your oven and another at any given temperature. Oven thermometers marked at 5°C intervals can be read more accurately than those marked at greater intervals. See also *oven thermostats*, page 19.

Sugar and deep fat thermometers If accurate, see above, one of these is an investment because it rules out all guesswork. Successful cooking is sometimes a matter of doing the right thing at the right time at the right heat.

■ The most practical thermometer is one which will clip over the edge of a pan – not disappear into the contents – and which you can use for either a sugar syrup or for deep fat. A sugar thermometer for instance may register only up to 420°F/216°C and might break if used for deep fat, while others may register up to 525°F/273°C.

■ As with a meat thermometer, it is vital to follow any instructions given with your instrument. To quote Brannan again (concerning their own sugar thermometer):

It is quite critical that the instrument be immersed up to the immersion line shown on the instrument and if the instrument is in fact immersed to a greater extent the thermometer would tend to read a temperature too high, and if it is immersed to a lesser extent the thermometer will tend to read too low, thereby implying in the case of jam that the setting point has not been reached and indeed may never be reached without burning the jam onto the bottom of the pan.

■ With care, a thermometer will last a lifetime. To avoid severe changes in temperature and danger of breaking, stand it beside the cooker in a large pan or heavy jug of hot water before putting into or after taking out of a very hot syrup. Alternatively, allow it to heat with the contents of the pan, particularly deep fat, when a wet thermometer would be dangerous and cause spluttering.

■ Should you have reason to query the accuracy of your thermometer, try first putting it into hot water, brought gradually to the boil. It should, of course, then register 212°F/100°C.

TIN OPENER

This piece of equipment has a busy time in some homes and is indispensable in all – or would you never, for instance, eat tinned pineapple or follow a recipe containing things like anchovies, condensed milk or tinned tomatoes?

■ A *good* wall-type opener is quick and efficient, easy to use and doesn't play hide and seek. Surely the best long-term investment of the lot. Think before you fix it though, choosing a practical position (not one above the dog basket) before drilling holes in your wall.

TINS

Bread tins Extra-strong, with a reinforced bottom, but not vital to have. I prefer loaf tins (below) for bread-making because I think the bread cooks faster and more evenly in them. If without either type, a stoneware dripping or Oxford marmalade type of jar (straight-sided, no neck), or even a small/medium-sized clay plant pot makes an interesting loaf. Failing all else, you can always mould your dough into a cottage loaf or cob by hand and bake on a baking sheet.

Cake tins Good quality tins are a long-term investment because how a cake bakes will to some extent depend on its tin. Aluminium tins are high on my shopping list. Rightly or wrongly, I think the outside of a cake made in some of the original non-stick tins is less good than that made in conventional or the latest non-stick tins. Gingerbread will bake in a roasting tin but I'd suggest these tins are basic for anyone with a family:

> 2 × 7in/18cm or 1 × 8in/21½cm sandwich cake tins
> 1 × 6½in/16½cm ordinary cake tin
> 1 × 8in/20cm ordinary cake tin
> 1 or 2 sets bun tins
> 1 Swiss roll tin

and I wouldn't be without these too:

> 3 moule à manqué tins, 7, 8 and 9in (18, 20 and 23cm) top diameter (see below)
> 1 × 9in/23cm cake tin for a larger fruit cake

Loaf tins Longer and shallower than bread tins, these come in two standard sizes

> *large* 9 × 5 × 2¾in (22.5 × 12.5 × 7cm)
> *small* 8 × 4 × 2¼in (20 × 10 × 5.5cm)

Used particularly to make tea-breads because such mixtures cook better in a shallowish tin (less risk of a soggy centre), the finished bread not only *looks* nicer but is also easier to slice than when made in a bread tin. If you make bread often, I'd buy three large tins and at least one small. With care, they will last not one, but two lifetimes.

■ For bread-making there's also an excellent, similarly-shaped clay mould – if you can track one down – called the original Suffolk breadmaker.

Moule à manqué May be plain or fluted, round or square, but always with sloping sides. Cakes and sweets turn out easily and the former are child's play to ice because the slides slope outwards when the cake is turned out.

■ Use a large plain one (at least 9in/23cm) for gâteaux, and one or two smaller tins are useful for other cakes or for a wider range of dishes like a steamed soufflé, crème caramel, 'upside-down' cake or other puddings.

Tart tin One with a removable base is excellent for a flan – more expensive, but easier to use than a fluted flan ring if you've never used either before. They're made in various sizes from about 4in/10cm in diameter upwards: all sizes from individual to huge.

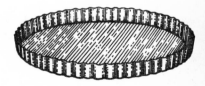

Yorkshire pudding tin Should be the correct size for the quantity of batter used, if you want a really perfect Yorkshire. For ½pt/250ml batter, use a tin as illustrated below, about 10 × 7 × 1¼in deep (25½ × 18 × 3cm). This is much better than a roasting tin, which may be larger and is certainly deeper.

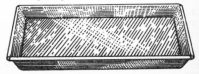

■ Alternatively, why not use individual Yorkshire pudding tins?

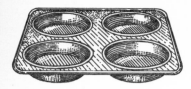

TRUSSING NEEDLE

This is essential if you like or have to draw and truss your own birds. If you can do them properly there are several advantages over the oven-ready bird: you can pull the sinews out of the legs, sew in stuffings and make sure the bird will rest steadily on the dish when carved.

■ You may want a lesson in drawing and trussing, the technique being difficult to grasp from a book. See page 252.

TUBES

Icing tubes May be of metal or plastic. Plastic tubes are much cheaper and less easily damaged but, due to the nature of plastic, you don't get the range of beautiful shapes available in metal. Choose these carefully when you buy. I don't know whether it's because of careless customers or shop assistants, but too many are faulty in some shops. Treat all with kid gloves to prevent damage, because the slightest imperfection produces a blurred result.

■ Fussy about all my equipment, I'm a real crank about metal tubes! They're not things to bury amongst the washing up, or to leave someone else to dry. Wash them under a warm tap the moment you've finished icing and, if necessary, soak rather than poke before drying in a warm place and putting carefully away.

■ Although a professional may have a complete assortment of over a hundred tubes, those of us less ambitious can accomplish quite a lot with a few simple ones:

No. 1 writing tube, to make thin lines, fine stems, scrolls, stamens on large flowers, and particularly for fine writing on a cake.

No. 2 writing tube, for bolder writing than above, for thicker lines and for the centres of certain flowers etc.

One or two *open star tubes* – easy for a beginner – to pipe stars, scrolls, border designs, floral sprays, etc.

Writing tube

Open star tube

One or two *closed star tubes*, say a six-point and an eight-point star, to pipe stars, shells, lettering or a bold border, etc.

Closed star tube

Meringue tubes A larger edition of an icing tube, in metal or plastic – the type you need to pipe things like duchess potatoes, large stars of whipped cream, certain petits fours, butter cream fillings on cakes or, of course, meringues and anything similar.

■ You could get by with three: one *star* tube, one *rope* and one *plain* ½in/1¼cm tube, the plain one for things like éclairs or macaroons.

TWEEZERS

Those from your dressing table drawer are perfect for decorating a cake with small, non-sticky things like silver balls or mimosa, to place each precisely where you want. Culinary tweezers (more like miniature sugar tongs) keep your fingers clean while hulling strawberries, or may help you pluck the strong wing or tail feathers of a pheasant, for instance.

VEGETABLE MILL

See *mills*, page 32.

WEIGHTS

See *scales*, page 41.

WHISKS

Are of all shapes and sizes and for all sorts of purposes. The serious cook will want several different types. The more wiry they are, the more air they will entangle, which explains why the balloon and coil-rim whisks are so excellent. Here are some of the well known:

Balloon whisks Generally acknowledged to be the best for egg whites, giving greater volume than most others and consequently making lighter dishes. The 10 or 12in/25 or 30cm size is manageable and efficient for 6 egg whites but a 9in/23cm whisk may be more generally useful. Modern stainless steel whisks are light and so easy to handle compared with the heavy, old type. If difficult to track down, try a catering equipment shop.

Coil-rim whisks The type illustrated is *my* favourite. If I could only have one whisk, this efficient, inexpensive, nearly all-purpose design would be my choice.

Electric hand-mixer Invaluable for whisking eggs and sugar (or other mixtures) over a pan of hot water. Also to whisk mixtures into which a hot syrup is poured from a height, e.g. crème au beurre mousseline, American frosted icing.

Electric (fixed) whisk Not in the same class as the best hand whisk, producing a dense mass of egg white rather than a light fluffy one – so you can't make such feather-light mixtures with it. It is also less good than an electric hand whisk, which can be circulated round the bowl to incorporate more air. I wouldn't be without one, though, because at times one is too busy or too exhausted to use anything else. See also *mixer*, page 33.

Rotary whisks Seems to be one of the most popular of the lot though it's difficult to know why – perhaps because they're so easy to use or because they're expensive, and people think they *must* be good! One can't compare results with those of a balloon or coil-rim whisk, which give far greater volume and much lighter egg white, cream, etc. Besides being inefficient, you need both hands, which is sometimes impossible, and sometimes – over boiling water, for instance – dangerous.

Whipper or batter whip Of strictly limited use. Although some people use one for everything, I personally wouldn't use it for anything because, due to its structure, you can't incorporate as much air with it as with many other whisks. You could use a wooden spoon for a batter, otherwise I can think of little for which a coil-rim whisk wouldn't be better.

Wire whisks Good for whipping cream as well as for mixing partly frozen ice cream mixtures, beating eggs, dried soups and lumpy sauces. Use also for sauce-making, to whisk hot liquid into the roux. They are made in various sizes from about 7½in/19cm upwards; a simplified form of the balloon whisk.

ZESTER

More efficient than anything else for scraping the zest off citrus fruits. See also *zest*, page 85.

2

Terms and techniques

A child can ride a bicycle if he's taught; an adult may still be walking if never taught. And so it is with cooking: there's no real magic in it but you'll get there faster if you're skilled, whether rolling pastry, chopping parsley, whisking egg whites or folding them, when correctly whisked, into another mixture.

If your creamed mixtures *will* curdle, you're afraid to use deep fat, you're not sure why some foods are blanched or others are given names like 'à la lyonnaise' or 'à la diable', I hope you may find the answer here.

AGITATING

Is just what it sounds like – gently jerking a saucepan up and down and round and about, to make sure that the contents are moved about enough to cook evenly without being stirred. When agitating a *frying* pan, the movement is a backward and forward slide.

AL DENTE

Is an Italian term meaning, literally, 'to the tooth', i.e. with a little bite, slightly crunchy. It is used to describe foods, particularly rice, pasta and certain vegetables, which should be cooked until firm to the bite, but not soft.

ANTIPASTO

'Before the pasta', this is the Italian name for *hors d'oeuvres* or appetizers.

BAKING

Baking and roasting are really the same things these days, even if we do seem a little crazy to talk of baked ham, but roast beef, lamb and everything else. Baking, the term we apply mostly to cakes, pastry and so on, is, of course, cooking in a current of air by dry heat.

■ Bread, pastry and things like scones and small cakes which need a hot oven are best cooked near or at the top of a traditional (unfanned) oven; fruit cakes and meringues, etc., which need a much cooler oven, are best baked at or near the bottom. According to British Gas 'the middle of the oven is equivalent to the thermostat setting'. Fan-assisted ovens have an even temperature throughout (see *cookers*, page 20).

BAKING BLIND

Means baking empty, like flan cases which are baked first, and filled later.

■ A double layer of tissue paper filled with haricot beans (preferably), dried cherry stones or split peas, is softer and damages the pastry less than greaseproof paper. Crumpled-up foil can be used alone, quickly and easily, but I don't like it because it so easily spoils one's carefully fluted flan.

BARDING

A way of protecting lean meat and the breast of dry birds with slices of fat – preferably pork fat – before braising or roasting, to keep the meat juicy and tasty. The fat – bacon fat if you like – needs tying on, otherwise it falls off when it cooks and shrivels.

BARQUETTES

Are boat-shaped tartlet shells, very tedious to cut if you don't know how, easy when you do:

1 Line up several boat-shaped tins just touching each other.

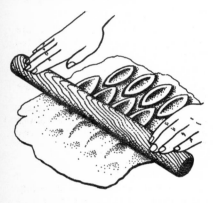

2 Lay the rolled out pastry on top of them – a strip wide and long enough to cover the whole line.
3 Roll carefully from one end to the other with a rolling pin, to cut each boat on the sharp edges of its tin. Place pastry neatly inside.

BATTER

Comes from the French word *battre*, to beat. Batter for Yorkshire pudding or pancakes is lighter made with half milk and half water instead of all milk.

■ A batter will rise better if it is chilled in the refrigerator rather than used at room temperature, because, when heated, cold air expands more than warm air – and air is its sole raising agent.

BEURRE MANIÉ

This sounds more elaborate than the simple butter and flour mixture it is. Used to thicken sauces, soups or the liquor from cooked foods. It's useful too if, by mistake, you make a soup or sauce too thin: just work together with a fork equal quantities of butter and flour, drop small balls of it one at a time into the sauce or soup, and whisk it continually with a wire whisk to blend it in rapidly. Then boil the liquid for a minute or so, to burst the starch grains in the flour and so thicken the liquid.

■ If a dish contains fish or meat, blend in the beurre manié by gently shaking and turning the pan, otherwise you may end up with fish purée.

BIND

To bind is to add egg, flour, potato flour or cornflour, etc. to a liquid to thicken it, *or* to hold a mixture of foods together with egg, melted fat, mayonnaise or other sauces. Fish cakes, for instance, if made without egg, disintegrate when fried, but those made *with* egg will stay whole because the egg coagulates when heated, binding the mixture together.

BLANCHING

Involves using boiling water in various ways for various purposes.

To remove fruit skins, by covering fruit for a given time with boiling water, sometimes aside from the heat; e.g. tomatoes 10 seconds, peaches 10 – 30 seconds, almonds 1 – 2 minutes if boiled, or 3 – 4 minutes aside from the heat, stirred well.
To cook or partly cook a food, prior to cooking by another method, by putting food into boiling water for a limited time, e.g. potatoes before roasting or sautéing, cauliflower florets before making fritters, sweet peppers before stuffing.
To have a cooked vegetable almost ready to serve, see *refreshing*, page 77.

To remove the strong flavour and smell of some foods, also to make some of them more digestible, by bringing to the boil in cold water and then discarding water, e.g. tripe, or by plunging into boiling water and boiling for a limited time, e.g. sweet peppers, celery, onions, turnips.

To clean and remove saltiness, by bringing food to the boil in cold water, then discarding water, e.g. salt pork, smoked bacon joint.

To make firm before cooking, by bringing to the boil in cold water before plunging into more cold water, e.g. sweetbreads.

To prevent deterioration of foods in a freezer, by plunging into deep, fast-boiling water for a limited time before 'refreshing' and sealing in containers, e.g. numerous vegetables.

BLENDING

Has various meanings. It may mean mixing things together in a liquidizer or blender, or variously combining different ingredients or mixtures smoothly together.

■ A basic rule in cookery is that mixtures should be of a similar consistency if they are to blend successfully together: neither whisked egg white nor over-whipped cream, for instance, will combine properly with a mixture which is much more liquid. This explains why a cold sweet recipe often directs that a mixture should be showing signs of setting before the whisked whites are added.

■ Dry ingredients blend best if sieved together. If using a spoon, the back of a tablespoon does in seconds what the tip of a teaspoon may take much longer to do.

■ To blend a liquid into sieved flour and other dry ingredients, make a well in the middle of the flour, pour the liquid into it – not too much at a time – and gradually draw in all the surrounding flour by stirring in an increasingly larger circle. If you're using a very small amount of flour, as for flour and water thickening, it's quicker and easier to use a fork than a wooden spoon.

BOILING

Doesn't always mean exactly what the word implies. Water, if boiling, is turbulent on the surface with bubbles breaking all over it, but meat and fowl harden, and fish breaks up and becomes watery if boiled like this throughout the cooking time. This is why boiled beef, for instance, is actually boiled for only 5 minutes, then simmered for the remaining time; and why stews are *simmered*, the liquid showing only the slightest movement on the surface.

■ Most foods, including vegetables, are tenderized in a given time by boiling slowly in a covered pan, bubbles breaking gently all over the surface.

■ Rice and jam, which boil fast, are, of course, cooked without a lid, because they would boil over if covered.

■ Liquids to be reduced are also mostly boiled fast and uncovered, otherwise they'd take ages to evaporate. See *reducing*, page 77.

BONING

Boning a bird is a tedious and rather difficult process until one knows the ropes – or should I say the bones – and is one of those jobs I'm happy to watch someone else do! You need a short sharp knife to *scrape* the flesh off the bones rather than cut it off, to avoid piercing the skin. It's quicker and easier to do too if the bird is drawn after it is boned. The drumstick bones are sometimes left in, to keep a bird a better and more realistic shape when stuffed. See also page 252.

BOUILLON

The French term for stocks or broths, from *bouillir*, to boil.

■ Bouillon, or stock, is used as a basis for soups and sauces, and bouillon cubes are just well seasoned stock cubes.

BOUQUETS GARNI

Are exorbitant to buy, and not nearly as good as a fresh one made from herbs in your garden, or even partly from dried herbs in your store-cupboard. It surprises me that even people with a garden will buy them, when basically all one needs are three herbs – ½ bayleaf, a spray of thyme, 3 or 4 sprigs of parsley – and a small square of clean cloth, about the size of a baby's handkerchief, easily cut, several at a time, from a piece of old cotton sheet.

■ Be sure to include the parsley stalks, because they carry more flavour than the leaf: simply roll the herbs up in the cloth, knotting the ends tightly.
■ Vary as you like by adding other herbs, a clove of garlic, or the odd spice, especially a clove.
■ Adjust the proportion of herbs to the nature of the dish, but use thyme and bayleaf sparingly because they're strong, and may dominate rather than improve the flavour of a dish.
■ Use a bouquet garni in soups, sauces and stews, but be sure to remove it before serving the dish – or before liquidizing soup. If you're likely to forget, tie it with thread to the pan handle.

BRAISING

The French equivalent of English pot-roasting; a combination of a type of stewing, and roasting. It is a good way to cook choice cuts of very lean meat, cheaper cuts of meat, elderly game or poultry, whole fish and certain vege-tables. Meat, particularly beef or any-thing tough, is often marinated first to tenderize and flavour it. Generally speaking, these are the how's and why's:

The pan A French braising pan is ideal, otherwise use a cast-iron casserole, or other dish or pan which has a tight-fitting lid and in which one can both fry the meat over direct heat and then cook it in the oven. If the lid doesn't fit tightly, flavour-ing juices will escape.

Meats Are fried for a minute or two in very hot fat – ends as well as both sides of a joint – to seal in the juices. (This is a vital part of successful braising.) The meat afterwards cooks (in steam) on a bed of vegetables in a small amount of liquid, with seasoning and other flavourings.

Vegetables Act as a base for the meat to stand on, and to flavour the meat and cooking liquid (used later for the sauce), not themselves to be served. To prevent them going mushy during cooking, slice onion thickly, carrots longways in half, cut a leek in half, and a celery stem into pieces. The prepared vegetables are then fried (after frying and removing meat) for just a few minutes, to flavour them and to absorb the fat. See also *mirepoix*, page 75.

Liquid Wine, stock, cider, or whatever the recipe calls for, is added and heated to simmering point before placing the meat on top. There should be just enough to cover the vegetables, and to baste and keep the meat moist, and finally to use in an accompanying sauce.

The oven Should be slowish, about gas 3, 325°F/165°C. This all-round heat is better than direct heat under a pan on top of the cooker because the meat cooks more evenly. Cooking time is about 25 per cent longer than for roasting. Finally the heat is increased for a short time and the pan lid removed, to 'roast' the meat.

■ If you feel it's too extravagant to heat your oven for a very small bird or piece of meat, cook it over direct heat but turn the meat over occasionally, to cook evenly.

BREAKFAST

Means 'break fast', and that's what the whole family needs after a gap of 10 – 12 hours or more since the last meal. The blood sugar and other blood nutrients will have fallen to base level, so if you start off the day empty, it's like trying to start an engine without fuel.

■ If you want your children to do their best at school – and what parent doesn't? – the first step is yours. Give them a proper breakfast because without, it is more difficult to concentrate. Besides, nearly all of us look better, feel better and work more efficiently when we have, literally, broken our fast.

BROILING

Is the American term for grilling. A broiler for instance is a chicken young enough to be grilled, hence its name.

CALORIE

Is simply a measurement of heat or energy which the body can obtain from a given amount of food. If the body takes in more calories than needed or used, then the surplus is stored as fat. The principle of wise slimming is, therefore, to reduce the intake of calories and force the body to use up its excess store of fat.

■ Foods like green vegetables, radishes, cucumber, gherkins, celery and unsweetened fruit juices are very low in calories, so some of these may be useful for snacks and nibbling, if nibble you must. On the other hand, if you feel like feasting on a bag of peanuts, you may think again when you know each nut means 5 calories down the hatch. Below, in case you're interested, are just a few more foods and their calorific values:

Food	Quantity	Calories
biscuits .	on average, each	50
bread, small loaf	3 thin slices	100
butter	½oz/15g	100
cheese, Cheddar	1oz/25g	100
chocolates	average, each	50
cream, double	1 tablespoon	100
eggs, boiled or poached	each	100

eggs, fried	each	200
jams	1 rounded tablespoon	100
milk, fresh	1 small tumblerful	100
pork chops, lean	average, each	200
potatoes, chipped	6, average size	100
potatoes, boiled or jacket	medium size	100
sherry or vermouth	small glass	100
spirits	1 'nip'	100
sugar	¾oz/20g	100
tea	without milk or sugar	nil

CANAPÉ

French for a sofa or settee – something to sit on. That's what canapés are: small 'platforms' on which sit tasty cocktail snacks, *hors d'oeuvres* or savouries. They may be shapes of pastry, or of buttered, fried or toasted bread.

■ Fried bread canapés to be served cold are better fried in oil than butter because it doesn't congeal when cold; and if you want a filling to sit on top without falling off, make a hollow in the middle of each while they're still hot – using the end of the handle of a wooden spoon, press down the middle in up-and-down movements.

CARVING

Said to be one of the least understood of the arts of the table, and I can believe it. Earlier generations thought skilful carving so essential that it was looked upon as an indispensable part of a well-born man's education. Nowadays, with large joints of meat so expensive, and with so much cut-up meat sold by supermarkets, many young people lack any real opportunity to learn.

■ To make the best of any joint or fowl, you shouldn't underestimate the value of good carving: you'll get more and better servings from the meat, it will be more tender and will have better flavour. Bad carving wastes and spoils good food.

■ To carve well, you need two things: a really sharp carving knife and some knowledge of anatomy. As a general principle, nearly all meat is carved *across* the grain, because this shortens the meat fibres, making each slice more tender. Leg of lamb or mutton is the exception: it can be carved either parallel to *or* at right angles to the bone.

■ The slices should be as large and of as even thickness as possible, some meats being carved thicker than others to provide their perfect flavour:

■ *Lamb and mutton* (and as a general rule *venison*, depending on the cut) are sliced ⅛–½in/3mm–1¼cm thick, thicker than *beef* or *veal* which are sliced thinly, at the most ⅛in/3mm. Though it depends on the cut, *pork* is generally sliced as beef. *All cold meat* should be cut thinly and evenly. *Duck* (page 260) and *goose*, because of their different structure, are carved quite differently from a bird like *chicken* or *pheasant*. A small *turkey* may be carved like chicken but a large bird is carved differently because the limbs also must be carved, being too large to eat whole (see page 273).

CHALAZAE

Plural of *chalaza*. The chalazae are the two 'threads' which hold an egg yolk in the middle of the white, so preventing the yolk being broken easily. See *eggs*, page 143.

CHAMBRÉ

Means 'at room temperature', the temperature at which red wines are served, and to which they are brought gradually, over a period of hours, from cellar temperature.

CHOPPING

Can take various forms according to the food in question. Onions (page 189), jelly (page 67), chives and parsley, for instance, all require different techniques.

■ You only need a sharp knife – preferably a French cook's knife (page 31) – and a chopping board for herbs, for *most* of which the action is basically the same as for mint or parsley.

Chives As if to defy what I've just said, these are chopped easily and quickly with scissors: bunch several tightly together, break bunch in half to shorten, and then cut across finely with sharp scissors.

Mint Pile several leaves up on top of each other, roll them tightly together (like a magazine for the post) and slice finely first one way, then the other, before sprinkling lightly with a pinch of granulated sugar to make them easier to chop. Now hold your knife at both ends: using the heel of the knife to chop, hold the point down on the board with the left hand and move the right hand in rapid up-and-down movements, and at the same time backwards and forwards in an arc-like direction. Scrape the mint continually into a heap again with the knife, chopping it until very fine.

Parsley For best flavour and to make an attractive garnish, parsley should be very finely chopped. Bunch the washed, dried parsley heads tightly together on the chopping board with your left-hand thumb and fingertips. Keeping the point of the knife firmly on the board, move the right hand up and down and at the same time backwards and forwards in an arc-like direction. All the time, still with your thumb and fingertips, keep the parsley bunched until in much smaller pieces. Now change your grip and hold the knife at both ends as for mint above, and continue as for mint. Coarsely cut parsley is literally unpleasant to eat – the reason no doubt why so many people say they dislike it.

CLARIFYING

Means, of course, to purify.

Butter Mainly because of salt in it, butter browns and burns at a lower temperature than many other fats (see page 88) so, even if you're frying or sautéing in it the tenderest or most fast-cooking of foods such as croûtons, par-boiled vegetables, fish fillets or lamb's liver, it is still likely to turn brown before cooking is completed. Clarified or saltless butter, both of which you can heat to a considerably higher temperature *without* browning, are therefore of paramount importance to good cooking: and for certain dishes may be absolutely essential. Clarified butter, rid of the elements (salt, sediments and residue of buttermilk) which cause butter both to burn readily and to go rancid is, therefore, not only a good cooking medium but also keeps a long time, so it's worth doing a quantity while you're about it, refrigerating any surplus. Although by clarifying salted butter, you lose roughly 25% of it, whereas with salt-less butter there's neither waste nor work, you may still like to know how to clarify butter. Here's one way:

1 Melt a lump of butter (however much you want to do), cut into smallish pieces, in a frying pan or strong saucepan over low heat.
2 Meanwhile, line a strainer with a piece of wet butter-muslin and rest it over a basin.
3 When the butter is hot, skim off any foam with a spoon as it appears, and when the foam starts to subside – but before the butter changes colour – strain it.
4 Transfer to a suitable storage jar and leave to cool. Cover and refrigerate.

■ Use any sediment left – in pan or on muslin – to flavour and enrich soups and sauces.
■ Clarified butter also makes an airtight, edible and effective seal for preserving potted meats and fish pastes. To use, stand the jar in a saucepan of water and heat it gently just until the butter is liquid enough to pour over the well-chilled pot-

ted food. Leave to set, cover and refrigerate.

Margarine May need clarifying for frying, should you particularly prefer it to oil or a cooking fat, because the milk products in it burn at high temperatures.

Dripping Needs clarifying for deep fat frying especially, because the impurities in it burn at high temperatures. It also, of course, keeps longer when purified. See *dripping*, page 96.

COATING

Coating foods evenly with sauce is easy if you start at one end of one side, and pour the sauce rather quickly over the food in up-and-down lines.

■ For coating foods which are to be fried, see *frying*, deep fat and shallow, page 64.

COMPÔTE

Stewed fruit with a refinement: the shape of the fruit is preserved. While stewed apple may, for instance, simply be sliced apple cooked with sugar and a small quantity of water until tender, compôte of apple implies whole, halved or quartered apples poached in a previously made syrup until *just* tender. (A little lemon juice in the syrup – 1 teaspoon per ¼pt/125ml – helps to prevent fruit breaking up.) Thicken the syrup after the fruit is cooked if you like, using arrowroot (page 87), cornflour or potato flour: 2 level teaspoons/10ml to ¼pt/125ml syrup. Pour over the fruit while hot, then leave to cool and set.

CONCASSER

French term meaning to chop roughly or to break up by pounding in a mortar: tomato concassé for instance is the roughly chopped up flesh of a tomato which has been peeled, seeded and juiced. You may need it like this for a garnish, as an omelette filling, or for any dish which would be spoilt by a tomato's wateriness and rather bitter seeds.

CONSISTENCIES

Play a much more important part in cookery than many people realize, because it is frequently upon just this that the success or failure of a dish depends. Knowing the right consistency – what a mixture should look like or feel like – is one of the main skills of a good cook, and something most of us can only learn by experience.

■ Over-thick soups and sauces are just as unappealing as runny. The latter take longer to adjust but the remedies are all there – beurre manié, egg yolks and cream, flour and water thickening, arrowroot, cornflour or potato flour – whichever is appropriate.
■ Cold sweets, especially creamy ones, ice creams, puddings, cakes, scones, pastry and doughs, etc. are affected for better or worse by the amount of liquid used, or by the amount of beating, whisking, whipping or kneading done to acquire the right consistency at each stage.
■ Mixtures won't combine successfully if of different consistencies: flour and water thickening for example will only blend properly with a liquid if it is liquid itself, and half-whipped cream blends more evenly with cold dessert mixtures than fully-whipped cream, because the latter is much stiffer than the mixture itself.
■ *Coating consistency* usually implies a sauce just thick enough to coat the back of a wooden spoon smoothly.
■ *Dropping consistency* would be better described as flicking consistency because it implies a mixture which can be *flicked* off a spoon, not one which is soft enough to drop off without help.
■ If you want to know any more about consistencies, see *blending*, also *ribbon, to the*, pages 53 and 78.

COURT BOUILLON

An aromatic liquid used mostly to poach whole or large pieces of fish: to give flavour they would lack if simply poached in water. It may contain wine, lemon juice or vinegar, sliced onion and carrot, herbs and spices, garlic, salt, etc. As its name implies, it is a type of bouillon (or stock).

■ Here is a simple recipe, to be prepared in advance and set aside ready to use:

4pts/2 litres water
1lb/450g carrots, sliced
2 medium-sized onions or 3 shallots, sliced
1 bayleaf
3 or 4 sprigs parsley, washed
1 sprig thyme
1½ozs/40g cooking salt
¼pt/125ml wine vinegar or cider vinegar
12 peppercorns

Method

Put everything except the peppercorns into a saucepan, bring slowly to the boil and simmer for 1 hour. Add peppercorns 10 minutes before end of cooking. Strain and cool.

■ It's a pity to waste the liquid from the cooked fish. Strained, it will easily keep a week in the refrigerator, or will freeze well, as ice cubes. Then you can use it to cook more fish, or you could make a tasty sauce with it.

TO CREAM

To cream is to soften or beat a mixture until it has the consistency of whipped cream. Creaming generally means beating a fat by itself, or with sugar, to trap air and make the fat or mixture smooth and fluffy enough to blend easily with other ingredients.

■ Caster sugar blends with fat better than granulated, because it is finer, smoother and more like the fat in texture. That's why a creamed cake made with caster has a more even texture than one made with granulated.
■ When creaming fat and sugar, the sugar won't fly about so much if you cream the fat by itself first.
■ It saves time and energy – and you'll

probably end up with a better cake – if your butter or margarine is soft; which either means thinking in advance, to have the fat at warm-room temperature, or using a soft type of margarine. When soft, it is then just a matter of minutes to cream it with the sugar as above. Only when they are completely blended, will they accept the gradually added whisked eggs without the mixture curdling. (As long as the eggs are warm, and the fat and sugar are properly creamed, as many as a dozen eggs can be added to a pound/450g of fat without the mixture curdling.)

■ If a mixture looks like curdling – curdled, it will make a heavy cake – beat in a spoonful or so of the measured, sieved flour. This may correct it.

■ Be sure to clean down the sides of the mixing bowl and the wooden spoon (or beater) from time to time, otherwise there'll be lumps of unblended mixture. See also *cakes, creamed mixtures*, page 317, and *all-in-one-mixtures*, page 318.

CRESCENTS

Usually made of fried bread or puff pastry, and used as a garnish. Cut quickly with a plain scone cutter, like this:

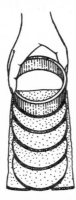

CROÛTE

French for a crust. A small round or other shape of fried or toasted bread, used to garnish or as a base for a savoury mixture. (Croûtons, page 163, are tiny croûtes.)

En croûte In a crust, this crust being of pastry: food wrapped in pastry before being baked, e.g. lamb chop en croûte, pâté en crôute.

DECORATING

See *garnishing*, page 65.

DEGLAZE

To deglaze is to add liquid – wine, stock, lemon juice, water or cream – to a pan or roasting tin in which food has been fried, sautéd or roasted: scrape into the liquid all the tasty particles and juices sticking to the bottom and sides of the pan, then use this as the perfect complement to the food.

DÉGORGER

A French word which doesn't exactly translate in culinary terms, but means 'to clear' or 'to purify'. Sweetbreads for instance are soaked in cold water to remove impurities like blood; aubergines, courgettes and cucumbers are sliced, put in a colander, sprinkled with salt, covered with a weighted plate and left to stand about an hour, to make them less watery and bitter. Shake them afterwards and dry if necessary.

DEGREASE

To degrease is to skim the fat off liquids such as stock, sauces, soups and gravies. Fat floating about on the top of any of these can spoil an otherwise lovely dish, so skim it off with soft absorbent kitchen paper or with paper tissues if you haven't anything else.

■ Better still, refrigerate stock overnight and lift the fat off in a sheet the next day. Whatever you want it for, you then know it is fat-free. (*Most* fats solidify.)

■ A quick way to degrease a hot liquid is to put a piece of butter muslin in a colander or a large strainer, fill it with ice cubes and pour the liquid over them into a bowl below.

DICING

See *slicing and dicing*, page 81.

DREDGING

Similar to dusting, but implies a heavy coating instead of a light sprinkling.

DUSTING

Dusting foods, cake tins or a pastry board, etc. with sugar or flour implies a light sprinkling, not a coating. Too much can easily spoil the consistency, flavour and/or appearance of whatever it is you're making or doing.

ENTRÉE

Literally the 'entry' to a meal; a dish served before the main course. Complete in itself, it is all served on one dish, usually with a sauce, and artistically garnished with flavourful, colourful vegetables, etc.

■ Dishes which in days gone by were served only as entrées, are frequently served nowadays as the main course. There's no need to say why.

FAGGOT OF HERBS

The English term for a bouquet garni, but now seldom heard of.

FARCE

Just another word for stuffing, used to give foods extra flavour, to offset fattiness (say of goose or pork) or dryness (say of turkey), to make food go further, or sometimes to make a main dish out of a minor ingredient, e.g. Dolmas.

■ While many of us are adventurous if we stuff veal or plaice with forcemeat, or loin of pork with sage and onion stuffing, the French use a vast variety of stuffings to bring new life to all kinds of food. They bring a fresh dimension to eating and it's fun to experiment with new combinations.

FATS

Saturated, polyunsaturated fats and cholesterol are words we often hear these days. Medical research has shown that many people who have suffered from heart attacks have a high level of certain types of fat in their bloodstream, including the fat-related substance, cholesterol. On a long-term basis, the cholesterol level in the blood can be lowered by avoiding foods high in saturated fatty acids and using foods high in polyunsaturated fatty acids instead.

■ All the different fats we find in foods contain these substances called fatty acids, which are of two main types:
Saturated fats are the fats which contain a high proportion of saturated fatty acids and are usually solid at room temperature. (Some vegetable oils are exceptions, e.g. coconut oil and groundnut oil, which solidify when refrigerated.) Foods of animal origin and some other foods contain saturated fats. All hard margarines contain saturated fats. In fact the very process of hardening the fat in the manufacture of margarine from vegetable oils involve the 'saturation' of the fat. The physical and chemical changes taking place during hardening mean that the fatty acids are converted to the saturated form. See chart below.
Polyunsaturated fats are those which contain a high proportion of polyunsaturated fatty acids and which are very soft or even liquid at room temperature. They are often called oils rather than fats. These are found naturally in many seeds and nuts, or in products made from them, such as corn oil, sunflower oil. Polyunsaturated fat is usually of plant origin. Margarines and oils which contain a high proportion of polyunsaturated fats are clearly labelled.

■ Olive oil and groundnut oil are *mono-unsaturated fats*. They are regarded as neutral in terms of coronary heart disease, i.e. neither harmful nor beneficial.

■ The type of fat eaten doesn't affect the body weight in any way: all fats and oils, whether of the saturated or unsaturated kind, have the same calorie content.

Food guide for those with heart problems	
Foods high in saturated fat	Foods high in unsaturated fat (*high in poly*unsaturated fat*)
butter milk yoghurt cream hard cheeses, e.g. Cheddar, Stilton	
fatty meats such as pork, sausages, duck, goose	
	*oily fish such as herring, mackerel, tuna

dripping
lard
all hard margarines
most soft margarines
most white cooking fats
oils: coconut
    solid
suet
	*sunflower oil margarines
	*sunflower oil white cooking fats
	
	oils: *corn
	    *cotton seed
	     groundnut
	     olive
	    *safflower
	    *sesame
	    *soya
	    *sunflower
	    *walnut

coconut cashew nuts	*most nuts, e.g. almonds, walnuts
egg yolk (particularly rich in cholesterol)	
chocolate	

baked foods made with butter,
  margarine or egg yolks, e.g. pastry,
  cakes, biscuits
	baked foods made with corn oil and
	  without egg yolks or chocolate

FÉCULE

Particularly implies potato flour – *fecula* is a very fine flour usually extracted from potatoes – but is sometimes loosely interpreted to mean other starches like arrowroot, rice flour or cornflour. Fécule is used to bind and thicken soups and sauces.

FLAMBÉ

Means 'in flames', and indicates the flaming of brandy or other spirits, used to flavour foods.

■ Warm the spirit or liqueur in a spoon, ladle, or very small pan (copper or cast aluminium if you have one) so that, when lit, it bursts into flame instantly, otherwise it won't ignite. Shake and rotate the pan so that the flames spread.
■ The reason for flaming is to burn up the alcohol (and take away the rawness) and concentrate the flavour, which will permeate the food.
■ Follow any other given directions.

FLEURONS

Small shapes of puff pastry, usually crescents, used as a garnish. It isn't worth making pastry specially, because they take so little – better to cut a strip off some partly thawed frozen puff pastry, and pop the rest back into the freezer. See *crescents*, page 59.

FLOUR, SEASONED

Flour mixed with a generous amount of salt and pepper, used to coat fish, meat, poultry, etc. It gives flavour, protects food from heat when frying, makes egg and breadcrumbs adhere better to foods, or acts as a slight thickening in stews, etc.

■ To give seasoned flour more pep, there's nothing to stop you adding a hint of cayenne, ground mace or nutmeg, etc.

FOLDING

Quite different from stirring, and is the customary term used to describe quite a complicated skill which many recipe books take for granted, but which many of us may not know how to do.

■ You may be adding sieved flour to beaten eggs and sugar, whisked egg whites to a soufflé, or sugar to whisked egg whites: whichever it is, the movement is always the same. It's best to use a tablespoon or metal spatula because, unlike a wooden spoon, these have a thin sharp edge which will cut through the ingredients without expelling any of the air just beaten in. That's why it is sometimes called cutting in the egg whites.

■ Hold the spoon so that its sharp edge cuts down through the mixture. Instead of going round and round as when stirring, stir once round the outside, then bring the spoon sharply through the middle, towards you, turning it 'bowl' upwards and lifting it right out. Continue doing this until the two mixtures are blended.
■ The mixture at the bottom of the mixing bowl is thus brought up over the egg whites, flour or whatever it is, which is literally folded inside.
■ Whisked egg white blends more easily and evenly into a mixture if you first fold in just one tablespoonful of it; loosened slightly, the rest of the white then blends in more quickly.

FREEZER BURN

This happens when frozen foods become dried by surface evaporation. The tissues of such foods as meat and poultry, for instance, develop dry white patches, and the foods become tough and spongy through dehydration. Not even the best of cooks can recapture a food's original flavour and texture once this has happened. All sorts of things can cause freezer burn: air in the packages; foil torn or too thin; polythene bags either too thin or perhaps pierced; seals broken. See also *water*, page 129.

FREEZING

The ideal way to preserve many foods because it simply arrests their life cycle and holds them in their natural state until you are ready to use them at the moment of your choice. The nutrients are unaltered, and apart from any watery foods such as jellies, fruit and vegetables whose texture changes, freezing changes neither the structure nor the flavour of food to any significant degree.

■ Excepting those foods which can be cooked while still frozen, the golden rule is *freeze quickly, thaw slowly*. Jill McWilliam in her book *Freezing* (Woodhead-Faulkner Ltd in association with Bejam Group Ltd, 1974) explains why:

All foods have an interior cell structure which can be destroyed if freezing is done too slowly. As food freezes, ice crystals form within the stucture – the faster the food is frozen, the smaller the crystal formation, keeping the interior structure intact as far as possible. Slow freezing produces large ice crystals which destroy the structure both internally and externally. Foods with a high water content such as strawberries, cucumbers, etc. never freeze very successfully as even the tiniest crystal formation breaks down the very delicate structure. On thawing they go rather soft and mushy but can be utilized in dishes, or for cooking, as the flavour is unchanged. Food frozen

slowly is disappointing in texture and flavour, but of more importance is the loss of nutrients when defrosting or cooking. The correct use of the fast-freeze device is important.

Open freezing Means freezing foods as they are, uncovered, for a short time, until firm enough to seal in a polythene bag or other container without damaging or squashing; spread and separate them out on a small tray or biscuit tin and leave until firm.

■ You may, for instance, have some butterfly cakes or 'nests' of duchess potato you want to pile into one bag, or a gâteau piped with crème au beurre. Twenty to thirty minutes is usually all they'll need to firm up.

FRYING, DEEP FAT

The greatest danger in the home for anyone who is either careless, or unaware that fat will burst into flame spontaneously at very high temperatures, even without being anywhere near a flame. A neighbouring family of mine lost their whole home within a space of an hour or two, because the mother left the kitchen while the fat was heating. Do, for your own and your family's safety:

1 Use a *thermostatically controlled* hot plate or plugged-in fat pan if you can. Failing this, use a thermometer. (See *ignition temperature*, page 67.)
2 Keep a rug or heavy blanket handy. This is a fire to smother – never one to throw water over.

The pan See *pans, deep fat*, page 35.

The fat Should be of the best quality for best results. The more refined it is, the higher will be its smoke point:

■ Oils. Solid vegetable oils (page 115) are excellent, as is a highly-refined corn oil. Alternatively, you can use a sunflower oil or a good vegetable oil. Olive oil *isn't* suitable: its smoke point is too low (quite apart from its cost).
■ Pure lard or white cooking fat of top

quality also gives excellent results.

■ Dripping can only be used if you clarify it, otherwise its impurities cause it to break down at high temperatures.

■ Have the pan a third to half full. If deeper, the fat may bubble up and boil over when you lower food into it. If too shallow, floating foods can't float, and others – like Scotch eggs, for instance – will spoil if not completely submerged.

■ Dry thoroughly any wet foods like chips before cooking, to prevent the fat spluttering and bubbling over.

Coating Foods need coating with something – egg and breadcrumbs, batter or pastry – before frying in deep fat, to:

1 Protect them from the intense heat;

2 Prevent certain foods disintegrating, when watery ones might make the fat bubble over;

3 Prevent flavour and juices escaping into the fat – which spoil both food and fat;

4 Give flavour, colour and a crisp texture.

■ Sweet and savoury foods can follow each other in the same fat because, providing each is properly coated, and the fat hot enough, no flavour or juices will pass into it.

Frying temperatures Vary from about 340–400°F/170–205°C according to the food in question. (A thermostatically controlled hot plate on the cooker should be set slightly above the recommended temperature for the fat, because without a lid on the pan, there is considerable heat loss.) Pre-cooked foods such as fish cakes are fried in hotter fat than raw foods, which have to be *cooked* at the same time as being crisped outside.

■ If the fat is too hot, the outside of foods will brown and burn before the inside is cooked; if too cold, the food will absorb the fat, becoming greasy and indigestible. In addition, some coatings may burst. It's important to avoid over-filling the pan with food too, otherwise the fat's temperature will drop too low.

■ Reheat fat before frying a second batch of food, to bring back to the required temperature.

■ Oil only smokes when it is too hot to use. If *any* fat becomes too hot, turn off the source of heat at once, and leave the pan to cool: more lard or cool oil, as the case may be, will lower the temperature immediately.

Frying basket Not used for foods coated with batter because the batter may stick to the wire, exposing the raw surfaces of the food, which the fat then penetrates. Foods such as doughnuts, aigrettes and parsley aren't fried in a basket either, because they'll stick to it.

■ Drain all foods on absorbent kitchen paper, to make sure they aren't fatty and indigestible.

■ Avoid covering fried foods with a lid while keeping them hot, because the trapped steam will make them go soft.

■ Heat fat after use, until all bubbling stops, to drive off any water, which would hasten decomposition.

■ Strain fat though butter muslin after use, to remove even the smallest crumbs, which if left in, may cause decomposition and will burn when next the fat is heated. Thus darkened it will give anything fried in it a bad colour and a bitter flavour.

FRYING, SHALLOW

Isn't as tasty a way of cooking as deep fat frying, and foods like fish are more likely to break up because they aren't sealed by the fat in the same way, and because they need extra handling.

■ Coat foods with such things as egg and breadcrumbs, seasoned flour or seasoned oatmeal to protect them from the intense heat, as well as to give flavour, colour and a crisp texture.

■ Butter gives foods a heavenly flavour but it burns easily unless saltless or clarified. Adding a dessertspoon of oil to 2oz/50g butter allows it to reach a higher temperature without burning.

■ Preheat the fat, of whatever kind, to

seal the surface of the food and prevent flavourful juices escaping into it. If not hot enough, the food will absorb the fat, making it greasy, indigestible and in some cases soft instead of crisp.

■ Avoid overfilling a frying pan, first because it cools the fat too much and secondly because, without air space between each piece of food, things will steam rather than fry and will consequently be soft instead of crisp.

■ As with deep fat, avoid covering fried foods with a lid, because they'll go soft in the trapped steam.

FUMET

The liquid left from cooked fish, meat or game, boiled down rapidly to a syrupy consistency, for addition in concentrated form to the accompanying sauce.

GARNISHING

Savoury foods are 'garnished', sweet ones are 'decorated'. Both should make a dish look more attractive and will almost invariably add extra, complementary flavour. Some provide contrasting texture to the food with which they are served, while others add moistness to a dry one or richness to a plain. Some on the other hand *counteract* richness. While their purpose is, therefore, varied, their presence is always pleasing if carefully and thoughtfully carried out.

■ Many classic dishes are so called because of their garnish (see page 71), but it's often up to your own imagination to provide that final touch which makes the difference between dishes which look dull and uninteresting, and those which are tempting – sometimes even a work of art.

■ Here are some examples of what one food can do for another:

Aspic jelly Used to coat things like cold salmon cutlets or certain cocktail snacks, secures the position of a garnish like hard-boiled egg or green pepper, gives flavour and a glistening appearance, and

prevents the food itself becoming dry.

Butter, savoury Such as maître d'hôtel (see pages 169 and 171) gives an enticing appearance, flavour, moisture and richness to grilled foods like fish, steaks or lamb's liver.

Cayenne pepper This or paprika gives colour and flavour to lots of savoury dishes, especially egg or cheese.

Cream, soured Adds a dash of colour to the centre of a plateful of beetroot soup.

Croûtons Look nice, taste nice and give both richness and a crisp texture to a vegetable purée soup (see page 163).

Cucumber Finely sliced and perhaps decorated with a fruit decorator, cucumber makes lots of cold dishes look colourful and complements the flavour of salmon particularly.

Eggs Hard-boiled, and sliced, quartered or cut into shapes with aspic cutters, eggs often give a lovely splash of colour. Used to glaze, egg gives a shiny appearance and may help a garnish like poppy seed to stick to dinner rolls or a milk twist.

Fleurons These or small shapes of fried bread or toast look attractive, give flavour and a crisp texture to a dish without 'bite', like mince.

Herbs Especially the brightly coloured ones like chives or parsley (page 103), with flavours which also combine well with other foods, can be used to garnish almost anything, whether egg dishes, cheese, soups, vegetables, fish, meat or poultry.

Lemon butterflies And/or lemon quarters look lovely, give additional flavour and counteract the richness of foods like fried fish. See page 69.

Mushrooms Cooked, give flavour more than anything else to many meat or fish dishes. See page 187.

Nuts Whether chopped, grated or flaked, they give crunchiness to soft foods like fish. If browned (in the oven, under the grill or by frying), they also contribute enormously to the flavour of a dish. Delicious, too, with fried chicken or with curry.

Onions Cooked pickling onions are mainly to give flavour to meat dishes. Batter-dipped rings of a larger onion will give richness and a crisp texture in addition.

Peas It goes without saying that they cheer up many a dull looking dish. Because of their perfect yet rather mild flavour, they're a good partner with many kinds of food.

Potato straws Look enticing, add richness, flavour and a crisp texture when accompanying something like grilled steak or fried fish.

Tomatoes Look bright and cheerful whenever they're used, besides adding flavour to many savoury dishes. Make tiny ones yourself from larger (see page 195), for a particular purpose, like replacing the stalk of a stuffed green pepper. Tomato quarters, juiced and seeded, make a better garnish than slices, which tend to disintegrate and make a dish watery.

Vegetables Cooked and diced (page 81), they give colour, flavour and food value to many dishes, especially if a mixture of, say, carrot, turnip, peas and celery.

GAS FLAMES

Are hottest at the tips, so if they're licking up the sides of a pan you're wasting gas, not getting as much heat as you may think.

GLAZE

Glaze, meat See page 343.

Glaze for pastry, rolls, etc. Use egg yolk if you can spare it, mixing a pinch of salt and teaspoon of cold water with it, which make it easier to brush on and give better results than whole egg.

■ Glaze sweet pastries with egg white if you like, sprinkling them with caster or icing sugar before baking.
■ Use milk if you can't spare egg – though it's not as good.

GOULASH

Comes from the Hungarian national dish, *goulasch*, generally a kind of beef stew made with diced onions and seasoned with Hungarian paprika.

GRATINER

Means to brown the top of a dish under the grill, or in a hot oven, after sprinkling it with breadcrumbs and melted butter, or with grated cheese – and perhaps breadcrumbs, too.

GRILLING

Is suitable for only best cuts of meat because only they will cook so quickly and yet so perfectly under such intense heat. Other foods grill deliciously too, of course – like small whole fish, fish steaks, lamb's or calf's liver, lamb's kidneys, bacon, sausages and certain vegetables.

■ Slash the fat round beef or gammon steaks, or the fat of bacon rashers before grilling, otherwise the meat curls up and cooks unevenly because the fat sizzles and shrinks faster than the lean.
■ Score whole fish two or three times across the top thick part, to allow the heat to penetrate to the middle, and to let out some of the surface fat so that it will cook crisply.
■ Salt on grilled meat? Some people say you shouldn't use it because it draws out the flavouring juices and hardens the meat. I'll settle for salt and flavour – the meat will still be juicy unless overcooked.
■ Brush the surfaces of the food with oil or melted fat, to keep moist and prevent charring. (Butter gives the best flavour.)
■ Preheat the grill, making it red-hot before you start. By first grilling meat fast for just one minute on each side, the

surface juices rapidly evaporate, sealing in those which would otherwise escape in the grill pan. This is what gives grilled meat its characteristically delicious flavour.

■ Turn meat over with tongs or two tablespoons, and fish with two fish slices or a fish slice and a pallet knife. If you pierce meat by using a fork, some of the juices will escape.

■ The time foods take to grill depends on their type and thickness, the maximum heat of the grill, the distance between food and grill, and upon your own taste – whether you like meat rare, medium or well done.

HANDS!

There are times when you're cooking when two hands just aren't enough, as when making mayonnaise in a basin. With a large tea-towel folded diagonally and tied firmly round the top of the basin, you can then twist the ends together and grip them between your body and the table, leaving both hands free to work; the basin held steadily in front of you.

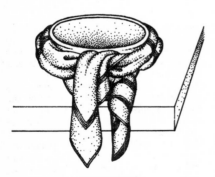

ICE CUBES

Can speed things up when mixtures are slow to cool or set, especially in hot weather. Decorated moulds and cooling mixtures will respond quickly if surrounded by ice in a larger bowl.

■ Make ice cubes in advance and transfer them to the freezer when a large party is likely to be a strain on a smallish refrigerator. Set a mint or borage leaf, a maraschino cherry or a sliver of lemon peel in some of them if you like.

■ Use an ice cube tray to freeze and store such things as stocks, lemon juice, orange juice, chopped fresh herbs, court bouillon, meat glaze or cream.

IGNITION TEMPERATURE

Is that at which oils and fats burst into flame spontaneously, without any flame being applied. Beware, therefore, when deep fat frying. This temperature varies according to the type of fat – oil, lard, cooking fat, clarified dripping – and even to particular types and brands of oil. The more refined each oil or fat is, the better, because the higher the ignition temperature will be. *Most* ignite between 685 – 800°F/365 – 425°C.

JELLY

To chop jelly requires a spot of know-how. Whether aspic or sweet jelly, it won't sparkle if you either finger it or chop it too small. Make it stiff, either with rather less liquid or rather more gelatine than usual. Chop the jelly on wet greaseproof paper with a long wetted knife, then it won't stick to either. Hold the knife by each end, cutting coarsely in up-and-down movements. Use to decorate (aspic for a savoury dish, sweet for jellies, creams, etc). It will make a dish go further besides dressing it up.

To decorate with jelly To decorate the bottom of a mould is easy when you know the ropes but the most sophisticated dish can look amateurish if you don't. Here's some help:

■ Have the jelly cool, but still liquid, so that it can find its own level yet not melt anything already set. If necessary, *keep* it liquid by warming its basin in a larger one of warm water.

■ Set a thin layer of jelly in the bottom of your chosen mould, surrounding the mould with ice cubes in very hot weather, or to speed things up if in a hurry.

■ Whatever you are using for decoration – cherries, angelica, grapes, banana, peas, prawns, cooked carrot, chives – pierce each in turn with a hatpin (or very fine skewer), dip it in the liquid jelly and place where you want it, sliding it off the first hatpin with a second. Put in refrigerator and leave to set, otherwise the decorations will float when you add more jelly.

■ *Spoon* a little more liquid jelly over the decorations, just to cover, and now leave *this* to set. (If poured from a jug, the decorations may be dislodged by the force of the jelly's fall.)

■ Now add your mixture and leave it to set.

KNEADING

Is very difficult to learn effectively from a book. If I were you, I'd have just one lesson from an expert. Many people find it difficult to learn even after seeing how to do it. You need to *do* it, putting the strength of your whole body behind your hand (or hands).

KNIFE SHARPENING

To sharpen correctly is all-important in the care of knives. Skilful sharpening before use will keep the blade razor-edged. Sharp blades should be honed (sharpened) with a fine steel; a coarse steel should be used only when knives are really blunt.

■ Hold the steel firm, as illustrated, and draw the knife blade down it: ensure that the full length of the blade is sharpened by drawing the knife from hilt to tip down the full length of the steel on both edges, as shown in figs 1 and 2 below:

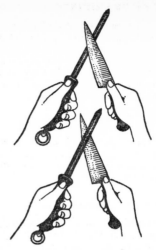

KNOCKING UP

Knocking up the edges of pastry ensures that you open up and free the layers, enabling the pastry to rise properly. Just before glazing a pie, plate pie, sausage rolls, or whatever, work your way all round the cut edges with the sharp edge of a knife blade, tilted slightly backwards (see illustration). It's a matter of almost brushing the blade lightly against the edges in an upward movement, from the lower part of the edge to the upper. Steady the pastry with the fingers of the other hand and turn the pie round gradually as you work, so that you're always knocking up the edge furthest away from you.

LARDING

A way of giving some fat (before roasting) to very lean joints of meat, and dry types of poultry or game, to make them moist and juicy. Thread thin strips of firm dry pork fat or bacon fat into the surface of the meat or bird with a special needle, see *Larding needle*, page 31.

LARDOONS

The actual strips of pork or bacon fat used in larding, varying in length and thickness, according to the meat for which you need them.

LEMON BUTTERFLIES

An attractive and quickly made garnish, used largely for fish or veal. Use the lemon as it is, or decorate it first with a fruit decorator. To make, see page 105.

LIAISON

May be a roux, flour and water, fécule, beurre manié, egg yolk, or egg yolk and cream – any of them used as a thickening or binding for soups, sauces and other liquids.

LINING A CAKE TIN

Lining a cake tin properly is particularly important when you want a well-shaped fruit cake. Tins sometimes have to be lined for other cakes as well.

Square or rectangular tins Shallow or deep.

1 Grease tin, preferably by brushing with a pure fat such as melted lard or white cooking fat.
2 Stand tin on a sheet of greaseproof paper, ABCD, at least the size of the tin plus the depth, plus about 1in/2.5cm for a collar to stand above the rim of the tin. Mark round the tin with a pencil. See illustration.
3 Cut diagonally, accurately, from A to E, B to F, C to G and D to H.

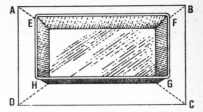

4 Fit paper in tin, the pencilled lines precisely along its bottom edges. Overlap paper at corners, cutting off the points if they get in the way.
5 Brush all surfaces with fat again.

Round tins To line bottom only.

1 Grease tin with fat, as square tin.
2 Stand tin on piece of greaseproof paper, mark round with a pencil and then cut just inside the line. Fit disc precisely in bottom of tin.
3 Brush all surfaces with fat again.
4 Dust out lightly with flour, giving tin a sharp knock, upside down, to remove any surplus.

Round tins To line fully. Use more than one layer of paper for a rich fruit cake.

1 Grease tin with fat, as square tin.
2 Stand tin on a doubled sheet of greaseproof paper, to make *two* discs, as above. Fit one of these in bottom of tin.
3 Cut a strip of greaseproof paper at least 2in/5cm longer than the circumference, and 1–1½in/2.5–4cm wider than the depth of the tin, fig 1 below.
4 Fold over a good ½in/about 1.5cm of the paper along the whole length, fig 2.
5 Open out the fold and cut slanting lines through the narrow piece, exactly to the fold line, fig 3.

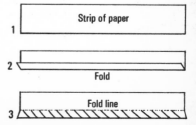

6 Fit into tin, the narrow slashed strip fitting round bottom.

7 Fit second disc in bottom to cover and hold down all slashed edges.

8 Brush all surfaces with fat again.

Round tins To line bottom quickly. Put a small square of greaseproof paper on the bottom of the greased tin. As long as two thirds of the base is covered, the cake should turn out easily. (Cut several squares of paper while you're about it, then they're handy when wanted.)

MACERATING

Like marinating, but concerns fruit instead of meat and fish. It is as simple to macerate as to breathe, and yet the result is delectable enough for a banquet.

■ Ripe, fresh fruits are flavoured and softened by caster sugar sprinkled over, together with a liqueur in which they are soaked for a limited time, according to the kind of fruit: use both liqueur and sugar to taste, (approx ½ – 1 tablespoon of liqueur per serving).

■ *Cover* fruits like bananas, pears or peaches (which discolour easily) while they are soaking, and don't leave too long – bananas and pears about half an hour, peaches about an hour.

■ Use two wooden spoons to turn fruit over once or twice in the 'syrup', to make sure the liqueur permeates it completely.

■ Serve the fruits just as they are, preferably with crème chantilly, cream or crème anglaise, etc.

■ Use macerated fruits also to make fritters (see *fritters*, page 290).

■ Some good combinations are:

Fruit	Preparation	Liqueur
apricots	skin, cut in half, stone	kirsch, apricot or peach brandy, any orange liqueur
bananas	slice thickly, diagonally	rum, kirsch

Fruit	Preparation	Liqueur
cherries	stone	kirsch, cherry brandy, sloe gin
figs	cut into quarters	cognac, any orange liqueur
guavas	peel, slice and de-pip	poire william, any orange liqueur
kiwi fruit	skin and slice across	apricot or peach brandy, cognac
mangoes	skin and slice or cut up	apricot or peach brandy
nectarines	as peaches, below	as peaches
oranges	cut off rind and pith in spiral; from between skins, ease out segments of flesh; remove pips	any orange liqueur, rum
peaches	skin and cut in halves, quarters or slices	peach or apricot brandy, cognac, rum, any orange liqueur
pears	skin and cut in halves, quarters or slices	cognac, kirsch, rum, calvados, poire william (best of all)
pineapple	peel, slice, remove core cut as liked	kirsch, rum, gin, cognac
plums	skin, cut in half, stone	quetsch, kirsch, cognac, rum
raspberries	nil	eau de vie de framboise, cognac, any orange liqueur
strawberries	hull	kirsch, any orange liqueur

MARINATING

Means soaking meat, fish or game and sometimes vegetables, in a highly seasoned liquid – a marinade. It can transform cheaper cuts of meat into the luxury class. Marinating flavours foods, tenderizes tough meat, gives moisture to dry meat, or helps to preserve meat or game which you may have to keep a day or two longer than desirable.

■ A marinade may be cooked or uncooked, simple (like French dressing for salad vegetables or lemon juice for fish), or complicated, with up to a score of ingredients, as for venison. Marinating may take half an hour or several days, according to size and texture of the food, and whether it is hot or cold weather.

■ A cooked marinade works more quickly than an uncooked, even though the ingredients may be identical, because cooking brings out their aroma and flavour. The ingredients may include wine, vinegar, brandy, oil (preferably olive oil), onion, garlic, carrot, herbs and spices. To cook a marinade, fry the vegetables lightly in the oil to bring out their flavour, then add the other ingredients and simmer for half an hour. Use cold because, if hot, it would amongst other things encourage rather than discourage the growth of bacteria.

■ Use a deep dish for large joints of meat, or for venison, so that you can baste and turn it over from time to time, as necessary.

■ After the food is marinated, add the strained liquid, if you like, to an accompanying sauce, freezing any surplus as ice cubes, and transferring them to the freezer for use another time.

MENU

A restaurant menu can be a teaser if you have no idea what's what and are too shy or embarrassed to ask the waiter – though you needn't be. When food is served, doesn't another diner's choice sometimes look twice as good as ours, and don't we occasionally regret a choice we would never knowingly have made?

■ Given that a certain name implies a particular method of preparation, or certain foods (either cooked in the dish, as a garnish, or perhaps with an accompanying sauce), you should be spared disappointment. By being informed, you'll for instance be able quietly to ignore florentine if you don't care for spinach, steer clear of marinière or nantua if shellfish bring you out in a rash, or make a mental beeline for provençale if you're a garlic and tomato fan. Here are some well known names, but first *à la carte* and *table d'hôte*.

À la carte The type of menu on which each dish is individually priced. Because special dishes are cooked to order, they're always more expensive than a set meal, where cooking, serving and choice are restricted to a few dishes.

Table d'hôte French for 'the table of the host' – or landlord – and is a set luncheon or dinner menu at a fixed price.

Restaurant menus

Name	Method of preparation or principal components	Comments
argenteuil	asparagus: as in potage à l'argenteuil	The asparagus of Argenteuil has no rivals.
bonne femme	cooked in some homely way, which often includes potatoes: as in poularde à la bonne femme	
bourgignonne	red wine, mushrooms and tiny onions: as in boeuf à la bourgignonne	
brochette	the food is cooked and served on a skewer: as in brochettes de sole à la duxelles	Brochette is French for skewer.
chasseur	white wine, mushrooms and shallots: as in tournedos chasseur	
darne	a thick slice of a large fish; poached, grilled, braised or sautéd: as in darne de saumon à l'ancienne	
daube	a kind of stew, of meat, poultry or game: as in boeuf en daube	The meat has usually been marinated and is cooked in the same marinade.
diable	to cook by grilling with mustard: to devil it, as in poulets grillés à la diable	Diable is French for devil.
duxelles	a mixture containing mushrooms and shallots: as in pommes de terre farcies à la duxelles	The name is thought to have originated where the dish was first created, in the household of the Marquis d'Uxelles.
fines herbes	chopped fresh herbs, especially chervil, chives, parsley and tarragon, together: as in omelette aux fines herbes	
florentine	spinach, and mornay sauce: as in sole à la florentine	Usually fish or egg dishes.
forestière	morels, diced potatoes fried in butter: as in entrecôte à la forestière	Morels are an edible fungus.

Name	Method of preparation or principal components	Comments
grecque	dish should be of Greek origin in the method of preparation: as in concombre à la grecque	In practice, the name is often given to dishes of French origin.
hollandaise	a rich sauce made with egg yolks and butter: as in fonds d'artichauts à la hollandaise	Served with eggs, fish or vegetables.
hongroise	paprika flavoured cream sauce: as in soufflé à la hongroise	
indienne	curry: as in hachis de boeuf à l'indienne	
italienne	finely diced or chopped mushrooms: as in oeufs à l'italienne	The name is also given to a method of preparing pasta.
jardinière	neatly cut, separately cooked vegetables, as garnish: as in escalopes de veau à la jardinière	
julienne	garnish of vegetables cut in thin strips, especially carrot, turnip, celery and leek: as in consommé julienne	May also apply to any foodstuff which is shredded, e.g. julienne of mushrooms, julienne of chicken breast.
lyonnaise	onions: as in tripe à la lyonnaise	
marinière	shellfish, especially mussels: as in moules à la marinière	Fish dishes only. Loosely translated means 'fishwife' style.
ménagère	a 'household' dish – something simply made: as in crème au beurre à la ménagère	Ménagère is French for housewife or housekeeper.
meunière	fish fried in butter, served with lemon juice and chopped parsley: as in raie à la meunière	Fish only (see also page 222).
milanaise	food is dipped in egg and breadcrumbs (often mixed with grated Parmesan cheese): as in côtes de porc à la milanaise	May also imply a method of preparing macaroni.
moka (or mocha)	coffee: as in crème au moka	Called after the famous coffee beans grown in Mocha (Yemen).

Name	Method of preparation or principal components	Comments
montmorency	cherries: as in bombe montmorency	A famous French variety of cherry.
nantua	crayfish tails or a covering of crayfish purée: as in potage velouté de volaille à la nantua	
niçoise	tomatoes and garlic, also often anchovy fillets and black olives: as in salade niçoise	
normande	mainly for fish braised in white wine, or may sometimes imply cider and/or calvados: as in sole à la Normande	Used also for small cuts of meat, chicken or winged game, prepared quite differently. This often also includes cream.
parmentier	potatoes: as in boeuf bouilli sauté parmentier.	Antoine Parmentier (1737–1813) introduced the potato to France.
paupiettes	thin slices of meat, or fillets of fish, stuffed and rolled up into cork-shaped parcels: as in paupiettes de veau à la grecque	Beef olives are paupiettes.
périgourdine	black truffles: as in omelette à la périgourdine	The finest truffles are found in the Périgord district of France. (Piémontaise, after the Italian white truffle of Piédmont, also implies truffles.)
polonaise	hard-boiled egg yolk and chopped parsley: as in choufleur à la polonaise	
provençale	tomatoes and garlic: as in courgettes à la provençale	
ragoût	a stew of fish, meat, fowl or vegetables: as in ragoût de champignons	Ragoût is French for stew.
saint-germain	french green peas, usually as a garnish: as in tournedos saint-germain	May also describe a thick soup made with peas.
soubise	a purée of onion and rice, or an onion sauce: as in côtelettes d'agneau soubise	

Name	Method of preparation or principal components	Comments
suprême	implies the best part – breast of fowl or game, or a choice piece of fish: as in suprêmes de faisan	Suprême may also describe a rich, white, creamy sauce.
véronique	white grapes: as in sole à la véronique	

MENU PLANNING

An important part of the cook's work, whether you are arranging family or special-occasion meals. Subconsciously you probably think about most of these things anyway but here are the main points to consider:

1 For whom is the meal? Young children; ravenous adolescents; overfed businessmen or a ladies' lunch?

2 How much time and money can you spare to make the meal?

3 The need for balanced meals – that means being sure that at some time during each day you serve all the nutrients (see below).

4 People's likes and dislikes. It's not really fair to give your friends shellfish, hare or curry as a main course, unless you know they like and can eat it. If you don't know them well enough to ring up and ask, it's kindest to choose something else.

5 Variety of texture. Supposing you want to serve soup, fish and then a caramel custard, do think of making croûtons to go with the soup, chips or sauté potatoes to go with the fish, or perhaps meringues to go with the soft sweet.

6 Variety of flavour. Avoid serving, say, mushrooms, tomatoes or a milk sauce in more than one course.

7 Variety of colour. Use green vegetables to cheer up a brown or white dish, and avoid following, say, gammon with strawberries.

8 The capacity of your cooker, both hotplates and oven.

9 The weather. Chilled soup may be lovely in July but probably not in December.

10 Variety of cooking methods. Avoid overdoing the frying, the boiling or the stewing for instance.

11 It isn't wise to mix homely and elaborate courses at the same dinner party. If you start off in Ritz style, that's the standard you're setting for the whole meal.

METRIC QUANTITIES AND MEASUREMENTS

Those given in this book are as follows: 1oz = 25g (although in fact 8ozs = 225g and 1lb = 450g). For convenience, particularly when exact quantities are unnecessary as for vegetables, they may be rounded up to 500g or 1kg. ¼ pt = 125ml (although in fact ¼ pt is 1 tablespoon more than 125ml and nearer 150ml – a quantity sometimes quoted).

MIREPOIX

A cooked mixture of coarsely diced vegetables, bacon and herbs. Its purpose is to give flavour and it is used mainly as the foundation on which meat, fish or fowl are braised. If the vegetables are diced smaller, it is sometimes used as a garnish for cutlets or for a fish dish. It should consist of such vegetables as carrot, onion, celery and leek, in quantities balanced so that no one flavour predominates.

NUTRIENTS

All vital to good health, they are:
proteins   minerals
fats   vitamins
carbohydrates   water
Roughage is also essential, although it isn't a nutrient.

TEMPERATURES

)kers, temperatures vary
ir numbering according to
make, but in the majority, number 4 corresponds to 350°F and each number up or
down represents 25°F more, or less – i.e.
350°F = gas 4, 375°F = gas 5, and 325°F
= gas 3.

■ Oven temperatures throughout this
book are based on these figures, *approximate* equivalent temperatures being given
also in degrees Celsius (centigrade).
Speaking generally, a

slow oven is gas 2, 300°F/150°C
moderate oven is gas 4, 350°F/175°C
hot oven is gas 6, 400°F/205°C
very hot oven is gas 8, 450°F/230°C.

■ Celsius, the scale in general use in
Europe, and called after its Swedish
inventor, Anders Celcius, now replaces
the unit which we have called centigrade.
The reason for changing is to avoid confusion with a unit (in some other countries) having the same name, but used to
denote fractions of a right angle.

PANADA

A very thick sauce. The base of a savoury
soufflé, a panada is also used to bind
croquettes and similar mixtures.

PARBOIL

Just as it sounds: to partly cook by
boiling, prior to completing the cooking
by another method, see *blanching*, page
52.

PARE

Simply another word for peel – to remove
the outer skin from fruit and vegetables.
Strips of lemon or orange peel are best
taken off with a potato peeler, to take the
minimum of bitter pith with the rind.

PINCH

A pinch of any dry ingredient is the
amount which you can pick up between
your thumb and forefinger. In fact, a
pinch of salt, as so often called for, is
frequently totally inadequate to bring out
the flavour of a food.

PIPING

Piping attractively and successfully comes
only as a result of practice: an excellent
way to acquire this is with hot sieved
potato. You can pipe it over and over
again, either to improve your skill, or to
plan a design; using something like an
inverted breadboard as a dummy flan or
cake.

■ Piping is a difficult skill to learn from a
book. It would pay dividends to have just
one lesson if you've never had one.

PIPING BAGS

Most easily filled like this, a cuff turned
over at the top, leaving both hands free to
work. Only three-quarters fill the bag,
then turn back the cuff and close bag up.
Pockets of air need to be pressed out with
a pallet knife before piping, otherwise it
is difficult, if not impossible, to pipe an
unbroken chain.

POACHING

Is done in 'shivering' – barely simmering
– water (see page 81). Only delicate foods
such as eggs and fish will cook at such low
temperatures, consequently this method
of cookery is restricted.

POINT

A point of anything, e.g. a spice, is the minute quantity which can be held on the point of a knife.

PROVING A DOUGH

The second raising of a *yeast dough*, see page 309.

PROVING A GIRDLE

Proving a warmed girdle or iron omelette pan, implies cleaning it with salt and rubbing it with soft paper instead of washing it with water. This prevents rust forming, and ensures that scones or omelettes will not stick.

PURÉES

Fruit or vegetable purées are made in seconds in a liquidizer. Failing this, a vegetable mill is usually quicker than a sieve, but seedy fruits may still need sieving.

RAISING AGENTS

May be chemical or otherwise. These are they:

baking powder, see page 87;
bicarbonate of soda with *cream of tartar* or another acid, see *bicarbonate of soda*, page 87;
bicarbonate of soda alone, in certain circumstances, see page 87 again;
yeast, see page 130;
air, see page 86.

RÉCHAUFFÉS

Dishes made up from cold cooked fish, meat, game or poultry. These will be tough and indigestible if the meat is re-cooked rather than reheated. Cold foods usually lack flavour and nourishment when reheated, so these are introduced by using such things as onions, herbs, spices, batter, egg and breadcrumb coating, or by accompanying sauces.

■ All flavourings are precooked, because quick reheating allows no time for raw ingredients to cook.

REDUCING

Boiling a liquid down rapidly (with the exception of wine, which should be just simmered) in an uncovered pan, to thicken the consistency and concentrate the flavour in a very small amount of liquid. This is an important step in the making of many delicious sauces.

■ Any salt you add will also become concentrated, so use sparingly until after the liquid is reduced.

REFRESHING

Is *making* vegetables go cold, instead of *letting* them do so, by running cold water through, or plunging them straight into deep cold water for 2 or 3 minutes – or long enough to cool them – after they've been blanched (or boiled) and drained. This abruptly halts their cooking, consequently they don't lose any of their colour, flavour, texture or nutrients, as they do if just left around simply to cool. Few people seem aware of the advantages and convenience of refreshing, on occasions such as these:

1 When you're serving vegetables cold, as in salads, e.g. asparagus, peas, sweet pepper, sweetcorn, cauliflower sprigs, French beans.
2 When you've blanched vegetables for some particular reason, page 52.
3 When for some reason you don't want to serve a vegetable immediately, but you want it to be nearly cooked, so that you can serve it within a few minutes:
   a You're going out, and want to serve the meal a few minutes after you return.
   b The vegetable is in the pan when a telephone call comes, asking you to delay the meal.
   c Mealtime is uncertain. If you have guests you can't spend too long in the kitchen.

RENDERED FAT

Is fat melted down from pieces of solid fat cooked either in the oven or on top of the cooker until the dripping runs freely and the pieces of fat are shrunken and golden. It needs straining through butter muslin, otherwise the tiny particles will burn when the fat is heated and used.

TO THE RIBBON

The term used to describe the consistency of eggs and sugar whisked until a ribbon-like trail forms on the surface of the mixture when you trail some back into it off the whisk. Only if the mixture is thick and fluffy enough to support this 'ribbon' will it support the other ingredients to be folded in.

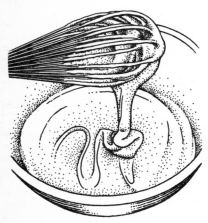

■ You can beat the eggs and sugar quickly and easily with an electric hand-whisk over very hot but not boiling water, or less quickly with a good hand-whisk. With certain food processors one can also whisk a sponge mixture. See *Soufflés*, page 298.

ROASTING

Strictly speaking, roasting is cooking in a current of air in front of or over a fierce glowing heat. What we today term roast meat is in fact baked, because it is cooked in a current of air by dry (or radiant) heat in an enclosed oven. The rôtisserie (page 40) is the modern return to true roasting.

■ Roasting is traditional for cooking *tender* joints of meat, poultry or game: they are too large and too thick to be grilled. Some people like to set their joint or bird on a wire meat stand in the roasting tin. Others prefer to set it on a bed of roasting vegetables (say a peeled onion and/or a large carrot cut into three or four thick slices), because when these caramelize as they do during cooking, they give a delicious flavour to the gravy.

■ Initially, roast meats need a preheated hot oven to seal the outside surfaces. The flavouring juices will then be kept *in*, instead of escaping into the tin, with the result that the meat will be moister, will have more flavour and will shrink less.

■ Cooking a joint or bird in a roasting bag or baking pan (page 35) does not give as good results as does an open roasting tin: when, with the heat of the oven, the juices in meat or fowl turn to steam, the steam is trapped, so this food is cooked by moist rather than by dry heat – which isn't really roasting. Even though you remove the covering towards the end of cooking, you can't, for instance, expect a chicken to become as crisp and golden as it is after roasting in an open tin throughout its cooking time. Your oven will be clean and meat will shrink less, but it's unlikely it will taste as good and the texture will be less firm.
See also individual meats and birds.

Pot roasting A simpler but less good version of *braising*, see page 54.

ROLLING PASTRY

Quite an art; the aim is to elongate the dough, away from you, not simply to enlarge it by squashing! With a cool dough, and with pastry board and rolling pin lightly floured, the dough shouldn't readily stick to either.

■ Hold the rolling pin (page 40) *lightly* at

each end, fingers over the top, and the thumb ends almost pointing towards each other along the pin. In this position, you can roll it and then pick it up, repeatedly.

■ Roll the pin sharply yet lightly forwards, until it is under the upper part of the hand, then roll it backwards and lift it up. Continue like this, lifting the pin up after each short forward and backward roll, until the dough is the size, shape and thickness you want. See also page 134.

ROUX

Can be made with butter, margarine, dripping or oil, depending upon the purpose for which it's needed. There are three kinds:

1 *A white roux*, used for white sauces and soups, when a white colour is important. Make with butter, margarine or oil – preferably butter, for its flavour – and cook it 2 or 3 minutes. For perfection, use clarified or saltless butter, so that you can cook the roux a minute or two longer, to give extra flavour without also colouring it.

2 *A blond roux*, used ideally for velouté and piquant sauces. Use butter rather than margarine because margarine doesn't colour so well, and burns more readily if overheated. Cook this a few minutes longer than a white roux, until pale straw colour.

3 *A brown roux*, used for brown sauces and soups. Make it with dripping, oil, saltless butter or clarified butter. (With salted butter, the sediment will burn during the long cooking, giving the sauce a bitter flavour.) With beef dripping, the roux will go brown more easily than with oil or clarified butter, but delicately flavoured dishes sometimes call for a particular fat. Cook a brown roux about 15 minutes, or until a golden nut-brown colour.

■ Equal quantities of fat and flour are normally used, but those who guess rather than weigh their ingredients are better to have a tiny bit too much fat than too little. (Too much fat can cause a

greasy sauce, but at the same time it is difficult to incorporate the liquid when a roux is too solid.)

■ A roux seems so straightforward and easy to make, yet it isn't. If the fat gets too hot, either because you *heat* it instead of just melting it, or because you don't set the pan aside from the heat while stirring in the flour, the starch in the flour will turn into tiny pellets which you can't get rid of. As a result, the flour will lose some of its thickening properties.

■ If tempted to dodge cooking the roux, do have second thoughts, otherwise your sauce won't be anything to write home about. This is why:

1 Cooking the roux gives a sauce or soup extra flavour.

2 Cooking the flour at this stage prevents the sauce having a floury taste, and also prepares the flour to absorb the liquid; as a result of which the liquid will thicken more readily when it comes to the boil. (As laundry starch bursts when boiling water is poured on to it, so the starch grains in flour burst, thickening the liquid when it boils.)

3 You can't make a blond or brown roux *without* cooking it.

■ A roux is cooked over *low* heat and stirred at regular intervals, to prevent the flour burning. If it burns, it not only gives the sauce a nasty taste, but may prevent it thickening properly as well.

■ Liquid is added to a roux aside from the heat because it is easier to incorporate that way. If you want to prepare a sauce in advance – leaving it ready just to boil up later when required – stir in the cold liquid gradually, with a wooden spoon. To add a nearly-boiling liquid to a roux, whisk it in all at once with a wire whisk, as soon as the roux has stopped bubbling.

■ You can make a roux hours before needed, even the day before if you want to: melt it again slowly when ready for it, but be careful not to leave any congealed on the spoon, or you'll probably end up with a lumpy sauce.

SALPICON

A preparation of one or more diced ingredients, bound together with a tasty sauce. There are endless varieties. Use them to fill such things as vol-au-vent cases, bouchées, tartlets or croustades.

SAUTÉ

From the French *sauter* – to jump (some foods jump about when fried). Small pieces of fish, meat, poultry or game – liver, kidneys, tournedos, salmon, chicken, etc. – are browned initially in a small quantity of pre-heated very hot fat in a sauté pan, or very strong frying pan, to seal in the juices.

■ Ideally one should use either a mixture of butter and olive oil (the oil allowing the butter to reach a higher temperature without burning), or saltless or clarified butter.
■ One can cook the food completely, in which case lower the heat after browning, or one can just brown it prior to cooking in another way. Some vegetables are sautéd in hot butter from start to finish. Others are blanched first.
■ Be sure the food is quite dry and the pan not overcrowded, otherwise the food will steam, not brown.
■ Use the juices left in the pan to make a sauce, see *deglaze*, page 59.

SAVOURY

Served as the last course at dinner, this is intended to clean the palate after the sweet, before serving port.

SCALDING

Means either bringing a liquid to just below boiling point, or pouring boiling water on to a food, like blanching.

SCRAPING

Scraping cut or chopped-up food off a chopping board into a pan or bowl, isn't just a combination of good aim and luck when you have the board overlapping the front of the table: hold the pan or bowl underneath it, and guide the food into it with a knife.

SEARING

This means browning meat quickly under high heat, or in hot fat, to seal in the juices. If the fat isn't hot enough, the juices will escape into it – and with them, flavour.

SEASONING

The name we give to salt, pepper and other dry ground spices when we add them to food during cooking. If added at table, we call them condiments, from the Latin *condire*, to season or pickle. See also *salt*, page 117, and *pepper*, page 120.

TO SEPARATE AN EGG

You need two basins or cups. Tap the middle of the side of the egg lightly but sharply on the edge of one basin to make an even, crosswise break. Now take the egg, cracked side upwards, in both hands, hold it over the basin and tip the egg so that it is blunt (wide) end downwards. Hold the edges of the crack with the tips of your thumbs and open it up by pulling apart the two edges until the shell is in halves. (Some of the white will drop into the basin as you do this, while the yolk and remaining white will stay in the blunt end.) Now pour the remaining egg from one half of the shell to the other, letting more of the white drop into the basin each time until only the yolk is left. Break off the chalazae (page 56) over the edge of the shell if necessary, and drop the yolk into the clean basin.

TO SET THE SPONGE

Applies to the making of certain yeast mixtures; a method used to speed up the action of yeast. For instance, a yeasty liquid (say yeast mixed with milk and egg) is poured into a well made in the flour, then a little of the surrounding flour is sprinkled over it and the bowl is covered and left. When bubbles of yeast start bursting through the floury surface – usually about 20 minutes if in a warm place – the sponge is set.

SHIVERING

An even lower temperature than simmering; no bubbles on the surface, 180–190°F/82–88°C. This is poaching temperature.

SIMMERING

Boiling *very* slowly in a covered pan on top of the cooker or in a covered dish in a very slow oven, the liquid showing only the slightest movement on the surface. Simmering temperature is around 200–210°F/93–99°C.

SITTING DOWN

Sitting down to cook, wash up, dry up and iron is a technique worth cultivating because it greatly reduces physical strain.

■ Like becoming accustomed to a thimble or rubber gloves, what at first seems impossible, soon becomes natural, even essential. A high stool – and some determination initially – are about all the average-height (or taller) person needs. Many sink units have an unshelved cupboard underneath, with sliding door. With your feet in the cupboard, you can work completely at ease – there are few jobs you can't do easily, and just as well.

SLAKING

Is blending a small amount of liquid with a thickening agent such as arrowroot, potato flour, cornflour or custard powder, prior to thickening soups, sauces or gravies with it.

SLICING AND DICING

Is an art, especially to do fast, evenly and without cutting your fingers. Given ten minutes, a chef will probably cut almost as many pounds of vegetables as most of us could cut ounces. It's worth watching if ever you have the chance – a case of 'practice makes perfect'.

■ To acquire this professional technique needs time, patience and perhaps weeks of practice. The art is to keep the tip of the blade on the chopping board, raising and lowering the knife handle to slice as you feed the vegetables under the blade. The amateur's way of cutting potato chips or diced vegetables is simpler:

1 Using a sharp knife (preferably a French cook's knife, page 31) gripped as illustrated, and keeping the fingertips of your left hand all the time tucked *under*, slice off thinly the rounded sides of a potato (or carrot or turnip) to make a more-or-less rectangular block.

2 Slice the block lengthwise, to the required thickness, each slice the same.
3 Reassemble the 'block' and give it a backwards or forwards quarter roll, the slices now lying neatly piled up on top of each other.
4 Control them, still as one block, with your thumb at end of potato nearest to you, small finger at far end, and your remaining three fingers on top, tips turned under. Then the slices can't slide about and you can't cut yourself, see illustration:

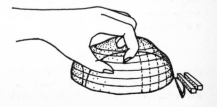

5 Slice the potato the same thickness as before, this time into chips.

6 *To cut dice* (for which you'll need thinner slices than for chips), give the block a quarter turn and slice *across* the chips, again the same thickness and with the same grip as before, to produce even-sized cubes.

SMOKE POINT

The temperature at which oils and fats begin to break down and give off a blue vapour. The temperature varies according to the type of fat, and the more refined it is, the higher the smoke point will be. Pure lard, for instance, has a high smoke point, while olive oil and unclarified dripping both have low smoke points. This explains why these two fats are unsuitable for deep fat frying, where the *lowest* temperature ever required is higher than their smoke point.

SORBET

Sometimes also called sherbet – a water ice, preferably served in a special 'cup' or glass. Often flavoured with lemon, its original purpose was to clear the palate between a rich entrée and the roast in a long Victorian dinner. Nowadays we make sorbets from many fruits, serving them whenever the occasion seems right: as a palate clearer; as refreshment during an evening party; as a thirst quencher on a hot day – lovely for instance at a tennis or children's summer party.

SOUFFLÉ

Comes from the French *souffler*, to blow up. The mixture is blown up by the air whisked into the eggs. See also *savoury soufflés*, page 150, and *cold soufflés*, page 298.

SPOONFULS

The standard measuring spoons (see page 43) which belong to a set and which are used by most manufacturers and maga-zine writers, are used level. However, a spoonful of a dry ingredient always used to mean (and still does in some books, this one included) *rounded* spoonfuls, so when following a recipe from an old book, i.e. pre-metric days, rounded spoonfuls will be implied unless the author says otherwise, see illustrations:

1 *teaspoon* means as much above the bowl as in it, not a heaped or mounded one.

½ *teaspoon* means a teaspoon levelled off with a knife.

¼ *teaspoon* means half a level teaspoon.

⅛ *teaspoon* means quarter of a level teaspoon.

■ A liquid spoonful means a *full* spoonful, whatever its size, not about ¾ or ⅞ of it! Especially when a recipe calls for 3 or 4 spoonfuls of an ingredient, that imbalance can make the difference between the perfection or otherwise certainly of some dishes, if not many.

STEAMING

Cooking by the vapour from boiling water, which must be kept boiling just hard enough for steam to escape continually (except for egg dishes when the water should just simmer). The lid must fit the steamer tightly, and the steamer must fit the pan, to prevent too much steam escaping.

■ Allow steamed foods about half as long again as boiled. There's less danger of overcooking, and of foods breaking up, because they're cooking more slowly.
■ Not all foods steam as well as they boil, however, green vegetables especially.

STEWING

Long slow cooking in a small quantity of liquid in a covered vessel, either in the oven, in a plugged-in slow-cooker or in a pan on top of the cooker. A close-fitting lid is essential, to prevent evaporation.

■ It's an economical method of cookery because it utilizes cheaper, tougher kinds of food.
■ See also *stews*, page 247.

STUFFINGS

See *farce*, page 60.

SWEATING

Plays an important part in the tenderizing of vegetables, especially of finely sliced onions before other ingredients are added. They are softened without being browned, by being partially cooked in fat, usually butter or oil, in a strong covered frying pan or saucepan over low heat.

TALMOUSE

A kind of cheese tartlet, served as an hors d'oeuvre or savoury.

TASTING

Is a must if you want to be a good cook. No sauce or soup should go to the table without tasting, nor should anything else you can easily sample. All your efforts may be wasted if you fail to taste, perfection often depending on it.

■ If it breaks your slimming rules, be strong-minded and taste without swallowing.

TOASTING

Toasting thinly sliced or frozen sliced bread is neither difficult nor impossible. The bread won't curl up at the corners and burn if you first grill each side until dried out but not coloured. Toasting in this way draws the moisture *evenly* out of both sides, helping the bread to stay flat when then toasted in the usual way.

UNMOULDING

Unmoulding creams and jellies, etc. can be tricky if you don't know how. A few drops of water smeared over the serving dish will make it easier to slide and centre the mould if it falls slightly to one side. Dip the mould for a few moments (not seconds) up to the rim in a large bowlful of water almost as hot as your hand can bear (no more, no less) to break the seal without also melting the jelly. Now use the tips of your fingers to loosen the top of the mould round the edges. Place the serving dish upside down on top, so that you can invert them both together, and then give a few firm shakes to release the jelly. If they refuse to part company, go back to the hot water stage.

■ Some people prefer to invert a mould over their flattened palm, carefully withdrawn as the mould slides out on to the dish.
■ See also *moulds*, page 33.

VANDYKING

A way of garnishing and can refer to various things, including the edges of fruits.

It is attractive but time-consuming, earning its name from the small pointed beard made famous by Van Dyck, the painter. The points must be fairly even if not to look amateurish.

Grapefruit It's quicker to use scissors

than a small stainless steel sawknife but you may ruin your scissors in the process. Cut just deep enough to show up, but not so deep that any juice will run out. I like to do it when the fruit is empty, see page 155.

Tomatoes Are done while whole, preferably with the tip of a small vegetable knife: hold fruit up in front of you in left hand, and work round in a circle until the ends meet:

1 Stick the knife point in the middle and make a small gash AB.
2 Turn point downwards and make the next gash CA to meet the first at A. The next gash is from D to C – and so on.
3 When circle is complete and ends meet – you hope – slip knife into middle of fruit to cut through the core, then ease and gently pull the two halves apart.

Apples Are easily done with a small pair of scissors after the fruits are hollowed out, before stuffing. Do the edge of the lid as well, dipping the cut edges in lemon juice to prevent discoloration.

WHISKING

Whisking egg whites successfully depends largely upon four things: the freshness of the eggs; your skill; the type of whisk (page 49) and bowl (see *mixing bowls*, page 16) used. Upon effective whisking and prompt correct folding, depends the volume and the lightness of whatever you are making. Avoid an *aluminium* bowl: its gives whisked whites a grey cast. On the other hand, should you have the luck to own a *copper* bowl, that's the best of all. Traces of copper combine with the albumen in the egg white, resulting not only in a greater volume of firm 'snow', but also in keeping it firm longer, even if by mistake you overbeat it. Two good and much less expensive alternatives to this (both using a spot of acid) are:

1 Rub the bowl round with a cut lemon before putting in the egg whites.
2 Add a pinch of cream of tartar per egg white when the whites start to look foamy soon after starting to whisk.

■ The tiniest trace of egg yolk or a greasy bowl or whisk will spoil perfect results.
■ Whether whisking by hand or with an electric whisk, you get the best results by whisking slowly at first, increasing gradually to a moderate speed when the whites start to foam.
■ If you whisk egg whites properly, they should be about 7 or 8 times their original volume, but just how stiffly you should whisk them depends upon what you want them for. You can easily over-whisk them, making them difficult to incorporate into a mixture.
■ These are the different stages to which recipes may tell us to whisk them:
Stiff: as you need egg whites for such things as soufflés and mousses. Whisk until you can *almost* safely turn the bowl upside-down, when the white is still very light and frothy.
Like cotton-wool is self-explanatory and it's quite a lot stiffer than stiff! This is the way you need them at the half-way stage for meringues, before you add the first of the sugar.
Rocky is much stiffer still, when the whites are shiny like satin, and as you need them for meringues, meringue toppings and for decorating. If you're whisking by hand, it may take you 5 minutes hard work between the cotton-wool and rocky stages, but only if you've whisked whites really stiff like this will they support the sugar when you fold it in, and keep a perfect shape when piped.

WRINGING

Wringing things out may be something to which you never give a thought if you have normal hands. If you haven't, however, and you don't know that there's an art to it, you may not even be able to wring out a dishcloth to wipe down your cooker, draining board, pans or anything else. Here's an easy and most effective way – a help for bulky things like towels even if you're nimble fingered:

First squeeze out as much surplus water as possible, then form the dishcloth (or whatever) into a shape long enough to stretch across both your hands when held palms upwards, and with your little fingers held close together. Now grip the cloth firmly in one hand – probably the left, unless you're left-handed – holding it still while the other does the twisting, towards you. Let go of the cloth with the 'twisting' hand when you can twist it no further and then, palm upwards again, take a new grip of the cloth and twist it towards you again. Continue doing this until all the water is wrung out, as it will be – quickly. Once you've got the knack, it's done in seconds.

ZEST

Is the outer part of the skin of citrus fruits – lemons, oranges, limes and grapefruit. It contains the essential oil of the fruit, and is used to flavour such things as creams, whipped creams, ices, butter creams and custards. All the bitter pith is left on the fruit.

■ Scrape it off with a *zester* or remove it by rubbing a serrated knife up and down against the fruit. (So fine are the shreds, using a zester, that they disappear into the cooked dish, leaving virtually nothing but their flavour in their wake.)
■ You can also take zest off with sugar lumps, rubbing them one at a time up and down against the fruit. When impregnated, crush them, and allow to dissolve in the mixture.
■ Some graters have an extremely fine section which *may* act as a zester.

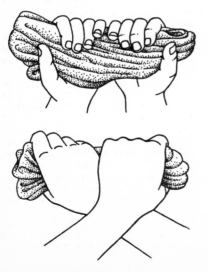

3

Ingredients

Successful cooking and the enjoyment one may have from it often depends on oddly varied scraps of knowledge so I'm not going to apologize for the hotch-potch of facts you'll find here.

There are some well-known and some little-known bits of information about the best-known as well as the not-so-well-known ingredients. I just hope that by filling in some of the missing pieces in the cookery jigsaw, they'll stimulate your interest and bring greater success to your results.

AGAR AGAR

The Malayan word for a species of red algae, used primarily to mean the trade product made from that particular algae or seaweed. The vegetarian's equivalent of gelatine – and hideously expensive – it is the oddest stuff to use, and is unlike gelatine in every way, except that both gel when combined with liquid.

■ A little goes a long way, because agar has enormous gelling power – though this is destroyed if it is heated with even a small amount of anything acid.
■ You must boil to dissolve it, and it forms a firm jelly without refrigeration, setting some mixtures even before they're cool. It makes a more chewy jelly than one made with gelatine.

AIR

The intangible ingredient which every good cook incorporates by sieving flour and other dry ingredients, by whisking egg whites, by whipping cream, or by folding and rolling pastry. Without it there would be no soufflés, sponge cakes, or even pastry as we know it, because air is their *only* raising agent.

■ A cupful of flour, for instance, becomes 1¼ cupfuls when sieved, and egg whites will, if correctly whisked, multiply their volume by 7 or 8 times.
■ The tiny particles of trapped air expand when heated. The colder it is the more it will expand, which explains why cool pastry and chilled Yorkshire pudding batter rise better than when at room temperature.

ALMOND ESSENCE

This may seem unnecessary when a recipe already contains ground almonds, but it brings out the flavour of the almonds.

ANGELICA

Candied angelica is the stem or leaf stems of the angelica plant. See also *herbs*, page 101.

■ When using angelica to decorate, thick slices or chunks look clumsy, so wash it under the hot tap (to make it pliable), dry it, then cut into long, thin slices. It's easy to cut slices, with the minimum of waste, into several leaves (like pastry leaves) or whatever shape you want, as below:

ARROWROOT

Comes from the roots and rhizomes of a tropical plant, taking its name from the American Indian word for flour-root, *araruta*.

■ Its great advantages over cornflour are that it is tasteless and it gives a clear finish when used to thicken certain soups, gravies, fruit syrups and fruit sauces. For glazing a fruit flan for instance, cornflour would obscure the fruit and give a distinctive flavour whereas arrowroot simply makes the fruit shine.

■ Slake it (blend with a little liquid) before using – 2 level teaspoons to ¼pt/125ml fruit syrup. Unlike cornflour which needs cooking to get rid of its raw taste, arrowroot is ready to use as soon as it clears and thickens.

■ If you overheat (boil or nearly boil) the liquid before pouring onto the slaked arrowroot, it won't clear and thicken properly.

■ Grocers don't usually sell arrowroot – it's a chemist's item.

ASPIC

Ready-made aspic lacks that homemade flavour, but is useful when one only wants a small quantity, or when its bought flavour will be masked by others which are stronger. See also page 153.

BAKING POWDER

Made from bicarbonate of soda and a mild acid. When moist and warm, these chemicals react and give off carbon dioxide, causing foods to rise.

BICARBONATE OF SODA

Will also combine with other acids as well as cream of tartar to act as a raising agent. This is why vinegar may figure in a simple fruit cake recipe which omits baking powder, and why you can make scones with bicarbonate of soda and sour milk. The strength of these acids is not constant, however, so they are not as reliable as the pure chemicals.

■ Bicarbonate of soda used alone with plain flour will give off carbon dioxide when wet and warm, but it leaves sodium carbonate (washing soda) as a residue, which not only has an unpleasant taste but makes mixtures brown. When this strong flavour can be disguised, therefore, by other strong flavours such as mixed spice, ground ginger or black treacle, and when a brown colour is *wanted*, as in gingerbread or soda cake, bicarbonate of soda used alone with plain flour is *better* than other raising agents.

■ Use bicarbonate of soda in the proportion of 2 parts cream of tartar to 1 part bicarbonate of soda, otherwise the bicarbonate of soda will dominate, spoiling both the flavour and colour of whatever you're making.

■ Bicarbonate of soda should always be sieved with other dry ingredients because any tiny lumps of it cannot unite with the acid.

BREAD

Keeps fresher and remains good longer if in a polythene bag in the bread bin; longer still in the refrigerator. If you have a deep freeze, you can have fresh bread continually, by putting part of a new loaf straight into it.

■ Sliced bread can be fried while still frozen, and even thinly sliced can be toasted without curling up, if you dry out both sides before toasting either until golden, see page 83.

■ Soft bread and rolls freeze perfectly for months, but the crusts of *crusty* loaves and rolls soon shell off.

■ One can rejuvenate a loaf of bread by wrapping it in foil and cooking, direct from the freezer, in a hot oven, gas 6, 400°F/205°C for about ¾ hr. Hot, crisp and new again, it needs eating quickly, because it soon dries out. See also page 307.

BREADCRUMBS

Dried white breadcrumbs A must for perfect results when coating delicately flavoured foods, such as fish, with egg and breadcrumbs. If crumbs are golden before you fry food, they will be too dark, if not burnt by the time it's cooked.

■ Dry fresh white breadcrumbs thoroughly, without colouring, in a very cool oven, then sieve and store them in an airtight jar. They'll keep for months – it's moisture which makes bread go mouldy.

■ 4 level tablespoons dried breadcrumbs weigh 1oz/25g.

Fresh breadcrumbs Will keep for months sealed in a polythene bag in the freezer, or for a long time in the refrigerator, so it's worthwhile making a quantity while you're about it. (Use *dry* bread.)

■ Sieve them for special things, such as coating foods with egg and breadcrumbs, but for less important purposes such as stuffings, bread sauce, or a queen of puddings, you can easily make crumbs in a liquidizer.

■ If you haven't got a sieve or a liquidizer, you can crumble stale bread between your hands, if the worst comes to the worst.

■ 4–5 level tablespoons fresh breadcrumbs weigh 1oz/25g.

Fried breadcrumbs See page 262.

Golden breadcrumbs Also known as *raspings*. Made from oven-dried bread crusts, etc. they are sieved and used to sprinkle over dishes cooked *au gratin*, to coat the fat of cooked ham, or they're lovely fried, to serve with roast game. They'll keep almost indefinitely in an airtight jar.

Bought breadcrumbs They're a sham. You must be very short of time to use *them*!

BUTTER

Butter is the fat with which I most love to cook, mainly because of its flavour. I would usually rather use the cheapest butter than the most expensive margarine.

■ In French cookery, butter, eggs, oil, cream, cheese and wine are all considered essentials, but outside France the true qualities of butter seem often to be neither realized nor understood. If you fry, sauté or otherwise cook in butter such foods as eggs, vegetables or small pieces of fish or meat, they seem to taste twice as good as those cooked in other fats. Cakes made with butter both taste better and keep fresh longer than those made with margarine.

■ When you fry or sauté with butter, it needs to be *hot*, the condition of the foam indicating the right moment to start cooking: as the butter melts, there is no foam and nothing would brown in it. As it heats, the liquids in the butter begin to evaporate, making it foam. It is as the foam subsides – when the liquids have almost evaporated – that you should begin to cook. If you fail to catch this moment, the butter starts to change colour. The hotter it becomes, the darker brown it turns, until at 278°F/137°C, it burns.

■ Salted butter – that's most kinds of butter – goes brown and burns at a lower temperature than saltless butter, discolouring food cooked in it. This is why some recipes call for saltless or clarified butter (see page 57) when a good colour and flavour really matter.

■ If you're frying foods such as chicken, which need longish cooking, add 1 dessertspoon of oil to 2oz/50g butter. The oil allows the butter to reach a higher temperature without burning.

■ Avoid sprinkling salt over foods while they're frying in butter, because salt makes them stick to the pan. Foods fried in saltless butter won't stick as they do in salted.

■ Butter congeals on fried or roasted foods served cold, unlike cooking oil (and some white cooking fats). It pays, therefore, to fry or roast in oil those foods which you intend to serve cold.

■ Butter tastes best when chilled, so for the table serve it slightly chilled when you can: put the pats straight into iced water, then cover and refrigerate them until needed.

■ If frying bread in butter (or any other fat), fry both sides momentarily before frying until golden: less butter is absorbed, and less is needed.

■ When a recipe directs you to melt butter, it *means* melt, not heat it. It is usually melted over minimum heat because, if overheated it separates and goes oily, and will not then amalgamate properly with other ingredients, spoiling things like Genoese pastry. If you overheat saltless butter, it loses its fresh flavour into the bargain.

■ Some brands of butter are slightly firmer than others. Firm (though not actually hard) butter is best for things like pastry which require manipulation, but soft butter makes lighter cakes because more air can be beaten into it. If by putting butter in a warm place (you mustn't let it oil) you can get it to a texture similar to that of a soft margarine, you can use it in the same way to make an all-in-one mixture (see page 318) – even a Dundee cake, for example.

■ Saltless butter will keep for 6–8 months in a freezer, salted only 3–4, but it's hardly worth storing in bulk unless you can buy it cheaply, because it keeps so well in the refrigerator.

■ While most countries cook by weight, the Americans cook by volume, which makes the use of their recipes tricky to say the least of it. To measure butter, here is some guidance:

American	approximate imperial/ metric equivalents
1 tablespoon	½oz/15g
¼ cup	2oz/50g
⅓ cup	scant 3oz/70g
½ cup (or 1 stick)	4oz/100g

CANNED FOODS

Let's face it, canned foods are often radically different from the original because, unlike freezing, preservation or canning alters their nature. It's sometimes hard to remember that canned peaches once smelt and tasted of the sun, that salmon tasted of the sea, or that peas came out of crisp green pods. Whilst we'd undoubtedly find catering more difficult if deprived of canned foods, many families would surely feed better with fewer.

■ If you can be bothered, mark cans with the date before storing, you'll bless your discipline later. Though it will give no indication of time spent on a shop shelf before finding their way to your larder, it's a reminder of their purchase date, which will help you to use them in rotation.

■ Canned foods and vegetables are harvested in their prime and immediately prepared and canned. The majority are cooked foods which can be eaten straight from the can or used in various recipes. The canning company, Metal Box, say that once the can has been opened and only part of its contents used, it's perfectly in order to cover and put it in the refrigerator, using as you would cooked food. Fruits, fruit juices and evaporated milk are the exceptions and should be decanted when opened, otherwise they tend to alter slightly in flavour.

■ All blown or leaking cans should be discarded – the former are distinguishable by bulged ends. Small dents on the body of a can are not significant, but cans with severe dents affecting the end seams should not be stored, which is why a supermarket will usually sell them at a reduction.

■ The length of time a product will keep after manufacture depends both on the conditions under which it is stored and the type of packaging materials used.

■ Metal Box's list below gives times ot keeping during which the product will remain in good condition if stored in a cool, dry place – but never in a freezer. It doesn't mean that after the times stated the foods will be inedible, but certain changes in colour, texture, aroma or flavour will start to occur. However, any products with a storage life of *less than one year* should be used within the year.

Product	Storage life in good condition
cocoa and drinking chocolate	1 year
coffee, instant	1 year
cornflour	1 year
custard powder	1 year
drinks, carbonated	6–12 months
fish in oil	up to 5 years
fish in tomato sauce	1 year
fruit (most fruits) prunes and rhubarb	1–2 years 9 months
fruit juices	1 year
hams, pasteurized, over 2 lb/1kg (if pasteurized, it will be stated on the label)	keep refrigerated and use in 6 months
hams, sterilized, 2lb/1kg and under	2–3 years
jams and marmalades	1–2 years
meats, solid – see also hams, above	up to 5 years
milk in cans	1 year
milk, dried, skimmed and full cream	9–12 months
pasta foods in sauce	2 years
soups	2 years
vegetables	2 years

CARMINE

Made from the dried bodies of female cochineal insects after they've been fertilized, but before the complete development of the eggs. See also *food colourings*, page 97.

CEREALS

Strictly speaking, cereals are cultivated grasses and their seeds or grain. These include wheat, oats, barley, rye, rice and maize, the word cereal being derived from Ceres, the Roman goddess of the harvest.

■ Wheat is known to have been used as human food for at least 6,000 and possibly 10,000 years. The ability to farm cereals, of which wheat was apparently the first, is probably one of the chief causes which led man to live in communities rather than to live a wandering life, hunting and herding cattle and other animals. When man discovered cereals, he found a food which could be grown in quantity during the warmer months of the year, and stored successfully through the colder. You could even say that with the discovery of cultivating wheat and other cereals, civilization began. They are the most important of all food plants – we eat more cereal food than any other.

■ See also *gluten*, page 100.

CHEESE

Cheese is almost as old as man, records going back to at least 4,000 BC. David was delivering cheese to Saul's camp at the time of his battle with Goliath. Cheeses travelled with the armies of Caesar. Marco Polo returned from his travels with reports of cheeses as made in the East. Its discovery was undoubtedly an accident: a simple matter of milk curdling.

■ It isn't just from cow's and goat's milk that cheese is made. Depending on the part of the world, it may be made of ewe, yak, llama or even reindeer milk. Not only does cheese differ according to the type and quality of the milk, but also according to the seasons and the mineral salts in the pasture land on which the animals have fed, to the way a cheese is made, and the skill of the cheesemaker.

■ On average, cheese contains one-third protein, one-third fat and one-third water – but, unlike milk, it contains no carbohydrates. This is because in cheese-making the milk sugar (lactose) is converted into lactic acid. It's mainly because of this concentration of fat that cheese is difficult to digest unless properly cooked – yet it would seem so simple that one couldn't go wrong. It's sometimes the cook's fault that people can't eat cooked cheese so here are a few tips just in case you want them:

1 *Always* grate cheese very finely, to melt quickly and completely in a mixture. See *mouli grater*, page 30.

2 Add cheese to a sauce *after removing pan from heat*, so that it isn't in fact cooked at all. Providing the sauce is boiling hot and the cheese finely grated, it will melt without being heated.

3 Add mustard, vinegar or a piquant sauce to cheese mixtures, to stimulate the digestive juices as well as to give flavour. Accompanying a cheese dish with a dressed salad serves the same purpose – say a green salad, tomato or even cucumber salad. As cheese is salted in manufacture, use salt sparingly.

4 Always use a preheated red-hot grill, to brown cheese rather than cook it through. If you cook it slowly, it becomes leathery and indigestible. If the food is too close to the grill, however, it may go black in patches.

5 Reheated cheese dishes are only for those with an iron constitution.

6 Use the right kind of cheese. Soft cheeses are unsuitable because one can't grate them like hard and, if even only slightly over-mature, they can irritate the digestive system.

■ *Cheddar* is probably the best of the English cheeses for cooking because it's flavourful without being acid, and also hard enough to grate finely.

■ *Parmesan* and *Gruyère* – or *Emmenthal* – are often used together, the Parmesan for its flavour, the other for its creaminess. Another advantage of a dryish cheese like Gruyère is that it is less inclined than many others to become oily in hot mixtures. (Emmenthal has larger holes than the true Gruyère.)

■ Cheese and red wine are natural partners, so cheese is always welcome somewhere in a dinner menu.

■ Refrigerating and freezing spoil the texture of soft cheeses, so it's better to buy little and often.

■ Most cheeses will keep fresh and moist longer when wrapped in foil than in other wrappings, because both light and air are excluded.

■ Mouldy cheese is quite edible once you've cut off the mould – cheese mould isn't harmful, so there's no need to waste any more of the cheese.

■ A catering pack of grated Parmesan cheese is a cheaper way to buy if you can store most of it in the freezer, keeping a little in the refrigerator for general use. Freshly grated Parmesan naturally has more flavour than ready-grated.

■ See also *Cheeseboard*, page 342.

CHERRIES, GLACÉ

Glacé cherries which are preserved in a very thick syrup should, for a cake, be washed in hot water, dried in a cloth and lightly dusted with a little of the weighed flour: otherwise, due to their weight, they'll probably sink before the cake mixture sets and can support them.

■ For decorating, cherries are daintier, just as colourful, and much nicer to eat when cut in small pieces.

■ Glacé cherries are incorrect for grapefruit because they have the wrong flavour and texture. You need *maraschino* for these.

■ See also page 276.

CHOCOLATE

As we all know, chocolate starts life as cocoa beans, but the fat present in the beans, cocoa butter, is less well understood. It is quite hard at ordinary room temperature but melts at just below body temperature – which explains why chocolate melts so easily on a hot day or in a child's hand. This enables chocolate to be used for bars, or as a coating for sweets and biscuits, where it remains solid until one eats it, but makes it less good as a cake icing (because of its 'snap' when cut) unless you add a little oil and sugar to soften it (1 teaspoon bland oil, 1oz/25g caster sugar, 2¼ tablespoons/45ml water to 4oz/100g chocolate).

■ UK legislation as to what may or may not be called chocolate has recently changed: what was formerly called cooking chocolate may no longer be, and is now labelled 'cake covering'.

Cake covering Contains an alternative fat in place of cocoa butter. Besides its lower price, the main advantage of this softer product is its ease of handling, in easy melting and in re-setting without any bloom appearing on the surface. The melting and setting properties of cake coverings are all important, but achieved very much to the detriment of the flavour. Therefore, although the flavour is much weaker than and greatly inferior to that of a dessert chocolate, a cake covering is considerably easier to use.

Dessert chocolate This may be either plain or milk.
Plain. A top-quality brand such as Bournville or Menier contains no other fat except cocoa butter, and is the best to use when flavour really matters as in a chocolate soufflé, a fine sauce, chocolate crème au beurre, truffles or in *anything* special. It is made from cocoa beans selected to have the desired flavours, and roasted to bring out those flavours to the extent required.
Milk. A variety such as Cadbury's Dairy Milk tends to be softer then plain chocolate because butterfat present in the milk, which replaces some of the cocoa butter, is softer than cocoa butter – the major fat in plain chocolate. Milk chocolate is usually less good for cooking than plain because, containing less cocoa, it doesn't give such a strong chocolate flavour. There is also the danger of the milk fats breaking down if the chocolate is overheated (see point 2 below).

■ The hardening or 'scrambling' of chocolate when overheated is usually due to too rapid heating and can result from:

  1 caramelization of the sugar;
  2 breakdown of the milk fats, in the case of milk chocolate – which is one reason why so many recipes call for plain chocolate;
  3 condensed steam getting into the chocolate, such as can happen when one uses a double saucepan;
  4 you can't 'unscramble' it if caused by 1 or 2 above, so the only remedy is to start again – if remedy you can call it. Unless you've got the patience of Job, I wouldn't bother to try and recover it from 3 either. It requires long-continued stirring and gentle warming.

■ Chocolate *is* tricky to melt without liquid. The vital thing is to do it really slowly in a thick china basin and to be sure that the water over which you're melting it is neither actually boiling, nor deep enough to touch the bottom of the basin. It's sometimes easier, depending on how you are going to use it, to melt a small quantity on a plate, resting on top of a pan containing 'shivering' water.

■ A Mouli grater grates chocolate finely and quickly – more quickly than doing it against an upright grater.

■ To make curls of chocolate quickly when decorating a cake or sweet, take a bar of cake covering or milk chocolate (both are softer than plain chocolate) and scrape down the edge of it with a potato peeler.

■ Chocolate flavoured cold sweets have more flavour when served at room temperature than chilled, from the refrigerator.

Drinking chocolate This is cocoa with sugar. It is not recommended as a substitute for either cocoa or chocolate in cooking, except as a coating, say for truffles.

CIDER

Made from special apples, sweet and sour, the varieties of which, differentiated by cultivation, have given a reputation to certain localities in which cider is produced, like Somerset in England, or Normandy in France. In general, cider is made with about one-third sweet apples and two-thirds sour.

■ For cooking, cider teams up in flavour with and counteracts the richness of pork, gammon and bacon in just the same way as apple does. Use some as part of the liquid when braising or boiling gammon, for instance.

■ Flat, left-over cider is excellent for cooking (as long as it hasn't fermented of course). The art of cooking with cider is to reduce it (see page 77) by half, then cool, bottle, cork and refrigerate it. Used in this way, the alcohol is evaporated and the flavour strengthened.

CITRIC ACID

A sharp-flavoured crystalline acid, made from lemons and other citrus fruits. If a lemonade recipe includes citric acid,

don't imagine it's unimportant, because it helps to give a concentrated flavour without using too many lemons.

■ For a delicious recipe for such a lemonade, see page 338.

COCOA

See page 335.

COFFEE

Coffee essence In the 19th century, Scotland led the world in producing the first coffee in concentrated form. Easily bottled, it was shipped abroad in large quantities to Queen Victoria's forces all over the British Empire. Along with beef cubes, it was in fact one of the very first 'convenience' foods.

■ According to the manufacturer, 'Camp' is prepared by a special process, known only to the proprietors. It is made 'from the finest coffee procurable, cane sugar and a proportion of chicory. All the nutritive and stimulating properties of the coffee are retained'.

■ Used in cookery, coffee essence gives concentrated flavour to cold sweets (coffee junket, mousse, cream, soufflé, etc.), cakes, icings and fillings, ice creams and milk shakes, or in fact to anything which would be spoiled by the wateriness of real coffee.

Instant coffee powder or granules Can sometimes be used to give coffee flavour, made with a very small quantity of boiling water to concentrate the flavour in the minimum of liquid. It's also useful when, for instance, a recipe calls for sponge cakes dipped in coffee-flavoured milk.

■ See also page 335.

COOKING FATS

Those of good quality are 100 per cent pure fat and made with refined oils which aim to be colourless, flavourless and odourless. They keep well, even without refrigerating, so there's certainly no need to deep-freeze them.

■ They are good for deep-fat frying, and though more expensive than lard, are mostly less expensive than a good oil.

■ The cost of a cooking fat is usually determined by the oils used. All are fully refined but some sources that can be used are cheaper than others, and a greater proportion of these cheaper oils are present in the cheaper brands, which are often made from a blend of oils which can include animal, marine and vegetable oils.

■ A blend of pure sunflower oil together with other refined vegetable oils is primarily designed for pastry-making (see instructions on packet for the method) but is also good for roasting or frying. Since no animal matter is included, it is useful for vegetarians – and it contains no more than a minute trace of cholesterol. Just enough hardened vegetable oils are blended in to make it useable direct from the refrigerator (like a soft lard) to make shortcrust pastry. If you enjoy fried food, this is a more 'healthy' fat to use than many others.

■ Good brands of white vegetable fat can be used at all times in place of lard, over which they have certain advantages:

1 They don't smell, as most lards do, when frying.
2 Refrigerated, or at room temperature, some brands are easier to rub into flour than lard (unless a soft one) of similar temperature. This is because they're slightly aerated.
3 Cooking oils and some white fats do not congeal on fried or roast foods when served cold, because they solidify at a lower temperature, and so the fat or oil can be more thoroughly drained on to absorbent kitchen paper.

■ See also *lard*, page 104.

CORNFLOUR

Milled from maize, not nearly as good a thickening as potato flour (see page 116). Cornflour needs more cooking, makes a cloudy sauce (unlike arrowroot) and – more important still – has a distinctive flavour, which may dominate a delicately flavoured dish.

■ One part cornflour to four parts plain flour makes light sponge cakes, because cornflour contains no gluten. It therefore lowers the overall gluten content, when one wants a light, soft mixture. If using regularly, it's easiest to blend a quantity of flour and cornflour while you're about it, sieving them together twice, before storing as other flours, ready for use.

CREAM

Cream comes in three different thicknesses, double, whipping and single. Sometimes one has particular advantages over another, sometimes they are interchangeable. It can also be made in a liquidizer or cream machine, but its use is limited, see page 342.

Double cream Good for vegetables, and usually best for a cream dressing, a gâteau or for anything like meringues, brandy snaps or éclairs which would be spoilt by the wateriness of thinner cream. This is also the cream for piping and decorating.

Whipping cream If you can't buy this, make it by mixing together equal quantities of double and single cream. Whipping cream is better and also cheaper (especially if you make your own) than double cream when cream has to be half-whipped, as for a cold soufflé, a mousse or ice cream. This is because it is less easily over-whipped and gives dishes a smooth light texture.

■ It will whip quite thick enough to be served separately with a sweet – makes lovely crème chantilly (see page 303), for instance – but not thick enough to pipe well.

Single cream Ideal for vegetables and for many soups and sauces, and for anything which has to be thinned down with cream.

■ As long as you're not a weight-watcher, and have a deep purse, it's just the thing for quiche lorraine or, used instead of milk, can take a down-to-earth dish like egg custard into the luxury class.

Half-whipped cream Should be thick enough to leave a trail, which sinks fairly quickly without trace, when dropped from the whisk back into the cream.

■ When adding half-whipped cream to a mixture, if one whips it to roughly the same consistency as that mixture, it will blend perfectly without forming snow-flakes, as it does if too stiff. Be sure the mixture is cold though when you add the cream, otherwise cream will lose its stiffness and thin out.

Whipped cream Cream, whether double or whipping, gives greater volume (and in hot weather is less likely to go buttery before you can whisk air into it) if the cream is chilled, also if possible the bowl and whisk. Use a mixing bowl (page 16) rather than a pudding basin and, if you have one, a coil-rim or balloon whisk, *not* a rotary whisk (see *whisks*, page 49). When perfect, whipped cream should be light, airy and about doubled in volume. If overwhipped, it ends up as butter – and jolly little of that.

■ Should double cream look buttery in hot weather, lightly stir in 1 tablespoonful milk per ¼pt/150ml before starting to whip.
■ If to be used for decoration, whip cream until just thick enough to stand in light peaks.
■ If whipping cream to fold into another mixture, for perfect blending whip it to roughly the same consistency as that mixture.
■ If adding a flavouring, such as brandy or a liqueur, to double cream, add it before whipping. (Added to *whipping* cream, the consistency may be too thin then to whip well.)
■ Gelatine adds bulk to whipped cream and will prevent separation of the water and fats in the cream for an indefinite period, even in very hot weather. Simply

sprinkle in the dry gelatine while whipping: ¼oz/10g gelatine to 1pt/600ml double cream.

Frozen cream Some makes are so good that, unless compared with Channel Islands cream, they are impossible to distinguish from fresh cream, especially when whipped. Some are very easy to measure too, coming in cork-shaped pieces, 6 making ¼pt/150ml. If freezers had been invented only for cream, I would have a freezer! Frozen cream is less expensive than fresh (no risk of waste for producer, retailer or housewife); you can use as little as you like when you like to put in soup, coffee or, say, to make a salad dressing; it is easily and quite quickly thawed; its freezer life is usually 6 months; cream is always at hand.

Long life cream Something my refrigerator never lacks. Less good than fresh or the best frozen cream, it's nonetheless an indispensable reserve, especially when you have no time, or forget, to thaw frozen cream.

Soured cream This is single cream, commercially soured, with a thick but soft consistency and a sharp flavour. For its thickest consistency, spoon it from its carton without stirring.

■ Fresh cream which is pasteurized will not sour naturally, but you can sour it by adding 2 teaspoons lemon juice to ¼pt/150ml double cream, leaving it covered, at room temperature, for 15 minutes.
■ Use soured cream as a base for dips, spoon it over fruit pies, stir it at the last minute into sautéd vegetables, vegetable soups or into some bland sauces. (When adding it to soups and sauces, stir a little of the hot liquid into the cream before adding the cream to, and heating it with, the remainder.)
■ Soured cream doesn't separate.
■ Blend a little with mayonnaise to sharpen and lighten it.
■ Use to replace some or all of the oil in a salad dressing.
■ Soured cream doesn't suit everybody:

it is too acid.

■ See also *cream, sour*, page 302.

CREAM OF TARTAR

A purified form of the deposit from fermented wine. It is used in the proportions of two parts cream of tartar to one part bicarbonate of soda, so that the flavour of the latter won't dominate, or make a cake or scones too brown.

■ One can sometimes substitute other acids for cream of tartar, such as sour milk, buttermilk, vinegar or lemon juice; see *bicarbonate of soda*, page 87.
■ A small pinch of cream of tartar acts as a stabilizer to egg whites when whisking, see page 84.
■ Cream of tartar acts as a deterrent to the crystallization of sugar – when a recipe calls for it in a syrup heated to a high temperature.

CUSTARD POWDER

Like cornflour and cornflakes, it is made from maize (corn).

DRIED FRUITS

Currants Take their name from Corinth, from where they originated – *raisins de Corinthe*. They are of course very small, seedless dried sweet grapes.

Dates See page 277.

Prunes Dried plums with a particularly high sugar content, and firm flesh.

Raisins A special variety of grape, dried in the sun or by artificial heat, to crystallize their sugar, and so preserve them. Besides being full of goodness, they are valuable in cookery for their flavour and texture.

Sultanas Also a special variety of grape, similar to raisins: seedless, golden-yellow and very sweet. The Americans call them seedless white raisins.

DRIPPING

Must be the downfall of many a cook, who pours any kind of fat, whatever has been fried or roasted in it, into a jar labelled *Dripping*. This awful mixture, possibly strong with age, is used to cook anything and everything from eggs to game. Full of impurities, which irritate the digestive system – often guaranteed to *cause* indigestion – it spoils the true flavour of anything cooked in it, unless first clarified.

■ Beef dripping is of course the right fat to use for roast beef or something like a beef stew; pork dripping for pork and gammon, etc., but each needs a jar of its own, and should be used soon.
■ Rendered chicken fat has a fine and delicate flavour. When using chicken stock for a soup, you can sweat the vegetables in chicken fat first, or use it to make a roux for a sauce – as long as the flavour isn't too strong for the dish concerned. It has a semi-liquid consistency, only partially solidifying if refrigerated or in a very cold larder.
■ The jelly under solidified meat dripping (or thoroughly chilled chicken dripping) gives lovely extra flavour to soups and sauces. The day after roasting a turkey, for instance, I always cut into pieces the jelly which has set under the (chilled) dripping, wrap each piece in Cling-film, and then freeze all in a container for future use. Alternatively, you can use the jelly as a stock cube, in any recipe calling for stock.
■ Dripping must be clarified for deep fat frying, because the impurities in it burn at high temperatures, giving food a bitter taste and a bad colour.
■ One can use clarified dripping for a plain luncheon cake.

EGGS

See pages 142 to 151.

FLOUR

White flour should always be sieved for

things like pastry, cakes or scones, however fine it is. Sieving traps air, blends together dry ingredients and gets rid of even the smallest lumps in any of them.

■ Water absorption depends on the type of or mixture of wheats so, of course, flours vary in the amount of liquid they'll absorb. This explains why recipes can't always give precise quantities, and why it is such an advantage for a cook to know what a mixture or dough should look or feel like, at different stages of its making.

White plain flour Has dozens more uses than self-raising, and is the one to use unless a recipe directs otherwise. With the addition of various raising agents, one can use it to make almost anything.

White or brown self-raising flour Is plain flour with a raising agent (bicarbonate of soda plus an acid) added, so it has limited uses. Its raising agent often conflicts with others which one may want or have to use, giving inferior results in various ways.

■ White self-raising flour is fine for things like a sponge pudding or a sandwich cake, but it has too much raising agent for rich cakes with a high egg content, and not enough for scones. It's not impossible to make a yeast dough with it, but such bread very quickly goes dry.
■ The advantages of self-raising flour seem to be few, as far as I can see: it's convenient; one can't forget to add the raising agent; it isn't essential to cook immediately certain cakes or puddings made with it.
■ These plain and self-raising flours which we use are *soft household flours* produced from winter wheat, which is sown in the autumn and harvested the following summer. Soft flour has a lower gluten content than strong so makes poorer bread, but better and lighter pastry and cakes.

Strong flour Rich in gluten so makes the best bread, and one can't make real croissants or perfect puff pastry without. It is made mainly from spring wheat, which is grown in cold climates like North America, Canada or Russia, where winter wheat can't be sown because it would be frozen in the ground; it is sown in the spring, and harvested in the late summer. In Britain there is not usually enough sun in the spring and summer months for it to grow fast enough – but some is grown.

100 per cent stoneground wholemeal or wholewheat flour Contains the whole of the wheat grain, without separation, ground between stones. It contains all the natural richness of the wheat and is, healthwise, the most valuable of all flours. It provides a balance of nutriments to give staying power, and helps to prevent constipation. At the same time, it is a lower calorie flour than white or brown

Roller milled wholemeal A similar flour, but during milling the wheat constituents are separated by the roller and have to be mixed together again at the end of the process, to make the meal up to 100 per cent extraction.

Wheatmeal or brown flour Terms used to describe flours which are not wholemeal. The rate of extraction can vary, but officially 'shall contain not less than 0.6 per cent of fibre calculated by dry weight'. (Wholemeal or wholewheat contains about 1.8 per cent.)

Granary flour A sort of hybrid flour, including malted wheat and rye. It is coarse, has 'bite' and a strong nutty flavour which, when this bread is toasted, is accentuated. You can make bread with this flour alone; with a mixture of this and another brown flour, or the way I like it best, with a small proportion of strong (or plain) white flour – say seven-eighths granary, one-eighth white.

FOOD COLOURINGS

Edible food colourings will last for years so it's common sense to buy good quality. Essential for much cake decorating and confectionery, they'll also cheer up the dullest things if used discreetly. As usually only a drop or two is needed, one can avoid some hideous results by dipping the point of a skewer into the bottle and shaking a drop or two of dye off into whatever one wants to colour.

■ A drop of colour will cheer up junket or a milk jelly, for instance. A dash of green added to the syrup glaze will spotlight the pears in a flan. A drop of yellow makes cream look extra rich for meringues and takes away the all-white look at the same time.

■ Coloured milk may tempt children to drink it, especially if you give them straws as well. For a young children's party, you could even let them choose the colour they want, mixing it as they watch. One only needs imagination. See also *carmine*, page 90.

GARLIC

A member of the lily family, the bulbs varying very much in size, as do the number and size of their cloves.

■ Use just as much or as little garlic as you like, but one clove, a segment of the head, is often enough. Keep it in a dry airy place. Its strong smell and flavour are weakened by blanching, but one can also use it so subtly that one may find friends claiming to dislike it while unwittingly enjoying it! Add a crushed clove to a bouquet garni for certain dishes, to give an elusive and lovely flavour; or put a cut-up clove on top of a roast or, sliced, on beef or gammon steaks before grilling them.

■ Fried garlic tends to be bitter and pungent. Some people prefer to add it to onions and other foods after they've been fried.

■ The reason why the smell of garlic hangs around for hours after we eat it is because it is expelled through the lungs.

■ To crush garlic, first pull a clove off the head, then remove its outer skin and squash it in one of these ways:

1 In a garlic press, see page 29.
2 Under the blade of a heavy, flat knife, pressing it down hard with the heel of your hand – the quickest way if you're strong enough.

3 With a sharp round-ended knife – slice the clove very finely, sprinkle it with salt and then squash it in up-and-down movements with the end of the knife until soft and mushy.

■ Garlic is sometimes called the vanilla of vegetables.

GELATINE

A material extracted from the colagen present in the bones and tissues of animals. It is obtained from selected hide pieces and bones taken from sheep and cattle killed for the meat industry. It is a tasteless, odourless, transparent, brittle solid, very faint yellow in colour.

■ According to Davis Gelatine Ltd:

> The introduction of jelly into England undoubtedly took place from the observation that when using bones to make soup, the liquid gelled, and by gradual clarification a reasonably clear jelly could be obtained. Mention is made in the household chronicles of Charles II that His Majesty delighted in 'jelleys made of the juices of fat capon, rich wines and ye finyst of herbes'. It was not until the early part of the nineteenth century that gelatine manufacture emerged as an industry.

■ One of the most important aspects of cooking with gelatine is its economy: gelatine gives bulk by converting liquids into solids, semi-solids, or thick liquids, depending on the quantity of gelatine added. It helps you to 'extend' foods, especially canned fruits and vegetables, the nutritious juices of which you can gel, at the same time reducing waste. Rather similarly, of course, you can *thicken* a canned fruit syrup to give it more bulk and body, say with either arrowroot or cornflour. Foods such as butter, cream, cheese, fillings, spreads, thick sauces, mayonnaise, etc. are also, in fact, all extremely amenable to extension with gelatine, which can be a help if you cook for large numbers.

■ *Gelatine can be dissolved* by either of two methods. Whichever you use, always add gelatine to the liquid, not the other way round.

1 For small quantities of gelatine up to approximately ½oz/15g by sprinkling on to very hot but never boiling water in a cup, stirring as you do so.

2 By pre-soaking and applying heat, suitable for any quantity of gelatine. Although you can use up to 1oz/25g without soaking it first, it is better to soak it. This way, it goes into solution more rapidly than unsoaked, owing to the solution occurring from the outer and inner surfaces, whereas if gelatine is used unsoaked, swelling is retarded to a certain degree and solution takes place from the outer surface only.

■ Perhaps the safest way to dissolve gelatine – soaked or unsoaked – is in a basin over a pan of hot water, though I personally prefer to dissolve it over very low heat in a small saucepan. If you use a metal spoon to stir it, you can see when it's dissolved and ready to use because there'll be no sign of granules on the spoon.

■ Sprinkle powdered gelatine over the liquid so that the granules can easily absorb it, swelling and softening quickly. (Done the other way round, the liquid poured over a little heap of granules, the liquid can't penetrate them so easily.)

■ Avoid boiling gelatine at all costs, unless a recipe calls for it, because this reduces its setting power. When it *is* necessary almost to boil it, say for a cleared jelly, a higher proportion of gelatine than usual is used to counteract its loss in strength.

■ *When adding dissolved gelatine to a partly cooled mixture* in a cold basin, pour it slowly from a height into the middle of the mixture. It may go ropy if you don't do it carefully, whisking to blend it at once.

■ *When adding gelatine to refrigerated or very cold liquids*, always add a little of the cold liquid to the concentrated gelatine before combining both mixtures. This will prevent instantaneous setting or 'stringing' of the gelatine. (Should stringing occur, however, remove gelatine, re-melt, and add again as directed above.)

■ *When milk is heated with gelatine* or gelatine is added to hot milk, the separation of milk solids takes place and a curdled appearance results. It is not a true curdle because the milk, or custard as the case may be, is perfectly sweet. For *milk jelly*, see page 294.

■ The strength of a jelly is influenced by its temperature, so it may not set in hot weather unless you use more gelatine or less liquid. For most purposes, ½oz/15g gelatine will set 1pt/600ml liquid.

■ A smaller proportion of gelatine can be used for small individual moulds or when serving a mixture in the dish in which it is to set. A larger proportion is needed for a very large mould, or when heavy things like shellfish or fruit have to be supported in it.

■ Raw pineapple and kiwi fruit contain an enzyme which liquefies gelatine mixtures, so be sure to cook either of these before putting in jelly, or in any mixture containing gelatine.

■ Gelatine dissolved in sherry or Madeira gives subtlety to a sweet such as a chocolate soufflé.

■ Gelatine is a protein food. As it also helps the digestion of foods with which it is combined and is itself so nutritious and easily digested, it's ideal for old people, invalids or children. The blandness and monotony of a semi-liquid diet for instance can be livened up by using gelatine and flavourings to alter the consistency and flavour of things like milk, cream, eggs or fruit juices.

■ *Freezing gelatine dishes*. With the exception of ice cream, all should first be allowed to set in a cool place. Cover them closely while thawing, to prevent condensation forming, causing the jelly to liquefy. Generally speaking, gelatine dishes which are water-based, and are of a predominantly jelly nature, are unsuitable for freezing. When thawed, the dish loses its jelly-like composition. In ice cream, gelatine prevents the formation of coarse crystals and helps to stabilize the mixture.

■ In whipped cream, gelatine prevents the separation of the water and fats, even in extremely hot weather, see *whipped cream*, page 95.

■ The weight of a powdered gelatine may vary marginally according to manufacturer, but Davis Gelatine give this possibly useful information: 1 envelope or 3 level teaspoons (or four 5ml metric teaspoons) sets 1pt/600ml liquid.

■ Davis Gelatine also produce a booklet of recipes for diabetics. If you're one of those unfortunate enough to be on, or cooking for, such a diet, why not write to them – their address is on the packets.

GLUCOSE

Liquid glucose, like cream of tartar, acts as a deterrent to the crystallization of the sugar in syrups heated to a high temperature, the amount used depending upon the purpose for which the syrup is required. Stir it in after the sugar has dissolved, but before the syrup comes to the boil.

■ If you can't get glucose out of its jar, run your fingers under cold water and pull it out.

■ You can easily measure a level spoonful if you first heat the spoon.

GLUTEN

Being, so to speak, the invisible part of an ingredient, gluten deserves mention because it is a key factor in the choice of flour for bread, puff pastry and croissants on the one hand, and cakes, scones and all other kinds of pastry on the other. It is thanks to the gluten in wheat – and so in flour – that it forms a paste, and makes an elastic dough when mixed with water. If rice, oats, barley or maize contained any gluten, we could make a paste and a type of bread with them too – but they don't.

■ If you've never seen gluten, and if you have the time, energy and interest to do a short experiment to isolate the gluten from some flour, it might just help you to make better bread and pastry, because you'll understand the need for gluten, and also why bread has to be kneaded, and pastry rolled and re-rolled.

Here's what to do: mix about 3 rounded tablespoons of flour – preferably strong flour, because there's more gluten in it – to a stiffish dough with water, and leave it to soak in cold water for half an hour. Now squeeze and press it under slow-running cold water until all the starch is washed out. You'll be left with the gluten which looks rather like chewing gum in colour, texture and elasticity. If you then bake this wet gluten, you'll find that the steam and air inside blow it up like a balloon. On further baking the gluten sets to a light crisp sponge, like a slimming roll. This dry gluten is the 'skeleton' which supports the body of the loaf, cake or pudding.

■ When a wheat flour dough is heated, the gluten in the dough is blown up in the same way.

GRAVY BROWNING

A good make of gravy browning (Parisian essence is the finest quality) is indispensable for colouring gravies and sauces – unless you have loads of time on your hands to brown a roux to perfection. Gravy browning is based on caramel; you can make it at home if you have a recipe.

GRENADINE

A cordial made from pomegranates, but they don't come from the Grenadines. A very little adds colour and flavour to long cool drinks.

GUM ARABIC

Comes from acacia trees. The yellowish or reddish fragments are soluble in water, and if left long enough acquire a viscous consistency. It is an important ingredient in the art of confectionery, for jujubes, marshmallows, etc. Buy it at the chemist. See also page 333.

HERBS

Plants whose stems die down annually, which is why we call such an array of flowers a herbaceous border. Given even a small garden, one can grow quite a selection of herbs, because just one or two plants of some varieties will meet a whole family's needs. Freshly-picked, when you want them, homegrown herbs have more flavour than most bought ones.

■ Many of the aromatic herbs originate from the Mediterranean, and have been used for centuries for their flavouring, health-giving and preservative qualities. Always to be used with subtlety, to complement and enhance the flavour of other foods, the right herb (or mixture of herbs) can often add an almost magical fragrance to the simplest dish. Herbs can be delightful if knowledgeably used, overpowering if clumsily used. Too much sage, for instance, in a sage and onion stuffing can be off-putting for life.
■ The finer one chops or pounds herbs, the more oil is released, and so the greater the flavour.
■ If substituting dried herbs for fresh in any recipe, use only about a quarter of the given quantity: with the moisture removed, the flavour is more concentrated.

Preservation I prefer to freeze rather than to dry my own herbs because it changes their flavour less. If washed and dried thoroughly, they will keep through the winter without blanching. Chop them, and either make into little foil parcels or, easier still, freeze with a little water in ice cubes. Alternatively, tie the herbs in small bunches, interleaved with foil or polythene for convenience, and store in a rigid container. Make up bouquets garni, single herbs or whatever you like.

Angelica The 'angelic herb' or 'herb of the angels', is so called because of its medicinal properties. Angelica was supposed finally to have dispelled the plague, and protected all those who used it.

■ Angelica is grown mainly for its beauty, but the leaves may be used to flavour a sweet sauce or a wine drink. See also *candied angelica*, page 86.

Basil Sweet basil, much used in Mediterranean cookery, is the natural and classic partner of any tomato dish – soups, sauces, salads, omelettes, etc. Try it with buttered carrots, too. Its flavour fades with long cooking, so don't add too soon.

■ Dried basil has a less attractive flavour than fresh.

Bay One of the three basic components of a bouquet garni. Use to flavour stock, a court bouillon, marinades, soups, sauces, fish and casseroles, not to mention sweet dishes like stewed prunes and egg custards. A small, perfect leaf also makes a pretty garnish for things like terrines, pulse vegetables or a mixed hors d'oeuvre.

■ A bay tree in the garden provides leaves all year round.
■ Dried bay leaves are usually cheaper at a chain-store than in a clever little pack from a specialized kitchen shop.

Borage You have probably enjoyed this lovely herb floated in a Pimms, fruit punch or lemonade, but have you used it (chopped very finely, because the leaves are hairy) in a fish sauce or a salad, or used the very smallest leaves as a garnish for such dishes?

Camomile Good in meat soups and stews. According to Alan Titchmarsh, the gardening expert, the non-flowering variety makes a lovely garden 'seat': sown in a small, raised, walled-in bed, it forms a cushion, the lovely fragrance of which is strengthened by being sat upon (and compressed)!

Capers The pickled, bullet-like, bottled flowerbuds of the caper-bush, which grows wild (and is also cultivated) around the Mediterranean particularly, hence the frequent use of capers in sauces and for flavouring in Provençal cookery.

■ While the British by and large may not find much use for them beyond boiled mutton or tartare sauce, some love their piquancy with fish, meat or poultry, and others will eat them with almost anything.

■ Capers *aren't* the same thing as pickled nasturtium seeds.

Caraway If you like its flavour, crush the leaves of this herb very finely and add to cabbage, sprouts or salads, or add a leaf or two to a bouquet garni for a soup or stew.

Celery Chop the smallest and most tender leaves finely, and use to flavour all kinds of things: soups, stews, sauces, vegetables, salads, etc.

■ Celery salt is a powdered form, combined with salt.

Chervil A more important herb in French and Italian cooking than in British. With its delicate aniseed flavour, it is a herb to be added at the last, like chives, not used in dishes which require long cooking. Use it in chilled soups, salads, sauces, or with eggs, cheese, chicken, veal or beef.

■ Dried chervil has very little flavour. Grow your own chervil if you can.

Chives Are a 'must' if you like a subtle hint of onion. If I didn't have a garden, I'd have to grow chives in a pot, because they pep up the blandest of dishes, as well as the more tasty: macaroni and other cheese dishes, scrambled eggs, omelettes, soups, sauces, potatoes, and, of course, sautéd vegetables and salads.

■ Cooking spoils and alters their flavour, so bunch and chop them finely with scissors, and then stir into whatever you're making at the very last minute.
■ In your garden, break off at the bottom any stems on which buds form, otherwise they harden, shortening the life of the plant as well.

Coriander An aromatic herb of the carrot family (sometimes called Chinese parsley) and the plant from which we get the lovely spice. Use the leaves only – no stems – and don't chop them. Float them in pea or chicken soups and in stews.

■ The fresh leaves of this plant are called *cilantro* in the Caribbean, *kothamille* in Mexico and *dhuma* in India.

Dill The herb for fish dishes, and for potatoes or a cucumber salad. Though a member of the parsley family, it isn't used nearly as much in Britain as in Sweden, for instance, where you're almost lucky to escape from it. Dill water, the cure for babies' wind, is made from its seeds.

Fennel Florence fennel, with its flavour of anise, is traditionally used, like dill, to flavour and garnish fish. Chop and use it in salads too, try it instead of parsley to make a sauce, or use in a marinade.

■ Fennel leads a double life, because it is both a herb and vegetable, see page 186.

Garlic See page 98.

Marjoram A little goes a long way: use it with great discretion in terrines, omelettes, a green salad, or with fish, beef or pork dishes; or sprinkled over grilled mushrooms or tomatoes.

■ Add marjoram sometimes to a bouquet garni to give soups and sauces a subtle 'something'.

Mint Probably brought to Britain by the Romans, who used it a lot in their cooking. Of the many kinds of mint grown, there are: *spearmint* which is ideal for sauces, jellies, salads and cool drinks, and *peppermint* which is, of course, the species from which oil of peppermint is distilled.

■ To chop mint, see page 56.
■ Better still, pound the chopped leaves to release even more flavour. Do this in a basin, with the end of a rolling pin if

necessary, but better still in a *suribachi* – a Japanese type of pestle and mortar.

■ Finely chopped mint makes a welcome change from parsley with new potatoes or green peas.

■ Mint vinegar is a good way of introducing mint to a salad; or it makes an extra-minty sauce.

■ A mint leaf set in an ice cube gives a pleasant tang to a cool summer drink and looks lovely and cool too. Do several at a time, and pop in the freezer.

Oregano A wild marjoram. Stronger than sweet marjoram, it needs using with discretion – a great favourite in Italian cookery.

Parsley The stalks are even more important in a bouquet garni than the leaf: they carry more of the flavour.

■ Parsley is used by many cooks as if to camouflage rather than to garnish a dish, as if something *had* to be hidden! Tiny pieces give just as much colour, and don't have a strong flavour.

■ If you want to garnish a dish perfectly (or in advance) with finely chopped parsley, it is easy to sprinkle, and won't lose its colour so quickly if you gather it up in a corner of fine cloth, hold it under a cold tap for a minute or so, and then twist it tightly, to squeeze dry.

■ To chop parsley, see page 56.

■ A decorative straight line of parsley looks tidier and is quicker than a random zig-zag:

1 Make a furrow on the surface of the food with a skewer.

2 Wash the skewer, and while it's still wet, dip it in the chopped parsley.

3 Lay the skewer back in the furrow, and lift it out – leaving the parsley behind.

■ *Parsley fried in deep fat* makes a tasty and crisp garnish with savoury fritters or fried fish. Be sure to dry it very well before frying, then turn off the heat – after everything else is fried – and fry it without a basket (otherwise it gets entangled).

■ *Parsley wine*, see page 130.

Savory With its faint suggestion of sage, savory is the classic herb to use with broad beans – in fact it's good with any kind of bean. If you grow it between the rows of broad beans, they shouldn't be troubled with black-fly – not infallible, though, as I have learnt for myself.

Tarragon One of the great herbs. It is very pungent fresh, but if you thread the leaves on to a fine, short skewer, and blanch them for 30 seconds, they'll have a milder flavour.

■ Tarragon is the classic partner with chicken, and is an essential flavouring in sauce béarnaise or sauce verte.

■ Tarragon vinegar is a good way of introducing the flavour to salads, sauces and savoury dishes – easily made with fresh tarragon and white wine vinegar, see page 128.

■ Tarragon butter (butter, tarragon, seasoning and lemon juice) is delicious with grilled fish, chicken or steaks, or to enrich certain sauces.

Thyme One of the three basic components of a bouquet garni: essential to flavour soups and sauces. Thyme goes with poultry, meat, game and vegetables, and is especially good with rich foods like shellfish or pork.

HONEY

Before the days of sugar, honey was the main sweet food of ancient times. Its flavour, aroma, quality and consistency vary according to the type of flowers most widespread in the region where it is gathered. Some of the finest French honey for instance is that of Narbonne, which owes its distinctive flavour to the nectar of the rosemary flower. In Greece, where it is widely used, the prized honey is that of Hymettus. I myself often think nostalgically of the honey gathered from the Northumberland moors, in which one can almost smell the heather from which it is collected.

■ Honey is a rich and concentrated food, high in calories and slightly laxative. While it is generally more readily digested than sugar, and its effect in cooking is very similar, its flavour is more distinctive than most types of sugar. Because it so easily dominates the flavour of other ingredients, honey's use in cookery is therefore much more limited. It is, for example, sometimes used as the sweetness in a sweet-sour sauce, to glaze some kinds of meat after roasting, and to make certain spiced cakes, biscuits and breads.

■ Honey is easiest to measure in a hot tablespoon, 1 level spoonful equalling approx 1oz/25g.

HORSERADISH

Hardly justifies taking up garden space when its uses are so limited and its need therefore so small. The root, rather like a huge brown carrot, white inside, has a sharp and piquant flavour and a very penetrating smell. All parts of the horseradish which grow above the ground are said to be poisonous so don't try eating the top! One can use horseradish grated, as a condiment, to serve with boiled or cold meat; to make a savoury butter, good with grilled steaks; or of course to make horseradish sauce to serve particularly with roast beef. You may find it easier to buy grated, in a bottle, than fresh.

KIRSCH

An ideal flavouring to combine with lots of fruits – apricots, cherries, plums, pineapple or strawberries. Use it to flavour the syrup glaze for a cherry flan, in a sweet custard sauce, in crème au beurre or particularly to macerate fruits, see page 70. You don't always have to put sherry or rum in a trifle either – why not try different liqueurs for a change? See also page 129.

LARD

The melted and purified fat of a pig.

Although top quality compound cooking fats undoubtedly have their merits and can be used in place of it, I prefer lard because I find it gives better results – particularly in pastry and bread. It is also simple to use, whatever you're doing with it. What kind of lard to buy, though? Just as butter, olive oil and other fats may vary according to the country and area of origin so, more surprisingly, do lards. The degree of hardness or softness also varies widely, depending on the climate in which the pigs are reared as well as on their diet. While the best traditional lards are certainly pure and almost flavourless, the one real drawback of this fat is its smell when heated. Pure, super-refined *soft* lards now available don't smell when heated, and for pastry-making they are soft enough to rub in or roll out direct from the refrigerator, so making lovely light pastry. A soft lard is, in fact, primarily intended for pastry. Multi-purpose and so good, I now buy no other.

■ Unlike butter and margarine, lard contains no water or curd. You can't, of course, compare it with the lovely flavour of butter for shallow frying, but lard has no complications and is hot enough for frying when a smoky haze starts to float above it. For general use, it is miles better than dripping, which besides having a strong flavour of its own, tends to make anything fried in it indigestible.

■ It is a false economy to buy a cheap lard for deep-fat frying. Top quality gives the best results and can be used and re-used repeatedly (providing you always strain it).

■ Lard or cooking fat alone makes beautifully light pastry or scones, but as both these fats are virtually flavourless so, it goes without saying, must the pastry (or scones) be. This explains why lard and butter (or margarine) are so often used together: for the lightness of the one and the flavour of the other.

■ Pure, melted lard is my first choice (because foods don't stick) for brushing and greasing cake tins, bread tins and pudding basins, etc. before dusting them out with flour. Only cakes with a high sugar content (like a Genoese sponge or gingerbread) or fruit cakes which require long cooking usually need to be in a lined tin – unless it's a poor quality tin. See also *cooking fats*, page 93.

LEMONS

Owe much of their powerful aroma and flavour to the zest, the outer part of the skin or rind.

Lemon rind Thinly pared with a potato peeler, rind contains less of the bitter pith than when grated. This explains why pared rind is so often used to flavour liquids, and why zest is better than grated rind. In large pieces, one can also remove it from some liquids without straining.

■ Any surplus thinly pared peel needn't be wasted. Freeze it in ice cubes, to use in drinks another time.
■ Grated rind contains both zest and pith. Finely grated lemon rind, as so often called for in recipes, is therefore less bitter than coarsely grated rind, giving a finer flavour to whatever one is making.

Lemon quarters Served especially with fish, are cut lengthwise from the fruit, so that when one squeezes it, one directs the juice downward over the food, not everywhere else!

Lemon juice Usually added to dishes after they are cooked, whenever it's possible to do so, to avoid loss of vitamin C.

■ If you squeeze a refrigerated lemon, you won't get much juice out of it – better to let it reach room temperature first.
■ Lemon juice does numerous other things besides giving flavour:

1 Added to fruit while it's stewing, it prevents the fruit breaking up or losing shape. Allow 1 teaspoon to ¼pt/125ml syrup – but omit it if you want a purée.
2 It keeps boiled rice, poached fish or poached eggs a good colour. Add a spoonful to the cooking water if you want to.

3 It can replace vinegar in salad dressings.
4 By counteracting the richness of foods, lemon juice helps digestion, whether in a salad dressing, hollandaise sauce or with fried fish, etc.
5 The acidity of lemon juice with other fruits (say added to a syrup, as it often is) not only counteracts general sweetness, but also enhances a fruit's own flavour.
6 It delays the discoloration of certain fruits and vegetables: for example, sprinkle some lightly over sliced banana, or add a tablespoonful of it to both steeping and cooking water for Jerusalem artichokes or celeriac.
7 It provides the pectin lacking in strawberries used for jam. Allow the juice of 1 lemon per 1lb/450g of fruit.

Lemon butterflies. To make as a garnish:

1 If you have a fruit decorator (see page 28) and the time, 'stripe' the lemon before cutting it in half, crosswise.
2 With a stainless steel saw knife (preferably), cut fairly thinly as many slices as you need, starting at the 'cut' end of each half lemon.
3 Cut each slice in half, to make two butterflies.

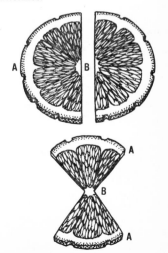

4 Cut the rind only, at point A, hold one end in each hand and gently open up the half slice to form the butterfly. Avoid cutting or breaking it at centre.

5 Place on the food and garnish centre of butterfly with a minute piece of parsley, for extra colour.

To freeze lemons Whole, they don't freeze well. Because they are so watery, they go soft when thawed, making them difficult to squeeze – much better to freeze rind and juice separately. For convenience later, put the rind of each half lemon in a twist of Cling-film, then put them all together in one large bag for easy finding in the freezer. Freeze the juice as ice cubes, say a quarter lemon to a cube, keeping a few handy in the refrigerator in the ice tray.

■ If you buy and prepare lemons when they are plentiful, perhaps from a market stall, there should be no need ever to cut a whole one for a spoonful of juice. If you're doing several, de-rind them all, then just divide up the rind equally into separate bags.

LIMES

Although only about half the size of the average lemon, limes contain about a third more citric acid. Don't, therefore, be deceived into thinking that, as a flavouring, the juice of two limes would equal that of one lemon. Judge by taste as well as by measure when substituting lime for lemon juice. Here are a few hints:

1 Remembering the above, lime is usually interchangeable with lemon for things like smoked, fried or cooked-almost-anyhow fish; in salad dressings, hollandaise sauce or mayonnaise; in forcemeat stuffings for veal, chicken or turkey; in syrups, sweet sauces or with pancakes; in cocktails or long cool drinks, when a twist of sliced lime also makes a colourful and nice change from lemon.

2 Lime juice, like lemon juice, not only counteracts general sweetness of poached fruits, but also enhances the flavour of many fruits themselves.

3 Make lime butterflies as lemon butterflies, above. See also page 279.

MARGARINE

The discovery of margarine was not just a commercial enterprise; it grew out of the social and economic needs of Europe at a time of considerable upheaval. From about 1750, Europe was experiencing a population explosion. The greatest food scarcity to feed these extra people properly was in protein and fats. At the same time, the Industrial Revolution, which began in Great Britain in 1760 and then spread to Europe, also brought about social change. People moved to towns to find industrial work, and there were few people working on farms and in the countryside.

To provide energy and warmth, fats were an essential food for the working population and the demand for butter resulted in high prices and serious shortages. From about 1850, France particularly was short of food. The threat of the growing power of its neighbour, Prussia, caused Napoleon III to realize that if it came to war, food shortages would be a major problem both for an army on the move and for the population as a whole. The lack of butter and other fats was a vital issue, and transporting what they had an additional one. Refrigeration and fast transport hadn't yet been invented and the fats didn't keep well on a long journey. All this prompted the Emperor to ask food scientists to produce a reasonably priced, wholesome butter-alternative which could be spread on bread, would be easy and inexpensive to manufacture and would keep well. In 1869, a French food research chemist, Mège Mouriès, finally patented margarine – named after the Greek word for pearl, *margaron*, because his new fat had a pearly shine to it. The main ingredients of it were beef suet and skimmed milk – both inexpensive because by-products of an already considerable meat industry, and universally available.

■ Thanks to constant research, today's margarines are vastly superior to that original discovery: a wider variety of natural products are used in its making and when a way of solidifying oils to various degrees was discovered, it meant that a wide range of vegetable oils (some of which contain no cholesterol) and fish oils could be used; a turning point in the manufacture of margarine.

■ Margarines vary so much in flavour, quality, texture, cholesterol content and cost that it can be puzzling to know which brands are best to meet particular needs. The top quality brands are a very superior blend, and their cost is usually determined by the oils and fats used. All the oils are fully refined, but some sources that can be used are cheaper than others, and a greater proportion of these cheaper oils are present in the cheaper brands. Edible vegetable oils are the more expensive variety. They are more costly than marine oils and animal fats, so products made only with vegetable oils – such as sunflower margarines – are usually among the more expensive. Legally all table margarines must conform to certain nutritional standards, which accounts for a weight-watcher's fat, which does not conform precisely to the regulations, being call a 'low fat spread', not a margarine.

■ The difference between a soft and a hard margarine is that soft products contain a higher proportion of oils which are liquid at room temperature than the harder products. Although their uses often overlap, one type is sometimes unquestionably better than the other; in pastry, for example, or when the fat has to be rubbed or rolled in, soft margarines are too soft. Unlike a soft lard which is primarily intended for pastry-making, a soft margarine makes a dough difficult to manipulate and won't trap as much air, so the pastry cannot be as light. (Their extreme softness is obvious in the way they are packed: soft margarines come in tubs, so that they can't run away; soft lards are simply parchment wrapped.) On the other hand, soft margarine is quite

marvellous for making an all-in-one-mixture, the modern version of a creamed mixture. Surely no other modern product has done so much to take the hard work out of cooking as this has. (For an *all-in-one-mixture*, see page 318.)

■ Soft margarine is, of course, wonderful for creaming because it's so easy to beat until light and fluffy, trapping air as you do so. Van den Berghs, Britain's biggest domestic margarine producer, claim that under standardized conditions, any margarine is easier to cream and has greater creaming power than butter – that is, it can hold more air.

■ I'm not so enthusiastic about all-in-one-pastry or white sauces as I am about the 'mixture' (see page 318): the results seem to me inferior to the conventional ways, and the time saved (if any), minimal.

■ Margarine contains more vitamin D than butter and, from the health angle, some people prefer it, especially margarine based on sunflower oil. There's roughly the same amount of water in butter as in margarine: in margarine, controlled at not more than 16 per cent of the product.

■ Margarine can often, but not always, be used instead of butter in a recipe. Should you wonder when and why, the following may give you some guidance:

1 No margarine so far produced has (or can give) the flavour of butter. Therefore, where flavour is vital, and is not masked by a strong one like ginger or mixed spice, use butter.

2 Cakes and certain bread doughs keep fresh longer and taste better made with butter.

3 If a recipe calls for *saltless* butter, margarine can't be substituted.

4 Used when grilling foods, margarine fails to give the flavour and gloss given by butter.

5 Used to fry – unless for something quick like a slice of bread – margarine needs clarifying. Even then, it burns at a low temperature.

6 Besides flavour, butter gives a

smoothness and gloss to such things as soups, fine sauces and butter fillings not given by margarines.

7 Margarine can't be substituted for butter in a sauce of the hollandaise family: it won't emulsify with the egg yolks.

8 In savoury butters and hard sauces, etc., margarine does not absorb a flavour in the same way as does butter.

MILK

Easily digested if you sip, eat some food with, or use it in cooking, but if gulped down, it forms one difficult-to-digest clot inside you.

■ It boils at 196°F/91°C, a lower temperature than water, at 212°F/100°C.

■ You can prevent hot milk from changing its flavour, and a skin from forming on top, by heating it *fast* in a *covered* pan – but don't forget it!

■ A liquidizer makes hot milk drinks deliciously frothy – skin and all – and milk shakes are a wonderful way of encouraging children who don't like milk to take it. This is important because milk contains every type of nutrient and is the most complete single food we know. Make sure the milkman doesn't leave it on your doorstep in sunlight though, because it loses up to two-thirds of its vitamin B content within 2 hours.

Skimmed milk Now widely available and popular with those who want to cut down on fats.

Dried milk Pasteurized fresh milk from which almost all the butterfat has been skimmed off, and the water removed. The fat-soluble vitamins A and D which occur naturally in milk are, of course, lost with the fat. There are different categories of dried milk, the following being the most important:

Low-fat spray-dried skimmed milk Some brands have the vitamins A and D replaced as it may say on the label. This is important if you're wanting to cut down your intake of fat whilst still having the goodness of milk.

Fat-filled dried milk powders Skimmed milk powders with vegetable fat added, also small quantities of other ingredients such as lactose, dextrose or dried glucose syrup. Thus, when reconstituted, they contain quite significant quantities of fat. This type of product is generally sold in plastic bottles.

■ You can use a good dried milk in almost any recipe where milk is required, except (as far as I know) for junket when fresh milk is essential. If using it for a savoury sauce, you'll have extra goodness and flavour if you mix it with vegetable water, if any is handy. To enrich a milk pudding, double up on the amount of fat used with fresh milk.

■ Heated dried milk, because fatless, will stick to a pan base: use a non-stick pan if you have one.

■ Splendid for camping or boating.

Long life milk See *ultra-heat treated milk*, below.

Homogenized milk Smooth and creamy because the milk and cream are so completely emulsified that the fat stays suspended evenly throughout the milk, instead of rising to the top and forming a cream line. I buy more of this than anything else: it's good to drink, on cereals, in milk puddings and for any milk-based sauce.

■ Homogenized milk freezes better than pasteurized because the cream and milk don't separate. Beware of freezing milk in a bottle though: put it in a plastic container, with room to expand.

Pasteurized milk The favourite of most households, whether the rich, creamy Channel Islands kind, or the milk from cows of more ordinary breeds. The milk is heated to a temperature (162°F/72°C) which kills harmful bacteria, without destroying any of the nutrients.

Sterilized milk Homogenized, bottled, and then heated to an even higher temperature, so that it remains fit for consumption for at least seven days without refrigeration – as long as it isn't opened. Despite having rather a 'cooked' flavour, it is all right for cooking.

Ultra-heat treated milk (UHT) Homogenized milk heated to 270°F/132°C for just one second, so that it will keep perfectly (unopened) for several months without even being refrigerated.

■ Because the milk and cream are emulsified, it gives sauces a creamy smooth texture one doesn't get with pasteurized milk – ideal for a custard sauce, for instance, or to make yoghurt (see page 300).
■ This kind of milk is a splendid larder stand-by when short of milk for cooking – and who isn't sometimes? Two or three cartons on the shelf seem just as necessary as spare fats, flour or sugar.

Evaporated milk Twice as rich as fresh milk, from which it's made. Fresh milk contains approximately 12.5 per cent solids (protein, fat, milk, sugar and minerals) and 87.5 per cent water, but evaporated milk must conform to a legal standard requiring 31 per cent solids, so the product is concentrated 2.5 times (by heat under vacuum) to remove nearly 70 per cent of the water. After concentrating, the milk is homogenized to form a permanent emulsion. Later, vitamin D is added and the milk is sterilized – which accounts for its long shelf life.

Full cream sweetened condensed milk We are indebted to Napoleon for this idea too. He asked his scientists to find a method of preparing milk in a concentrated form to simplify the feeding of and to nourish his army on the march. In fact, these scientists were beaten to the post – but following Napoleon's instigation, it wasn't many years before it was produced commercially. Not only that, Captain Scott took it with him on his Antarctic explorations. It's a valuable product healthwise: all the natural vitamins are preserved.

■ Amazingly, approximately 2 tons of sugar are added to every 3,000 gallons of milk. In more comprehensible terms, that's about 2oz/50g sugar to 13½fl oz/400ml milk.

Buttermilk The liquid remaining after butter has been churned from cream. Buttermilk is also made from pasteurized skimmed milk to which a culture is added for flavour and to give it 'body'. Commercial buttermilk may have added cream or butter particles.

■ Buttermilk (or sour milk) makes excellent scones: in place of some of the cream of tartar – another acid – they together neutralize (as does cream of tartar on its own) the very strong flavour of the bicarbonate of soda, also helping this to act as the raising agent.

MOLASSES

The thick non-crystallizable dark syrup which drains from raw sugar during manufacture: the thickest kind of treacle.

MUSTARD

Strongest when absolutely fresh, so dry mustard gives a dish more flavour than tired made mustard. Some recipes call for one, some for the other, but a spoonful of made mustard is more than a spoonful of dry.

■ Mustard helps the digestion of rich dishes, especially cooked cheese, so it has more importance than simply its flavour.
■ French mustard, with its piquant flavour, makes much better mustard butter than English mustard.

Mustard seed Makes a hot and unusual garnish for some savoury dishes. If you've never tasted it before, do bite a seed, to understand why they need to be used with restraint.

NUTS

Often have to be shredded, flaked or chopped, and it is important to do whichever a recipe says because the flavour, texture and appearance of a dish will to some extent depend upon this.

■ Nuts tend to go rancid because of the very high proportion of fat in them. They'll keep longer in an airtight jar in the refrigerator if you have room for them, or longer still in the freezer.
■ It's unwise to give tiny children nuts, because they can easily cause choking.

Almonds One of the most important ingredients of the French pâtissière, and probably one of the main reasons why their pastries are so 'moreish'! Chopped and roasted or toasted, their flavour is even better.

Almonds are of two main types:

1 *Jordan*, the long narrow and more expensive variety which are used particularly when whole almonds are called for, as for the top of a Dundee cake, macaroons, or to serve salted (see page 343). They do not in fact, come from Jordan: the name is a corruption of *jardin*, a garden. The variety is grown round Malaga.

2 *Valencia*, the shorter, wider nuts, irregular in shape, but with an equally good flavour. This is the kind to have in store for flaking, shredding, chopping or making into ground almonds.

■ For almonds at their best, with the strongest flavour, buy them unblanched, skinning and preparing them just before use.

To skin almonds – either boil them for a minute or two, or cover with boiling water, stirring once or twice while soaking for 3–5 minutes. Pinch off the skins.
To flake – skin as above and then, while still hot and soft, flake them quickly with a potato peeler or small vegetable knife, paring off the *side* of the nut. (They go brittle if left to go cold and dry.)
To shred – as flaked above, but split each through the middle and then cut finely longways.
To roast – skin, chop, spread out on a baking sheet and bake in a slow oven until golden, turning them over at least twice with a fork.
To toast – skin, chop, spread out on a baking sheet and put for a few minutes under a slow grill, turning them several times with a fork, and watching them carefully, to avoid over-browning.

■ *Ground almonds* can be made in a liquidizer from chopped or flaked blanched almonds – not too many at a time. If ground almonds are used in a fruit cake, their purpose is to help to keep it moist, as well as to give flavour. Using almond essence with ground almonds in a cake helps to bring out the flavour of the almonds. It isn't an unnecessary extravagance.
■ *Almond nibs* save a lot of time when one needs almonds for decoration or texture. Brown them lightly in a slow oven to extract their true nutty flavour.

Brazils Come from the gigantic brazil tree, native to Brazil and from which trees that country takes its name. Each nut is only one part of a huge (often head-sized) woody shell at least ½in/ 1¼cm thick which falls to the ground when ripe, sometimes from as high as 100 feet up. Inside the shell are four divisions, in each of which fit – in almost jigsaw accuracy – *lots* of nuts. When fresh, they have an ivory smoothness and rich flavour; when stale, they lose both sheen *and* flavour.

■ Shell and eat as they are, dipping the end in salt. (Children love them dipped in melted chocolate, left to dry off.)
■ To use as decoration, say for a trifle, shave slices longways with a potato peeler and then toast them (see *almonds* above): the shavings curl up, colour and taste delicious.

Chestnuts Lovely roasted, preferably in a chestnut pan (like a long-handled, holey frying pan) over a glowing fire. First split them with a knife (there's also a special chestnut knife) to prevent bursting, and turn them at intervals until your nose tells you they're done. Peel and eat while hot, dipped in salt.

■ Top quality, large nuts are the best buy: too much waste with many others.

■ Use to make soups, pastries, desserts, stuffings, etc.

■ *Dried chestnuts* lack the flavour and texture of fresh. You should find them in some shops during November and December.

■ *Chestnut purée* – French, canned – I unashamedly buy this each Christmas to stuff my turkey: it's time-saving, easy and delicious. Use it as well for other dishes calling for purée.

Coconut Desiccated coconut has lots of uses: coconut ice, a coconut cake (one of my favourite cakes) or coconut pyramids; to sprinkle over and decorate an iced cake; browned, to serve as an accompaniment to curry. I also like it (browned) sprinkled over certain salads, sautéd vegetables and even fish dishes, to which it gives both flavour and a crunchy texture.

■ To brown desiccated coconut, spread it out on a baking sheet and put in a slow oven or toast it under a slowish grill, either way turning it over at intervals with a fork, to brown evenly.

■ Colour it for a cake decoration in the same way as sugar (page 334) or, probably more quickly but less effectively, shake it in a covered jam jar with the colouring.

Coconut milk As a substitute for real coconut milk, to use in a curry sauce for instance, make an infusion with water (some people make a milk infusion, which is 'heavier') and fine desiccated coconut. One quick way is to boil 1oz/25g coconut – more to make it stronger – in ½pt/300ml water for five minutes, then strain, squeeze it well and make the liquid up to ½pt/300ml again.

Hazelnuts Rich in oil, they are delicious in cookery and for this reason often used in confectionery as well as in things like cakes and sweets. The cob and filbert are simply cultivated varieties of the hazel, the filbert having a very full husk which completely conceals the nut, and the cob

being much larger than an ordinary hazelnut.

To skin hazelnuts, spread them on a baking sheet, put in a hot oven for a few minutes and then rub together in a clean cloth to flake off the skins. To get rid of any lingering fine shavings, shake the nuts over a sieve or in a strainer.

To chop whole, skinned hazelnuts, use a Mouli grater (page 30) failing which a knife. (They are difficult to chop with a knife but, in a blender, may become oily and form a paste unless very quickly done.)

Peanuts The same thing as groundnuts and monkey-nuts. Nutritional as they are, and eaten raw or roasted (or as groundnut oil, below, or as peanut butter) they have a rather dominant flavour which limit their use in cookery more than, for instance, almonds, walnuts or hazelnuts.

■ Add them chopped (unless tiny) to coleslaw, rice dishes, a chicken or fish salad, etc., preferably at the last to ensure they're crisp and crunchy. Peanuts are an economical way of adding protein to various dishes.

■ Because of their high oil content – think of groundnut oil – peanuts form a paste when finely ground: peanut butter.

Pistachio nuts Have a sweet and pleasant flavour, for which they are mainly used. If very fresh, very green and very finely chopped after blanching (like almonds), they are also most decorative on something like a lemon soufflé or meringues which need something simple but colourful to dress them up. Alternatively, one can thinly slice a blanched pistachio and arrange the pieces like clover leaves, with stalks cut from another nut. (Place them with 2 hatpins, see page 30.)

■ Pistachio nuts grow in pairs inside a thin husk about the size of an olive, reddish-brown in colour. Serve (in their husks) in little dishes, as cocktail snacks.

Walnuts Add crunchiness and flavour to many dishes, either as an important ingredient or as a decoration. Use the shelled nuts whole, chopped or finely grated, as called for by a recipe. They're lovely in a coffee cake or coffee gâteau; in a rum gâteau or shortbread; sprinkled at the last in certain salads or sautéd vegetables; in a savoury butter to serve with fish; mixed with cream cheese and pineapple on canapés or in sandwiches.

To chop – use scissors, or cut with a sharp knife on a wooden board.

To grate finely – use a Mouli grater (see page 30).

■ Walnut pieces are the most economical buy, and answer most cooking needs, decorating apart.

■ Like nearly all nuts, walnuts are rich in fat (walnut oil), so will go rancid if kept too long. In their shells, they also shrivel in time.

■ Use if necessary as a substitute for pecans. Though different (and less good, I think) they're of the same family, have a not-too-different flavour, can be bought everywhere all year round, and are less expensive.

See also *devilled* and *salted nuts*, page 343.

OATMEAL

Oatmeal, bread and ale were for centuries the three great dietary staples of the British Isles. It is hard to believe today, when one cannot even buy oatmeal in some parts of the country, that oatmeal porridge was at one time celebrated as the national dish. It was used then – as it no doubt still is by some people – as basic nourishment, and to sustain. It was used to thicken, coat and make foods go further, never mind to give comfort and warmth. It offers a balance of protein and carbohydrate, with a lot of vitamin B and iron, not to mention other essential minerals.

OIL

Cooking oils are less versatile than those fats which can be used in both solid and liquid form, but are the only choice for dishes where other fats of similar temperature would congeal. We wouldn't, for example, contemplate making French dressing with butter, or a marinade with dripping. As most oils solidify at a considerably lower temperature than other fats, this is the fat to use when a mixture must remain completely liquid. This explains why it is better to fry or roast in oil dishes which are to be served cold: a roast chicken for example, or fried canapés for buffet snacks.

■ Oils naturally have a multitude of uses besides these: some kinds (see list below) are excellent for deep as well as for shallow frying and if for some reason or other you don't want to fry with butter when it is called for, oil is often the best substitute. Mixed with butter to fry or sauté foods – approximately 1 dessertspoonful oil to 2oz/50g butter – it allows the butter to reach a higher temperature without burning. This is an advantage should the food you are cooking need more than just a few minutes to fry.

■ Oils can also be used to sweat sliced onions or shallots, to make roux for soups and sauces, in certain batters and, if you like the results (which I do not), in cakes and scones.

■ A solid vegetable oil, grated rather than rubbed in (page 115), brings variety to pastry.

■ Some kinds of oil are more suitable than others for particular dishes, their flavour (or lack of it) usually being the deciding factor. The flavour of an oil is to some extent dependent on the refining process: the more highly refined, the less flavour and odour it will have, which explains why for most purposes it pays to have a good one. The level of refining is set by a manufacturer's specifications, so naturally even the same types of oil can and do vary. An unbranded supermarket corn oil, for instance, is not necessarily of the same high quality as a good branded corn oil.

■ A kitchen cupboard, where the temperature is neither too hot nor too cold, and where light is excluded, is a good place to keep oils. So stored, they should generally keep, unopened, for at least six months. If you do store oil where it is too cold, and the oil goes cloudy, stand the bottle in a jug of hot water until clear again. A canned oil has the advantage over a bottled oil that light is automatically excluded, but the former tend to be in larger quantities, and could go rancid if too long open.

Some other uses for oil

1 Mixed with egg yolk – 1 or 2 teaspoons oil per yolk – for an economical and excellent coating when 'egg and breadcrumbing' foods: the oil makes the yolk go further and, more important still, the emulsion so formed gives a thin, even, easily brushed-on coating.

2 Quick and easy to use for greasing bread tins, cake tins, baking sheets, pudding basins, greaseproof paper, etc. For any form of meringue, I prefer oiled greaseproof paper on oiled baking sheets to anything else, even Bakewell paper: I also like to use oil (or melted lard) to grease both tin and lining for a Christmas or wedding cake.

3 As a tonic for all wooden kitchen equipment: treat your salad bowl, servers, cheeseboard, toast-rack (or anything else made of wood) to a shiny new face with a tissue lightly dipped in oil.

Corn oil Pure corn oil is bland in flavour, thus making it a very versatile product. You can use it in almost any recipe which calls for oil: salad dressings, marinades, shallow or deep-fat frying, roux-based soups and sauces, and in a wide variety of baking – if you think oil is a good fat for baking. Because they dislike the fruity flavour of some olive oils (possibly because they haven't found one they like, see below), some people almost unbelievably prefer corn oil to olive oil even in mayonnaise, completely tasteless though such mayonnaise is.

■ The recommended temperature for deep-fat frying with corn oil is 375°F/190°C. The smoke point is 440°F/227°C. and the flash point 575°F/300°C.

■ Pure corn oil contains no cholesterol and is high in polyunsaturated fats.

■ Corn maize is of American origin, where it was first used 10,000 years ago.

Groundnut oil Comes from the nuts better known as peanuts or monkey-nuts. They are the oily edible seeds of a trailing plant, ripening underground in very brittle pods – hence their name. Different grades of groundnut oil vary considerably, but at its best it is light and bland in flavour and liked by some people for salad dressings. It is widely used by manufacturers, blended with other oils to make what we buy as 'vegetable' oils, and also in prepared dressings, etc.

Olive oil Has been used for thousands of years. As early as 2500 BC in Crete, forests were felled to make room for olive groves. Trade in 'liquid gold' as they called it, formed the basis for much of Greece's maritime and imperial expansion. The Romans grew even richer by planting huge orchards throughout their empire. In the ancient world, the olive was the richest source of their necessary oil. It flavoured and cooked food, lit lamps, formed the base of medicines, and was the ritual liquid used for anointing priests and kings.

■ Olive oil is as essential to cooking as butter if you enjoy good food. Virgin oils are the finest, delicate and aromatic, giving flavour to anything made with them. For mayonnaise and salad dressings, this oil has no equal, unless of course, as already mentioned, you dislike its fruity taste. Use it also for marinades, casseroles, shallow frying, sautéing, grilling and roasting, to pour over pasta or to toss with vegetables. Do *not* use it, however, for deep-fat frying: it has such a low smoke point that if heated to the temperature necessary to fry foods in deep fat, it will break down and give off a blue vapour.

■ The best olive oils are always expensive

because so costly to produce. Like wines, they vary with climate, country (and even area) of origin and from year to year. Many different varieties of olive are grown for oil, so the range of oils is wide. They vary in colour, flavour, aroma, consistency and character and come mainly from France, Italy (these two considered the best), Spain, Greece (whose oils are widely sold in this country, presumably because they cost less, but which are thick, heavy and in my opinion horrible), Turkey, Morocco and Tunisia. Spain is known for its oil 'lake', but Spanish oils are heavier and more fruity than the French and Italian, generally making food cooked in them less digestible. It may take time to find your ideal oil, because even if you can afford what is classified as the finest, you may prefer the flavour of another which comes from a different area or country. I think most of us would agree for example that just because we may dislike some kinds of chocolate (bitter, milk, orange or coffee-flavoured), we would not say 'I dislike chocolate'. From the hundreds of olive oils there are, it is simply a case of finding one that you like.

■ Good wine merchants will be as selective in their choice of an olive oil as of wine and will sell an oil infinitely superior to anything obtainable at a chemist – even though the latter is labelled 'pure olive oil'. For medicinal use, flavour and aroma don't matter, whereas purity does. You may also find fine oils in health food shops (too many, alas, only sell Greek), delicatessens and any shop selling high-class groceries. Supermarkets are more likely to sell a pure but blended oil (not a virgin oil) because it will be cheaper.

■ French and Italian labelling laws ensure that you know exactly what you are buying because, even among virgin oils, there are several qualities, depending on their acidity. As few shop assistants (or even managers) will have the knowledge to advise you in detail, be your own expert and learn to interpret the label yourself:

Virgin oil This is cold-pressed (first pressing), the first to be pressed out of the olives. It is natural and pure, without further treatment and without the admixture of any other oil, of whatever origin. Besides stating *huile d'olive* and *vierge* (virgin), the label must give further qualifications to indicate the quality. The different grades are shown in the table below.

In addition, a label may also give a grower's name, the site of pressing, the method of pressing and a descriptive adjective such as *fruitée* or *douce*. Given all these facts, not only can you be sure of buying a genuine natural product, but also it is simple to repeat (or avoid) the same oil when you want more. My own favourite is a 'fine' virgin oil from Provence, 'Emile Martin'. To me, a flavour I like is more important than a ruling about acidity.

Refined olive oils (huiles d'olive raffinées) These are obtained from the refining of oils which fail to qualify for the grades of virgin oil given above, either because of defective flavour or excessive acidity. The residual dryish pulp from the first pressing is pressed again (second pressing), this time using heat, to yield a fattier and more acid oil which is often blended with first-pressing oil to make commercial,

French oils	Italian oils	Maximum allowance of oleic acid
vierge 'extra'	olio 'extra' vergine	1 %
vierge 'fine'	olio 'soprafino' vergine	1.5%
vierge 'semi-fine' or 'courante'	olio 'fino' vergine	3 %
—	olio vergine	4 %

branded, but still pure olive oils of a standard flavour (if any) and quality.

■ From the health angle, virgin (cold-pressed) olive oil, when eaten uncooked as in salad dressings, is one of the world's most nutritious foods. Of all fats, it is the most easily digested, and the closest in chemical composition to the fat in mother's milk. It is also slightly laxative and full of valuable mineral salts and vitamins. It is only cooked for gourmet reasons and is not harmful to those with heart problems, because low in saturated fats and rich in unsaturated (see page 61).

■ Although at their best in the first year, good olive oils will keep a long time if properly stored (page 112). Cold will make the oil congeal and too much heat or light can adversely affect flavour and colour. Once opened, olive oil will still keep for months in such conditions, longer if there is not a large head-space in the can or bottle.

Rapeseed oil This has rather taken the place of soya oil in the manufacture of blended cooking oils because rape is now grown more widely in Europe.

Safflower oil This is quite expensive but it has a bland flavour which makes it a versatile product. It is extremely rich in polyunsaturates, so one can usually find it in health-food shops.

■ A type of thistle, it was cultivated by ancient civilizations along the Nile, down into Ethiopia. Now it is mainly grown in Mexico, the USA and Australia.

Sesame oil Sesame oil has been known for thousands of years in the Far East. It is used in oriental cooking, giving an attractive nutty flavour to food cooked in it. It's expensive compared with most other similar oils, but doesn't go rancid easily – a great advantage in hot countries.

Soya oil Made from the soya bean, this is one of the cheapest oils. It has a rather marked backtaste, a flavour associated with soya which is difficult to diffuse, even in refining. Pure soya has its limit-

ations, therefore, although it is used in many blended cooking oils.

Sunflower oil High in polyunsaturates, so for those with heart problems this is a safe choice in any recipe calling for oil – or for that matter, as a possible substitute for other fats. I find sunflower oil almost unpleasantly bland, but it's good for deep-fat as well as shallow frying and has a highish smoke point.

■ The sunflower is now grown in many parts of the world, from the USSR and Turkey, to southern and central Europe, and all the Americas.

Vegetable oils Usually blends of various oils selected by a manufacturer. They may include sunflower, groundnut, soya and rapeseed, but not usually corn because of its cost. Blended oils aren't necessarily highly refined as this would add to their cost. Some vegetable oils may be restricted in use largely to frying or roasting as their backtaste would be unacceptable mixed or cooked in things.

Walnut oil Use for salad dressings, not for cooking. It has a distinctive nutty flavour as you would expect, but does not keep as long as most oils.

Solid vegetable oil Quite unsuitable of course for traditional oil-based things like dressings and marinades because it solidifies when cold, but it has many other uses. In case you haven't used this comparatively recent addition to the larder, here are a few tips:

1 It will keep at least six months without going rancid if correctly stored, i.e. properly wrapped, in a refrigerator or cool, dry larder.

2 Used refrigerated, the oil is difficult to cut because excessively brittle but, if you need to grate it (in a Mouli grater for speed), it is much easier to handle.

3 It is excellent for deep-fat and shallow frying: you can use and re-use it for months because of its keeping qualities – providing of course that you strain it after use, preferably through butter muslin; it is almost odourless and flavourless

(though I personally have reservations about the smell of some brands when heated); its smoke point is fairly high (approximately 425°F/220°C), as is its flash point (approximately 610°F/320°C); compared with most liquid oils, it leaves a much less rubbery (and difficult-to-clean-off) deposit on the pan; it is less costly than many other fats you might use.

4 When melted, a 1lb/500g packet of oil equals approximately 1pt/600ml liquid oil.

5 It is safer and more convenient than a liquid oil for campers and caravanners.

6 Grated, this oil is a good substitute for suet, should you not have or never eat suet. Use the same quantity as you would of suet to make stuffings, shortcrust-type pastry, mincemeat or a Christmas pudding (neither of the two latter quite as good as with suet I find). Use only half the quantity to make suetcrust-type pastry for things like dumplings or a steak and kidney pie.

7 If on the wrapper it is claimed that a vegetable oil is 100 per cent pure without additives of any kind, this is a versatile and useful fat for vegetarians. The nature of the oil is not disclosed, however.

8 Because of its vegetable origin, it is low in cholesterol (0.003% compared with lard at 0.1% and butter at 0.18%) but, being a solid oil, it is high in saturated fat (see page 60).

OLIVES

Used mainly for their oil, olives grow in hundreds of varieties in the great olive-producing countries like Spain (with some 200 million trees), Italy (with 185 million), France and Greece. Generally speaking, green olives are the unripe fruit, black the ripened, but there are emerald olives, purple olives, thick black juicy olives, some very small, others lush as plums. A tree is probably 15–20 years old before it produces a paying crop but some still bear fruit 400–500 years later. (The average age of today's Mediterranean olive trees is 200 years.) Not surprisingly, olives figure often in Mediterranean cookery – in salads, stuffings, sauces; as an essential ingredient in the garnish for many dishes, pickled, etc.

■ If you buy olives loose, they keep best in a jar, covered with olive oil. See also *olive oil*, page 113.

ORANGE FLOWER WATER

This doesn't sound nearly as fragrant as orange *blossom* water, its other name. A few drops will flavour, amongst other things, almond paste and confectionery. Buy it at a chemist.

PORRIDGE OATS

Will keep indefinitely in an airtight container away from any contamination, according to a producer. Although there used to be a tendency for them to go rancid, because of enzyme action, the big millers don't expect it to happen nowadays with modern processing.

■ Some brands make smoother porridge than others, due to different processing, but if you prefer a slightly rough porridge, try sprinkling the oats into *boiling* liquid instead of adding them to cold.

POTATO FLOUR

A powdery-fine flour prepared from cooked, dried and ground potatoes. It is both expensive and often difficult to find.

■ This is the thickening particularly intended when a recipe calls for fécule, it is much better than cornflour for this purpose.

■ Slake it, and use as arrowroot, using 2 level teaspoons to thicken ½pt/250ml thin liquid. It is flavourless.

PULSES

See page 197.

RASPINGS

Golden breadcrumbs, the word meaning,

literally, scrapings or gratings. See page 88.

RATAFIA

A liqueur or cordial distilled from almonds, peaches, apricots or plums, etc. and flavoured also with the crushed kernels of the fruit. This is why ratafia essence is so full of flavour, and so often used instead of almond essence. To quote *Larousse Gastronomique*, 'All homemade liqueurs are made by steeping fruit and other basic ingredients in alcohol or spirits . . . Liqueurs made in this way are often called ratafias.'

Ratafia biscuits Sweet biscuits flavoured with ratafia – hardly surprising if they don't all get as far as the trifle!

RENNET

An extract from, or preparation of, the inner membrane of the stomach of the sucking calf.

■ When rennet is used to make junket, the milk is warmed to blood heat, since this is the temperature at which rennin – a substance in our stomachs which makes milk clot – is accustomed to working in our stomachs, and those of calves.

RICE

See page 201.

RICE FLOUR

Rice flour, often sold by health food shops if you can't find it elsewhere, is milled rice ground into flour. It is considerably finer than *ground rice* which, like cornflour, is also sometimes used with plain flour to vary the flavour and texture of a cake: in shortbread, for instance, to keep it flat and give it a close texture.

RICE PAPER

Used especially for macaroons, and made from the pith of a Formosan tree.

■ Have you ever thought of using it as place names for a birthday tea? It's a novelty for children to be able to eat their names, even if it doesn't taste all that good! Pipe names in icing sugar on a sheet of it, and cut (with pinking scissors for a decorative edge) into 'cards'.

SAGO

The starchy pith of certain kinds of palm, particularly of Malaysia. Our word comes from the Malay word, *sagu*. Besides making a pudding, it is used for cooking as a liaison element, often also to prepare thick or thin soups and dishes recommended for special diets.

SALT

A necessity of life itself, the most important seasoning in the world. Precious enough once to have been used as money in some parts of it, salt was the origin of our word *salary*, from the Latin word *salarium*, 'money paid to a soldier in lieu of his allowance of salt'.

■ There are two sorts of salt: sea salt, the purest, which is distilled from sea-water, and rock salt, the kind most of us use, which is found in the earth in crystalline form.

Table salt Refined to make it run easily, but it isn't the kind for cooking because it doesn't bring out the natural flavour of the food as cooking salt does.

Cooking salt Infinitely preferable to table salt for cooking because it is both purer and stronger, never mind less expensive. Salt is extraordinary stuff when one thinks about it because nothing tastes of anything without it, whether a succulent steak, fried fish, a cake, a milk pudding, scones, pastry, or simply a plate of porridge. Its true magic is in bringing out the flavour of the food itself, when cooked with it. That's why one can never, at the table, make up for a cook's shortcomings.

■ Salt raises the boiling point of water (to 224°F/106°C), therefore vegetables boiled with a good quantity of salt cook more quickly than when boiled without, and there is consequently less loss of vitamin C. For the same reason, if one adds salt to the water when boiling an egg – misguidedly thinking that because the water goes off the boil, the egg will boil more slowly and therefore won't crack – the water will in fact get hotter still! See *egg pricker*, page 25.

SEMOLINA

Made from hard wheats, rich in gluten. The grains are granulated into coarse particles, but not crushed enough to reduce them completely to flour. Some wheats of hot dry countries, such as France and Italy, are especially suitable for its preparation. It is used to make soups, puddings and various other dishes.

SPICES

Mostly of tropical origin and said to have brought the world together, spices were at one time the world's most profitable trade, some literally being worth their weight in gold. So precious indeed was a cargo of spices that the loss of several hundred men on a voyage was not considered too high a price to pay.

■ For their full aroma and flavour – beautifully described once as perfumes trapped in glass jars – it is ideal to buy spices in small if not minute quantities; to store each in a small, airtight container in a dark and cool place; to replace ground spices annually.
■ Like herbs, spices should also be kept in a handy place in one's kitchen and used with subtlety: be careful rather than generous when using one with which you are not familiar. Spice tolerances vary from person to person, family to family and nation to nation, so you may want to use more, or less, of any given spice in any recipe.
■ As a general, but certainly not un-

broken rule, whole spices are tied in a scrap of butter muslin or white cotton cloth, which can easily be found and removed before a dish is served; ground spices are, when possible, sifted with other dry ingredients to ensure all blend completely; crushed spices are sprinkled (sometimes rolled) into or on to foods they are to flavour.
■ It is often less expensive to buy the more common spices at a chain-chemist (where they are very simply packaged) than at a health food shop or grocer's.

Allspice Name for the seeds of Jamaica pepper: so called because they combine the flavours of cinnamon, cloves, nutmeg and juniper berries. Smoother and larger than black peppercorns (but otherwise not unlike them), they can be ground similarly in a mill, giving a delicious flavour – alone or in a combination with other spices – to grilled pork chops, pâtés, soups, certain meat casseroles (especially beef) and to cakes and steamed puddings which contain dried fruit.

Caraway We must all know caraway, even if only because of having – or avoiding – it in seed cake. In Sweden it may turn up in almost anything: cabbage, ice cream, brown bread, potato soup, cucumber salad.

■ Seeds fresh from one's own garden have a stronger and more lasting flavour than bought. I have a feeling this is a spice that most people either love or can't bear: not one to give to the unsuspecting guest.

Cardamom The seeds of a plant belonging to the ginger family, with a unique flavour and strongly-scented aroma, especially when freshly crushed. Buy cardamom in three different ways: whole (in their tiny pods, which one can grind along with the seeds), as seeds, or ground.

■ Cardamom is used particularly in pickles, curry powders, a barbecue sauce and, in some European countries, to flavour cakes and confectionery.

■ With a light sprinkling of freshly crushed cardamom added to a cup of after-dinner black coffee, one is temporarily transported to some foreign land!

Cayenne pepper Not in fact from any peppercorn, but a red, fiery-hot powder ground from the dried seeds and pods of red chillies. Positively pungent in flavour – often only a 'point' (see page 77) of it is needed – it is a lovely flavouring for savoury dishes of eggs, cheese and seafoods.

■ Its colour (but not flavour) soon fades so, for garnishing especially, buy cayenne in microscopic quantity.

Cinnamon The dried inner bark of the cinnamon shrub, grown in the East and West Indies. It is peeled off, rolled into thin quills or sticks and allowed to dry. Ground cinnamon gives character and a lovely flavour to certain cakes, puddings, seafood and meat dishes, while cinnamon stick (removed on completion of cooking) adds fragrance to mildly flavoured stewed fruits such as plums and pears, as well as to sweet pickles, cider cups or mulled wines.

■ 1 level teaspoon ground cinnamon sieved with ½lb/225g flour makes delicious spicy pastry for a baked jam roll, an apple pie, apple dumplings or mince pies.
■ See also *cinnamon sugar*, page 126.

Cloves Named from the Latin *clovus*, a nail, because of their nail-like shape, these dried unopened buds of the clove tree give flavour and fragrance to soups, sauces and curries as well as to sweeter things such as stewed apples or pears and to hot wine punches. I also love to add one (or more) to the syrup for a fruit salad, to a bouquet garni sometimes, or to press several into the scored fat of gammon when glazing it.

■ An onion stuck with 3 or 4 cloves is a classic addition to stocks and stews, just as it is to bread sauce: about 2 per ½pt/250ml milk.

■ However you use cloves, do count how many you put into anything, so you can take the same number out.

Coriander The dried fruit of the coriander herb, the flavour of which is said to resemble a mixture of sage and lemon peel (if one could think up such a combination!). Crushed or ground, coriander gives a subtle flavour to sweet or savoury dishes: to flavour a fruit salad, the syrup for a savarin, orange marmalade, gingerbread, curries, pickles, cheese dishes.

Cumin Acrid and spicy seeds not unlike the warm flavour of caraway. They are used in spicing cheeses, salads, sauces, curries and drinks, and especially to make the liqueur kummel (the German word for cumin).

Curry powder This consists of finely ground spices – some may contain as many as 50 different varieties – the mixture differing according to where and for what it is made. In their countries of origin, spices are freshly ground each time a curry is made so, when buying ready-made, it pays to buy the best and use while fresh.

■ People who make their own, generally use their own special combinations of spices to go with various dishes: sometimes these call for mild seasonings, other times for hotter.

Ginger The root of a tropical plant.
Root ginger, dried Tied in a piece of cloth for easy removal later, root ginger is used solely for its flavour. Bruise it first with a hammer, to release its strength, preferably enclosing it in a scrap of cloth to prevent it flying about. This is more a workbench or floor job than kitchen table – it is *very* hard.

Ground ginger is made from the dried roots. Besides all the traditional ways of using it in cakes, puddings, curries and chutneys, etc., have you tried it sprinkled very lightly over cooked carrots or sautéd chicken?

Crystallized ginger comes from the fresh green roots and is used in cakes and puddings as well as a sweetmeat.

Stem ginger also comes from the fresh green roots and is sold bottled in syrup. If you like ginger, it is delicious diced finely and served with some of its syrup over sliced bananas or vanilla ice cream; with a dessert apple, or stirred into crème chantilly for a quick and quite sophisticated sweet.

Juniper berries From a small evergreen bush with an aromatic blue berry which is used in the distillation of gin and to make juniper wine.

■ Crush the berries to release their resinous flavour, and use especially in marinades for venison and game, also in certain bean dishes, sauces and stuffings.

■ ½ teaspoon of juniper berries, crushed and soaked for a long time in a marinade, or cooked for hours in a casserole, is said to give a seasoning equivalent to 2fl oz/65ml gin.

Mace The dried shell of the nutmeg, with a flavour of both nutmeg and cinnamon, mace is fragile and very beautiful: almost like starched, unbleached lace.

Whole mace is used to flavour things like marinades and syrups, and to make infusions for fish dishes, stews and sauces – in dishes where ground mace would not be suitable.

Ground mace is used, always sparingly, to flavour vegetable dishes, certain sauces, buns, cakes, mincemeat, etc., sometimes being mixed with other ground spices.

Mixed spice A combination of ground spices, as the name implies: allspice, cloves, cinnamon and nutmeg. Used especially in buns, cakes and puddings – a really lovely flavouring.

Nutmeg The seed inside the membrane of mace, this is a versatile and powerfully flavoured spice, which goes equally well with sweet or savoury dishes: finely grated over green vegetables, especially spinach or sautéd courgettes; very lightly sprinkled over cream soups, milk puddings or a baked custard; mixed with minced beef in a meat loaf, meat balls or beefburgers; to flavour a sauce for cauliflower or to give character to certain cheese dishes. Whatever you use it in, go carefully with it.

Paprika The Hungarian name for a sweet pepper. The powder made from it is red and looks like (but should not be confused with) cayenne. Paprika has a much milder but slightly pungent flavour and is an important seasoning in the Hungarian dish goulash. Use it to garnish cheese canapés, grilled fish and other savoury dishes, or to flavour savoury sauces and meat dishes. I love it added to the seasoned flour in which to toss pork chops before frying them in butter or mixed with crushed cornflakes and seasoning as a coating (after oiling and egging) for oven-fried chicken joints.

■ Like cayenne, paprika loses its brilliant colour, so buy in minute quantity.

Pepper and peppercorns
Ground white pepper Not a thing to buy at the corner shop: if of poor quality, it is likely to contain additives which spoil both its flavour and appearance. Ground from white peppercorns of course, it is less pungent and less aromatic than black pepper and is the kind we use most: in soups, casseroles, sauces and savoury dishes of all kinds, particularly where the colours would be spoilt by black pepper.

Ground black pepper More spicy than white, and loses its flavour during cooking, which explains why it is usually added to a dish just before serving, and also, in a mill, at table. Ideally, have two mills: one beside the cooker, another in the dining room.

Black peppercorns The unripe green berries of the tropical climbing pepper shrub, which turn black when dried. Use them loose when a liquid is to be strained, otherwise tie with other spices and herbs as required in a small twist of cloth. (Occasionally they are left loose.)

■ For a really hot, lingering, spicy (and lovely) flavour and some bite, crush some with a rolling pin, then press or roll them into the surface of meat before grilling it. Also grind them in a mill at the last moment into meat soups, sautéd vegetables, meat casseroles, etc. Use milled, too, for French dressing, sprinkled over salads, or as a flavouring garnish on any savoury dish which would be enhanced by its spiciness.

White peppercorns From the same shrub as black, but the berries are riper when picked, and the outer husk is removed.

■ Use them particularly to flavour special white sauces or soups, the colour of which would be spoilt by using even the finest *ground* white pepper.

Green peppercorns Although black and white peppercorns have been used for centuries, the idea of a Madagascan pepper grower of preserving (by canning) the unripe green berries is a comparatively new one. Less powerful than black and white, and with a lovely fresh aroma, they combine well with the sweeter spices of oriental cookery such as cinnamon, coriander, ginger, saffron and sesame, etc., as well as with our own more everyday flavours like garlic, bay leaves, shallots or mustard. (Unlike black and white peppercorns, dried green ones can be broken up by hand.)

■ Shellfish, salmon, chicken, pheasant, beef steaks, lamb and pork all seem to combine well with this flavour, the full potentials of which are yet to be discovered.

Poppy seed Although we see more of this pretty garnish than formerly, it is not a modern idea – the Egyptians used poppy seed more than 35 centuries ago.

■ To give a thoroughly professional finish to dinner rolls, milk bread or a milk twist, etc., brush the surface completely with egg glaze (page 66) and sprinkle lightly, while still wet, with poppy seed just before baking. (Sometimes I like to use sesame seed instead, for a change.)

Saffron A frightening price, but that's hardly surprising when one knows it takes thousands of the orange-red stigmas of the saffron crocus to make 1oz/25g. The stigmas contain a volatile oil and a colouring substance, which give the familiar musty flavour and saffron-yellow colour to rice or anything else in which they are cooked. Use it with restraint: only about 9–12 stigmas for ½lb/225g rice, a tiny pinch of sugar making them easier to pound. Mix with a spoonful or two of stock or water from whatever dish the saffron is to flavour, soak until the liquid is bright orange and then strain it in.

■ Widely used in the Mediterranean countries, saffron is delicious in many chicken, shellfish or rice dishes, though I think it is an acquired taste.

■ Saffron was at one time extensively cultivated in England, particularly at Saffron Walden, from which the town took its name. In the west of England, traditional foods include saffron bread and saffron cake.

Sesame seed The seeds of an East Indian herb, used largely to flavour and decorate buns and breads. Try sprinkling them (toasted or roasted if liked) over salads and cooked vegetables as well. See also *sesame oil*, page 115.

Turmeric One of the ginger family, though in taste quite different. The dried tubers are ground to a fine powder, which has a bright, deep-yellow colour. Its chief use is to give colour in the making of any curry powder, but it is also widely used in pickles, chutneys and relishes. Some people like to add a pinch of turmeric to mayonnaise and to chicken and egg dishes.

■ Turmeric is sometimes used as an economical substitute for saffron in rice and other dishes. (Its flavour is totally different so no one knowing saffron would be deceived.) I prefer to serve white rather than turmeric-coloured rice.

STOCK

One of those details a good cook really cares about. It is the very fabric of good gravies, soups and sauces, just as milk is the fabric of a milk pudding. Without it, there is neither body nor flavour.

■ Anyone with a freezer can store stock in cubes, like ice, to have a constant supply. If pressed for space in the freezer, reduce the stock to concentrate it (see page 77). Concentrated, it can even be stored in the ice tray of a refrigerator.

■ Quite good stock comes from bones alone, but the best stock includes meat – raw or cooked beef or veal bones, with fat-free meat, or meat scraps – or the carcase of a bird, with scraps and giblets. Break up and cut up both bones and meat, to expose maximum surface, and so draw all the goodness out of them. Use a variety of vegetables – strong ones sparingly – to achieve the right balance of flavour, without any of them dominating. Put meat, bones and vegetables into *cold* water, bringing gradually to the boil. (Pouring boiling water over them doesn't draw out the flavour in the same way.)

■ Cloudy stock is unfortunately much easier to make than clear. To make it clear:

1 Cut vegetables into largish chunks. Slices or small pieces go to pulp.

2 Avoid using cooked vegetables, or starchy ones like potatoes. Besides making stock cloudy, they also tend to make it go sour quickly.

3 Blanch raw veal bones – a knuckle bone makes lovely jellied stock – before using to make stock for a special white sauce or soup, otherwise there'll be masses of scum.

4 Skim off any scum (impurities) when it forms, and then again occasionally during cooking.

5 Always *simmer* stock. Boiling causes the scum to combine with any fat there may be.

■ If stock lacks flavour, *reduce* it to concentrate its strength (see page 77).

■ Strain stock as soon as it is made, leaving it to cool uncovered, so that it will do so rapidly and keep fresh longer.

■ Whatever one wants it for, one needs fat-free stock. The easiest way to make sure of this is to refrigerate it overnight, because one can then lift the fat off it the next day. See also *degrease*, page 59.

Brown stock Used for meat dishes where its strong flavour and dark colour will improve, but never dominate or spoil a dish. See above.

Fish stock Quite different from meat stock because it's made so quickly and, made with white fish, is fat free. If simmered longer than 20–30 minutes it goes bitter.

■ Use it for anything fishy – soups, sauces and of course fish dishes – for special occasions make it with fresh fish (not oily), bones, trimmings and perhaps a little wine, or otherwise quite simply with the head (minus eyes), bones and trimmings of the fish you are cooking. (You need onion, salt and parsley stems as well, but not the leaves because they'd darken the stock.) You may be surprised, if you refrigerate it overnight, what good jellied stock it will make.

■ The important thing is not to leave the fish carcase and trimmings with the fishmonger. If nothing else, one is losing some very tasty soup.

■ Fish stock doesn't keep like meat stock. Use it quickly, or transfer it to the freezer as ice cubes.

White stock Made with veal or chicken, for use in these and any other dishes where a light colour and a delicate flavour are important. See beginning above.

Stock cubes Useful for convenience and emergencies, but the stock may need degreasing.

SUET

One of the most natural fats used in cooking, suet is the hard white fat which surrounds and protects the kidneys. Fresh (when it should be hard and white, not soft and yellow), it is also one of the cheapest. Beef suet is used rather than any other, having the mildest flavour and adapting as well to sweet dishes as to savoury. (You would, I feel sure, sense something strange about the taste of a jam roly-poly made with lamb suet, even if you couldn't identify what was wrong.)

Packet suet This is clarified, ready-shredded suet mixed with a trace of flour to make it easier to handle, and blend more easily with other ingredients. The only effort required is to weigh and add it to a mixture. Store it in a cool, dry place, perhaps refrigerating it in extremely hot weather, to prevent shreds of suet sticking together. A highly purified and deodorized brand should keep for a year unopened, and for six months opened, though obviously the fresher any suet is when used, the better the end product. RHM Foods, the makers of Atora, claim that not only has a top quality packet suet superior storing and eating qualities, but that a Christmas pudding made with it will have a better flavour and keep far longer than a pudding made with fresh suet.

Fresh suet Grate this very finely, preferably in a Mouli grater (page 30), or shred it finely on a floured board – otherwise it will be indigestible and will take even longer to melt (see below). To store, cover and refrigerate or freeze it, making sure there are no traces of blood. Render it down if you like and use it as required, or freeze it as it is. If wanted at once, it can be grated direct from the freezer.

■ Suet needs a high temperature for melting to occur. Cook it well too otherwise it will be indigestible. When baking, use a hot oven; when steaming or boiling, have the water already boiling and allow time for long, slow cooking.
■ Use to make suet-crust pastry (which can be baked as well as boiled and steamed), stuffings, forcemeat balls, puddings, mincemeat, as a crunchy topping for certain baked dishes or simply to use, rendered down, for roasting or frying, particularly any cut of beef.
■ The normal rule of thumb is to use half

suet to flour (self-raising) in pastry, half suet to breadcrumbs in stuffings. For the best results, cook suet pastry as soon as possible after making.
■ Although it has more limited uses than most other fats, there is nothing easier than packet suet to mix in with other ingredients: you need neither skill nor utensils, and the job is done in seconds.
■ If you're without, or unable to eat, suet, solid vegetable oil is often a good substitute, see page 115.

SUGAR

Has a long history, although it has only been known in Britain for the last 900 years. According to Tate & Lyle, no one knows who first discovered sugar or began its cultivation, but Polynesian folklore suggests that it was first used in the South Pacific. The fame of sugar took some time to travel westwards from the Orient. People in Europe heard about it, but due to its primitive processing, there was no means of preserving it during long voyages. Only in the sixth century, when the cane was introduced into Persia, did sugar come within range of the Mediterranean countries. From Persia, in time, it reached Venice – then the greatest commercial centre of Renaissance Europe – soon becoming a major article of Mediterranean trade. The first recorded shipment of a large quantity of sugar to arrive in Britain was in 1319. At £20 a pound, nicknamed 'white gold', only royalty and the nobility could afford it for the next 200 years or so, and even then it was something only for the well-off.

■ Through the Portuguese and the Spaniards, however, who were developing their Empires in the East and West Indies, cane sugar was planted and grown in such quantity that by the eighteenth century the West Indies were supplying the whole of the Western world. The boom of coffee houses in Charles II's reign added to sugar's popularity, and sales rose dramatically.
■ Sugar beet was first grown in England

by a group of Quakers in 1832, as a protest against slave labour being used on the West Indian plantations, but it wasn't until the First World War, when necessity demanded it, that beet became an established crop in Britain.

■ Of all the plants which contain sugar, two of them – cane and beet – contain so much that it is commercially worthwhile to extract it. Sugar is made from their juice. Here are some of its qualities:

1 Stored in a dry place, sugar keeps well for years. In addition, it helps us to preserve all kinds of other foods – preserves, confectionery, frozen fruits and simple things like cakes and icings.

2 Sugar has a constant level of sweetness. Weight for weight, all refined sugars are equally sweet. The finer the sugar, though, the more quickly it dissolves, which explains why icing sugar may seem sweeter than others when we add it to something like cream.

3 We absorb sugar readily, which explains why a sweetened hot drink is a better pick-me-up (especially when suffering from shock) than one without sugar.

4 Sugar acts as an odour fixative, helping to preserve the balance of the aroma components of many delicate foodstuffs.

5 In low concentration, sugar speeds the action of yeast, so bread doughs will rise faster with than without it. Without sugar, and despite a raising agent (page 77), even a cake will not rise. (If you've ever forgotten to put the sugar in a sandwich cake or drop scones for example, you'll know this: the former ends up as a board, the latter as rubbery pancakes. I've made both!)

6 Sugar preserves the flavour, texture and shape of frozen soft fruits and berries: if one freezes them without, their liquid turns to particles of ice, which break up the structure of the fruit and make it disintegrate when thawed. With sugar, whether dry or in syrup form, the ice particles are prevented from forming. Don't, however, freeze fruit immediately

after adding dry sugar. In a strong polythene bag, give them about 30 minutes together first, turning the bag over at intervals to let the juices run, and to allow the sugar to penetrate all the fruit. If freezing in syrup, make it strong – about 1¼lb/500g sugar to 1½pt/750ml water, boiling it about 5–7 minutes, for extra concentration.

■ Most of us eat far too much sugar. As (of the nutrients) it only provides carbohydrates, and we get plenty of those anyway in things like potatoes and bread, there's no need for any: it's just that we like and want it! For the sake of your health, especially teeth, it's wise to cut down on the sweet foods.

■ Varying types of sugar give varying flavours and textures to foods: some dishes can be made with several kinds, all producing a perfect, yet slightly different, finished product, as, for example, meringues. Other dishes may need one type in preference to another, as explained with each type of sugar below:

Brown sugars

Demerara took its name and came originally from the old colony of that name, now a part of Guyana. Today, it comes from various cane sugar producing countries and, although originally a raw sugar, may now also be fully refined, mingled with molasses to give it a distinctive flavour.

■ Because of its syrupy flavour, demerara is many people's chosen partner for coffee, porridge, cereals or grapefruit. It's also the ideal choice to caramelize on top of a sweet like crème brûlée.

■ Because of its coarse crystal, one can usually only use demerara successfully in a cake or pudding when it can be dissolved and added in liquid form, as in gingerbread. Meringue shells are an exception.

■ 'London demerara' is the first demerara to be produced from fully refined sugar in Britain. Tate & Lyle called it by this name partly to distinguish it from the more traditional demeraras which are not fully refined. I myself find it flavourless.

Golden granulated sugar A natural unrefined cane sugar. As long as you like its flavour, and its darker colour will not spoil whatever you are making, use it at any time instead of ordinary granulated sugar. Some people like it in tea.

Soft brown sugars are sometimes called moist, soft, sugar pieces, or 'foot' sugars. It is occasionally even called sand sugar, because it looks like damp sand.

■ The most important thing about brown sugar is the very individual flavour that it gives to cakes, puddings, biscuits, stewed fruits, chutneys and pickles, toffees and fudges, to sweet and sour sauces, and to bastes for hams.

■ Brown sugars may range in colour from a creamy golden beige to a warm dark brown, the degree of colour depending on how refined it is. As a rule, the darker the colour, the richer the flavour.

■ These soft brown sugars are so fine that they will cream and blend as well as caster sugar with fat, or can be used for rubbed in as well as melted mixtures – as long as the flavour is acceptable, of course.

■ If you're caught without brown sugar at any time, try using a teaspoon of black treacle with 4oz/100g white sugar.

■ Brown sugar makes an 'Oxford' type of marmalade. Cut the fruit slightly thicker than usual and substitute brown sugar for not more than 25 per cent of the white – adding about 1 level dessertspoon of black treacle for every 3lb/1.5kg total sugar.

■ If brown sugar goes lumpy because not in an airtight jar, pop it in a large plastic bag and roll out the lumps with a rolling pin. If the sugar has gone rocky, it's better to use it in a recipe where it is dissolved. Alternatively, put it in a bowl, cover with a damp cloth and leave overnight.

Brown loaf sugar is available for those who like a measured quantity in a cup of coffee.

White sugars

Caster sugar has the smallest crystal of all boiled sugars. It is the best for creamed mixtures because it blends so smoothly with fat, consequently giving this type of cake an even and perfect texture. Use caster for whisked sponge mixtures as well.

■ Caster, or better still icing sugar, will sweeten a fresh fruit purée well because it dissolves more readily than granulated without heat – unless one makes and sweetens the purée in a liquidizer, when granulated is just as good. Most recipes for meringues call for caster sugar, but perhaps surprisingly, one can also make meringues with other sugars – icing, demerara, and lovely ones with granulated.

Coffee crystals are the largest and slowest dissolving sugar crystals. They were originally intended for the coffee connoisseur who likes the first sips of coffee to be bitter. As the crystals dissolved, so the coffee would gradually become sweeter. The custom then was to eat any remaining crystals with the spoon.

Cube sugar has succeeded the sugar we used to call 'loaf' – pieces taken off the large loaf. Only brown loaf sugar is now sold.

■ Cube sugar is produced from selected granulated sugar which is moistened and moulded into neat shapes. This is obviously first choice, therefore, for all hot drinks, because one can add a measured quantity of sugar to each cup every time. Use cubes as well for picnics, and for crushing coarsely to sprinkle over cakes and tea-breads before baking them.

■ Many old caramel recipes call for loaf sugar because at one time that was the purest white sugar. Granulated and caster, being less pure, were less suitable because impurities in sugar are one of the causes of it crystallizing. Nowadays, icing, caster, granulated and cube are each as pure as the other, so one may just as well use granulated which is cheapest.

Granulated sugar, the main product of the normal refining process, is best used in recipes where the liquid content and cooking time are such that the crystals dissolve completely. While too coarse for creamed mixtures, it blends easily with the fat for rubbed in mixtures. Because it is as pure as, but considerably cheaper than, the other white sugars, this is the best one to use for syrups. See also *golden granulated* (brown sugars) above.

Icing sugar wasn't even thought of until towards the end of the nineteenth century. It began as a by-product of loaf sugar – the sievings of the rough-shaped nibs that fell from the early form of cut cubes.
■ It is made nowadays by grinding sugar crystals to a fine powder. This is the ideal sugar for cold drinks, fresh fruit purées, whipped cream, icings, butter-cream fillings and uncooked sweets like truffles because it is so fine that it dissolves quickly, even without heat.
■ If ever you're short of caster sugar, icing is better than granulated for flan or French flan pastry, or for shortbread. Granulated tends to caramelize when these things are baked, giving a speckled appearance.
Preserving sugar is specially designed for making jams, jellies, marmalades and preserves. As the slow-dissolving crystals don't settle in a dense layer at the bottom of the pan, it doesn't need so much stirring to prevent burning, so the final preserve is clearer and brighter – important particularly for delicately coloured jellies such as apple or gooseberry, and for anyone seeking perfection.
■ Another plus about preserving sugar is that it produces very little froth when it dissolves. This means it needs less skimming than other sugars, so there's less waste of preserve and less work into the bargain.

Vanilla sugar is as easy to make as it is expensive to buy. Ideally, have two jars, one with caster sugar to use in sauces, cakes and desserts; the other with icing sugar to flavour whipped cream – because

this dissolves most quickly and sweetens the cream immediately, making it *appear* sweeter than say, caster.
■ Be sure the vanilla pod is fresh when you buy it. Simply break it into pieces, then split and bury in up to 1lb/500g of sugar in an airtight jar. Top up the jar when you use the sugar – or whenever you think about it – and you'll never be without vanilla sugar.
■ A pod will give flavour for months and months. There's no need to replace it until its aroma fades.
■ In just the same way, you can make *cinnamon sugar*, burying two broken up sticks of cinnamon in the sugar. It's delicious with almost any apple dish, or is an easy way to make *cinnamon toast*, see page 345.

Sugar hints from Tate & Lyle:

1 Sprinkle a spoonful of sugar over a chicken or duck before roasting, to help make the skin crisp.
2 Rub a spoonful of sugar and a knob of fat into very dry or dirty hands. The fat softens them and the sugar draws out any ingrained dirt.
3 A spoonful of sugar added to the water when cooking vegetables will improve their flavour, especially peas and carrots.
4 A light sprinkling of sugar over tomatoes before grilling or frying will give them more flavour – because it caramelizes.
5 A spoonful of sugar sprinkled over mint makes it easier to chop *and* gives mint sauce a better flavour.

SYRUP

Golden syrups vary in flavour and colour according to the different refineries. They are made from selected refinery liquor after the refined sugar has been crystallized.

■ Syrup won't leave a sticky trail if, when taking it out of the tin, you keep turning the spoon steadily over and over.

Measuring hints

1 To obtain level measures, warm the syrup slightly in cold weather – perhaps just standing the tin in a warm place for a while.

2 Rinse cups and spoons in very hot water first, so that you can scrape the syrup off cleanly, without waste.

3 When accuracy is important, for recipes using syrups melted with other ingredients, weigh the empty pan first, then add the required amount of syrup to it. In other recipes, put a weighed cream carton or something on to the scales, and weigh into this. Here are some easy measures for syrup – all used level:

One tablespoon holds approx 1oz/25g syrup by weight

¼pt measure/125ml holds 7oz (*about* 200g) syrup by weight

¼pt measure + 1 tablespoon holds 8oz/225g syrup by weight

½pt measure/250ml holds 14oz (about 400g) syrup by weight

TABASCO SAUCE

Takes its name from a red pepper introduced into the United States from the state of Tabasco, Mexico. It's so hot that it takes only a few drops to give soups and gravies some zest.

TAPIOCA

Comes from the roots of a tropical shrub – it's not a cereal.

TARTARIC ACID

An acid (commercially extracted) which is found in many fruits.

TEA

Can't be described as an ingredient, but see page 338.

TREACLE

The thick syrupy substance which drains out of sugar in the process of refining – use it in baking and confectionery when you want its strong flavour.

■ See also *syrup*, page 126

VANILLA

Vanilla essence The extract obtained from vanilla pods, usually added to a mixture after it is cooked, preferably when it has cooled. Vanilla has an alcohol base so, if added while a mixture is still hot, the instant aroma, though glorious, is very much at the expense of the flavour.

■ Use it in almost anything containing chocolate or cocoa, to flavour custards of almost any kind, in sweet sauces, cold sweets, certain puddings, cream, ice cream, certain cakes and cake fillings. In some dishes it is used in addition to another flavouring.

■ To make your own wonderful vanilla essence, soak a split, halved vanilla pod in a tightly sealed glass phial (or anything else suitable) of vodka for at least three weeks, shaking it occasionally. (The vodka, a virtually flavourless spirit, becomes vanilla powered – and vice versa!)

Vanilla pods The dried, rather liquorice-like pods of a Mexican orchid, which give the true flavour of vanilla. Use to make vanilla sugar (page 126), or break a piece off, split and drop it into heating milk to flavour sauces, milk puddings or whatever you like. If rinsed in warm water after use, dried carefully, and kept buried in sugar, one can use it several times before its aroma fades.

VEGETABLE FATS

White cooking fats, thought by many people to be purely of vegetable origin, do in fact mostly contain other fats as well – unless they claim to be pure vegetable.

■ Some low fat spreads are completely free of milk products, and can therefore be used by strict vegetarians who wish to avoid the whey normally present in margarine. See also oil, page 112.

VINEGAR

Takes its name from *vin* and *aigre*, meaning 'sharp wine', so let's hope this may remind you, if you are in doubt, that for most purposes wine vinegar – made by the fermentation of diluted wine – is better than malt or cider vinegar.

■ The difference in the flavour, quality, colour, price and most importantly in its use, naturally depends upon what vinegar is made of. Cheap vinegars taste harsh and spoil good food, but a selection of good vinegars can bring new life to eating, and each is child's play to make (see below). Some recipes may call for mixed vinegars, say a spoonful each of chilli, tarragon and wine. This is the way in which you can introduce flavours to something like aspic jelly without making it cloudy, or introduce them quickly and easily to whatever you are making.
■ If hard pressed on the housekeeping, you can stretch out the vinegar by topping up a half bottle with cold boiled water, and leaving it for 3 days. If not quite what it was, it's still surprisingly strong.
■ Vinegar is versatile stuff. Use:

1 In marinades, to tenderize cheaper cuts of meat as well as to flavour.
2 To give piquancy to rich foods. By stimulating the digestive juices – with a dressed salad, for instance – the food is more easily digested.
3 To soften and dissolve the smaller bones in fish, as soused herring.
4 To wash strong-smelling meat, using a vinegar-soaked cloth.
5 Instead of lemon juice in a savoury dish if you've run out of lemons, or want a change of flavour.
6 To rinse out a jar still smelling of earlier contents.

Garlic vinegar Easy to make and gives instant flavour of garlic to a salad dressing or anything else. Bring ½pt/250ml white

wine vinegar just to boiling point – this brings out the flavour of the garlic better than cold vinegar – and pour it on to 4 largish cloves of crushed garlic. Cover it as it cools (to keep out the vinegar fly), then bottle and store it for 2 to 3 weeks before straining.

Herb vinegars Usually best made with white wine vinegar so that one can use them for anything. It's generally just a matter of having about 1pt/500ml of loosely packed leaves – basil, dill, fennel, mint, savory, tarragon or thyme – and covering them with, and soaking in, the same amount of vinegar. Cover the jar and leave for 2 to 3 weeks, or long enough for the flavour to develop.

Malt vinegar Used mainly for pickles and for some kinds of chutney, but it is not the vinegar for salad dressings. Malt vinegar doesn't cut through oil as wine vinegar does, so the oily taste dominates, spoiling both the salad and the food it accompanies. It's a pity to be miserly over using wine vinegar, because it only takes a spoonful or so to make a dish – or the same amount of malt vinegar to spoil it. In fact if you use malt vinegar to make French dressing, it *isn't* French dressing – it's something quite, quite different.

■ Distilled malt vinegar is the white one, the sort one needs when brown malt vinegar would spoil the colour of something, like pickled pears.

Wine vinegar Best for cooking, and also for salads, because unlike malt vinegar, it cuts through the oil in a dressing – so preventing the oil from dominating – and sharpens the taste. To make the real thing, French dressing *must* be made with wine vinegar.

■ White and red wine vinegar are often interchangeable, but it naturally depends upon what you're making as to which you use. You'd spoil the colour of a cucumber salad, mayonnaise or white fish for instance by using red vinegar, but how monotonous food would be if we only had white. A green salad is lovely made with red.

■ High-class grocers or good wine merchants are usually a reliable source of supply. Good vinegar should have a light delicate taste (no unpleasant sharpness) and be bright and clear, even if months old.

WATER

Keeps us alive – we can't live more than a few days without it, in fact – about 1–1½pt/0.5–0.75 litre a day coming from solid foods. Water is the medium in which the body's reactions occur.

■ It is in nearly every food we eat, roughly as follows:

40 per cent in bread
33 per cent in cheese
75 per cent in eggs (whole)
67 per cent in oily fish
80 per cent in white fish
87 per cent in milk

And even more than this in some fruits and leafy vegetables; up to 97 per cent in lettuce.

■ It's because of water in foods that one needs to pack them carefully and effectively before freezing. It is converted to ice within their cell structure, and if it isn't maintained there the foods dry out, losing both nutrients and flavour as they do so.

Ice cold water Better than tap water to make pastry and batters rise well. The colder the trapped air, the more it will expand when heated.

Salt water Boils at 224°F/106°C, which explains why boiling water appears to go slightly off the boil when one adds salt to it.

WINE

While as a drink, a wine should complement the food and the food enhance the wine, in cooking, wine has further functions: to give flavour to bland dishes; to blend other flavours together; to give food a lovely aroma and stimulate the digestive juices; to bring out the flavour of a food with which it is cooked; to give 'fullness' to a dish; to tenderize tough meat (as well as flavour it), in a marinade. To use wine is, in fact, like waving a magic wand over even the simplest of dishes. It should be all but undetectable *as* wine – simply enhancing and enriching a dish so subtly that it could never taste the same without it. Table wines used in fish and meat dishes are usually cooked long enough for the alcohol to evaporate and for the flavours of wine and cooking liquor to amalgamate. Although it need not be of the best, a wine must have a good flavour: whether a good or a poor one, that flavour will be stronger when a wine is reduced (page 77), to vaporize the alcohol and concentrate the flavour and fragrance, as it is for many dishes.

■ Generally speaking, a (dry) red wine is used for meat and game; a (dry) white wine for fish, white meats and chicken dishes. A dry white vermouth is often a good substitute and, more concentrated than wine, can be diluted with up to an equal quantity of water. Alternatively, a rosé can sometimes be substituted or, failing all else, it is generally better to use a dry cider in a recipe calling for wine than nothing.

■ One of the easiest ways to use wine is after frying, sautéing or roasting, see *deglaze*, page 59.
■ If using wine often in cooking, a (good) wine box is handy and almost certainly less extravagant.
■ An unfinished bottle of wine will keep longer if you decant it into a smaller bottle, then cork and refrigerate it. Rather than make it into ice cubes, as some do, I prefer to make beurre bercy or beurre marchand de vins, freezing the butter until I want it. This way, the flavour is held and the wine is kept almost perfectly. See *butters, savoury*, page 169.

Fortified wines, spirits and liqueurs Used particularly to flame foods (see *flambé*, page 62) and to macerate fruits (page 70), also often in such things as gâteaux, desserts and buttercream fillings.

Cognac – if a recipe calls for this, it is usually just a way of indicating a brandy of that quality. For many purposes, e.g. for most pâtés, a Christmas cake or pudding, peaches in brandy or a sponge gâteau, an ordinary (and less expensive) grape brandy will suffice.

Kirsch – a white eau-de-vie distilled from cherries – wild ones because of their acidity and the bitter almond flavour of the stones which are crushed in with the fruit. Use particularly for macerating and to flavour dishes containing fruit, as it blends superbly with so many other flavours. Although normally it is expensive to buy liqueurs in miniature bottles – probably enough only for one dish – a double-miniature bottle of kirsch de cuisine works out less pro rata than a half-bottle. See also page 104.

Madeira – lovely in consommé: use very discreetly, adding it (for its direct flavour, to taste) at the last moment. Use also in sauce madeira (page 170), certain soups (mushroom particularly) or sometimes as a substitute for sherry in desserts.

Pernod – if you like the flavour of anise, use just a few drops to flavour a fish sauce or simple fish soup.

Port – especially good in terrines and sometimes used to flavour, say, a game sauce, a dessert or rich fruit cake.

Rum – originates from cane sugar, hence the rums of Jamaica and Guyana (formerly British Guyana), the home of demerara sugar. As long as one accepts that the flavours are different, one can usually substitute cognac for rum, or vice versa. Use in gâteaux, creams, custards, pancake batters, etc.

Sherry – little used in French cookery but, stirred in at the last, is the making of some soups. In addition, it is lovely in many desserts: trifles, sponge gâteaux, or in a chocolate mousse or soufflé, for instance, when it's tasty to melt the gelatine in sherry instead of in water.

Whisky – try using it to flame (page 62) lobster dishes, chicken and pheasant. It is sometimes also used as an alternative to calvados in certain specialities of Normandy.

Home-made wines Parsley and elderberry can be good in cooking if their flavour goes happily with whatever one is making. Instead of putting parsley into a bouquet garni for instance, I prefer very often to add a tablespoonful or two of parsley wine to the liquid. Elderberry gives lovely flavour to a meat stew or soup – and is surprisingly good (and powerful) mulled.

■ The recipe I like for parsley wine uses bruised ginger root, orange and lemon as additional flavourings.

YEAST

Today's fine, powdery, fast-action, easy-blend, dried yeasts are as simple to incorporate with other ingredients as sugar or salt. Compared with fresh yeast, they are also so handy and easy to store that I now seldom use any other: nobody need be afraid nowadays of using yeast.

There is nothing I enjoy making more than a yeast dough: it smells lovely, feels lovely and looks lovely – and the aroma while baking is glorious too. As for the end product, no shop can produce anything as satisfying as your very own (well made!) bread and rolls.

The quantity of yeast needed varies both with the type of dough you're making and yeast you're using. Dried fruits, eggs and sugar, for instance, delay its action, slowing down fermentation, so a rich dough with these needs more yeast than an ordinary bread dough.

Fresh yeast Should have that lovely strong yeasty smell, should be a good even colour – no dark patches – and it should be in large pieces which crack rather than go crumbly. Stale yeast won't become liquid when mixed with a teaspoon of sugar. A pinch of fresh yeast will dissolve quickly on your tongue.

■ Yeast's life depends upon temperature: it is dormant when frozen, flourishes in

Imperial weights	Metric
½oz yeast to ½–1lb flour	15g yeast to 0.25–0.5kg flour
1oz yeast to 1–3lb flour	30g yeast to 0.5–1.5kg flour
2oz yeast to 3–6lb flour	60g yeast to 1.5–3kg flour

warmth, but is killed by too much heat. This explains why it can be deep frozen for months, why a warm dough rises faster than a cold, and why bread needs a hot oven to stop it rising through the roof.

■ If you have a freezer, fresh yeast is considerably cheaper by the lb/500g than in smaller quantities, because it is an easier and more economical way for a shopkeeper to sell it. It's a lot easier for you, too, because it's always there, fresh when wanted. (You may have to buy it by the kilo.)

■ Cut the yeast into equal-sized pieces *before* you freeze it – 8, 16, 32, according to the weight you generally use – and parcel each up before packing them into a freezer container to protect well. When you want it, it acts more quickly if thawed for an hour or so first (say in a covered basin), because it doesn't cool down the liquid when mixed with it. Once again, you can't then cut it into pieces because it liquefies when thawed.

■ Given three things, warmth, moisture and suitable food, you can't stop yeast growing. The warmth I've mentioned above, the liquid is obvious, and its foods are the sugars and other carbohydrates in the flour. This explains why there's no need always exactly to double the quantity of yeast in a recipe when using double the amount of flour – because the more flour there is, the more food there is for the yeast cells to feed on and so multiply. For bread, the proportions required of yeast to flour are approximately as shown in the table but you can step up the yeast slightly to make a dough rise faster.

■ Creaming (mixing) the yeast with sugar is an outdated method because it is said now to inactivate some of the yeast cells, slowing down rather than speeding up fermentation. Simply add the warm liquid (⅔ cold, ⅓ boiling water gives the right temperature) to the yeast, then stir to dissolve it.

Dried active (drum dried) yeast Kept cool and dry, this will keep for very long periods, but deteriorates if kept in warm, humid conditions. Buy it where there's rapid turnover. In use, this type of yeast differs from 'fresh' as follows:

1 1oz/25g dried yeast=2oz/50g fresh.
2 Dried yeast needs slightly hotter liquid (110°F/43°C) than fresh (about 85°F/30°C) for good results.
3 Reconstitute by sprinkling on top of the warm liquid in which you've dissolved 1 teaspoon of sugar. (This yeast does need sugar to activate it.)
4 Leave for 10 minutes or until frothy in a warm place. (If it fails to froth, it's dead and useless.)

Dried easy-blend (or fast action) yeast All you have to do is sprinkle this yeast from its foil sachet over the other ingredients: no previous mixing, frothing or anything else. Follow the instructions given for the quantity required and stick to the usual basic rules for yeast mixtures as mentioned above.
A few points to note:

1 Using this yeast, the fat should be *rubbed* into the flour, before adding the yeast. Otherwise the fine particles of yeast become coated with fat, which prevents them reconstituting when mixed with the water.
2 These yeasts are approximately 30 per cent more efficient than drum-dried, so you need less: approximately half the quantity of drum-dried, quarter the quantity of fresh.
3 Some of these yeasts include ascorbic

acid (see page 307) in their ingredients. If it mentions this (on the outer packet), don't add more.

4 Some of these yeasts contain two permitted bread improvers – potassium bromate as well as ascorbic acid. With these, the dough needs only one rising: quite a saving of time. (Look on the outer packet to see if they're mentioned.)

YOGHURT

A form of curdled milk – and not only cows' milk, of course – which dates back centuries and probably originated in the Balkans. Like yeast, the activator in yoghurt is a living organism sensitive to temperatures: for the dos and don'ts of how to make it, see page 300.

■ Should you like yoghurt, and not be upset by its acidity, it can add interest and variety to many dishes besides being eaten neat. Here are some suggestions:

1 Sprinkle it with the sugar of your choice and serve with stewed fruit or compôte. Alternatively, stir sugar into it, to make a creamy consistency, and serve with a fruit pie or fruit crumble.

2 Add a spoonful or two at the last minute to soups, sauces or sautéd vegetables, cooking the mixture just long enough for the flavours to blend together. (You can also swirl it over the top of chilled soups, as you would cream.)

3 Make mayonnaise lighter by mixing it with an equal quantity of yoghurt.

4 Mix with an equal quantity of whipped double cream (whipped to a similar consistency as the yoghurt) to serve with, or top, strawberries or to serve with a fruit flan or pie.

5 Substitute a spoonful of yoghurt for some of the milk when making scones, to give them a lighter texture.

■ If you're a yoghurt addict, it may be worth investing in a yoghurt maker – in which case I'd investigate the alternatives. (Some makes are much better than others.)

4
Pastry

GENERAL INFORMATION

Pastry would be flat as a board when cooked if it wasn't for the particles of air trapped in the making. These expand when heated, and the cooler they are to begin with, the more they expand, so the lighter the pastry. This explains why everything has to be cold – flour, fats, water (iced if possible), hands, and finally the dough itself. It's the main reason for sieving the flour, for using a large mixing bowl, for using a knife to mix it with, and for lifting your hands well above the bowl when rubbing fat into flour. The success of all pastries depends on air – on trapping and retaining it.

■ The variety and texture of a pastry is determined by the proportions of flour, fat and water, and the way in which they are incorporated.

Flour Use plain flour: self-raising gives a spongy, cake-like texture. Apart from suet-crust pastry, which is heavy, pastry neither needs nor wants the chemical raising agents present in self-raising flour, because air is pastry's raising agent. Strong flour, which contains more gluten, is used only for really rich pastries, soft household flour giving a better texture for all others.

Fats Vary according to the kind of pastry being made. Butter (which gives the best flavour) or margarine provides the flavour and crispness of pastry, while lard or cooking fat provides the lightness. That's why a combination of the two is used in some pastries. Pastry made with lard or cooking fat alone may well be light as air, but it will also be utterly tasteless.

■ Cold butter or hard margarines make better pastry than soft and the pastry is easier to manipulate, but neither should be refrigerator-hard if they are to be rubbed into flour, because they won't blend properly. Ideally, they should be cold and firm.

■ A soft lard is preferable to traditional lards because you can use it, chilled, direct from the refrigerator, where it is always soft enough still to rub in or roll out. Because it is cold, it makes lighter pastry than a hard lard at room temperature. (See *lard*, page 104.)

Water Can be the cause of success or disaster in pastry-making, depending on whether you get the dough the right consistency or not. Some pastries are drier than others (e.g. shortcrust is drier than flan), but basically pastry should neither be too dry nor too wet, and certainly never sticky. If too wet it is difficult to handle, tough and hard when cooked. If too dry, it's also difficult to handle but for different reasons – some kinds of pastry crack, and others aren't pliable enough to roll successfully.

Salt Used in the proportion of 1 level teaspoon to 8oz/225g flour, in *all* kinds of pastry. Without it, one might as well eat straw.

Lemon juice Used in some kinds of pastry to give greater elasticity to the gluten, which makes the pastry rise better. It also slightly counteracts the richness. If called for in a recipe, results won't be as good if you omit it.

Egg yolk Makes pastry crisp, full of flavour, rich and golden when cooked, as for instance in flan, cheese, or French flan pastry. It also helps pastry to keep a sharp shape, as round the edge of a flan.

Heavy handling or over-handling Knocks the air out of pastry, so the more you can do with a knife, the less you have to use your hands. This is why it is better to cut the fat up into smallish pieces amongst the flour, before starting to rub it in. If it's either very hard or very soft, or if the proportion of fat to flour is high, it is more important than ever to do this.

■ It's important, too, that you should just lightly brush your fingertips and thumbs against each other when rubbing fat into flour, because squashing them together expels air. If you're one of those unfortunates with permanently hot hands, cut the fat extra small, and see if it's easier to use your palms instead of your fingers, just lightly brushing them against each other, with the flour and fat between.

Rolling pastry A floured pastry board may be old-fashioned, but it is still better than formica or melaware. This is because it keeps cooler, and also because you can't distribute flour evenly over formica – which makes it more difficult to roll the pastry well.

■ Use the minimum of flour on a board (preferably sprinkled from a flour dredger), otherwise a dough which was soft and perfect in the mixing bowl may become dry, heavy and difficult to roll – and then it won't rise well. The same sort of things will happen if you sprinkle the pastry itself with flour.

■ If you're not sure how to roll, see page 78, because heavy rolling makes heavy pastry: the aim is to extend pastry in whatever direction you want, not to flatten by squashing it. Many people unconsciously put more pressure on the rolling pin with one hand than the other, the would-be rectangle ending up either with a waist or, perhaps even worse, shapeless. To correct a waist, roll the pastry diagonally wherever it has narrowed. To avoid shapelessness, consciously roll more firmly with the weaker hand wherever the pastry is thicker. Unevenly rolled pastry will rise unevenly, the thinner parts perhaps burning before the thicker are cooked.

■ Flaky and puff types of pastry are rolled and folded – some kinds 5 to 7 times – for two main reasons: first to produce lots of wafer-thin layers of pastry, which give it its characteristic flaky texture; secondly to trap more air (see illustrations) and then to distribute it, together with the fats, throughout the pastry. If it is rolled *too* often, the fat simply mixes with the dough instead of remaining in layers.

■ The usual way to fold a strip of pastry ABCD is like this, dividing it in your mind's eye into thirds, see dotted lines.

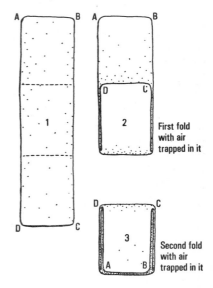

First fold with air trapped in it

Second fold with air trapped in it

Keep the second fold (DC, fig 3 above) to one side, either to your right or left, so that each time you roll the pastry, it will have done a quarter turn. In this way, if your pressure on a rolling pin *is* uneven, the extra pressure will come on each of the four sides in turn, distributing the weight evenly in the end. If your memory is as bad as mine, it's probably best to make a habit of *always* turning the fold to the same side: for me, that's to the left.

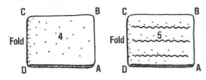

Before actually rolling out the pastry (fig 4), distribute the air trapped at folds by pressing down gently right across pastry (with your rolling pin) in about 3 places, see wavy lines, fig 5, *then* start to roll.

■ Here are a few general tips:

1 Some pastries are intended to rise more than others: there's a right or wrong thickness for them all – and the latter may easily spoil results, e.g. puff pastry for a vol-au-vent will not, if rolled too thin, rise high as it should; cheese straws made from cheese pastry rolled too thick will have a cake-like rather than a nice crisp texture.

2 No pastry tolerates being turned over during rolling. This makes it tough.

3 Roll pastry larger than required size, to allow for shrinkage before cooking. If you stretch it to fit a dish, it will inevitably shrink later – that's its nature.

■ It is better and easier to lift a large piece of rolled-out pastry over the rolling pin than with your hands, especially if it's thin. It is much less likely to tear or break, because the weight is evenly distributed over the length of the pin, and if you're lining a flan ring or covering a pie, it's easy to centre the pastry precisely above it.

Relaxing pastry A period of 15–20 minutes – in the refrigerator if possible – between rollings, and after the final rolling, is a vital but frequently neglected process in pastry-making, because there's no apparent reason for it. Here's why you should do it:

1 It allows the gluten, stretched during mixing and rolling, to relax. If it isn't given time to do this, the pastry is difficult to roll out and will also shrink badly when cooked – like stretched elastic suddenly released. See *gluten*, page 100.

2 The fat has time to firm up, making the dough easier to handle.

3 The pastry will rise better when cooked because, chilled in the refrigerator, the cold air in it expands more than warmer air would.

4 After the final rolling, relaxing gives the pastry the opportunity to shrink on the board rather than on the pie, plate, or whatever.

■ To keep it moist and prevent it from cracking while relaxing, put it on a floured plate, and cover it with foil or a polythene bag. If pastry is refrigerated too long, the fat may have hardened more than the dough, so will break through when rolled – best then to leave it at room temperature for a while first.

Cutting pastry Use a sharp floured knife or cutter, to free the layers and so allow it to rise properly. If either is blunt, or if you twist a cutter instead of making a clean cut, this drags and seals the edges.

■ The edges of pastry are 'knocked up', page 68, to help ensure they are open, allowing the pastry to rise perfectly when cooked.

Glazing pastry This needs care. If you brush any cut edge with egg, the egg coagulates immediately in the hot oven, causing a seal, which stops the pastry rising there – fatal for vol-au-vents and patties, and not very good for a pie or anything else. See also *glaze*, page 66.

Steam Must escape, otherwise, sealed in, it makes the inside of pastry soggy. An escape is usually made by making a hole in the middle of a meat pie, by slightly raising one corner of the pastry on a fruit pie, or by pricking the top of a plate-pie in 2 or 3 places with the prongs of a fork. The more water there is in a dish, the more steam there is, so obviously a meat pie needs a bigger outlet than a plate pie.

The oven It must be preheated and hot,

and the richer the pastry the hotter the oven. This makes sure that the starch grains in the flour will burst and absorb the fat before it can melt and run out. (If you've ever found a baking sheet running with fat, it's probably because the oven was too low.) A hot oven also helps pastry to rise quickly, and form a crust which will hold its shape.

■ To allow a dish to cook inside, one can lower the heat or, once it has set, lower the position of some kinds of pastry in the oven.

■ A pastry like puff, with very high fat content, is baked on a *wetted* baking sheet. The moisture prevents the bottom of the pastry from browning too quickly, and consequently from burning in the necessarily very hot oven.

SHORTCRUST PASTRY

Must be short and light, but it won't be if you add too much water. 1 teaspoon/5ml to each 1oz/25g flour gives about the right consistency with most flours.

Proportions Normally half fat to flour, but of course you can make a richer melt-in-the-mouth version – *rich shortcrust pastry* – by using a higher proportion of fat to flour, and an egg yolk in place of some of the water. You need 4oz/100g shortcrust pastry for a 1pt/500ml pie dish.

■ If you shake the mixing bowl lightly after rubbing the fat into the flour, any remaining lumps will come to the surface. If the fat isn't properly rubbed in, the pastry may end up blistered.

■ Some cooks say that the water should be added by sprinkling all at once over the surface, to give an even texture and avoid blisters in the cooked pastry. I prefer adding it to a well in the flour, because it distributes the water more evenly.

■ Once the dough has formed into a few large lumps, it's best to draw them together with your fingertips into one big ball, when the sides of the bowl should be quite clean. Then you can feel if the consistency is right.

■ Kneading shortcrust pastry is quite different from kneading bread. It simply means drawing up the edges very lightly into the centre, to bring it to the required shape – round, square or rectangular – and to make a smooth, even dough.

■ If you cut portions of dough off a batch of pastry to make different dishes, put the *cut* side uppermost on the board before kneading it to the required shape. It's easier to roll the pastry evenly this way, than when the pastry is cut side downwards.

■ *To roll a circle of pastry*, first knead the dough lightly into a round lump, then turn it upside down (smooth side up). Turn the pastry round little by little each time you roll – in other words avoid rolling it twice running in the same direction.

CHEESE PASTRY

A crisp, rich, savoury form of shortcrust pastry. If some of the cheese can be Parmesan, so much the better for the flavour – and do remember a pinch of cayenne.

Proportions Are half to equal quantities fat to flour; half to equal quantities cheese to flour; 2–4 egg yolks to each lb/450g flour. If one uses equal quantities fat and flour, the fat has to be very cool, and is easier cut in with a knife than rubbed in. This is because so much fat tends, with warm fingers, to form a dough with the flour, even before one has added the water.

■ The fat should be either butter or margarine, never lard or cooking fat, which would give the pastry the wrong texture.

■ Too much water makes cheese pastry tough, not short, so it's better to err on the dry side if in doubt. It may crack, and be difficult to roll and handle, but at least it will taste good.

■ A delicious melt-in-the-mouth cheese pastry (suitable for straws and canapés, but not for moulding because it cracks too easily) can be made by using equal quantities of flour, margarine, cheese and fresh breadcrumbs, salt and cayenne –

but no egg yolk or water. 2oz/50g of each ingredient makes quite a stack of straws. Rub or cut the fat into the flour and seasonings, then add the cheese and breadcrumbs, and knead it lightly to a dough. Rolled to ¼in/6mm thick, straws take about 7–10 minutes in a hot oven, gas 6, 400°F/205°C.

FLAN PASTRY

Made with butter or margarine, never lard, then, (unlike shortcrust, which may become tough and hard) its crisp short texture isn't spoilt by a filling.

■ It's important not to make this dough too wet, otherwise the pastry won't be crisp. The amount of water needed may vary according to the size of the egg yolk.

Quantities For a 7in/18cm flan ring, one needs:

  4oz/100g plain flour
  ½ level teasp salt
  2oz/50g butter or margarine
  1 egg yolk
  2–4 teaspoons cold water
  1 level dessertspoon caster sugar, for a sweet flan

■ Caster or icing sugar is used rather than granulated because granulated caramelizes during baking, so the flan ends up speckled. Too much sugar, and the pastry will be heavy.

FRENCH FLAN PASTRY

Also called *pâte sucrée* or sugar pastry, this makes the most delicious flans ever – but then I have a sweet tooth! Its crisp, short texture depends upon the careful blending of the right ingredients in an unusual way, as well as upon very light handling. It isn't too easy to make.

■ Butter gives a better flavour than margarine, but if it isn't fairly soft, it is difficult to blend with the yolks, sugar and flour.

Proportions Some recipes call for 2 egg yolks to 4oz/100g flour, or 1 yolk and 1

dessertspoon of water. Whether you use one or two yolks, the texture is crisper and lighter without any water. 1 small whole egg can take the place of 2 yolks, but because of the wateriness of egg white, once again the pastry isn't as crisp.

■ Caster or icing sugar are used for the same reason as for flan pastry, but caster keeps the pastry a sharper shape than icing.
■ Work the dough just until smooth, shiny, pliable and soft. If overworked, it tends to become a sticky mass, which is difficult to roll out without using extra flour, which spoils the texture.
■ Unlike most other pastries, it is very malleable, and easily patched if it breaks during rolling or moulding. It doesn't shrink in the same way either, so can be rolled to the exact size required.
■ Brush both baking sheet and flan ring with oil or melted lard, otherwise the pastry, because of its high sugar content, will stick.

FLAKY PASTRY

Should rise more, and be lighter than shortcrust, because of all the air trapped during folding and rolling.

Proportions Are two-thirds fat to flour. One needs 6oz/150g pastry for a 1½pt/750ml pie-dish.

■ If one mixes the lard and margarine together on a plate with a knife while they're at room temperature, then refrigerates them until firm, but not too hard, they'll be evenly distributed when one comes to using them.
■ After rubbing in a quarter of the cooled fat, cut the rest into large sugar-lump-sized chunks. Like this, air will be trapped between them each time the pastry is folded over.
■ Most of the water is added at once, to prevent the dough getting a flaky appearance. It should be soft to the touch, without sticking to the fingers.
■ Seal the edges of the folded dough with the rolling pin, to *trap* the air. If you then

press the dough in ridges 2 or 3 times with the rolling pin (see page 134), this distributes the air more evenly throughout, before re-rolling.

■ Keep the edges straight and the corners square, to ensure even thickness when folding, and avoid rolling over the ends of the pastry if you can, because this forces out the air.

■ Lay any trimmings flat on top of each other, rather than kneading them into a lump. This keeps the pastry in layers.

ROUGH PUFF PASTRY

A richer version of flaky.

Proportions Are three-quarters fat to flour. One needs 6oz/150g pastry for a 1½pt/750ml pie dish.

■ Margarine and lard (or cooking fat) are best mixed together on a plate with a knife while at room temperature, then refrigerated until firm, but not too hard. If you then toss walnut-sized lumps of the fat lightly in the flour, this makes the pastry easy to handle.

■ Add the water and lemon juice (see page 133) almost all at once – *all* at once if you're sure of the quantity, because this ensures an even texture.

■ Keep the edges and ends straight during rolling, and the corners square, to ensure even thickness when folding. After folding each time, seal the edges with the rolling pin to trap the air caught under the fold.

■ Rough puff is flakier than flaky as it happens. Because it's rolled more times, there are extra layers to rise, with more air trapped between.

PUFF PASTRY

Called *pâte feuilletée* in French (pastry of leaves) because of the way it is folded and rolled so many times, to produce the numerous layers.

Proportions Equal quantities of butter to flour. Margarine doesn't make good puff pastry. The texture of the butter is impor-

tant because ideally it should be the same consistency as the dough, so that they will blend together evenly. If too soft, it keeps bursting through the dough when rolled, but if too stiff it won't distribute easily. The firmer they both are though, within reason, the more easily they will roll out. If butter is too hard, press it with your hands in a floured cloth to make it more pliable.

■ Rubbing one-eighth of the butter into the flour makes the dough slightly easier to roll out, before enclosing the remaining seven-eighths.

■ You can't make real puff pastry without strong flour – it's a waste of time and materials with 'soft'. Only strong flour has the high gluten content needed to construct thin layers which won't collapse in the oven.

■ Rolling is done with quick short rolls, lightly but firmly backwards and forwards. If you push the rolling pin, the butter is likely to go sideways, and the pastry won't rise properly.

■ Relaxing between rollings is necessary for all the usual reasons (see page 135), and absolutely essential to keep this large amount of butter firm. Otherwise it will come through both top and bottom of the dough, making it impossible to roll without using extra flour, which spoils it.

■ I find rolling and folding puff pastry seven times (in envelope form as illustrated on page 134), gives better results than rolling it four times in the 'double folded' method. The pastry is so thick the latter way that it's difficult to roll it evenly – and any unevenness is greatly exaggerated when puff pastry rises.

■ Good shaping when rolling – straight sides and square corners – is still more important with puff pastry than with flaky or rough puff, for the same reasons. It must be rolled evenly to rise evenly.

■ The large amount of rolling toughens the gluten in the flour, and develops the strength of the pastry, counteracting the softening effect of so much fat.

■ A cutter dipped in boiling water gives the sharpest cut, and helps the pastry to rise best.

■ A vol-au-vent or patties are better turned

upside down to cook because the side which was uppermost when rolled shrinks more than the side which was against the table – they'll be a better shape and less likely to topple over.

■ If one side of your oven happens to be hotter than the other – it shouldn't be, but sometimes is – the pastry at the hotter side rises more quickly than the other, giving yet another cause for toppling.

■ 8oz/225g flour is the easiest quantity for most people to handle. It isn't easy to make a larger amount successfully at one time.

SUET PASTRY

Needs self-raising flour, or baking powder with plain flour, because air isn't a strong enough raising agent when using suet. The proportion of baking powder to flour is higher than for cakes, the pastry being hard and tough if too little is used. Using self-raising flour, there is less urgency to cook suet pastry as soon as it is made. It can easily wait an hour or so.

■ Use either fresh or packet suet, see *suet*, page 122.

Proportions Are a third to a half of fat to flour, but a quarter of the flour can be replaced by fresh breadcrumbs, if liked, to make extra-light pastry.

■ A suet pudding – meat or sweet – will be very solid if not well protected from condensed steam during cooking: cover it first with greased greaseproof paper – a butter wrapper is handy for this – and then with foil.

■ A very similar end result is achieved by using solid vegetable oil instead of suet, see page 116, **6**. (Grate the oil very finely and if making the pastry for, say, a beefsteak pudding, use only a quarter of fat to self-raising flour. Use enough water to mix to a dry dough.)

CHOUX PASTRY

As quick and easy to make as a sauce, for that's all it is; a very *thick* sauce (called a *panada*, see page 76) into which egg is beaten. Quite different from all other pastries, choux is the basic mixture to which various flavourings and other things can be added to make dishes like cheese aigrettes, quenelles or gnocchi. It's no bother to do and it widens one's range of cooking in all sorts of ways.

Proportions Opinions vary about the proportion of flour, butter and water used to one egg, but this is *my* favourite recipe, followed by *why* it's better to do one thing than another:

1oz/25g butter
4 tbsp/80ml water
1½oz/40g plain flour
pinch of salt
1 egg
few drops vanilla essence, if for cakes

Method

1 Melt butter, add water and bring to boil.
2 Sieve the flour and salt on to a clean sheet of paper and when the butter and water boil, stir in the flour all at once, still over the heat. Reduce heat to low and beat mixture until it leaves the sides of the pan clean, probably in seconds.
3 Cool mixture two or three minutes, beat in half the lightly mixed egg (using a wooden spoon still) and when amalgamated and quite smooth, add remainder, beating again until smooth.
4 Leave to cool before using, and then pipe or use as required.
5 If baking, bake in a hot oven on a greased baking sheet, gas 7, 425°F/220°C for 15 minutes, then lower to gas 4, 350°F/175°C until crisp and golden, *probably* 25–35 minutes altogether, according to whatever one is making. (After 20 minutes, when the choux is set, puncture small things like éclairs with the point of a knife to let steam escape, or slit large puffs.) Cool on a cake tray.
6 Remove any uncooked part in the centre of puffs, etc. as soon as they're cool, slitting open with a sharp knife or a pair of scissors.

■ Why it's better to do one thing than another:

1 Butter gives the best flavour. Neither oil nor margarine is a patch on it.

2 With the flour and salt sieved on to paper, you can shoot the whole lot at once into the boiling liquid.

3 When the *panada* leaves the sides of the pan clean, this indicates the flour is cooked. If you continue to cook it beyond this stage, the choux won't rise properly and will have a heavy cake-like consistency.

4 If you add the egg to the boiling mixture without allowing the mixture to cool at all, the egg will cook immediately, which it mustn't. Then it won't be able to blow up the mixture when it's baked (or otherwise cooked).

5 The lightness of choux pastry depends on thorough beating of the mixture after the egg is added, to incorporate air.

6 Choux, like other pastries and for the same reasons, is used cold (but not chilled) – unless otherwise specified. (Some cooks like to use it warm but I never think it makes such good pastry.)

7 A preheated hot oven is essential to raise and set choux, and if you take it out of the oven before it's firm to the touch, it will collapse.

8 If you don't puncture (or slit) the nearly cooked choux, the trapped steam will make it go soggy when cold.

9 Any uncooked centre, if not removed, will spread its dampness to the outside, which *should* be crisp, firm to the touch, and tender and dry to eat.

■ And here are a few more general tips:

1 A filling shouldn't be added until the last possible minute because any moisture in it will make choux go sad.

2 Deep fat, if used, should be 320–40°F/160–171°C – not too hot. If much hotter, the outsides of the choux harden before the insides can expand, so the mixture can't rise – making cannonballs instead of featherweight puffs. The heat is increased slightly during cooking.

3 For perfection, choux pastry should be no more than a few hours old. If you freeze things like éclairs or puff shells, bake them for 3–4 minutes in a hot oven, gas 7, 425°F/220°C to thaw and crisp them just before using.

4 Any left-over uncooked choux will keep, refrigerated, for a few days: put it in a basin, brush the surface with oil and cover closely with foil to prevent a skin forming. Don't expect it to be quite so good though.

HOT WATER CRUST PASTRY

Odd man out, as it sounds. Everything has to be warm instead of cold, otherwise it's almost impossible to manipulate. Few doughs are more quickly made.

Quantities One needs 4oz/100g pastry for a small pie (see page 34) to serve 2, or 6oz/150g for a 1¼pt/625ml oval loose-bottom tin, to serve 3 – i.e. about 2oz/50g pastry per person. Proportions are one-third fat to flour. Lard or cooking fat is the only fat which gives a raised pie (the kind like a bought pork pie) its characteristic texture.

■ One can't stop midstream to make the filling for a raised pie. This must be ready before one starts to make the pastry, because the dough has to be rolled and moulded while still warm, before the lard has time to set, making it brittle and difficult to handle.

■ Use a wooden spoon to mix it – it's warmer than a knife – until cool enough to use your hands. The boiling lard and water partially cook the starch grains in the flour, forming this lovely-to-handle, warm, soft, pliable dough. (It's quite different from other doughs and rather greasy by comparison.) Knead it for just a few moments, until free of cracks and absolutely smooth.

■ Any pieces of pastry cut off, say to make a lid or a second pie, should be kept warm in foil. Even then you need to work fairly quickly.

■ If you add an egg yolk, the dough cracks more easily, but the flavour is better and the pastry keeps fresh longer.

FROZEN PASTRY

Can be thawed, made up into dishes, and refrozen. A filling is often pre-cooked, but the pastry is usually better cooked fresh when needed.

■ Some commercial frozen pastries are so good that a busy person would have to be a perfectionist never to use them. One particular make of puff pastry is probably better puff than the great majority of people can make anyway – and lots of people can't make it at all. I find it a must for the occasions when I'm short of time. One can't really compare it, though, with the *best* home made puff, nor with rough puff or flaky pastry for such things as a meat pie or sausage rolls, because puff isn't the right kind of pastry for them.

■ Left-over scraps of pastry, bought or homemade, are best made up into a dish if possible, but otherwise one can wrap them in foil and freeze, to use later.

■ When making your own pastry, if you have a freezer, it's not much extra trouble, while busy, to make two or three times as much of some kinds as you need, lining two or three foil plates with it, instead of just one. A future quiche or flan is about three-quarters made when the case is ready, while jam rolls and other simple dishes can be ready for the oven.

■ Some of the juice from stewed apple, etc. in plate pies, tends to seep into the pastry during freezing. Brushing the inner side of the pastry with egg white seals the surface and prevents this happening.

■ Frozen pastry must be allowed time to thaw enough to roll it evenly, otherwise it will rise unevenly. Like others, however, it will rise better if chilled, than if at room temperature.

5

Eggs and egg dishes

GENERAL INFORMATION

Eggs are packed with goodness, and worth understanding. They look so simple, and are such an everyday food that their complexities often go unnoticed. It is difficult to realize, because the shell hides an egg's changes, that they deteriorate if improperly stored, or with age, giving gradually worsening results when used for cooking.

■ Because we don't know exactly when shop eggs were laid, although an egg box gives a lot of information, anyone who has their own hens scores over everyone else, qualitywise. Next best to having one's own, if one can buy them, are fresh farm eggs: two new-laid can be better than three, or even four older (or badly stored) eggs. It depends on what one is making.

Storage How eggs are kept is of even more importance than their age. For instance, a week-old egg which has been kept in warm conditions is likely to be in a worse condition than a three-week-old egg which has been kept cool from point of lay to cooking.

■ It's on account of the air chamber (see below) that eggs are always stored point downwards, because they keep better when the yolk rests on the white, rather than on the air chamber. If the other way up, the yolk will in time press against, and stick to the shell; then it soon goes bad.

Structure of an egg The *shell* is not as elementary as it looks: it is porous so one should avoid storing eggs near strong-

smelling foods like kippers or cheese. It also has an invisible protective coating, so if you wash an egg, you wash this off, shortening its life as you do so. If an egg is dirty, just wipe it carefully, unless you are about to use it.

■ An *air chamber* at the blunt end increases in size as an egg deteriorates, either through age or bad storage conditions. When one boils an egg, the shell often cracks, as the air expands with the heat, so the staler the egg, the more likely it is to crack. It's easy to prevent a fresh egg cracking, by giving the expanding air an outlet: simply prick the egg at the blunt end with an egg pricker, see page 25. A thoroughly stale egg will actually float in a bowl of salted water, being so full of air.

■ The *egg white* is thin when an egg is fresh from the nest, most of it becoming thick and jelly-like within 48 hours. So it will remain for the next few days, then very gradually it becomes thinner and more watery as the egg ages. This explains why, if you compare a new-laid

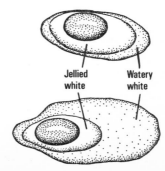

Jellied white   Watery white

with an older egg, each on a saucer, the former will be compact – with the yolk standing high, on the thick jellied white – while the older yolk will sink down amongst the spread-out, more runny white.

■ Before poaching or deep frying an egg, it pays, for reasons explained with each recipe, to examine it first.

■ The yolk of a new-laid egg doesn't break as easily as that of an older one when you drop an egg into a basin or pan. This is because the jelly acts as a cushion for it to fall on.

■ Because of its glutinous nature, you can whisk egg white into a froth which is almost permanent. New-laid whites, correctly whisked, will increase their volume by 7 or 8 times – one-eighth egg white, seven-eighths air – so is it surprising that something like a savoury soufflé will rise so magnificently without any other raising agent being added? If on the other hand you have oldish whites, is it any wonder that a soufflé may hardly rise at all?

■ The *membrane* surrounding the yolk is strong and firm when the yolk is fresh, but weakens as it ages. This is often why a yolk breaks when you separate an egg – even though done carefully.

■ The *yolk* is held and protected in the middle of the white by two 'threads' or bobbles, called the *chalazae*. To do their job, they cling so hard to it that you may actually have to break them off over the sharp edge of the shell, when separating the white from the yolk. They're a curse when it comes to cooking, because they are the main cause of curdling in cooked mixtures, and therefore the main reason for straining beaten raw eggs before making a custard or sauce.

Cooking Nest-fresh (1- or 2-day-old) eggs are unsuitable for hard-boiling (they won't shell), whisking (they won't whisk properly) or cake-making (a cake won't rise as it should) due to a chemical change in the egg which has yet to take place.

■ Eggs begin to coagulate (set) at 140°F/60°C – a temperature well below boiling point. Apart from omelettes and fried eggs, great heat or long cooking make eggs hard and indigestible, which explains why they are 'boiled' *below* boiling point, and why the best scrambled eggs are made over low heat. Most other kinds of food wouldn't cook at all at such a low temperature. It's not surprising then that such lightly cooked food is good for invalids, tiny children or old people.

■ Eggs are most easily digested when the white is just set, and the yolk still liquid.

■ 'Eggy' cutlery, plates and dishes are washed clean more easily if first soaked in cold water: this releases the egg protein, whereas hot water glues it on.

■ *Refrigerated eggs* are tricky to cook with because they crack easily when boiled – the colder the air inside is, the more it expands – or curdle easily when added to creamed fat and sugar. It's better to keep most of them in the larder – and a few in the kitchen at room temperature, if you know you're going to be making a creamed cake or pudding.

■ If you aren't yet convinced that you will cook better with new-laid than with age-less eggs – supposing you *could* get new-laid – here are some more advantages:

1 They have more flavour, passing this on to any dish made with them.
2 The yolk is more golden, so gives things made with them a better colour.
3 They make bigger and better omelettes, lighter and bigger cakes, more and better meringues.

Separating To separate an egg, see page 80.

Egg whites If eggs are fresh when one buys them, whites will keep well in a covered container in the refrigerator for some time – you can even add to them day by day within reason. This is because they are virtually fatless – unlike the yolk – and contain 87 per cent water. You can also freeze them, of course. Should you lose count of how many eggs you have put in a container, here are two ways of calculating:

1 Weigh them: the white of an average-

sized egg weighs approximately 1¼oz/
35g. (The make-up of an egg is roughly
one-eighth shell, five-eighths white, one-
quarter yolk.)

2 Pour them very slowly into another
container, counting each as it drops in:
their viscous consistency keeps them more
or less separate.

■ Egg whites kept at room temperature
for about an hour will whisk to a greater
volume than when chilled. (To take the
chill off them quickly, put in a china pudding basin and stand that in a bowl of
hottish water for a short time.)

■ Egg whites can be used up in various
ways besides meringues and meringue
toppings:

1 Meringues cuites, macaroons, coconut
pyramids, royal icing, crème au beurre à la
meringue, fritters, or to make mashed
potatoes lighter, whipped cream go
further (page 302) or a fool lighter.

2 To glaze sweet pastry – but they give
no colour.

3 To bind a mixture – but they give
neither flavour nor colour.

4 In certain liquidized drinks, e.g. lemon
foam.

Egg yolks If eggs are fresh when you buy
them, yolks will keep easily two or three
days in the refrigerator. Either pop an odd
one into an egg cup, lightly cover it with
water and then with foil, or mix the yolk
with one teaspoon water and cover closely
with foil, to exclude air.

■ However you use up an egg yolk, it is
always nutritious, and you never need
wonder what to do with them. Here are
some suggestions:

1 Make a custard – baked, boiled or
caramel. Whichever it is, it will be
creamier, richer and better than when
made with whole egg.

2 Use to glaze pastry, rolls or scones,
etc., see page 66.

3 Use for egg and breadcrumb coating –
much better than whole egg.

4 Bind a mixture, like fish cakes or meat-
balls.

5 Use as a liaison, to make soups and
sauces thicker, richer and more creamy.

6 Make mayonnaise or hollandaise
sauce, etc.

7 Enrich creamed potatoes or shortcrust
pastry. Make French flan pastry.

8 Add an extra yolk to a ground rice or
semolina pudding.

9 Make French toast, see page 345.

10 Make chocolate truffles.

■ Egg yolks are much less likely to cause
curdling than the whites. This is the main
reason why only yolks are used as a liaison
in soups and sauces.

■ If you want egg yolk to form an emulsion with fat, as for mayonnaise, either
liquidize it or beat it very hard with a
whisk, to break it down to a condition
when it will readily absorb the fat. It will
take a minute or two by hand, or about 30
seconds in a liquidizer. The yolk will turn
pale yellow.

Egg shells Are used in consommé and
cleared jellies, because the impurities
cling to them when the whites are whisked, heated and begin to coagulate.

■ Half an egg shell makes a much more
efficient scoop than any utensil if you let a
spot of yolk escape into the white when
separating an egg.

Deep freezing Eggs are one of the few
things which don't deep-freeze successfully. This is because the contents expand
like any other liquid, when frozen, and the
shells crack. Worse still, eggs don't
recover their natural state when thawed.

■ Two or three eggs mixed together – with
a big pinch of salt to prevent coagulation –
and stored in a covered container, are
more successful, but even they have limited
use. One can't use them for anything
which calls for whisked or beaten egg.

Goose and duck eggs These have a denser
white and a stronger flavour than a hen's
egg, so they don't whisk well – either
whole, or just the whites – so aren't suitable for things like a mousse, soufflé, true
sponge or meringues. On the other hand,
the richness of the yolk (which is more oily

than a hen's) makes them excellent for custards, pastry, butter creams, breadcrumb coatings and glazing.

■ If you know what these birds have been fed on and that the eggs are absolutely fresh, there's little danger of salmonella poisoning, otherwise, be careful. In any case it pays to cook them well, e.g. hardboiled rather than soft-boiled and in cakes which require long cooking.
■ An average-sized goose egg is about three times the weight of an average-sized hen's (2oz/50g) and a duck egg about 1½ times the weight. A recipe calling for 3 medium-sized hen eggs might therefore be made (if a duck or goose egg is suitable) with 2 duck or 1 goose egg.

BOILED EGGS

Aren't so ready to crack if you prick them at the blunt end to let the expanded air escape, see *egg pricker*, page 25.

■ Eggs are 'boiled' – a misnomer – in *simmering* water over low heat, to prevent the white becoming tough and indigestible, as it does when an egg is boiled fast or for too long. By adding salt to the water, you ensure that any escaping white coagulates, though you also make the eggs boil faster, not slower, as many people seem to think (see page 118).
■ If you crack the shell at the pointed end after an egg is boiled, this helps to halt further cooking if anyone is late for breakfast.
■ Use a frying basket when boiling several eggs if without a special holder, to lower into and take them out of the water all at the same time. Give them an extra minute or so, too, because they'll cool down the water if in a small pan.
■ It evidently isn't dangerous, according to the British Egg Information Service, to use the boiled water for something else. If the shell's dirty, however, then things are of course different, so it may be this rather than anything else which has given rise to the opinion many people hold that such water is harmful. Apart from campers and others like them, anxious not to waste *any*

really hot water, I can't see why anybody would want to. Used to make tea for instance, the water would be completely flat after such long boiling, so that 'cuppa' would be horrid.

EGGS EN COCOTTE

Simply eggs in ramekins. To make a quick light meal, it's more economical and usually quicker to cook them in ¾in/2cm *simmering* water in a frying pan than in the oven:

■ Melt a good knob of butter in the ramekins, in the hot water, before sliding an egg into each. If you put another knob of butter on *top* of each as well, this helps to keep the yolk moist, and avoids that hard skin forming.
■ 3–5 minutes is all they'll need to set the white without hardening the yolk, but the pan needs to be covered, to trap the heat.
■ Ring the changes by putting something tasty into the melted butter before popping the egg into each ramekin: finely chopped fresh herbs, cooked chopped mushrooms, asparagus or shellfish, etc.

CODDLED EGGS

Look after themselves while you dress, or set the breakfast table.

■ They're just like boiled eggs except that you *cover* the pan, set it aside from the heat – to a warm place if possible – and forget about it for the next 7 or 8 minutes.
■ If you use an *egg coddler* (page 25), the water has to be hot enough to penetrate the coddler, so they're usually simmered for about 7 minutes rather than set aside from the heat – but instructions usually come with the coddler.

EASTER EGGS

Are unique when dyed in the brown outer skins of onions, with a few coffee grounds, and a flower head or two as well, to vary the colours.

■ Prick each egg at blunt end, and wrap it

– with coffee and flower – in the onion skins, inside a small square of white cloth. Parcel each up in a piece of newspaper, tie with thread and simmer them in a covered pan for 20 minutes (25 if doing several eggs) to dye well. Unwrap them when cooked, put straight into cold water and, to make them look nice, rub shiny with salad oil when cold. The colours can be so beautiful that it's worth overlooking the faint taste of onion and the rather tough egg! What matter if you never eat them, they're so ornamental – and just right for an Easter picnic.

FRIED EGG

Will stay compact if you slide it off a saucer into a tilted pan, because the fat – if as hot as it ought to be – will set the white immediately. Use enough fat to baste the egg, so that it cooks top and bottom simultaneously. Fry an egg on one or both sides, as you like.

■ If you fry an egg in butter – if you never have, you've missed something – it shouldn't be quite as hot as lard, bacon dripping or oil, because butter burns at a lower temperature.

Eggs fried in deep fat Are used mainly for an entrée, and should be almost egg-shaped if perfectly done. If anxious about doing them, use soft hard-boiled eggs instead, see *oeufs mollets*, page 147.

■ Deep fried eggs can be dangerous to cook – and *will* be if they're old and watery – because the hot fat may splutter and bubble over, just as if one had poured water into it, not an egg.

■ The eggs *must* be very fresh, the yolk standing high on the jellied white (see illustration, page 142), so it's safest to examine each on a saucer first. Fry just one at a time.

■ The egg will be oval, as it should be, if you slide it off the saucer, held close to the fat, into a whirlpool made by stirring the fat fast but carefully with a tablespoon. Keep it whirling until the white completely envelopes the yolk – in a matter of seconds. The heat is so intense that each egg takes only about a minute.

HARD-BOILED EGGS

These are only easy if you know the idiosyncracies of an egg:

1 Prick them at the blunt end, like boiled eggs, to prevent the shell cracking. To hard-boil already cracked eggs, wrap each (closely, to prevent bubbles forming between shell and wrapping) in a good-sized piece of Cling-film, tie with thread and cook eggs in a covered pan allowing 2 minutes extra.

2 Put into boiling water, so that the yolk will set instantly in the *middle* of the white. If brought to the boil in cold or warm water, the yolk is gradually drawn to the side by the heat. A lop-sided yolk of course spoils Scotch, stuffed, or any sliced egg.

3 'Boil' the eggs for 10 minutes in simmering water, because they become tough and rubbery if boiled fast, or for too long.

4 Put the eggs straight into cold water when boiled. This halts cooking at once, makes them easy to shell, and should prevent that unpleasant black rim forming round the yolk. (The rim is due to a chemical change of the sulphur in the egg white and the iron in the yolk, but can also be caused by over-cooking, or by the egg being stale.) See also *nest-fresh eggs*, page 143.

5 Hard-boiled eggs are almost impossible to shell hot. If you want to *serve* them hot, the shells will come off more easily if you pop the boiled eggs into cold water for a few minutes first – you can always heat the eggs again by putting them into a basin of hot water for one minute.

6 To shell an egg easily, give it a sharp knock, and then roll it gently between the palms of your hands, to crack and help the shell to come off in large pieces.

7 Put shelled eggs straight into a basin of cold water, to keep them moist, if preparing them in advance of a meal.

■ A vegetable mill chops several eggs in a trice.
■ Sieved hard-boiled yolk makes a lovely garnish for a savoury dish, but it dries and discolours quickly.

OEUFS MOLLETS

These eggs – one can't really translate the name – can easily end up in the dog's dish, unless you know how to cope with painfully hot, squashy boiled eggs that need shelling.

■ Used particularly for egg entrées and as a substitute for deep fried or poached eggs, they are a cross between a soft and a hard-boiled egg – the whites set and the yolks still just runny. It's important to try and choose eggs all of similar size, and put them all into the water at the same moment, because small eggs need exactly 5 minutes, medium 5½ and large 6.

■ Instead of trying to shell them while agonizingly hot, pop them straight into a basin of cold water for a few minutes to set the white, and to make shelling possible. If you then tap them carefully all round with the back of a teaspoon or the blade of a large knife, the shell will come away more easily.

■ Put them straight into a basin of warm water if for a hot dish, or into cold if for a cold dish. This prevents the whites becoming tough, through being exposed to the air. If necessary, for a particular hot dish, put them into a bowl of *hot* water for one minute, when all of them are shelled.

■ If fragments of shell persistently cling to the white, it's usually quicker to wash off the bits than to pick them off.

POACHED EGGS

Are tricky, and difficult to cook successfully unless the eggs are very fresh, with the yolk standing high on the thick jellied white (see illustration, page 142). Older or badly stored eggs are watery, and a watery white simply disintegrates when poached, drifting about in the water in uncontrollable wisps – unless you have a poaching ring to make things easier (see page 25).

■ Eggs aren't poached in a poaching pan, despite its misleading name – poaching is done in, not over water – and the easier, if less professional, way to do them is in a deep frying pan, or a sauté pan.

■ To cook them perfectly, the shivering (barely simmering) water should be deep enough to cover the eggs completely. If the water is too hot, the eggs will cook too fast and will be tough. If too cool, the white may not set. They need about 4 minutes over low heat to set the white lightly.

■ If you slide the egg very gently into the water, off a saucer held close to it, you can easily direct it into the poaching ring; or can control it at once with a wooden spoon, if loose in the water. Simply spoon the water gently over the yolk, until it sets, a few seconds later.

■ With a large frying pan, you can cook 3 or 4 eggs at the same time, but you may need to raise the heat slightly, to keep the water at shivering temperature.

■ It's easy to lift the cooked eggs out of the water in a draining spoon.

■ You can if you like poach your break-fast eggs the day before: put them straight into a basin of cold water to halt the cooking, and all that needs to be done in the morning is put them into a basin of very hot water for one minute. (If an egg is perfectly poached in the first place, it will still be almost perfect the next day – as long as it's left in the water.)

■ Older eggs will sometimes poach better if first boiled for 20 seconds. This usually makes the whites just firm enough to cling to the yolk.

SCRAMBLED EGGS

Just don't have the same flavour made with margarine instead of butter. A creamy texture is their other important characteristic, so to make them creamier still, use a dessertspoon of cream instead of milk per egg – or stir in a spoonful of cream or nut of butter at the last minute.

■ Scrambled eggs are best if cooked over very low heat, and stirred frequently, or better still constantly, if you can spare the time. If you cook them too fast, or over-heat the eggs by leaving unstirred in the hot pan bottom, you'll end up with a leathery mass, not a soft creamy mixture which will almost pour out of the pan. Avoid overcooking too, because even while taking a plate out of the oven, they'll continue to cook in the hot pan.

■ Pep them up, by adding at the very last moment chopped chives, garlic powder, finely sliced chopped green peppers, or chopped anchovy fillets, etc., and serve in bouchées, hollowed-out vegetables, or croustades, as a change from the time-worn hot-buttered toast. (One famous chef serves them with stewed rhubarb!)

OMELETTE, FRENCH

One of the most nourishing meals to put on the table within minutes of starting and no problem to make well, if one knows the ropes. Serve the moment it's cooked, because it can become sad and leathery if kept hot. You'll enjoy it all the more for a light lunch if you serve some crisp rolls or crusty French bread and a dressed salad with it.

■ If not an omelette expert, you'll probably find it's easier to make two small omelettes using 2 or 3 eggs each, than one 4 or 6 egg omelette, for two people. Small ones are often the lightest and best anyway.

Pans To start with, one needs the right-sized pan, because the eggs shouldn't be more than about ¼in/6mm deep, otherwise they won't cook fast enough – they shouldn't be too shallow either. These are about the pan sizes required:

Bottom diameter	No. of eggs
7in/18cm	2–3 large
8in/20cm	4 large
9in/23cm	6 large
10–11in/25–8cm	8 large

■ One should avoid washing an omelette pan – unless of course it's nonstick – because the eggs will stick more easily, especially if it gets rusty. Just clean it round with soft paper, or, if stuck with a little egg, heat a sprinkling of salt in it

before rubbing it out with the paper. See also *pans, omelette*, page 36.

■ Lots of people have their own way of making omelettes but these are the basic guidelines.

Ingredients Should be ready before starting to cook, because it's a one-minute operation when you do so.
Butter is best, giving an omelette its characteristic flavour, and preventing the eggs from sticking to the pan. Oil and margarine lack flavour, and margarine burns at high temperatures – unless clarified – *and* may make the eggs stick to the pan.
The eggs will make a better omelette if new-laid and large. Just mix them lightly together with a fork, because they shouldn't be frothy.
Water – one dessertspoon per egg – helps to make a light omelette. Milk on the other hand makes it heavy.
Seasoning is essential: plenty of it, to bring out the flavours.
Flavourings like finely grated cheese, chopped fresh herbs and finely sliced spring onions are simply mixed in with the raw eggs.
Filling, if any, mustn't be watery, and should be in small proportion to the eggs. Simple fillings, such as chopped mushrooms or tomato flesh, can be just lightly cooked in butter.

Method From the time you mix the eggs until the omelette is on the plate, you only need one utensil – a fork. One can't easily give an omelette its characteristic formation with anything else.

■ The butter has to be very hot – likewise the heat under the pan. The right moment to add the eggs is when the butter's foam has almost subsided, and when the butter is on the point of colouring – but just before it does so.

■ Use the *side* of the fork, drawing it along the bottom of the pan, to draw the eggs from the sides to the centre, where they set, while liquid egg fills the gaps round the sides again. This is the movement which gives an omelette its almost veined appearance.

■ An omelette should be moist, so it is better to take it off the heat before the top is quite set. When folded, the under-cooked part will be surrounded by the part which was on the hot pan bottom, which will quickly set it.

Folding an omelette Shake the pan so that about one-third of the omelette overhangs the edge opposite the handle. If in any other position, it's very difficult to turn out a perfectly-shaped omelette.

■ Put the filling, if any, into this hollow, fold the overhanging piece back over it, and then envelop the filling with the remaining omelette in the pan.

■ An omelette is traditionally kidney-shaped, taking this shape from the curves of the pan, in which it is now lying.

■ To turn an omelette out without doing contortions, put the pan down and change your grip, your thumb up the front of the handle, see illustration.

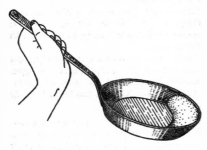

Omelette variations Vary omelettes however you like. They're delicious filled even with such unlikely companions as fried onions and garlic croûtons (fried separately in butter). You can serve omelettes *au gratin*, topped with whipped cream and a sprinkling of Parmesan cheese before grilling, or you can fill and coat them with a sauce, like omelette à la florentine.

OMELETTE, SPANISH

Is really made with finely sliced onion and chopped potatoes, which are fried in olive oil and generously flavoured with garlic. In practice, people often make it with other cooked vegetables in place of the potatoes, it being a quick and tasty way of using up leftovers. It's a more solid affair than a French omelette and is served flat, cut into wedges, like a cake. (I'm afraid I like to fry the onion in butter, but that's not then a true Spanish omelette!)

PIPÉRADE

This Basque speciality is neither quite French nor quite Spanish; neither quite an omelette nor quite scrambled eggs. It's a good recipe if you'd like it.

■ The quantities given serve 2 generously: in 2 tablespoons olive oil sauté for a few minutes 1 small, green de-seeded pepper and 1 small onion (both thinly sliced), 1 clove crushed garlic and 1 large tomato, previously skinned, seeded and chopped. Add 2 tablespoons chopped ham, then simmer over lowest possible heat about 15–20 minutes until vegetables are tender. Stir in ½–1oz/15–25g butter, and when melted make very hot over increased heat. Pour in 4 lightly beaten seasoned eggs. Stir just two or three times, let the eggs set and serve very hot direct from the pan.

SCOTCH EGGS

Excellent with a salad for a picnic, or one can serve them hot or cold for a buffet lunch, or for a light lunch or supper. Be sure to put the eggs into boiling water, to have the yolks in the middle of the whites (see page 146).

■ The sausage will crack if you flour the eggs too heavily – better just to dust them lightly.
■ Coat the eggs twice in egg and bread-crumbs for a perfect result. It's best to use dried breadcrumbs, not golden, because the latter would burn by the time the sausage is cooked.
■ The halved eggs won't stand up when

served unless you flatten both ends of each egg after breadcrumbing.

■ The eggs will be firmer – and will fry better as a result – if refrigerated for fifteen minutes after coating.

■ The fat *must* be deep enough to cover the eggs completely, otherwise they'll burst. The temperature should be about 340°F/170°C. If too cool, the sausage will burst and absorb the fat, or if too hot the crumbs will brown and burn before the sausage is cooked. Fry without the basket: the eggs will stick to it, and the wire may break the egg and breadcrumb seal.

■ If serving Scotch eggs on croûtes of fried bread, it's quickest to fry these in the deep fat too.

■ A fine stainless steel saw-knife makes it easy to cut Scotch eggs in half.

SOUFFLÉS, SAVOURY

Are either baked or steamed. Serve individual ones, if you possibly can, for an *hors d'oeuvre* or savoury, using a large dish if the soufflé is for lunch or for a supper.

■ Soufflés aren't really the feat which some fear and others think they are – they're reasonably easy in fact. It may simplify things if you know there are two main parts:

1 *The base* is a thick sauce called the *panada* (page 76). This carries the flavour, which may be something like finely grated cheese, vegetable purée, cooked mashed fish (not a watery tinned fish), minced or finely diced cooked chicken, or sweetbreads.

2 *The egg whites*, holding the air which blows up the mixture and gives a soufflé its name. Large fresh eggs and skilful whisking to the correct stiffness, needless to say, play a big part in the 'blowing'. If over-whisked, the whites are difficult to incorporate. (You can prepare a soufflé mixture in advance – up to the point where the egg whites have to be whisked.)

Baked soufflés The oven must be preheated, because nothing much will happen to your soufflé if it isn't! Give it the oven to itself if you can, and be sure the temperature is right, ideally gas 5, 375°F/190°C. If too hot, a top crust will form, which will stop the soufflé rising and prevent the inside cooking. If too cold, it won't rise properly either.

■ To rise perfectly, a soufflé should have heat simultaneously from top and bottom. If put in the middle of the oven, this avoids too much heat being concentrated on the top of the soufflé, and if you stand the dish on a hot baking sheet – pop one into the oven when you turn it on – this gives the instant bottom heat needed.

■ Don't be surprised to find your perfect soufflé has grown through the oven shelf above it – it will, if you don't raise or remove that shelf when turning on the oven.

■ If you forget to preheat the oven, or if the telephone rings just at the wrong moment, cover the soufflé closely with an upturned mixing bowl. The mixture will hold surprisingly well for 20 minutes or more, providing the whites were properly whisked.

■ The dish is important, see *soufflé dishes*, page 24. The size needed depends on the freshness of the eggs, and how well one whisks the whites, as well as on the quantities used. For a well risen soufflé, the uncooked mixture should come to within about ½in/1–2cm of the top. It is better not to grease a soufflé dish: the mixture clings better and rises higher. The sizes of dish given below are just a guide because, as I've said, so much depends on the eggs and their whisking:

No. of eggs	Size of dish
2 large new-laid	1pt/500ml
3 large new-laid	1½pt/750ml
4 large new-laid	2pt/1 litre dish

■ The mixture needs lots of seasoning, to avoid the soufflé being tasteless. The whisked whites need flavouring just as much as the *panada*, so allow for them as well. (Incidentally, a little shallot or garlic give extra flavour to a vegetable soufflé: sauté very finely sliced shallot or a halved clove of garlic in the butter over low heat for 2 or 3 minutes before making the roux. If garlic, now remove it.)

■ Whisked egg whites can only raise a *light* mixture, so it's important to drain a vegetable purée well, before you add it. Soggy purée makes a soggy soufflé.

■ The *panada* to which the egg yolks have been added, should be just tepid when you fold in the whisked whites. If it's too hot, they'll start to cook before you can get the soufflé into the oven.

■ Some people like a soufflé to be firm throughout, others prefer it to be slightly soft in the centre. A slightly undercooked soufflé flops faster than ever once taken out of the oven, but an overcooked one is hardly worth eating because, more than likely, it will be dry, tasteless and shrunken.

Steamed soufflés Although basically the same as baked, there are some important differences:

1 An oval or round (charlotte) tin mould is preferable to a cake tin because it has a wider top than base. When inverted, the wide part will become the bottom, so the soufflé is less likely to collapse. To three-quarters fill it, you'll need about a 1½pt/750ml tin for a 3-egg soufflé.

A band of doubled foil, or three-fold band of greaseproof paper to stand about 3in/7½cm above top of tin is needed to support a steamed mixture when it rises: tie it on tightly, otherwise the mixture will run down the sides when it rises.

As a steamed soufflé is turned out, it's wiser to line the bottom of the tin, and essential to brush with oil or melted lard (or saltless butter) all inside surfaces, band included.

2 A steamed soufflé is covered with greased greaseproof paper to protect it from condensed steam during cooking.

3 The base is usually uncooked; fish, liver, chicken or veal. Fish should be finely shredded, the others finely minced.

4 The pan must be full of steam (just as an oven must be preheated) before the soufflé is put in, then the most gentle steaming is essential: if the heat is too high, the soufflé will rise very rapidly like a blown-up balloon, then will collapse when that air is expelled. For good measure (or should I say bad measure?) a 'burst' soufflé is tough and close in texture.

Should you move the soufflé, or lift off the steamer lid before the mixture has set, or should you overcook it, these are more causes for collapse. Reckon on about 40 minutes to 1 hour to cook, when it should be firm to the touch in the centre. (When pierced with a skewer, the skewer should come out quite clean.)

5 If you remove the band and wait half a minute after taking the soufflé out of the steamer, it will have time to shrink, so making it easier to unmould. To unmould, allow the weight of the soufflé to pull it away from the sides of the mould, by moving it round very gently while slightly tilting it.

6 It's best to hold an inverted dish over the top of a soufflé without actually touching it. Then carefully turn dish and soufflé over, allowing soufflé to slide out gently, holding the mould so that its weight doesn't press on the soufflé.

7 A steamed soufflé must have a tasty sauce, otherwise it is both dry and uninteresting.

6

Hors d'oeuvres

GENERAL INFORMATION

Hors d'oeuvre, translated, means 'outside the main work'; in this case before it. It should enliven one's appetite, never spoil it, so do be sure your hors d'oeuvre *is* appetizing – fresh, light and attractive – and a carefully thought-out forerunner to the main course: try to choose something different in flavour, colour, richness and texture.

■ Hors d'oeuvres fall into three groups, *plain, dressed* and *mixed*. Although this chapter consists mainly of old favourites because these will give you the basics, you can be much more adventurous yourself, especially if prepared to explore the possibilities with fruits, salads and vegetables. Here are some examples of each group.

Plain: asparagus, globe artichoke, melon, smoked salmon, whitebait.

Dressed: egg mayonnaise, prawn cocktail, ratatouille, tomatoes in aspic.

Mixed (hors d'oeuvres variés): a selection of at least six, preferably eight different dishes (see page 156).

■ Ideally make and serve something like cheese soufflé or prawns in aspic in individual dishes rather than in a large one, so that everybody has a perfect and complete portion of their own, rather than an untidy helping. An attractively arranged individual hors d'oeuvre, served directly on the plates, can work wonders as table decoration.

■ You can *prepare* everything in advance for an hors d'oeuvre, but it's best to assemble a dish at the last minute, especially if serving it chilled.

■ Serve thinly sliced and generously buttered fresh brown bread with those hors d'oeuvres which need it. It's best crustless, cut into triangles or fingers; or you can roll up each slice like a baby Swiss roll. If you have one, use an electric saw-knife because rolls will crack unless the bread is very finely sliced.

ARTICHOKE, GLOBE

Is a variety of thistle, cultivated for centuries in various parts of the world. Not many people seem to grow them in Britain, probably because they don't compare in flavour with those grown in sunny climates; but they are decorative enough to grow in the flower rather than the kitchen garden, even if you never eat them! The hairy 'choke', or inedible part in the middle of the artichoke, develops into a flower if allowed to grow.

■ Washed well under the cold tap to flush out any grit, an artichoke must be so prepared that it is perfect to eat and will stand upright when served. To do this, lay it at the edge of the table, stalk overhanging, and bend the stalk first one way and then the other, until it breaks off – bringing with it the coarse fibres from the base. (If you cut off the stalk, which is much easier, these fibres are left in.)

Some other tips:

1 To prevent discoloration, rub the cut stalk with lemon juice.

2 It is easier to eat if you cut the tips off the inner circle of leaves (when preparing).

3 An artichoke is better soaked for 1–2 hours in cold water to soften it before cooking, and a lump of sugar in the cook-

ing water improves the flavour.

4 Boil for 20–45 minutes according to variety, size, recipe and taste – in water deep enough to cover.

5 A draining spoon makes it easy to lift them out of the pan without damage. Turn upside-down to drain.

■ In case you're not sure how to eat them, the edible parts are the *fond* (bottom) and the fleshy base of each leaf; detach each leaf separately by hand, dip its fleshy base in a butter sauce and draw off the pulp between your teeth.

ASPARAGUS

If prepared and cooked properly, asparagus is one of the most heavenly of all vegetables, especially when eaten within an hour of picking.

■ There's a tender moist green stem inside a spear of asparagus, which many people never find. One can eat the whole spear if, when preparing, you cut off all the lower, outer, hard skin; holding it as if sharpening a pencil, and cutting deep enough to bare that stem.

■ If you tie the spears in bundles near each end, either with cotton tape or string, this protects the tips during cooking, and also makes it easier to lift the bundles out of the boiling water without breaking the tips, with a fork slipped under each tape.

■ If you have to prepare asparagus in advance, either refrigerate the bundles, standing them in a jug of shallow cold water, covered with a polythene bag, or wrap in foil, to exclude light and air. Allow about 8–10 stems per person, according to size.

■ Be sure not to boil asparagus too fast – the tips tend to break off.

■ I think it's difficult to improve on melted butter with asparagus, but ring the changes if you like with beurre noisette, hollandaise, maltaise or mousseline sauce (see *sauces*, page 171).

■ *Cold asparagus* can be a disappointment if boiled and then allowed to go cold, instead of being *made* to go cold:

refresh it for a minute, to halt cooking, and to preserve its glorious colour and flavour (see page 77).

■ Tinned asparagus spears are tasty for a buffet meal, each one rolled in very thinly sliced new brown bread, spread generously with butter and home-made mayonnaise.

ASPIC

The name of the pale-coloured savoury jelly in which fish, meat, poultry and vegetables are often served. It is a classic garnish, used for some of the most sophisticated dishes because of its flavour, transparency, and ability to keep foods moist. In addition it makes a delicious savoury mould, or can be mixed with certain sauces to coat a huge variety of cooked foods served cold. If one just wants a very small quantity as a glaze, or if its flavour will be masked by other stronger ones, one can easily get away with bought (to which you can add a little sherry to taste), otherwise it's much better to make your own. It is troublesome though, because unless you're careful, it won't be crystal clear. Here, I'm afraid, are a lot of dos and don'ts:

1 Have the pan, bowl and jelly bag scrupulously clean, never washing the bag in soapy water.

2 Use absolutely fat-free stock (see *degrease*, page 59).

3 Cut the carrot and onion into largish pieces, then they won't break up.

4 Peel the washed lemon very finely with a potato peeler, so avoiding the bitter pith one gets with grated rind.

5 Wipe the eggs before separating them and crushing the shells. All the impurities in the liquor will cling to the shells like metal to a magnet when the mixture you're whisking becomes hot enough for the egg whites to coagulate. There's a snag though, if you don't stop whisking just before it reaches boiling point, the impurities will be released back into the liquid.

6 Let the liquid go through the jelly bag

without helping it, however tempted you are to press or squeeze, otherwise the jelly will be cloudy. Providing it is hot, it will go through, so *keep* it hot by standing an ovenware glass of very hot water in the middle of all the contents.

■ Here are a few more hints:

1 An electric hand-mixer saves effort.

2 If you boil the jelly bag just before using it, and also rinse the bowl out with hot water, they won't cool the liquid so fast – important if it has to go through the bag a second time.

3 One can make a Heath Robinson contraption with a calico jelly bag and a large liquidizer jar: stand the jar (no other part of the liquidizer) in the clean hot mixing bowl, fitting the jelly bag into the jar.

4 If you're surprised by the amount of gelatine in aspic, it's not a mistake. There must be extra, to allow for it losing strength when almost boiled. Besides, aspic is used slightly stiffer than a sweet jelly.

5 Don't skip the soaking time (about 10 minutes) before pouring everything through the jelly bag: just as tea infuses in a teapot, so extra flavour is drawn out of these ingredients into the liquid.

6 When using aspic as a glaze, it should be cold but just runny. Should it show signs of setting before you want it to, stand its basin in a pan of warm water.

7 Use twice as much mayonnaise to aspic for *aspic mayonnaise*.

8 Use twice as much sauce to aspic for *chaud-froid sauce* (see page 170).

9 To chop aspic jelly, see page 67.

AVOCADO PEAR

As abundant in countries where they grow as are apples in Britain, the avocado is one of the most nourishing of all fruits: a nearly all-in-one food for vegetarians! They contain more protein than any other fruit, up to 25% oil, various minerals and vitamins A, B, C, D and E.

Choosing, storing and preparing

1 The best are shiny and weigh between ½–1lb/225–500g.

2 Cradled in the palm of your hand, they should 'give' everywhere to gentle pressure, with an extra softness around the stalk: soft, but without being mushy, and easy to cut, peel or slice.

3 If buying in advance, choose firmer fruits. In a warm kitchen, they'll ripen in a few days and can then, if necessary, be kept for a few more in the salad box of a refrigerator or, on the floor of it, in a thick polythene bag.

4 To halve an avocado, use a stainless steel knife to cut down from the stalk, penetrating to and going round the stone. Now separate the halves by twisting them gently in opposite directions. Remove stone. (To save half until next day, leave the stone in it, wrap first in Cling-film and then in foil and refrigerate as above.)

5 To prevent discoloration, moisten the cut surfaces with a wedge of lemon, otherwise with another citrus fruit or with French dressing.

6 To serve most simply, pour a well seasoned, rather sharp French dressing (adding at the last a little finely chopped parsley and chives if you like them) into the cavities. Accompany with thinly sliced brown bread and butter, and with more dressing in a sauce-boat.

7 Serve chilled, for extra flavour.

■ Prawns (preferably cold-water, page 224) in a piquant cream dressing are a very tasty alternative.

■ *To skin an avocado* for, say, a cocktail or salad, put the halves cut-side down on a chopping board, score the skin down the centre with a sharp, pointed, stainless steel knife and carefully pull back the skin in sections. Dice, cut across – to make curved slices – or cut longways as required. See also *salads*, page 204.

■ *To freeze*, make into a purée, because unsuccessful whole: remove flesh from skin, as above, then mash to a pulp, adding 1 teaspoon of lemon juice per fruit and seasoning to taste.

BOUCHÉES

If true to their name, *bouchées* are only a mouthful, the word coming from the French word *bouche*, mouth.

BROCCOLI, PURPLE SPROUTING

This and some varieties of calabrese are almost as good as, and surprisingly like, asparagus if you cook, serve and eat it with your fingers in the same way, with melted butter or one of the sauces given with asparagus.

■ Allow about 6–8 oz/150–200g per person, tie the sprigs together in bundles (the head, a finger's length of stalk and the smallest leaves), boil about 8–10 minutes, drain well and serve piping hot. (Cut or slit thick stalks as slender as the small tender ones.)
■ Homegrown, this must be one of the most delicious of all winter vegetables.

EGG MAYONNAISE

A quick and good prelude to various main dishes – it doesn't have to be dull. One can introduce variety by adding green herbs to the mayonnaise, by garnishing the coated eggs with capers and strips of drained anchovy fillets, or with shrimps or prawns, etc. Alternatively, one can liquidize or finely chop asparagus spears or lobster before adding to the mayonnaise, while garnishes such as cayenne pepper, chopped chives, watercress, tomato quarters, or finely sliced cucumber or radishes will make a lovely colourful dish.

■ The eggs won't be tough if slightly undercooked: boil only 9 minutes to make the white firm, but to leave the yolk still just moist (see page 145).
■ Served cut in half lengthwise and arranged round-side up, they are easier to coat perfectly, look more professional when finished and take less mayonnaise.

GRAPEFRUIT

Grapefruit should be juicy, fleshy and properly prepared – which calls for a grapefruit knife (page 31). If you like them nice and sweet, as I do, prepare several hours before serving, sprinkling with caster sugar to taste. If on the other hand their vitamin C is more important to you than their flavour, do them at the last: once cut, deterioration soon begins. Eating a grapefruit should be neither a bath nor a battle. Here is one way of making their eating as easy as melon balls – as it should be. If it sounds fiddling, you'll find that, with practice, it takes only about 2 minutes:

1 Using an up-and-down sawing movement, cut all round between the flesh and skin of each half, sides first and then the bottom, taking care not to puncture the skin at the bottom (otherwise the juice will escape), then lift the whole lot out bodily on to a plate.
2 Slip the knife point between the segments and the bitter white membranes, easing out each piece of flesh until only core and membranes remain. Squeeze these, to extract any juice.
3 Replace the segments in the halves just as they came out and garnish with a maraschino (*not* glacé, which is wrong both in flavour and texture) cherry.

■ You may like a spoonful of kirsch, grand marnier or even crème de menthe sprinkled over. See *macerating*, page 70. See also page 277, for general information.

MELON

Not many things look more tempting and decorative on a dinner table than sliced honeydew melon prepared quickly in the following way: cut the flesh from the skin, slice it in about finger-width pieces and arrange in zig-zag pattern, with a maraschino cherry and a crescent of orange on a cocktail stick to give a splash of colour.

■ Melon balls are another lovely way to serve melon, will cheer anyone up and aren't much bother to make because the flesh is so soft (see page 14). If sprinkled with caster sugar and soaked about half an hour in a little port (failing which, madeira, marsala, sherry or kirsch), one can serve them in glasses as a fruit cocktail or, if made from a tiny melon put them back in the skin. (If you haven't got a baller, cut the flesh into smallish even-sized dice.)

■ Do you like ground ginger with melon? It won't catch in your throat if you moisten it well in the melon juice before popping each piece into your mouth.

■ See also page 280.

MIXED HORS D'OEUVRE

A dish one seldom seems to meet in people's homes, though I never know quite why. It's expensive and can be time-consuming, but doesn't have to be complicated – just carefully chosen, fresh, well seasoned and nicely arranged. It's supposed to be an appetizer, not an appetite killer – with at least 6 dishes – so serve rich foods in moderation.

■ If there are 6 dishes, it is usual to have two meat (one can be egg), two fish, and two (or more) others which can be all vegetable if you like. Aim to serve something bland like rice salad or a salad of cooked vegetables; something raw like a salad of mushrooms, cucumber or tomatoes; and something salt like anchovy fillets or salt herring.

■ Piquancy is introduced with various kinds of dressings – mayonnaise, oil and vinegar, or cream dressing – while thinly sliced brown bread and butter rounds everything off.

NIÇOISE, SALADE

See *salads*, page 210.

PÂTÉ OR TERRINE

Nowadays both names apply to the same thing when it is cooked and served cold. Pâté en croûte is moulded in a pastry case and served hot or cold.

■ Fowl or game pâtés are usually made basically with pork, veal and the chosen game, the proportions of each depending on the richness or otherwise of the game. Hare for instance, which is dry, needs a higher proportion of fat pork than domestic duck, which is fatty.

■ *Pâté maison*, despite its name, isn't necessarily the speciality of a restaurant: you may find the same thing called *terrine de campagne*, *terrine du chef*, or simply pork and liver pâté. Whichever the name, it is usually made basically from pork belly, lean veal and pig's liver.

■ To make a successful pâté requires a certain amount of know-how, so here are some tips:

Ingredients Providing the flavours blend and the final texture of the pâté is right, you can vary the proportions of meat and seasonings according to your own taste. The correct proportion of *fat* meat is the important thing, because with too little, the pâté will be dry.

■ For pâté to have the right texture, mince the meats finely together, twice. Warned in advance, your regular butcher (even possibly a supermarket) will probably be willing to do it for you. If mincing the meats yourself, they are easier to do if not too soft and squashy: harden them slightly by putting in the freezer for about 40–60 minutes beforehand.

■ Marinating the meats in wine, spices and seasonings for 2–3 hours before cooking, makes the pâté more tasty because the flavours penetrate the meats better. Marinating (overnight) also tenderizes tough game.

■ The right kind of firm pork fat plays an important role, and comes from the belly or from the back of a fat pig (hog) next to the skin. When cut into dice, it is these squares of fat which are characteristic of a homemade pâté and, unlike fats from other parts of the animal, this particular fat doesn't distintegrate when cooked. In addition, it helps to keep the pâté moist and gives it a smooth light texture.

Again, ask your butcher in advance, otherwise he may not have any.

■ Brandy helps pâté to keep well, in addition to giving flavour.

■ Breadcrumbs, if used, are to give a firm texture.

■ If you use bacon rashers instead of thinly spread out pork fat to line the terrine, they should be very fatty and preferably not smoked, because the flavour is too strong.

Cooking Use a 2½pt/1.5 litre terrine (see page 44) for 2½lb/generous 1kg meat. Using two smaller terrines for that quantity instead of one large you'd need more fat or bacon rashers to line them because there's a bigger surface to cover.

■ Avoid over-cooking. Pâté is cooked when it begins to leave the sides of the dish, and when the surrounding juices are clear yellow, not pink. Cooking time is determined by the depth and shape of the terrine, not the surface area. A narrow rectangular shape for instance will cook faster than a round or oval shape.

Cooling When pâté is cooked, you'll save a mess if you stand the terrine on a large plate, to catch any overflow of fat and juices.

■ Compressing the pâté properly as it cools plays an important part in it acquiring the right texture. After removing lid, cover pâté with foil or greaseproof paper, then a close-fitting pan, pie-dish, casserole or plate. Into or on this put a 3–4lb/1.5–2kg weight. Allowed to cool completely in this way, preferably overnight, at room temperature, there'll be no air spaces in the meat, so the pâté will be easier to slice and serve as well as good to eat.

Serving Pâté is often served in its dish. If sliced in advance for a party, it *looks* untouched, but at the same time pieces can easily be lifted out. Otherwise unmould and serve it on a dish, or directly on to plates.

■ Do remember to serve something of contrasting crisp texture with pâté, like Melba toast (page 345), fresh crusty rolls or French bread.

Freezing or refrigerating? You can freeze pâté if you don't mind spoiling the texture slightly, but it's much better sealed and refrigerated. If you want to keep it more than a few days, unmould it when cold, wipe the meat jelly off the surfaces and it will keep well for some time: return it to the terrine, and seal it with barely melted pure lard. (If too hot, the lard may penetrate the pâté.) Alternatively, one can unmould the pâté, wrap it in greaseproof paper and seal completely in foil.

PRAWNS IN ASPIC

Look mouth-watering if you're willing to spend some time on them, and make individually in darioles. If not, the quickest way is three-quarters to fill a plain mould with liquid aspic (page 153), adding the prawns, seasonings and anything else as the jelly begins to set.

■ After garnishing darioles or a large mould (see page 67), be sure to allow each alternate layer of prawns and aspic to set before adding the next, otherwise the prawns will float, landing up on the bottom when unmoulded.

■ Everything will glisten if you set a film of aspic on the bottom of the serving dish and use any remaining aspic chopped, as a garnish. (See *jelly, to chop*, page 67, also *prawns*, page 224.)

PRAWN COCKTAIL

Really *must* be served chilled, in chilled glasses, to have tip-top flavour. This is definitely an hors d'oeuvre to be assembled at the last minute, otherwise the lettuce goes slimy and the whole thing looks unfresh. The mayonnaise-based sauce needs to be piquant and well seasoned. Numerous recipes contain curry powder and something like Worcestershire sauce, while others may be flavoured with things like soured cream, fresh cream, tomato purée, lemon juice, etc. Here's a quick and very tasty example, to serve 6, which you can prepare and chill at least two days ahead of time:

Mix together ¼pt/125ml each of mayonnaise and tinned tomato soup, ½ level teaspoon curry powder, 1 teaspoon Worcestershire sauce, 1 teaspoon lemon juice, salt and pepper. Pass them through a strainer to blend properly, pour into a jug, cover with foil and chill in refrigerator until required. Shred the lettuce finely (with a stainless steel knife) for prawn cocktail, otherwise it's difficult to eat with a teaspoon and in addition looks clumsy. Serve each in a wineglass on a small plate, preferably on a small plain doyley, to steady the glass, and put the teaspoon beside each, rather than on the dinner table.

■ See also *prawns*, page 224.

RATATOUILLE

A ragoût or stew of vegetables, ratatouille is one of the famous dishes of the Mediterranean, everything tasting of the sun.

■ Although there are various versions, they differ more in the quantity of the ingredient used than in their content – aubergines, sweet peppers, onions, tomatoes, courgettes and garlic being the principals.
■ Dégorgé the aubergines and courgettes to make them less watery and bitter. This concentrates their flavour too, and prevents the stew being watery. (See dégorger, page 59).
■ Use olive oil to cook it in the traditional way, but if you haven't got any, use another vegetable oil.
■ Be careful just to sweat the onions enough to soften them without browning, which spoils their colour, and changes the flavour of the dish.
■ Serve it hot or cold today, or tomorrow when the flavour is even better. Reheat slowly if serving hot.

SHRIMPS, POTTED

Are finest when made with the tiny brown shrimps – if you can buy, and have energy to peel them. No other local shellfish are said to match their flavour.

■ Warm the butter, shrimps, spices and a touch of lemon juice just enough for the shrimp flavour to permeate the butter, without at the same time allowing the butter to become hot enough to oil and separate.
■ Youngs Seafoods, famous for their potted shrimps, say the flavour of the shrimps and spices comes through best when one serves them slightly warmed; just until the butter melts enough to lose its hardened state. Arrange on lettuce leaves and serve at once, or if you have a fondue pan, warm them at table if you like.

SMOKED FISH

A wonderfully easy and delicious hors d'oeuvre, as long as it's fresh and moist. This means removing the skin of a fish like mackerel or eel at the last minute. Serve the fish – or half a fish if large – direct on the plate with some greenery for colour, and a wedge of lemon to counteract the richness as well as to give flavour. Don't forget the brown bread and butter, and the pepper mill.

■ Have you tried serving smoked mackerel or trout warm? Some people think this is the best way to eat them: simply wrap in foil and pop in a cool oven, gas 2, 300°F/150°C, for about 15 minutes. Horseradish sauce gives piquancy too.
■ See also page 227.

TOMATOES, STUFFED

Good either cooked or raw as an hors d'oeuvre. The latter are often spoilt by a stuffing becoming watery because the tomatoes themselves aren't prepared properly. This is the best way to draw all excess juices out of them:

1 Slice off a shallow lid at end opposite

to stalk, and with a teaspoon to help, gently squeeze out the seeds and juice without splitting at rim.

2 Cut out flesh and core, keeping flesh for stuffing.

3 Dégorgé: sprinkle salt inside and turn the tomatoes upside down in a colander or on absorbent kitchen paper, to drain. Leave 15–30 minutes before stuffing.

■ Here are a few ideas for stuffings, each to include any chopped tomato flesh removed from inside, seasoning and chopped herbs of your choice, especially basil:

mayonnaise and cold, cooked, re-freshed vegetables (see page 77);

mayonnaise and shrimps or prawns;

mayonnaise mixed with sardine, hard-boiled egg, a few chopped capers, chives and a squeeze of lemon juice;

curry mayonnaise (page 175), and cooked chicken;

scrambled egg and chopped anchovies;

taramasalata (smoked cod's roe, olive oil, lemon juice, chopped parsley, finely chopped shallot and seasoning).

WHITEBAIT

So called from their former use as bait, these are said by some authorities to be the 'fry' or young of the herring or sprat, while others equally categorically say this has never been proved. Whatever they are or were, they are an inexpensive luxury at their price. It's time they take, not money. Allow about 3oz/75g per person.

■ If not dried thoroughly, or if you try to toss too many at a time in the seasoned flour, the flour forms a paste and all stick together in a mass. The secret is to keep them separate.

■ Shake off any surplus flour before frying in hot deep fat, 380°F/190°C, for a few minutes until golden. For tip-top results, they need frying twice: reheat the fat and fry them another minute or two, to become crisp.

■ Garnish with fried or fresh parsley, and served well drained, piping hot and with a wedge of lemon to counteract their richness. Don't forget the brown bread and butter as well.

■ Speed things up if you like by thawing frozen whitebait in cold water. Bought frozen, they're good value.

7

Soups

GENERAL INFORMATION

Soup. What a warming welcoming start to a meal on a cold wintry day, or alternatively what a lovely cooling start it can be to dinner in summer time. Whether the homely 'filler-upper' for a light lunch, or the opening to a formal dinner, nearly everyone enjoys a good homemade soup. Imaginatively garnished and served with something crunchy like fried croûtons, crusty French bread, garlic bread, newly baked dinner rolls, or perhaps Melba toast, who *couldn't* feel cheered up?

■ When choosing a soup, there are other considerations besides the occasion, weather, cost and time you can spend on it. Your choice should also depend on the richness, flavour, colour, texture and bulkiness (or otherwise) of the following courses – because soup must harmonize with them all.

Ingredients A well flavoured soup starts with good ingredients.
The stock is the foundation of the whole thing: the more gelatinous it is from meat, bones, fish trimmings (for fish soup), or whatever it is made from, the better its flavour and the better the soup. It simply must be fat-free as well, because nobody wants soup floating with grease (page 122).
Vegetables, meat or fish should be very fresh and in correct proportion to the amount of stock used. Vegetables should be finely diced, shredded or cut into julienne strips, to ensure quick cooking, good flavour and easy eating. Finely sliced onions, shallots, leeks, etc. are usually sweated until soft without being

coloured, otherwise they may spoil the flavour and colour of a soup.
Butter or olive oil make twice as good a thickened soup as any other fat, so use one of these, not margarine. So little is needed that the difference, spread over 6–8 helpings, is enormous in flavour but marginal in cost.
Herbs and garlic should be used with subtlety. A bouquet garni, containing extra herbs for a particular soup – say basil for tomato, tarragon for chicken, or dill for fish – can make all the difference to a soup's final flavour.
Salt, plenty of it, is a must, and so usually is pepper – or peppercorns, if ground pepper is likely to spoil a soup's colour. Without enough salt to draw out the flavours, the most expensive soup is hardly worth eating.
Cream and egg yolks make the simplest soups luxurious. There's nothing to beat this liaison for a smooth, rich, creamy, bursting-with-flavour soup. Use about 3 yolks and ¼pt/125ml single cream to each 2pt/1 litre of soup. Be sure to add a little of the hot soup to the mixed yolks and cream before adding them to the soup. This way, the egg is gradually warmed, instead of suddenly scalded, and it can then bind and make the soup creamy and delicious. If by mistake you now boil the soup, instead of just reheating it, the liaison will curdle unless the soup contains a starch thickener like potato flour or arrowroot. (You may be able to correct a curdled mixture by liquidizing it in small amounts.)
Cream by itself, stirred in at the last minute, gives soups a glorious flavour besides making them rich and smooth. It

doesn't take much to tranform a soup. Have you ever experimented with single cream to invent your own versions of chilled vegetable purée soups, like vichyssoise? You may be amazed at your success. Simply stir about ¼–½pt/125–250ml cream into 2pt/1 litre soup, chill it until the last minute, and sprinkle in finely chopped fresh herbs just before serving. Cucumber, pea, celery, tomato, etc. are all lovely.

Soured cream or yoghurt stirred into a vegetable soup at the last minute makes it piquant.

Savoury butters, stirred in at the last moment, can enrich and flavour many soups. See page 169 for how to add.

Sherry can do miracles for many a soup based on meat stock, like oxtail or kidney – or even in something simple like pea soup. It only takes the odd spoonful to make family or guests inquisitive. Sherry, after all, is often drunk *with* soup, so it stands to reason it's good stirred *into* it at the last minute.

Wine is the making of some soups, especially white wine in fish soups.

Other necessities There's more to making a good soup than just good ingredients.

1 It isn't practical to make a tiny quantity, because so much is lost through evaporation; better to make it for at least 6–8 while you're about it.

2 Simmer soups slowly, to extract all the flavour and goodness from the ingredients.

3 The right consistency is important. Thickened soups should be 'flowing', not thick – just thick enough for diced vegetables, if any, to be held in suspension. Adjust a soup before you serve it if necessary, adding a little cream or stock if too thick, or a liaison if too thin.

4 Take care that a skin doesn't form on top, or you'll soon have lumpy soup if you stir it in. If you keep hot soup covered with a lid or foil, there'll be no evaporation from the surface, which is the cause of skin. (A liquidizer will of course cure it.)

5 A liquidizer purées soups in a jiffy, the result being creamy, smooth and delicious. If you find the texture characterless for some kinds of soup, try using a vegetable mill instead.

6 If soup is supposed to be hot, then hot in hot plates it must be. If on the other hand it's cold, keep it chilled up to the last minute at the bottom of the refrigerator.

7 Soup is intended to stimulate the appetite, to help you digest whatever is to follow; not to kill your appetite for the rest of the meal. It's a mistake to serve too much.

■ Soups, very broadly speaking, fall into two main groups: thick and thin. The former may be thickened in various ways; with a roux or a starch such as potato flour, arrowroot or cornflour; by the starchy purée of a vegetable like potato; or very often with a cream and egg yolk liaison. Some very rich soups may have a roux base *and* a final binding of yolk and cream.

Thin soups These consist of consommés, and also homely soups like broths. The latter have a relatively large amount of garnish cooked in them. They are served without being sieved or liquidized, so the garnish should be cut into neat, even-sized pieces.

Thickened soups Purées made with a vegetable base such as lentils, cauliflower, pea or potato, are made with stock, or stock and milk. It may not be traditional but I prefer to thicken these soups with a roux (*when* flour thickened), the flour stirred into and cooked with the sweated onion rather than mixed to a liquid with stock, and added at the end. The well cooked flour gives the soup more flavour, and in addition there's no last minute thickening to bother with, or danger that if careless, the soup will go lumpy.

■ In case you'd like the basic recipe for a vegetable purée soup, here it is – to serve 6 generously:

1 medium-sized onion
1oz/25g butter or 3 dessertspoons oil
1oz/25g flour
2pt/generous litre fat-free white stock, or stock and milk
salt and pepper
¾–1lb/350–450g prepared fresh vegetables or 4oz/100g pulses
bouquet garni
croûtons, fried, to serve separately

Method

1 Sweat (fry over low heat with lid on) the finely sliced onion in the fat in a strong saucepan for about 10–15 minutes until soft but not coloured, agitating pan occasionally.

2 Remove pan from heat and stir in flour. Return to low heat again and cook this oniony roux for 2–3 minutes, stirring occasionally.

3 Away from the heat again, add the stock, very gradually at first as for a sauce, stirring in each addition before adding more. Season generously with salt and pepper.

4 Bring to the boil (over high heat now if you like), stirring continually. Add the fairly thinly sliced or cut-up vegetables (or pulse, soaked if necessary, see page 197) and bouquet garni and bring back to the boil.

5 Reduce heat to minimum, cover with lid (beware of a milky soup boiling over) and simmer until vegetable is tender, usually about 10–20 minutes, according to type, or to thickness sliced.

6 Remove bouquet garni. Liquidize, sieve or put soup through vegetable mill, and then reheat.

7 Taste, adjust seasoning if necessary and serve piping hot with fried croûtons.

■ Here are a few tips that may be of help:

1 The thicker you cut or slice a vegetable, the longer it will take to cook, and the poorer the flavour of the soup – just like any overcooked vegetable.

2 You can vary the proportion of stock to milk as you like: cauliflower, courgette or mushroom soup, for instance, are good made with equal quantities stock and milk; potato soup with three-quarters stock and a quarter milk; pea, split pea or lentil soup with seven-eighths stock and one-eighth milk.

3 If a vegetable purée soup contains something starchy like a large potato (this of course includes potato soup itself), it probably won't need a flour thickening if you're going to liquidize it; and this sort of soup freezes splendidly.

4 Liquidized soups are blended better and are lighter and smoother than sieved – but you may prefer the different character of a soup which has been sieved or put through a vegetable mill.

5 If a milky soup separates after freezing, liquidize it. Made with homogenized or long life milk, it won't separate though.

Cream soups These are basically a purée of vegetable, fish, shellfish or poultry thickened with a béchamel or velouté sauce. The soup is enriched at the last minute with cream, or in the case of a velouté, with a cream and egg yolk liaison, using 3 yolks and about ¼pt/125ml single cream to 2pt/1 litre liquid. Béchamel and velouté differ in that the former is made with milk and the latter with the liquor in which the fish or poultry was cooked. (It would be silly not to use such liquid since it contains so much of the flavour of the main ingredient.) A vegetable velouté soup can be made with chicken stock.

■ A cream of vegetable soup is the sophisticated version of a vegetable purée soup. Although differently made, its main advantages are that it is smoother, richer, has more body and is much more tasty. This is mainly due to the milk (for a béchamel based soup) being previously flavoured (see page 177) and to the presence of the cream, or cream and egg yolks as the case may be.

ARTICHOKE SOUP

Is one of the best ways to enjoy Jerusalem artichokes, either as a purée soup (page 161), or as 'cream of artichoke'.

ASPARAGUS SOUP

Needs straining if liquidized, otherwise it is stringy.

BEETROOT SOUP

Made with raw beetroot for the best flavour and colour. Peeled and diced or cut into thin strips, say together with a sliced potato, it doesn't matter how much the beetroots bleed because they'll be flavouring the stock.

■ A blob of double or soured cream in the centre of each serving takes away the dead look of beetroot soup, doing wonders both for looks and flavour.
■ *Borscht* (or various other spellings) is the famous beetroot soup of Russia and Poland. According to one author, 'there may well be as many versions of it as there are Russians'!

BISQUE

The sort of soup it's less costly to dream about than eat nowadays – so dream about it I do. Made usually with lobster or crayfish, and with wine, brandy, spices and cream amongst other things, could anyone ever think up a more heavenly dish than this? Even the shells will make stock from which you can make a very tasty soup.

BOUILLABAISSE

There are all sorts of variations, but the real and authentic soup is one made within a small radius of Marseilles. It originated as a simple fisherman's soup, made from several varieties of the day's catch, or its unsaleable leftovers, cooked in water or perhaps white wine, and flavoured with many of those heavenly products of Provençe, such as olive oil, tomatoes, onions, garlic, parsley, bayleaf and saffron. The classic dish includes fish only found in the Mediterranean.

CAULIFLOWER SOUP

A purée or cream soup very few people seem to make, yet it's quick and delicious. It is just as good made with frozen home-grown cauliflower as with fresh, so you can make it all year round if you like (see page 161).

CHOWDER

Often with a milk base, chowder is a thick, nourishing soup, frequently made basically with fresh fish or shellfish, or both. Bouillabaisse for instance is a chowder. The name is a corruption of *chaudière*, a large heavy pot or cauldron used by French country people and fishermen to make their regional soups and stews.

COCKIE-LEEKIE

Is just what it sounds like: a soup made basically from an old cock or hen, and leeks. At one time this was a favourite dish of the Scots – probably still is with many families.

CONSOMMÉ

The French name for meat stock which has been enriched, concentrated and clarified. Beautiful as it is, how many people will appreciate all the work and expense involved? Innumerable versions as there are, it's never the sort of soup one can make in a hurry. Like aspic, it must end up sparkling, whether one wants to serve it hot or jellied. For the latter, be sure to make the stock with something like a knuckle of veal, which will *make* it gel; and give the consommé 12–24 hours to do so. Taste it for salt too – cold foods nearly always need extra. See also *aspic*, page 153.

CROÛTONS

When fried, croûtons make a vegetable purée or cream soup absolutely tip-top, garnishing and enriching it as well as giving crispness. The bread dice should be dainty, not clumsy, so that one can sip them off the side of the soup spoon without appearing to make a meal of them!

■ You can't look after anything else while frying croûtons. If not turned over continually, over lowish heat, they're more likely to burn than to colour evenly. Shoot them all at once off a sheet of paper into hot lard, oil, garlic butter or butter – preferably clarified or saltless, for a perfect golden colour.

■ Drained well, first on the draining spoon used to stir them, and then on absorbent paper, a plain doyley on the small serving plate will absorb any surplus fat and ensure they won't be indigestible – unless of course the fat was only semi-hot when you put them into it.

■ Croûtons are best when freshly made, but if you're going to have half a dozen other things to look after when making the meal, fry them earlier in the day, and reheat them in a low oven while the plates are warming.

FISH SOUPS

Those such as bisques or bouillabaisse are the real thing, but one doesn't need a deep purse to enjoy some sumptuous fishy soups. Instead of using white stock in purée soups like potato, tomato or pea, why not use fish stock (page 122) made from the head, bones and trimmings of the sole, plaice, halibut, skate, trout or other white fish you bought for lunch or dinner? It's a real loss to waste so much flavour and goodness.

GARLIC SOUP

The very thought of it may appal you. If you've ever boiled garlic, though, you'll know that it loses all its pungency, so it isn't overdoing things to use a whole head of cloves in soup for six people. Even though you're a garlic-lover, you may be unable to define its flavour if you've never had this soup before.

GAZPACHO

A speciality of Andalusia in Spain, it is an excellent forerunner to a rich main course on a hot day.

■ Its delight is in all the fresh vegetables: cucumber, sweet peppers, tomatoes, garlic and Spanish onion. (You could use shallots but not the average British onion because it's too strong and raw.)
■ Serve well chilled, with ice cubes in each plate. The other ingredients are white bread, olive oil, wine vinegar (preferably red), seasoning and water.

LENTIL SOUP

It may sound plebeian, but can vie with the most luxurious soups when made with the best chicken or veal stock, and served with fried croûtons. There's no need to steep the lentils, which will be tender after 20 minutes simmering.

MINESTRONE

From *minestra*, the Italian word for a thick soup, which in turn derives from the Latin *ministrare*, to serve. In the days when there were great distances between inns, travellers often found food and shelter in a monastery. The monks, ready to 'minister' to them at whatever hour they arrived, would serve them at once with a meat and vegetable soup, which was kept simmering for the purpose.

■ Non-Italian minestrone may contain no meat. (For the agricultural and manual workers, in the north of Italy particularly, it makes a nourishing one-course meal with meat in it.)
■ Made in the Italian way (but without meat), there should be just enough stock to float the large mixture of vegetables and pastas (or rice).

MULLIGATAWNY

An Indian soup by origin. The name is a corruption of the Tamil *molegoo tunee*, pepper water. It is made with a boiling fowl or breast of lamb cooked in water until tender – with garlic, onions, herbs, spices, etc. Rice and slices of lime or lemon are usually served as a garnish along with the meat, sliced small.

MUSHROOM SOUP

Has more character I think when you chop the mushroom finely, rather than liquidize the soup. Alternatively, use a vegetable mill. Frozen mushrooms make excellent soup because freezing concentrates their flavour.

ONION SOUP, FRENCH

Isn't the sort to choose if you're short of time. It's not that the soup is laborious to make, but rather that the actual cooking is so long. It will only have its characteristic flavour if the large quantity of finely sliced onions are first sweated (to soften them), and then fried in butter and oil over very low heat until deep golden colour. This may take 1–1¼ hours, stirring frequently.

PARSNIP SOUP

An unusual and excellent variety of a vegetable soup (see basic recipe, page 161), adapted as follows:

1 If the parsnips are young, slice them fairly thinly; if old, quarter or cut them into eight, and core, buying extra to allow for the waste.
2 Sprinkle 1½ level teasps curry powder over the sweating sliced onion.
3 Use only ½oz/15g flour to thicken: parsnips are themselves starchy.
4 Allow an extra ¼pt/150ml liquid. (I like to use 1¾pt/1 litre chicken stock and ½pt/300ml milk.)
5 Add the juice of an orange when cooking is completed: added earlier vitamin C will be lost.
6 Croûtons and cream perfect it: ¼pt/150ml, stirred in just before serving.

PEA SOUP

Can be made almost in a flash if you use frozen peas and have a liquidizer. It's twice as good if you stir in a little sherry at the last minute – and three times as good if you add single cream as well!

POTATO SOUP

Potato soup has lots of character and flavour made with fish stock for a change.

VICHYSSOISE

Comes in my top 5 soups. Basically the most humble of purée soups – leek and potato – cream and chives are its making.

■ Here's the recipe, to serve 8. Make the soup at least several hours before you need it, preferably the day before, to serve it well chilled:

¾–1lb/350–450g *white* of leek (to make sure the soup is white)
1 large onion
1oz/25g butter or 3 dessertspoons olive oil (or a mixture of the two)
¾–1lb/350–450g potatoes
2pt/generous litre fat-free chicken stock
salt and white pepper (black pepper will spoil the soup's colour)
½pt/250ml single cream
2 tablespoons chopped chives
Melba toast, to accompany (see page 345)

Method

1 Sweat (see page 83) the prepared and finely sliced leeks and onion in the butter and/or oil until soft but not coloured, agitating pan several times.
2 Add the peeled and thickly sliced potatoes, stock and seasoning, bring to the boil and simmer until tender, about 15–20 minutes.
3 Liquidize, sieve or put through finest cutter of a vegetable mill. Leave to cool, cover and chill at bottom of refrigerator.
4 Shortly before eating, stir in the chilled cream, and at the very last minute (for their finest flavour), stir in the

chopped chives. Taste before serving.

WATERCRESS SOUP

Rather good if you've never had it before, but the watercress must be really fresh, you should cut off the thick part of the stalks, and the soup *must* be sieved (even if liquidized), otherwise it's stringy.

■ I like to add some thinly sliced potato when making watercress purée soup, to give it a little more body, but there's no need for it in cream of watercress because this gets its body from cream, or a cream and egg yolk liaison.

8
Savoury sauces

GENERAL INFORMATION

Sauces tend to be an absent art in the cooking of some nations, often spoiling the most expensive dishes either by their dullness or by their complete absence. What a waste! With a little bit of extra know-how and trouble, a sauce-minded cook can transform the simplest dish into a remarkable one.

■ So many people seem to think a simple white sauce (maybe with cheese, parsley or mushrooms, etc. added) meets every need. How characterless – and how boring! Some will even wash down the sink those heavenly juices stuck to the bottom of a frying pan or roasting tin rather than use them to make a sauce or delicious accompaniment to serve with the food.

■ Lots of even quite enthusiastic cooks don't appear to realize that sauces can give endless variety to simple everyday meals, are a splendid medium for using up cooked foods, enhance flavour, can enrich plain foods, or make rich ones more digestible. There is in fact little better or much easier than a good sauce to uplift something otherwise rather tasteless.

■ A sauce may sometimes be in direct contrast to the dish it accompanies, subtly blending two flavours in one. If partners are traditional, like pork and apple sauce, or lamb and mint sauce, there's generally a gastronomical as well as 'tasty' reason for serving them together.

■ The egg yolk and butter sauces, like hollandaise, and the savoury butters come into their own when there aren't any trimmings with which to make a sauce, as for instance with grilled meat or boiled vegetables.

■ Flavour is what matters most. Good stock scores over poor, butter over margarine, béchamel milk (page 177) over ordinary milk, wine vinegar over malt, fresh herbs over dried.

■ Roux, liaisons and stock are discussed in earlier chapters; they all play their part in good sauce-making.

■ The right consistency follows close behind good flavour, because however good the sauce, one can ruin it by making it either too stodgy or too runny. It's child's play to adjust a thick sauce with extra stock, milk, or perhaps cream, but it's more bothersome to correct a thin one. This may involve using a liaison such as beurre manié, fécule, or egg yolk and cream, or it may be better to reduce it by evaporation.

■ If a sauce thins out during cooking, this is caused by a chemical change in the flour used to make it, when a sauce cooks too long.

■ Lumpy sauces can often be corrected in a liquidizer. If you don't have one of those marvellous gadgets, then you'll have to whisk the sauce vigorously (preferably with a balloon or wire whisk), or pass it through a sieve and simmer it a few minutes.

■ If a skin forms on top of a sauce kept hot, this is due to evaporation from the surface, and can be prevented in various ways:

1 Float a film of stock over the top of brown sauces, or of white sauces made with stock, e.g. velouté-based sauces.
2 Float a film of milk or melted butter over white sauces made with milk.

3 Cover a sauce closely with a disc of foil, or wet greaseproof paper, and then with the pan lid.

■ A bain-marie (page 13) is invaluable for keeping sauces hot or warm, as necessary, especially sauces which separate if overheated, like the egg yolk and butter ones.
■ Apart from a number of unrelated miscellaneous sauces such as apple, bread, horseradish, tomato, etc. the classic French sauces largely belong to 6 definite groups. As long as you know how to make the basic or mother sauce of each group, therefore, you can make dozens of others without difficulty. The technique remains the same, while varied ingredients and trimmings are added or changed, to give a different flavoured sauce with a different name, suitable for all kinds of fish, meat, poultry or game. The Family Tree on pages 170–1 shows how simple it in fact is.

APPLE SAUCE

Add a pinch of ground cinnamon, or some finely chopped chives or mint to make an interesting variation.

BÉCHAMEL SAUCE

See page 177.

BREAD SAUCE

Tastes good if you flavour the milk first, by heating it slowly with the onion (stuck with cloves) and a small piece of bayleaf. When nearly boiling, and infused, take out the flavourings and add the breadcrumbs, butter and seasoning. To give the sauce extra last-minute flavour, add a spoonful of cream and a pinch of cayenne.

■ It's worth remembering that if you're over-generous with the breadcrumbs (failing to weigh them or measure the milk), simmer the sauce more than 3 or 4 minutes, or keep it hot long after it's made, you'll end up with a poultice, not a sauce. Use 2oz/50g breadcrumbs to ½pt/250ml milk.

BROWN SAUCE

Can take either several hours to make, about an hour, or about 5 minutes (if you have some good stock at hand), according to the method. Demi-glace sauce, itself based on a sauce base called an espagnole, is the traditional 'mother' of the brown sauces, but the espagnole is such a performance, so specialized and so little used except by the professional that I'm only mentioning, not describing it.

■ A simple roux-based sauce is much quicker, or it's quicker still to thicken a really good brown stock with a starch such as potato flour, arrowroot, cornflour or rice flour.

Roux-based brown sauce Brown stock is necessary, for its strong flavour and basically dark colour. If the sauce is to be fat-free, the stock certainly has to be.
The fat can be oil, cooking fat or clarified dripping – or saltless or clarified butter if the sauce is accompanying something with a delicate flavour. If you use any old dripping, or unclarified salted butter, it may burn during the long cooking of the roux, spoiling both the colour and flavour of the sauce. See *roux*, page 79.
The vegetables – onion, carrot, celery – should be finely diced, to extract all their flavour. If you sauté them gently in the fat before making the roux, the sauce will have much more flavour than it would have by adding them to the liquid later, unfried. After making and simmering the sauce as your recipe directs, you'll extract flavour from the vegetables if, when straining the sauce, you lightly press their juices out.
A bouquet garni simmered in the sauce gives subtle flavour. A herbless sauce is a characterless one.

■ The sauce, degreased if necessary, can now be used just as it is, or you can use it as the base for the brown sauces on the Family Tree, page 170.

■ You may just as well make extra if you have a freezer, then it's there when wanted.

Starch-thickened brown sauce The brown stock should be top quality as well as fat-free, because this sauce is simply thickened stock, and is only good if the stock is good. See *stock*, page 122.

■ Potato flour or cornflour are generally used unless the sauce needs to be very clear, when arrowroot is better. A sauce made with cornflour needs to simmer a few minutes longer than one made with either of the other two thickenings, to cook it, as well as to thicken the sauce lightly.

■ This sauce can also form the base of the brown sauces on the Family Tree, page 170.

BUTTERS, SAVOURY

One of the easiest yet most delicious ways of flavouring food that I can think of. I love having a selection of them in the freezer, to use in any of the ways described below.

■ Individual recipes, if necessary at all, may vary slightly, but basically all you have to do is cream some butter and seasoning together until soft enough to blend with the flavouring of your choice. This may include such things as crushed garlic, finely chopped herbs, French mustard, finely sliced shallot, cut-up shellfish, juiced and seeded tomato flesh, anchovies or wine (see Family Tree). You can use a combination of these flavours if you like; say mustard and parsley, or garlic and tomato. If you're in too much of a hurry to cream the butter properly, simply make sure it is soft and squash it on a chopping board with a round-ended knife, then blend the flavour with it, gradually if something moist like mustard. (A liquid flavouring such as wine, previously flavoured and reduced, needs blending in a bowl, of course.)

■ Here are some ways to use them:

To add flavour, richness and moisture to grilled fish, meat, poached eggs, etc. Put a pat of chilled savoury butter on top of each piece of fish or meat just before taking it to table. The food must be hot enough to melt the butter before you eat it, so that its flavour is spread everywhere. Anyway, who wants to eat a lump of chilled butter?

■ The sort of butters you may want to use include anchovy (for fish dishes), bercy, colbert, herbs, horseradish, garlic, maître d'hôtel, marchand de vins, mustard, tarragon or tomato.

To enrich sauces Cut the *soft* savoury butter into small pieces, and stir it into the boiling hot sauce aside from the heat, just before serving it. If added over heat, or if the sauce is re-boiled, the butter will oil and lose its flavour.

■ ¼–½oz/10–15g butter will flavour ½pt/250ml of, say, simple white sauce. If the sauce then has to be kept hot, use a bain-marie.

■ Butters to use include anchovy (for a fish sauce), bercy (white sauces), garlic, marchand de vins (brown sauces), mustard, shallot, shellfish (shellfish sauces), tomato (white sauces) or tarragon.

To enrich soups Add the savoury butter as for sauces, above. Butters to use include garlic, shallot, shellfish (bisques, and tinned or frozen shellfish soups), tarragon or tomato.

To toss with boiled vegetables Chive, garlic, mint, parsley or tomato butter are good with certain vegetables.

To baste fish, meat, tomatoes or mushrooms, etc. while baking or grilling Butters to use include chive, garlic, mustard, tarragon – or anchovy butter for fish.

To garnish appetizers, cold dishes and canapés If you want to pipe a savoury butter, it will need sieving – and possibly also chilling slightly if too soft to use. If on the other hand you want fancy shapes, spread it fairly thinly but evenly on a plate, refrigerate it until hard, then cut with a cutter dipped in boiling water.

THE FAMILY TREE OF SAUCES

Mother sauces		
White		**Brown**
Béchamel sauce	*Velouté sauce*	*Brown sauce*
anchovy	allemande	bercy
aurore	(egg yolks and butter or	(white wine and shallots)
(tomato)	cream)	bigarade (bitter orange)
caper	aurore (tomato)	bourgignonne (red wine,
cardinal	bercy	mushrooms and onions)
(lobster)	(white wine and shallots)	chasseur
crème (cream)	chaud-froid, white (aspic or	(white wine, mushrooms and
curry	gelatine)	shallots)
egg	fennel	chaud-froid, brown (aspic or
mornay	(allemande+fennel)	gelatine)
(cheese)	hongroise	diable
mustard	(suprême+paprika)	(white wine, very peppery)
poulette	normande	duxelles
(shallots,	(white wine, for fish)	(mushrooms)
mushrooms,	parisienne	italienne
egg yolks	(another name for allemande)	(mushrooms, ham and
and cream)	poulette	herbs)
ravigote	(allemande+shallots and	lyonnaise
(white wine,	mushrooms)	(onion, white wine)
onions,	ravigote	madeira
herbs)	(white wine, onions, herbs)	orange
soubise	suprême (cream)	piquante
(onion purée)	tarragon	(diable+pickles and capers)
tarragon	vin blanc	poivrade (peppery)
		robert (onions, mustard)
		tarragon
		venison
		(poivrade+red currant jelly
		and cream)

Egg yolk and butter sauces	Egg yolk and oil sauces	Oil and vinegar sauces	Flavoured butters
Hollandaise sauce	*Mayonnaise*	*French dressing*	(1) *Savoury butters*
béarnaise (white wine, shallots, tarragon)	aïoli (garlic)	anchovy	anchovy
choron (béarnaise + tomato)	andalouse (tomato, sweet red pepper)	aurore (tomato)	bercy (white wine, shallots)
colbert (béarnaise + meat glaze)	cardinal (lobster)	cream	colbert (tarragon, meat flavouring)
maltaise (orange)	chantilly (whipped cream)	marseillaise (garlic)	egg yolk
mousseline (whipped cream)	collioure (anchovies)	mint	garlic
noisette (browned butter)	curry	mustard	herb
paloise (béarnaise, with mint instead of tarragon)	fines herbes (chervil, chives, parsley, tarragon)	ravigote (onion, herbs, capers)	horseradish
vin blanc	indienne (curry)		maître d'hôtel (parsley, lemon juice)
	remoulade (anchovies, pickles, capers, herbs)		marchand de vins (shallot butter with red wine)
	tartare (pickles, capers, herbs)		mustard
	verte (green herbs)		paprika
			shallot
			shellfish
			tarragon
			tomato
			(2) *Hot butter sauces*
			beurre blanc (shallots, wine)
			beurre au citron (lemon)
			beurre noir (or noisette) (browned butter)
			melted butter

■ Butters suitable for garnishing include anchovy, egg yolk, paprika, sardine, shellfish or tomato.

To fill hard-boiled eggs or to use as a quick sandwich spread Butters to use include anchovy, egg yolk, sardine, shellfish or tomato.

BUTTER SAUCES, HOT

Serve them with fish, chicken or turkey breasts, asparagus, sprouting broccoli, or poached or fried eggs. These are some of the quickest and easiest sauces.

■ The important thing is just to melt and warm the butter with the seasoning, not to overheat it – because it then 'oils' and loses flavour.
■ A few drops of lemon juice added at the last moment, help to counteract the richness.

Beurre noir This is really a misnomer because if allowed to become black, it will be burnt. See Family Tree, page 171.

■ A good beurre noir should be clear, unspeckled, and golden nut-brown; and needs to be made with clarified butter because the milk solids in ordinary butter turn black and bitter.
■ Use for certain egg dishes, calf's brains, fish (especially skate), chicken breasts and certain vegetables.

DEGLAZING SAUCE, BROWN

An incredibly simple, useful, delicious and quickly made brown sauce using the coagulated juices left, after straining off any excess fat, from foods cooked in a roasting tin, sauté pan or frying pan. It's perfect with something like, say, roast chicken or steaks.

■ All you need do is add wine or stock to the pan, scrape into and dissolve in it these tasty crispy bits, then reduce the liquid until syrupy. If, aside from the heat, you then stir in a little softened, cut-up lump of butter, it will act as a slight liaison as well as flavouring and

making the sauce creamy.
■ To make the sauce even better still, if the flavour goes well with the dish the sauce is accompanying, fry a little sliced shallot or spring onion in a spoonful of retained fat, before pouring the wine or stock into the pan.

GRAVY

Originally this meant only the natural concentrated juices which come out of a roast. Nowadays the word is more loosely used, indicating a sauce made from them. It's made in the tin in which the meat, poultry or game has been cooked, largely (if not sometimes entirely) from these juices extracted during cooking.

■ Serve thick gravy with a stuffed roast, thin with others, for the simple reason that these make the best partners when it comes to eating them.
■ It's quite tricky to make good gravy so here are a few tips:
1 You need stock (made from the giblets, if a bird), a stock cube or vegetable cooking water, such as onion or potato.
2 The sediment, meat juices and tasty crisp brown bits stuck to the tin and caught by the sieve when straining off the fat, are a gravy's essential flavourings. Without them, your gravy will be tasteless and characterless.
3 Be sure to cook the roux (fat and flour) for 2 or 3 minutes if you're using flour to thicken it, scraping into it with a metal spoon all those tasty bits stuck to the tin.
4 Make sure a thick gravy is just thick, not coating consistency! Use 1oz/25g flour and 1 tablespoon of the fat to 1pt/500ml stock.
5 Taste, seasoning generously with salt and pepper.
6 Use a few drops of a good gravy browning to colour it if necessary. At all costs avoid using a flavoured gravy powder, unless you like every gravy to taste of that and nothing else.
7 Before serving in a sauce-boat, skim off any fat that rises to the surface.

HOLLANDAISE SAUCE

A warm relation of mayonnaise, the difference being that hollandaise is a lemon-flavoured emulsion of butter and egg yolks, while mayonnaise is an emulsion of oil and egg yolks.

■ Simple flavourings like finely chopped herbs or puréed asparagus tips can be stirred into it, and the classic sauces on page 171 (see Family Tree) are only slight variations of this, the 'mother sauce' of its group.

■ Anyone can make it in a liquidizer, it's so easy, though the texture is slightly different from handmade, which is slower and more chancy for a beginner.

■ However you make it, hollandaise is served lukewarm, preferably the moment it's made. If it has to be kept warm, but is in fact heated, it will thin out and curdle. It will hold for some time in a sauceboat, standing in a pan of warm water – the water replaced as it cools – or in a pan in a bain-marie containing lukewarm water.

■ If too thick, thin it down with a tablespoon of cream or hot water, but it *is* a thick sauce.

Made in a liquidizer *The butter* should be cut into small pieces and heated in a small saucepan until foaming hot, but not coloured. A smaller amount is used than when making the sauce by hand, because the emulsion becomes so thick that the cutters can't rotate. You can slowly beat in some extra butter later though, if you transfer the sauce to a bowl.

The egg yolks should be at room temperature, fresh, and free of all egg white, including chalazae, to avoid risk of curdling. Liquidize them with the strained lemon juice and seasoning at maximum speed for 30 seconds, to break them down and so prepare them to absorb the butter.

■ With liquidizer at maximum speed, and the central cap removed, you can now pour in the hot butter, in a very thin steady stream – there's no need to add it drop by drop, as long as the yolks were well liquidized in the first place. (Beware

of the mess if your liquidizer has no central cap, and you have to take the whole lid off. Replace it with a funnel, see page 28.)

■ If the yolks and butter do fail to emulsify, pour the mixture into a jug and add it gradually to the liquidizer again, *very* slowly to start with. As the butter cools, it should begin to cream and will form itself into a thick sauce.

Made by hand There are numerous ways to do it but all must accomplish the same result, that of forcing egg yolks to absorb butter and hold it in creamy suspension. *The egg yolks* should be as for liquidizing, above. The smaller the yolks, the less butter they will absorb, one yolk taking about 2–3oz/50–75g butter. It's easier to make a sauce with 2 or 3 yolks than just one, because there is more yolk to beat, initially.

■ If you beat the yolks with a small wire whisk for at least a minute, until thick in consistency and pale yellow in colour, they will absorb the butter much more readily. Beating them for a further ½–1 minute when the lemon juice is added, is an extra precaution worth taking.

■ Adding a very small fraction of the butter (cut into tiny pieces, and in addition to the lemon juice) to the well-whisked yolks before putting these over heat prevents them coagulating (setting) before they and the larger quantity of the butter could possibly emulsify. Also, for the mixture to emulsify, the butter must – until the emulsion process begins – be stirred in by driblets to the warming yolks. (Incorporate each addition of butter completely before adding more.)

■ For the yolks to thicken into a smooth cream, slow and gradual heating is essential: they'll become granular if the heat is too sudden, scrambled if overcooked. Stir them over the lowest possible direct heat or, better still, in a double pan with lukewarm water to start with, raising the temperature of the water gradually to shivering. Beware though! If the water isn't hot enough the yolks won't thicken; if too hot, the sauce will curdle.

■ If you've never made hollandaise before, and are wary of overheating the yolks, it pays to run some cold water into the sink before you begin, so that you can plunge the bottom of the pan into it at the slightest sign of curdling. This will cool the yolks instantly, even more so if you beat them as well. When recovered, return pan to heat and carry on as before.
■ If your recipe tells you to add another fraction of the total butter, cold, to the heated creamy sauce, this is to cool the yolks and halt their cooking instantly.
■ Melted butter, if called for, means *melted*, not *hot* butter.

Curdled hollandaise sauce Can sometimes be rectified by beating in a tablespoon of cold water. Failing this, and using a small wire whisk, beat a tablespoon of the sauce with a teaspoon of lemon juice in a warmed basin until they thicken, then beat in remaining curdled sauce, just one dessertspoon at a time.

Left-over hollandaise Can be refrigerated for a short time, or you can pop it in the freezer if you like. To use again as hollandaise, beat a tablespoon or two of it in a pan standing in a bain-marie containing hottish water, then gradually beat in the remainder, a spoonful at a time. Alternatively, use it to enrich a béchamel or velouté sauce: simply beat it into the sauce, a tablespoon at a time, aside from the heat, just before serving. Avoid boiling the sauce because the butter will oil and lose its flavour.

MAYONNAISE

According to one theory, mayonnaise may take its name from the very old French word *moyeu*, meaning yolk of egg. According to another it comes from mahonnaise, celebrating the capture of Mahon, in Minorca, in 1756.

■ Mayonnaise, the 'mother sauce' of the egg yolk and oil sauces (see page 171, Family Tree) is the best possible reason for having a liquidizer. A tricky and long operation by hand if you've never made it

before, even an inexperienced cook can conjure up mayonnaise in the space of a few minutes with a model which will run at low speed.
■ Making mayonnaise by hand is more difficult and quite a different operation from making it in a liquidizer, but they have various things in common:

1 *The oil*. Only olive oil (see page 113) will give mayonnaise its true flavour. If too costly, or if too strong, try a mixture (say 50/50) of, say, olive oil and corn oil. The emulsion may thin out and curdle if you try to add too much oil, because the binding properties of the yolks break down. 6fl oz/about 160ml per large egg yolk is the ceiling.
2 *The vinegar*. Use white wine vinegar or lemon juice, preferably the former, for the finest flavour and colour. Malt vinegar is too harsh and gives mayonnaise a bad colour, unless distilled. See also *vinegar*, page 128.
3 A tablespoon of boiling water per egg yolk beaten into the made mayonnaise helps to make it lighter, and also acts as an insurance against curdling.
4 If the mayonnaise is too thick, stir in a spoonful or two of cream just before you need it. This corrects the consistency and flavours and makes it creamy-smooth all at one stroke. On the other hand, if you'd rather cut *down* the richness, use soured cream or yoghurt instead of fresh cream.
5 Curdled mayonnaise can be remedied by starting back at square one with a new yolk. Simply add the curdled mixture to the well-beaten yolk in the same way as you added the oil to the original yolk.
6 Finely chopped herbs, if used, are added at the last minute, otherwise they lose their colour and will in due course turn sour. Alternatively, if you want to add them in advance, blanch them for one minute, refresh, drain, squeeze dry and chop.
7 It's important to taste mayonnaise before serving it, to make sure it's both well seasoned and well flavoured.
8 If mayonnaise thins out in a very cold larder, you can thicken it again by adding

it very gradually to 1 teaspoon of made mustard. First beat the mustard and 1 tablespoon of the mayonnaise with a wire whisk until they cream and thicken together, then beat in remaining mayonnaise, a teaspoonful at a time.

Made by hand *The egg yolks* should be large ones if they are to absorb all the oil. They should also be fresh, entirely free of egg white (including the chalazae) and at room temperature, because the mixture is more likely to curdle if they're cold. It's easier to make up 2 or 3 egg yolks than 1, because there's a greater bulk of egg yolk to beat initially.

■ *The mixing bowl* is better for being warmed in hot water, to avoid chilling the yolks.
■ *A small wire whisk* is better than a wooden spoon to beat and break down the yolks – it takes a minute or two before they're thick and pale yellow, as they should be. Then they need beating again for another 30 seconds or so after adding the vinegar and seasonings, to break them down even more. Only then are they ready to absorb the oil.
■ If you don't add the oil drop by drop to start with and if you don't beat the yolks and vinegar *constantly*, they won't emulsify – there's no time for a nap in the middle!
■ It's important to watch the oil rather than the mixture as you drop it in. The lip of the oil bottle (see oil *dropper*, page 34) or a jug is easily steadied over the edge of the bowl, and you can tie a cloth round the bowl to steady it, see page 67. It's best to stop pouring about every 10 seconds, while continuing to beat, to make sure the oil is being absorbed.
■ Once the yolks and oil emulsify, the real danger of curdling is over and you can beat in the remaining oil a tablespoon at a time.
■ If the mayonnaise is too thick and difficult to beat before all the oil is added, thin it out with a few drops of vinegar or lemon juice, but if you've never made it before, it's probably safer not to try and add more than ¼pt/150ml oil per egg yolk.

Made in a liquidizer Some people like to use whole egg, other prefer to use yolk, but whichever you do, it's easiest with a normal household-sized liquidizer to make up only one egg or one yolk at a time. Made with whole egg, I personally find it so poor as to think it not worth while making, whereas the yolk alone produces an emulsion unmistakably like, if not as good as, handmade mayonnaise.

■ Success hangs upon the complete breaking down of the yolk with the vinegar. Liquidize these together with the seasonings for 30 seconds at maximum speed. This makes them ready to absorb the oil, now easily poured in from a jug. Next, turn on liquidizer at slowish speed, remove the central cap (or lid, if no cap – see *funnel*, page 28) and pour in the oil, in a thin steady stream – there's no need to worry about adding it drop by drop. Any worries you may have are over when the whirring noise of the liquidizer changes to a quieter one, which it does suddenly, when the egg and oil emulsify.
■ When using yolk only, you may find the emulsion is so thick that the blades will stick before you've added all the oil. If so, switch off, stir in a tablespoon of very hot water, and off you go again.
■ Whole egg will absorb about 3 tablespoons more oil than egg yolk will, to reach a thick consistency, so if you add all that, you're bound to need a spot more vinegar and seasonings to counteract the extra oil's richness.

Curry mayonnaise This particular version is so good with chicken, fish or an egg salad that you may like to have the recipe. It serves 4. Sweat a finely chopped small onion in 1oz/25g butter until soft and transparent, but not coloured. Stir in 3 rounded teaspoons curry powder and fry for about 2 minutes with the onion. Add a pinch of salt, 1 level tablespoon honey and 2 level tablespoons mango chutney sauce, stirring over low heat for 2 or 3 minutes until thick. Sieve and cool it, then mix with ¼pt/150ml homemade mayonnaise.

MINT SAUCE

Can be varied by making it with brown sugar instead of white, and/or lemon juice instead of vinegar. It's better made with wine vinegar than with malt, because the former cuts more effectively through the richness of a roast and its accompaniments.

■ Mint sauce has an extra-minty fresh flavour if you chop and then pound the leaves, rather than just chop them finely (see page 102).
■ Make the sauce at least an hour or two in advance, to develop its full flavour, making it thick with mint, not watery.

OIL AND VINEGAR SAUCES

See page 207.

SALAD CREAM

A commercial salad cream differs from a commercial mayonnaise in that it contains a lower proportion of oil. A thickening agent is used to give the required consistency.

SWEET-SOUR SAUCE

A Chinese (soy sauce flavoured) sauce which seems to have 'caught on' and taken root in Western cookery as well – and rightly so, because of the character and new life it gives to pork particularly, but also to other meats. The sweetness may come from either honey or sugar – soft brown sugar gives much more flavour and colour than does granulated – and the sourness from vinegar.

VELOUTÉ SAUCE

See page 177.

WHITE SAUCE

This sauce, made simply with butter or margarine, flour, milk and seasoning is *the* basic white sauce. So basic is it in fact to all cooking that for the sake of the non

sauce-makers, here are precise details:

Coating consistency
1oz/25g butter or margarine
1oz/25g flour
½pt/250ml milk
salt and pepper

Pouring consistency
½oz/15g butter or margarine
½oz/15g flour
½pt/250ml milk
salt and pepper.

Method

1 Make roux:
   a Melt fat slowly, without really heating it, then set pan aside from heat. Stir in the flour and blend with a wooden spoon until absolutely smooth.
   b Return pan to low heat and cook roux for 2 or 3 minutes, stirring at intervals.
2 Set the pan aside from heat again and stir in the milk, very gradually at first, blending in each addition until smooth before adding more.
3 Season with salt and pepper. (*If you want to, you can prepare as far as this earlier in the day.*)
4 Heat and bring sauce to the boil, stirring constantly, then boil about a minute to thicken it properly and to make sure the flour is cooked.
5 Taste, and correct consistency if necessary. (A coating sauce should coat smoothly the back of the wooden spoon.)

■ See also *roux*, page 79, for other hows and whys.
■ You can now give this sauce flavour by enriching it with a nut of savoury butter (see page 169), or you can add a variety of flavourings such as grated cheese, chopped parsley, cooked chopped mushrooms or cooked sliced onion. Whatever you add, though, nothing will make such a tasty sauce as that same flavouring stirred into béchamel sauce (see below), the 'superior' white sauce made in exactly the same way but with milk which has been

previously flavoured. It's so little extra trouble, yet transforms the dull into the subtle.

■ Certain foods, crushed garlic or finely sliced shallot, for instance, are sometimes cooked lightly in the roux because this way their flavour is more pronounced.

Béchamel sauce This, and velouté, see later, are the two 'mother sauces' of the white sauces, the aristocratic relations of the simple white one above. The only difference between them and the basic white sauce is that for béchamel you flavour the milk first, and for velouté you use well flavoured stock *instead* of milk – usually the liquor in which the meat or fish has been cooked. These are the two, which with additions or slight alterations, can be made into any of the sauces in their group (see Family Tree, page 170).

■ With the addition of cream, for instance, béchamel becomes cream sauce (sauce crème), while velouté with cream becomes sauce suprême. With the addition of cheese, an ordinary white sauce becomes just a cheese sauce, but a béchamel sauce becomes mornay sauce.

■ Anyone with time on their hands may want to make béchamel the perfect way, with carrot, onion, celery and leek, etc. but the rest of us must probably settle for the lightning alternative, which for reference elsewhere in the book I'm going to call *béchamel milk*.

Béchamel milk All you need do to make ½pt/250ml sauce is put the following ingredients together in a small saucepan:

Ingredient	Remarks
½pt/250ml milk	be generous with it, to allow for evaporation
1 sliced shallot or small piece of onion, sliced	use dried onion if in a hurry
1 small bayleaf	

Ingredient	Remarks
a few white peppercorns	ground pepper may spoil the appearance of a sauce (salt is added later when you make the sauce)
1 clove	not official, but *I* think it's the making of the sauce
pinch of celery seed	if available, and if it won't spoil the appearance of the sauce

1 Bring the milk slowly to the boil – the slower the better, to extract all the flavours.
2 Set pan aside from heat, cover with a lid and infuse for 10–15 minutes to draw out even more flavour.
3 Strain, make up to ½pt/250ml again with extra milk if necessary, and use hot or cold, as ordinary milk.

■ A good roux is the foundation of a good sauce (use a white roux for a béchamel sauce), affecting flavour, colour and consistency for better or for worse (see *roux*, page 79).
■ Having made the sauce as an ordinary white one, with the roux, flavoured milk and some salt, you can make it better still by enriching with butter, cream, or a cream and egg yolk liaison. (See *butters, savoury*, page 169, if adding butter.)
■ Sauces such as these are served with fish, chicken, veal, eggs or vegetables, and may also be the base for savoury soufflés, hot hors d'oeuvres or cream soups.
■ White sauces containing wine or egg yolks tend to become discoloured if made in an aluminium pan; and a pan in which a starchy sauce has been made, is more easily washed if first soaked with cold water rather than hot.

Velouté sauce Is like béchamel (see

above, and also *white sauce*, page 176), but made with stock – chicken, veal or fish – instead of milk. The liquor in which food has been cooked and from which the sauce may be made, is often flavoured with wine, and the sauce may also include cream or milk. When enriched with a cream and egg yolk liaison, velouté sauce must be one of the most delicious of any quickly made sauce.

■ Velouté used to be called *sauce blonde* because, ideally, it's a white sauce made with a blond roux (see *roux*, page 79) instead of a white roux.

9

Vegetables

GENERAL INFORMATION

In France vegetables are delicious enough to merit being highlighted as a separate course rather than being served as a nutritious necessity or as a main course filler-up.

Where French shoppers are discerning about their choice of vegetables, selecting and rejecting with meticulous care, we will often take what we are given. We'll even pick up the discoloured limp rubbish ourselves in some supermarkets, and pay full price for it too. Just as tender veal would become beef, or lamb become mutton so, with age, tender beautifully flavoured young vegetables turn into something quite different. How crazy can we be to encourage people to think that the largest are the best at the village show, when in fact nothing about them makes good eating? Some gardeners actually plan their vegetable digging or picking round their local show, allowing everything to grow huge in order, at the right time, to produce six perfectly shaped giants.

Vegetables help protect the body from illness, and are best when eaten fresh and raw, when nothing is lost by cooking. Next best is to prepare and cook them perfectly. Most of us know the smell and flavour of a freshly picked tomato, but many people don't seem to realize that the flavour of a freshly picked green vegetable is no less rewarding, although there's usually no glorious smell to advertise it.

One can't see vitamins disappearing any more than one can see an egg going bad, but this is just what begins to happen when you pick or dig up a vegetable, especially greens. The longer they are stored, the greater the loss, and the further from the meal they are prepared, and the more they're cut up, the more that loss is accelerated.

It's often easier said than done, but if one wants the flavour of garden vegetables at their best, one should aim to cook greens within an hour of picking. If you must prepare in advance – we all must sometimes, especially in winter – the important thing is to exclude light and air. Wrapped in foil or polythene, and refrigerated, deterioration is greatly slowed down.

While the British mainly simply boil most of their vegetables, the French are more imaginative. By blanching them first – either for just a few minutes or until nearly cooked, according to whatever you're going to do with them – you can vary their flavour and texture in all sorts of ways by sautéing, glazing, roasting, stuffing, or by making fritters or a purée (see later).

You can blanch and refresh a vegetable earlier in the day if necessary, and cook it in the same or another way later, when ready for it. See *refreshing*, page 77.

Deep-freezing vegetables Vegetables to be deep frozen are blanched in order to kill the enzymes which cause deterioration in colour, flavour, and to some extent, food value. An authority on the subject says the maximum acceptable storage time in the freezer for unblanched vegetables is – to take just 2 or 3 examples – 1 month for runner beans, 3 weeks for broad beans and 3 days for

Brussels sprouts, compared with 12 – 14 months for blanched vegetables. The enzyme which breaks down vitamin C is destroyed by blanching, so more of the vitamin is retained when vegetables are blanched than if stored unblanched for several months. (See *refreshing*, page 77, and *blanching*, pages 52–3.) When you cook a frozen vegetable, allow less than half its normal cooking time after the water has returned to the boil. The longer you cook it, the poorer the flavour and texture.

Boiled vegetables They keep their goodness and cook best in a covered pan large enough for the vegetable to be in one layer, not piled up in a small pan. This way, if you choose vegetables of the same size – or cut them into equal-sized pieces – they'll cook quickly, and will all be ready at the same time. The fewer outer green leaves removed the better because that's where most of the goodness is.

■ Use shallow well-salted water to retain flavour and nutrients, because there's a heavy loss of mineral salts with deep water.

■ Put vegetables into fast-boiling water over maximum heat so that the water can come quickly back to the boil – from when cooking time starts. Only then should you lower the heat, allowing a vegetable to boil slowly for its allotted time. The shorter the cooking time, the greater the food value and the better the flavour, colour and texture.

■ Many vegetables are fatless so if you're not worried about your waistline, do enrich and flavour them when you can by serving a sauce, or by tossing with chopped herbs and butter, cream or soured cream. It makes all the difference in the world.

Sautéd vegetables So tempting and so basically simple to prepare that they put even the common spud, carrot, turnip, parsnip or swede into another class. Just as fried onions taste like a different vegetable from boiled, because the sugar in them caramelizes, so it does in lots of other vegetables, given the chance. An

unpleasantly strong flavour is mellowed, a characterless texture becomes almost crunchy, and pale-coloured vegetables turn golden.

■ While some vegetables are sautéd in hot butter from start to finish, others – in particular root vegetables and potatoes – are previously blanched. Sliced or quartered as necessary, they are boiled until nearly but not quite cooked, and then sautéd in hot butter until turning golden. When tossed with flavourings such as freshly milled black pepper and chopped herbs just before dishing, it puts an edge on the dullest veg.

■ If you haven't sautéd vegetables in this way before, a few more guidelines may be helpful:

1 Allow 1–1½ozs/25–40g butter for 4 people, and rather more of a watery vegetable than usual, because it will shrink as the moisture is drawn out.

2 Evaporate excess moisture from a hot blanched drained vegetable by returning it to the empty pan, and tossing over moderate heat for a minute or two – uncovered. If you don't do this, it will splutter and make the butter watery. Otherwise refresh the vegetable after blanching, if for some reason you aren't going to sauté it straight away. If watery, like courgettes, cover in a colander with a weighted plate until required.

3 Turn the whole mass of vegetables over occasionally, using a fish slice for potatoes, to prevent breaking up, or two wooden spoons for most other vegetables.

4 Add salt when the vegetable is nearly cooked (about 5 – 20 minutes according to type). Having been blanched in salted water, the vegetable won't lack flavour, but will stick to the sauté pan if you add salt to the butter.

5 A minute or two before dishing, enrich and vary a vegetable's flavour by stirring in and blending a pinch of a spice like nutmeg and 2 or 3 tablespoons of cream, soured cream or yoghurt. Herbs are added at the last second. There's no end to the permutations you might think up.

6 As a change, mix with another vegetable: fried onions, for instance, go well with French or runner beans, or with potatoes. Tomato flesh or mushrooms, lightly fried in butter, are other good mixers.

Fritters Can be made with florets of cauliflower or sprouting broccoli, with celery or with sliced aubergines, Jerusalem artichokes or courgettes, etc. The important thing here is to blanch the cut-up or sliced vegetable first, just enough to partly tenderize, but not so long that it becomes soft and difficult to handle. Make sure too that a vegetable is compact – no stalks sticking out – otherwise such pieces are difficult to coat completely.

■ To give extra flavour, some vegetables are marinated, and others may be mixed with or coated in béchamel sauce before being dipped in the batter. The sauce should be thick enough to coat the back of a wooden spoon fairly thickly but smoothly, and used while just hot enough to set smoothly on the vegetable. Give the coated vegetables plenty of time to cool and set firmly, before dipping in the batter on a fork, otherwise you'll end up in a mess. Serve a savoury sauce with fritters when serving them as a separate course, e.g. mornay, mushroom or tomato, etc.

Purées Quickly reheated with butter or a little double cream, purées will be richer and twice as good as those served plain.

Roast vegetables Such as potatoes, Jerusalem artichokes and parsnips, are blanched for a few minutes first, to tenderize them partly, as well as to soften the outside and make them more fat absorbent. After draining and drying them, prick them all over with a fork.

Glazed vegetables Such as carrot, turnip and onions make an attractive garnish, because they're so shiny, colourful and tasty. Rather a lot of butter and sugar are used in the stock in which they're cooked so that the liquid, during the long slow cooking, reduces to a syrupy glaze in the bottom of the pan.

■ Roll the vegetables about in the glaze to make them shiny, then sprinkle with finely chopped herbs for additional colour and flavour.

Bought frozen vegetables These shouldn't, as a rule, come to too much harm before you get them home, because slight thawing won't spoil them, especially if they're still frosty.

■ Even if completely thawed, there's no health hazard, though freeflow, flavour and texture suffer. The 'do not re-freeze' instructions on packets protect manufacturers, who naturally and rightly want you to eat their produce while in tip-top condition. At the same time, it stops thoughtless people from thawing and re-freezing indiscriminately, which one must not do.

■ Vegetables fall into 7 main groups. Here are our most popular vegetables:

Roots	Tubers	Bulbous	Green leaves	Blanched stems	Flowers or heads	Fruits and seeds
beetroot	artichoke	garlic	Brussels	asparagus	artichoke, globe	aubergine
carrot	(Jerusalem)	leek	sprouts	celery	broccoli	avocado pear
parsnip	potato	onion	cabbage	chicory	broccoli,	beans
radish		shallot	chard, Swiss		sprouting	corn-on-the-cob
swede			and ruby		calabrese	courgette
turnip			kale (winter		cauliflower	cucumber
			greens)			peas
			lettuce			pepper, sweet
			mustard and			tomato
			cress			vegetable
			spinach			marrow
			watercress			

ARTICHOKES, GLOBE

see page 152.

ARTICHOKES, JERUSALEM

Really the tubers of a species of sun-flower, not artichokes at all. 'Jerusalem' is a corruption of *girasole*, Italian for sun-flower.

■ Artichokes are beastly to peel, and such an irregular shape that I prefer to slice them first – but you may like to eat them whole?

■ A tablespoon of lemon juice or vine-gar, added to both steeping and cooking water, helps to prevent rapid dis-coloration.

AUBERGINES

Also known as egg plant or egg apple, these have been used for centuries, and are one of the great vegetables of the world, varying widely in shape, size and colour. Though the pear-shaped fruits are most common, they may also be long and thin like a sausage, or round like a large ball. The colour ranges from ivory-white to yellow, and from the palest mauve to the deepest purple.

■ They must be fresh to be good: glossy, firm and of uniform colour. To make them less bitter and watery, see *dégorger*, page 59.

■ The skin is full of flavour and prevents them breaking up when cooked, so aub-ergines aren't usually peeled except for a salad or purée.

BEANS, BROAD

Can be one of the horrors of the British table. It may seem extravagant to pick them when no longer than your little finger, and when the flower is just with-ered, but that's the gourmet's broad bean, eaten complete with pod. (Extrav-agance is when one wastes a mountain of pods, to eat but a handful of their leath-ery contents.) Top, tail and wash them while tiny and tender, boil for about 10 minutes, and toss in butter with chopped savory or parsley.

■ The second stage for beans is when they're about as big as a good-sized pea. Boil them until tender, or blanch a few minutes before cooking in another way.

■ The third stage is the potentially grim one because so many people fail to blanch and skin them. How can anybody eat and swallow anything with such a flavour and texture? You can prepare them in advance of a meal if necessary, refrigerating them in a polythene bag: just a minute or two's blanching makes them firm and easy to handle, then after refreshing for another minute or two, they'll pop out of their skins (like almonds) when pressed.

■ Broad beans should be married to savory as peas are to mint: add a sprig to the cooking water, or chop the leaves finely to toss with the cooked beans and butter.

BEANS, FRENCH

Also called *haricots verts*, these are heavenly when young and small enough to eat whole; not more than ¼in/6mm thick, the seeds inside immature. If buying, be sure they're fresh and firm enough to snap crisply, too.

■ However one is going to cook them, French beans are usually boiled first until tender, or nearly tender, according to need.

■ French beans take an even greater trouncing than most other vegetables, in flavour, colour and texture, if either overcooked or kept hot.

BEETROOT

This and sugar beet are both members of the same family.

Beetroot 'bleed' and lose their flavour if you cut the roots, cut the stem too close to the top, or scrub them instead of just rubbing clean with your hands.

■ If you've never eaten tiny beetroot boiled for about an hour, and served hot (with butter or parsley butter and plenty of salt), you've missed something. (An unusual use is as a main breakfast dish in Sweden, but for the more conventional of us, they make an excellent hors d'oeuvre.)
■ Have you ever had beetroot au gratin, made with mornay sauce? It's good with something like hot-pot or a beef casserole.

BROCCOLI

The winter and early spring cauliflower.

BROCCOLI, SPROUTING

Like a cauliflower, but lots of small undeveloped flowering heads instead of a single large one. To eat at its best, serve as a course on its own rather than as an accompanying vegetable (eating it as asparagus with your fingers), with melted butter or one of the hollandaise family of sauces (page 171), e.g. hollandaise, maltaise, mousseline.

■ The very dark green variety, sometimes called calabrese, mainly from Italy and Spain, has clusters of quite large florets – and very little leaf.
To prepare, slit any thick stalks into two or four, to cook in the same time as the heads and thinner stalks – usually just about 8 minutes.
■ The florets make delicious fritters (page 181). Be sure to undercook them when blanching, otherwise they'll be too soft to handle.
■ Makes a lovely cream soup too.
■ See also *purple sprouting broccoli*, page 155.

BRUSSELS SPROUTS

A variety of cabbage brought to Britain from Belgium in the nineteenth century. How they're ill-treated – though I can't help feeling market gardeners and retailers (keener on size and weight than

on flavour) may be just as much to blame as we cooks. If everyone asked their greengrocer for small sprouts (and insisted on having fresh ones), we might eventually get the best. Meanwhile, nobody can stop those of us who have a garden from growing a small variety. In view of all this, it's hardly surprising that these monsters taste, look and smell as foul as they often do by the time they're tender if you don't cut them in half, or cut a cross in the stalk of any smaller ones left whole. This way, the heat penetrates them faster, so they cook quickly. Allow small garden or cut ones 6–8 minutes, slightly larger 8–10, to keep a brilliant green colour and slightly crunchy in texture. At all costs avoid overcooking or keeping them hot more than a few minutes – for I guarantee they'll be nasty to look at, smell and eat.

CABBAGE

Cabbage has been grown for its leaves for many centuries in many lands. There are two main classes, the smooth-leaved and the curly-leaved, or savoys. There are early and late varieties and although the majority we grow are green, there are white or purple ones as well. One can eat cabbage cooked, pickled or raw.

■ Cabbage is a mine of mineral salts, one of which is sulphur – the cause of its nasty smell when cooking. If you prefer varieties which don't smell when cooked – because the sulphur is hybridized out of them – they are of course inferior dietetically.
■ Though notorious among British vegetables, it isn't the fault of the poor cabbage! When properly cooked, it's a lovely colour, has a slightly crunchy texture and is full of flavour.
■ Cabbage needs the minimum of water (because it contains plenty of that already), fine shredding, lots of salt and the shortest possible cooking time to make it *al dente:* 8 minutes at the most.
■ After draining and pressing hard with the back of a wooden spoon or vegetable

184 1001 Ways to be a Good Cook

press in the colander, one can toss it with butter and flavour with chopped herbs, grated nutmeg, caraway seeds, or whatever you like.

■ If you're a health fan, serve red or white (Dutch) cabbage raw. Coleslaw ranks amongst the best of salads, see page 206.

Chinese cabbage Has some good qualities, others not so good, I think.

1 It takes up less room in a small vegetable garden than most other varieties because it grows tall and thin, like a huge cos lettuce.
2 Finely shredded, it boils in about 4 minutes – half the time most varieties take – but despite this is insipid. (Use lots of salt and flavour it in similar ways to ordinary cabbage.)
3 You can cook and eat the ribs like asparagus, and use the leaves raw in a salad if, unlike me, you enjoy its rather strange texture and flavour when used in these ways.

Red cabbage Flavourless if boiled, and loses its colour into the bargain. It may be an acquired taste, but red cabbage is usually considered best when braised with sour apples, or something acid, to flavour it and hold its colour. Long, slow cooking is essential to develop its full flavour, which some people find better still when reheated the next day, and yet again on following days.

■ Serve it with rich or strongly flavoured foods such as sausages, roast pork, venison, hare, roast goose or duck.
■ Makes excellent coleslaw.

Spring greens Young spring cabbages, before the heart is properly formed.

CALABRESE

A type of sprouting broccoli (see pages 183 and 155), with an abundance of green florets.

CAPSICUM

See *peppers, sweet*, page 190.

CARROTS

Contain precious vitamins and mineral salts. As so much of this goodness as well as flavour is in and close to the skin, it's much better just to scrub young ones well than to peel or even scrape them. One can peel old ones before or, more thinly, after cooking.

■ Carrots so often smell and taste almost nauseating, when they can (with a little know-how) just as easily be delicate and delicious, as, for instance, when sautéd (see page 180). A trick with old carrots is to slice them really thinly, or to cut them lengthways into six or eight pieces instead of four, to avoid that nasty strong flavour which develops during prolonged boiling or stewing.
■ *Fines herbes*, chives or basil buck up cooked carrots as a change from the eternal parsley garnish, and they are both tasty and cheerful when mixed with finely sliced mushrooms (previously cooked a few minutes in butter) and sprinkled at the last moment with a chopped herb of your choice.
■ Given time and patience (housewives can probably find neither, students may have to find both), one can make four small carrots from each of three or four large, to serve glazed as a garnish. Cut each one longways into quarters, then shape each quarter into a realistic looking carrot with a potato peeler.

Vichy carrots Carrots glazed in Vichy water in place of the usual stock. Carrots are supposed to be good for liverish people, the dish taking its name from Vichy, whose waters are considered particularly good for liver complaints.

CAULIFLOWER

A variety of cabbage grown for its undeveloped flower rather than for its leaves. Its name seems to derive from *cole flowers*, *cole* being the generic term for the Brassica family. If you grow cauliflowers, you may know that one picked with the morning dew still on it has a finer flavour than one uprooted later in the day after the sun has dried it up.

■ Cauliflower is at its best when cut into sprigs, because it cooks so quickly that both flavour and texture are perfect – boiled for just 5–10 minutes according to size.
■ If you prefer to cook it whole, cut a chunk out of the middle of the stalk, so that the heat penetrates the 'flower' quickly and speeds up cooking.
■ Blanched, refreshed cauliflower can be cooked in all sorts of ways, because it's bland enough to mix with other foods, yet has itself got lots of flavour and character. If you are likely to be short of time when actually cooking a meal, you can cook and refresh cauliflower earlier in the day, then reheat by steaming in a covered colander over boiling water for 2 or 3 minutes. It's not ideal, but is sometimes useful if you don't want to cut it into sprigs.

CELERIAC

Turnip-like in appearance, celery-like in flavour and unusual in texture, this ugly but interesting and good-storing vegetable has lots of uses: in salads (page 205); to flavour stocks, soups, sauces and stews; served in various ways as a vegetable. (I use it less as a vegetable than in salads and for flavouring.)

A few tips about its idiosyncrasies:

1 The smaller roots are usually less woody and you can peel them with less waste than big and/or knobbly ones: choose smooth ones if possible.
2 Unless you're for some reason cooking the whole root, scrub it, slice thickly or cut into pieces *before* peeling: peeling is easier and less wasteful this way.
3 Once cut, it discolours very quickly: before even reaching for a knife, prepare some acidulated water (1 tablespoon

vinegar or lemon juice to 2pt/generous litre water) into which to put the cut pieces straight away.
4 For the same reason, and in the same ratio, add vinegar or lemon juice to the cooking water as well.

■ Stored in a cool dark place, and if in good condition when bought, a root should keep at least a fortnight. See also page 205.

CELERY

Served raw with cheese, celery should have the root left on because this is one of the best parts: remove the coarse outer stems, and the leaves of all but the smallest heart stems, and trim the root to a slight point. Now cut the head into quarters, right down through the root.

■ However celery is to be cooked, most varieties need blanching for about 10 minutes first, to mellow the strong flavour.
■ Braised celery – especially good to serve with rich foods like pork or duck – needs long slow cooking to allow the flavours to blend perfectly together.
■ Celery loses its crispness in a freezer, but still makes a useful flavouring for soups, sauces or casseroles.
■ See also pages 205 (*salads*) and 102 (*herbs*).

CHARD, SWISS

Two vegetables in one. Grown essentially for its chards or mid-ribs, the outer green leaves one tears off can also be cooked, as spinach. Though I think you're unlikely to want it as often as, say, cauliflower, beans or peas, it makes (when young) an interesting change of vegetable for those with a garden, and space to grow it.

■ An easy (and my favourite) way to eat it is sautéd: first pull any strings off the chards, just as with coarse celery, cut the ribs into 2½–3in/6–8cm lengths, and then blanch or steam them, partly to

tenderize, before sautéing.
■ See also page 180.

COURGETTES

A great vegetable to have in the garden, at their best when small and tender, as the flower fades. They grow as fast as weeds – almost as you watch them – can be cooked in lots of different ways and freeze satisfactorily, sliced, halved or whole to make excellent soup.

■ Their skins are colourful and full of flavour so leave them on unless coarse, when pare off the ridges in stripes with a potato peeler.
■ Sliced or halved courgettes are sprinkled with salt and left to drain for an hour or so in a colander, to make them less bitter and watery (see *dégorger*, page 59). By the way, they're more attractive when sliced diagonally than cut straight across.
■ Despite their rather pronounced flavour, courgettes are amazingly versatile so for heaven's sake don't just boil them and coat with a white sauce! They make a lovely purée, are good *au gratin*, stuffed, sautéd or frittered, besides combining splendidly with other things like onions, tomatoes, herbs, spices, mushrooms, cream or nuts.

EGG PLANT

The American name for *aubergine*.

FENNEL, FLORENCE

A large bulbous root which looks like a monster head of celery, and is used similarly, though it tastes of anise. British grown fennel isn't always suitable to eat raw, due to its need for the right soil, as well as for sun and moisture.

HARICOTS VERTS

See page 182, *French beans*.

KALE

From the generic name of the Brassica family, *Cole*, kale is believed to be the original form of the great cabbage family. It has sprouting, curled, finely dented leaves which never form a solid heart or head.

■ Of different varieties, mostly with a strong flavour, it is often sold as 'winter greens'. Cook it like cabbage, or if you like it raw, you can shred and then wash it well and serve it as a dressed green salad, with or without lettuce, etc.

MARROW, VEGETABLE

Best eaten when so young that the seeds have hardly formed and the skin is tender enough to eat. When very small you can use them as courgettes, and the more you pick them the more you'll get.

■ For speed, to cut the seeded centre out of a sliced marrow, use a plain scone cutter, or slit it longways and scoop the centre out with a spoon.
■ Like other vegetables, you can blanch and cook marrow in all sorts of ways, but if you're thinking of boiling it, think again: steaming is better because the marrow is less watery, firmer in texture and has more flavour.

MUSHROOMS

Cultured mushrooms should be white, firm, fresh and crisp enough to eat raw when finely sliced. Don't allow yourself to choose or be fobbed off with limp and leathery ones, which neither fry nor grill well, however long you cook them in an effort to make them tender. One trouble is that mushrooms fried more than a few minutes develop a nasty strong taste and smell: watch what you're buying, and if you don't like the look of them, ask for fresh. (There are often better ones tucked away out of sight.)

■ Mushrooms go through three stages of growth, at each of which they may be better for one purpose than another:

1 *Buttons* haven't got much flavour, but are ideal for garnishing, since small, and best for sauces because they cause least discoloration.

2 *Cups*, half open, are best for salads and for general use. Cut the stalks off level with the caps when frying or grilling, then they won't shrink as much as when stalkless.

3 *Flats*, wide open, usually have the best flavour and are good for soup, casseroles and duxelles (a mixture used in stuffings, patties or a quick sauce).

■ Wipe rather than peel mushrooms unless very coarse, because the skins, like the stalks, contain lots of flavour. Slice the stalks finely before frying, sweating or stewing them with the mushrooms, or using them to flavour anything. Mushrooms are so watery that a few minutes cooking will reduce a pile of them, chopped, to 2 or 3 spoonfuls, so it's essential to get rid of some of this water before cooking them, when making something like a soufflé, duxelles, or stuffings: simply chop the mushrooms small, and squeeze the water out, by twisting them up tightly inside a clean piece of cloth.

■ Butter is the fat to give mushrooms a good flavour. They don't need much and, apart from bacon dripping, there's nothing to match it. Sautéd or sweated in butter, and flavoured with such things as shallots, herbs, spices, cream, or other vegetables, there are countless ways to serve mushrooms, not only as a vegetable or garnish, but as an important flavouring in innumerable dishes.

Mushrooms as a garnish Here are two easy ways to prepare them:

1 If without button mushrooms, make mushrooms of different sizes the same by using a scone cutter the size of the smallest. (Use up the trimmings in the main dish if suitable, or to flavour something else.) Incidentally, a scone cutter is a good way to make large mushrooms uniform in size too, say to serve stuffed.

2 Cut a large mushroom in half, through both cap and stalk, see below,

then slice each half finely from the centre outwards, to give several leaf-thin slices, as in fig 2. Use them raw on salads, or heat momentarily in butter to garnish something like a mushroom omelette or, say, fillets of fish.

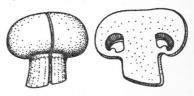

To freeze mushrooms While perfectly *safe*, it is not ideal because, being such watery things, they go mushy when thawed. Freezing concentrates their flavour, however, so though much too soft and squashy to fry or grill, they make a tip-top soup or sauce, or are excellent for a risotto or casserole, etc.

■ Wiped first, they'll freeze well for up to 6 months if blanched, only 3 months if not blanched.

■ If faced with a real glut of rather poor or very dirty field mushrooms, why not liquidize them and freeze the runny purée either in suitable quantities to make soup, or in ice trays? You can transfer the iced cubes to a polythene bag in the freezer and use them in the weeks ahead to flavour meat or fish dishes, sauces, vegetables, etc, or to make soup. (They'll lose out slightly on flavour if you haven't time or can't face wiping them individually by the bucketful, but in this case break the rules and wash them under a cold tap before liquidizing.)

OKRA

Native to tropical Africa but now grown in other parts of the world, these five-sided tapering bitter-sweet pods (known also as lady's fingers and gumbo) are probably best known for their use in Mediterranean and American stews, the sauce of which acquires an almost jellied smoothness from their gummy juices. The names okra and gumbo both derive from West African names of the plant which, like the first users, crossed the Atlantic with the slave trade. However you're going to cook them, they need a little know-how:

1 The pods (about 4oz/100–125g per person) should be firm and fresh-looking, a good green colour and small – not limp, large, coarse and brown down the edges. (Buy from a shop with quick turnover, e.g. where there are West Indian communities.)

2 To prepare, slice off the top of the stalk end, taking care not to cut into and expose the seeds, otherwise the pods will disintegrate when cooked. Wash well in a colander under running cold water.

3 To extract at least some of their gummy juices, either dégorgé (see page 59) okra for ¾–1 hour or, better still I think, soak them for ½–¾ hour in a vinegar/water solution: 4fl oz/125ml vinegar to ¾pt/500ml water (to cover about 1lb/400–500g pods). Rinse and dry, unless blanching or boiling.

4 Cook gently, to keep the pods' shape intact.

■ This is another vegetable I like best sautéd (blanched 5 minutes) and finally tossed in cream, black pepper, etc. (see page 180).

■ Good partners with okra, individually or together, are onions, shallots, peppers, aubergines and (especially) tomatoes.

■ Canned okra, for use in various ways, make a good larder store. Depending upon what you're going to do with them, it's generally best to rinse them under the tap to get rid of excess gumminess.

ONIONS

A native of Asia, and used the world over, onions are one of the basic aromatic vegetables of all European cookery. Anyone who doesn't like or can't eat them misses some of the greatest dishes there are: grounds for divorce, I think!

■ Many British onions are so pungent

that some people really can't digest them, so why not try a milder variety? I wonder why recommendations in gardening catalogues are usually about yield, size, shape, colour and storing qualities, but say so little about flavour? I'd put flavour and storing qualities first.

■ For anyone who finds onions indigestible, you can change their nature by boiling. Blanched for just 3–5 minutes before cooking in another way, they lose all their pungency. If you want to fry an onion after blanching, slice it finely first, blanch only one minute, then drain and dry.

■ Before mixing them with other ingredients, onions are frequently fried, to bring out their flavour. If fried with other watery vegetables such as courgettes or tomatoes, however, they tend to steam rather than fry so their flavour and aroma in the finished dish are less pronounced.

Spanish onions The large ones with a shiny golden skin, mild enough in flavour to eat raw in a salad and one of the best varieties to boil or braise. A *very* mild British onion can be used as a Spanish but shallots are better still.

Shallots Famous in French cookery, shallots are another garden vegetable I'd hate to be without. Delicate in flavour, they grow abundantly, store splendidly and one can use them all year round for sauces, stuffings, salads and general cookery. Usually more easily digested than onions, they also go squashy when cooked, which makes them ideal for certain sauces, and in preparations like duxelles. So if it's the stringy texture of an onion that you don't like, why not try shallots instead? They're splendid in salads too because, unlike other onions, one's palate doesn't retain the taste of raw shallots and spring onions.

■ When a recipe calls for shallots, you can often use spring onions instead, or sometimes even a finely sliced onion – blanched one minute, refreshed and drained.

Pickling or button onions The best for garnishing because they're small. They are always served whole.

■ A speedy, tearless way to peel them is by blanching in fast-boiling water for 15 seconds, not too many at a time. Drain and refresh them, drain again, and then trim the ends sparingly so as not to loosen the layers when slipping off the skin.
■ To tenderize them slightly, blanch for 2 minutes instead of 15 seconds.

Chopping onion or shallot finely is quick and easy as long as you don't cut the root off – that's what holds body and soul together. In case you're not sure how to do it, this is the way:

1 Remove skin, cut top off, and cut onion in half from top to root, and put cut side down on a board, root end to your left.

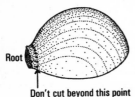

Root

Don't cut beyond this point

2 Slice it vertically, lengthwise, almost but not quite to the root, as illustrated.
3 Slice it horizontally, starting at the bottom and working up to the top – but still not through the root.

4 Cut it *across*, downwards, into dice, starting at right hand end.

■ Sliced onions are often sweated (see page 83) to soften without colouring them before cooking with other ingredients which take a shorter time to cook.
■ The reason why fried onions are so delicious and turn golden is because the sugar in them caramelizes.
■ If you can't get rid of the smell of onion on your hands, wash them in cold water and rub with salt. Now rinse under cold water again and then wash in the ordinary way.
Onion rings need to be small for a garnish. If you haven't got a small onion, simply remove the outer layers of a larger.
Dried sliced onions are not to be scorned. They're a useful standby to flavour something like béchamel milk for a white sauce when you're pressed for time, or if a dish only needs a hint of onion and it means cutting a whole one.
Frozen sliced onions are sometimes convenient too. One can either buy, or slice and freeze them oneself, raw or blanched. Store for only 4–6 months if raw, and be sure to seal them in a thick polythene bag, to isolate.

■ Tears seem to go hand in glove with sliced onions, unless you have some pet solution like standing a lit candle close by, slicing them under cold water or out in the fresh air, or refrigerating the onion an hour or so before you cut it to chill the juices which cause the tears. It's all apparently due to a chemical called *allyl isothiocyanate*. The eyes are particularly sensitive to it, so protect themselves by flooding with tears, to wash away the chemical.

PAPRIKA

The Hungarian name for a sweet pepper. See also below.

PARSNIP

An acquired taste perhaps – but worth acquiring. Unless sliced fairly thinly, it must be cored if not (when boiled) to be stringy.

■ Delicious roasted, like potatoes (page 193), or makes a most lovely soup (page 165).

PEAS, GREEN

They don't seem worth freezing unless from your garden. Bought by the sackful (time of picking usually unknown), their flavour after freezing may be indifferent, the economy is marginal compared with the cost of a large bag of frozen peas, and it's certainly a time-consuming and wearying job. The professionals, like Birds Eye, freeze their peas within 90 minutes of picking. If not processed within this time, peas evidently lose their sweet taste and green colour. Few of us can in addition be expert enough to know, as they do, even to the hour, when peas are at their most perfect to harvest – and also do so.

■ Really fresh peas will be crisp, bright green and smooth, 2lb/1kg yielding about 1lb/500g of small tender peas, or 1½lb/750g large.

■ Peas can be cooked in different ways according to their size and tenderness. Small garden peas cooked in the French way (sweated in butter with lettuce and spring onions), make a heavenly course on their own. Larger peas can be rejuvenated by blanching 5–10 minutes before cooking in another way, say sautéd, or sweated in butter. Peas are lovely too when tossed in mint butter.

■ Be sure to refresh (page 77) peas you plan to serve cold, say in a rice salad, to retain their flavour, texture and brilliant green colour.

PEAS, SUGAR

Also known as *mangetout*, these are a wonderful vegetable to grow, and are as easy to freeze as other peas are troublesome: they don't have to be podded.

■ Unlike other varieties which have a tough lining, this pea has a very tender pod so one can eat the whole thing, like asparagus, serving them as a separate course with melted butter. If you've never had them before, this is the technique:

1 Pick them when very young, before the pigeons want them, when the peas have just formed in the pod. Wash.

2 Boil in heavily salted water for 10–12 minutes until tender but still slightly firm – best to test one by eating.

3 Eat with your fingers, holding each by the stalk. Dip into salt and melted butter and pop into your mouth without leaving go of the stalk. Now close your teeth on it, pulling away the stalk, which will bring the two pod strings with it.

PEPPERS, SWEET

Also called pimientos or capsicum. They should be glossy, firm and free of wrinkles. Be choosy – why pay the same price for poorer?

■ If you're lucky enough to have your own greenhouse as well as enough sun, peppers make most attractive pot-plants, especially when some of the fruits turn red. They're almost too beautiful to pick.

■ If you only want quarter or half a pepper for a dish, interleave the remaining quarters and pop them in the freezer, without even blanching. Bought frozen sliced peppers are an excellent buy, and usually much better value than buying fresh peppers to freeze yourself.

■ People with an iron constitution seem to be able to eat peppers raw without suffering, while others enjoy them so much that they think the suffering is worthwhile. The considerate cook however may 'temper the wind' by blanching them for 2 or 3 minutes (and refreshing) before use as a garnish or in a salad, or before cooking them in another way. This not only makes them more digestible, but also takes the edge off their very strong flavour.

■ The tiny South African peppers, light as a feather, varied in shape and very beautiful, are extra hot.

POTATOES

Take their name from the Spanish *patata*, that name originating from the American word *batata*. They were first introduced to Ireland, and thence to Britain, from America in the late sixteenth century.

■ Potatoes can be one of the dreariest or one of the most exciting foods we eat, depending upon their variety and upon the cook! How incredibly lucky we are that this staple part of our diet is so bland that it will go with meat, fish or poultry – however cooked – and that the potatoes themselves can be cooked in literally scores of different ways as well. It's because of their mild flavour that we don't tire of them, and that we can cook them in a rich way to go with a fatless dish; in a simple way to go with a rich; make them crisp to serve with soft foods; colourful to partner colourless foods and flavourful to accompany bland ones. Practically anything one wants to do with potatoes one can do – but nothing is more boring than always boiling or mashing them.

■ Blanching often precedes cooking them in another way, just as with other vegetables. Potatoes can be blanched with their skins on, skins off, halved, sliced, or cut into balls with a baller. They should be tossed and dried off for a minute or so in the empty pan over very low heat if you're then going to put them into hot fat.

■ Lots of their flavour and food value is in and next to the skin, so more of both is retained if you blanch or boil potatoes before peeling. The skin then pulled away is much thinner than peel cut away with a knife or peeler. The main reason why jacket potatoes are so tasty, without even the addition of salt, is because nothing is lost, as into boiling water, and because we eat the whole thing.

■ New potatoes are a great source of vitamin C, so it's important not to prepare them hours before you need. What better or more delicious way anyhow than new potatoes dug, cooked and eaten within the hour? What worse potato than a variety such as Pentland Dales which, however good their yield to a farmer, are really no good to a cook – not unless you'll put up with a flavourless sodden mush whatever you try to do with them? The variety of potato you buy or grow does indeed make a difference to what you eat. My personal favourites for all-round use are Lincolnshire Whites, Maris Pipers, Wilja, Estima and the pink-skinned Desirée – though I find Desirée less good for deep-fat frying than for, say, baking or roasting.

■ Whether you're boiling old or new potatoes, they're best put into fast-boiling water, and the less they're cut up the better as this will save them breaking up when cooked.

■ To wash a potato pan, soak it in cold water rather than hot: hot tends to glue on rather than release starchy foods.

Potatoes fried in deep fat Irresistible to lots of us, even if they do mean an extra inch round the waist – chipped, croquettes, dauphine, Dunkirk, game chips, gaufrettes, knots, matchsticks, ribbons, potato puffs or anything else you can think of. All of these are worth trying if you haven't come across them before.

■ Besides knowing how to fry in deep fat (page 63) potatoes themselves have some peculiarities:

1 Raw cut-up potatoes need soaking in cold water for at least 30 minutes to get rid of some of their starch, otherwise the pieces stick together when fried. If you can only spare about 15 minutes, stir them round with your hands in a large bowl of water, changing it 2 or 3 times. You'll see how starchy it is.

2 Chips, etc. are dangerous to fry unless well dried, because the fat so easily foams up and bubbles over.

3 Thick potatoes, like chips, are best fried twice, the fat reheated in between; first to soften without colouring them, the second time to make crisp and golden.

4 Deep fried potatoes are salted after cooking, and of course, like other fried foods, go soft if you cover the serving dish.

Anna potatoes A little tricky to prepare because the potatoes have to be sliced to just the right thickness; about that of a new penny. If too thin, they curl up and won't overlap evenly, but if too thick they may not tenderize by the time the outside is golden.

■ Dry them very thoroughly, too, otherwise they'll cook in their own steam rather than in the butter – and *do* use butter, not margarine, for a lovely golden finish and perfect flavour.

■ Be generous with the quantity of potatoes you use because they shrink a lot when cooked.

Croquettes Made with duchess potato, these are difficult to cope with if the purée is too soft: dry off the potatoes in the empty pan for a minute or so over minimum heat after boiling, and mix the purée with egg yolk rather than whole egg, which is too watery for croquettes.

■ Let the purée go cold before rolling it into cork shapes because it's too soft and difficult to shape when hot.

Dauphine potatoes A mixture of choux pastry and duchess potato, these are potatoes at their most scrumptious. They make a heavenly garnish and accompaniment to grills or steaks. In case you haven't got the recipe, here it is, briefly, to serve 5–6:

> 12oz/375g duchess potato (see next entry)
> choux pastry, using 1 egg (page 139 if you need a recipe)
> seasoning and deep fat

Method

1 Heat deep fat to 360°F/180°C. (If too hot, the outsides will harden before the choux can expand, preventing them rising, as they should, to about the size of a large walnut.)

2 Slide rounded teaspoonfuls of the mixture carefully into the hot fat, frying several at a time but taking care not to overfill pan. Fry for about 6–8 minutes, or until golden all over, turning them after a few minutes.

3 Drain well on absorbent kitchen paper, serve very hot – and don't cover your vegetable dish with a lid.

Duchess potato Must be firm enough to hold its shape when piped, so it's important to beat the hot mashed sieved potato with egg, preferably just the yolk, rather than with milk. In addition, the egg binds and flavours it. Pipe the potato as required while still hot, otherwise it goes solid.

■ These are the approximate proportions: 1lb/500g potatoes, 1 egg or 2 yolks, 1½oz/40g butter or margarine, salt and pepper, pinch nutmeg.

Dunkirk potatoes Taste rather like a sophisticated version of roast. To be sure they're tender inside by the time they're crisp and golden outside, choose smallish potatoes of even size, blanch about 10 minutes, dry them off in the hot empty pan, and then deep fry about 20 minutes.

Game chips Have to be cut wafer thin, to curl up when fried. Slice them with the potato peeler illustrated on page 37 (if you have one) or by machine. If by hand, make sure they are so thin that you can see the knife blade through the slices.

■ Deep fat is used hotter than for ordinary chips, because game chips are so thin that by the time they're golden, the potato is cooked.

Jacket potatoes About the best of all healthwise, because there is no loss of goodness – or of flavour – into water thrown away. They are crisper than ever if you rub the skins with salt after washing them; or if you prefer them soft, rub the skins with oil before baking.

■ Jacket potatoes cook evenly and more quickly if impaled on a spike murphy, or with a couple of short metal skewers run through each. This is because the metal conducts heat through the middle, cooking the potatoes from the inside as well as from the outside. See page 42.
■ If not served fairly soon when cooked, jacket potatoes develop a nasty strong smell and taste. If necessary to keep hot, cut a cross in each, to help to keep them sweet longer.

New potatoes These contain lots of vitamin C so if you don't want to lose this, it's better to scrape them just before a meal than hours earlier. They are much easier to scrape when freshly dug – it's often this rather than the variety which makes new potatoes 'good scrapers'.

■ If the potatoes are tiny, it's quicker to skin them after boiling them than to scrape before – some people enjoy eating them in their skins, of course. Dried off in the empty pan and skinned when cool enough, they're lovely sautéd in butter, or make the best potato salad.

Potato puffs Made from smallish round potatoes sliced slightly thicker than a matchstick, and fried three times in deep fat. If either too thick or too thin, they won't blow up the third time they're fried, as they should. The fat should be about 380°F/190°C, the potatoes fried for 5–10 minutes the first time, until ten-

derish but not coloured, and a few minutes the second time until light golden. The third time they should be puffy and golden.

■ See also page 191.

Potato ribbons or knots Prepared differently from game chips, but fried in the same way. To make *ribbons*: slice a large peeled potato about ½in/1¼cm thick (the slices of a small potato are too difficult to handle), trim off any projecting points, then peel thinly round and round with a potato peeler (the old kind), making the ribbons as long as possible. Make *knots* the same way, but cut shorter ribbons, and tie a single knot in each. Dry them carefully, especially knots, otherwise they break easily. See also page 191.

Roast potatoes Often seem to take a hammering, poor things. There's more to roasting them than just laying potatoes round a joint, basting now and then. In case yours aren't exactly Ritzy, here are some tips:

1 Avoid using small potatoes because roasting dries them out too much.
2 Potatoes cook better if first blanched (boiled) for 5–10 minutes in well-salted water. Drain well in a colander, return to pan and dry them off a minute or two over minimum heat, to make them floury, agitating pan two or three times meanwhile.
3 Pierce all with a fork, in several places, to help them absorb a little of the fat and so keep them moist inside.
4 Put them into hot fat (oil makes them crispest I think), basting immediately. Baste and turn two or three times during cooking.
5 If a joint is likely to be 'watery', especially a frozen one which hasn't thawed out completely, roast the potatoes separately. Though potatoes get much of their delicious flavour from the roast, they'll be soft rather than crisp outside if cooked in fatty liquid instead of fat containing limited meat juices.

Sauté potatoes Aren't at all the same

thing as fried, being cut up and cooked *en masse* in hot butter for 15–20 minutes, the whole lot occasionally turned over with a fish slice.

■ New potatoes sauté best: boil them in their skins until nearly but not quite cooked, drain through a colander, return to the pan and dry them off for a minute or two over minimum heat, then allow to cool before skinning. If you want to skin them while very hot, spear them with a fork or protect your hand by wearing a rubber glove. Whether skinned or not, avoid covering the potatoes before they're cold because any trapped steam will make them wet.
■ It's best not to sprinkle sauté potatoes with salt while cooking because this makes them stick to the pan. If previously boiled in well-salted water, they won't lack flavour if you add a little more salt after sautéing.
■ Chopped herbs and freshly milled black pepper are also added at the last minute, their flavours being spoilt by cooking.

Storage A sackful of potatoes will probably keep better in an outshed (if protected from frost) than in a cellar, where the higher temperature is likely to make them shoot earlier and faster, so making them go soft before they should. It's essential to keep the shoots pulled off once they do start to grow – or the potatoes will go soft.

POTATOES, SWEET

A favourite of many South Americans, if not of mine! At a luxury price and with a very ordinary flavour (thought by some to taste of chestnut), these irregular-shaped tubers with a thick reddish skin and pinky-yellow flesh become, when cooked, more like a swede than a potato (to which they are in no way related). Although large and solid-looking, they tenderize more quickly than an ordinary potato and are easier to peel after than before boiling.

■ You may like to try them mashed – and beaten with butter, freshly milled black pepper and a sprinkling of nutmeg. After parboiling, you can roast them like potatoes (see page 193) or slice and fry them.
■ I've never had them, but I'm told the white-fleshed, red-skinned potatoes are good puréed, then mixed with butter and sherry.

RHUBARB

Really a vegetable, though regarded and used as a fruit. The leaves contain a toxic element, making them unsafe to eat.

■ In some parts of the world, rhubarb has long been used medicinally for its purgative qualities, and only comparatively recently has it been used in Britain as a food.
■ Many arthritics won't eat it – afraid of its acidity.

SPINACH

Must be washed and re-washed until there's no sign of earth; the water clinging to its leaves is all it needs to cook in.

■ Spinach can be puréed in seconds in a food processor or with the coarsest cutter of a Moulin-légumes, either of which are much quicker than a liquidizer. If you find spinach too bitter, or don't care for it, have you tried adding a pinch of sugar? As for butter or margarine, it will absorb almost any amount one cares to add; or is richer and creamier still with double cream – single tends to be too watery.
■ Spinach purée goes twice as far, and is delicious, stirred into a creamy béchamel or mornay sauce.

SWEDE

A purée of swede is less watery with some potato purée and a little butter or margarine beaten into it. Swede is quite good sautéd too, this again making it less watery, besides giving a dull vegetable some character. See page 180.

SWEET CORN

Grown as a vegetable, sweet corn contains both sugar and starch, differing from field corn, which isn't sweet, and is more starchy. Nobody need explain the difference to you if you have ever tried eating field corn as sweet corn!

■ Grown in your garden, just turning yellow, and eaten within an hour of being picked, sweet corn is a magically different vegetable from the beautiful-looking golden, but over-ripe corn cobs we see lined up in the shops. Do try growing it, if you haven't already. The tiny end-of-season ones are sometimes the best of all – you may even be able to eat the whole thing, cob as well.

■ Frozen sweet corn-on-the-cob is one of the few vegetables which need thawing, completely, before being cooked.

TOMATOES

Tomatoes keep fresh longer, look more cheerful and are easier to eat for a picnic if you leave the stalks on. They really mostly need skinning though, and it's important just to loosen the skins without spoiling the flesh – which happens if blanched too long. Cover with boiling water for only 10 seconds, before plunging into cold water and skinning.

■ Tomatoes are too watery, and the seeds too bitter, to use as they are for such things as an omelette, tomato purée or ratatouille. If a recipe calls for tomatoes to be juiced and seeded, therefore, cut them in half and squeeze gently, to leave only the flesh.

■ The bitterness of tomatoes can be counteracted easily in soups, sauces and sandwiches, etc. by adding a spot of sugar; and if you've never fried in butter, tomatoes sprinkled with sugar as well as with seasoning, you have a treat in store. The sugar caramelizes and gives them a completely different flavour, as well as sweetening.

■ Halved tomatoes are grilled round side up first, while still firm, and cooked long enough, altogether, to soften them without also losing their shape.

■ Skinned tomatoes freeze well for some purposes: either open freeze them before sealing and freezing, or cut them up and freeze in an ice tray.

■ *As a garnish*, quartered tomatoes are usually better than sliced, because slices tend to disintegrate. If one cuts the core out of each quarter with a sharp knife, it will take the seeds with it, and the tomato won't spoil the appearance of a dish by its wateriness.

■ You can make a *miniature tomato* from each seeded quarter if you put them, one at a time, round side down in a piece of butter muslin, then draw the tomato up into a ball, by twisting the muslin tightly around it. They look attractive in an hors d'oeuvre, glazed with aspic, or for a tomato salad, sprinkled with French dressing. Heat lightly in butter if required hot, say to garnish a sweet pepper in place of the stalk, or in a potato nest.

■ Unripe tomatoes deteriorate at temperatures below 50°F/10°C, the damage being progressive. After this, even if they redden, they'll never develop a true tomato flavour. To ripen green tomatoes *not* exposed to such cold, simply lay them on top of your refrigerator at normal room temperature for a few days.

TRUFFLES

The finest black truffles are found in the Périgord district of France; the best 'white' (in fact they're really pale brown and beige) in the Piedmont region of Italy. Scarce even there, because they defy cultivation, they are (at £100 per lb/500g) a food for the gourmet. Besides needing the right soil, climate, air and light, the truffle has a symbiotic relationship with certain tree roots, principally the oak, and is snuffed out by piglets or dogs trained to the smell of truffle-flavoured meat. (A fully grown pig is too strong to pull off before it guzzles them itself.) People own truffling rights in the same way as we may own fishing or shooting rights. This hard, knobbly, pungent, subterranean (a few centimetres down) fungus is used essentially for its pervasive fragrance and elusive flavour, which far exceed its actual taste. Its aroma even penetrates unbroken (porous) egg shells, enabling one to make truffle-flavoured scrambled eggs without using even a fraction of the truffle just by keeping them in a sealed jar together for 24–48 hours. Very fine slices (of a thoroughly washed truffle) placed on food and stored overnight in a closed container in the refrigerator will also pass on their fragrance. In addition to scrambled eggs and omelettes, they are used particularly to flavour foie gras, certain soups, sauces and stuffings, salads, risotto, and as a garnish.

■ If not used as above, or raw, black truffles are added to a cooked dish at the last minute. White truffles, which have a distinct peppery taste I am told, are usually sliced (there's a special slicer, which cuts razor thin) raw directly on to the dish when it comes to the table – or at most just heated through by the food they garnish.

■ Even in Paris, people may order just one truffle for a special occasion: costing perhaps £25 (as I write) each, it's not so surprising!

■ There's no substitute for fresh truffles. Canned ones have only a fraction of the aroma, and may never originally have been of the highest quality.

■ See also *périgourdine* and *piémontaise*. page 74.

TURNIPS

Traditionally served, and at their best, with fatty meats such as pork, sausages, ham, mutton, goose and duck, because when cooked in or with fat they can absorb large quantities of it. If turnips are

simply boiled, it's the lack of fat which makes them so unappealing.

■ Except the small tender early ones, turnips are better blanched, before being cooked in another way. Sliced or quartered, this helps to tenderize them and gets rid of their very strong flavour at the same time.

■ Have you tried glazed turnips? They're delicious. See page 181.

WINTER GREENS

Another name for *kale* (see page 186).

YAMS

The large bulbous root (there are about 250 different species) of a tropical plant with white flesh not unlike that of a Jerusalem artichoke. From all I have read, they are declared tasteless, while the only instructions given for their cooking seem to be (as Jane Grigson points out in her *Vegetable Book*) 'cook in most ways as potatoes or sweet potatoes'. In fact, I find boiling them – the most obvious method of all – to be horrendous. Even mashed with butter and pepper they are unpleasant because of their extraordinary texture and complete lack of flavour.

■ After peeling deep enough to expose the white flesh, and trying them in various other ways as potatoes, a long story can be cut short by saying that the only ways I personally enjoy a yam are sautéd (see page 180), or boiled, sliced and fried in butter: the unpleasant texture of the boiled or creamed yam becomes an interesting one – reminding me somewhat of a roast chestnut.

ZUCCHINI

The Italian name (also used by the Americans) for courgettes.

10

Pulses, pastas and rice

With potatoes, fish and meat all rising astronomically in price, and a greater awareness of the relationship between wise eating and good health, more and more of us are looking for new alternatives. Seeing the demand, health food shops have sprung up in almost every town, and display such an array of specialized and 'whole' foods that, knowledgeably used, they have given a new dimension to the diet and table of many. For those seeking detailed information, these same shops also often sell specialized recipe books.

PULSES

These, the seeds formed in the pods of leguminous plants, have been grown throughout the world for over 10,000 years, and include dried peas, beans and lentils. When the potato and maize arrived in Europe from the New World in the sixteenth century, pulses came to be regarded as the poor man's diet and fell out of favour. The revival of their popularity in recent years is not only because people are eating fewer animal foods but also because pulses are comparatively inexpensive and very nutritious, with valuable (if incomplete) protein, B vitamins, calcium, iron and a high roughage but low calorie content. They also store well for months, some indefinitely, and can be used as a main dish, as an accompanying vegetable, in casseroles, soups, salads, spreads, desserts and, the more colourful ones, for garnishing other dishes.

■ After soaking and cooking, most pulses

rather more than double in size and weight, the soya bean and chick pea trebling. Generally speaking, allow 2oz/50g per person.
■ Pre-packed beans usually only need rinsing before soaking but, if you don't want to risk breaking a tooth sometime, cast your eye through the cheaper loose beans sold directly from the sack. (Foreign bodies may include anything from grit to stones, not to mention pods and twigs, etc.)
Soaking After rinsing, all pulses (lentils and black-eye beans excepted) should be soaked in at least twice their volume of water in a large basin for at least 8 hours, preferably overnight. Avoid adding anything to the water: salt, lemon juice or vinegar, for instance, prevent its absorption by the pulse, so the object of soaking is partly defeated. Unsoaked beans, even after long cooking, are too hard and indigestible to eat – and also cause flatulence.
■ With a pressure cooker, only 6 hours soaking is necessary – apart from soya beans which need 24 hours.
■ If soaking the previous day slips your memory, there is a short cut: put the washed pulse in a pan with plenty of cold water, bring to the boil and simmer for 15 minutes. Set aside from the heat and leave for 1–1½ hours, tightly covered. Finally, boil in clean water.

Cooking – hows and whys

1 The simplest method is by boiling: strain off and throw away the soaking water, rinse the pulse again and, covered generously by fresh cold water, bring slowly to the boil in a covered saucepan.

Type of pulse	Approx. cooking time after soaking	Pressure cooking	Comments
Beans aduki	40–60 mins	10 mins	One of the smallest beans, reddish brown in colour and grown throughout the Far East. A strong nutty flavour which enhances both savoury and sweet dishes.
black	1–1¼ hrs	10 mins	Widely used in South American and Caribbean cookery. Use at any time in place of red kidney beans, e.g. in soups, casseroles, salads. (Boil 10–15 minutes.)
black-eye	30 mins	8 mins	Smallish creamy-white beans with a black spot on the hymen. You can cook them without soaking (allowing ½ hr longer) because thinner-skinned than most other beans.
butter	1½-2 hrs	15 mins	Soak at least overnight. Much better to eat if skinned. (After quick blanching, or after cooking, 'pinch' them out, like almonds.) Traditional partner of boiled bacon.
cannelini	1–1½ hrs	10 mins	Pinky-beige in colour and one of the haricot bean family – in place of which they can be used at any time.
flageolet	1–1¼ hrs	10 mins	Pretty pale green beans (haricots harvested while young and tender), but expensive – unjustifiably so for such a dull flavour, I think. Use as a salad vegetable or serve hot with meat (especially lamb) or a firm-fleshed fish such as monkfish. (I find them too flavourless for soup.)
haricot	1–1½ hrs	10 mins	Immortalized (in tomato sauce) by Heinz! Use in casseroles or as a vegetable: especially good when tossed in butter and mixed with a little fried onion and (juiced, seeded, chopped) tomato flesh.
kidney, red	1–1½ hrs	15 mins	Very colourful in salads and rice dishes. Boil rather than simmer for the first 10–15 minutes.
mung	40–60 mins	10 mins	Very small olive green beans. Use cooked or sprouted. Rich in vitamins A and B, but five times *more* nutritious when sprouted, then containing vitamins C and B 12 in addition (the only source of these vitamins to be found in pulses).
pinto	1–1½ hrs	10 mins	Pretty speckled beans which change to a pinkish colour when cooked. Good for salads.

Type of pulse	Approx. cooking time after soaking	Pressure cooking	Comments
soya	3 hrs	25 mins	One of the world's most important foods, for 5,000 years a vital part of the diet of millions in the Far East, especially China: they contain about 40 per cent protein and include all except one of the essential amino acids. Allow extra-long soaking (in the refrigerator during hot weather, as they ferment easily) because they are one of the hardest of all beans.
Lentils brown	30 mins	8 mins	Good with game. Cook to a purée, or just to the point of tenderness and eat whole. Sometimes used to extend meat, e.g. in a meat loaf or cottage pie. Can be cooked without soaking, but allow 45 minutes.
green	30 mins	8 mins	Rather insipid, so enhance their flavour with onion, seasonings, herbs or whole spices. Cook as brown lentils above, allowing 45 minutes if unsoaked.
red	15 mins	6–8 mins	Egyptian lentils – the most generally used. The inner starch part of the whole lentil, they disintegrate very quickly when cooked, which explains why they make lovely soup and are suitable for dishes based on a purée. Unsoaked, cook 20 mins.
Peas black-eye			See *beans*, black-eye, above.
chick	2–2½ hrs	25 mins	Used widely in the Middle East, North Africa and Southern Europe. Nutritious but very hard, they need long soaking and long cooking. These creamy-coloured round knobbly peas are mainly used in casseroles, or are served as a separate dish.
marrowfat	1½–2 hrs	10 mins	Large, dried, pale green peas. Make a purée, use in casseroles or make soup. Soak at least overnight.
split	30 mins	8 mins	Like the red lentil, the inner part of the whole pea. Yellow or green (often sold in health food shops), use them in soups, casseroles or as purée. Pease pudding is the classic partner of boiled pickled pork, or is excellent with baked gammon or bacon. Use herbs, spices and onions etc. with subtlety to complement their flavour. Unsoaked, cook ¾–1 hr.

The boiling/simmering time required by different pulses to tenderize depends upon their type (see chart), on how long they were soaked, and how they are cooked.

2 Salt is added during the last few minutes of cooking: put in at the beginning, it retards the absorption of the water, and so inhibits tenderizing.

3 Add a flavouring to the cooking water if liked, e.g. a skinned shallot or onion, a carrot, piece of celery, bouquet garni.

4 Bicarbonate of soda in the cooking water speeds up the softening process but kills the B vitamins: never use it.

5 Beans are boiled rapidly for 10 minutes initially to kill their harmful enzymes. This therefore rules out the use of a slow cooker.

6 Test for tenderness by pressing a bean between your fingers and, for the larger varieties, by biting: although they may feel soft outside, they may still be hard inside.

7 A pressure cooker greatly reduces cooking times, see chart, but it is more complicated to test when a pulse is tender. The pan should not be more than half-filled, including liquid, as some pulses may bubble up through the safety valve while under pressure. (Adding a tablespoon of vegetable oil to the ingredients helps to prevent this.)

■ Use any remaining liquor as stock for soups, sauces or casseroles. It's full of flavour as well as nutritious.

■ Soaked or cooked beans can be stored a few days in the refrigerator. If necessary to keep them longer, they freeze well.

For a salad To be perfect, beans must be *just* tender, still retaining their shape. The appearance and texture of a salad may be spoilt if the beans disintegrate when tossed with other ingredients. Use a sharp French dressing – about equal parts oil and vinegar – and toss the cooked beans in it while still hot, to absorb flavour from it as they cool. Because of their mealy texture, beans make the best salads when mixed with crisp and crunchy

things like celery, raw cabbage, nuts, etc.

For casseroles and soups Overcooking matters less and may even improve the dish, thickening and adding flavour to the liquor as beans then do.

PASTA

The Latin name for a paste. Probably invented about 6,000 years ago by the Chinese. Made from durum wheat – a very hard wheat grown in North America and Italy – pastas now come in all shapes and sizes, some flavoured with tomato or coloured green by spinach: alphabet, shells, whirls, spirals, tubes, wagon wheels, quills, stars, bows, noodles of varying sizes (e.g. thread, baby, broad), lasagne, cannelloni, vermicelli, spaghetti, macaroni, and so on. In addition, there are wholewheat pastas which have a slightly nutty flavour and are popular with weight-watchers and the health conscious: nutritious, low in calories and more satisfying than pastas made with refined ingredients.

■ Basically bland, dry and starchy, pastas need other foods to complement them. These may take the form of a rich sauce (from which a dish often takes its name, as in spaghetti bolognese), or in simpler flavourings and fats such as herbs, spices, fried bacon rashers, butter, olive oil, Parmesan cheese, cream, etc.

■ Although many people today make their own pasta, most people buy it (fresh or dried) ready made. When well cooked, it can form the basis of many quick, nutritious and yet reasonably priced meals – or may be included in soups, salads and even, in some cases, desserts. If a substantial dish, there may be no necessity to serve anything before it, while with it, a tossed green salad may be quite enough. To follow, I like usually to serve fruit in some form, e.g. baked apples, compôte, sorbet or even just fresh fruit.

To cook

1 Use a large, strong pan about two-

thirds filled with well-salted water. This allows not only for the pasta to expand but, more importantly, for it to keep moving.

2 Add the pasta gradually to the fast-boiling water, so that the water never goes off the boil – then it can't settle on the pan bottom. Cook without a lid, and keep the heat under the pan as high as possible without letting the contents boil over. If the water does go off the boil, use a fork to keep the pasta moving until boiling again.

3 Cooking time is nearly always stated on the pack and depends upon the type and thickness of the pasta and upon whether it is fresh or dried. Spaghetti, whirls and many other varieties for instance take 10 minutes, while smaller and thinner types may take as little as 6 minutes and some fresh pasta as little as 30 seconds. Pastas (like lasagne) may sometimes be only partially cooked by boiling, the remaining time being completed by baking.

4 A tablespoonful of oil in the cooking water works magic, preventing pasta from sticking either to itself or to the pan.

5 To put spaghetti into boiling water, hold it upright – like a bunch of flowers in a jug – and coil it round the inside of the pan as the lower ends soften in the water.

6 Drain pasta immediately it is cooked (see *al dente*, page 51), otherwise it continues to cook – and goes soft – even though the pan has been set aside from the heat. Overcooked pastas are heavy and glutinous.

7 If serving pasta hot, pour scalding water through it after draining to take away any glueyness – unless you're just about to toss it in butter or a really good olive oil. If serving it cold, say for a salad, cool it quickly under cold water, forking it occasionally as it cools again to prevent it sticking together.

8 Tongs are useful for lifting lasagne out of the boiling water, and a special pasta spoon eases the serving of long stringy kinds.

9 Use a warmed dish and eat without delay.

■ An easy alternative way to cook spaghetti is to boil it fast for 2 minutes, stirring continuously, then set it aside from the heat, cover with a tight-fitting lid and leave for 10 minutes.

RICE

Known to have been cultivated in China as long ago as 5,000 BC and in different countries for century after century, rice has meant life for millions, the only source of food for many. Though there are said to be 7,000 different types – and all rice-eating peoples have varied ideas about how it should be cooked – the rice we buy is mainly of two kinds: long grain and short grain. Various other kinds are available, of course, some only if one is prepared to hunt for them.

■ Rice will keep indefinitely as long as it's dry.

Long grain rice The long thin grain variety which originally came only from Patna, is used for things like curries, salads or kedgeree, which require the grains to be kept separate.

■ Many people think that because it is more expensive than short grain, it will make a better rice pudding. It won't, however, because it doesn't absorb the milk, nor does it go so creamy.

■ Long grain rice like 'Uncle Ben's' is a high quality rice with grains which remain separate when cooked, but it takes longer to cook than the above. Follow directions given on the packet.

Short grain 'pudding' rice The type needed for rice puddings and other sweet dishes, because it absorbs the milk well, is very white, and goes creamy when cooked.

Brown rice The whole unpolished grain, with only the husk removed. It is eaten by peoples whose principal nourishment is rice, because it's a vital source of the vitamin B complex – which we in the West can get from other foods in our traditional diet: brown bread, eggs, milk, cheese and so on.

■ Brown rice has a nutty, stronger flavour than polished, so is served with things like steaks, stews, game or roast duck. Use it too in stuffings, or substitute it for polished rice where its brown colour doesn't matter. It should be chewy, not soft, when cooked, taking about 35–40 minutes – a little less if soaked for an hour first.

■ As it's about twice the price of polished rice and takes nearly four times as long to cook, I myself can see no reason to buy it unless one lives on a special diet or enjoys its flavour.

■ *Short grain brown rice* can often take the place of short grain pudding rice above but, like long grain brown rice, needs longer cooking. If using it in a milk pudding, for instance, soak the grain for at least an hour in the milk before baking, and even then cook the pudding longer – otherwise it won't have time to absorb all the milk, and will end up runny. I'm not too sure that I like its flavour, but it makes an interesting change.

Italian rice A thick stubby grain with a hard central core: the kind to use for risotto, see below. It absorbs at least twice its volume of liquid (i.e. 1 cup rice, 2 cups liquid) and becomes creamy during long slow cooking (25–30 minutes), although still retaining a little 'bite'.

■ Use rice in soups; as a vegetable entrée; as an accompaniment to fish, meat or other vegetables; as the basis of a main dish; as a salad, sweet, pudding or savoury.

Boiled rice A problem to many cooks, unless they use 'packet' rice, when one should follow the instructions given. I make no claims to the expertise of anyone native to a rice-growing country, but I do know the grains must be separate, so here are a few tips:

1 *Ordinary long grain rice* needs washing thoroughly, to remove the mill flour which, if not washed out, makes the cooked rice gluey: hold it in a strainer for a minute or two under a fast-running cold tap.

2 Use a large strong pan and deep, generously salted water, so that the swollen rice has plenty of room to boil fast without boiling over.

3 Shake the rice from the strainer into the fast-boiling water – gradually, so that it never goes off the boil – and now boil it fast enough to keep the rice continually 'dancing'. (Don't cover with a lid, or the water will boil over.)

4 Boil the rice for 10 minutes until *al dente* (page 51): test either by eating a grain, or press one between your thumb and finger.

5 Drain thoroughly, then pour either boiling or cold water through, according to whether it is to be served hot or cold, to separate the grains.

6 When rice needs stirring, use a two-pronged meat fork (page 26): you're sure to make it mushy by using a spoon.

7 Dry it out if you like in a colander over a pan of simmering water, covered with clean, dry, loosely folded cloth.

To freeze cold boiled rice, put in an ice tray, without dividers, to quick-freeze in a shallow block. Remove from the tray and seal in a thick polythene bag before returning it to the freezer.

Rice in the Persian way From a friend who spent many years in that country, I have learnt this easy-for-entertaining and lovely way to serve rice:

1 Boil it as above (but several hours or even days before needed), running cold water through it when boiled. Cover and refrigerate.

2 Using a strong saucepan, melt – without heating – 2oz/50g butter (not margarine) for each 8oz/225g rice previously boiled.

3 Aside from the heat, add the rice and some extra salt. Stir with a two-pronged fork until every grain glistens, then cover and leave it until required.

4 At least an hour before you want to serve it, stand the pan over low heat, cover the rice with only a loosely folded

clean tea-towel and leave it, untouched, until time to serve. The crunchy golden rice on the bottom of the pan is the high-spot, while every grain is separate and delicious.

Kedgeree See page 220.

Pilaff This takes its name from the finest Indian rice known as pillau, of which pil-law and pillaff (amongst others) are varieties. Any of these names, and more besides – pilaf, pilau, pilaw, for instance – are now commonly used in culinary terms and always imply a dish prepared with rice.

Risotto Takes its name from the Italian word for rice, *riso*. For the authentic dish, none other than Italian round grain rice is perfect. Its excellence is that dur-ing long slow cooking, and in a small amount of liquid, it manages to remain *al dente* while at the same time becoming creamy. See *Italian rice*, above.

■ Rice for risotto is cooked in a totally different way from boiled rice. It isn't washed because there's no need to remove the mill flour, and because it must be dry, to fry in the hot butter or oil.
■ If you can't buy Italian rice, it is better to use short grain pudding rice than long grain, because it absorbs the stock better.

11

Salads, salad components and salad dressings

GENERAL INFORMATION

The great thing about salads is their freshness – their fresh flavour, crisp texture and colourful appetizing appearance.

■ *The flavour* depends upon using tender young vegetables (whether raw or cooked), salad plants or fruits, and tossing them in various piquant dressings. Some vegetables need to be marinated longer in the dressing than others to develop their full flavour, while certain cooked vegetables will have more flavour if turned over in the dressing while still hot – and left in it to cool.

■ *The texture* of a cooked vegetable salad depends upon the vegetables being perfectly cooked and, if not left to cool in the dressing, upon being refreshed – plunged straight into cold water after being cooked and drained, as before deep freezing. The texture of salad plants depends upon them being well dried and unhandled after washing (see *salad basket*, page 15), upon being crisped in the refrigerator if appropriate, and upon being dressed at the last moment to avoid sliminess.

■ *Colour* is no problem if cooked vegetables are refreshed, and as long as foods are not prepared too soon. Tomatoes, especially, go dull, and green vegetables lose their fresh colour when left too long in a dressing. Contrasting colours like those of beetroot, tomato, radish, carrot and red pepper should be used in moderation.

■ From a health point of view, raw vegetables and salad plants are as good, if not better, sources of vitamin C than fresh fruit. Dressings make up for vegetables' deficiency in fat, as well as giving piquancy and helping the digestion of rich foods they may accompany.

■ It's surprising how many vegetables normally eaten cooked are good raw, when properly prepared and dressed. As in a fresh fruit salad, so many of their flavours mingle well together. Finely sliced mushrooms or green of leek, wafer-thin sliced courgettes, very young peas, tiny broad beans, finely sliced Brussels sprouts, or green or red cabbage are just a few examples.

■ Salads, besides being served with cold dishes, may be the backbone of a mixed hors d'oeuvre, or just the right thing to serve with a grill or roast. With hot fish, meat, poultry or game, a piquant salad not only clears the palate but enhances the flavour of the main dish too. Served individually and eaten direct from a salad plate, there's no chance of the hot meat plate spoiling the salad's crisp texture, nor of the salad dressing spoiling the main dish and its accompaniments.

■ Vegetables à la Grecque are highly flavoured cooked vegetables. They're sometimes combined with others in a mixed salad, or served in a mixed hors d'oeuvre.

AVOCADO PEAR

Prepare (see page 154), then mix the sliced or diced avocado in a sharp French dressing with, say, chopped dessert apple and/or walnuts, orange and/or grapefruit segments, tomatoes or any other suitable fruit or vegetable.

BEANS, BROAD

Delicious raw in a salad if they're really young and tender, marinated about half an hour in a vinaigrette dressing. Alternatively, cooked beans are equally good as long as they're refreshed straight away after boiling, then marinated as raw. See also page 182.

■ Chopped savory, added at the last minute, is a good partner for beans.

BEANS, FRENCH AND RUNNER

Keep their firm texture, lovely flavour and brilliant colour best if you refresh them immediately after boiling, drain well, and then marinate them in a dressing for about half an hour. I like them better this way than allowing them to go cold in the dressing, as some people recommend.

BEETROOT

Needs to be marinated and turned over several times in dressing for at least 3 or 4 hours after it has been cooked, otherwise it tastes dead, just like cold beetroot in fact!

■ The way you cut beetroot has an extraordinary effect upon its flavour: served chilled, and sliced wafer-thin, diced or cut into strips, it makes quite a different salad from thickly sliced beetroot served at room temperature.
■ Beetroot makes a bad garnish because it discolours anything it touches. *For* beetroot, as a last-minute colour-giver, chopped chives, parsley, or finely sliced shallots or spring onions both relieve its redness and give extra flavour.

CAULIFLOWER SALAD

Just about uneatable if you allow a cooked cauliflower to *go* cold, but it's a totally different thing if you boil its sprigs for a few minutes until tender but still firm (see page 185), refresh and drain them, then marinate an hour or two in the dressing.

■ Bouquets of cauliflower make a change in a mixed hors d'oeuvre: simply press 3 or 4 cooked refreshed florets lightly together to form a well-rounded surface, which you can then coat evenly and easily with mayonnaise.

CELERIAC

Like celery, this is a super addition, both for its flavour and texture, to all kinds of salads. Unlike celery, however, celeriac is not at its best raw unless prepared at the very last minute, because it discolours so quickly when cut. Unless you prefer simply to grate it at the last moment, this is a good way to deal with celeriac for a salad:

1 Prepare as on page 185.
2 Slice each thick piece to matchstick thickness, putting straight into the acidulated water. One by one, now dice or cut each into matchstick-sized strips or as wanted.
3 Blanch for 2 minutes in acidulated boiling water, drain, refresh (see page 77) and drain again to mellow the flavour and keep it white. Cover and chill until needed.
4 Use as required, e.g. in coleslaw, in a fish salad, mixed with other refreshed vegetables in mayonnaise or a cream dressing, etc.

■ As even a small root is often more than I need for a salad, I freeze the remainder and am never without it. Slice it thinly as above, blanch, drain, refresh and drain again, and then open-freeze (page 63) for 20–30 minutes, or until firm. Seal and freeze in the usual way and use in salads or to flavour.

CELERY

Gives a crunchy texture and lovely flavour to almost any salad, combining well with salad vegetables and many fruits, including nuts. With something like an oil and vinegar dressing, a cream or soured cream dressing, or mayonnaise thinned down with cream, the delicious sort of mixtures which come to mind are:

coleslaw (below);
waldorf salad (celery, dessert apple, walnuts, raisins);
rice salad (rice and, say, peas, sweet corn, celery, peppers, etc.);
celery and orange salad;
celery, tinned pineapple, sultanas (soaked for 10 minutes in hot water).
See also *celeriac*, page 205.

CHICORY

The names endive and chicory are muddling because the French call our chicory *'endives'* and our endive *'chicorée'*. It's high time we sorted this out because a French menu may mislead some of us.

■ Avoid buying chicory heads which are beginning to turn green, because they're bitter. The plump white ones are best. Chicory usually only needs wiping as it's seldom dirty inside, but do slice it with a stainless steel knife, otherwise you'll spoil its flavour.
■ Chicory is mild enough to mix well with lots of fruits and vegetables when sliced finely or cut into ½in/1¼cm chunks and then separated out. The larger leaves make good 'boats', filled with a dressed salad, say the remaining chicory, finely sliced and mixed with chopped apple and dates.
■ French dressing with a clove of garlic is the classic partner for chicory and endive, but you may prefer a cream dressing.

COLESLAW

Sounds infinitely more tempting than cabbage salad, which is what it is. *Cole* is the generic name for any plant of the Brassica family, and *slaw* derives from the Danish word for salad. This explains why it's never called coleslaw salad. We have the Americans to thank for thinking up this scrumptious recipe which, with a little imagination, you can concoct in various ways with different fruits and dressings.

■ White Dutch cabbage or red cabbage make the best coleslaw, because of their nutty flavour, crispness, and because either is so solid that, with luck, they won't need washing. This is a big plus, because if you have to wash the cabbage, you've also got to dry it jolly well, otherwise it dilutes the dressing, making the whole salad watery and tasteless.
■ You only need about 2oz/50g cabbage per person because, being uncooked, there's no shrinkage. Be sure to shred it finely, to make it delicate and to avoid the salad tasting too strongly of cabbage. It's a mistake to skimp on the other ingredients like apple (or well-drained pineapple chunks), celery or celeriac, walnuts, etc. because the salad's crunchy texture and lovely flavour depend on this sort of thing.
■ Be wise and make the dressing first, to prevent the chopped apple discolouring. A good cream dressing (page 207) subtly blends everything together, but don't substitute single cream, soured cream or yoghurt for the double cream in coleslaw because they all make it too watery. For quite a different result, you can toss and chill the vegetables in French dressing then, just before serving, turn them over in a mixture of equal quantities of mayonnaise and double cream.
■ Taste coleslaw before you serve it, especially for sweetness. Then chill it for half an hour to tenderize the cabbage.
■ If you like mung, aduki or any other beans, add some of these too. See *pulses*, page 197.

COURGETTES

If used raw in a salad, they should be very young, sliced wafer thin and dégorgéd, for about half an hour before marinating in dressing, also for half an hour to tenderize and flavour them. Leave the skin on, to give colour, and cut them diagonally to make them look nice

CUCUMBER

A native of the East Indies and has been cultivated in China for 3,000 years.

■ Cucumber salad looks cooler and more colourful if you leave the skin on, or better still if you stripe it with a fruit decorator (page 28). Should you find the skin indigestible though, a potato peeler will take it off thinly and quickly.

■ All cucumbers are very watery and some are sweeter than others: cut paper-thin, as it should be, you'll find it has a much better flavour if you dégorgé it half an hour or so before covering with dressing (see page 59).

■ For the dressing, use lemon juice or white wine vinegar rather than red wine or malt vinegar, either of which will spoil the colour of the cucumber. Alternatively, you could use distilled (white) malt vinegar. It's better to make a slightly oily dressing like this one, than a sharp: stir 3 tablespoons cream, one by one, into a dessertspoon lemon juice mixed with salt, paprika and a good pinch of sugar.

■ Chopped chives, parsley, chervil, finely sliced spring onions or caraway seeds make a good garnish if you like any or all of these flavours.

DRESSINGS

Make or mar salads, and there's no doubt that most of them are best freshly made. Besides sometimes binding together the ingredients of a salad (for example, rice salad) and making the whole thing more moist, and tasty, they have another vital role: to make more digestible the rich sort of dishes which salads often accompany, like roast chicken, roast duck, or salmon.

■ Use two wooden spoons, wooden salad servers or your hands to toss and turn over salad plants and vegetables in a dressing, or vegetables in a marinade. They break up the food less than metal utensils and can't pass on a metal flavour. Marinating vegetables need turning over now and then to make sure the flavour penetrates throughout the food.

Cream dressings Really just a kind of oil and vinegar dressing, see below, using cream, soured cream or yoghurt instead of all or some of the oil, and lemon juice in place of the vinegar if you like. In case you'd like me to cross the 't's and dot the 'i's, here's a delicious recipe: Mix a tablespoonful each of lemon juice and oil with seasoning and a pinch of sugar, then stir in 3 tablespoons double cream, one at a time. Stir again just before using.

Mayonnaise See page 174.

Oil and vinegar sauces or dressings Also called vinaigrette sauces.
French dressing (or sauce vinaigrette). This is the 'mother sauce'. It is also often used for a simple marinade.

■ The right ingredients for French dressing are simple but important, though the proportion of oil to vinegar depends upon how sharp or bland you like it. This is the proportion most people like:

1 tablespoon wine vinegar or lemon juice – or a mixture of both
3 tablespoons oil, preferably olive
salt and freshly ground black pepper
⅛ teaspoon dry mustard, optional
1–2 level dessertspoons chopped green herbs in season, optional

■ Either shake the vinegar, oil and seasonings vigorously together in a screw-top jar, *or* mix the vinegar with the seasonings until the salt is dissolved and then add the oil. Either way, add herbs at the last minute, for perfect flavour and colour.

■ The vinegar is more important than lots of people realize. A dressing made with wine vinegar comes from a different world from one made with malt. Just as wine cuts through rich foods, so wine vinegar cuts through the oil in a dressing.

■ Herb vinegars are a good way of introducing other flavours to a salad.

■ See also *vinegar*, page 128.

■ The ideal oil for dressings is olive, but it is expensive, and in addition some people dislike its sometimes strong fruity flavour, preferring to use another oil. See *oils*, page 112.

■ Heresy though the French consider it to add sugar, some people prefer it that way.

■ For variations of French dressing, see page 171, the Family Tree of sauces.

ENDIVE, CURLY

Looks like a frilly, curly lettuce. Separate and wash the leaves well, using them like lettuce in mixed green salads etc. or to garnish almost any cold dish. See also *chicory*, page 206.

'FRUIT' SALADS

Served with a hot or cold main dish, fruit salads really come into their own in winter when many salad plants are out of season. They also liven up a mixed hors d'oeuvre, or make a cool, fresh starter for a summer lunch.

■ Fruits take on a new flavour when mixed together and dressed with a cream, or oil and vinegar dressing. They blend perfectly with raw winter vegetables like finely shredded cabbage, chopped celery or chicory, also with some cooked vegetables. You might, for instance, like orange segments and celery, banana and peach with raw grated beetroot and lettuce, or California salad – lettuce, celery, cucumber, tomatoes, apple and banana.

■ Just as orange salad is good with roast duck, so are such combinations as apricot or pineapple salad with baked gammon or grilled gammon steaks; cherry salad with poultry or game; pear and grape salad with cold ham or roast chicken.

■ If you use tinned fruits, drain them well and use a rather sharper dressing than for fresh, to counteract the sweetness. On the other hand, you're almost sure to want to use a little sugar with some sour fresh fruits.

■ Lemon juice is sometimes better than vinegar in a dressing, a cream dressing going superbly with many salads (see page 207).

■ Experiments with fruit salads don't often go wrong: with lettuce or watercress, even the unlikely mixture of black grapes and sliced banana bound with mayonnaise is delicious with something like cold chicken.

GREEN SALAD

Goes perfectly with such things as roast chicken, turkey or game, as well as with grills, omelettes, some cheese dishes and many cold. It can consist of any green salad plant and herbs – nothing of another colour – and is dressed with a vinaigrette sauce.

■ Ideally, the torn-up coarsest lettuce leaves go at the bottom, the heart in the middle surrounded by the smaller leaves, so that the salad looks like a fresh head of lettuce – whether in individual bowls or in one large one. Arrange sprigs of watercress, endive, land cress or anything else green that you like, amongst the lettuce, sprinkling it all lightly at the last minute with dressing.

■ Alternatively, simply toss the crisp green salad plants in dressing at the last moment.

LAND CRESS

American land cress is a good garden substitute for watercress. It's a hardy perennial plant which hardly gives up even in the winter. The tender young leaves are the best, used whole or chopped up with scissors together with chives, say, for a salad. A sprig also makes a cheery and tasty garnish for lots of savoury dishes.

LETTUCE

One of the most rewarding things to grow if you have a garden, for with very little shelter, you can eat it almost every month of the year. With seeds sown at regular short intervals and the thinnings transplanted, to extend their maturing period, anyone with a vegetable patch can at least produce lettuces without a break, from spring to autumn.

■ This isn't a seedsman's catalogue, so I'm just going to suggest you look out for some of my different-season favourites:

Buttercrunch
Kloek
Kwiek
Premier
Tom Thumb
Valdor
Webb's Wonderful
Little Gem – my *most* favourite ⎤
Sugar Cos   ⎬ Cos
Winter Density   ⎦

Mixed lettuce Somebody certainly had a brainwave here, to help the smaller household. Packets contain seeds for both cabbage and Cos types, which mature at different times instead of bolting together. For good measure, there's a varied mixture of lettuces to eat. (Cos take their name from one of the Aegean Islands, from which they were introduced.)

■ Whether you buy or grow lettuce, wash and dry it thoroughly at least an hour before the meal, and put in bottom of refrigerator to make it crisp (see page 39). If without, store lettuce in a covered saucepan: with light and air excluded it will deteriorate less quickly than in a vegetable rack.

■ It's important to dry lettuce properly. If you don't, the leaves won't become crisp, the dressing won't adhere to them, and in addition the dressing is diluted. See *salad basket*, page 15.

■ A steel knife makes lettuce slimy, so tear up rather than cut any leaves too big to eat whole. If you have to shred them, for something like a prawn cocktail, use a fine stainless steel saw-knife.

■ You can't freeze lettuce any more than you can hope to go on picking it in arctic conditions outside. As up to 97 per cent of it is water, there's no need to say why.

Iceberg lettuce Although seemingly expensive, they really aren't. Developed in and imported first from California, this crisp, very compact and excellent lettuce is no extravagance because there's virtually no waste and, wrapped in Cling-film and stored in the salad box of a refrigerator, it may keep as long as 3–4 weeks: an invaluable store and one which I would not be without in winter. The growing demand for Iceberg is leading to their wider cultivation elsewhere.
To use, just pull off and discard any limp or discoloured leaves, then pull off as many more as you need, using as ordinary lettuce. No washing is necessary, but do cut off any brown part at the stalk, to keep it fresh.

■ Home-grown are, from my personal experience, disappointing – they seem to bolt just when I think them 'hearty' enough to pick: very different from the professionally produced imported ones.

Radicchio The leaves of this purply-red, marbled-with-white Italian lettuce have a rather bitter taste not unlike (but hotter than) chicory. Shredded and mixed with other salad plants, or in a mixed salad, they add flavour and colour.

■ Cling-film-wrapped, a head will keep for weeks rather than days in the salad box of a refrigerator: another marvellous store.

MIXED SALADS

Also called combination salads or *salades composées*, they are of several categories. They may be based on mixed cooked vegetables, like salade niçoise and some rice salads, or they may consist of things like chicken, turkey, ham, tongue, fish or shellfish with salad plants and mixed vegetables. Into the latter group comes such a comparatively simple dish as cold beef salad, as well as the much more sophisticated ones such as salmon and lobster mayonnaise.

■ If a salad contains fish or poultry coated with aspic or chaud-froid sauce, then strictly speaking it's a cold entrée rather than a mixed salad.

MUSHROOM SALAD

Good with cold chicken, cold meats, or in a mixed hors d'oeuvre, but it has to be perfect to be good. The day before yesterday's mushrooms are unlikely to be crisp enough to eat raw, so this means making sure they're fresh and firm when you buy them. See page 186.

■ The mushroom caps need slicing paper-thin if they're to tenderize and develop flavour in ½–1 hour while marinating in a French dressing. In a shorter time, they'll taste of nothing, left longer they'll largely turn to water.
■ Red wine vinegar makes a good French dressing – which for this salad seems best slightly on the sharp side.

SALADE NIÇOISE

A Mediterranean dish, with lots of variations. It's composed chiefly of Mediterranean foods which traditionally include cooked French beans, tomatoes, boiled potatoes, black olives, finely sliced green peppers, anchovy fillets, lettuce, hard-boiled eggs and perhaps tinned tuna fish.

■ Chopped fresh green herbs are added to the French dressing, which usually contains garlic, and needs lots of freshly ground black pepper. Serve this lovely dish as an hors d'oeuvre or as a main course mixed salad, with the tuna.
■ Cut the beans in small diamonds before boiling and refreshing them, and dice the potatoes after they're boiled. Stone the olives of course, and quarter the tomatoes (juiced and seeded, otherwise they'll make the salad watery).

ORANGE SALAD

Traditionally served with roast duck, but oranges make lovely salads to go with other dishes as well. When mixed with oil and vinegar, they don't taste the same as when fresh, and combine delightfully with sliced chicory or finely sliced shal-

lots, spring onions or Spanish onions and black olives. The orange segments must be absolutely free of pith as well as skin, otherwise they will be bitter (see page 282).

POTATO SALAD

All the better for a little know-how, not to mention waxy new potatoes (not a dish to use up left-over or cold potatoes). If you mix the hot, very slightly under-cooked, diced potatoes in the dressing and allow them to cool in it, they'll absorb the flavour and acquire character they'd never otherwise have.

■ Main-crop potatoes break up less when steamed than boiled, and if you cook potatoes in their skins, they'll have lots more flavour than if peeled beforehand. Toss them a few moments in the hot empty pan over low heat to dry them off, then skin and dress them.
■ Large quantities of thick mayonnaise give potato salad a cloying effect. It's much nicer made thinner, or with a well-seasoned French dressing, either of them flavoured with finely chopped shallots or spring onions, and chopped fresh green herbs.

RADICCHIO

See *lettuce*, page 209.

RADISHES

Grow in all shapes, sizes and colours: round, oval, olive-shaped, small, large, long and tapering; scarlet, white, white-tipped, pink, black, purple; mild, nutty and peppery in taste; early or late growing. There are three main classes:
Summer – all are small, grow quickly (as many a child will know) and are eaten raw.
Main crop summer and autumn – later and larger varieties.
Winter – larger, firmer and more compact. Some are black and round, or long, like carrots; others are white, grey, pur-

ple or scarlet. These are mostly used finely sliced and grated, but you can cook them in any way suitable for young turnips.

■ Radishes are traditionally used to clear the palate for food or drink. To prepare summer ones, top them (leaving on a finger-nail length of stem by which to pick them up), then, 'tail', rinse and serve in a small dish or bowl. Homegrown, young and tender, and eaten within an hour or so of picking while fresh and firm, are totally different from most bought. (If limp, put for a couple of hours in a basin of cold water with ice cubes to crisp them up.) You may – or may not! – like radishes with a good dab of butter on the end, dipped in sea salt and eaten with bread.
■ To garnish, radishes look pretty sliced wafer thin – when they're also much easier to digest.
■ Should you want to make radish roses, choose the long thin variety: they open up better than round ones. Cut about three-quarters of the way down (from root to stem end), first one way, then the other, and perhaps twice more, as below, and leave to soak about ½ hour in cold water.

■ If growing your own, a packet of mixed seeds has advantages: they mature over a longer period instead of all together; you get variety of colour, flavour, size and shape.

Black (Spanish) radishes A rather coarse winter radish, with white flesh of good flavour. Peel and use grated or finely sliced, in salads and with cold meats. Homegrown, you can usually leave them in the ground, lifting as required from autumn onwards.

White radishes (mooli) A long tapering radish with a mild or pungent flavour,

according to variety – again better home-grown, so that you can lift and eat them while young and tender. Peel and grate or slice very finely, to use in salads.

RICE SALAD

Splendidly colourful and easy for a winter party, or as the base of a mixed salad with left-over fish, shellfish, meat or poultry. It can be just as good as it looks, too, if the long grain rice itself is properly cooked (page 202) and allowed to cool in enough French dressing to glaze it. Stirred together with a two-pronged fork, the rice will absorb the flavour of the dressing as it cools, and the grains will remain separate instead of forming a stodgy mass.

■ All sorts of things besides the well-tried peas and pineapple chunks help to give rice salad flavour and colour:
Vegetables, such as chopped red or green peppers (quickly blanched and refreshed), sweet corn, shredded celery or blanched celeriac, finely sliced shallots or spring onions. Cooked vegetables which have been left to go cold are second-rate. It's much better to cook, refresh and drain them, then they'll retain their fresh flavour, colour and texture.
Fruits, such as tomatoes (juiced and seeded, see page 195), tinned mandarin segments, orange segments, chopped apple, sultanas or chopped browned nuts – added at the last minute, to make sure they don't go soft.
Herbs and flavourings, such as chopped parsley, chives or dill, instant garlic powder or a pinch of cayenne.
Dressings may consist of more French dressing or say a soured cream dressing (soured cream replacing oil in a French dressing) or a dressing made with equal quantities of mayonnaise and double cream. I like a sharp French dressing for this salad: equal quantities of oil and vinegar.

SHALLOTS

See page 188.

SPRING ONIONS

If you serve them whole, they should have about 1½–2in/4–5cm of the top left on, to make them easy to pick up. Finely sliced spring onions can often take the place of shallot if necessary, either in a salad or in a cooked dish.

SUMMER SALAD

An English summer salad can include almost anything one can think of in the salad line – lettuce of any kind, chicory, endive, watercress, land cress, cucumber, tomatoes, radishes, spring onions, finely sliced shallot, chopped herbs, hard-boiled egg or cheese (grated, sliced or cubed).

■ As tomatoes and egg tend to disintegrate when sliced, it's nicer to quarter them, and salad plants should be tossed in an oil and vinegar dressing.

TOMATO SALAD

Much less watery if you quarter rather than slice the fruits (serving them points upwards) and if you make and dress it more or less at the last minute.

■ Basil is wedded to tomatoes as mint is to peas, or you can garnish tomato salad with other finely chopped herbs such as parsley or chives, as well as with finely sliced shallot, spring onions or Spanish onion. See also page 188.
■ See also tomatoes, page 195.

WATERCRESS

Makes a lovely colourful, fresh-looking garnish for a hot dish like roast chicken, baked ham or game, as well as for something cold, or in a salad.

■ Take off any white rootlets high on the stem, as well as discoloured leaves, but don't cut off all the stem – just the bottom coarse parts.
■ If you want to arrange watercress sprigs in tiny bouquets, you'll probably find it easiest to dip each bunch head down in a well-emulsified oil and vinegar dressing, then shake gently to flick off any surplus.

12

Fish

GENERAL INFORMATION

Fish cookery is largely influenced by the flavour or lack of flavour of particular fish. While salmon, for instance, is naturally so succulent and delicious that it could almost cook itself, white fish depend much more upon the cook enhancing their flavour, if not actually providing it.

■ Fish, like meat, takes flavour from the bones during cooking, hence fish on the bone tends to be more tasty than fillets. That is why fish like halibut are better cut into steaks on the bone in preference to being filleted; it is the main reason why small fish, flat or round, have more flavour when cooked whole than when filleted; it is also why it is important, if possible, to use the head and bones, when cooking fillets, to make good cooking liquor, or to make stock for a sauce. Why leave the trimmings with the fishmonger when fish stock makes superb soups, even if you don't want it for the fish itself? If without better use for it, it makes tastier potato soup than does many a white stock. See *stock, fish*, page 122.

■ From the cook's angle, fish are usually divided into three groups because each group has similar characteristics, requiring a similar approach.

Oily fish Those such as salmon, mackerel, sardines and the herring family are basically flavourful, rich (12–20 per cent fat) and not always easily digested, because most of their fat – oil – is distributed throughout their flesh. That's mainly why these fish are more nutritious

and darker in colour than white fish, whose fat is largely stored in the liver, which we discard. It's also why cod liver oil and halibut liver oil can be produced, but not mackerel or herring liver oil.

■ One can poach, steam, grill or fry oily fish fairly successfully without much fuss, knowledge or extra flavouring, counteracting the richness with accompaniments such as a dressed salad or a piquant sauce, rather than accentuating it by rich methods of cookery or rich accompaniments.

■ Most oily fish make a good cold meal, too, whether it's an elaborate dish like salmon in aspic, or a simple one like soused herring.

■ Brown bread and butter, which contain carbohydrates, are often served with oily fish so that the valuable protein in the fish isn't used up to give energy, instead of being used for body-building.

White fish They lack the richness and strong flavour of oily fish, but you can make up for these in the kitchen in almost dozens of different ways. Some fish are, in fact, so bland that, like potatoes, they can be cooked in such varied ways that you need never tire of them. You can enrich or flavour them, for instance, by such simple means as frying, or by such sophisticated accompaniments as béarnaise sauce.

■ The 'musts' for cooking fish are few and far between: one can cook fillets of all such fish as dab, brill, flounder, plaice, sole, turbot, trout and whiting in similar ways, as one can most small whole flat fish and most large fish, whether whole, sliced or filleted. Due to the unique qualities of many fish, however, there are methods of preparation and numerous dishes specific to certain types.

■ White fish is nourishing (17 per cent protein) without being fattening (0.5 per cent fat) to those who worry, or ought to worry about their weight. One can also cook it so lightly, and it's so digestible, that it makes one of the best foods there are for tiny children, old people or invalids.

Shellfish are divided into two groups, *crustaceans* and *molluscs*:
Crustaceans – e.g. crab, crayfish, lobster, prawns – take their name from the Latin word *crusta*, a crust or shell. Unlike other fish, and mammals, their skeleton is on the outside, their flesh inside.
Molluscs are themselves divided into two main groups: *univalves* (e.g. winkles, whelks, snails) and *bivalves* (e.g. mussels, oysters, scallops, cockles).

■ In addition, there are the fish with tentacles, like the squid or octopus.
■ Even if you squirm at the thought of cooking it, you can't fault the fish in countries where they sell it live, tasting as it does of the sea. Freshness, important for all fish, is absolutely vital for shellfish, both for safety and flavour.
■ Some shellfish, like crab or lobster, for instance, are as often served hot as cold because they can be just as good either way, yet taste quite different. To counteract their richness generally, and to make shellfish more digestible, serve accompaniments like a piquant sauce, a dressed salad, lemon quarters and brown bread and butter.
■ It's hardly surprising that the French and English names of certain types of shellfish confuse some people. Anyone could be excused for thinking a Dublin Bay prawn was a kind of prawn, and some might be surprised to find that (seawater) crayfish, crawfish and *langouste* are one and the same thing. If you're in a muddle, this table of the more familiar fish may help you to unravel it.

English name	French name	Comments
crab	*crabe*	See also page 218.
crayfish, sea-water	*langouste*	Also called crawfish.
crayfish, fresh-water	*écrevisse*	
Dublin Bay prawn	*langoustine*	Not in fact a prawn, but of the lobster family – sometimes up to 8in/20cm in length. Culinary name 'scampi' comes from Italian word *scampo*. See also *scampi*, page 226.
lobster	*homard*	See also page 221.
mussel	*moule*	See also page 223.
oyster	*huître*	See also page 224.
prawn	*crevette rose*	See also page 224.
scallop	*coquille Saint-Jacques*	Also commonly known as the pilgrim shell. Pilgrims finding empty shells on the shore used them as cup, spoon and dish. *Coquille* is French for shell, see also page 226.
shrimp	*crevette grise*	See also page 226.

Preparation of fish While many cookery books give instructions for choosing and cleaning fish as well as for cooking it, a few offbeat tips may be helpful:

1 It's easiest to scrape the scales off fish with a sharp knife if you hold the fish upside down by the tail. You can then wash off any loose scales under running water.

2 Dip your thumb and fingers in a small heap of salt so that you can grip fish firmly, and keep it under perfect control. Salt is useful too to rub off any black film still remaining after cleaning, washing and drying a fish.

3 Rolled or folded fillets of fish such as sole and plaice *must* be skinned because, quite simply, they are unpleasant to eat otherwise. The white skin's texture is no nicer than the black, so skinned fillets always score over unskinned, because one can eat the lot.

4 Rolled fillets will look larger, will stand firmly and will not unfold if you lay each fillet skinned side upwards, and roll it from head to tail round a thick raw potato chip: the chip should be flush with the bottom of the fillet when the roll is standing up, and long enough to stick out at the top, to pull it out easily when the fish is cooked. The chip also makes a handle when coating the rolled fillet with egg and breadcrumbs.

5 If you're cooking small flat fish whole, and dislike the constant battle on your plate with the tiny bones down the sides, then trim the fish to the edge of the flesh with scissors before coating or cooking it. It makes the fish look small, but it's easy and good to eat.

6 Scoring, mostly of round fish, is only necessary when one cooks fish whole: it prevents the skin from bursting, and it looks attractive. It also helps both the heat and the flavourings (from seasonings and sauces) to penetrate the fish.

Methods of flavouring fish The most insipid of fish can swim into the luxury class as long as it's really fresh, for even these one can make distinctive in various ways.

1 *Poaching* Poach the fish in wine (or wine and water, or vermouth and water), fish stock, or a court bouillon (page 58). Generally speaking, you need just enough liquid to cover the fish, but if you boil rather than poach it, it will break up and become watery: poach it in the oven or a frying pan, but be sure to grease whatever you cook it in, to prevent the fish sticking to it.

■ If you poach it in wine, flavour it with finely chopped shallots or spring onions as well as with seasoning, and use the strained wine afterwards to make a velouté sauce (page 177). This is a delicious way to cook fillets of white fish – and doesn't take much wine.

■ *Fish stock* (page 122) may ideally contain wine, but you can also make it quite simply with the head, bones and trimmings of the fish you're cooking. Reduce the fish stock after the fish is cooked, to concentrate the flavour, and then use it as wine above, to make a velouté sauce.

■ *Court bouillon* (page 58), a herby spicy liquid, is used mostly for whole fish or large pieces of fish.

■ If you poach in milk, the fish will have more flavour if fried first for a minute or two in a little butter.

2 *Marinating* Marinate the fish before you cook it. Even a simple marinade like lemon juice will give fish some zip if soaked in it for half an hour, first one side and then the other.

3 *Using herbs* Use parsley, thyme, bay leaf, dill or fennel to flavour poaching water, or in a sauce which will enhance the flavour of the fish. Alternatively use a herb butter or add a little parsley wine to the poaching water, or sprinkle chopped herbs on top of the cooked fish. You'll be able to think of other ways of introducing herbs too.

4 *Stuffings* You can stuff almost any kind of white fish, skewering the fish, or tying the stuffing in with thread if necessary.

5 *Coating* Coat the fish with egg and breadcrumbs, batter, seasoned oatmeal, or seasoned flour: egg and breadcrumbs will stick better, and the fish will have more flavour, if dipped first in seasoned flour. Fine, dried white breadcrumbs give a better and more professional finish than fresh or golden breadcrumbs.

6 *Frying* If you fry fish, especially in deep fat or butter, it gives a marvellous flavour. Deep frying is ideal for small whole fish, fillets and small pieces of larger fish. Shallow frying is good too, as well as for thicker slices (steaks) of fish which need longer cooking.

■ After frying fish in butter, counteract the richness and make it really tasty by deglazing the pan with lemon juice, which you can then pour over the fish. See page 222, *meunière*.

■ Alternatively, fry some chopped nuts in the butter after the fish is cooked, and when nicely browned pour everything over the fish.

7 *Grilling or baking* Baste the seasoned fish with a savoury butter – orange, for instance, is excellent with some white fish. If the fish is too large to grill whole, cut it into slices (steaks) 1–1½in/2½–4cm thick, and cook them as whole fish: the smaller the fish the hotter the grill should be – larger fish need slower cooking so that the heat can penetrate the flesh gradually.

8 *Steaming* The fish can lie between two plates or in foil, with butter, to retain all the fish juices and flavour.

9 *Serving with a sauce* Make a fish velouté from the poaching liquid or from fish stock. Other suitable sauces include a béchamel such as mornay made with the milk in which you've poached the fish, and also sauces made independently of the fish such as hollandaise, tartare, savoury butters or hot butter sauces.

10 *Serving fish 'au gratin'* Either sprinkle the cooked fish with golden breadcrumbs before dotting it with melted butter and grilling it, *or* coat the fish with a sauce, say aurore, then sprinkle it with grated cheese and breadcrumbs before grilling.

11 *Garnishing* Serve tasty and attractive garnishes such as lemon quarters, capers, fried parsley, chopped herbs, mushrooms fried in butter, shrimps, grapes or matchstick potatoes.

Hints about cooking fish

1 A long flexible fish slice is essential because fish lacks the connective tissue of meat, so (for this and for other reasons) breaks up more readily when cooked.

2 Place fish fillets boned side down first

when you fry them in shallow fat: that way you only need to turn them once, reducing the risk of their breaking up. Another advantage is that the first side fried is usually the more golden: (butter for instance may brown before the second side is fried).

3 Fillets of fish or small whole flat fish fried in deep fat will remain flat if you fry them between two frying baskets – if you have them.

■ If frying fillets in shallow fat, they'll keep flat if, at the beginning, you hold them down with a pallet knife or a long fish slice. Otherwise they tend to curl up and fry unevenly.

4 Fillets of fish such as lemon sole, plaice and whiting, which tend to flake after poaching – unlike Dover sole and brill which do not – are best cooked, sauced and served in the original poaching dish to avoid their breaking up.

5 Correct cooking times really matter. Undercooked fish is uninviting, to put it mildly. Overcooked fish looses flavour and also breaks up: fish is cooked when it is opaque, when the flesh has shrunk slightly from the bone, if any, and when the flakes – if flaked type of fish – are just beginning to separate.

■ Fish is usually cooked according to thickness rather than weight, but sometimes both apply, especially in the case of large whole fish. Always test fish at the thickest part.

6 When making such dishes as salmon mayonnaise or chaud-froid of halibut, and preparing the cooked fish, that's the time to remember that compact neat pieces help the general appearance of the finished dish: each piece will be easy to coat with sauce if you wrap it tightly in butter muslin while still hot. Pressed flat, the fish will firm up as it cools, making it easier to handle too. When quite cold, cover it with foil or damp greaseproof paper until ready to coat it.

Serving fish

1 Serve fried fish on a plain doyley,

which helps to absorb excess fat not already absorbed by draining.

2 Never keep fried fish hot in a covered dish, because the trapped steam makes it go soft.

ANCHOVIES

To the ancient world they were what the herring has been to ours. For all we know of the anchovy, though, they might be caught in tins; they don't travel so can only be eaten fresh where found, e.g. the Mediterranean. Anyone who has once tasted them straight from the sea, however, will know what an unrecognizably different fish the fresh anchovy is from the tinned.

■ Wash anchovy fillets in hot water and dry on absorbent kitchen paper if you dislike their saltiness or oiliness, or if for a particular purpose you want them fat-free.
■ If anchovies go hard, as they may if you don't use the whole tinful at once, you can soften them and at the same time get rid of their saltiness by soaking in milk for a few hours.
■ If you have a freezer, you can pop any unwanted ones in there for use another time, then they won't go dry.
■ Use them to make amongst other things:

1 Anchovy butter (see page 169), to cook or serve with fish, or to add to a sauce served with fish.
2 Anchovy toast, see page 345.
3 Anchovy sauce, by adding (dare I suggest it) anchovy essence, if you can obtain it, or anchovy paste to a white or béchamel sauce.

BLOATERS

Are smoked ungutted herring, unlike kippers which are split, smoked and usually dyed.

■ Yarmouth bloaters became famous because the herring was in prime condition when the shoals arrived off Yar-

mouth in the autumn, before they cast their roe. It's so essential to eat bloaters at once (they keep no longer than fresh fish) that in days gone by the epicure would go to Yarmouth – not allowing the fish to do the travelling – and even there, would eat them before going to bed rather than waiting for breakfast!
■ Fry or grill them, or, if you can be bothered with all the bones, make bloater spread.

BRILL

With light and delicate flesh, it is allied to the dab, plaice and sole, and belongs to the same family as the turbot. Cook fillets as sole, or a whole fish as turbot.

BRISLING

Small seafish of the herring type, of North European waters, canned in oil like sardines, though unlike them in other ways.

COCKLES

Small bivalve molluscs, which make a tasty fish soup and are good with sauce poulette (page 175 of Family Tree), or in fish sauces in place of oysters or mussels, when these aren't available. (Cockles are, in fact, often more difficult to buy than oysters or mussels, depending on where one lives.)

COD

First introduced to Europe by the Basque mariners, who came upon it on their frequent whaling expeditions to Newfoundland.

■ Cod steaks, sometimes difficult to buy in these days when so many people want everything simplified, are twice as good as fillet. This is because, during cooking, so much flavour from the bone goes into the flesh. See also *general information*.

Cod fillet, smoked Is less overpowering if soaked overnight in cold water before cooking. Even then, I find it unlikeably strong.

COLEY

'Leave it for others' is the only advice I feel able to offer with any enthusiasm. Soak it in water for hours, marinate or make it into fishcakes, fry it, poach it in wine – *nothing* disguises its (to me) strong and rather unpleasant flavour. I have friends who like it, so perhaps I'm spoilt!

CRABS

Like lobsters, the male is known as the cock and the female as the hen. Crabs are quite tricky to select because the shell hides the meat – or lack of it. Medium-sized crabs, which are heavy in relation to their size, are usually best because they're both fleshy and 'sweet'. It's wiser to avoid:

1 Crabs with missing limbs – one is losing good flesh.
2 Very large crabs, which may be coarse.
3 Those stuck with barnacles, which are probably old.
4 Any which rattle when shaken, because they'll be watery rather than fleshy.
5 Tiny crabs, unless you're adept at preparing them, because the small amount of meat hardly justifies the fiddling work.

■ Lots of books tell one how to cope with a crab but here are a few tips:

1 Use tongs to pick up live crabs if you're squeamish or not used to handling them.
2 Lay a cooked crab on its back to remove the claws, first the big then the smaller ones, twisting them off inwards.
3 Separate upper shell from lower by placing both thumbs under tail flap (the big part) and pushing up until the body breaks from the shell.
4 Have one small basin for the white meat, another for the brown (mainly the liver and roe) and something else for the inedible parts: the spongy gills known as the dead men's fingers; the stomach, a little sac which lies near the head; and the twist of intestines with the greenish matter.
5 To crack round the natural line on the underside of the shell, tap gently with a skewer and small hammer, when it will break off easily.
6 The shell (and any claws used for garnish) will glisten and look lovely if rubbed over lightly with salad oil after scrubbing and drying.

EEL

The most nourishing of all fish, fresh-water eel even more so than sea-eel (conger), salmon, mackerel or herring. It's so rich in fact that you may want to remove the layer of fat between the skin and flesh to make it more digestible.

■ Eel's blood may poison you if it gets into a wound, but cooking and the action of the gastric juices make it harmless.

Smoked eel Delicious, and superior in many people's opinion, to smoked salmon. See also *smoked fish*, page 227 and page 158.

FISH CAKES

Have more flavour when made with haddock than with cod and are delicious using other fish like bream, halibut, salmon or even tinned mackerel.

■ One can't make fish cakes without egg, which coagulates when heated, binding everything together. Without, they'll disintegrate when fried: whole egg tends to make the mixture too soft, white of egg alone gives neither flavour nor colour, so it's better to use just the yolk which binds, flavours and makes fish cakes golden at a stroke.

FISH PIE

Doesn't have to be made with parsley sauce, though few appear to make it with anything else. Whether you make cheese sauce, mushroom, mustard, anchovy or egg, the pie will be more tasty if you use a béchamel sauce base (page 177), or if you include the liquid in which the fish was cooked, or use some stock made with its bones and trimmings (see *fish stock*, page 122).

HADDOCK

One of the more aristocratic members of the cod family, but why must so many fishmongers only sell it filleted when it's so much better on the bone? Everything nowadays has to be made easy for us, though on balance we must often lose out.

■ Haddock excels when smoked, which explains why there's such a variety to choose from: golden cutlets, finnan haddock, smoked fillet and smokies. See also *smoked fish*, page 227.

Golden cutlets Very small haddock filleted in a special way, dyed and cold-smoked.

Haddock fillet, smoked Is often from a large fish, and too strong by far. Soaked overnight in cold water before cooking, its flavour is slightly mellowed.

Finnan haddock Undyed and cold-smoked, this has a finer flavour than golden cutlets, chiefly because the flesh takes flavour from the bone.

■ Finnan is a corruption of Findon, the name of a place near Aberdeen, famous for the finest smoked haddock.

Smokies Small haddock smoked closed, instead of split, like finnan haddock.

HAKE

Another close relation of the cod, with flesh which is tender, white, flaky and easy to digest. Cook similarly, remembering steaks will have more flavour than fillet. See also *general information*.

HALIBUT

From *hali* and *butt*, meaning 'holy fish', supposedly because it used to be eaten on holy days. The largest of the world's flat fish, weighing anything from 1½–400lb/0.75–180kg, the most enormous on record (landed at Grimsby in 1957) weighed 504lb and was thought to be over 60 years old.

Chicken halibut The very young fish weighing 2–4lb/1–2kg have the finest flesh, larger halibut being coarser.

■ Cook halibut on the bone for the finest flavour, or cook fillets in almost any way you like (see page 215).
■ Halibut, like cod, is a wonderful source of vitamin D – halibut liver oil – but we don't of course eat the liver when we eat the fish. See also *general information*.

HERRING

These fish move around Britain in a clockwise direction, which explains why at certain seasons of the year they are caught off different parts of the coast, and why those caught at some places are better than others, so much depending on the season.

■ Though the once 'penny herring' now costs a fortune by comparison, they're still as nutritious, tasty and bony as ever. In case you're not sure how to cope with them, here's the remedy for boniness:

To clean and bone

1 This is a slightly gory (though not too time-consuming or horrible) operation, so it's sensible to collect the gear you need before embarking on surgery: a sharp filleting (or similar shaped) knife, a pair of sharp, pointed scissors to cut off the fins, cooking salt to help you grip the fish firmly, a scrap of clean cloth or some absorbent kitchen paper to dry the fish and, on top of your chopping board, several layers of torn-up newspaper in which to wrap and get rid of the emerging mess.

2 Hold herring upside down by its tail,

head on board, and scrape off any loose scales with the sharp edge of your knife. Cut off all fins.

3 Lay herring along board, head to your right, underside downward, and (at a slanting angle) *almost* cut off the head. Now pull if off where still attached by the uncut skin at the bottom. Hopefully, the innards should come away with it.

4 Using knife or scissors, slit right down the underside and open fish out, taking care of any roe if still inside. Take out such roe, and remove any black film by rubbing with salt.

5 Remove backbone: open fish out as much as possible and lay it slit part downwards on chopping board. Now with the palm of your hand stretched right along it, press and flatten the herring against the board. Turn fish over. Slip knife under backbone at head end and gently lever bone out, taking as many as possible of the small bones with it. Pull out any other bones you see.

6 Wash and dry fish well before cooking, e.g. dipping in seasoned flour or oatmeal to fry, or sousing, etc.

Herring, soused Better if cooked the previous day because the liquid has a chance to gel slightly, and the fish firms up and absorbs more flavour from the liquor if allowed to cool and soak in it overnight. Vinegar not only counteracts the richness of oily fish like herring and mackerel, but, combined with long slow cooking, softens and dissolves the smaller bones. That's why roll mops are no problem to eat, even for children.

■ As soused herring tend often to receive rather unfair treatment, here's what to do:

1 When cleaning and boning herring as above, leave on the back fin which, sticking up, acts as a herring's own garnish.

2 Dip fish in liberally seasoned flour, and roll from head to tail, skin side outwards, then they won't unroll.

3 Pack fish tightly in an ovenware dish, fins upwards, sprinkling over them a finely sliced shallot (or a little onion),

salt, a few peppercorns, a clove and a broken-up bay leaf. Just cover with a mixture of equal quantities wine vinegar and water. (Wine vinegar gives a finer flavour and cuts through the richness of the fish better than malt.) If you swamp the herring with vinegar and water, there's no chance of the liquid gelling, and both fish and liquid will be insipid.

4 Cover with lid or foil and bake in a slow oven, gas 2, 300°F/150°C for about 1¼ hours. Allow to cool and set.

5 Serve with a little of the liquid over the fish, and with brown bread and butter, a wedge of lemon and a salad, all of which help to make it digestible as well as tasty.

HUSS

A member of the shark family, it was once called dogfish but people were put off by its name, so it was re-christened rock salmon. Now the law says 'no' to that too, presumably because the fish is nothing like salmon, except perhaps in its pinky flesh. Sold skinned, in long, double, rather thick fillets, huss has a thin, narrow and extraordinary backbone with the minimum of waste. It's firm, fleshy and filling, has quite a distinctive flavour and doesn't separate into flakes or disintegrate when cooked. It's good fried, can be cooked in the same way as cod, and is used to make soups and stews, especially curries.

■ Healthwise, this is a valuable fish.

KEDGEREE

A corruption of the Hindustani name *khichri*, a favourite Indian dish, and one often served at Anglo-Indian breakfast tables. Though the British version is different from the Indian, it's one of the most savoury breakfast or supper dishes imaginable, when properly made. This involves:

1 Using fish and rice, not rice with a dash of fish! One needs at least 8oz/225g cooked flaked fish to half that quantity of

long grain rice.

2 Using really tasty fish: to me, no other fish except salmon compares with finnan haddock, but some people like to use a mixture of this and white fish, or smoked haddock fillet and white fish.

3 Boiling the rice properly (see page 202), and stirring it (or the made kedgeree) always with a two-pronged fork, to make sure the grains are kept separate.

4 Seasoning the kedgeree generously. Do be sure to taste it before serving, adding chopped parsley or chives at the very last moment, without cooking.

■ If you want to make it in advance, for convenience, try heating it like boiled rice, in the Persian way (see page 202): stir the cooked fish, hard-boiled egg and seasonings along with the rice into the melted butter, allowing a little extra butter. Cook for one hour as directed for this rice, sprinkling with chopped parsley or chives at the last minute. It's delicious, unusually crunchy and, in the refrigerator the night before, you can have it all ready for breakfast the next morning, if you put the pan over heat as soon as you get up.

KIPPERS

If properly smoked and well cooked, kippers are a delicacy – this you're sure to know if you've ever eaten either Craster or some of the finest small Scottish kippers. Some people prefer to grill them (brushed first with melted butter), others prefer to fry them, but either way if you cook them until dark brown and crisp, their smoky flavour is drawn out. One can also bake, poach or steam them.

Variations on a kipper!

1 Make kipper spread, if you have time to cope with the bones, to use as a sandwich filling, spread on canapés, etc.

2 Serve marinated (raw) kipper fillets as an hors d'oeuvre, with brown bread and butter and lemon quarters. (Be sure to marinate them for several hours to tenderize and flavour them and counteract their richness.)

3 Make *Yarmouth straws*. Lay a tiny sliver of raw kipper between two uncooked, rather long cheese straws, pinch together the ends of the straws then twist each three-layer straw into a spiral before baking.

■ Kippers aren't only a breakfast dish: if you want to serve them for high tea or supper, they and malt whisky go hand in hand.

LOBSTERS

Around 2lb/1kg in weight is the best size for eating, and should produce about 12oz/375g meat. The hen is thought to be more tender and delicate than the cock but there's less meat on it and it's not so firm when cooked.

■ Cooking or killing a live lobster always makes me shudder but, mercifully for anyone like me, there are others who don't seem to bat an eyelid. *Homard à l'américaine*, for instance, calls for the lobster to be split alive, while for other hot dishes requiring uncooked meat, one can kill the lobster in a painless way first. It all depends what you're going to make as to what method you settle for.

For recipes using cooked lobster The lobster will have a finer flavour if you put it into *boiling* liquid (e.g. court bouillon, or court bouillon and seawater) rather than cold because the former seals in the juices.If you bring it gradually to the boil in cold – possibly the more humane method – the flavouring juices in the lobster are drawn out into the liquid as it heats. (Be sparing with the vinegar in a court bouillon, otherwise you'll spoil the colour of the shell.) After simmering for 10–15 minutes to the lb/450g let the lobster cool in the liquid.

For hot dishes using uncooked lobster Just before cooking, either plunge the point of your knife into its head, between the eyes, or sever the spinal cord by making a small incision in the back of the shell at the juncture of the chest and tail.

■ When cutting a *boiled* lobster in half, there's less risk of breaking the shell when the tail is tucked underneath than when the lobster is stretched out.

■ The inedible parts of a lobster are: *The gills*, otherwise known as the dead men's fingers; *the stomach*, a hard sac or bag in the right side of the head; the *intestine*, a thin grey or black line runing down through the tail meat. (This can poison one if eaten.)

■ Coral, the roe of the hen lobster, is greeny black when raw, bright red when cooked, while the green or creamy part of a lobster is the liver – and shouldn't be discarded. Should there be water inside, include it in the sauce if making one, to give it extra flavour.

■ Lobster and sherry have the same sort of affinity as say, duck and orange, or chicken and tarragon, so it's always safe to marinate cooked lobster for a short time in dry sherry before finishing and serving. See also *shellfish*, page 214.

LUMP FISH

Eaten smoked, is also called *lumpsucker*, *henfish*, *sea-hen* or *paddle-cock*. If you've never heard of any of those names, you'll at least know the fish for its roe – salted, dyed black or red and sold as mock caviar.

MACKEREL

These go off more quickly than almost any other fish, which explains why, at one time, it was the only fish allowed to be hawked in the streets in England on Sundays. With present-day freezing methods, of course, everything is different, but be sure the eyes are protruding, and the skin is iridescent. Dull, limp fish with sunken eyes are indigestible, unpleasant to eat and may be poisonous.

■ Hot or cold, mackerel is one of the best fish. If you've never eaten it for instance à la meunière or soused, there's a treat in store. Smoked mackerel is good too.

Soused mackerel Clean and bone, pre-pare and cook as soused herring (page 220), but cut each fish into two fillets (if large) before rolling up, and bake for 1½ hours instead of 1¼ hours.

■ See also *oily fish*, page 213.

MEGRIM

A rather flavourless but otherwise nice flat fish of the flounder family: giving it flavour is up to you. Cook it as sole or plaice, see *general information*, page 213–16.

MEUNIÈRE, À LA

Meaning 'as the miller's wife would cook it', this is a classic, easy (and heavenly) way of cooking and serving small whole fish, fish steaks or fillets. Here, briefly, is the method:

1 Dip fish in seasoned flour.

2 Fry on both sides in a generous quantity of *hot butter* (saltless or clarified, ideally, which don't burn so readily) until cooked and golden. Transfer to a warmed dish and keep hot.

3 Lightly brown any remaining butter (if not already brown), deglaze the pan with a dessertspoon or two of lemon juice, and pour this piping hot, lemon-flavoured butter over the fish before sprinkling it with chopped parsley.

MOLLUSCS

See *shellfish*, page 214.

MONKFISH

Also called angler fish, this is a weird-looking but interesting and good – if rather insipid – fish, of which only the tail end is sold, the extraordinary bony head end being cut off at sea. Normally sold skinned, because the skin also is coarse and ugly, monkfish is said to have a flavour of lobster – but I wonder? It certainly isn't unlike scampi in texture, however, and, again like scampi, does not separate into flakes when cooked. To give it flavour, cook in a tasty way, season it generously and cheer it up with colourful, flavourful garnishes and accompaniments such as wedges of lemon, a savoury butter, tartare or tomato sauce, a tossed green salad. I like it best grilled, fried or poached in wine. Here, briefly, are three ways of preparing and cooking it.

1 Kebabs – marinate the fish for at least half an hour on each side, either in a sharp French dressing, or in lemon juice and water – 4 spoonfuls water to 1 of lemon. Dry well, remove flesh from bone, cut into bite-sized pieces, spear (alternating with, say, prawns or thick slices of banana) on kebab skewers, brush with melted butter, season and grill. Garnish with walnut (or some other suitable) savoury butter and with wedges of lemon.

2 Remove from the bone, cut into scampi-sized pieces (the thicker parts cut in half), coat with egg and seasoned breadcrumbs and shallow or (preferably) deep fry.

3 Prepare as above, but coat with batter and deep fry.

■ A fish often used to make bouillabaisse and other fish soups.

MULLET, RED

Costing more (as I write) than a salmon steak of equal weight, less waste and infinitely finer flavour, this pretty little fish – *rouget* to the French – with its silvery pink and red skin and its unusually firm flesh, is outrageously priced here. Though it's a fish I have enjoyed countless times on the Mediterranean, I refuse to pay more per lb/500g for *rouget* than for almost any other fish: at half its cost, it would still be overpriced. For those more enthusiastic than I, however, and for others who are tempted to try cooking it in different ways, here are some tips.

1 The connoisseurs neither clean nor de-scale it. Others prefer to clean it very carefully, drawing out the gills and with

them the intestines, but leaving the liver – a great delicacy – inside.

2 Mullet is more often cooked whole than filleted: to cook whole, remove the fins and eyes, wash, dry and then score the fish.

3 *Methods of cooking*
   a Fry in butter, e.g. à la meunière, page 222: filleted, dipped first in seasoned flour, then in egg and breadcrumbs, and served with wedges of lemon.
   b Grill, see page 216, and serve with maître d'hôtel or bercy butter, pages 169 and 171.
   c Bake – (in a well-buttered roasting tin or dish) – sprinkle with fresh breadcrumbs, seasoning, a little finely chopped parsley and a little lemon juice. Dot generously with butter and allow about 15–20 minutes in a moderate oven, basting at least twice.

MUSSELS

Full of protein and rich in vitamin D, mussels aren't nowadays associated with danger the way they used to be, due to the scrupulous care taken in rearing. If you never buy them, do you really know what you are missing?

■ The chore of getting mussels to the table lies in their preparation:

1 Make sure they're alive, discarding any that are open, broken, or remain open after you have tapped them sharply on the sink. Keep in cold water up to the last minute.

2 Scrub and clean them meticulously, shaving off their beards (with which they cling to the rocks) and scraping off any barnacles. If you just give them 'a lick and a promise' kind of wash, the delicious juices, which pour out of the mussels as they open during cooking, will be fouled by the slime and dirt on the shells, almost certainly making the liquor unusable.

3 Soak mussels for an hour or two in a pail or large bowl of fresh water, giving them time to disgorge some of their sand, and to make them less salty. Gritty

mussels are as bad as gritty leeks.

4 Lift carefully out of the water, to avoid taking any sand with them.

■ One can sometimes substitute tinned mussels for fresh, using the liquid to make a sauce. Laced with a little white wine or vermouth in addition, such a sauce is excellent.

■ The water inside the shells of live mussels plays a vital role in their flavour. Lack of this is the main reason why shelled mussels are usually only suitable for something like garnishing, or to include in another dish. See also *shellfish*, page 214.

OYSTERS

Were once plentiful enough to be amongst the cheapest foods in the British diet, records showing that 36 million of them were landed on the coasts of England and Wales in 1898. At four old pennies a dozen they were eaten freely by the poorest families in Britain, only becoming a food of the rich later, when they grew scarce.

■ The native British oyster is too good to cook, which accounts for the British mostly eating them raw, just with lemon quarters, cayenne and brown bread and butter. Oysters must be absolutely fresh, shells tightly closed, and not opened until shortly before eating. To open, slide an oyster knife in at the hinge, snap the ligament which attaches the fish to the top, or flat shell and serve the oysters each in their own tasty, salty liquor in the deep shell embedded in crushed ice.

■ Today, to meet demand both in Britain and on the Continent, an industry practised by the Romans is passing from the hands of the fishermen to the culturists, from the natural oyster beds to artificial farms (such as on the Alderney coast), whence a fast-maturing Pacific type may reach the table 2 or 3 years earlier than native oysters. See also *shellfish*, page 214.

PLAICE

The skin is coarse and clings very hard to the flesh, so it's easier to cut the skin off fillets individually, than to pull the skin off the whole fish. When skinning plaice to cook whole, pull the skin off from head to tail rather than from tail to head – it comes off more easily that way. See also earlier pages regarding methods of cookery.

PRAWNS

Those from the cold seas of the world are very different from those of the warm seas, which explains why they don't all look alike on a fishmonger's slab.

Cold-water prawns First choice for any cold prawn dish because they have a finer flavour and firmer texture than warm-water prawns. Blindfold, you'd know what you were eating, so although more expensive, they're worth it for something like melon and prawns, prawn cocktail (page 157) or prawns in aspic (page 157).

Warm-water prawns Grow much faster and are in far greater supply than cold-water prawns, and are the staff of life of Chinese restaurants. Use them in hot dishes where their poorer qualities aren't so obvious as in a cold dish, and where one can enhance their flavour with other tasty ingredients cooked with them.

■ 1lb/450g fresh prawns yield about 6oz/150–175g peeled.

REDFISH

Formerly called sea-bream, but now (under EEC regulations) renamed redfish or Norwegian haddock, this fish deserves more customers than it seems to have because, though it looks coarse, it has good flesh. One can just about pull the rough pink skin off the fillets before cooking as cod or haddock, etc.

ROES

A marvel of nature for their delicacy and

sometimes sheer beauty, roes are the eggs of fish in the breeding season, bringing to the table a novel range of flavours, textures and colours not usually found in other foods.

Caviar The most famous of all roes comes from various members of the sturgeon family. Black is the finest. Eat caviar well-chilled (with well-chilled vodka?), with hot toast, butter and lemon quarters.

Mock caviar The roe of lump fish (see page 222) which when dyed black – and remember, dyes can run – looks (but doesn't taste) like caviar. The same roe is sometimes dyed red.

Cod's roe, smoked This, mullet or tunny fish roe, is the main ingredient of the Greek dish *taramasalata.*

Coral Greeny black when raw and going brilliant red when cooked, it is the roe of the hen lobster. Use to garnish, or sieve it finely to make lobster butter which one can use to flavour and colour a soup or sauce.

Crab's roe With the liver, this makes up the soft brown meat of a crab, which explains its very different texture from the firm, fleshy white meat.

Orange tongue of a scallop Corresponds to the roe in fish, which accounts for its requiring shorter cooking than the white meat. See page 226.

Soft roe The sperm or milt of male fish. I've never tasted it, but carp roe is said to be the most delicate, then herring and mackerel. Wash them in cold water and strip off the tiny blood vessel that runs down one side. Use to garnish fish dishes, to make fritters, serve them in patties, in tartlets or on canapés, etc., as well as on toast.

SALADS, FISH

Best made with types of fish which have as much flavour hot as cold. These include the crustaceans; nearly all the oily fish; and white fish such as halibut and turbot. You may want to counteract their richness by a sharp dressing, or by sousing; or perhaps complement others with a rich sauce like mayonnaise. See also *mixed salads*, page 209.

SALMON

One of the few fish one can't really fault. Its glorious colour, delicate flavour, firm texture, suitability for cooking by almost any method, and its perfection when served hot or cold, smoked or potted, make it a magnificent fish for the table.

■ Whatever you plan to do with it, make sure that the salmon is fresh, with bright silvery scales. Wipe rather than wash it, rubbing any bloody parts with salt.
■ *Boiled salmon* would be better described as *poached salmon* because fish breaks up and becomes watery if, after putting it into boiling water, you allow the water to continue boiling. Cooking time depends partly on the thickness of the fish, but you won't go far wrong by allowing 10 minutes to the lb/450g and 10 minutes over, in plain, salted, 'shivering' water, 180–190°F/82–88°C. Vinegar in the poaching liquid, whether water or court bouillon, spoils the colour of salmon. If after cooking there's a thick creamy curd between the flakes, this is just because the salmon is river-fresh.
■ The difference between tinned red and pink salmon is simply one of species. Nearly all tinned salmon comes from the Pacific where there are five major species.

SARDINES

The fry of the pilchard, taking their name from Sardinia, round whose coasts they abound.

■ In tins, sardines vary in flavour and quality according to the oil used, and to how long they are matured. Their bones are packed with calcium, so do eat rather than pick them out.

SCALLOPS

Coquilles Saint-Jacques, are at their very best in January and February when the roe is full and a bright orange colour. One of the most nutritious and delicious of all shellfish, one famous chef (amongst other gourmets) rates them the finest of *all* fish. A discerning friend of mine when last in Brittany – it seems remarkable enough, amidst no doubt such tempting alternatives, to mention this – chose scallops cooked in four different ways (one twice, it was so delicious) each of five evenings at five different restaurants. The *most* lovely, she thought, were served in a cream sauce subtly flavoured with pernod. (See *pernod*, page 130.)

■ The roe is the pearl in the oyster, so to speak: so delicate that, when possible, you should cook it a shorter time than the white meat, even if you've cut that in half.

■ If you buy closed scallops, you can be sure they're fresh. In addition they'll be moist, not desiccated as they tend to become when left about opened on the fishmonger's slab. If you prefer to buy them open, remember to ask for the other, deeper half of the shell should you want to serve the fish in it. There isn't enough room in the shallow half for fish, sauce and garnish.

■ When you've washed and scrubbed them, put scallops round side down in a warm place, say on a plate rack or in a very low oven, to open. (*Shallow* shell down, the messy water runs out.) Remove the black part and gristly fibre before you cook them.

■ If preparing scallops au gratin in the shells, support them in an ovenware dish to prevent them tilting, otherwise some of the sauce is almost bound to escape over the edge when grilled. See also page 214.

SCAMPI

The accepted culinary name for the tail-meat of what we call a Dublin Bay prawn (see also page 214). The tail is the only part we eat.

■ Unlike prawns and lobster, scampi don't change colour when cooked. The fish is naturally pink, darker red in parts.

■ Fresh, scampi have a sweeter taste and more delicate texture than lobster. Frozen? Well, blindfold, they might be difficult to recognize.

SHRIMPS

Either pink or brown when cooked. The tiny brown ones so much prized by the Romans make much the best eating but, nearly 2,000 years later, they're still hell to peel!

■ Use shrimps to garnish fish or egg dishes, in a mixed hors d'oeuvre, au gratin, on canapés, potted, etc. See also page 214.

SKATE

Such a weird looking fish that, if you're unfamiliar with it, it's worth asking your fishmonger if he can show you one. The only really fleshy parts are the fins which, understandably when you know what they look like, are called wings. A wing usually weighs about 1½–2½lb/700g–1.1kg, the smaller ones serving only two people. Ask the fishmonger to skin it, or do it yourself after rather than before cooking, having first scrubbed and rinsed it well.

■ To prepare, trim off the fringe of the gristly bone round the edge, and cut the fish longways into wide strips 3–4in/7.5–10cm long and 2–3in/5–7.5cm wide.

■ The pieces are usually poached (20–30 minutes according to thickness) in a simple court bouillon (water enough to cover the fish, a finely sliced shallot or small onion, a bouquet garni containing also a few peppercorns, salt and 1 tablespoon white wine vinegar – previously simmered together for 5 minutes and used while hot) or in milk (also flavoured with onion, a bouquet garni and salt), then finished off tastefully. *Raie au beurre noir* (skate with black butter) is one of the best known: put the cooked skinned fish in a warmed serving dish and cover generously with well-browned (nut brown) butter. Deglaze the butter pan with 1–2 tablespoons wine vinegar, adding a teaspoon each of chopped capers and finely chopped parsley before pouring this, too, over the fish.

■ Considering the waste – easily 50 per cent, in the form of their gristly bone – one is paying an almost luxury price for a rather poor-flavoured if interesting and unusual – in appearance, structure and texture – fish.

SMOKED FISH

Either cold-smoked like salmon, eel, kippers, bloaters, cod's roe and haddock (finnan, fillet, golden cutlets and smokies), or hot-smoked like mackerel, sprats and buckling.

■ All fish are brined before being smoked over oak or other hardwood shavings or sawdust, but while the cold-smoked fish are smoked to just a high enough temperature (86°F/30°C) to impart flavour, the hot-smoked fish are, at about 200°F/93°C, slightly cooked as well. Apart from smoked salmon, into which rock salt is rubbed, cold-smoked fish therefore keep less well than hot-smoked, and should be eaten soon after one buys them, like fresh fish.

■ See also *smoked fish*, page 158.

SMOKIES

See *haddock*, page 219.

SOLE, DOVER

Has an almost lacy-thin skin; so thin and so easily detached from the flesh that it is easier to pull it off the fish while it is whole than to cut it off when filleted. Unlike lemon sole and plaice with their tough skins almost glued to the fish, Dover sole is skinned from *tail to head*, that being the easiest way to do it. (Lots of cookery books give the method.) Not

only does the skin of the Dover sole separate easily from the flesh, but also the bone from the flesh, after the fish is cooked. This is why it's essential to have Dover sole, not lemon sole, for sole colbert – an egg and breadcrumb-coated, deep-fried whole fish, with its backbone removed after cooking and the cavity so formed filled with maître d'hôtel butter. Incidentally, it's easier to cut the bone at each end of the fish with scissors than with a knife.

Soles, slip Dover soles weighing less than ½lb/225g. Though cheaper than the larger fish, these small soles have an even better flavour and make a delicious meal, whole, for one person. They're worth looking for.

SOLE, LEMON

See *general information*, page 213.

SPRATS

Don't seem as popular as they ought to be, perhaps because they're so cheap, or because people don't know how to cook them. One can grill them and serve with mustard sauce, dry fry for 5–10 minutes, or dip in batter or seasoned flour and deep fry. (I like quickly to split and clean the larger ones.) Allow about ¼lb/100g per person.

Smoked sprats Served with lemon quarters, freshly milled black pepper and brown bread and butter, they make a delicious hors d'oeuvre. Allow 3 or 4 per person. See also *oily fish*, page 213.

TROUT

Have white, pinkish or 'salmon' flesh, according to the waters in which they live. 'Salmon' (sea) trout differs from other types in that it (like the salmon) lives a greater part of its life in the sea. As a rule, treat this and large trout as salmon. The smaller river or lake trout are excellent smoked, fried, grilled, poached or otherwise prepared in many different ways.

TURBOT

These fish certainly assure their future – the female will lay up to 10,000,000 eggs in the spawning season!

■ This is one of the best white fish, its flesh white, firm and delicate in flavour. Avoid skinning or trimming turbot because its skin, fins and bones are full of flavour. (Gastronomes prize the skin, also the gelatinous matter in the fins.)
■ Turbot is often served with shrimp, lobster or anchovy sauce, whether poached (in plain salted water or in a court bouillon), baked or fried.

Chicken turbot A small turbot weighing under 4lb/1.75kg – delicious cooked à la meunière (see page 222).

WHITEBAIT

See page 159.

WHITING

Belongs to the cod family but many of us fight shy of it without perhaps knowing what we're missing. Gastronomically, it is an important fish because its flesh, though tasteless, is also very light and easily digested. The fact that it is tasteless means one can cook it by almost any method one likes (see *general information*) to make it tasty. It is often served with its tail between its teeth, in which position one can also stuff it.

■ Whiting used to be very cheap – so cheap and plentiful that it was often fed to cats. The memory of that price is no reason to dismiss this silvery, fine-textured little fish.

WITCH

Also called Torbay sole, this fish is very similar to the megrim – both of them quite nice but unexciting flat fish of the flounder family. Cook as sole or plaice, add flavour to it and cook in various ways (see *general information*, page 213).

13
Meat

GENERAL INFORMATION

Meat is a major item in most family budgets so it's essential to know what you're looking for, to shop wisely and to buy where the standard is consistently high. There's often nowhere to beat the small family butcher who rears his own beasts, feeds them on what he knows produces the best quality meat, kills them at the right age and understands the importance of proper hanging. If not careful, one can pay nearly as much, if not just as much, for second-quality meat as for first. It is, for instance, mainly because of the feeding that the best Scotch beef is famous for its flavour and texture, and that the best lamb is always so succulent and delicious. This explains why a prime cut is not necessarily a guarantee of prime quality, which depends on so many factors.

In addition to selling good meat, your butcher (even if in a supermarket) should know his stuff: a good one will actively enjoy advising you, and amongst other things will know how to cut meat for specialized dishes like beef olives or wiener schnitzel (and will be able to cut it), will sell you chops without bone splinters, and will without being asked trim away gristle and excess fat on meat.

The parts of an animal which do the least muscular work produce the prime cuts, while the working parts – mostly from the forequarters of the animal – make up the cheaper cuts of meat. They are of similar quality to prime cuts from the same carcase, but usually have a high proportion of bone, fat and muscle fibre, which means they depend for their ten-derness upon the cook.

Cheaper cuts of meat more often than not involve long slow cooking and should often include marinating the meat before you cook it, see page 71. (Besides a marinade giving meat extra flavour, the acids in it break down connective tissue and fibres.) As a general rule, the tougher the cut of meat, the slower and longer you should cook it: here a moist method of cookery such as braising or stewing is ideal. During the process, the meat tenderizes, and the goodness from all the connective tissue, etc. goes into the cooking liquor. Other ways to break down fibrous tissues are by beating the meat with a rolling pin, or, of course, by mincing it.

Meat is basically of two kinds: flesh and offal. The unusual textures and flavours of the latter give variety to our meals, most offal is easily digested, and some of it is of great nutritional importance.

The main reasons for cooking meat are to tenderize and make it digestible, to destroy bacteria, and – naturally – to make it taste and look good. Meat, like fish, takes flavour from the bone, so although you gain from the easy carving of a boned, rolled joint, you lose out on flavour and goodness. This, for instance, explains why something like best end of neck of lamb is so sweet and delicious and why rolled ribs of beef will have less flavour than ribs on the bone.

A good-sized frozen joint needs 36–48 hours to thaw out, slowly, in the refrigerator. If thawed faster, at room temperature, more juices will run out of it – and with those juices, a lot of flavour. People who roast small joints which are still frozen, can't know what they're missing in terms of goodness, but to cook a rolled joint in that condition is to risk salmonella poisoning. This is because the bacteria causing surface contamination of meat are normally destroyed by heat, but when meat is boned and rolled, the 'surface' is inside, and the heat may not penetrate enough to kill the bacteria.

ROASTING A JOINT

Roasting a joint isn't simply a case of sticking it in the oven with some dripping and basting it occasionally. If you want meat to be really succulent and tasty, and not to shrink out of sight, you need a little bit of know-how and must be prepared to go to a little bit of trouble as well. Here, in case you'd like them, are a few hints:

Choice of meat

■ A large joint is in fact much more economical than a small one because, pro rata, it shrinks much less. Even though you may only want to buy 2–3lb/1–1.5kg, it will be cheaper in the long run to buy 4 or 5lb/1.75–2.25kg and get the extra servings from it either as cold meat, or in made-up dishes. It is also labour-saving because you probably won't have to cook again for the next day or two – or at least will have cold meat to put in the freezer for another time.

■ For a joint *with* bone, allow 8–10oz/225–275g meat per person. In addition to meat on the bone having more flavour, it roasts better because the bone conducts heat through the centre of the meat.

■ For a joint *without* bone, such as rolled ribs of beef, allow 6–8oz/175–225g meat per person.

■ Fat is an important part of a joint because any natural covering of it means the meat will be more tender and succulent. This is because a good top layer of fat bastes the joint automatically, and does away with spoon-basting, which by comparison dries the meat up and makes it shrink. Really lean meat doesn't roast well unless you lard it (page 69), bard it

(page 51) or enclose it in a flour and water paste, page 235.

Storage of joint Covered loosely with waxed paper or foil, and put at the bottom of the refrigerator, it will keep in near-perfect condition for 3–4 days – or you could marinate it for 24 hours.

Preparation

■ Weigh meat and calculate cooking time, remembering that a thin joint needs less cooking than a thick one of the same weight. (See different kinds of meat for oven temperature and roasting times, also *roasting*, page 78.)

■ A little seasoned flour rubbed into the surface of a joint makes the outside slice taste extra good, absorbs surplus fat and gives a lovely golden finish to the meat.

■ A few slivers of garlic here and there give subtle flavour. Do try it, even if you think you don't care for garlic.

■ Stand the joint, with the thickest layer of fat on top so that it will baste itself, either on a meat stand in the roasting tin, or perhaps better still on a bed of roasting vegetables, which are heavenly served with the joint: slice one or two large onions in two or three slices each, also a large carrot or two, and rest the meat on top. During cooking, the sugar in them caramelizes, giving a lovely flavour to the gravy in the by-going. (If you stand the meat itself in the hot fat and baste with it as well, this tends to draw out the juices, shrinking and drying the meat in the process.) I myself like to spread an over-lean joint (if not otherwise protected, as above) with a good layer of lard or dripping (whichever appropriate) before roasting, and then spread it again at half-hourly intervals with a little more, to keep the meat moist. (The juices in meat are essential to its flavour, moistness and non-shrinkage, so at all costs must be kept in, and not allowed to escape.)

The oven Have the oven hot before putting the meat in, usually gas 7, 425°F/220°C for the first 15 minutes, to seal the surfaces of the meat and prevent the juices escaping. Once again, everything you do is concerned with retaining the juices to keep the meat moist and full of flavour.

■ Avoid using a fork to lift a roasting joint because juices will escape. It's better to use two spoons.

■ For consistently perfectly cooked meat, a meat thermometer should remove the guess-work, see *meat thermometer*, page 45. Otherwise make sure the meat feels springy when pressed with the back of a spoon, not spongy. Also press the meat with the back of a fork to see the colour of the emerging juices. If you like beef rare or medium done, the juices should be red or pink, whereas for well done meat they should be clear. Pork and veal juices should never be pink because both must be well cooked to be palatable. Lamb you may like slightly underdone, in which case the juices will be just tinged with pink.

■ Allow roasted meat a resting period of about 15 minutes, longer if a very large joint, in the partly-cooled oven. This gives time for the juices to reintegrate into the flesh – instead of pouring out onto the dish, as they do if the meat is carved as soon as it's cooked – making it not only more succulent and tender, but firmer and also easier to carve. (Despite the oven being off, the interior temperature of the meat in fact goes on rising.)

Accompaniments Do serve the right ones, because they nearly all have a purpose: either to add richness, to counteract it, or to give complementary flavour or contrast of texture. Serve thick gravy with a stuffed joint, thin with others.

COLD ROAST MEAT

If planning to serve roast meat cold for a particular occasion, you should, for perfection, cook it specially and let it go quite cold before carving: juices run out if you cut into a joint while it's hot, so the meat ends up drier, with less flavour and a poorer colour.

To carve cold meat An electric saw-knife will carve cold meat easily, thinly, economically and in good-sized slices which will have the maximum of flavour – different in every way from poorly carved meat.

To boil meat, see *boiling*, page 53.
To braise meat, see *braising*, page 54.
To fry meat, see *shallow frying*, page 64.
To grill meat, see *grilling*, page 66.
To stew meat, see *stewing*, page 83, and *brown stews*, page 247.

FOR THE FREEZER

Meat will not keep indefinitely in a freezer. According to the UK Meat Promotion Executive, their maximum recommended storage times are:

beef	8 months
lamb	6 months
pork	6 months
mince and offal	3 months
sausage and cured green bacon	3 months
smoked bacon	1 month

BACON

Bacon cuts come from the middle and forequarters of the pig, differing from gammon which is the hind leg. As with other meats, it pays to shop where the quality is reliable. This, in turn, depends on the breed, age and feeding of the pig, and the way in which it has been cured. It also varies according to the cut. Danish bacon for instance is specially cured to avoid over-saltiness, which explains why small cuts of this can be cooked without pre-soaking.

■ Whether you plan to boil, bake or braise bacon and gammon, allow about 30 minutes per lb/450g, longer if a very thick rolled joint. Should you want to bake a very lean joint, the old-fashioned way is still difficult to improve upon: enclose the meat in a flour and water paste (page 235) to keep it moist, prevent it from shrinking and retain its glorious flavour.

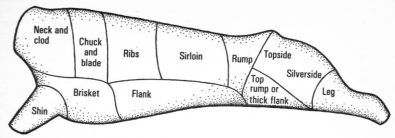

*Beef carcase showing what comes from where
By courtesy of The Meat Promotion Executive*

■ To *store* bacon or gammon, replace the shop wrapping with kitchen foil, and refrigerate it. For larger storage of both cooked and uncooked meat, put it on a clean plate, cover loosely and keep it as cool as possible.

■ To *freeze* bacon, it should be vacuum packed and stored no longer than the stated time. The drying action of freezing is intensified by salt, used in curing, the meat becoming dehydrated and hard unless so protected. See also *gammon*, page 235.

Green bacon Bacon which has been cured but not smoked, hence its much milder flavour.

Bacon rashers They won't curl up if you slash the fat before you grill or fry them; otherwise they do because the fat cooks and shrivels faster than the lean.

■ Back rashers fry best overlapping each other like slates on a roof, the lean lying on top of the fat of the rasher under it. The fat becomes crisp and the lean keeps moist. Reverse the process for grilling, and have the fat on top of the lean, where it will baste and keep it moist. Whether grilling or frying, therefore, the fat always protects the lean from the fiercest heat.

■ Unless you like the fat fried to a crisp, you can't leave the rinds on because their texture makes them inedible. Rather than fiddle around with a few rashers each time you want them for breakfast, it's quicker to cut them all off with scissors when one buys the bacon. Fry the rinds first, make the pan greasy, then when frizzled you can crush them with a rolling pin, cool and store in an air-tight jar to sprinkle over savoury things like scrambled egg, macaroni cheese, cooked vegetables etc.

■ In a covered container in the refrigerator, rashers store better unwrapped than wrapped.

Bacon rolls These cook faster and the rashers go further if you stretch them before cutting into 2 or 3 pieces each, and rolling up: lay rashers on chopping board and elongate each with the blade of a knife, with firm stroking movements away from you.

BEEF

Beef can be cooked in so many different ways that, if you want to save expense and disappointment, it's worth knowing what all the cuts look like. Cut and quality determine the cooking method: if, for instance, you want to stew steak, it's silly to buy a prime cut which not only costs more but also makes a poorer stew, because it lacks all the gelatinous matter that makes the liquor so good. If you want to roast, fry or grill beef, it's useless to buy anything *but* a prime cut, because only these will tenderize quickly enough in the greater heat required for these methods of cookery. These are some of the signs of best quality beef:

1 It should be a good colour. (Beef cuts which have been pickled ready for boiling will be grey in colour. The colour change is caused by the brine, and the meat will turn a nice pink during cooking.)

2 Lean meat, particularly cuts intended for grilling or roasting, is best when marbled with fat. The flecks of fat melt into the lean, making it tender, succulent and full of flavour.

3 The fat should be creamy white, firm and dry. (Yellow, oily fat comes from an old or poorly-fed animal.)

Roasting See also *roasting a joint*, page 230, and *roasting*, page 78.

1 Allow 15 minutes per lb/450g and 15 minutes over for a nicely underdone joint on the bone, or 20 minutes per lb and 20 minutes over for a similarly cooked thick, boned and rolled joint. Roast in a preheated hot oven, gas 7, 425°F/220°C for the first 15 minutes to seal in the juices, then reduce heat to gas 5, 375°F/190°C for remainder of cooking time, allowing 20 minutes resting time in addition, see page 231.

■ Traditional accompaniments are Yorkshire pudding (page 301), roast potatoes, horseradish sauce and thin gravy.

2 For fillet (which, if you are serving it rare, need not be barded because of the very short cooking time, but only needs brushing liberally with oil or melted butter), allow 5–7 minutes per lb/450g in a very hot oven, gas 8, 450°F/230°C for the first 15 minutes, then lower to gas 3, 325°F/165°C for remainder of time, allowing 15 minutes resting time in addition, see page 231. If you prefer it not quite so rare, then bard it in order to protect and keep the meat moist, and cook it for up to 10 minutes per lb/450g, still allowing 15 minutes resting time in addition.

■ The filet mignon, the narrow tip of the fillet or tenderloin, is folded double and tied to equalize the roast's thickness.

■ Accompaniments for fillet are pont neuf potatoes (potato chips all of the same size – 2½in/6.5cm long and rather less than ½in/1.25cm thick), dressed watercress to garnish and the meat's own gravy: made with the drippings and a little beef stock.

The prime and better cuts are:

Sirloin Roast either on the bone or boned and rolled – or bone and braise.

Sirloin steaks Grill.

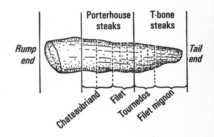

Loin and wing-end section

The fillet (If separated from sirloin.) See drawing above. On the inside of the sirloin bone, the fillet is the most tender of all cuts and, when roasted, one of the most choice of all beef dishes.

■ Fillet steaks are enough to confuse any of us: different parts of the fillet are called by different names, according to whether they're cut from the rump end, the middle or the tail end. In some cases, a steak is named according to the thickness or portion of a particular cut. *Châteaubriand*, for instance, corresponds to the undercut or fillet portion of a porterhouse steak. It is 2in/5cm thick, should weigh at least 1lb/450g before trimming – and is always grilled. A thinner steak cut from this same portion is called a *filet*. What the French call *filets*, *tournedos* and *filet mignons*, we often refer to more generally as fillet steaks.

■ Although I myself like them best

grilled (see *grilling*, page 66) – with a sprinkling of salt, plenty of freshly milled black pepper, a sliced clove of garlic on top and served with a savoury butter – fillet steaks are more often sautéd. Cook them quickly in hot butter to a nice brown on the outside and a juicy red inside, saucing and serving them according to your recipe.

Rump steak Grill or fry. Although not as tender as fillet steak, lots of people prefer it for its fuller flavour.

■ Use also for beef olives (lean, and thinly cut) and for beef strogonoff.

Ribs Roast fore ribs and wing ribs either on the bone or boned and rolled. If preferred, bone and braise. Back ribs and top ribs can be braised or pot-roasted, back ribs can be roasted.

■ Grill (preferably) or fry entrecôte steaks. (The entrecôte, by definition, is the part of the meat between the bones of the ribs of beef. An entrecôte minute steak is a very thin one which, as long as you like it rare, should cook in one minute on each side.)

Topside This is a lean cut usually sold rolled with a layer of fat tied round it. Roast, pot-roast, braise or boil.

■ Use thinly cut for beef olives.

The cheaper cuts are:

Top rump (Also called thick flank.) Fry, grill or braise if sliced. Braise or pot-roast a joint.

Brisket Sold on the bone or boned and rolled. Requires slow, moist cooking to prevent shrinkage, so braise or boil rather than roast. Is often salted or pickled for pressed beef.

Silverside Very lean and contains no bone. Boil, fresh or pickled (boiled beef and dumplings).

■ Some people like to roast silverside but I think it's better braised.

Shin (Called hough in Scotland.) Stew and use in dishes like hot-pot, beef steak

and kidney pudding, a pie, etc. Lots of people don't seem to realize what superb meat this is: there's hardly a scrap of waste on it, it is one of the cheapest cuts, has a lovely flavour and, given long slow cooking, makes the most delicious gravy – due to the muscle in it turning to gelatine. This is why, when cooked with the shin bone, it makes jellied stock.

■ Make soup and potted hough with it as well. In addition, shin is the traditional cut for making beef tea.

Leg (Also called hough in Scotland.) Not always quite so good as shin, I think, but one can use it in the same ways, see above. (How gelatinous it is varies according to an animal's muscle.)

Neck and clod Like shin, good for hot-pot and stews, but has less flavour and is less gelatinous.

Flank Boil (salted or pickled) for pressed beef. Braise or pot-roast on the bone. Stew.

Chuck and blade (Sold as shoulder in Scotland.) Braise or stew. In my opinion chuck steak and skirt (which comes from inside the ribs and the flank), are inferior to shin for dishes where the meat is stewed.

BEEF-STEAK AND KIDNEY PUDDING

Much better made with shin (see above) than with a more expensive cut of (braising) steak such as skirt or chuck. Long slow cooking, 3½–4 hours, is essential if the meat is to be cooked, the gravy rich and dark and the suet crust pastry its characteristic golden colour: *not* a dish for the pressure cooker.

■ It is very difficult to line a basin perfectly with a round of pastry: the easy way is to roll all the pastry into a round large enough to line and slightly overlap the basin, then cut out one third of it for the lid, see illustration.

Form the larger piece into a kind of cone inside the basin, damping and overlapping the cut edges. Re-shape the cut-out piece to make the lid.

BRAWN

Made from the pig's head or the trimmings of the animal together with either trotters or a cowheel, which provide the gelatine needed for the liquor to form a jelly when cold.

■ It is easier and the job is less macabre if you ask your butcher to prepare the head (or half-head) for brawn. Although there's lots of it, the meat (apart from the cheek) is rather tasteless, so be generous with seasonings and spices, subtle with herbs.

■ You'll need ingredients of this sort:

half a fresh pig's head, prepared
1 or 2 pig's trotters, well washed
1 onion
20 peppercorns
1 blade mace
4 cloves
12 allspice
bouquet garni
enough cold water just to cover meat

■ The tongue is simmered a shorter time (2–3 hours) than the other meat (3–4 hours), which should be just falling from the bones when cooked.

■ Use brawn for hors d'oeuvres, supper, sandwiches or as a main dish with salad in summer. Because it is served sliced, it is better to set brawn in a square or rectangular mould than in a round one.

FLOUR AND WATER PASTE

An old-fashioned method which is still just as good today for baking very lean joints of meat like gammon or venison. Sealed up inside and protected, the meat juices are retained so the meat shrinks very little, keeps nice and moist and is full of flavour. Gammon and bacon should first be soaked, a chicken should be brushed with oil, and venison is better if previously marinated (see page 273).

■ Briefly, here's what to do:

1 Make a dough just firm enough to roll out by stirring approximately ½pt/300ml water into 1lb/450g sieved flour. Turn the dough on to a floured board and knead lightly, before rolling roughly to the shape and size of the joint, and large enough to enclose it. (For a very large joint, you may need half as much again.)

2 Lay joint upside down on dough before damping the edges and sealing in the meat, then the joins are sealed underneath the meat when you turn it the right way up to bake.

3 Bake in a greased roasting tin for usual roasting time plus 15 minutes extra, to allow heat to penetrate the paste. There's no need for fat as a rule because the paste prevents any drying of the meat but if the crust looks like getting too brown, cover it with foil or oiled greaseproof paper.

4 When the meat is cooked, crack open and break away the crust. A joint is then usually returned to the oven for 10–15 minutes without the crust to glaze, brown, or otherwise finish it off, according to recipe.

GAMMON

Gammon comes from the hind leg of a bacon pig, bacon from the fore or shoulder cuts. The main difference between gammon and ham is that gammon is cut from the carcase after the whole side has been brine-cured, whereas ham is the whole hind leg removed from the carcase at the fresh pork stage, and cured separately to ensure its special flavour.

■ For a number of people, you may want to buy a whole gammon. For a family meal, I'd buy a smaller joint, e.g. corner, middle gammon, slipper or hock. These can be boiled or baked, and do remember that larger joints shrink less than small (pro rata) when cooked. As gammon is good sliced and eaten cold, it is more economical in the end therefore to buy a joint at least 3½lb/ 1.5kg. If cooking it specifically to serve cold, allow the meat 12–24 hours to cool before slicing.

■ Unless otherwise instructed, soak gammon or bacon 12–24 hours in cold water, to cover, otherwise the meat may taste over-salty. If time simply won't allow for this, at least bring the joint to the boil in cold water and then throw that away before bringing the meat to the boil in more cold water, again to cover.

■ Weigh the meat and calculate cooking time well in advance, allowing approximately 30 minutes per lb/450g (up to 40 minutes for a large, thick, rolled joint), whether to bake or boil.

■ *To boil*, place the meat in a large pan, skin side downwards and with water to cover, adding an onion and a bay leaf or a sprig of rosemary to the water – and topping up with more boiling water as required.

■ *To bake*, wrap the joint loosely but completely in foil along with a bay leaf and a sprig of rosemary and put in a roasting tin with a little water in the tin. Bake at gas 5, 375°F/190°C.

■ On a meat thermometer, bacon and gammon are cooked when the internal temperature reaches 180°F/82°C.

■ Sometimes it is nice to use cider in the cooking water: add about ¾pt/450ml 1 hour before the meat is cooked, bringing the liquor quickly back to the boil.

■ The rind is removed when the meat is cooked. If sprinkling it with golden breadcrumbs (raspings), they will stick on better now than when the meat is cold.

■ Glazing gives extra flavour and a glorious aroma to the cooked joint: first score the de-rinded hot fat in a criss-cross pattern, then cover with any of the following, baking the meat (whether baked or boiled) for an extra 15 minutes or so, until it caramelizes, in a hot oven, gas 6, 400°F/205°C.

1 Spread (not too thickly) with French mustard, and then with a covering of Demerara sugar, pressed on.

2 Press on a mixture of fresh brown breadcrumbs and Demerara sugar: about 1oz/25g of each. Now stick about 10–12 cloves into the fat at intervals, removing them before serving.

3 Spread with apple or redcurrant jelly, or with warmed apricot jam.

■ *Accompaniments and/or garnishes*. These vary slightly according to whether the gammon is baked or boiled, but either way you will probably want to serve potatoes, a colourful vegetable (e.g. green peas, French beans, creamed spinach, sautéd courgettes) – or individual salads (say green, or apricot and pineapple) if the meat is *baked* – and a tasty sauce such as Cumberland or parsley, the latter preferably made with béchamel milk (see page 177). A large baked joint also looks and tastes splendid if you spear heated pineapple rings or peach halves all over it with cocktail sticks. Other suggestions are watercress, pease pudding, dhal, a savoury butter, e.g. mustard, parsley, marchand de vins. With cold sliced gammon, pickled peaches are unusual and delicious.

■ The cold fat-free liquor left after boiling a piece of gammon makes good lentil, split pea or flageolet bean soup – but beware of adding more salt before you have tasted the soup.

■ See also *bacon*, page 231.

HAMS

A speciality of many countries. The wide differences between them depend on things like the breed of pig, the particular foods on which they may be fed, how the hams are cured and smoked, where and how long they are matured, etc. The main types are:

American hams These include famous types like *Kentucky* and *Virginia*.

Continental hams *Parma*, *Bayonne*, *Westphalia* and the French country (locally cured) hams. If you have the opportunity, do try and compare them, and see which you like best.

Irish hams These are dry-salt cured and,

after being boned, are peat-smoked.

English hams *Wiltshire* and *York* for instance. York ham is famous the world over because it is so consistently good in flavour, texture and appearance, due mainly to the cure. The meat is a lovely colour, firm and yet tender, mild without being in any way insipid.

HAMBURGER

Implies either a flat cake (or patty) made of minced meat, or the same thing served in a split roll with various garnishes such as a slice of tomato or fried onion, pickles, ketchup or indeed almost anything the roll will hold.

■ It's better to choose a lean cut of meat and have it minced than to buy fatty mince because the hamburgers will shrink less, taste better and won't be so indigestible. A little egg yolk or whole egg is included to bind the mixture and prevent the cakes disintegrating when fried or grilled.

KEBAB

The Turkish name for various dishes whose principal feature is skewered meat, traditionally lamb. Kebabs originated in the Caucasus where the mountain people impaled meat on their swords, roasting it outside over an open fire.

■ Kebabs are a splendid way of tickling a jaded appetite for they combine the best of everything on a single spike: an unlimited variety of flavour combinations, prime pieces of meat (nothing tough will cook in so short a time) and the natural succulence of all grilled or spit-roasted meat. It's worth telling your butcher you want the meat for kebabs, then he knows just what to give you.

■ If possible, use proper kebab skewers (see page 42). If you first run these through a piece of suet, everything will slip off more easily, or if you like garlic, why not run them through a clove of garlic instead?

Marinated lamb kebabs These are such a

favourite of mine that I'm going to spell out the details. Give yourself a 24 hour start.

To serve 4

1lb/450g fillet or boned shoulder of lamb
3 dessertspoons pineapple syrup
2 dessertspoons soy sauce
3 level dessertspoons clear honey
⎫ marinade, to flavour and tenderize the meat ⎬ ⎭

1 medium-sized can pineapple chunks – about 6 per person
about 12 spring onions or tiny shallots
salt and black pepper
10oz/275g boiled long grain rice, see page 202
large tin baked beans in tomato sauce – plebeian, but easy and very good!

1 *First day* Trim excess fat and any skin from meat and cut it into largish bite-sized pieces. Put in a basin.

2 Make the marinade. Mix together the pineapple syrup, soy sauce and honey. Pour over the meat, mix well, cover with foil and refrigerate for 12–24 hours, turning meat over occasionally to flavour it fully.

3 *Second day* Drain meat and reserve marinade, also drain the pineapple chunks well. Thread meat, prepared spring onions and pineapple chunks on to 4 kebab skewers, alternating so that the onions flavour the meat. Season well with salt and freshly ground pepper. (Be sure to pierce the food in the middle, otherwise it won't cook evenly, and won't rotate evenly if on a spit.)

4 Grill kebabs 1 minute on each side under preheated red-hot grill, at least 3in/8cm from the heat. Now spoon over them a little of the retained marinade and grill under reduced, moderate heat for about 20 minutes or until the meat is cooked, turning kebabs every 3–5 minutes and basting them each time with more of the marinade. (If uncertain whether the meat is cooked, cut a piece to test it.)

5 Serve the hot boiled rice in a 'wall' on a side-dish, put the heated beans in the centre and lay the kebabs on top. Scrape up all the juices and marinade in the bottom of grill pan and pour over rice, to flavour it. Serve piping hot.

LAMB

The meat of an animal under one year. Mutton, with its firmer flesh and stronger flavour, generally comes from an animal under two years. Spring lamb is from a lamb 3–4 months old.

■ Some cuts are expensive but make a glorious roast, while the more economical cuts make good stews. Whichever you're buying, look for fine-grained lean with a bright colour. The fat should be crisp and white, but not brittle. Leg and loin have a reasonable layer of fat covering the lean, which in turn is covered by a thin paper-like skin. This skin should be pliable to the touch, not hard and wrinkled: remove it from chops before cooking because, being on the side, it doesn't get cooked properly, but don't remove it from a roasting joint as it helps to retain the juices in the meat, and to cook it evenly.
■ Both lamb and mutton are more wasteful on the whole than beef because so much fat is embedded in the lean, as well as around the joints. It is the fat, though, which makes lamb so tasty and juicy – apart from stewing cuts – so if you cut too much off, you'll spoil your meat – just trim off any excess.
■ Use herbs to enhance the flavour of lamb roasts and casseroles: rosemary is a traditional herb for cooking with roast lamb, or if you're stewing it, you may like rosemary, marjoram or basil added to a bouquet garni.

Roasting See also *roasting a joint*, page 230, and *roasting*, page 78.

1 Seasoned flour rubbed into the surface of lamb helps to absorb surplus fat. Also, if you like the flavour of rosemary, make a few slits in the covering skin of a joint, slipping a wee sprig of the herb into each.

2 Lamb is best when slow-roasted so calculate cooking time (after stuffing) and allow 25 minutes per lb/450g and 25 minutes over. Allow a thick leg cut slightly longer.
3 Given a joint with a moderate or good layer of fat on top, you shouldn't baste it: before you cook it, simply brush the joint with oil or melted lard or cooking fat, or spread the top with fat.
4 Roast in a preheated hot oven, gas 6, 400°F/205°C for the first 15 minutes to seal in the juices, then reduce heat to gas 4, 350°F/175°C for remainder of cooking time.
5 If you like lamb's sweetness accentuated, and the skin crisp and tasty, spread its fatty surface with redcurrant or mint jelly half an hour before the end of the cooking time. The sugar in the jelly caramelizes, making the lamb scrumptious.

■ Traditional accompaniments to lamb are: roast potatoes; stuffing, optional, to give extra flavour, to counteract richness and to make a joint go further; mint sauce to counteract richness (mint jelly is also delicious if you like its sweetness); thick gravy if the roast is stuffed, otherwise thin.

The prime and better cuts are:

Leg (Known as gigot in Scotland.) Leg is often divided into fillet end and shank end. It is more economical and preferable, however, to buy the whole leg, basically because it cooks better: when roasting, it will lie where you put it (unlike the fillet end which is apt to tilt over) and, with its good covering of fat, is self-basting. Given these advantages, the meat shrinks less and is more juicy and tender than a smaller joint cut from it. Roast on the bone, or boned, stuffed and rolled. Fillet end: roast. Shank end: roast or casserole.

Loin Usually divided into loin end and chump end, unless you want a big joint. Roast in the piece, or boned, stuffed and rolled. Loin chops: Grill or fry. Chump chops: These are to lamb what rump is to

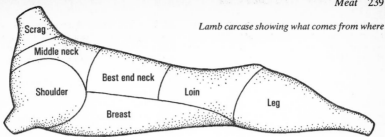

Lamb carcase showing what comes from where

By courtesy of The Meat Promotion Executive

beef – one of the finest cuts available for tenderness, meatiness and flavour. Grill or fry.

Best end of neck Roast, like loin, either on the bone, or boned, stuffed and rolled. It has more flavour than loin but is much less meaty.

■ A *crown roast* is made with two best ends of neck, but in my opinion never seems to taste as good as it looks, or ought to taste after so much work. Cutlets: grill or fry.

Saddle The whole back (two loin joints) left together – delicious, but too big for small families or small ovens.

The economy cuts are:

Shoulder (Not cut like this in Scotland.) Shoulder is sometimes divided into blade end and knuckle end. Roast on the bone, or boned, stuffed and rolled.

■ Braise or casserole.

Middle neck Usually cut into chops, then stewed, as in hot-pot or Irish stew.

Scrag end Nearly all bone, and better for soups than stews.

Breast A very fat cut which can be roasted (boned, stuffed and rolled), braised or stewed.

MINCE

Isn't worth buying when as fatty as some butchers sell it: the fat in it melts when cooked so the meat both shrinks and is indigestible.

■ Mince should be lean, red and preferably finely ground: if your butcher hasn't got this on the counter, ask him for it, perhaps choosing the steak you'd like minced, even if slightly more costly – it depends what you want it for.

■ Use mince for things like galantine, meat loaf, meat balls, moussaka, lasagne, cottage pie, Cornish pasties, hamburgers, spaghetti bolognese, mince on toast, or steak tartare.

■ Butchers nowadays are mincing lamb, veal and even steak and kidney as money-savers, so it's worth experimenting with some of these for a change.

MIXED GRILL

A dish complete in itself. It consists of grilled meats garnished with grilled fruits and vegetables such as tomatoes, banana and mushrooms, and served with maître d'hôtel butter, watercress, and chipped or other similar deep-fried potatoes. A grill does not include fried foods when you can't fit everything on the grill!

■ Meats may include fillet steak, lamb chop, lamb's kidney, fillet of veal, sausage, bacon rolls, etc. The skill is in knowing the varying lengths of time which different things take to cook, and having everything done to perfection at the same time. Cooking times depend on the thickness and type of the meat, one's personal taste for rare or well done meat, the distance from the grill and the intensity of the heat. Here's a rough guide for some of the more popular foods, about 3in/8cm from a red-hot grill:

fillet steak 4–8 minutes; lamb chop 10–12 minutes; lamb's kidney 6–8 minutes; sausages 10 minutes; bacon rolls on skewer 5 minutes; mushroms 5 minutes; halved tomatoes 3–4 minutes. See also *grilling*, page 66.

MUTTON

Though mutton is eaten much less nowadays than lamb, it makes a better stew (such as ragôut of mutton or Irish stew) because of its fuller flavour. When buying, the lean should be a dull red colour, of fine texture and firm to the touch; the fat creamy white, firm and hard.

Roasting See also *roasting a joint*, page 230, and *roasting*, page 78.

1 Trim a joint of excess fat, rendering down the trimmings for dripping.

2 A few sprigs of rosemary in the roasting tin help the flavour, as do thin spikes of garlic stuck into the fatty part of the joint and near the bone.

3 Marinating (see page 71) an older and larger piece of mutton helps to tenderize it as well as giving extra flavour. If you then enclose the joint in a flour and water paste (page 235) before roasting, it is delicious: put on a meat stand in the roasting tin so that the crust won't absorb any dripping and, after cooking and breaking away the crust, return meat to hot oven, baste, then leave for about 15 minutes to brown the surface.

4 Cook mutton well: the juices should be clear when it is done. Allow 20 minutes per lb/450g and 20 minutes over.

5 Roast in a preheated oven, gas 7, 425°F/220°C for the first 15 minutes to seal in the juices, then reduce heat to gas 5, 375°F/190°C for remainder of cooking time.

■ Traditional accompaniments to mutton are: stuffing, optional; onion sauce or onion purée (soubise) is correct with shoulder; redcurrant or other sharp-flavoured jelly such as mint, crab-apple, cranberry or gooseberry with leg, loin or neck; thick gravy for a stuffed joint, otherwise thin; slices of fried pineapple are also good with mutton.

■ The cuts of mutton are the same as lamb (see page 238).

■ Best for roasting are saddle (the prime joint), leg, shoulder, loin and best end of neck.

■ Joints suitable for boiling are leg and middle neck and, for braising, leg, shoulder and stuffed breast.

■ For stewing and the making of ragoûts use breast, middle neck or head – scrag end as well if you think it's worth bothering with.

OFFAL

Derived from 'off' and 'fall' or 'waste parts', as the dictionary describes it. In fact offal is anything but this, for it plays an invaluable part in our diet, besides giving us a welcome, occasional change from flesh. Veal offal is the most delicate, delicious and digestible of all.

■ Offal, or 'variety meats' as the Americans more wisely describe everything, includes all the extremities like head, tail, trotters and tongue, as well as the inner organs such as liver, kidneys, sweetbreads, heart, brains and tripe.

Brains More delicate than sweetbreads, though similar in texture and flavour. Because they're so alike, both are prepared in virtually the same way to purify and whiten them (see page 243). When blanching is necessary, the time you blanch brains depends on the type of animal from which they come: calf, lamb, sheep, ox or pig. Calf's and lamb's brains are delicate and equally as good, but some people prefer sheep's, so it partly depends on preferences as well as on how you plan to cook them as to which type you should use. Whichever it is, it's essential to cook brains the day you buy them because they must be fresh. If impossible to do so within 24 hours of purchase, at least soak and blanch them.

■ Various ways to cook brains include

braised, sliced and sautéd, frittered, served in a cream sauce, or in a savoury sauce au gratin, e.g. mushroom.

Kidneys Once reserved for chiefs and warriors as it was believed they gave both courage and strength to anybody eating them. Gout sufferers, however, can't eat kidneys or liver because either is liable to lead to excess uric acid on digestion. This is because both are rich in proteins which are different from the proteins of lean meat.

■ Here are a few tips on preparing kidneys:

1 Kidneys can't be too fresh; they quickly lose their firmness, flavour and goodness, so it pays to buy them in their fat when possible, then it's much easier to tell the fresh from the stale. With frozen kidneys, one must hope for the best.

2 *Soaking:* lamb's and calf's kidneys tend to absorb water if washed or soaked, and there is nothing to be gained by doing so. Pig's kidney is less strong if soaked in milk (or even water) for about ½–1 hour before cooking. Ox kidney is less strong if soaked, thinly sliced, in water with a little vinegar for an hour or so.

3 After pulling off the fine skin and cutting a lamb's or pig's kidney in half longways (round side up, core side down), it's easiest to snip out the core with a smallish pair of pointed scissors.

■ Here are a few cooking tips:

1 When cooked, kidneys should be tender and slightly pink near the centre.

2 There are two main reasons why grilled, fried or sautéd kidneys easily go hard and dry:
  a Because a kidney is surrounded by fat, the meat itself is almost fatless. There is nothing to keep it moist, therefore, if you overcook it.
  b The juices pour out of a cut kidney (causing it to shrivel) unless, initially, your source of heat is very strong: if grilling, this means using a preheated red-hot grill and grilling the kidney for one minute on each side before

cooking either side fully. If frying or sautéing, the cooking fat or butter should be hot when you put the kidney in: as for grilling, cook it for one minute on each side before cooking either side fully.

■ Ox and calf kidneys are multi-lobed, the latter bought by weight and cut off the core by the butcher. Ox kidney is mostly only used in things like a stew, pie or beef steak and kidney pudding because, even when soaked, it is too strong alone. Unlike other kidneys, it needs long slow cooking. Kidneys play a vital role in these dishes because they both flavour and thicken the liquor.

Liver The most important of all offal, being rich in proteins (see *kidneys* above) and itself the storehouse in mammals of such essential nutrients as iron and vitamins. Because so valuable in the diet, and because many people dislike it on account of its unusual texture, it is important for most dishes to use liver which isn't too strong, like calf's (the finest of all) or lamb's, and to cook it properly. To start with, that means proper preparation, easing out the tubes and core with a sharp-pointed vegetable knife in one hand, and with the thumb and fingers of your other; also pulling off the thin outside tissue.

■ Liver is quite versatile meat but be careful not to fry or grill it too long because, being almost fatless, it easily goes hard and dry. Although I personally like it best grilled (brushed with fat, well-seasoned, scattered with a sliced clove of garlic and served topped with savoury butter), one can ring the changes in many ways like this:

1 Cut in thin strips, coat with egg and breadcrumbs and fry.

2 Make liver pudding – a light kind of steamed suet pudding in which the cut-up raw liver is mixed with the flour, breadcrumbs, suet and herbs, etc. (You need a sauce with it.)

3 Cook *en brochette* – pieces of liver threaded on a skewer alternately with

similar-sized (but thinner) pieces of rather fat gammon or bacon. (Don't forget to season and brush them with oil or melted fat before grilling.) Again, basted or served with a savoury butter, they're more tasty.

4 Cut liver in smallish pieces, dip in batter and fry in deep fat.

5 Make liver pâté, with calf's, lamb's or chicken's liver.

6 Include pig's liver in pâtés.

7 Use pig's liver to make stuffings.

8 Serve liver casseroled. Here's a quick, simple recipe to serve 3: Dip 8–9oz/say 250g prepared, sliced calf's or lamb's liver in 1 tablespoon of seasoned flour, and lay slices in a greased casserole. Mix together and then sprinkle over the liver 1½oz/40g fresh white breadcrumbs, 3 finely sliced mushrooms, 1 teaspoon each of finely chopped onion and parsley, seasoning and a pinch of nutmeg. Lay two thinly spreadout rashers of bacon on top (each cut in half) and pour over ½pt/300ml stock mixed with 1 dessertspoon Worcestershire sauce. Cook in a slow to moderate oven, gas 3, 325°F/165°C, for 1–1¼ hours.

■ Ox liver, if used at all, is best in a spicy sort of dish which is cooked long enough to tenderize the meat, and where its strong flavour will be masked. To mellow it, first soak overnight in milk or salted water.

Oxtail A tasty end piece which has been used for centuries to make one of the finest British soups and stews. Its excessive amount of fat – which gives the dish its character – means it must be cooked differently from other stews if not to be greasy, and so rich as to be indigestible. Make a two-day operation of it and you can't go far wrong. Here's a recipe, with some whys and wherefores:

1 Wash rather than wipe the jointed oxtail, to make sure the pieces are free of hairs, etc.

2 Using a fairly large saucepan, add enough cold water barely to cover the meat. (The less water used, the more concentrated the final flavour, so the size of the pan has a bearing on the result.) Add some flavourings like a bouquet garni, a whole onion (stuck with a clove), a blade of mace and plenty of seasoning before bringing to the boil, skimming and simmering gently for about 2 hours.

3 Cool, then refrigerate the meat and strained liquor. (If left overnight the floating fat will set firmly enough on top so that you can lift it off next day.)

4 Now continue as for other stews, briefly as below:

a Fry a finely sliced onion for several minutes in 1oz/25g dripping, then add a sliced carrot and fry a minute or two more. Stir in a heaped tablespoon of flour to make a roux.

b Make a sauce in the usual way with the cooked roux and 1pt/500ml of the (now jellied) liquor. Before bringing it to the boil, add 1 dessertspoon of vinegar or lemon juice to counteract richness, some more seasoning, a fresh bouquet garni, a spoonful of tomato purée if you like, and a few drops of gravy browning.

c Add the pieces of half-cooked oxtail, and when the sauce returns to the boil, reduce heat and simmer very gently either on top of the cooker or in the oven for about 2½ hours, or until the meat is just leaving the bones.

5 Serve sprinkled with finely chopped parsley.

Ox tongue Expensive to buy cooked, so it's not only more economical but also much better to cook your own. In addition, sliced as and when needed, it doesn't go dry. Serve it hot with a savoury sauce, or boil, press and allow to go cold.

Pressed ox tongue Ideally, use a tongue press because it will cope best with any size of tongue which can be easily turned out when cold and jellied. Otherwise, you'll probably have to manage with a deep cake tin, 6in/15cm in diameter for a largish tongue, and a heavily weighted, fitting plate or dish of some kind on top.

■ Soak a salted or pickled tongue in cold water for about 24 hours, changing the water once or twice, to get rid of the strongest flavour. Then after bringing the tongue to the boil in cold water, drain off that water as well, and re-cover with fresh. Put in an onion (stuck with a couple of cloves) and a whole carrot or two, and skim off the scum (impurities) from time to time during cooking. Allow the tongue to simmer for 40 minutes per lb/450g and 40 minutes over, topping up with extra boiling water, if needed during cooking, to keep the tongue covered.

■ To test when a tongue is cooked, pierce the tip with a pointed skewer or knife. If tender here, then the rest of the tongue is cooked and, when plunged at once into cold water, the skin will easily come off and you can readily remove the duct, gristle, fat and tiny bones from the root. Now curl the tongue round and fit it tightly into the press or cake tin, cover and weight it and leave overnight to cool. There should be plenty of jelly to keep it moist.

Carving Slice cold, pressed tongue very thinly across the top of the round. As you cut off the first two or three slices, gently incline the knife, so that the top of the round has a slanting surface. This helps you to slice the whole tongue very thinly, without waste, down to the last small piece. If serving tongue hot, carve thicker slices, against the grain of the meat. Carve glazed slipper of tongue similarly, for each helping taking slices both from the centre and from the root end.

Sweetbreads These are glands – the pancreas and the thymus of the calf, lamb or ox, and are only found fully developed in young animals. The thymus, or 'throat' sweetbreads, are elongated in form and neither so white nor so fat as the others, which are superior.

■ Calf and lamb sweetbreads are considered the most delicate of all the products of butchery, in flavour, texture and digestibility, but they must be cooked the day one buys them to make sure they're fresh. Ox sweetbreads are coarser,

stronger, and bear no comparison with calf's and lamb's.

■ Sweetbreads, like brains, are dégorgéd (soaked in cold water to purify them) for 3–4 hours before cooking. This is primarily to whiten them by drawing out the blood, though at the same time it softens their covering membrane which is then easier to pull off: leave them under a dripping tap if you aren't going to be around to keep changing the steeping water until it is clear (no longer turning pink).

■ Sweetbreads and brains are blanched and then plunged into cold water if to be sliced or sautéd, to firm them up and make them easier to cut. They aren't blanched before braising because there's nothing to be gained, and quite a lot to be lost, in flavour and delicacy.

Tripe The stomach of ruminants, the best tripe coming from the ox. Depending on which stomach it comes from – which explains the differences in appearance and texture of tripe – it is of three kinds: honeycomb, blanket or thick seam. The flavour of all three is the same.

■ Tripe contains a large amount of connective tissue which is changed into gelatine during long slow cooking. It lacks flavour, hence the necessity to provide this with onions, herbs and spices, etc. Tripe is a valuable and easily digested food: in addition to protein, it contains an appreciable quantity of calcium from the lime used in its preparation. It shrinks a lot during cooking, so allow at least ½lb/225g per person.

■ While in Britain the popular way of cooking it is with onions, the classical way in France is *tripe à la mode de Caen*, a time-taking and complicated dish on which to embark. The tripe (some of each type), cooked with cow heel or calves' feet, leeks, carrots, onions, seasoning, cloves, thyme, bay leaf, garlic, cider and calvados is simmered very slowly in an earthenware (preferably), fireproof dish for at least 10 hours.

OX

A fully grown, neutered male of domestic cattle. A young neutered ox is a bullock or steer.

■ Besides the flesh we eat, there's all the offal: kidney, heart, liver, tail, tongue, tripe, sweetbreads. (See under *offal*.) In addition there are its suet and bones, some of which are particularly valuable for stock and for cold dishes like potted hough.

PORK

Takes its name from the Latin *porcus*, a pig, and is the fresh, uncured flesh. The meat would be darker in colour, and the flavour less good if the pig wasn't hung by the hind legs immediately after killing. The blood is drawn off and used to make black puddings.

■ When buying pork, look for firm, dry lean of a good pinkish colour. The fat should be firm and creamy white. Because pigs are killed young, every joint can be roasted and all the individual cuts from them are suitable for grilling or frying.
■ Bay leaf, basil, marjoram, parsley, thyme, sage and mixed herbs are all suitable for savoury stuffings and casseroles because they enhance the distinctive flavour of pork. Other good flavourings for pork dishes are cayenne, paprika, cloves, garlic, curry powder, mustard and chopped chives.

Roasting See also *roasting a joint*, page 230, and *roasting*, page 78.

1 Make sure the joint has a good rind and that your butcher scores it for you, preferably deeply and evenly. If a frozen joint of pork is not scored, you'll be able to do it more easily while the meat is still frozen, than when it is thawed, and soft.
2 To make the crackling really brown and crisp, brush the scored rind with oil or melted lard before rubbing in a generous amount of salt. If you like, you can give the pork additional flavour by mixing

a little pepper, dry mustard and dried sage with the salt. Alternatively (or as well), if you like the flavour of cloves, push a few into the scored rind, taking them out again just before serving.
3 Avoid covering the rind with foil or anything, otherwise the crackling won't get crisp.
4 Make sure pork is properly cooked, because underdone, it is unpalatable and makes some people ill. Weigh a joint after stuffing, allowing 30 minutes per lb/450g and 30 minutes over for a thinnish joint on the bone; 35 minutes per lb/450g and 35 minutes over for a thick joint, especially when boned, stuffed and rolled.
5 Place pork, rind uppermost, on a meat stand in a dry roasting tin. If without a meat stand, put the joint in the roasting tin, or straight on to an oven rack with a tin on the shelf below to catch the drippings – good but messy!
6 Roast meat in a preheated hot oven for the first 20 minutes to seal in the juices, gas 7, 425°F/220°C, then reduce heat for remaining time to gas 5, 375°F/190°C. If a joint is small and the crackling not quite crisp enough when the meat is almost cooked, raise the heat for the last 15 minutes. It is better not to baste pork: the thick layer of fat on top will automatically baste the lean below.

■ Traditional accompaniments to roast pork are: roast potatoes; sage and onion or other suitable stuffing, to counteract the richness of pork (see also savoury pudding, page 246); apple sauce – unless you prefer, say, a sharp cranberry sauce; thick gravy.

The better cuts are:

Leg (Called gigot in Scotland.) Leg is the prime roasting joint, but is often divided into *fillet end* and *knuckle end* because a whole leg is so huge – and expensive. The whole leg roasts better and works out more economically than either joint cut from it because it stays where you put it during roasting, basted by its own fat, unlike the tender fillet end which so easily

Pork carcase showing what comes from where

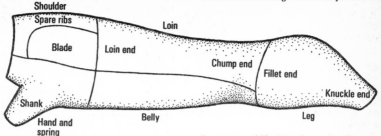

By courtesy of The Meat Promotion Executive

tilts over so that the lean is then on top.
Fillet end is a thick slice from the top of
the leg. Roast, or slice into steaks for
grilling or frying.
Knuckle end Roast this. It's also excellent
boned and stuffed.

Loin Roast on the bone, or boned, stuffed and rolled.
Loin chops, sometimes sold with the kidney in. Grill or fry.
Chump chops are large and meaty, coming from the chump end of the loin. Grill
or fry.
Chump end of loin Roast.

Tenderloin Also known as the pork fillet,
but don't confuse this with the fillet end
of the leg, see above. Tenderloin is a
lean, very tender cut on the inside of the
loin bone. It's ideal for slicing and frying,
especially if you coat the slices with egg
and breadcrumbs and fry them in butter.

The less expensive cuts are:

Shoulder Roast. It's especially good
boned and rolled.

■ Shoulder is often divided into blade
and spare rib. Blade is good roasted,
being excellent boned and stuffed. You
can also braise or stew it. Spare rib can be
roasted, or used for raised pork pies.
Spare rib chops can be grilled, fried or
braised – best braised I think.

Hand and spring Roast.

■ Often divided into hand and shank.
Hand can be boned and roasted, or can

be boiled, fresh or pickled. Shank is good
stewed.

Belly (Also called flank.) Roast thick
end, stuffed. Braise, stew or boil, fresh or
pickled.
Sliced belly Grill (crisp) like bacon
rashers, or fry if you prefer.

Head and trotters Make *brawn*, see page
235.

SAUSAGES

A wonderfully convenient food for the
cook because the variety is great, yet preparation may be almost nil. Made usually
of pork, beef, veal or liver – or a mixture
of some of these – one can buy them
cooked or uncooked, spiced or unspiced,
fresh or smoked. Many of the cooked
continental sausages can be served with
other cold meats and a salad, are delicious with crusty French bread or rolls for
a quick snack or make a tasty addition to
an hors d'oeuvre.

■ Here are some of the familiar kinds:

Beef sausages Sausages and sausage meat
made of beef are less expensive than pork
sausages and sausage meat mainly
because they contain a smaller proportion of meat. Whereas pork sausages
must by law contain a minimum of 65 per
cent meat, the minimum for beef is 50 per
cent.

Bierwurst A lightly smoked sausage of
German origin as are many of the best

sausages. Made from finely minced pork and flavoured with mustard seeds and a touch of garlic, it is cooked and ready to serve.

Black pudding A rich, strong and to some people rather indigestible cooked sausage containing chopped pork fat and blood. You can eat it cold, or may prefer to slice and fry it to eat with bacon, or, to counteract its richness, with mashed potatoes and a vegetable.

Chipolata A corruption of the Italian word *cipollata*, a chive. As originally made, they were small chive-flavoured sausages. This is the best size to serve with chicken or turkey: a garnish, not a meal in itself!

Frankfurters Like *wienerwurst* (Vienna sausage) and *bologna*, frankfurters take their name from the city in which they were invented so that, strictly speaking, the genuine sausage only comes from that town or its immediate surroundings. The ancestor of the American hot dog, frankfurters are made basically from high quality lean pork, smoking giving them both flavour and colour. One can use them in lots of different ways, such as cut into slanting pieces for a mixed hors d'oeuvres, with savoury spaghetti, in risotto – and, of course, to make hot dogs. Canned frankfurters must have a minimum of 70 per cent meat, others not less than 75 per cent meat.

Garlic sausage, French Cooked and smoked in the skin. It is made from coarse-cut ham and pork, with a subtle flavour of garlic.

Liver sausage This varies widely – there is liver sausage and liver sausage as anyone who has eaten the best of the German and the worst of the British will know. Generally, continental liver sausage is a spreading sausage, containing minced pork and liver. The delicious Strasbourg variety, for instance, is very smoothly blended, is surrounded by a thin layer of pork fat, and one can spread or slice it. On German black

bread, this is at its best.

■ Serve liver sausage with freshly-made toast, Melba toast (page 345) or black bread, on canapés, in buttered rolls or in really fresh, generously buttered sandwiches. Alternatively you can slice and include it in an hors d'oeuvre or salad.

■ You can also make characterless and unspreadable (or nearly unspreadable) liver sausage spreadable, richer and infinitely more delicious by liquidizing 6oz/150g of it with 2oz/50g softish butter, 2 cloves of crushed garlic and plenty of fresh milled black pepper. (Cut sausage into thinnish slices and blend only a little to start with, gradually adding remainder.) Put in a larder or other cold place.

Pork sausages See *beef sausages*.

Salami A highly seasoned and salted Italian sausage, differing from province to province, in the kind of meats used, in flavourings added, in shape and size, and in the salting and maturing.

■ Other countries make salami as well: *Danish salami*, for instance, is a smoked sausage made with finely minced pork and veal. Bright pink in colour, it has a hint of garlic and a distinctive salty flavour. *Hungarian salami* is a matured type made of finely minced pork.

SAVOURY PUDDING

This can eke out a joint of roast lamb, mutton or pork besides counteracting the richness and being very tasty with any of them, or with sausages. Regard it as a stuffing and serve thick gravy. Here, briefly, is the recipe to serve 3–4: Sieve 2oz/50g self-raising flour with plenty of salt and pepper. Add 2oz/50g each of fine or medium oatmeal and grated suet, 1 lightly rounded tablespoon of finely chopped onion or shallot, 1 heaped teaspoon of chopped parsley and a pinch of mixed herbs if you like them. Mix all together, then stir in about 4 tablespoons of milk and water mixed, to make a stiff batter. Using a pallet knife, spread the mixture evenly in 8 individual bun tins or a small shallow tin about 9×6in/23×15cm and bake for approximately half an hour in a hot oven, gas 6, 400°F/205°C or until crisp and brown both top and bottom. (If your joint is cooking in a slower oven, you'll probably have to cook the pudding for about 10 minutes longer at the lower temperature.) Serve cut into squares.

STEWS, THICKENED BROWN

These need never be monotonous because one can vary them endlessly by using a different combination of ingredients. Here's a real opportunity to forget about recipes and use your own imagination, as long as you know the basic needs for a stew, like:

1 Long slow cooking, to allow the cheaper cuts of meat such as shin to become tender, and to make the sauce good. (See *shin*, page 234.)

2 Using stock rather than water.

3 Frying the onion, to bring out its flavour. Also fry things like sliced carrot or chopped mushrooms for a minute or two for the same reason.

4 Dipping the meat in seasoned flour before frying, to flavour and brown it, also to help thicken the sauce.

5 The subtle use of herbs.

■ Here are the sort of things to use:

1 *Fresh vegetables:*
carrot
chopped celery or celeriac
sliced leek
chopped mushrooms
a little sliced turnip or swede
chopped sweet peppers, fresh or frozen
pickling onions
whole shallots
sliced courgette
frozen sweetcorn
a little chopped fennel

2 *Fruits:*
skinned tomatoes, plus a teaspoon of sugar
soaked prunes (for beef or rabbit stew)
whole peeled chestnuts (for beef stew)
canned pineapple
stoned cherries

3 *Flavourings:*
bouquet garni, including herbs of choice and most suitable for type of meat
crushed garlic, or a clove of garlic in the bouquet garni
tomato purée
a twist of fresh orange peel
little wine, parsley wine, cider or beer, to replace some of the stock
a spoonful of vinegar or sour cream, stirred in at the last
dry mustard, curry powder, paprika or chilli powder added to seasoned flour
a spoonful of chutney
good beef dripping (for a beef stew), to make the roux
freshly milled black pepper, stirred in at the last.

TENDERLOIN

The American name for the fillet – of beef, veal or pork.

VEAL

Veal depends for its whiteness and flavour upon a calf being correctly fed, killed at the right age and properly slaughtered. It is lean and tender with a delicate pink colour, but the small amount of fat in the meat is the reason why many people prefer to braise it rather than roast, and why a joint for roasting should first be larded. Unlike beef, which so many of us prefer underdone, veal should be well cooked because it is immature meat.

Roasting See also *roasting a joint*, page 230, and *roasting*, page 78.

1 Lard (page 69) or bard (page 51) leg or loin with pork fat before roasting so that the joint will cook without being basted.

2 Give veal additional flavour either by stuffing or by rubbing seasonings, etc. into the joint, e.g. small spikes of garlic and tiny sprigs of fresh herbs slipped into the lean or fat; salt and pepper to which for variation one can add mixtures of: paprika, ground cloves, ginger, thyme,

rosemary, tarragon, grated lemon rind. A typical mixture is salt and pepper with ½ level teaspoon dried thyme and half a grated lemon rind.

3 Allow 35 minutes per lb/450g on the bone, 40 minutes per lb/450g off the bone, stuffed weight.

4 Roast in a pre-heated hot oven, gas 8, 450°F/230°C for the first 15–20 minutes to seal in the juices, then reduce heat to gas 4, 350°F/175°C for remainder of cooking time when the juices should be clear, not pink or red.

■ Traditional accompaniments to roast veal are: forcemeat stuffing or forcemeat balls, fried or baked in the oven; roast potatoes; bacon rolls; lemon; thick gravy.
■ The different cuts can be cooked in ways like this:

Leg Roast or braise.

Loin Roast on the bone, or off; or braise.

■ Use as chops.

Shoulder Better boned, rolled and braised than roasted.

■ Use to make things like blanquette, fricassée or, minced, to include in pâtés.

Breast Bone, stuff and braise.

■ Stew. Use for galantine.

Knuckle Braise or stew, e.g. osso buco, blanquette. (This is, like shin of beef, superb meat for stewing because it is so gelatinous.) Cooked with the knuckle bone, it makes delicious and nourishing jellied stock.

Calf's feet Used mainly for their gelatine, as is knuckle. Use for calf's foot jelly and include in a braise such as boeuf à la mode.

Head Braise or boil. This includes the tongue and brains, the latter often incorporated in the accompanying sauce. It's better to ask your butcher to prepare it, as with pig's head.

14

Poultry and game

GENERAL INFORMATION

Although poultry and winged game are often apparently so closely related, they may be poles apart when it comes to preparation for the table.

We can more or less take it for granted today that chickens, turkeys and ducks will be young and tender, but this isn't always so with game, many kinds of which depend for their tenderness and flavour upon being hung for the correct length of time. Where chicken, fish or butcher meat would be inedible at such a stage, pheasant and grouse, for instance, only become perfect when they are 'gamey', 'high', or by some people's standards slightly 'off', perhaps with a greenish tinge on the thin skin of the abdomen. When hanging game, therefore, and deciding how long to give it, it is essential to take into account personal taste as well as the type of bird and the weather – cold, hot or possibly thundery. Also older birds, which one can usually tell amongst other things by their hard scaly feet, need to hang longer than young. For most people's tastes, game birds are mature enough when one can pluck the tail or breast feathers easily.

■ Where chicken has such a bland flavour that one can cook it in scores of ways with all kinds of flavourings, each game bird has its own distinctive flavour. This is a flavour to be complemented, not altered or lost. A wild bird's flavour will to some extent depend on what it feeds on, the quality of its flavour also reflecting the quality of the food on which it has fed. Why else the fame of, say, the Scottish grouse?

■ Whereas chickens are plucked immediately after killing – because it is easier to do this while the bird is still warm, and makes no difference to the flavour – game birds are hung with their feathers on. Again, while chickens are plucked head hanging downwards and hung by the feet so that the blood will drain into the neck-skin and keep the flesh white, game birds are hung by the neck, tied tightly to prevent air entering by the mouth.

■ Both poultry and game are simply wiped inside; washing takes away their flavour. Some types of bird are so dry that they may need larding or barding to make them moist and juicy (see page 69 and 51), while others are better still for a piece of butter slipped inside.

■ Young game is nearly always roasted, for the simple reason that this is the way it tastes and eats best, especially when cooked in butter. Old game on the other hand usually ends up better used for soup or pâté, potted, or in something like salmi, a raised pie or a casserole. Venison, or an old hare, rabbit or game bird is improved by marinating, which not only flavours but also tenderizes tough meat (see page 71).

■ The other principal way to flavour is by serving the right accompaniments and, for poultry, with stuffings. The classic accompaniments nearly always complement the flavour and may have some additional purpose like counteracting richness, providing richness, giving moisture, colour or perhaps contrast of texture.

■ After hanging, you can freeze game with fur or feathers on or off, as you like, but you can't safely hang it after freezing because it deteriorates too rapidly when thawed. The important thing is to use a thick polythene bag – or strong foil and then polythene – to prevent freezer burn (page 63) which destroys flavour besides making the flesh dry. Feathered game particularly should be thawed gradually in a cool place, otherwise it is difficult to pluck without tearing the skin. Oven-ready game and poultry will also lose less of its juiciness and flavour if thawed slowly, about 36–48 hours in a refrigerator.

■ It's unwise to cook a frozen bird. Salmonella, a common cause of food poisoning, can lurk in the intestines of all animals, birds and fish. It is usually destroyed quickly by heat but when you roast a bird, the body cavity – where bacteria can linger – is slightly insulated by all the surrounding flesh, so if this is frozen, the heat may never penetrate enough to destroy the bacteria.

Seasons for game in Britain

Species	Season	Comment
Mammals		
deer, red (males)	1 Aug–30 Apr	England and Wales
	1 Jul–20 Oct	Scotland
deer, red (females)	1 Nov–28 Feb	England and Wales
	21 Oct–15 Feb	Scotland
roebuck	all year	England and Wales
	1 May–2 Oct	Scotland
roedeer	1 Nov–28 Feb	England and Wales
	21 Oct–28 Feb	Scotland
hare, brown and blue mountain	all year	no close season but must not be sold between March and July

Birds		
grouse	12 Aug–10 Dec	
partridge	1 Sep–1 Feb	
pheasant	1 Oct–1 Feb	
ptarmigan	12 Aug–10 Dec	
snipe, common and jack	12 Aug–31 Jan	
Wildfowl		
mallard, teal, widgeon, wild goose	1 Sep–31 Jan / 1 Sep–20 Feb	inland / foreshore

Roasting a bird This is a different proposition from roasting a joint of meat because a bird is complete in itself, not a cut from something larger, usually with areas of unprotected flesh. The flesh of a bird is completely covered by and protected by skin (unless unhappily this is torn), usually with a layer of fat underneath. During roasting – providing you don't enclose the bird in a roasting bag or wrap it in foil where it will, as it were, steam-roast – the flesh becomes firm and remains nicely moist while the skin, thanks to basting (which tends to dry and spoil meat) becomes crisp and golden. If before roasting, you brush a bird with oil or melted butter, results are even better.

■ Unlike meat, which is cooked throughout its cooking time in the same position, fat uppermost, most kinds of bird are best placed first on one side, then the other and finally, for the longest time, breast upwards. Thus any juices dripping into the cavity flavour and keep moist alternating parts of the flesh, instead of collecting in the bottom of the carcase. Any bird not too large to manipulate, such as chicken and most game birds, will benefit from such treatment. To avoid damaging a bird's skin, use two wooden spoons to turn it – or, for a small bird, one can use tongs. (Continual rotation is one reason why a spit-roasted bird is so succulent and delicious.)

■ 'Frothing' the breast makes a bird look and taste delicious. About 10 minutes before it is cooked, remove the barding fat (if any), baste the bird with the hot dripping, dredge it with flour and baste again. Return the bird to the oven until it is a good brown colour and frothy.

■ Use a small roasting tin for a small bird, then you won't need as much fat, there's less surface from which the tasty juices can evaporate, and less likelihood of butter (if that's the fat you're using) burning.

To draw a chicken, or other fowl Collect your tackle before getting into a mess: chopping board, trussing needle, a clean damp cloth, two good lengths of strong thin string, some newspaper for the unwanted parts, and a sharp, pointed knife, preferably a French cook's knife.

1 Singe the carcase (after plucking) over a low gas or other clear flame, when possible, in preference to singeing it with a taper or long match, either of which can cause charring.

2 Draw the leg sinews – one of the great advantages of drawing a bird yourself, because it makes such a difference to the tenderness and enjoyment of the drumsticks:

a About 1in/2½cm below hock joint, cut through to bone at the front of the leg, but only through the yellow surface skin at the back, where the sinews lie.

b With the bird breast side up on the chopping board, its feet dangling over front of table, break each leg off where already cut. (Hold bird down with one hand, knock its foot sharply down with the other.)

c Twist the foot well, then pull it away from the leg, hopefully bringing all the sinews with it – one for each toe. Use a damp dish cloth to grip the foot if easier, or, with a skewer, to pull out any straggling sinews. (If a bird is old and the sinews tough, you may have to pull them out one by one in this way with a skewer.)

3 Trim extreme end of wings and cut off 'thumbs' with a knife or scissors.

4 Cut off head, leaving as much of the neck as possible, to have plenty of loose skin to tuck under bird later.

5 Place bird on a chopping board, breast down, neck towards you. With one hand, pinch up a portion of the skin along the back of the neck; with other hand, slip point of knife under the skin down to bottom of neck and slit skin full length of neck to expose the neck bone. Sever this at shoulders.

6 Still at neck end, ease out the crop, windpipe and gullet. Insert your long finger into the body cavity along the backbone, loosening the lungs and any other organs you can reach and loosen. (If all the internal organs are loosened, first from the neck end then from the other, almost everything should come away together later, without breaking, and therefore with the minimum of smell and unpleasantness.)

7 Stand the bird on its shoulders, breast towards you, grasp the parson's nose and make an incision between vent and tail, taking care not to cut into the intestines. Hook up the last portion of these with your first finger, and, inserting knife into body, between the intestines and the uncut skin, cut out the vent.

8 Place bird on its back, tail more or less towards you. Leave vent attached to intestine, but move it temporarily away from aperture. With your longest finger, now loosen everything possible from the inner walls of the carcase before gripping gizzard and easing it out, with all the other organs following it.

9 Make sure the pink spongy lungs are out – they're near the ribs.

10 Wipe bird inside with a clean damp cloth. (Don't wash it because this spoils its flavour among other things.)

11 Cut giblets away from organs, and use to make stock for gravy or a sauce:

a The liver Cut gall-bladder away from it, carefully, without breaking. (This is a longish, narrow, dark-coloured sac to be discarded.)

b The heart Cut off the fat and tubes.

c The gizzard Cut up the centre,

through outer part only, so that you can then pull it away from its horny yellow lining without spilling lining's messy contents. Wash well.
d The neck.

To truss a chicken or turkey for roasting

1 Fold loose neck skin down over the opening and tuck it underneath the bird. Double the wings back to hold it in position.
2 Thread trussing needle with string, knotting other end.
3 Lay bird on its back, tail to the left. Take both legs in the left hand and draw them down back over the breast as far as possible. Pass the needle through the body between the body and the thigh, catching in a tip of the wing when pulling string through. Turn the bird on to its breast. Stick the needle through the folded wings from the outside of the elbow to the tip of the wing as it lies on the shoulder. Pass the string over the back. Reverse the stitch down the other wing, and tie the ends tightly under the elbow. This completes front part of bird.
4 Thread needle with other piece of string. To secure legs in correct position, hold the skin tightly over the tip of the breastbone, passing the needle through underneath. Unthread needle.
5 Using your first finger as a hook (palm upwards), put it inside the bird, feel for the string under the breastbone and pull the string out. Loop it over your finger, turn your hand over (palm downwards) and put the now twisted loop over the parson's nose. Pull both ends of the string to close up the hole, pass the ends round the hock end of the 'drumsticks' and tie tightly so that the legs are pulled down over the opening, and the breast muscles pushed up to give a plump finish. The bird should, if properly trussed, now lie quite steadily on the table – and in due course for carving.

To joint a chicken This is easier when you have a fresh rather than a thawed frozen bird because the latter is more squashy and difficult to handle. All you

need is a chopping board and a very sharp knife – preferably a French cook's knife – to cut the bird into 8 good-sized joints: 2 pieces breast, 2 wings each with a piece of breast, 2 thighs and 2 drumsticks.

■ Here's one way to set about it:

1 Lay the bird first on one side then on the other to cut off each leg – drumstick and thigh – pulling the thigh bone back at the bottom to expose the joint, and cutting off the 'oyster' in one piece *with* the thigh. (The oyster is a small delicate piece of meat on each side of the back; almost scoop it out with the point of the knife.) Cut each leg at joint, to separate drumstick from thigh.
2 Turn chicken, breast towards you, and carefully cut down one side of the breastbone. Lifting the flesh away, continue cutting and scraping with the knife to remove flesh from bone, taking wing with it. Lay this on chopping board and cut diagonally into two pieces – it looks nicer that way – so that the wing has a section of breast with it. Repeat operation on other side of breast.

■ Use the carcase to make stock, the bones from limbs as well, if cooking chicken off the bone.
■ Many dishes call for chicken joints to be skinned: if too slippery to hold easily, a damp, clean dishcloth will give you a better grip.

To bone a chicken or other fowl This isn't easy to follow from a book and, even with understanding, is a time-consuming and fiddling job for anyone lacking experience. If you don't feel like tackling it yourself, some butchers will bone a bird for you, but you reap in the dining room what you sowed in the kitchen because there's nothing simpler to carve than a boned, stuffed bird.

■ The aim is to remove the flesh with the skin from the carcase bones without piercing the skin except where you *have* to cut it. The skin (with flesh) then acts as a container for the stuffing called for in a recipe.

■ It's unnecessary work and makes boning more difficult if you draw the bird first. You need a small sharp knife, e.g. a vegetable knife, to work close to the bone, mostly scraping rather than cutting the flesh away. To avoid tearing the skin – so easily done at the ridge of the breastbone where skin and bone meet – the cutting edge of your knife must always face the bone, never the flesh. The method of boning depends on what you're making:

To bone, for stuffing and reshaping, as a bird

1 Draw the leg sinews. Cut off the end joints of the wings and remove head, neck and crop, all as described on page 251. Cut legs off at hock joint.
2 Pull loose neck skin well back and scrape the flesh off the wishbone. Place the knife at the back of the wishbone and force it out.
3 Place the bird on its tail end and cut between shoulder bones. Scrape the flesh off the wing bone to the first joint and remove the bone. This is the only bone removed from the wings.
4 Skin down the back very carefully about half-way down, removing the 'oysters' from the hollows.
5 Cut away the two cutlets from the breastbone and remove the flesh from the trunk right down to the leg joints, rolling it back as you work.
6 Push up and bend back the leg, to make it easier to cut between the joints, and remove the bones. Alternatively, leave *in* the drumstick bones. They make the bird easier to stuff and give it a more realistic shape, but the drumsticks will have to be set aside (for the family!) when carving.
7 Pull the flesh well down, taking care not to puncture the skin. Cut from the end of the breastbone right through the vent.
8 When all the flesh is off the carcase, turn everything right side out and stuff according to your recipe (see one suggestion below). Position the breast cutlets, and shape the creature as far as possible to resemble a chicken. Truss it with wings and neck skin underneath, legs close to the body, so that it later presents an easy surface to coat evenly with chaud-froid sauce and aspic.
9 If you tear the skin while boning, stitch it up with a needle and thread.

A suitable stuffing for a boned chicken

1 Half a small tinned tongue, turned round side up, to form the breast – with the breast cutlets on top of it.
2 8–12oz/225–350g sausage meat, to pack round tongue, fill thighs, pack at tail and neck end.
3 1 or 2 hard-boiled eggs, sliced, also to place round tongue.
4 Seasoning.

To bone, when the flesh is to be rolled, as for a galantine

1 Draw the leg sinews, also remove head, neck and crop all as described on page 251.
2 Cut a deep slit down the back of the bird from neck to tail, to expose the backbone. With your small, sharp knife, its edge always cutting against the bone, scrape and cut the flesh from the carcase bones down one side of the bird, pulling the flesh away from the carcase with your fingers as you cut.
3 When you reach the ball joints connecting the wings and the second joints to the carcase, sever them and continue down the carcase just until you reach the ridge of the breast where skin and bone meet. Take care here – and again when you reach the same place on the opposite side of the breast – because the skin is thin and easily slit.
4 Repeat same operation on the other side of the bird.
5 Lift carcase frame and cut very closely against the ridge of the breastbone to free the carcase, but not to slit the skin covering the breastbone.
6 Chop off the wings at the elbows, to leave just the upper wing bones attached.
7 Arrange this frog-like creature on a board, flesh side up. Scrape the meat from all the bones not yet removed and

pull out the bones.

8 Remove any bits of fat attached to the flesh and the bird is ready to stuff.

CHICKEN

Chicken's popularity must stem largely from its mild but lovely flavour – mild enough to blend wonderfully with a huge variety of foods – and from its own versatility. Providing it is properly cooked, one can make a feast of an old bird or a young, serve chicken just as deliciously cold as hot, cook it fresh or use it up, cook it whole; boned and stuffed; in individual joints or cut into pieces. Almost anything you want to do with chicken, you can do.

■ Tarragon is its classic flavouring.

Roasting a chicken See also *roasting a bird*, page 250, and *roasting*, page 78. Allow 15 minutes resting time, see page 231.

1 Veal forcemeat stuffing is traditional but many people prefer chicken without because forcemeat dominates and alters the flavour of the meat. Use 2–3oz/50–75g forcemeat or a mixture of forcemeat and sausage meat.

■ Use a different kind of stuffing if preferred, or to give variety.

2 Allow 20 minutes per lb/450g and 20 minutes over in a preheated moderate-to-hot oven, gas 5, 375°F/190°C. (As chicken is a delicately flavoured and rather dry meat, a hot oven such as is required for some types of meat tends to dry up a chicken's natural juices.)

3 Roast chicken for 15 minutes first on one side, then on the other, basting when you turn it, before placing breast upwards for remainder of time. (The legs take longest to cook so should be uppermost for the longest time.)

4 Brushing a chicken with oil or melted butter before roasting helps to protect the flesh and makes the skin crisp and golden. Also it is best to protect the breast initially with a rasher of bacon or

buttered paper, tucked in. Remove it later to let the breast brown.

5 A chicken roasted in butter has the best flavour. Other suitable fats are oil, white cooking fat or lard. Dripping, other than bacon or chicken dripping, spoils a chicken's true flavour. Baste regularly, to cook a bird properly.

6 If you haven't got a meat thermometer, a chicken is cooked when:

a The meat tends to shrink from the end of the drumsticks.

b A sharp fork runs easily into the thigh joint. If the escaping juice is pink, cook the bird a little longer.

7 Traditional accompaniments to roast chicken are: stuffing (optional, see **1** above); bread sauce; bacon rolls; sausages (preferably chipolata, as they're intended as a garnish, not a meal); thin gravy, unless the bird is stuffed, when it should be thick; game chips or boiled new potatoes (the modern substitute for chips is, alas, often warmed potato crisps); a dressed green salad. (You may prefer instead to serve a comparatively mild-flavoured vegetable such as peas, green beans, new carrots – or even coleslaw.) Pear purée makes another nice accompaniment.

8 *To carve:*

a Press thighs down outwards, away from the body, so that you can see the joint and cut the legs off. Separate drumsticks from thighs, unless the bird is *very* small.

b To cut off the wings, take a line from the top of the wishbone right down through the joint, to include a good portion of breast meat.

c Cut breast in two or three slices either side of the breastbone. If a bird is very small, cut off each side of the breast in one piece.

■ Game shears or saw-edged scissors are a great help at the joints.

Roasting a chicken in butter This is a French way and is a rich but positively sumptuous method of cooking chicken:

1 Make and put this stuffing into body

cavity: mix together 2oz/50g softish butter, a little chopped fresh or dried tarragon (essential to this recipe), a good pinch of salt and plenty of freshly ground black pepper.

2 Brush bird all over with melted butter – or you could use oil.

3 Put about 2oz/50g butter in a roasting tin and roast bird as described for *roasting a chicken* above, **2, 3** and **6**. Baste as usual.

4 Accompaniments to this type of roast chicken are: game chips – or, if you must, warmed potato crisps; a dressed green salad, essential to counteract the richness; the gravy (juices) and butter from the roasting tin (served in a 'grasmaigre' gravy boat – one with a hole near the bottom of one side – you can pour the tasty gravy out through the hole while *most* of the butter floats on top).

Cold roast chicken If planning to serve roast chicken cold, roast it in oil, which doesn't congeal when cold. The bird will remain moister and will taste better if not cut into until cold, because fewer juices will escape.

To boil a chicken See page 258.

To steam a chicken See page 258 for cooking time.

There is an almost infinite number of ways in which to serve a roasting chicken. Here are some of the popular dishes to be found in many recipe books:

Cold dishes
Boned chicken Stuffed, and coated with chaud-froid sauce.

■ To bone, see page 252.

Chaud-froid of chicken Cooked boneless portions of chicken, preferably breast, coated with chaud-froid sauce.
Chicken Calcutta Cold chicken portions – boneless – coated with curry mayonnaise (page 175).
Chicken mayonnaise Cooked, boneless portions of chicken coated with mayonnaise mixed with aspic jelly, with a final coating of aspic.

Galantine See page 260.
Potted chicken See page 268.
Chicken sandwiches or rolls Be generous with the butter and serve *very* fresh.
Chicken liver pâté One can often buy chicken livers at a supermarket.

Hot dishes
Blanquette of chicken Similar to fricassée, the main difference being that the cooking liquor is thickened (to make a sauce) *after* the chicken (or veal) is cooked. Finished with a liaison of cream and egg yolks, this is a delicious way to serve chicken.
Bouchées or patties Use frozen cases if you like. They come in different sizes. Fill with a tasty chicken mixture. (You could use the filling given below for chicken vol-au-vent – but making a smaller quantity.)
Casserole-roasted chicken e.g. poulet poêle à l'estragon.
Chicken casseroles Classic dishes such as coq au vin, poulet sauté marengo, poulet sauté chasseur. Chicken in a cream sauce such as chicken normande or chicken à l'allemande.
Fricassée of chicken Made with raw chicken, not cooked chicken stirred into a dull white sauce, as so many people seem to think it is. Basically, the meat is sautéd in butter before using the butter to make a white sauce with chicken stock, in which the chicken is then cooked. Lastly, it is enriched with an egg yolk and cream liaison.
Chicken and ham croquettes Minced cooked chicken and ham bound with a panada, coated with egg and breadcrumbs, formed into croquettes and fried in deep fat.
Chicken kromeskies Balls or rolls of croquette mixture or farce, rolled in a thin slice of bacon, dipped in batter (preferably a delicious yeast batter), and fried in deep fat.
Chicken pancakes Pancakes containing a savoury chicken mixture (such as used for croquettes for instance), lined up in a dish, coated with a tasty sauce and served au gratin.

Chicken pie Usually made with a boiling fowl. Be sure to make stock with the carcase before making the pie, unless you already have chicken stock on hand.

Chicken rissoles Similar to croquettes but enclosed in thin pastry before coating with egg and breadcrumbs and frying in deep fat.

Chicken risotto or pilaff See risotto, page 203.

Chicken risotto-stuffed green peppers.

Curried chicken Delicious if you include pineapple chunks in the curry. Serve at least six accompaniments, e.g. boiled rice (page 202); fried almonds or cashew nuts (page 343); browned coconut (cook in low oven or under grill, turning coconut over once or twice with a fork); sliced cucumber, sliced banana (sprinkled with lemon juice to prevent discoloration), melon balls and/or tomato salad (page 212); chopped hard-boiled egg; rings of fried onion, dipped first in seasoned flour, then fried in oil; mango chutney; poppadoms (see page 343 for how to cook but not to make).

Chicken vol-au-vent For a short cut, use a large packet of a good make of frozen puff pastry. If you haven't got oval vol-au-vent cutters (one large to cut it out, the other smaller to cut the lid) roll pastry to a rectangle about 8×6in/20×15cm, trim all edges cleanly with a sharp knife, and then cut a lid into the pastry with the knife. Glaze with egg before baking but be sure not to brush any cut edges, otherwise the pastry won't rise there. After baking, while still hot, carefully lift out lid and remove any doughy centre.

Vol-au-vent case before baking, using knife

├── 20cm/8in ──┤

├── 20cm/8in ──┤

Vol-au-vent case before baking, using cutters

■ For filling, make ¾pt/450ml béchamel coating sauce (page 177), to which add cut-up cooked chicken and, say, some sliced mushrooms previously fried in butter with a little seasoning.

Chicken stock Use this as a base for many white soups and sauces, see page 122. If you have a freezer, you need never be without stock, storing it in the form of ice cubes.

Poussins Baby chickens 4–8 weeks old, usually less than a lb/450g in weight and enough for one or, at a stretch, two portions, depending partly on how they're cooked.

■ Because *all* their flesh is so tender, they're ideal for grilling or frying – as well as roasting – but it's up to the cook to give them flavour. This explains why if roasted they're often stuffed, if grilled they're improved by marinating and, if fried, are best fried in butter – mixed with a little oil, to prevent burning.

To fry or grill, they must be opened out and flattened, otherwise they won't cook evenly, but if you take the flesh off the bone you'll lose flavour: use a sharp knife to cut along one side of the backbone, from the inside. To divide in half, use scissors or game shears to cut at breastbone.

■ Grilling, after marinating, is one of my favourite ways to eat poussin: cook them for 18–20 minutes about 3in/7.5cm from the heat under a preheated red-hot grill for just one minute on each side, thereafter under moderate heat for 8–9 minutes on each side.

Suggested marinade Well-seasoned French dressing made with lemon juice rather than vinegar, and flavoured with tarragon.

Suggested accompaniments Grilled rashers of bacon, cooked alongside the chicken for the last few minutes, tarragon butter (pages 103 and 169); game chips; dressed green salad.

Spring chickens or broilers From about 2–4 months old, therefore at 1½–2lb/

675–900g will serve three people at a stretch. You can roast (or spit-roast), or split, flatten and fry or grill them, like poussins.

■ Here are two ways to fry:

1 Dip the skinless cut-up chicken pieces in seasoned flour, coat with egg and fresh white breadcrumbs, chill for about an hour to firm up the coating, then fry in a frying basket in deep fat, 340°F/170°C for about 8–10 minutes. (If you use raspings instead of fresh white crumbs, they will burn; if the fat is too cool the chicken will be greasy and indigestible; if too hot the crumbs will brown and burn before the chicken is cooked.)

■ If necessary, see *deep fat frying*, page 63.

2 Dip flattened chicken halves (see *poussins* above) in seasoned flour, to protect and give them flavour before frying skin side down in a large strong frying pan in hot butter and oil over moderate heat. (Use 1 dessertspoon of oil to 2oz/50g butter.) When browned, turn chicken skin side up, cover pan now to tenderize them, add a pinch of dried or chopped fresh tarragon and cook gently for about 15 minutes, basting now and then. When cooked (the juices should be clear, not pink), deglaze the pan with a tablespoon or two of dry vermouth and pour all this tasty liquor over the chicken.

Capon A roaster, 7–10 months old, which has been neutered. Fat and full of flavour, capons weigh from 6–10lb/2.75–4.5kg undrawn.

■ The capon owes its existence to a curious Roman law passed when the city was at its height of glory and extravagance, the gluttony of the wealthy extreme. It was feared that the enormous consumption of hens would lead to their extinction, so by law it became forbidden to fatten and eat them. There was, however, no mention of the cock so, concerned to try and fatten *them* for the table, a surgeon experimented with gelding. Thus it was by chance found that the flesh was more succulent and tender than that of the forbidden hen, and that birds could be almost doubled in size. There's more flesh on a capon than on any other bird, the fat being marbled and worked through the lean tissue, rather than 'pocketed' as with other fowl. (Today's cock is neutered by modern methods!)

■ Cook and serve in any way as a chicken or turkey.

Poularde A *hen* which has been neutered to increase its size – a roaster weighing 4lb/1.75kg or over.

Boiling fowl A hen over 10 months old. Due to present-day mass production and to deep freezing, this old bird is much less in evidence that it used to be.

■ For serving whole, coated with sauce, a boiler is drawn in the same way as a roasting chicken but trussed slightly differently: to make the legs tender and to present a flat even surface for coating the legs are 'pocketed' – put under the skin – and the parson's nose is tucked inside.

To pocket the legs:

1 Place bird on its back, tail towards you. Starting just above the vent, separate the skin from the flesh until you can get two of your fingers between the skin and the flesh. Work these fingers under the skin towards the leg.

2 Loosen the skin round the drumstick, keeping your fingers between the skin and the flesh. Bend back the hock joint of the leg and cut through the skin and the tendon just below the joint.

3 Remove the shank and the wide tendon at the joint, leaving the round bone clear.

4 Put two of your fingers inside the skin above the vent and gather the loose skin into folds. Press your thumb on the end of the hock bone, pushing the drumstick towards the wing and close to the body. Then push the hock bone towards the end of the breastbone nearest the vent until it is pocketed between the skin and flesh.

5 Repeat with second leg.

To truss a fowl for boiling

1 Thread trussing needle with a 2ft/60cm length of thin string, and knot at other end.

2 Lay bird on its back, neck end nearest to you, holding the thighs close to the body. Pass needle through thigh, just behind the joint, through the carcase and out through the other thigh.

3 Turn bird over. Pass needle through the elbow of the wing, over the back to hold down the loose neck skin, and out through the other wing elbow. Unthread needle, pull ends of string tightly and tie a double knot between the wing and the thigh.

4 Press the parson's nose inside the body cavity, and tuck in the loose skin from the drumsticks.

5 Smooth the skin from the breastbone over the vent, and pull to the back of the bird.

6 Thread needle with a slightly shorter length of string this time and pass the needle through the flesh under the tip of the breastbone.

7 Cross the string under the bird and, holding the ends of the drumsticks as close to the body as possible, bring the string to the top of the bird and tie securely.

8 Tuck in any surplus skin under the drumsticks and smooth the skin all over the bird, making sure that the flap of skin under the body is held firmly in place by the string.

To boil a fowl

1 Tying slices of lemon over the breast (or rubbing it with a cut lemon) and wrapping a bird in a clean cloth, is an old-fashioned but good way to keep the flesh white. If you don't do this, be sure to skim the water from time to time, otherwise both skin and flesh will go a nasty colour.

2 To make sure you put the bird into the right amount of boiling water, put the fowl in the pan first, cover it with cold water and then take the bird out again while boiling the water. (If you put the bird into cold water and bring it to the boil, flavouring juices will be drawn out of it into the liquor.) If necessary, top up with boiling water during cooking.

3 To give the cooking liquor and the fowl flavour, put plenty of salt in the water along with the prepared giblets, an onion stuck with 3 or 4 cloves, a bouquet garni and a chunk of carrot.

4 Boil fowl for 5 minutes then reduce the heat and simmer for 2–3 hours according to age of bird. (If you boil rather than simmer it, the flesh will harden.) Test with a fork near the thigh to see when it is tender.

■ If boiling a moderate sized roasting chicken, allow ¾–1 hour, a large one 1–1¼ hours, or a very large one 1¼–1½ hours.

■ Accompaniments to boiling fowl are: coating sauce to cover fowl, made with equal quantities milk and strained cooking liquor; sieved yolk of egg and finely chopped parsley, to garnish; creamed potatoes or boiled rice: a colourful but mildish vegetable such as Brussels sprouts, green peas or beans, courgettes or new carrots.

■ Should you want to *steam* a fowl, cook half as long again as for boiling, wrapping it in a clean cloth as for boiling.

DUCK

Duck, which has much more carcase and far less flesh than a like-sized chicken, is drawn and trussed in much the same way, but with these differences:

1 Cut legs off at hock joint – unless you prefer to leave on the scalded, scraped feet.

2 Cut wings off at elbow, because the lower part is mostly bone.

3 Cut out the wishbone, to make the breast easier to carve.

4 Minimize the richness by:
　a Removing oil sacs at base of tail – if still there.
　b Removing any loose fat from the cavity and around the neck.
　c Pricking the skin with a fork at

½in/1.25cm intervals along the thighs, the back and the lower part of the breast, to help let the layer of subcutaneous fat escape during cooking.

5 After stuffing or seasoning the cavity, sew or skewer the legs, wings and neck skin to the body to make the bird compact and plump-looking.

6 Sew or skewer a stuffed bird at vent, to keep the stuffing in.

Roasting a duck See also *roasting a bird*, page 250.

1 Only a duckling under 6 months is really perfect for roasting. (They tend to grow thinner as well as tougher after 8 months.)

2 Stuffing counteracts the richness of a duck and, because it keeps the flesh moister, also makes it more tender. If you're not a sage-and-onion fan, try another stuffing such as apple and walnut: sweat a finely sliced onion in ½oz/15g butter until nearly soft. Mix with 2oz/50g each of breadcrumbs and sausagemeat, ½ level teaspoon herbs, a few chopped walnuts, a chopped sour apple, seasoning and egg yolk (or half a small whole egg) to bind.

■ As a quick alternative to the more time-consuming stuffings, here are three easy ways to give flavour. *Either:*
   a Slip a peeled cored cooking apple into the cavity.
   b Season the cavity with salt, pepper, a pinch of thyme or sage and a small sliced onion or shallot.
   c Mix the chopped duck liver with a finely sliced shallot, a clove of crushed garlic, 1 tablespoon of chopped parsley, seasoning and a little mixed-up egg to bind.

3 *The roasting tin* Choose one just large

enough to hold a duck easily, then you won't need any dripping, just 2 tablespoons of water or stock: the duck itself provides the fat, *some* of which at intervals it is better to pour off – or draw off with a bulb baster. Although some people swear by basting a duck, there's no need to: with so much of its own fat beneath the skin, a duck is self-basting, which keeps its flesh moist and makes its skin crisp.

■ A duck roasts best, however, if you keep turning it: place it breast up for the first 15 minutes, then approximately 30 minutes on each side, then the last 15 minutes breast up again.

■ If you lay the bird on thickly sliced carrot and onion, these will give extra flavour to the gravy.

4 *Roasting time* In the centre of a moderate oven, gas 4, 350°F/175°C – depends, of course, on the duck's weight and whether it is stuffed or not. The table below is a guide.

■ To test when cooked, prick duck at fattest part of thigh or drumstick. If the juices that run out from there, and from the vent (when you lift and drain the duck) look pinkish, the duck is medium rare – the way the French like it. If the juices run pale yellow, the duck is well done.

■ If you want to have it ready in advance, a roast duck won't spoil if left for half an hour in a turned-off hot oven, door ajar.

5 Traditional accompaniments to roast duck are: sage and onion stuffing (but not too heavy-handed with the sage!); apple sauce; thick gravy if stuffed, otherwise thin: new or duchess potatoes, to minimize richness; green peas or other

Weight of bird when drawn	No. it will serve	Cooking time for medium rare	Cooking time for well done	If stuffed, add
3½lb/1.5kg	3 or 4	65–70 mins	75–85 mins	20–30 mins
4½lb/2kg	4	75–80 mins	85–95 mins	20–30 mins
5½lb/2.5kg	5 or 6	85–90 mins	95–100 mins	20–30 mins

vegetables such as braised celery, turnips or Brussels sprouts.

6 Carving a duck is different from carving a chicken, because its anatomy is different: cut through the crackling skin with the point of a sharp knife, and cut the meat from the breast in long, rather thin slices – in slivers. One way to do this is to turn the dismembered bird first on one side and then on the other, its tail towards you, cutting diagonally. You may find it easier to cut the wing joints with game shears rather than with a knife.

Other good ways to cook or use duck

■ Roasting in various other ways, including the famous duck à l'orange.
■ Spit roasting.
■ Braising or casseroling, perhaps after marinating the duck in a red wine marinade.
■ Make salmi.
■ Serve it cold, or make it into cold dishes the same as many chicken dishes, e.g. chaud-froid of duckling, galantine, pâté, pâté en croûte (boned, stuffed duck baked in a crust).
■ Make soup.

Duck fat, rendered Makes good dripping toast: spread it on hot toast, sprinkle lightly with salt and put back under grill again for a few moments, to help the fat melt and the toast to absorb it.

Duck, wild These (mallard, widgeon, teal) shouldn't hang longer than a day, the flavour becoming rancid rather than gamey like that of a well-hung grouse or pheasant. It is safer to eat wild duck without delay. Allow two birds for four people or, at a stretch, two mallards for five.

■ Because of their sometimes rather strong fishy flavour, depending on what they feed on, it's wise to take precautions before you roast them – mallard and teal especially.

1 Remove oil sacs near tail – their contents keep the feathers oiled.
2 Blanch the birds: put them in a roasting tin with a sliced onion and enough boiling salted water to baste thoroughly. Spend several minutes at the kitchen table just spooning the onion-flavoured water over them. (Alternatively, marinate them in a well-flavoured marinade or, less effective I think, stuff each bird's cavity either with a small peeled orange or two, or with a raw potato and an onion or an apple.)

3 Pour water away, drain birds well, wipe dry, rub the skin all over with salt, and then smear liberally with either softened butter or olive oil.

4 Bard or lard the breast. (Unlike the fattiness of a domestic duck, wild duck is by comparison dry.)

■ Roasting or spit-roasting are the best ways to cook wild duck, which should be underdone, and served hot. Roast teal or widgeon for about 25 minutes, mallard about 30 minutes – preferably in butter – in the middle of a preheated hot oven, gas 7, 425°F/220°C, basting 2 or 3 times to prevent the flesh drying out.

■ Accompaniments for roast wild duck are: orange salad, bigarade sauce (page 170); game chips or creamed potatoes; watercress, to garnish.

Other suggestions for wild duck, should you tire of eating it roasted: marinate it (e.g. in a liquid containing red wine and port) and then braise, pot-roast or casserole it, or make it into salmi, page 270. Use up cooked wild duck in things like risotto, savoury pancakes, patties, or just in a tasty béchamel sauce, served with croûtes of fried bread.

GALANTINE

Originally referred to a boned, stuffed and pressed chicken served in its own jelly, its name deriving from the Latin word *gallus*, a cock. Towards the end of the seventeenth century, however, other birds, and also meat and fish, began to figure in this dish, but the term galantine, by itself, still implies galantine of poultry. When made with something different, the main ingredient is always named, as in galantine of veal, or galantine of partridge or grouse.

■ The meat itself may be stuffed, or may be minced and combined with other meats and flavourings. It is very like pâté, the difference between them being in the cooking: if the meaty mixture is baked in a fat-lined terrine it is a terrine or pâté; if baked in a pastry crust it is a pâté en croûte; if *steamed*, it is a galantine.

■ A few hints:

1 The meats should be finely minced, preferably together, preferably twice, to blend perfectly.

2 To blend the mixture thoroughly and to give the galantine a light texture, beat the ingredients vigorously together with a wooden spoon.

3 Be generous with seasoning; a cold mixture of this sort tends to lack flavour.

4 A galantine needs very gentle cooking, tied in a clean cloth. If cooked too fast, the meat will harden and the surface may crack.

5 For the right texture, a galantine should be weighted and left overnight to cool.

6 If when cold, a galantine's surface is greasy rather than jellied, wring a clean cloth out in very hot water, fold it and place over the galantine for a few minutes.

7 If the meat hasn't jellied when cold, meat glaze or aspic helps both to keep it moist and to garnish it.

GAME

Plucking game It would be easier to pluck game if we didn't afterwards have to chase after the feathers. In the kitchen, you only have to sigh or sneeze for the downy ones to take off, so it's easiest to work on several layers of spread-out newspaper and from time to time clear the decks. Game is ready for cooking when the tail feathers come out quite readily when pulled – unless you like it very high.

■ In case you're flummoxed by the prospect of a feathered bird, here are some tips:

1 All the skin is tender, especially the breast and neck skin. To minimize the risk of tearing it – because a damaged bird roasts less well than a perfect one – grip the skin tightly between thumb and fingers of one hand while, close beside them, you carefully pull out the feathers with the other.

2 To have some sort of organization and to be able to see what you're doing, pluck in this order:
   a Underside of wings.
   b The tail. (Keep the best six tail-feathers of a pheasant to stick in the vent, giving the cooked bird a festive look on the serving dish.)
   c From neck to tail on breast side of bird, then from neck to tail on back.
   d Legs.
   e Upper side of wings, cutting off the wing tips.

3 Singe bird over a low gas flame, or other clear flame, to make it less whiskery.

Drawing game Draw as for *chicken* (see page 251), apart from some minor differences:

1 The leg sinews aren't pulled out, for it's a game bird's wings that are the hard-working part. The feet are in fact left on, so scald the legs and cut off the claws.

2 Snipe is roasted without being drawn or decapitated, see page 271.

Trussing game Truss game as *chicken* (page 252), apart from:

1 The wings: fold these up at the sides of the body instead of underneath.

2 Truss the legs so that the feet lean well back towards the breast. (To help set them in this position, lay a bird's feet against the roasting tin when you roast it, first on one side, then the other.)

Roasting game See *roasting a bird*, page 250, for general information, and individual birds for details specific to each.

Fried breadcrumbs These are so often a disappointment that it seems a pity not to spell out the simple details. This quantity serves 6:

> 1oz/25g butter (preferably but not essentially saltless or clarified, which burn less easily)
>
> 2oz/50g golden breadcrumbs (raspings) which, unlike white breadcrumbs, give a delicious nutty flavour

Method

1 Heat butter in strong frying pan over moderate heat until it foams. Wait until the foam almost subsides but *not* until the butter begins to go brown.

2 Stir in crumbs, reduce heat to low and stir frequently if not continually – to brown them evenly – for a few minutes until a darker golden colour. (If not cooked slowly and for long enough they will lack flavour, but if cooked too fast or too long the butter will burn.)

3 Serve hot in a warmed sauceboat with roast game – pheasant, partridge, grouse, etc.

GOOSE

Goose is drawn and trussed as duck, and in much the same way as a chicken (page 251), but with these differences:

1 Cut legs off at hock joint.

2 Cut wings off at elbow – because the lower part is mostly bone. (Even then, the remaining part makes poor eating.)

3 Cut out the wishbone, to make the breast easier to carve.

4 Minimise the richness by:

a Removing any loose fat from cavity and around the neck. (See *goose fat*, below, for what to do with it.)

b Pricking the skin with a fork at ½in/1.25cm intervals along the thighs, the back and lower part of the breast, to help let the layer of subcutaneous fat escape during cooking.

5 After stuffing or seasoning the cavity, sew or skewer the legs, wings and neck skin to the body, to make the bird compact and plump looking.

6 Sew or skewer a stuffed bird at the vent, otherwise some of the stuffing will escape during cooking into the fat in the roasting tin.

Roasting a goose See also *roasting a bird*, page 250.

1 A bird under 6 months old and from 9–11lb/4–5kg is best: smaller ones are largely bone, while larger tend to be tough, because usually older.   •

2 Stuffing counteracts richness and, because it keeps the flesh moister, makes it more tender.

■ Goose and prunes have an affinity with each other, so a prune and apple stuffing (or even a chestnut stuffing) is to many people a welcome change from sage and onions.

■ The goose's liver is often included in the stuffing because it gives so much flavour, but if you want something really quick and simple just to cut down its richness, try stuffing the bird with peeled and cored sour apples.

■ Although you can have the stuffing prepared, ready to put in, it's better actually not to stuff the goose until just before you cook it, otherwise it can spoil both bird and stuffing.

3 If before roasting you rub over the skin with flour, it helps it absorb some of the surface grease as well as making the skin crisp.

4 Goose isn't basted because, with so much fat of its own beneath its skin, it is self-basting. To protect it during the rather long cooking, cover the breast with a piece of foil or a sheet of greased greaseproof paper for the first 45 minutes. (Some people baste a goose with boiling water to help in the dissolution of all subcutaneous fat.) There is so much fat that you may at intervals need to ladle some of it out of the roasting tin, or better still, draw it off with a bulb baster.

5 *Roasting time* Goose should be 'done to a T' – 180°F/82°C, on a meat thermo-

Weight of bird (drawn)	No. it will serve	Approx. cooking time, unstuffed	If stuffed, add on:
9lb/4kg	6–8	about 2 hrs	20–40 mins
9½lb/4.25 kg	8–9	about 2¼ hrs	20–40 mins
10½lb/4.75kg	9–10	about 2 hrs, 20 mins	20–40 mins
11½lb/5.25kg	10–12	about 2½ hrs	20–40 mins

meter (but see *meat* and *oven thermometer*, page 45), the meat juices running pale yellow: if overcooked, the breast meat especially will be dry; if undercooked, goose is indigestible and unpalatable.

■ Cooking time depends on the weight of the goose and whether it is stuffed or not. Roast it in the centre of a preheated hot oven for the first 15 minutes, gas 7, 425°F/220°C, then reduce the heat to gas 4, 350°F/175°C, for the remainder of the cooking time. If you're unsure how long to give it, here's a rough guide. As you'll see from the table above the larger the goose, the less time per lb/450g it takes to cook.

6 Traditional accompaniments to goose are: sage and onion stuffing; apple sauce (pineapple isn't traditional, but fried pineapple rings makes a good variation); thick gravy, if stuffed, otherwise thin; watercress, to garnish.

7 Carve goose as duck, see page 260.

Braised goose Some people prefer this to roast, finding it more tender and flavourful, but less rich. Cook it at gas 3, 325°F/165°C, a lower temperature than for roasting, but for a similar length of time.
See 5 above.

Goose fat Rendered down from the loose fat inside the bird, goose fat is much too good to waste, being excellent for sautéing or basting. Once rendered, it will keep for weeks in the refrigerator. To prepare:

1 Cut fat into ½in/1.25cm pieces and simmer about 20 minutes in a covered saucepan with ½pt/250ml water, to draw the fat out of the tissues.

2 Remove pan lid and boil liquid slowly to evaporate the water. (The fat will splutter as the moisture in it evaporates. When it stops spluttering, the fat is pure, ready for use.)

3 Strain the pale yellow liquid through butter muslin.

■ Goose fat is also a delicacy smeared on soft fresh bread, sprinkled with salt and freshly milled pepper.

Goose liver A valuable part of a goose, both for its goodness and its flavour. The liver of other birds is just as good but the goose's is larger, and when the bird is grossly overfed and deprived of exercise, the liver may grow to as much as five times its normal size. This explains why geese in some countries, France particularly, have been bred and fattened for centuries especially to make pâté de foie gras, and why the *flesh* of these birds is inferior to the flesh of a bird reared specifically for roasting.

Goose stock Makes an excellent brown sauce: make it as chicken stock (page 122), using the gizzard, neck, heart and wing tips – the liver as well if you haven't used it in the stuffing or to make goose liver pâté, like chicken liver pâté. Simmer the stock about 2 hours.

Green goose A gosling under 3 months old. As its flavour is easily overpowered by a stuffing, it is better not to stuff it – or anyway not with sage and onions.

Michaelmas goose A young goose; tender, delicious and less rich than a mature bird because it hasn't had time to develop so much fat.

■ The English tradition, dating back to

the sixteenth century, of eating goose on Michaelmas Day appears almost to have died out. The custom originated with Queen Elizabeth who was at table when the news of the sinking of the Spanish Armada was brought to her. Because the principal dish that day was roast goose, and because it was a favourite dish of hers, she decreed that the glorious occasion should be commemorated by serving roast goose on Michaelmas Day (29 September) every year.

Wild goose A bird which I confess I've never either eaten or cooked, but it is said not to compare in flavour with a domesticated goose. Because it is so much leaner, one good way to cook it is evidently in a flour and water paste (page 235) in a slower oven and for a longer time than a farmyard goose – probably for about 3 hours. Remove the crust and froth the bird's breast (page 251) about 20–30 minutes before you expect it to be ready.

GROUSE

At their best young, and between mid-August and mid-October. This is probably the finest of all game birds and is, in the culinary sense, unique to the British Isles. The best come from Scotland, parts of Northern England, Wales and the West of Ireland. Grouse is equally good whether you eat it hot or cold.

■ Young birds are best roasted, old birds marinated and casseroled, or made into tasty dishes like grouse pudding (beef-steak and grouse actually), raised pie, pâté or potted grouse. They also make a good salmi.

■ Grouse should be well hung to develop its true flavour. Allow young birds about a week in warm weather – unless badly shot or in moist thundery weather – or up to a fortnight if cold, and if you like them high. (Use the tail feathers as a guide, see page 249.)

To roast grouse See also *roasting a bird*, page 250.

1 As the flesh is inclined to be dry, it's best to bard the breast and put a nut of seasoned butter inside the bird, as well as roasting it in butter.

2 The liver is almost too good to use in the stock: fry lightly, mash and spread it on an oval slice of bread, all ready to slip underneath the bird when you froth the breast about 15 minutes before the bird is cooked.

3 Make the giblet stock in advance – you'll need it to make thin gravy with the drippings in the roasting tin.

4 Allow *about* 35 minutes in the centre of a preheated hot oven, gas 6, 400°F/205°C. If a bird is very high, be sure to cook it well.

5 Accompaniments to roast grouse are: fried breadcrumbs (page 262); bread sauce; thin (giblet) gravy; game chips (page 192); a dressed green salad; water-cress, to garnish.

6 *To carve.* Young grouse are usually cut in half, allowing half a bird per person.

GUINEA FOWL

Though related to the pheasant, guinea fowl isn't as succulent and good to eat because it never runs to fat and the flesh is naturally dry. The bird takes its name from its homeland, the West African coast of Guinea, from where it was originally brought to Europe. Although in Britain it has been domesticated since the fifteenth century, in its native haunt it is wild.

■ The flavour isn't too unlike that of either a chicken or pheasant, and one can cook it as either, in almost any way – but it's better cooked according to pheasant recipes because of its lack of fat.

■ A few facts may help:

1 Hang guinea fowl for at least 2 days in warm weather, longer in cold. Pluck just before you cook (or freeze) it.

2 Stuff it or not as you like. A lump of butter in the cavity, for instance, will help to make the flesh moist, as will any stuffing containing fat.

3 Truss like game.

4 Bard the bird well, to protect, make moist and give the flesh flavour.

5 Roast as pheasant (page 266), allowing about 1 hour.

6 Accompaniments for roast guinea fowl are: bread sauce; redcurrant jelly; thin gravy; game chips; watercress, to garnish.

HARE

At its best in Britain in late December. Young hares are best for roasting or jugging – the two most usual methods of cooking hare – while the older are usually best marinated (to tenderize and flavour them) before braising or casseroling. In addition, one can make many tasty dishes like raised pie or potted hare, hare soup, pâté, pudding or brawn.

■ A hare is never eaten high. Hung head downwards, with a bowl to catch the blood, and without skinning or paunching (drawing), allow a fully grown hare up to 10 days in very cold weather, about 6–7 days when warm. A good-sized hare will serve 9–10 people, a leveret 6–8.

To skin and draw a hare

1 Cut off the legs at the first joint.

2 Slit the skin along the belly and loosen it from the body.

3 Draw it over the hind legs by pulling away inside out. Pull towards the tail.

4 Pull the skin towards the head and off the front legs.

5 Draw the skin towards the neck, then, with a sharp knife, remove it from the head. (You may want to cut off the head while you're about it.)

6 Slit the belly and pull out the internal organs, reserving the liver if you want it, to stuff a hare before roasting. Collect in a basin all the blood if you're roasting or jugging the hare. (It collects under a piece of membrane in the ribs, so take care when breaking this.)

7 Apart from the tail end, wipe rather than wash a skinned hare, to avoid it losing flavour.

Jugged hare When it is properly made, jugged hare is one of the best British dishes. The essential points are:

1 Long slow cooking, until the meat is completely tender – ready to leave the bones. Young or old, a hare must always be well-cooked. (It's better *over*cooked than undercooked.)

2 Port – a large glassful – to give flavour. Alternatively, use a glass of the red wine marinade if the hare was first marinated.

3 The use of the hare's blood as a liaison, to thicken the liquor after the hare is cooked: add 2 or 3 tablespoons of the hot liquor very gradually to the blood (as you would add it to a cream and egg yolk liaison), then stir this back carefully into the sauce. Reheat the sauce gently, to thicken it without boiling, otherwise it will be curdled by the blood.

■ Accompaniments for jugged hare are: fried forcemeat balls; redcurrant jelly.

PARTRIDGE

Young birds, which are best roasted (or can be split and grilled), are at their plumpest and best in Britain in October. Because of their delicate and perfect natural flavour, young partridge shouldn't be hung until high – give them just three or four days. In cold weather, older birds may hang up to a fortnight. These are better marinated and then braised or stewed rather than roasted, or one can make them into dishes like salmi, raised pie, galantine, pâté or potted partridge. Cold roast partridge with bacon makes a breakfast fit for Lucullus.

To roast partridge See also *roasting a bird*, page 250.

1 To help keep the flesh moist and to give flavour, cover the breast with a rasher or two of fat bacon and put a nut of butter (mixed with seasoning and a few drops of lemon juice) inside the bird, as well as cooking it in butter.

2 Make the giblet stock in advance – to make thin gravy with the drippings in the

266 1001 Ways to be a Good Cook

roasting tin.

3 Roast for about 10 minutes in the centre of a preheated very hot oven, gas 7, 425°F/220°C, then reduce heat to gas 6, 400°F/205°C, for the remainder of the cooking time – *about* 30 minutes altogether. (Baste and turn bird every 10 minutes to make sure it cooks perfectly.)

4 If liked, slip a slice of bread under a bird about 15 minutes before it's cooked, to catch the juices and become crisp. Accompaniments to roast partridge are: fried breadcrumbs (page 262); bread sauce; thin (giblet) gravy; game chips (page 192) or potato straws; a dressed green salad (avoid any overpowering vegetable, particularly one of the cabbage family); watercress to garnish.

5 To carve, cut in half, allowing half a bird per person.

PÂTÉ (TERRINE)

Made from the game or poultry of your choice, usually together with veal and pork, the proportions of these depending on the richness or dryness of the bird or animal in question. To make pheasant pâté, for instance, you may want about 1lb/450g each of lean veal and pork belly to the meat of one plump bird, but for duck pâté you'd need correspondingly less fat meat and rather more lean meat.

■ The ideal way to make these pâtés is with an uncooked bird, but as it's so much easier and quicker to strip the flesh off a partly cooked bird (say roasted about 20 minutes) than an uncooked, this is the way it's often done. A bird's liver, raw, is sometimes minced along with the flesh and the other meats.

■ See also *pâté*, page 156.

PHEASANT

The most beautiful of all our game birds, pheasant was in ancient times known as the bird of Phasis. Its name originates from the river Phasis, between the Black and Caspian Seas where the bird originated.

■ Young birds are best – and at their best in Britain from November to January – but must be hung long enough to taste of pheasant: in a cool place, preferably one with lots of fresh cold air, this means at least five days in normal weather, or up to about 12 days when very cold – unless they're badly shot. The hen is normally plumper, more tender and more succulent than the cock, but the cock is larger, even if not quite so good. This is why birds are usually sold by the brace and why, if the purse allows, it is better to cook a pair rather than a single bird.

■ As with most other game birds, young pheasants are best roasted; older birds should be marinated before stewing, casseroling, etc., or making into all the traditional things like galantine, pâté, raised pie, salmi, potted pheasant or soup.

To roast pheasant See also *roasting a bird*, page 250.

1 To help keep the flesh moist and to give flavour, bard the breast. Some seasoning and a few strips of juicy steak inside the bird will give it even more flavour.

2 Roast about 10 minutes in the centre of a preheated very hot oven, gas 7, 425°F/220°C, then reduce heat to gas 6, 400°F/205°C for remainder of cooking time – about 40–60 minutes altogether according to the size and age of the bird. (Baste it at least each time you turn it.)

3 A slice of white bread slipped underneath the bird about 15 minutes before it's cooked is unorthodox but delicious. Saturated by the bird's juices, and made crisp by the hot fat, my mouth waters even as I write about it.

4 If you want to stuff a pheasant, here's one very simple suggestion: 1oz/25g butter mixed with salt, pepper, a pinch of cayenne and a few wiped, chopped-up mushrooms.

5 To make chirpy, serve with six of the best tail feathers coming out of the vent.

6 Accompaniments to roast pheasant are: fried breadcrumbs (page 262); bread sauce; thin (giblet) gravy; game chips or potato straws; a dressed green salad;

watercress to garnish.

7 Carve as chicken. A pheasant's legs are quite a lot darker and more highly flavoured than the breast and wings, so some people prefer the dark meat to the white.

To serve a roast pheasant cold An old country custom which is still, I think, unequalled: the moment the roast pheasant leaves the oven, wrap it up closely in a cloth wrung out in cold water or cider. Cover it then with a clean sack or an old piece of blanket or rug and leave to cool. (Because the steam is kept in, the breast is moist and succulent, instead of dry, as cold pheasant tends to be.)

PIGEONS

The pigeon has been kept for centuries in semi-domestication in many parts of the world. Better known in biblical terms as a dove, it has for thousands of years had religious connotations. It was because of its prized flesh that this was the bird chosen for sacrifice.

■ Until the eighteenth century, before turnips and swedes were introduced to British agriculture, and we could keep cattle and sheep alive through the winter, non-breeding animals had to be slaughtered and preserved in salt. Pigeons in those days, therefore, supplied the wealthy with fresh meat during the months when little else was available. In castle, monastery and manor-house, the 'table' was the chief concern, so that by the middle of the seventeenth century, every house of importance had its own dovecote in which hundreds or even thousands of these prolific birds could be, and were, accommodated.

■ The dovecote originated in Rome. Some Romans were so impatient to fatten the squab that as soon as they were covered with down they were separated from the parent birds and fed on white bread already half-chewed by men specially hired for the work!

■ Pigeons are at their best from March to September, a young bird being recognizable by its small pink legs, fat breast, flexible beak and thick neck. Properly cooked, they make as good a meal as almost any game bird. See also *squab*, page 271.

Hanging, plucking and drawing

1 You can hang a pigeon a day or two or not at all, as you like, but to keep the flesh a better colour, the bird should be hung head downwards for at least an hour immediately after shooting. Otherwise, the meat is very dark.

2 If you can pluck a pigeon while it's still warm, the feathers will almost fly off. It's the easiest of all birds to do. (Scalding with boiling water may be a quick way to de-feather a pigeon, but it toughens both the skin and the outer layer of the flesh.)

3 Draw a pigeon when you pluck it. The liver contains no gall so you can either leave it in the bird for extra flavour, use it in a stuffing if you're roasting the bird or, if you have many birds, make pâté.

■ It's because cooks had to be imaginative if people weren't to tire of pigeon that old cookery books abound with pigeon recipes. Young birds are best roasted (see below) or grilled – in the same way as poussins (see page 256). Old birds are usually improved by marinating and can be braised, casseroled, stewed, curried, made into a pie, a pudding (with steak), a raised pie, salmi, pâté, soup or potted.

To roast pigeon See also *roasting a bird*, page 250.

1 Allow one plump young bird per person.

2 To protect the flesh and give extra flavour, either bard the breast with a fat bacon rasher or brush the bird with melted butter and dust lightly with flour. Best of all is to brush it with butter *and* bard it.

3 Stuffing – at the neck end, as a chicken – is optional. Here's one suggestion: sauté the pigeon's liver and a chopped mushroom in a walnut-sized piece of butter. Mash them when cooked and mix with 2 rounded teaspoons of fresh white breadcrumbs, seasoning and any remaining butter in the pan. If liked, add a touch of sherry or brandy.

4 Roast for 25–35 minutes according to size in a preheated hot oven, gas 6, 400°F/205°C, basting frequently.

5 A small slice of bread slipped under the bird about half time will absorb the juices, become crisp in the fat and is *delicious* with the bird.

6 Accompaniments to roast pigeon are: fried breadcrumbs – if no bread under the bird; thin gravy; bacon rasher used to bard bird – with a pigeon this is served; dressed watercress to garnish.

7 To carve. Cut in half down the centre.

■ However you cook pigeon, any fat used shouldn't be too intensely hot, otherwise it will spoil the delicate flavour of the flesh.

POTTED MEAT

Cooked, finely minced meat preserved in pots or jars, potted meat is so concentrated, compact and well preserved that in days gone by it was an ideal food for seamen and travellers to take on their journeys. Covered with a thick layer of butter to exclude air, and refrigerated, any meat's keeping time is greatly extended.

■ Potted meats are more or less the British equivalent of a French pâté or terrine. Their basic difference is that for potted meat, the meat is cooked before being preserved, whereas for pâté the meat is cooked in the dish in which it is to be stored and served.

■ Here's one tasty recipe, to serve 5 or 6:

    ½lb/225g cooked, boneless chicken or game
    2oz/50g cooked ham or streaky bacon rashers
    2oz/50g softish butter
    salt and cayenne pepper
    pinch ground nutmeg
    pinch ground mace
    1 clove garlic, optional
    saltless or clarified butter, as required to cover surface

Method

1 Mince the meats together.

2 Liquidize together – adding meat to liquidizer a little at a time, to prevent machine sticking – the meats, cut-up butter, salt, spices and crushed garlic.

3 Press into pots and cover with a ¼in/6mm layer of barely melted cool butter. Tilt pot carefully in all directions to seal in the contents. Leave butter to harden.

4 Cover with foil or Cling-film to store and refrigerate.

5 Serve with hot toast or crusty French bread or rolls.

■ A few tips:

1 Old game is better marinated before being cooked, to tenderize and flavour it. It won't then need quite such long cooking, so the flavour benefits in two ways.

2 A touch of garlic gives a subtle flavour. It's worth trying, even if you think you don't like garlic.

3 If without a processor, liquidizer, or chopper strong enough to cope with meat, pound everything together, then pass the mixture through a sieve.

4 If you overheat the butter to pour over the top, it will oil and separate: melt it over minimum heat. If it's too hot when you pour it over the meat, it will tend to penetrate rather than lie on top of the meat.

5 Saltless butter gives a better flavour and preserves the meat better than salted.

RABBITS

Best in Britain from October to February. Wild ones are paunched (drawn) immediately they are killed and shouldn't be hung longer than a day to be really fresh and good.

■ A good-sized rabbit weighs approximately 2½lb/1.25kg and will feed 5–6 people. A tame rabbit may weigh twice as much but is unlikely to have the lovely flavour of a wild one which may have been tucking into corn or your best garden lettuces. The doe is generally larger and has a better flavour than the buck.

■ It isn't always easy to choose a rabbit, but above all it must smell fresh: if the ear tears fairly easily, a rabbit is young, and if the kidneys are buried in fat, it is certain to be good.

■ To whiten and improve the flavour of a rabbit's flesh, also to make it more digestible, soak overnight in some vinegar and water – 1 dessertspoon vinegar to 1qt/1 litre water. Unless you are planning to roast it, joint it before soaking, then if you want to – or if the rabbit is old and needs it – you can marinate it afterwards.

To skin a rabbit See *hare*, page 265.

To joint a rabbit

1 Cut off all legs at joint and cut 'wings' away from the ribs.
2 Cut the back into three or four pieces according to size of rabbit.
3 Use the head (split, and minus eyes) to make stock while the rest of the rabbit is soaking.

■ There are many better ways of cooking a rabbit than roasting it – because roasting tends to make the flesh dry. If you *do* roast it, stuff and baste frequently in order to keep it all as moist as possible. You can grill or devil rabbit, stew, casserole or curry it; make it into galantine, a pie or soup – or you can substitute rabbit for veal in a recipe like fricassée or blanquette. As long as it is soaked to remove its strong flavour, you can even in some recipes use rabbit instead of chicken.

RAISED PIE

A pie moulded entirely from pastry – top crust, walls and bottom. Made basically with meats such as veal and ham, pork, gammon and hard-boiled egg, pigeon or any game meat (or perhaps a mixture of game meats) and served with a salad, it makes a delicious supper or light luncheon dish, or is ideal for picnics. One can serve it hot but I prefer it cold, freshly made, when the crust is crisp.

■ Though lots of people fight shy of hot water crust pastry (see page 140), it is easy to make. The other thing that puts people off can be the mould, but if without the correct kind of hinged raised pie type, you can make your own individual mould (see page 34) or use a loose-bottom oval mould, or even a loose-bottom cake tin.

■ Here are a few tips:

1 Small pies are easier to make than large.
2 Have everything ready for the filling before making the pastry so that you can then get on quickly before it cools and becomes difficult to handle.
3 Cut the meat up small so that it will cook in the same time as the crust. A tough bird should be marinated, and a bird may even be partly cooked.
4 Use enough stock just to moisten the filling without also making the pastry base soggy, i.e. about 1 tablespoon stock to meat for 4oz/100g pastry.
5 Fit the pastry into the mould carefully, without holes, otherwise there'll be an escape-hatch for the stock/gelatine liquor added after cooking, especially if too liquid when poured in.
6 After rolling out and moulding the pastry (to come marginally above top of mould), adding the filling (traditionally mounded towards the middle), covering with pastry lid and sealing edges, it is easier to trim the edges with scissors than with a knife. Use the trimmings to make small pastry leaves, each to span from pie centre to side.
7 Egg yolk makes the best glaze because it gives the pie a shiny golden finish.
8 A tiny funnel (made of card, and held in shape with a paper clip) stuck into the central hole in the lid of the pie, ensures steam can escape from within and that the nearly-setting stock can, after the pie is baked, be poured in.
9 Hot water crust pastry needs a pre-heated very hot oven for the first 10–15 minutes, gas 8, 450°F/230°C, reduced then to gas 4, 350°F/175°C for remaining

time, approx. ¾–1 hour *altogether*. About half-way through cooking time, when the pastry is set, carefully take pie out of its mould and brush the sides with glaze, to make them golden too.

SALMI (OR SALMIS)

An abbreviation of the French word *salmisgondis*, meaning a hotchpotch – and though time-consuming, this is one of the very greatest hotchpotches, mainly because of its lovely sauce.

■ The word *salmi* indicates a mixture of two processes: roasting (lightly, so that the flesh is slightly underdone), then casseroling, when the bird's cooking is completed in the sauce. The amount of sauce you need depends on a bird's size.
■ One can make salmi with any game bird, young or old, or with duck, goose or pigeon.
■ Here's one recipe:

Ingredients	Comments
1 lightly roasted pheasant (page 266)	Could use partridge or grouse, etc. first marinated if an old bird.
1oz/25g raw lean ham or bacon	
1oz/25g saltless or clarified butter	Margarine or salted butter would burn. (You could use 3 dessertsps. oil.)
1 small onion or 2 shallots	
½ small carrot, thinly sliced	
1oz/25g flour	
1 tsp tomato purée	
¾pt/375ml good brown stock	
salt and pepper	
bouquet garni	
4 tablespoons port	Use red wine if you like.
1 dessertspoon redcurrant jelly	
a few button mushrooms	
a nut of butter	
a few glacé cherries	Use stuffed olives if you prefer.
fleurons of pastry (page 62)	Baked fleurons, of course.
a little finely chopped parsley, to garnish	

1 In a strong saucepan over low heat, lightly fry the diced ham or bacon (rind as well) in the butter.
2 Add finely sliced onion and fry it just 2 or 3 minutes before adding the carrot, frying it also for a few minutes. Set pan aside from heat.
3 Stir in the flour, return pan to heat and cook roux over minimum heat for 15–20 minutes or until a good brown colour, stirring at frequent intervals.

(This long slow cooking of the roux gives the sauce extra flavour.)
4 Set pan aside from heat again and stir in the tomato purée, then the stock, gradually at first, as for any sauce. Season.
5 Bring sauce to the boil, stirring constantly, add bouquet garni, reduce heat, cover pan and simmer sauce very gently for about 20 minutes, skimming occasionally if necessary.

6 Meanwhile, joint the pheasant and lay the skinned (and preferably boned) pieces in a casserole.

7 Add port and redcurrant jelly to the *strained* sauce, simmer it for about 10 minutes and then pour over the pheasant.

8 Cook in slow oven until bird is tender, probably about half an hour after it starts to cook, depending, of course, on how old a bird is and how long you roasted it. (Alternatively, you *could* simmer it in the saucepan on top of cooker.)

9 Serve garnished with the mushrooms fried lightly in the nut of butter, the glacé cherries heated in boiling water, fleurons of pastry and parsley.

SNIPE

At its best in Britain in October and November, and should be eaten when fresh, some people thinking it most delicious when cooked straight after being shot. Its rather distinctive flavour is due to the snails and worms on which, mainly, it feeds.

■ Although one can cook snipe in other ways – for instance grill, casserole or make salmi – they are best roasted, or spit-roasted.

To pluck and truss for roasting

1 Don't, as for most other game birds, cut off a snipe's head: the beak is needed as a skewer, so simply pluck the head and remove the eyes.

2 When plucking, handle snipe with kid gloves – their flesh is very delicate.

3 Don't draw snipe either. Their entrails (or 'trail' as the internals are sometimes called) play an important part in a bird's flavour and, minus the gizzard, are to gourmets one of the most succulent morsels.

4 Truss as other game birds, but instead of using a trussing needle and string, twist the head round and pass the beak through the legs and body.

To roast snipe See also *roasting a bird*, page 250.

1 Allow one bird per person. (Snipe weigh between 2 and 10oz/50 and 250g.)

2 Brush with melted butter, and bard it with a fat bacon rasher to protect the flesh during cooking. For the best flavour, also roast in butter.

3 Put a slice of bread under the bird before roasting, to catch the drippings from the trail. Serve the bird on the bread, then crisp and tasty.

4 Roast in preheated hot oven, gas 6, 400°F/205°C for 12–20 minutes depending on whether you like snipe very underdone or just slightly underdone. Avoid over-roasting anyway, and baste several times.

5 Accompaniments to roast snipe are: fried breadcrumbs (page 262); clear gravy; game chips; orange or green salad; watercress, to garnish.

SQUAB

A young pigeon not more than 4 weeks old. At 28 days it is at its peak – a plump, tender and delicious meal for one.

■ Split and fry them in butter with a spoonful of oil, or in good olive oil, or grill, roast or cook as young pigeon (page 267).

TURKEYS

First introduced by the Spaniards to Europe from Mexico (where turkeys had long been domesticated) in the earlier part of the sixteenth century. Until then, the name 'turkey' applied to the bird we now call a guinea fowl – which is thought to have been introduced to Britain from Turkey, although originating in West Africa. One reminder we have of this is that when Shakespeare wrote of a turkey, he in fact meant a guinea fowl.

■ The turkey-hen is a better buy than the cock because, weight for weight, the hen is the fleshy one while the cock has the heavier bones. As a rule, the hen is also more tender than the cock, so if you're buying an oven-ready bird and can't tell which is which, it's wise to ask. Allow ¾–1lb/350–450g per person if a small bird (say under 10lb or 4.5kg); ½–¾lb/225–350g per person if a medium-sized bird; ½lb/225g per person if a large bird, say 20lb/9kg and over.

To draw a turkey See page 251.

To truss a turkey See page 252.

To bone a turkey See page 252.

To roast a turkey in the British way See also *roasting a bird* (page 250) and *roasting* (page 78).

1 Your chosen size of bird must obviously depend to some extent on the number of people you want it to serve, see above, but a medium-sized turkey is easier to cook than a very large, and fits better in the average oven. A very small bird, especially a cock, is uneconomical.

2 A frozen turkey will take 2–3 days to thaw slowly and completely in its vacuum-sealed bag, depending on the size of the bird, *where* you thaw it, and the weather. If you thaw it quickly, say in a hot room or by putting it in a bowl of cold water, an excessive amount of juices will drip into the bag, instead of remaining in, and flavouring, the bird.

3 Stuffing gives extra flavour, helps to keep the flesh moist and stretches the number of servings. Veal forcemeat in the neck cavity is enclosed by the loose neck-skin, folded and stitched under the bird when you truss it. Chestnut and sausagemeat stuffing goes into the body cavity, to be spooned out when the turkey is carved.

4 The most succulent way I know of roasting a turkey is in butter, the bird covered with butter muslin which absorbs the fat, only gradually letting it drip down into the roasting tin. (An additional bonus is that you have a clean oven afterwards!) Here are the details:

a Choose a roasting tin large enough to make basting possible, and brush all its surfaces with 1–1½ tablespoons/20–30ml oil.

b Rub salt over all the visible surfaces of the prepared, stuffed turkey – to flavour it and make the skin crisp. Place in the roasting tin.

c Slowly melt (without heating) about 3oz/75g butter. Brush all the bird's surfaces with it, pouring remainder round about. Cover now with a doubled piece of butter muslin, cut to the right size to protect the bird completely (about ½yd/45cm).

d Allow 18–20 minutes per lb (42–5 minutes per kg) stuffed weight for a bird over 12lb/5.5kg – the shorter time for a huge bird; 2 or 3 minutes more per lb (5 minutes more per kg) for a smaller bird.

e Roast at the bottom of a preheated slowish oven, gas 3, 325°F/165°C, basting hourly over the muslin (left on throughout the cooking time.) The breast cooks more quickly than the thighs, so if these are overcooked, the breast meat will be very dry.

5 However you roast a bird, test it for tenderness about three-quarters of an hour before the cooking time is up. If without a meat thermometer (but see this and *oven thermometer* page 45), guides to when a turkey is cooked are:

a When a trussing needle or sharp fork runs fairly easily into the thickest part of the thigh. If the escaping juices are clear and colourless, the leg is well done, the breast perhaps rather overcooked. If very pale pink, it may be just the way you like it – as I do. (For the breast to remain moist, the leg should retain a little pink blush at the joint.)

b When the meat starts to shrink from the end of the drumsticks.

6 Allow 20–30 minutes resting time, see page 231.

7 Accompaniments to roast turkey are: veal and/or chestnut stuffing; bread sauce; bacon rolls, thick gravy – thin if the bird isn't stuffed; cranberry sauce; chipolata, to garnish; watercress, to garnish; Brussels sprouts.

8 To carve a turkey is a different proposition from carving a chicken because the limbs are too big to serve in one piece:

cut off the drumstick, slicing it and the thigh, and serving some of this dark meat with each portion of breast. For a small bird carve the breast in single slices as for chicken, but carve a large bird in alternate ¼in/6mm slices as illustrated.

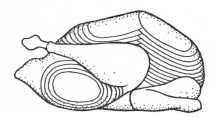

Cold roast turkey Can be used up in almost any way as cold chicken, often with the tasty stock made from its carcase. Here are a few recipes you'll probably be able to find in one of your own cookery books, under *chicken* if not under *turkey*: croquettes, kromeskies, savoury pancakes, patties, rissoles, risotto, vol-au-vent, turkey hash or potted turkey. Turkey is, of course, good added to a béchamel sauce and served with croûtes of fried bread, served cold with curry mayonnaise, or as a filling for fresh baps when you want an easy snack round the fire.

■ Freezing it is a good alternative for, once off the carcase, it doesn't take up too much space: interleave the limbs and sliced breast meat with foil or thick polythene, then you can easily take out later whatever quantity you want.

Turkey breast or joints Now sold throughout the year, breast or joints will make all sorts of dishes. Try coating the breasts in egg and seasoned fresh white breadcrumbs before frying in butter with a little oil. Off the bone, and cut into smaller pieces, you can make things like curry, fricassée or blanquette, or any kind of casserole for which you'd use a jointed chicken.

VENISON

The name comes from the Latin word *venari*, to hunt, and is the meat of any kind of deer. The flesh of the male, or buck, has a better flavour than that of the doe, but no venison has much fat and all is by nature dry and inclined to be tough; you can counteract the dryness by larding or barding a roasting joint, or alternatively by enclosing and protecting it inside a flour and water paste. You can make the meat tender by correct hanging and by marinating it well before you cook it. The custom of dredging venison with black pepper and ground ginger before hanging it in muslin is to help preserve the meat during its necessarily long hanging/tenderizing time. In cold weather allow about 12–20 days in a cool airy place. To test from time to time, run a skewer into it near the bone. When it smells slightly gamey, the meat is ready for marinating and then cooking.

■ The haunch, loin, saddle and fillet are the best parts so these are the most suitable for the faster methods of cookery like roasting, grilling, frying or sautéing. You can, if you prefer, braise the haunch, loin or shoulder, casseroling or stewing the cheaper cuts. Venison also makes a good galantine or raised pie, or – with minced *cooked* meat – a tasty cottage pie.

To roast a large joint of venison

1 It's better to weigh the joint before rather than after marinating, then you can calculate the cooking time and will know where you are: according to the thickness of the joint, allow 20–25 minutes per lb/450g and 20–25 minutes over.

2 Marinating venison for 24–48 hours (or longer in cold weather) is an important step in its successful cooking. A marinade not only helps to tenderize the meat by breaking down the tough fibres, but also flavours and makes it less dry. Make a good quantity of marinade – at least 1pt/600ml – to ensure the meat is well soaked; turn it over occasionally and baste it with marinade from time to time.

3 It's important to dry the marinated meat before roasting it, otherwise the fat in the roasting tin is going to get very watery and the meat will as a result cook in steam rather than in dry heat.

4 Some of the strained marinade can be used for venison sauce, the remainder saved for future use. (You can store marinade as ice cubes in the freezer.)

5 Before roasting, venison must be larded, barded or enclosed in a flour and water paste as it is too dry and fatless to roast without. Your butcher will supply the fat, and flatten barding fat if told what it's for.

6 Roast in a preheated oven, gas 7, 425°F/220°C for the first 15 minutes to seal in the juices, then reduce heat to gas 5, 375°F/190°C for remainder of cooking time.

7 Accompaniments to roast venison are: redcurrant or rowan jelly, or cranberry sauce, or better still if you can be bothered to make it, venison sauce (poivrade sauce plus redcurrant jelly and cream); roast or creamed potatoes; French beans; clear brown gravy.

15

Exotic fruits

With the advance of science on so many fronts, numerous fascinating, delicious and sometimes beautiful new fruits have been finding their way to our markets, shops and table. How do we choose, prepare and use these lovely things, and how can those of us on a tight budget enjoy their extravagance? In answer to the first of these questions, it would be difficult to stress too much the importance of shopping where the turnover is fast and the quality high – one third-rate fruit deftly slipped in amongst the others is a loss, not a saving – and of knowing what fruits should look like and feel like when in prime condition. In short, how to tell the fresh from the weary, the perfect from the imperfect. Generally speaking, self-service fruiterers have one great advantage over others – one can feel as well as see what one is buying. While the firmness or softness of a fruit may be as right for one variety as it is wrong for another, colour, bloom, size, weight, shape and aroma are all factors about which it is better to be informed than uninformed. It is not only costly but disappointing to be sold (or worse still to choose!) rubbish.

The lovely affinity in flavour, texture and fragrance of cooked fruits and *meats* – for instance, pineapple or banana with beef or gammon – is probably still to be explored with the less familiar fruits. The cost of some is almost prohibitive, however, so, to add a new dimension to eating and to make a little go a long way, it's worth experimenting with new combinations of fruits and other foods. For example, try adding cut-up pomelo segments (or other fruits) to a mixed or rice salad, or to coleslaw; add halved kumquats, at the last, to your favourite sweet and sour meat or poultry dish; cape gooseberries (small orange-red berries covered by a gauzy lantern-shaped husk) to a chicken casserole or a salad, or used as a garnish for salmi of game. These suggestions are purely to stir up your imagination! The permutations are unlimited.

APRICOTS

Not widely known in Europe until the fifteenth century and even now, more often than not, disappointing to buy in the UK. The trees blossom so early that of the fruit which does survive the frosts, much is apparently picked early, when hard, flavourless and with little fragrance. This explains why, with rare exceptions, we must usually cook rather than eat them fresh. Although there is little, if any, choice, look for ripeness: the stronger the apricot colour, the sweeter the fruit as a rule.

■ Almonds (chopped, whole, ground, browned – in jams, cakes, sweets and pastries, etc.) are almost married to apricots due to their affinity with the fruit's almond-flavoured kernel.
■ In confectionery and pastries, apricots are one of the most popular fruits. Of all crystallized fruits, for instance, could any surpass the apricot?
■ Apricot jam is one of the two finest cooking jams (raspberry the other). With its delicate flavour, pretty colour and thick texture, it is invaluable as a glaze (page 329).

■ Apricot brandy, like the jam, is versatile and combines superbly with many other flavours.

Some ways of using apricots

1 Sweets, e.g. compôte, omelette, flans, tarts, creams, ice creams, fool, mousse, soufflé, fritters, crumble – and the best brûlée of all I think (the purée of a 14½oz/411g can of drained apricots, 6 – 8 drops almond essence, ½pt/300ml double cream and approximately 3oz/75g soft brown sugar).

2 Apricots in brandy; or spiced, or pickled.

3 In stuffings or as a garnish for lamb (a lovely sweetness), chicken or duck.

Dried apricots Depending upon what one is making, the large, fleshy, sweet apricots sometimes give better results than the small, dark variety – or vice versa. Use them (always well soaked first) to make jam, stuffings, a winter fruit salad, sauces and puddings.

BANANAS

Bananas may not seem exotic, but of course they are. Thanks to their ripening and travelling qualities and to refrigerated ships, we've never known life without them – the first shipments to Britain from the Canaries were in 1882. What a lot so many of us miss though, in not cooking bananas more: grilled or split and fried with bacon for breakfast; grilled (brushed first with fat, of course) along with grilled chicken joints, beef or gammon steaks or white fish; fried (or baked) with roast beef; lots of sweets – among them fritters, banana chartreuse (a *glorious* sweet), macerated; banana bread.

■ Citrus juice, usually lemon, sprinkled over sliced banana prevents it from discolouring too quickly.

■ Favourite partners of banana are: browned coconut, cream, yoghurt, kirsch, rum.

CHERRIES

Are, in a general sense, of three different groups: the deliciously sweet dessert varieties, which may be 'white' or red; the bitter, dark red, cooking cherries, often labelled 'morellos'; the hybrids, which are slightly bitter. Morellos or the hybrid fruits are better for cooking than sweet cherries; bitter cherries are used for jam, and for meat dishes. When buying red dessert cherries, the certain way of avoiding disappointment is a request to eat one.

■ Cherry Heering and many other cherry brandies are distilled from the fruit, while the eau de vie, kirsch, is a white brandy distilled from wild cherries along with their bitter, almond-flavoured, crushed stones.

■ As with apricots, and for the same reason – their almond-flavoured stones – almonds, especially ground, are a classic partner of cherries. (One of my favourite of all sweets is Danish cherry flan.)

Some ways of using cherries

1 To give colour, and thereby decorate, all kinds of dishes, sweet and savoury.

2 To make many sweets, e.g. flans, pies, tartlets, compôte, coupe, fritters, sorbets.

3 In confectionery, e.g. crystallized, glacé fruits, chocolate-coated 'liqueur'.

4 In or with certain savoury dishes, e.g. gammon, duck, venison.

5 To make sauces, sweet or savoury.

Glacé cherries See page 91.

Maraschino cherries The kind we use in drinks and to decorate a grapefruit or slices of melon, etc. are supposedly the Amarasco cherry, bottled in a maraschino liqueur-*flavoured* liquid.

CITRON

A variety of the true lemon, originating in the Himalayan region. Like an overgrown lemon with a knobbly skin, we all know citron best as candied peel. Apart from this, the fruit is not used in any other way.

DATES

Called after the Greek word *dactylon*, meaning a toe or finger, this rich and nourishing fruit (one bunch of which can weigh 30lb/13.5kg or more) has for thousands of years provided food for tribesmen in the deserts of Arabia.

Boxed dates The way we buy them at Christmas time. Packed on the stem, these have a strong and good flavour and, when perfect, should be shiny and moist. Traditionally, we mostly eat them as they are, but they are also stuffed, or used to make glacé fruits (stoned and also stuffed, often with marzipan).

Large fresh dates from Israel Sold loose at what seems an exorbitant price. Less sweet and good, and with a much less distinctive flavour than the above, they at least make a change. At their best, they are shiny and moist – to be avoided if matt and dry-looking.

■ To remove their rather tough, papery skin if you don't care for it, simply snip off the stalk end, squeeze from the other, and the date will pop out. Better for stuffing than boxed dates, one can also slice and use them say, in a mixed salad, a fruit salad, or to garnish.
■ Covered and refrigerated, fresh dates keep moist longer than when in a fruit bowl.

Dried dates Small blocks of compressed dates: cut them up and use to make cakes, puddings and so on. In an airtight container, they keep well for months.

FIGS

If you have ever eaten a fig straight from the tree, you will know that unique aroma and flavour, so different from most bought figs. Once one of the four basic foods of Mediterranean eating, figs vary in flavour not only from country to country but also from region to region. There are over 160 varieties. Vine-ripened even when shipped, they should be soft to the touch, unbruised and have a sweet (never a sour) smell.

■ A fig is at its best when warm: leave the dish in the sun for at least an hour or two – if there is sun – and, if you can, serve them on some pretty leaves (vine or fig if available).
■ If serving figs in syrup, cook them *very* lightly – so as not to spoil their lovely shape.
■ Good partners with figs are fortified wines, orange liqueurs (see macerated fruits, page 70) and cream.
■ To serve fresh figs with Parma ham as an hors d'oeuvre, cut the figs down from the top into sections, opening these up like flower petals.

Dried figs Although primarily for dessert, they can be fattened back into a semblance of their old shape by steaming.
■ Used in puddings and cakes, their character changes – for the worse I think.

Canned figs A good larder store because, when served with cream (single, double, whipped, Chantilly, Devonshire – with a little orange zest), a luxurious sweet.

GRAPEFRUIT

So called because of the way the fruit hangs in 'grapes', or clusters. Depending upon their variety, the climate in which they grow and their state of maturity, they may be sweeter than an orange, or acid enough to make one's head spin. The best are usually firm, heavy for their size and have a shiny skin, although sometimes a softer fruit can also be both juicy and sweet.

Some ways of using grapefruit

1 In the traditional way, see page 155.
2 Use instead of vinegar or lemon juice to make salad dressings, or serve the segments in salads (together with other fruits and/or vegetables).
3 Cold sweets, e.g. a *lovely* mousse; jelly (probably with lemon and orange); caramelled.
4 A milk shake.
5 Candy, or use in jam, e.g. grapefruit

and pineapple, or with lemons and oranges.

To cut grapefruit into segments See *orange segments*, page 282.

To freeze Put the segments in a very sweet, chilled syrup, or in dry sugar (for both see page 124).

GRAPES

Basically they are of four main types, each being superior to the others for the purpose for which they are grown: wine (the great majority), dried fruits, the table and fresh grape juice. High quality grapes are wrapped in soft paper to prevent damage in transit; second-class are usually plastic-wrapped; the poorest simply boxed. This explains why bunches of cheaper grapes have often disintegrated. Choose them by bloom, colour, condition and – if allowed – taste.

Black grapes or white? Seedless whole or seeded halved black grapes are colourful and decorative in a fruit salad, savarin, brûlée or vegetable salad, etc., but if to be skinned for cooking, their outward colour matters little: the flesh is green whether black or white, and the flavour similar.

Preparation and serving Shop grapes should be washed (what may have been sprayed, or who may have coughed over them?), then dried gently on a clean cloth and, if possible, left in the sun to dry off completely. Scissors make it easy to cut off the clusters without spoiling the beauty of a whole bunch and without dislodging other grapes.

■ For cooking with pigeon or game, acid grapes are ideal, combining perfectly with other flavours.

Frosted grapes make a lovely decoration: brush small clusters with egg white, dip in caster sugar and leave – not for *too* long – to dry.

GUAVAS

So strong and beautiful is their aroma that many fruiterers sell guavas simply to attract customers into their shops. Their flavour is less exciting, but they have a higher vitamin C content than even many citrus fruits. When ripe and perfect, they should give slightly, like a pear, to gentle pressure – but at the round, not the stalk end. Avoid unripe (hard, green) or blemished fruits.

■ They are best eaten fresh: peel, slice, sprinkle with caster sugar and serve chilled, with cream. If you don't like the seeds, scoop them out with a teaspoon. In a fruit salad, guavas combine especially well with bananas and pineapple.

To use in cooking – a few hints

1 Poach them very lightly (they easily disintegrate), or purée to make a cream, ice cream or fool.

2 Bake (unskinned) for about half an hour in a moderate oven and serve with whipped cream.

3 Make jam, jelly or guava cheese (one of the finest of all fruit cheeses).

Canned guavas Have less flavour than fresh but bring variety to your larder. Served chilled with, say, crème chantilly or sauce diplomat, they're almost a delicacy.

KIWI FRUIT

Also called Chinese gooseberries because it was from China that the New Zealanders got their seed. Egg-shapped, egg-sized and hairy-skinned, beautiful when cut and sweet and delicate to eat, the kiwi is softly firm when perfect, giving slightly to gentle pressure, and stores well in a cool place.

To eat Cut in half and scoop out the flesh with a teaspoon; or skin and slice: starting at the stalk end, cut into and pull off the skin. (Blanching for a minute makes this easier, but not easy.) Slice across.

Some ways of using kiwi fruit

1 To get good value from just one (costly) fruit, slice and use to decorate a fruit salad, meringue gâteau, cheesecake or fool, etc.

2 Macerate (page 70), make compôte (setting the syrup with arrowroot), sorbet, tartlets, etc. (I'm sure they make a delicious ice cream, fool or flan as well if one doesn't live on a tight budget.)

■ The fresh fruit contains an enzyme which, like fresh pineapple, destroys the setting power of gelatine. It's therefore no good hoping that a jelly containing sliced kiwi fruit (or a cream or mousse made with them) will set, because it won't. The fruit must be poached first.

KUMQUATS

Another fruit native to China, where they have been grown for centuries, and which explains their other name: Chinese oranges. These miniature oranges are sharp as lemons – and some have almost as many (tiny) pips. Pick firm, glossy fruits and, if wanting to eat or use them whole, avoid the largest: they're quite a mouthful, thanks also to their acidity!

To prepare and use

1 Wash, dry and eat either whole (if you like eating the pips), or halved or sliced (de-pipped).

2 Poach (whole, halved or sliced) lightly in a syrup, to eat on their own, with vanilla ice cream or in a fruit salad; use also to decorate any dish likely to be cheered up by their colour and flavour. (Thicken the syrup, if you like, to give it body, see *compôte*, page 57.)

3 Use in, or to garnish, a sweet-sour dish.

4 Use in preserves and for confectionery (fondant especially) where the sweet-sour contrast is so effective.

LEMONS

See page 105.

LIMES

Look like very small bright green lemons. Although mostly about half the size of a lemon, they are infinitely more acid. Choose fresh, shiny (not dried up, matt) ones.

■ Lime juice cordial, is made from the much sweetened juice of the fruit. See also page 106.

LYCHEES

Oval nuts (known also as Chinese nuts, litchi and lichee) about 1in/2½cm in diameter, lychees have a fragile, reddish brown, scaly and beautiful shell. Although native to certain hot regions of China, the fruit is so perishable that, until recently, even the Chinese living away from those regions were never able to eat them fresh, only canned. (Millions are canned.) As with other nuts, it is difficult to assess the inside from the outside, so it pays to buy these where the quality is high and turnover fast. After picking, lychees are said to change colour in one day, lose their aroma in two, and their flavour in four.

To prepare Crack the shell with your thumb, peeling off the husk to reveal the fruit's translucent firm white flesh. Very aromatic, it is totally unlike any other fruit: slightly sweet-sour, chewy yet juicy in texture. Inside is a brown stone.

Some ways of using lychees

1 Best of all, eat fresh, either alone or in a fruit salad.

2 Macerate (page 70) and top with whipped cream.

3 Halve and use in a dressed salad.

4 Poach lightly in syrup and serve well chilled, with cream, crème chantilly or sauce diplomat. (Thicken the syrup if you like, see *compôte*, page 57.)

5 Make glacé fruits.

Canned lychees A lovely fruit to have in the larder. Chill and serve them with cream, or use in a fruit or dressed salad.

MANGOES

It is not difficult to understand why so many experts say the best way to enjoy a mango is in the bath or a bathing costume. How amazing that nature can produce anything so juicy and superb to eat: of many heavenly fruits at their best, the mango must surely be difficult to better. There are over 500 varieties of it too, those imported into the UK mostly golden (if ripe) with a red blush, almost as if rouge had been badly applied. Unless a green *variety* – some varieties are red, others golden freckled with red or black – avoid green fruits: they are usually unripe, and will never ripen properly. A huge stone runs the full length of the fruit, the golden-yellow, slightly acid-sweet flesh of which it is very reluctant to leave.

■ Use your hands as well as your eyes when choosing mangoes: ripe mangoes will give slightly all over to gentle pressure and often look as if a blob of glue had been applied at the stem end. If they are mushy, or have dark patches, as one too often sees them in the shops, leave them there.

To prepare and use

1 Pare away every bit of the skin – easily done with a potato peeler (page 37) – and eat whole.

2 Pare, cut into bite-sized pieces and use in various ways, e.g. in a fruit salad; macerate (page 70); make fritters; in a flan.

3 Make a purée, to use in many different ways. (The liquidized flesh of one large mango, 12–14oz/350g, plus 4oz/100g granulated sugar makes approximately ½pt/300ml sweetened purée.) So delicately and gloriously flavoured is this fruit that I must spell out in more detail than with other fruits some ways of making a little go a long way. Here are some ideas:

a *Make fool*, (page 290) or *ice cream* (page 292) using equal quantities of sweetened mango purée and half-whipped cream.

b *Make a milk jelly* (page 294) using about ⅜pt/225ml sweetened mango purée and ⅝pt/375ml room-temperature milk, set with 1 packet (scant ½oz/12g) powdered gelatine dissolved in 2 tablespoons water. To enrich it, replace (say) 2 – 4 tablespoons of the milk with cream and decorate with cream as well.

c *Make a milk shake* – lovely on a hot day, or if you're ill. Allow per person: 6 large ice cubes; 3 tablespoons/60ml sweetened (preferably chilled) mango purée; scant ¼pt/125ml chilled milk. *Method* Briefly: liquidize (to crush) the ice cubes, then add the purée and milk and blend for 30 seconds at maximum speed. Pour into a tall glass and drink without delay. To enrich and give extra flavour, replace some of the milk with cream. Use other fruit purées to make a milk shake in the same way.

d Use the sweetened purée as a sauce, e.g. spoon it over vanilla ice cream, peach halves or other delicately flavoured fruit of your choice – and top with a dollop of whipped cream.

4 *Make chutney* – the finest of all chutneys I think – and pickles.

■ Unripe fruits can be poached, baked, used in a curry or to make chutney.

MELONS

Much prized by the ancient Greeks and Romans, the melon is of Asian origin, being first transplanted to Italy and then to France well before the sixteenth century. Belonging to the cucumber family, they grow in warm and temperate countries, and are of two distinct groups: musk and water.

Musk Those we know best are the *cantaloup* (named after the castle of Cantaloupa, near Rome, where it was developed in the sixteenth century), the round, rough-skinned type with lovely sweet flesh, varying in colour from a pinkish yellow to pale green; *tiger melon*, similar to the cantaloup but with a smooth skin; *charentais*, a small melon with a delicious flavour and deep orange flesh; *honeydew*, sweet and fragrant, with greenish flesh not unlike a water melon. These are rugby-football shaped, many of the green ones coming from Spain, the yellow from Israel, amongst other countries. *Ogen*, green-skinned, with orange lines dividing it into sections, and with green flesh.

Water melons Are smooth-skinned, mostly with black seeds embedded in the centre of exquisite pinky, very juicy flesh. Lacking the lovely flavour of most musk melons, however, they are much less good – if worth eating at all – even when just harvested.

■ Have you ever travelled through Provence at melon time, the perfumed air even penetrating your car as you whizz past the roadside stalls? If only it could be bottled! Melons coming here seldom compete but, carefully selected and served chilled, they can still be very good.

To choose a melon They should be heavy for their size: hold two or three, and take the heaviest. If ripe, they'll give slightly at the stem end, and a strong aroma usually indicates a good flavour.

To cut a melon into sections Cut in half, scoop out the seeds and then slice the halves into equal-sized pieces.

To use as a container (for a fruit salad or macerated melon, etc.) Cut off the lid and scoop the seeds into a strainer over a basin – so as not to waste any juice.

■ Melons are as much at home with an oil and vinegar dressing as with sugar: in a salad (fruit or dressed) they have a great affinity with other fruits and vegetables.

To freeze Cut into balls (page 14) or dice, and freeze either dry with sugar, or in a strong syrup (both page 124).

NECTARINES

A smooth-skinned variety of peach, with a sharper flavour and firm flesh. As with peaches, paler-skinned fruits have a finer flavour than the prettier yellowy ones.

Eat, skin and cook as peaches.

NUTS

See page 109.

ORANGES

Introduced into Europe from China, and now cultivated in many parts of the world, we eat, drink the juice of and use them by the billion. Even then, we don't all seem to understand the difference between the zest, pared rind and grated rind – and why one is often to be preferred to the others.

The zest The very outside (see page 85) and, for its lovely flavour and fragrance, often (but not always) the best to use.

Pared rind Slivers of rind, easily removed with a potato peeler, taking with it the minimum of pith underneath.

Grated rind Taken off with a grater, this contains more of the bitter pith than either of the above. The finer the grater used, the better the flavour – whatever you are making.

The juice To avoid losing vitamin C, which is destroyed by boiling, add the juice after cooking rather than before whenever possible.

Choosing oranges – a few tips

1 Greenish fruits are usually just as ripe as bright orange ones.

2 Generally speaking, small fruits are juicier than large, and the heavier a fruit for its size, the juicier it too is likely to be.

3 A glossy skin indicates that the natural oils (which give the flavour and fragrance) have not dried out.

To skin an orange easily – taking most but not all of the pith with it:

1 Cut through the skin, in quarters, as one would for eating.

2 Put in a good-sized basin, cover with boiling water and leave for 5 minutes.

3 Put into cold water for a minute or so, then peel, scraping off any remaining pith with a knife.

To cut an orange into slices without rind or any pith:

1 Cut off each end of the orange just deep enough to expose the flesh.
2 Hold the fruit up in front of you and, using a small stainless steel knife (preferably) and a sawing action, cut off the peel in a continuous spiral – again just deep enough to expose the flesh.
3 Slice the orange across thinly or thickly, as required by recipe.

To cut an orange (or grapefruit) into segments:

1 Peel as above, for slicing.
2 Using a pointed knife, ease back the membranes to release the flesh.

To freeze oranges See *Lemons*, page 106.

To make orange-flavoured cream Rub a cube of sugar up and down all over an orange, then break up the sugar and add it to the cream.

Seville oranges Introduced into Europe from India. With their bitter, aromatic rind, juicy acid flesh and pips (which are full of pectin), these are the oranges essential for marmalade making. Use them also for Sauce Bigarade (its name taken from the variety, *Citrus Bigaradia*) and to make the classic orange salad served with wild duck and other rich dark meats.

PASSION FRUIT

Also called purple granadilla, this plum-sized fruit with its wrinkly, dark purple (when ripe) skin, is native to Brazil. Like guavas, its perfume fills the air – at a price: about a thimbleful of the flesh works out at the price of a good-sized lemon or orange!

A few tips

1 Sold individually, there is seldom much choice. Be greedy, and take the largest, which are just as delicate as the smaller.
2 To eat fresh: halve, or cut off the top and scoop out the fleshy, seedy pulp with a teaspoon. If liked, pour and mix in a spot of cream.
3 Add to a fruit salad, or use to flavour a syrup, or decorate another dish: the seeds particularly are very beautiful.
4 If a recipe calls for the fruit to be sieved – say for an ice cream or curd – warm the pulp very slightly (with a little sugar from the recipe, to add bulk) to help it part company with the seeds. Keep the seeds, to decorate.

PEACHES

One of mainland Europe's most delicious fruits – said to have originated from China, but introduced to Europe (via Iran) over 2,000 years ago. Familiar as we are with them, some tips may not go astray:

1 There are two main types of peach:
   a Slightly hairy, downy-skinned – this category is itself divided into those with a juicy flesh and a lightly embedded stone; fruit with a firmer flesh which clings to the stone.
   b Smooth-skinned, hairless fruits – with a firm flesh and a cling stone.
2 Bloom is not necessarily a sign of ripeness. Choose fragrant fruits which are yellow (not pale green) round the stem. Feel them gently too: they should give slightly to gentle pressure.
3 Harder, unripe fruits will usually ripen with time, or tenderize by cooking. Soft peaches (even though not obviously bruised or over-ripe) lack flavour, are often cotton-woolly in texture and do not, even with cooking, improve.
4 Peaches grown against a sheltered wall are larger, finer and more juicy and fragrant than those grown in the open.

To halve a peach Cut round the natural line of the fruit, then gently twist the two halves in opposite directions. Remove the stone.
To skin a peach Cover with boiling water for just 10 seconds if ripe, up to 30 if unripe, then plunge momentarily into cold water before pulling off the skin.

Use in innumerable ways

1 *Sweets*, e.g.: compôte (page 57, preferably skinning after poaching), macerated (page 70), flamed, ice cream, flan or fritters, grilled (brushed with butter and sprinkled generously with sugar, gentle heat at first), meringue gâteau, with raspberry purée.

2 Preserve in brandy, or make jam. (No breakfast could surpass some of the French: croissants, butter, home-made peach jam and café filtre. The *thought* of it is nostalgic!)

3 To garnish a savoury dish – baked gammon especially.

PINEAPPLES

A hardy herbaceous perennial plant native to America, but grown (on the ground) now in many hot regions of the world. When ripe and in perfect condition, the plume should be compact and fresh looking, an inner leaf easily pulled out. In addition, it should be fragrant and the eyes should protrude slightly.

To prepare Twist off the plume if your hands are strong enough, otherwise cut the top off, slice, peel and core – neatly and quickly done with a tiny scone cutter.

Some ways of using pineapple
Serve in all kinds of combinations, savoury and sweet, e.g.:

1 With cheese (in various ways); grilled, with grilled gammon or beef steaks; with duck, or with curried or other chicken dishes; on toast, grilled, with bacon (or in baps).

2 In desserts, e.g. meringue gâteau, savarin, sponge or creamed mixtures, fritters, macerated.

3 To make cakes, sauces, ices, jams and long cool drinks.

■ Raw pineapple contains an enzyme which destroys the setting power of gelatine. If making a jelly, therefore, either cook the pineapple first, or use canned fruit.

SATSUMAS, TANGERINES AND CLEMENTINES

Tangerines have seeds, the others are seedless. All are easily peeled and separated into segments, have sweet juicy flesh, tender membranes and, generally speaking, are best eaten raw. Use them in a fruit or dressed salad, to decorate, or to make lovely glacé fruits.

STAR-FRUIT

A waxy-looking rather beautiful sharp-flavoured yellow (when ripe) fluted fruit from Brazil. Eat skin and flesh together, unless the skin is too tough to eat, in which case peel it off.

To prepare Wipe, then slice across thinly to use, say, in a fruit or dressed salad.

UGLI FRUIT

A hybrid – a cross between a grapefruit and a tangerine. With pinkish flesh which is slightly sharper than a tangerine but much sweeter than most varieties of grapefruit, the ugli has distinct characteristics of both fruits. Those with easily removed rather baggy skin seem to have sweeter flesh than have firmer, heavier fruits. Like the tangerine and unlike the grapefruit, the membranes separating the segments are sweet and tender enough to eat.

To eat, preferably fresh:

1 Cut in half and prepare as grapefruit (page 155), or eat with a pointed teaspoon.

2 Peel and eat as a tangerine.

3 Macerate the segments in any orange liqueur, page 70.

4 Add the cut-up segments to a fruit salad, fruit cocktail or dressed salad.

■ The peel is good candied.

16
Sweets and puddings

GENERAL INFORMATION

Sweets and puddings are a forte of British cooking. Pâtisseries apart, this is one course where I think it can knock spots off French cooking. Most British people consider it an important part of any main meal, the repertoire is enormous, and high standards are expected when entertaining or being entertained.

■ Like savoury sauces, the majority of desserts are simply varieties of a few basic recipes, hence if you know how to make one, you can make any other version. To be successful, however, it's a good thing to understand the changing characteristics of *eggs* (page 142) and *cream* (page 94), the unusual qualities of *gelatine* (page 98) and the importance of *consistencies* (page 58). The latter especially play a vital role in the texture and volume of most light and airy sweets. When making such dishes as a cold soufflé, a cream or a mousse, whipped cream and any mixture to which it is added should be of similar consistencies, so that the two will blend perfectly together to give the dish its characteristic texture (see *whipping cream*, page 94). This is one reason why recipes frequently direct that a mixture should be left until cool and beginning to set before adding cream and/or whisked egg white – because it will by then be thicker. Another reason is that if whisked whites and whipped cream are added to a warm mixture, they will lose their stiffness and thin out, spoiling the texture and reducing the volume of the sweet. Egg whites should not be whisked before a mixture shows signs of setting, unless the bowl has been standing on ice, when the mixture is likely to set quickly.

■ Because intense cold tends to thicken a liquid, gelatine-based sweets which were perfect at room temperature will become (and remain) rubbery if long refrigerated. If, for instance, you refrigerate a soufflé overnight, it will become stiffer than if it is chilled for just an hour or two, or not at all. According to Davis Gelatine, recipes which actually call for the use of a refrigerator have their gelatine content adjusted accordingly.

■ In addition, overchilling masks and spoils many flavours, chocolate particularly. Unlike a spoilt texture, however, a flavour will recover at room temperature. See also *unmoulding*, page 83.

APPLES, BAKED

These need a little know-how if they are to be delicate and not dreary. It all depends on your choice of apple and what you do – or don't do – with them.

1 Choose the right type of cooking apple, not a dessert apple: large sour varieties such as Bramley's Seedling, Howgate Wonder, Grenadier or Lord Derby all bake beautifully because they're juicy as well as acid.
2 Choose even-sized apples so that, to become tender and cook perfectly, one apple doesn't need five minutes longer than another.
3 After washing and coring, run a skin-deep cut around the middle of each apple, making the ends of the cut meet. The apples will then puff up like soufflés, instead of bursting – and looking a mess.

4 Stand apples in a greased baking tin or ovenware dish before sweetening: with a rounded tablespoonful of sugar (mixed with a little ground cinnamon if you like) in each hole, a nut of butter on top, and a dessertspoon of water or orange juice per apple round about, they'll form a lovely, buttery, caramelized syrup – providing you don't cook them in too hot an oven.

5 Bake apples in the middle of a moderate oven, gas 4, 350°F/175°C for about 40 – 60 minutes according to size, or until tender when tested down the inside with a skewer. (The outside becomes soft before the middle.) If overcooked, your apple 'soufflés' will flop, which is the reason for using fruit all of a similar size.

6 Fluffy, liquidized custard and, if you can rise to it, some whipped cream as well, combine deliciously with the apples and their toffee-like syrup. Better still is sauce diplomate, page 305.

APPLE STRUDEL

This seems like a conjuring trick because the dough (made from only 4oz/100g strong flour, ½ level teaspoon salt, 1 small egg, 1–1½ tablespoons warm water and 2 teaspoons oil), is transformed into a lacy-thin, tea-towel sized sheet of paste. You really have to make this to believe it. Eat it hot or cold, with ice cream, crème chantilly or even single cream. If you've no need to slim, it's delicious also for elevenses or at teatime. I enjoy making it even more than eating it, and that's saying something.

■ To help solve the problems with the dough:

1 It must be soft but not sticky, otherwise it will be impossible to manipulate after kneading and resting. The kneading is to make it smooth and elastic. Resting the dough for half an hour – in a small basin, covered with a cloth – strengthens the gluten in the flour and increases the dough's elasticity so that it will stretch, as far as possible without tearing, to an enormous size.

2 The rolled-out rectangular-shaped dough is manipulated on a large clean tea-towel to which, unlike a pastry board or table top, it doesn't stick. In addition the tea-towel later facilitates the rolling up of the thin pastry.

3 Using initially the floured backs of your hands and knuckles, and working from the underside, you can pull and stretch the pastry in all directions providing you keep it spread out. (If it forms folds, the surfaces may refuse to part.) Work from the middle outwards because once the outer edges are very thin, it is more difficult to get at and stretch the middle.

4 When fully stretched, the original tiny lump of dough should be nearly the size of the tea-towel and lacy enough to see the towel's pattern through it.

■ The rest, with a recipe, is plain sailing but the strudel should be cooked soon if not immediately after it is made, before the apple juice starts to run, and spoil the pastry.

BATTENBURG CAKE

Bought Battenburg makes a quick, easy and delicious sweet. To serve in individual dishes:

Bottom layer A slice of Battenburg, soaked with a dessertspoon each of fruit syrup and sherry, madeira, rum or whatever you like best with the fruit you're using.

Middle layer Prepared fresh, or well-drained canned fruit, e.g. strawberries, peaches, sliced banana, fresh raspberries, apricots, lychees.

Top layer Crème chantilly (see page 303) or (though not so good) if you're dieting, the arrowroot-thickened fruit syrup (page 87).

BEIGNETS

French for fritters, in a wide sense.

BEIGNETS SOUFFLÉS

A type of fritter, made with choux pastry. The temperature of the fat is the tricky part: if too hot initially, the outsides harden before the choux can expand, so they don't rise. The fat should be hot but not smoking – 320–340°F/160–171°C – the heat being raised slightly while the beignets are frying.

■ Avoid using a frying basket because the choux will stick to it.
■ After the beignets are cooked, it's quicker and more efficient to toss them in caster sugar in a paper bag than on a sheet of paper.

BREAD AND BUTTER PUDDING

Should be made with egg and milk, not custard powder, and soaked long enough – about half an hour – before baking to allow the bread to absorb most of the liquid. (Made with powder, the custard sets on top of the bread instead of being absorbed, so the top layer of bread doesn't go crisp and brown and the pudding ends up quite different.)

■ Unorthodox as it is, bread and butter pudding assumes a delightfully different character when made with mincemeat in the middle, instead of dried fruit and a flavouring of nutmeg: simply spread the bottom slice of (buttered) bread lightly with mincemeat before cutting it up into pieces, then cover with the remaining pieces of cut-up bread and strain over them the warm milk/egg/sugar mixture.
■ In case you've never tried it, vanilla ice cream served with it makes bread and butter pudding twice as good.

CHARLOTTES

Probably take their name from Charlotte, wife of George III. The original charlottes were made of fruit, in a mould lined with thin slices of buttered bread – and served hot. The only thing these charlottes have in common with charlotte russe is their outward appearance.

Charlotte russe Prepared with Bavarian cream which is set in a plain round mould, lined sides and bottom with sponge fingers, this dish was invented by Carême, regarded even today as the founder of classic French cookery. Here are just a few tips:

1 To decorate the bottom of the mould with jelly, see page 67.
2 Line up the savoy fingers on a board to make them all the same length, trimming their edges to make them fit each other closely. As the mould is narrower at the bottom than the top, taper the fingers slightly, if necessary, to make them fit. (Bought savoy fingers are usually of a more regular shape than homemade.)
3 The Bavarian cream, or bavarois as it's sometimes called (basically an egg custard mixed with whipped cream and set with gelatine), must be just on the point of setting when poured into the mould; otherwise it will ooze out between the Savoy fingers. If on the other hand it is too set, it won't pour into and fill the mould evenly.
4 An unmoulded charlotte russe is very fragile. Handle it with care.

Fruit charlottes These are crisper and better when made in a charlotte mould (page 33) or tin pie-dish than in a glass or ovenware dish because metal is a better conductor of heat.

■ If the fruit is too watery, it will make the bread soggy and the charlotte will collapse when unmoulded. It may also disintegrate if you don't allow it to set for a few minutes before turning out.

CHRISTMAS PUDDING

Should be made well ahead of Christmas because, with maturity, the flavour improves. Generally speaking, the more sugar, fruit and alcohol a pudding contains, the longer and better it will keep. (Once it has matured, I tend nowadays to pop mine in the freezer where it's less in the way.)

■ A Christmas pudding cooked in a pressure cooker doesn't compare with one gently steamed: the traditional, naturally dark colour and lovely flavour of a properly made pudding are acquired during hours of slow cooking, not by the addition of gravy browning, very dark sugar, carrot or anything else.

■ If serving alight, see page 62, *flambé*.

COMPÔTE

See page 57.

CREAMS

Made, basically, with whipped cream and an equal quantity of either rich creamy egg custard or fruit purée. A custard is flavoured with such things as chocolate (melted in the milk), coffee essence or diced ginger, to give chocolate, coffee or ginger cream respectively. A fruit purée can be made from fresh, frozen or canned fruit. (A fruit purée freezes perfectly if you have surplus fruit: I like to liquidize about 3oz/75g sugar with ½lb/200g of, say, strawberries or raspberries before freezing. This makes ½pt/250ml purée.)

■ Use egg yolks in preference to whole eggs for a custard. They make it thicker, smoother and richer: allow 4 yolks to ½pt/300ml milk for this sweet (see page 303).

■ See also *gelatine*, page 98, and introduction to this chapter regarding cream and consistencies.

■ You can dress up a cream and at the same time make it go further by decorating the bottom of the mould first, with jelly, and by chopping up more jelly to serve round it (see page 67).

CUSTARDS

Are richer, smoother, have a finer flavour and colour, and are less likely to curdle if made entirely with egg yolks, two yolks replacing each whole egg given in any recipe. If this seems too extravagant or too rich, or if you prefer to use whole

eggs, do at least increase the proportion of yolk to white by adding an extra yolk. This will lessen the risk of a custard curdling and at the same time improve its texture.

■ After lightly mixing the warmed milk with the eggs, always strain them into the cooking dish. This is to hold back the chalazae, one of the main causes of curdling (see page 143).

■ If you boil, or even nearly boil, a custard, it will become full of holes, leathery and rather indigestible. This is because it has curdled, and explains why custards are always cooked at a low temperature: either very gently in a steamer or, if in the oven, in a bain-marie or roasting tin containing cold water coming about half-way up the dish. To avoid curdling, these custards are *never* cooked in direct heat.

■ All baked custards are better covered during cooking – with a lid or oiled greaseproof paper – to prevent the surface becoming dry and brown.

■ When cooked, a custard should be firm but slightly shaky. To test, stick the point of a small vegetable knife in the middle – always the last place to set – and press back a little of the custard. If cooked, there'll be no sign of liquid.

Custard, baked See above.

Crème brûlée The richest and most heavenly form of baked custard, made with cream instead of milk, and with a caramelled top, for which I, personally, like Demerara sugar most. Serve it well-chilled, with chilled stewed fruit, or just by itself, to enjoy its flavour fully.

■ Use 1pt/600ml single cream, 8 large egg yolks, 2oz/50g granulated sugar and a small teaspoon of vanilla essence for the custard itself, and another 2–3oz/50–75g Demerara or caster sugar later, for the top.

■ If you beat the yolks and sugar together until fluffy and pale yellow before stirring in the hot cream, the custard will be lovely and light.

■ Bake as custards (above), using something like a shallow soufflé dish, but at all costs, don't let it boil. Allow *about* ¾ – 1 hour according to depth, in a slowish oven, gas 3, 325°F/165°C, the covered dish standing in a roasting tin of water, of course.

■ It's important to cool and then chill the custard for several hours before covering the top with a thinnish layer of sugar, and caramelizing it under a hot grill. (If still warm, it may boil under the intense heat, ruining its texture.)

■ Two last thoughts:

1 It's safer to protect the rim of the dish with a strip of foil before putting it under the hot grill.

2 It's often easier to make the custard 24 hours before required. Covered, this allows plenty of time to chill it *before*, and for two hours *after*, caramelizing.

Crème caramel Another variation of a baked custard, but can equally well be very gently steamed. I like best of all to make it entirely with egg yolks, which make it creamy and delicious. One can always use up the whites in meringues – what better partner for this sweet anyway?

■ If serving crème caramel hot, allow the custard to cool and set for a few minutes before unmoulding it, otherwise it may collapse. If serving it cold, allow it to cool in its tin. Hot *or* cold, crème chantilly served with it makes this a red-hot favourite.

■ *A metal mould or tin* such as a charlotte mould or moule à manqué tin (or darioles) is the best thing to make it in because the heat can't break it, and the caramel will run freely and thinly on tin, coating it evenly and easily, *especially if you've warmed it first*. Caramel is apt to set quickly, thickly and unevenly on ovenware china, so although a French soufflé dish will usually stand up to the heat, it isn't as successful. Whatever you use, though, there's no time for daydreaming once the caramel is ready. Have the warmed tin standing on a thick wodge of newspaper, to protect your table top from the intense heat, and use

an ovencloth to protect your hands. (Caramel burns, like sealing wax, are real torture.) Pour the caramel into the tin all at once, tilting and circulating it quickly to cover all surfaces, then leave it to cool at room temperature. If you either refrigerate or pour hot custard into it now, the caramel will crack, not that this seems to alter its final appearance.

■ Don't wash the caramel pan! If you heat the milk for the custard in it, the caramel flavour will permeate the whole sweet – like deglazing a pan in which you have sautéd food.

■ *The caramel* itself is quite easy if you know how, but can be tricky if you don't. Here are a few tips:

1 It's unwise to use a non-stick pan, which may be scratched by the grittiness of so much sugar, or damaged by the great heat. Some people like to use a frying pan, but I find a small strong saucepan (in which I can see the colour of the caramel) is better because the sugar seems less apt to crystallize when deep than when shallow. (One can buy a special pan, called a sugar boiler.)

2 The proportion of water to sugar doesn't really matter. You can make caramel with a small amount of sugar and a panful of water if you boil it long enough, or with no water at all, because sugar caramelizes when all the water evaporates. It's easier with water than without, however, so for 1pt/600ml of custard, you won't go far wrong with 4oz/100g sugar and 4 tablespoons of water. Many old recipes call for loaf sugar because at one time this was the purest, and therefore least likely to crystallize. Nowadays icing, granulated, caster and cube are all equally pure so why not use granulated, the cheapest?

3 Follow the guidelines for making a strong syrup (page 343). The vital thing is to be sure the sugar is dissolved before the syrup boils and never to stir it after. Once the sugar *is* dissolved, boil the syrup rapidly until light caramel in colour, at which point the sugar now starts cooking quickly because the water has evaporated. All you need do now is keep an eye on it, not letting it get *too* dark because it will very quickly burn and go bitter, the sugar having lost its sweetening power. Even slightly agitating the pan at any time may cause the sugar to crystallize. When the sugar is brown, line the tin with it at once, as explained earlier.

■ Make the custard exactly as for a baked custard – 1pt/600ml very hot milk poured on to 8 yolks (or 4 eggs plus 1 or 2 yolks) mixed with 1oz/25g granulated sugar and about ½ teaspoon of vanilla essence. Strain it into the caramelled tin, cover and cook as *Custards* (see page 287), until set – not forgetting to stand it in water if you bake it, and using the middle of a slowish oven, gas 3, 325°F/165°C. (They're easier to bake perfectly than to steam because it's all too easy to let a pan steam too fast.)

FLANS

Can be made with French flan pastry (pâte sucrée) or flan pastry, the latter being simply a rich shortcrust pastry made with egg yolk and butter or margarine – no lard. See *pastry*, page 137.

■ Traditionally, a *fluted* flan ring is used for a sweet flan. Both it and the baking sheet should be greased for French flan pastry because, with its high sugar content, it may stick otherwise.
■ It's important for flan pastry to be the right consistency if it's to be crisp and light. If too wet, the pastry will be heavy. If too dry, the dough cracks and is difficult to manipulate without breaking.
■ Roll flan pastry about 1½ – 2in/4 – 5cm larger than the flan ring's diameter, to allow for the sides, and for shrinkage while it's relaxing after rolling. Otherwise, the pastry will shrink during baking, and may be too shallow in places to hold semi-liquid fillings. (There's no need to make allowance for French flan pastry shrinking.)
■ If you lift the pastry up over the rolling pin and centre it above the flan ring, you're less likely to tear it than if you lift it with your fingers. Slide the rolling pin out, fit the pastry close to lower edges of ring, and use your small fingers to press the pastry carefully but firmly into each flute.
■ Cut off the untidy bits of pastry at the top, with your rolling pin, not a knife: simply bend any surplus pastry over the sharp top of the flan ring and roll from middle to far side, then from middle to near side, and pull the trimmings away.
■ Prick flan pastry with a fork before baking it blind, otherwise the bottom may rise. See *baking blind*, page 51.

Fillings for flans These can be of many kinds, some cooked together with the pastry, others used in a flan case previously baked blind. Here are a few:

1 Coat attractively arranged, fresh or well-drained canned fruit with an arrowroot-thickened syrup. This, unlike cornflour, is the perfect finish, because it gives a clear, tasteless glaze (see *arrowroot*, page 87). If decorating with cream, allow the glaze to cool completely first, otherwise the cream will slide about.
2 Lemon curd and cream filling – delicious and very quick (see page 333).
3 Pour hot crème patissière (page 331) into the cold, baked flan case, and allow it to cool and set. Arrange fruit such as sliced banana on top, brushed with apricot glaze (page 329), to colour and to prevent the fruit discolouring.
4 Stir things such as desiccated coconut into hot crème patissière, used as above. Alternatively, flavour the crème patissière itself in various ways if you like. Topped with meringue and baked about half an hour in a preheated cool oven, gas 1, 275°F/135°C (or until crisp and golden), you can serve it hot or cold – nicer cold, I think.
5 Half fill an uncooked flan case, made of French flan pastry, with fruit such as stoned cherries or thinly sliced apple. Now cover the fruit evenly with frangipane, page 290, using 1 egg quantity for a 7in/18cm flan. (The frangipane is sweet,

so apple won't need sugar.) Bake for 30 – 40 minutes, or until firm and golden, then brush and glaze the top while still hot, with thin icing made of icing sugar and stock syrup (page 345), to make it shiny.

FOOLS

Probably got their name from the French word *fouler*, to press or crush. In culinary terms, *fouler* means to press through a sieve.

■ Ideally, fools are made with equal quantities fruit purée and cream, not purée and custard. Whipping cream is almost better than double because, if to blend perfectly with the purée, cream should only be half-whipped. See *cream*, page 94.

■ If dessert gooseberries are sweet, ripe and soft enough to use raw, like raspberries or strawberries, there's every reason to do so. Liquidized with sugar to taste, then sieved and blended with a similar quantity of cream, this is a fool you'll never forget.

■ Here are a few more assorted tips:

1 Unless you use a liquidizer – indispensable in my kitchen – icing sugar dissolves more easily than caster with raw fruits.

2 The purée and the half-whipped cream should be about the same consistency if to blend properly, so stewed or canned fruits must be well-drained. Watery raw fruits such as raspberries and strawberries naturally make a watery purée, the fool sometimes being more a drink than a sweet. I like to thicken such purées very slightly with arrowroot, using 1½ level teaspoons to ½pt/250ml purée (see *arrowroot*). To avoid cooking *all* the purée and so spoiling its lovely fresh flavour, heat and thicken only half the purée, then thin it down with the remainder.

3 If you use a proportion of cream and custard, liquidize the cold custard with the purée before blending with the cream. Custard made with custard powder is creamier and lighter if it is liquidized, but make it thicker than

required because it thins when liquidized.

4 You can fold a stiffly whisked egg white into a fool at the last minute if you like. Though not traditional, it makes the fool go further and is a good way to use up a spare white.

5 A few drops of lemon juice, or a spoonful or two of liqueur give a lovely flavour; and a drop or two of colouring may do wonders for the appearance.

6 Serve fool ice-cold, preferably in individual dishes. It's far nicer, and easier to eat than a helping from a large bowl.

7 Serve savoy fingers, tuiles or meringue fingers, for contrast of texture.

■ When one stops to think about it, the main ingredients of a fool, a cream or a fresh fruit ice cream are all the same – sweetened fruit purée mixed with half-whipped cream. A fool becomes a cream when it is set with gelatine; ice cream (page 292) when it is frozen.

FRANGIPANE

Said to take its name from its inventor, an Italian called Frangipani, who lived in Paris at the time of Louis XIII. It is used as a filling, with pastry of some kind, often in tartlets or a flan – heavenly it is, too. Frangipane is basically just a sandwich cake mixture using ground almonds in place of flour. A level dessertspoon of flour (to 1 egg) in addition to the ground almonds, slightly stiffens the mixture, and a few drops of almond essence helps to accentuate the almond flavour.

FRITTERS, FRUIT

Best made with fruits which are ripe enough to have plenty of flavour but firm enough to handle.

■ Fruits taste super when macerated because this both sweetens and flavours them (see macerating, page 70). Bananas and strawberries need only 15 minutes, most other fruits about half an hour. If soaked longer, they'll be too soft. Do be sure to drain and dry them before dipping in fritter batter, otherwise they'll make it watery and will splutter madly in the hot fat.

■ If not macerated, nearly all fruits (except things like bananas, dessert apples or canned sweetened pineapple rings) will at least need sweetening. Put them on a tray, sprinkle with caster sugar, leave for half an hour and then dry them. Who can forget the bitterness of a sour cooking apple inside that eagerly awaited and perhaps expensive apple fritter?

The batter This is easier to cope with if it's deep, so use a smallish basin in which you can submerge and coat the fruit completely.

■ Air, beaten into the whisked egg whites, is the only raising agent, unless the mixture also contains yeast, so the batter is therefore always made with plain rather than self-raising flour. (A *yeast* batter makes about the best fritters ever, I think – light, crisp and dangerous for the waistline.)

■ Another way to make them crisp is to mix 1 dessertspoon of oil with each 2oz/50g flour – though I'm not quite sure why it does so.

■ Leave a batter to rest for 30–45 minutes before adding the whisked egg white if you can. This gives it time to thicken, so it will coat the food better. (You can't achieve the same results by making a thicker batter because that means raising the proportion of flour, which of course produces heavy fritters.)

■ For perfect results the batter should just coat the back of a wooden spoon without running off. If the white isn't whisked stiffly enough, the batter may be thick enough to coat the first lot of fritters but may thin out by the time you can fry the second.

■ Some people like to dip each piece of fruit into the batter in the curves of a fork, but I find it easier to hold each in my fingers. Either way, you can easily slip the battered fruit into the hot fat – but beware of burning yourself.

The deep fat This should be about 360°F/182°C. If much cooler, the fritters won't float and will absorb the fat. If much hotter, the outside of the fritters will be burnt by the time the inside is cooked. There's also a danger in trying to fry too many at once, because the temperature of the fat will drop too low.

■ It's better not to use a frying basket because the batter tends to stick to the wire and the surface of the fruit becomes exposed to the intense heat. Turn them over when golden underneath, to brown evenly. If overcooked they'll burst. For further information, see *frying, deep fat*, page 63.

■ Fritters are usually tossed in caster or icing sugar, but 1 level teaspoonful of ground cinnamon sieved with 2oz/50g of sugar gives a spicy flavour to fruits such as apple, banana and peach.

■ Serve fritters on a fancy doyley (to absorb any excess fat) in an uncovered dish – if covered at any stage, they'd lose their crispness.

FRITTO MISTO OF FRUITS

The Italian name for a *variety* of fritters. Just as easy to make as fritters of one kind, except that you may need to macerate some of them separately.

FRUITS, STEWED

Stewed fruits such as apple quarters or unripe pear halves taste sweeter and don't break up so readily when put into a boiling syrup, as they do if simply brought to the boil with sugar and water. The larger the pan the better too, the fruit cooking evenly when in one layer, but apt to become mushy if piled up.

■ Use a metal spoon to make the syrup, but two wooden ones to turn the fruit over. They don't break it up so easily.

■ Ripe peach and pear halves don't usually need cooking; simply lay them in the boiling syrup, turn them over straight away to prevent discoloration, bring the syrup back to the boil and set the covered pan aside from the heat. After a few minutes, turn the fruit over to soften the other side, then leave to cool.

■ Soft fruits like raspberries and strawberries don't usually need cooking either, and are easier still: cover them in a basin with a small quantity of strong boiling syrup, and leave to cool.

■ Use a syrup with a smaller proportion of water to sugar for watery fruits such as rhubarb or apple, than for hard fruits such as quinces or unripe pears.

■ Lemon juice may be used for two reasons: to give flavour, and to prevent fruit breaking up. *Avoid* using it, of course, if you want a purée.

■ Stewed fruit can be made more substantial by thickening the hot syrup with arrowroot, potato flour or cornflour (see page 87).

■ See also *compôte*, page 57.

ICE CREAMS, FRESH FRUIT

Memorably delicious, easy (when one knows how) and surprisingly quick to make, good homemade fruit ice creams are a treat to friends and family alike, not to mention a valuable freezer store for even the most illustrious guest, expected or unexpected. For 7–8 servings, you need only ½pt/250ml each of cream and sweetened fruit purée.

The hows and whys, for perfection:

1 *Equipment and utensils* – all to be pre-chilled and kept in the refrigerator for everything to remain ice-cold:

a The refrigerator Leave at its normal setting. This is usually quite cold enough to freeze the mixture without also turning other foods to ice should you forget later to re-set it. Use the floor of the ice compartment. (Stacked on top of other things, freezing times are less predictable.)

b A mixing bowl is better than a basin, to allow for the proper whipping of the cream and later the thorough breaking down of any ice crystals. Return both it and whisk to refrigerator after every use.

c The whisk chosen should be strong

enough and wiry enough to crush any ice crystals forming in the freezing mixture. A wire whisk, page 50, is ideal for this. If without anything suitable, use a strong fork.

d The ice trays For ½pt/250ml each of purée and cream, use a shallow aluminium biscuit tin about 11 × 7½in/28 × 18cm, or two ice trays about 10 × 4in/26 × 10cm (or the equivalent). Well dried, pre-chilled and shallow rather than deep, the freezing process will start immediately the mixture reaches the ice compartment.

2 *Sugar* The right proportion of sugar to fruit is vital: if a purée is not sweet enough, the ice cream will be hard instead of velvety, and the flavour insipid. If you're without a blender or other suitable mechanical equipment, icing sugar will dissolve better and faster in a sieved purée than will granulated. (In a liquidizer, granulated dissolves perfectly.) A very acid fruit such as loganberries will need more sugar than, say, raspberries or strawberries, but generally speaking the right proportions are 3oz/75g sugar to 8oz/200g fresh fruit – to make ½pt/250ml purée.

3 *Fruit* Liquidize (preferably, or sieve) enough fruit with the correct amount of sugar to make the required quantity of purée. Those made from fruits with skins and/or seeds such as blackberries, *ripe* dessert gooseberries – a *glorious* fruit of which to make ice cream – and raspberries need sieving (ideally, a nylon or hair sieve) and if the waste is heavy, as with gooseberries or blackberries for instance, you may need up to 12oz/300g fruit – and a pro rata increase in sugar – to make ½pt/250ml purée.

4 *Cream* Use chilled double or whipping cream, whipped – for easy and perfect blending – to approximately the same consistency as the purée (marginally thicker when for very watery fruits like raspberries). See also *whipped cream*, page 95.

5 *Accompaniments and/or decoration* Serve something crisp-textured and mild

enough in flavour to enhance, never dominate, the fruit flavour of the ice cream. Meringues will partner any flavour, as do tuiles (page 326) or Askey's decorative, crunchy and delicious fan-shaped wafers.

6 *Freezer container* I like best to use a long narrow (bacon-rasher type) poly-thene box for the made ice cream. In this shape, it thaws evenly, and you can, if without an ice cream scoop, slice to serve it.

Method, briefly:

1 Blend the chilled whipped cream and the sweetened purée smoothly together. Using a rubber or plastic spatula (not anything metal), spread mixture flat in the ice trays and put on the floor of the refrigerator ice compartment.

2 About 15–20 minutes later, or when the edges of the mixture are starting to harden, turn the whole lot into the chilled mixing bowl. Using a whisk, crush and beat the mixture until completely smooth. Spread flat in the ice tray again and replace quickly in ice compartment – bowl and whisk back to refrigerator as well.

3 Probably about half an hour later, repeat above process – again, when the edges have hardened slightly.

4 About half an hour later still, look again. If the whole mixture is not by now freezing smoothly, crush and beat it yet again. Only when all the ice crystals have been broken down and the texture is creamy throughout, will the ice cream remain perfect (for months, in a freezer) to eat.

5 Transfer to the container, spread flat, cover with a strip of greaseproof or waxy paper and put on the lid. Store (several days if liked) in ice compartment of refrigerator, or put straight into freezer.

6 To serve, at a melt-in-the-mouth creamy texture, put container in middle of refrigerator for about 20–30 minutes (according to temperature of refrigerator or freezer) before required.

7 Serve in balls, on ice plates (if pos-sible) and decorated with an ice wafer.

■ Avoid touching the ice cream with your hands, the warmth of which will quickly melt it.

■ The time required for the freezing mix-ture to firm up will depend upon the size of the ice trays you use, the depth of the mixture and the temperature of your refrigerator.

■ Fruit ice creams can make a colourful ending to a meal.

■ Vanilla ice cream is also hard and flavourless if made with too little sugar.

■ If you serve homemade ice cream direct from the freezer, or ice compart-ment of refrigerator, not only is it too hard to eat and enjoy, but also it seems to lack flavour: it freezes (desensitizes) the taste buds.

JELLY, LEMON

Homemade lemon jelly, cleared with egg white and egg shell, certainly has a splen-did flavour, but so it should after such a long-winded process.

■ A few points need special care to make sure that nothing will make cloudy a sweet which should be crystal-clear.

1 Pan, bowl and jelly bag should be scrupulously clean, the bag never washed in soapy water. It pays to scald it just before using, to help the jelly run through more quickly.

2 Wash the lemons and peel with a potato peeler rather than use grated rind, which includes bitter pith.

3 Wipe the eggs before separating them and crushing the shells. All the impurities in the liquid will cling to the shells, like metal to a magnet, when the whisked mixture is hot enough for the egg whites to coagulate. It's important to stop whis-king *just* before it reaches boiling point though, otherwise the impurities will be released back into the liquid.

4 Let the liquid run through the jelly bag by itself, resisting all temptation to squeeze, press or help it, otherwise you'll make it cloudy again.

■ The liquid should be about one-third

lemon juice, two-thirds water, and a larger proportion of gelatine is used than for something like a soufflé or cream, because it loses some of its strength by being almost boiled.

■ The jelly acquires a stronger lemon flavour by being 'infused' for about 10 minutes in a warm place before being cleared. Don't skip that soaking period.

JELLY, MILK

Quite easy as long as you don't try to dissolve the gelatine in the milk, because it gives a curdled appearance. It is not a true curdle, however, because the milk is perfectly sweet.

■ The milk should be used at room temperature. Flavouring and sugar are added, and the gelatine is dissolved in a little hot water and added when cool; the gelatine is always added to the milk, not the milk to the gelatine.

■ If the milk is chilled, stand it in warm water for a few moments, otherwise the gelatine won't mix with the intensely cold liquid, but will set in globules or will string. Should that happen, strain out most of the milk and stand the container in a basin of warm water. As the milk warms, the gelatine will dissolve, when you can then stir in the rest of the milk.

JELLY, PACKET

This will set quickly on hot days or when you're in a hurry if you dissolve it in about half of the required quantity of nearly-boiling water, then top up with ice cubes, stirring until they melt.

JUNKET

A junket won't set if the milk is warmer than blood heat (see *rennet*, page 117), or if you disturb the milk after adding the rennet to it. This explains why junket is more likely to set if you add the rennet at the very last second – after the serving dish or sundae glasses are placed where you intend to leave them while the junket

is setting, and after you've stirred sugar and colouring (if any) into the milk. You can only safely move it when *set*.

■ If you like to flavour junket with ground nutmeg – heaven knows, it needs some flavour if served by itself – sieve it on to the set junket from a height. This way, you can sprinkle it on sparsely and evenly. Alternatively, serve junket with cream, a fruit salad or stewed fruit.

■ You can also dress up junket and make it a bit more appealing by decorating it with angelica leaves (see page 86) and cherry. Make them light and dainty, though, or they'll sink, and leave a liquid in their place.

■ Junket is often given to invalids because it's so easy to digest, the rennet having already got to work on the milk.

KEBABS, FRUIT

Besides making an unusual dessert (served with whipped cream), these make a delicious accompaniment to certain fish, meat and poultry dishes particularly anything grilled. Fruits which grill well with each other are: thickly sliced banana; fresh or canned (drained) pineapple cubes; halved canned (drained) apricots; quartered canned (drained) peaches; grapefruit segments; apple sections.

■ Before grilling the kebabs for two or three minutes on each side, macerate all the fruit for about half an hour in the following (or a similar) mixture, using it later to baste the kebabs, and turning the fruit over in it at least once while macerating:

> 8fl oz/225ml grapefruit or pineapple juice
> 4 level tablespoons clear honey, warmed, to blend easily
> 2 tablespoons cointreau
> 1 teaspoon finely chopped mint – for savoury dishes, optional

■ See also *skewers (shish)*, page 42.

MERINGUE

There are three principal types of meringue:

Meringue suisse The kind we make with whisked egg whites and sugar, for meringues and toppings for sweets and puddings, see below.

Meringue cuite Made with egg white and icing (or sometimes caster) sugar beaten over low heat until thick enough to stand in peaks, and used for things like piping, petits fours or smallish cakes, or as a cake filling. It doesn't collapse like Swiss meringue would for a cake filling, because of course the egg white has been coagulated and set by the heat.

Meringue italienne Made by pouring sugar syrup (boiled to 260°F/127°C) on to stiffly whisked egg whites, and whisking until thick. This can be used when cold for things like baked alaska, certain pastries, cake fillings, or to replace whipped cream. As above, the heat coagulates and sets the egg whites. You'll need to follow a recipe.

Meringues Such a popular and easily made sweet, whether for the family, a dinner party or for a crowd, that they're worth some concentration if you're not already a dab hand. If you can't make good meringues, it's probably because you trip up over one or more of these four things:

1 The eggs themselves may not be new-laid: if old, or if they've been badly stored, the whites will be too watery to whisk properly.

2 You may not be whisking the whites to the correct consistency at each stage:

a They should look like cotton wool before you add the first lot of sugar – about quarter of the total. The reason for adding this sugar now is to strengthen the whites so that they can then support the larger amount following.

b They should be 'rocky', shiny like satin, before you fold in the remaining sugar. (For details, see *whisking*, page 84.)

■ Beware of over-whisking too. This breaks down the structure of the egg white, which changes and collapses. Only when perfectly whisked, can meringue be piped in sharp shapes which hold that shape.

3 The sugar may not be properly folded and cut into the whisked whites (see *folding*, page 62). (I prefer granulated to caster for meringues, or one *can* use icing or even Demerara. Allow 2oz/50g per egg white.)

4 The oven may be too low when you put the meringues into it, or, because you may not have set the shelves where you need them beforehand – low down in a conventional oven – there's excessive heat loss at a crucial time while you do so. The oven should be preheated as well as prepared, gas ¼ – ½, 200°F/93°C. While most people know that meringues cook best in a very low oven, many seem not to be aware that it must be *hot enough initially* to coagulate and set the egg white before it melts and 'weeps'. If you've forgotten to preheat the oven, it's much better to leave the piped meringues on the kitchen table than to put them into too cool an oven. If despite doing everything apparently correctly, your meringues still either weep or get too brown, check that your oven is not at fault, see *oven thermometer*, page 46, also *gas ovens*, page 19.

5 Once the meringues have had time to set throughout, say after 15 – 20 minutes, the slower you cook them, the whiter and firmer they'll be. Good meringues will dry out in 3 – 4 hours: they should be firm when pressed underneath, but may need turning later on, depending mostly on their position in the oven. Those in the coolest part may not need turning. This is where a fan-assisted oven comes into its own because a whole batch of meringues will cook perfectly in the same time, in the same, constant temperature.

■ Some further tips:

1 Prepare the baking sheet/sheets before you heat the oven or start the

meringues. Best of all, I like a sheet of *oiled* greaseproof paper on an oiled baking sheet: it's easier to lift the cooked meringues off this than off foil, Bakewell or waxed paper. In days gone by, the technique was to use a thick wooden board because on wood, which is a bad conductor of heat, meringues don't turn brown underneath. Modern baking sheets, however, are thick, just as good and readily available in any home where there's a serious cook.

2 To fill the piping bag easily, see page 76. If you haven't got a bag, shape the meringues with two wetted dessertspoons.

3 After piping meringues on to prepared baking sheet/sheets, sprinkle with caster sugar to improve their texture, then pop them into the heated oven.

4 Cool the cooked meringues on a wire tray, then put at once into an airtight container. If left out, they absorb moisture from the atmosphere, quickly losing their crispness.

5 If you like eating them really crisp, avoid filling meringues before you must, because now they will absorb moisture from the cream as well as from the atmosphere.

6 Double cream is best, whipping cream being too watery.

7 To set them off well and help them to stand steadily, serve with the cream-filling upwards, in coloured paper cake cases. Use a fancy doyley underneath, and a dish which looks too large for them, to act as a picture frame.

8 Meringue halves will store a week or two if properly made and in an airtight container. (Some people like to freeze them.)

Meringue toppings Toppings for sweets and puddings only need about half as much sugar per egg white as individual meringues, say 1–1½oz/25–40g. The meringue is made in the same way but cooked slightly faster, for a shorter time.

■ Cook hot things like queen of puddings in the cooler half of a slow oven, gas 1, 275°F/135°C for about 30 – 45 minutes or until crisp, the peaks lightly browned, the centre still soft. If you cook the meringue faster, its flavour is less good.

■ Sweets such as flans or fruit crust – say canned peaches, with meringue on top – which are to be served cold, need longer, slower cooking to firm up the centre, otherwise they'll flop as they cool. Allow about ¾–1¼ hrs at gas ¾, 250°F/120°C.

Pavlova This featherlight dish was created in honour of Pavlova, in her day the leading ballerina of the Imperial Russian Ballet. A large, cream and fruit-filled meringue case with built-up sides, to represent a ballet dancer's tutu, it owes its soft marshmallowy interior to the teaspoonful or so of lemon juice or white wine vinegar added after folding in the sugar.

■ Cornflour – about 1 level tablespoon to 3 egg whites – prevents the sugar weeping and helps to dry out the meringue, which is cooked for a shorter time in a hotter oven than individual meringues. Fold it in at the last minute, with a little of the sugar. The more cornflour you use, the drier the meringue.

■ This is a recipe worth digging out, and excellent for a dinner party because you can keep the meringue at least a week in an airtight container.

■ For the perfect texture, assemble the meringue with its filling about 2 hours before serving – 1 hour on a very hot day – giving the meringue time to soften slightly. (If not assembled until the last, the meringue will be rocky; if done too soon it will flop.)

MILK PUDDINGS

These often do deserve the drab name they've got, yet I can't think of many puddings I like better than a creamy flaked tapioca or rice pudding served with stewed apple and softly whipped cream (preferably chantilly, page 303) to go with them.

To make milk puddings creamy:

1 Be sure to use the right proportions of

grain to milk. The creamier the milk the better, of course, but dried milk does just as well, if you double up on the margarine or butter.

2 Soak *whole* grain puddings such as rice or tapioca for at least half an hour before cooking. This softens the grain, helping it later to absorb the milk.

3 Use a slow oven – no higher than gas 2, 300°F/150°C.

4 Stir the pudding at least once, preferably twice, when a thin skin forms on top, after about half an hour and again after about another 15 – 30 minutes if you can remember, before the skin goes brown. Stirring prevents the grains sticking together in little heaps, consequently all can fully absorb the milk.

Chocolate cornflour pudding This changes magically from stodge to fluff if you liquidize it, skin and all, when cold. The consistency thins though, so it won't set again.

■ The skin on top of a cold blancmange is due to evaporation from the surface, so if you aren't going to liquidize it later, sprinkle the top lightly with sugar to prevent a skin forming – unless you like it, of course.

Rice pudding This is made with short grain pudding rice because it's absorbent, very white, and goes creamy when cooked, unlike long grain which is much less absorbent and doesn't go creamy. See also *milk puddings*, above.

■ One way of eating up *cold rice pudding* is to remove the skin, dredge the top with Demerara sugar and grill it to a caramel. Eat soon when cool, before the caramel melts. (Before grilling, protect the rim of the dish with a strip of foil.)

MINCE PIES

These freeze perfectly, the mincemeat usually being moister when they're frozen uncooked.

■ Freeze in their bun tins until stiff enough to pack in a covered container,

which gives better protection against damage than a polythene bag.

■ Small mince pies are often made with either shortcrust or a flaky type of pastry, but a large pie is best made with flaky or rough puff pastry – not with frozen puff pastry.

PANCAKES

Still traditional on Shrove Tuesday, even though we don't nowadays have to use up the milk, fat and eggs once forbidden during the Lenten fast.

■ They are just as light, if not lighter, when made with equal quantities of milk and water instead of all milk; and one egg to 2oz/50g flour makes much better pancakes than one egg to 4oz/100g flour, as called for in many recipes. Pancakes will be lighter, too, if the batter is chilled for a while, because cold air trapped in it will expand more than warm when heated.

■ Fat is used only to grease the pan well before making each pancake, to ensure each slides out easily; never actually to fry them in. They should be lacy-thin, and are lighter when turned over with a pallet knife than when tossed – sorry to be a spoilsport!

■ Lemon butter pats make pancakes sumptuous (see page 304). Make up to ¼–½lb/100–200g butter while you're about it, if you have a freezer. Alternatively, have you tried eating them with a lump of ordinary butter inside, along with the traditional lemon juice and sugar? This is a scrumptious North Country custom. (I find them deadly dull with only lemon juice and sugar.)

■ If you want to freeze pancakes – I don't, because nobody can persuade me they're as good – they'll be lighter with about a tablespoon of oil or melted butter stirred into 4oz/100g batter. Cool the pancakes quickly on a wire tray, to let the steam escape.

■ A strong frying pan about 8in/20cm in diameter may be just as good as a real pancake pan (galettière).

PIE, FRUIT

Lovely made with a melt-in-the-mouth rich shortcrust pastry (see page 136). 1 level teaspoon of ground cinnamon sieved with 8oz/225g flour gives a nice spicy flavour to pastry for an apple pie or mince pies, etc. – or you may like it in a pear flan.

■ It's better to put the sugar between the layers of fruit rather than over the top, then it won't make the pastry soggy underneath.

■ A little cornflour or semolina mixed with the sugar (2 rounded teaspoons to 4oz/100g sugar) makes the juice of fruits like apples, blackberries or rhubarb deliciously syrupy instead of watery.

■ There's no need to use a pie funnel in a fruit pie because there should be enough fruit to come above the level of the rim of the pie-dish, to support the pastry. By the time the fruit softens and shrinks, the pastry will have set, so shouldn't collapse into the middle.

■ Put the strip of pastry round the rim of the pie-dish with its *cut* edge outwards, because this edge is open, not sealed, and can rise perfectly when baked.

■ Raise the pastry slightly at one corner of a fruit pie, for steam to escape, otherwise the underside of the pastry will be soggy.

Plate pie Will be crisp underneath as well as on top if you make it on an aluminium or old-fashioned enamel plate – because metal is a better conductor of heat than ovenware glass or china.

■ If you freeze an uncooked plate pie, it's wise to brush the inner surfaces of the pastry with egg white. This seals the pastry, preventing seepage of fruit juice, which would make it soggy.

SABAYON

The French version of the Italian zabaglione, made with white wine instead of marsala. See page 301.

SOUFFLÉS

Cold soufflés such as milanaise (lemon) or chocolate are best the day they're made because then the texture is perfect, especially if you can use new-laid eggs (see *whisking*, page 84).

■ It's always tricky to try and advise anybody about the size of soufflé dish required, because so much depends on other things besides quantities: how fresh and large the eggs are; how well you beat the yolks and sugar, how skilfully you whisk the whites, etc.

■ A large doubled strip of foil to stand 2in/5cm above the top of the dish allows the soufflé to come 1in/2½cm above the rim. This is easy to fix on, and *far* easier to take off, without spoiling the edge, than greaseproof paper. Grip the ends together, first with a paper clip, then tie it on tightly with string to prevent any mixture escaping down the side, because this is difficult to wipe off when set.

■ Ideally, you need a large mixing bowl each for the yolks/sugar mixture, the cream, and the egg whites, because in none of these ingredients could you entangle enough air if using small basins. A soufflé depends on air.

■ The yolks/sugar bowl should be big enough to sit steadily on top of a pan of hot water without the water touching it. If it does touch, or if the water is actually boiling, you'll end up with cooked yolks instead of whisked. They need gentle, indirect heat to become light and fluffy.

■ You can't go wrong with the temperature of the water if, when it boils, you stand the pan in the sink and beat the yolks and sugar over it, there. It's a comfortable height at which to beat, and you can't easily scald yourself either. Beat the yolks and sugar 'to the ribbon' (see page 78), to give the mixture enough body to support the other ingredients when added. If not beaten enough, it will thin out.

■ If the mixture refuses to thicken – perhaps because the eggs aren't very fresh – try adding an extra yolk.

■ I prefer whipping cream to double

cream (see page 94) because, for a soufflé, the cream should be only half-whipped. To blend perfectly with the beaten yolks and sugar, you should whip it to their consistency. See also page 284.

SPONGE PUDDINGS

Made in a flash with an all-in-one mixture (page 318), these can be varied in innumerable ways, baked or steamed. You're bound to know lots of the following, but some you may not have thought of, or recognized their simple base.

Eve's pudding Bake the sponge mixture on top of the prepared fresh or canned fruit. With a name like this, the fruit is, of course, officially apple, very finely sliced – with sugar between the layers rather than over the top.

Castle puddings Bake in darioles and serve with jam sauce or, if chocolate, serve with chocolate sauce or a sweet white sauce.

Syrup sponge Put golden syrup (or jam for a jam sponge) at the bottom of a pudding basin or darioles. Steam. For variety, add a few chopped glacé cherries and a little chopped angelica to the mixture.

Lemon, chocolate, spice, ginger, fruit, date, pineapple, etc. pudding Add the necessary flavouring to the mixture – respectively lemon rind, cocoa, mixed spice, ground ginger, dried fruits, chopped dates and a spice, chopped canned pineapple. Steam. Serve a complementary sauce, such as egg custard, an appropriately flavoured sweet white sauce or a hard sauce (see page 304).

Upside-down pudding Use a shallow tin like a moule à manqué or sandwich cake tin, spreading its inner surfaces with creamed soft brown sugar and margarine – about 1oz/25g of each for a 1-egg pudding. Decorate the bottom with pineapple and glacé cherries, spread sponge mixture on top and bake for about 45 minutes in a slow to moderate oven, gas 3, 325°F/165°C. It tastes every bit as good as it looks when turned out, and served with cream, custard or better still, both.

West Riding pudding Bake sponge mixture in a pie-dish, first lining its sides with a thin strip of shortcrust pastry, and spreading jam or lemon curd in the bottom.

Plain steamed (vanilla-flavoured) pudding With this, serve a well-flavoured sauce such as sweet white, lemon, lemon butter, strawberry butter, arrowroot or cornflour-thickened fruit syrup, or differently flavoured custards made in the British or French way.

SYLLABUB

This fattening, delicious old-English sweet made with ½pt/300ml double cream, a large lemon, 3oz/75g sugar and 2 or 3 tablespoons of sherry (or sherry and brandy), has a finer flavour made with lemon zest than lemon rind. (If using rind, soak it for 2 – 3 hours in the juice, to give the juice extra flavour before straining and using it.)

■ Much depends upon the freshness of the cream – you can't make syllabub if it's buttery. Whip it to light peaks before gradually stirring in the other mixed-together ingredients, and then whip the whole lot until thick.
■ If made much in advance of the meal, the sherry may separate out, especially if not refrigerated at once.
■ Serve it well chilled in individual glasses – the cream can be chilled in advance – decorated with finely chopped pistachio nuts. Serve something with a contrasting crisp texture with it – like tuiles or savoy fingers.

TARTS

Pastry shells with a sweet filling, sometimes decorated with lattice. Unlike a pie, the filling is never completely enclosed.

TRIFLE

Trifle is well named – there's no knowing what one is going to find under many an inviting creamy top. It's not a sweet you can make in 10 minutes.

■ For the basics, you can't beat good homemade sponge cake soaked for at least 2 or 3 hours – to make it firm enough to support the cream – in plenty of *cooled* custard made with egg yolks. Make about a pint/600ml for 6 people, bearing in mind that if you use it while still warm, it won't have thickened fully as it should. (Custard made with custard powder is incorrect because it will set on top of the sponge cake, rather than soak into it.)

■ Sherry, rum or liqueur, not to mention jam, fruit and ratafia biscuits, are all traditional ingredients of the real thing.

■ Surely the most luxurious trifle of all is topped with syllabub rather than whipped cream.

YOGHURT

This calls for know-how if you are always to be successful, but homemade is worth making, for a family anyway, because it is much less expensive than bought yoghurt. A machine isn't necessary, but a thermometer should ensure that the milk is at the right temperature. If you don't have a thermometer, test the temperature by putting a drop of milk on your wrist; it should feel hot, but not too hot – slightly above blood heat.

The main causes of failure are:

1 Using out-of-date, sterilized or pasteurized yoghurt as a starter.

2 Using the wrong kind of milk:
Fresh is unsuitable unless first sterilized, because of bacteria other than those needed for the yoghurt.
Sweetened condensed is too sweet – so much sugar stops the bacteria growing.

3 Wrong temperatures:
 a Using chilled starter: it will cool the milk to a temperature too low for the bacteria to multiply.

b If the milk is too hot when you add the starter to it, yoghurt bacteria will be killed.
c If not warm enough during incubation, the bacteria won't multiply. Could you use your hot cupboard if nowhere better?

4 Adding a flavouring before the yoghurt has thickened. If nothing worse, anything like crushed fruit is likely to sink.

To make plain (or natural) yoghurt (for 6–8)
 2pts/1 litre UHT milk
 ¼pt/125ml *natural* yoghurt

Method

1 Heat the milk to 110°F/43°C, then set pan aside from the heat.

2 Meanwhile, lay a warmed serving bowl on top of a large, doubled, thick towel – large enough so that you can later wrap the bowl snugly in it – in a warm place where the yoghurt can be left to set.

3 Whisk (preferably with a wire whisk, page 50) the *room-temperature* yoghurt into the milk, then pour into the prepared bowl. Cover at once with a warmed plate and then wrap completely in the towel, trying not to disturb the contents. Leave for 6 – 8 hours to set.

4 When set, refrigerate as soon as possible for at least 12 hours, by which time the yoghurt should have thickened.

A few more hints

1 Thickened yoghurt, when stirred, becomes creamy. Now is the time to stir in a flavouring, e.g. mango, dessert gooseberry, raspberry, strawberry or (canned) apricot purée, well-squashed bananas.

2 It should keep well for at least a week. Longer, and separation into curds may occur.

3 ¼pt/125ml left-over yoghurt will start off another batch, but you can't go on indefinitely using starter from the last making because eventually it becomes too weak.

4 Yoghurt doesn't freeze well because its texture changes, but I none the less like

always to have some. Thawed, it's still good to make a dressing, to add to a sautéd vegetable or to stir into a soup or sauce for instance.

■ See also page 132.

YORKSHIRE PUDDING

This is lighter when made with half milk and half water instead of all milk. The batter, contrary to many an old recipe, is much better for being chilled than beaten, because trapped cold air (caught when sieving the flour) expands more than room-temperature air when heated, so it rises better.

■ The right-sized tin has a real bearing on results (see page 47) and a tin gives a crisper Yorkshire than an ovenproof dish, because metal is a better conductor of heat.
■ Heat is essential for success. You need a hot oven, hot lard (or cooking fat) in a hot tin, and a quick hand to keep things hot. The oven must be hot enough initially to make the batter rise and then hold its shape. Use the hottest part of it and have it preheated to gas 7, 425°F/220°C for the first 15 minutes, then lower to gas 5, 375°F/190°C for about another 45 minutes.
■ If you have a large family, and a restricted purse, one large new-laid egg will raise 6oz/150g flour – plain, of course. Use a tin about 12 × 9½in/30 × 24cm.
■ If you cut off the thick edges of any

left-overs, so that the remaining piece is flat and will cook evenly, Yorkshire pudding is lovely fried for 2 or 3 minutes on each side. Serve it with the cold beef, or as a pudding (fried in butter or oil) with golden syrup – or deep freeze it along with the sliced cold beef.

ZABAGLIONE

Can be served by itself in glasses, either warm or cold, or as a sauce poured over or accompanying certain hot puddings and sweets, such as Christmas pudding, sponge puddings or stewed fruits. The Italians use marsala, while the French use white wine and call it sabayon.

■ It's a little tricky to make. You need:

1 The right-sized basin for the quantity you're making. It's difficult for instance to beat 2 egg yolks and sugar properly if the basin is too big, while on the other hand it is difficult to entangle enough air as they thicken if the basin is much too small.
2 Shivering, shallow water in the pan under the basin. If the yolks are overheated because the water is too hot or too deep, they'll coagulate before you can beat air into them.
3 An electric hand-beater if you've got one, otherwise a good whisk (page 49), to beat enough air into the mixture to get the volume. It's never better than when just made – thick, warm and full of flavour.

17

Dessert sauces

GENERAL INFORMATION

Sauces can make or mar sweets and puddings, perhaps by their absence even more than by their presence. They can enrich and give flavour to the simplest pudding; by their sharpness counteract the richness of others; provide moisture with dry dishes, a soft creamy texture to partner a hard, or a dash of colour to cheer a dull. In addition, a hot sauce can make a contrast for ice cream, or a chilled sauce may be the perfect choice for something hot.

■ With a sauce one can dress up, vary and disguise the plainest sponge, or one can crown the most sophisticated sweet. Some of them require skill, few are very time-taking, nearly always they are a bonus.

CHOCOLATE SAUCE

To serve over vanilla ice cream, canned pears or sliced banana, etc., chocolate sauce makes a handy store in the refrigerator. I never make less than ½pt/250ml because, providing you keep it chilled and covered, it lasts for weeks. This recipe uses stock syrup, which helps to make the sauce shiny:

2½oz/65g plain dessert chocolate
½pt/250ml warm stock syrup (page 345)
½ teaspoon vanilla essence
about 1 tablespoon rum (optional)

Method

1 Melt the shredded or grated chocolate in a basin over a pan of shallow, very hot but not boiling water (see page 92 if necessary).

2 Set basin aside from the heat and stir the syrup into the chocolate, a little at a time to start with. Flavour with vanilla and, if liked, also with rum. Taste.

3 Allow to go quite cold, to thicken properly.

4 Cover with foil and refrigerate until required.

Note If the stock syrup is too hot it will turn the chocolate to rock. If cold, it's *difficult* (but not impossible) to mix it evenly with the chocolate before the chocolate cools and hardens.

CREAM, SLIGHTLY SOUR

Double or whipping cream is delicious if you whip about 1 level tablespoon of vanilla sugar (or icing sugar plus a few drops vanilla essence) and about 1 teaspoon of lemon juice with ¼pt/125ml of cream that has gone slightly sour. Taste, and adjust as you like it.

■ Surprisingly perhaps, an unpleasant acidity is transformed into a most likeable sharp flavour.

CREAM, WHIPPED

As an accompaniment, whipped cream goes further and isn't quite so rich if you fold a stiffly whisked egg white into ½pt/250ml whipped double cream.

■ I wouldn't use it for piping because it soon collapses – best made just before you need it too.
■ See also whipped cream, page 95.

CRÈME ANGLAISE

A sophisticated version of British boiled custard or custard sauce – the way it *ought* to be made! It is made with yolks rather than whole eggs and contains just enough cornflour or potato flour not to thicken it but to prevent the custard scrambling if marginally overheated. (Approximately 1 level teaspoon of starch to ¾pt/375ml milk.)

■ Vanilla is the basic flavouring: in addition you may like to stir into the finished sauce a spoonful or two of your favourite liqueur, add a spoonful of coffee essence, or, while heating the milk, melt a little shredded chocolate in it.
■ The sauce is served either warmed or chilled, depending on what it accompanies, e.g. fruit salad, a pudding or wherever it could take the place of cream.
■ With additional egg yolks and with double cream it becomes the custard used for ice creams. Also with more egg yolk, plus whipped cream, gelatine and flavouring, it is ready to be a Bavarian cream.
■ See also *custard, boiled*, below.

CRÈME CHANTILLY

More subtle and much more delicious than ordinary whipped cream and no extra bother for anyone who has a jar of vanilla sugar in their larder (see page 126). The term *chantilly* indicates a slightly sweetened vanilla-flavoured whipped cream.

■ You can use double or whipping cream, lightly whipped, to accompany a hot or cold sweet; more stiffly whipped double cream if to pipe or use in meringues, a gâteau or with pastries, etc.
■ Precise quantities aren't necessary: just whip about a rounded teaspoon of vanilla sugar (preferably icing sugar) with ¼pt/125ml cream, or more to taste.

CUSTARD, BOILED (CUSTARD SAUCE)

When made with whole eggs this is as unattractive as it sounds, besides having the most idiotic name imaginable for a sauce which at all costs must not be boiled. The French name *crème à la vanille* sounds so much more enticing, and so is the sauce if, despite a recipe stating '1 egg', you instead use 2 yolks. The sauce will have a finer flavour, is much less likely to curdle and will be richer, smoother, yellower and thicker – and thicker still when it's cold. (Use 3 large yolks to ½pt/250ml milk.)

■ It's because of the conflicting temperatures at which an egg white and egg yolk set that whole eggs curdle or at best make a wretched sauce: you can't win because the white coagulates (begins to solidify) at a lower temperature than the yolk, so if you heat the milky liquid enough for the yolk to thicken it, that's too hot for the white.
■ As yolks themselves coagulate well below boiling point, this explains why there's no need to boil a custard, and why it will be worse rather than better if heated above 165°F/74°C.
■ A few more tips:

1 It's better to stir the heated milk into the whisked egg and sugar in a thin stream rather than to tip it in all at once, especially if you've rather overheated the milk. This way the yolks are warmed gradually instead of being suddenly cooked.
2 Rinse out the pan with cold water after heating the milk and before straining back in the milk, eggs and sugar. Otherwise, if a pan is very hot, the eggs may start to solidify before you have a free hand with which to stir.
3 Hot custard left in a hot pan may, due to the heat of the pan, scramble. If serving it cold, therefore, pour the custard straight into a cold basin, stirring it from time to time as it cools. If serving it hot, cool slightly first by beating for a minute or two aside from the heat. If necessary

to *keep* it hot, use a bain-marie containing warm water.

4 If your luck is out and the custard curdles, try liquidizing it.

CUSTARD SAUCE 2

When made with custard powder, custard sauce can be creamy, fluffy and delicious, or thick, skin-covered and abhorrent, depending entirely on the cook.

■ Homogenized or long life milk makes extra creamy custard because with these milks the cream and milk are emulsified. Liquidizing (skin and all) when cold or nearly cold makes custard smooth and light – but it needs to be made slightly thicker, to allow for thinning.

■ If without a liquidizer, you can stop skin forming either by covering the hot custard straight away with a disc of foil, or by sprinkling the surface with sugar. (Either method prevents evaporation from the surface.)

FRUIT SAUCE

A fruit sauce to serve with ice cream or a light dessert should be made with very ripe fruit so that you can liquidize or sieve it easily to make a purée. Though the fruit needn't be perfect, it must, of course, be good.

■ If you're without a liquidizer, icing sugar dissolves more readily than caster or granulated, when you're making a sauce with something like fresh raspberries or strawberries. If you have a liquidizer, the sweetened purée will thicken slightly if you whizz it at high speed for 2–3 minutes.

■ Lemon juice perks up a fruit sauce. Cognac or kirsch, in addition, will pep it up even more.

FRUIT SYRUPS

Usually better when thickened with arrowroot than with cornflour. Arrowroot is both tasteless and clear – the correct glaze to show up the painstakingly arranged fruit in a flan, or the cherries in tartlets, etc.

■ 2 level teaspoons of arrowroot thicken ¼pt/125ml fruit syrup, the glaze being cooked the moment it thickens and clears. By contrast, cornflour must be cooked for several minutes after it has boiled if not to have a raw taste.

HARD SAUCES

Those such as rum, lemon, or strawberry butter give a fillip to certain sweets and many steamed puddings. They may have a similar or a contrasting flavour to whatever they are accompanying, but whichever it is, they make a pleasant change from the more conventional kinds of sauce most people serve.

■ Here are some ideas to start you off. Be imaginative and experiment with different combinations of butters and puddings:

Butter	Pudding
brandy	traditional with Christmas pudding and mince pies
chocolate	castle puddings, vanilla-flavoured plain sponge, chocolate, ginger
coffee	castle puddings, vanilla-flavoured plain sponge, chocolate, walnut
lemon	castle puddings, lemon sponge (canary), pancakes
orange	vanilla-flavoured plain sponge, marmalade, pineapple sponge.
raspberry	plain sponge, jam roly-poly, rice pudding
rum	baked apples, apple dumplings, grilled bananas, rich fruit pudding, mince pies, spiced jelly.
spice	fruit sponge, Christmas pudding (if you don't want a spirit), mince pies, apple (plate) pie, spotted dick.
strawberry	as raspberry.

■ These hard sauces are as good after freezing as before but they don't keep for ever, despite the sugar to preserve the butter. With a freezer it's worth making up this sort of quantity at a time, otherwise I'd make less:

Hard sauces (to serve about 8)

4oz/100g softish butter
4oz/100g sieved icing sugar, caster sugar or soft brown sugar, see tips, *4 below*
flavouring e.g.:
  brandy – 2 tablespoons or to taste
  chocolate – 2oz/50g melted plain dessert chocolate (added quickly, before it hardens, to the creamed butter and sugar)
  coffee – 2 teaspoons coffee essence, e.g. Camp
  lemon –⎤ zest of one large fruit and 1
  orange –⎦ tablespoon strained juice
  raspberry – 2 tablespoons fresh raspberry purée
  rum – 2 tablespoons or to taste
  spice – 1 level teaspoon (more to taste) ground mixed spice, preferably sieved with the sugar
  strawberry – 2 tablespoons fresh strawberry purée

Method

1 Cream the butter until soft, then gradually add about three quarters of the sugar, beating until soft as whipped cream.
2 Beat in flavouring: if a liquid, add a little at a time and blend in each addition thoroughly before adding any more.
3 Add and beat in remaining sugar.
4 Pile up in a dish and leave to harden, or make it into 'pats', pipe in stars, or chill and cut into blocks or shapes, using a cutter dipped in boiling water.

■ And here are just a few tips:

1 In order to harden, these sauces *must* be made in advance – so there's no last minute rush as with a sauce.
2 The fruit flavoured butters taste best when made with saltless butter.
3 If the butter is fairly soft, it's much

easier to cream it with the sugar. If not then beaten until soft as whipped cream, the mixture won't accept and blend with a liquid flavouring, which anyway must be added gradually for the same reason.
4 Choice of sugar depends on whether you like a smooth or gritty texture, or the flavour of brown sugar. As a general rule, I find icing sugar best.
5 Zest or *very* finely grated rind of a citrus fruit is much better than more coarsely grated rind. Zest has no bitter pith, just lovely flavouring oils.

JAM SAUCE

More economical if you simmer ¼pt/125ml fruit juice or water for a few minutes with 3 large tablespoons of jam, and then thicken this with 2 level teaspoons of arrowroot or cornflour, slaked and added in the usual way. A few drops of lemon juice, added at the last moment, counteract the sweetness.

SABAYON

This is a lovely sauce to serve with such things as fresh fruit salad, apple charlotte, Christmas or a steamed sponge pudding.

■ There are recipes for using it warm or cold, depending on what you're serving it with. To serve it warm, use your ordinary recipe for sabayon (*zabaglione*, page 301). One way of using the same recipe cold is to add an extra yolk – say 4 yolks instead of 3 – beating the sabayon frequently (over ice) as it cools. If just left to cool, the wine separates out.

SAUCE DIPLOMATE

An easy, absolutely delicious, economical and versatile sauce. Light in texture and not too rich, you can serve or use it with lots of dishes, e.g.:
As an accompaniment, say with fruit salad, jam tart, fruit pies or flans, jellies.
As a base for other flavours, e.g. to mix with fruit purée for a not-so-rich fool;

with lemon curd stirred into it as a flan filling.

As a light filling in meringues, choux pastry buns, vanilla slices, brandy snaps.

As a topping for trifles, compôtes, mousses, etc.

In case you haven't got this recipe, let me give it to you – to serve 6:

½oz/15g custard powder
½oz/15g granulated sugar
¼pt/150ml milk
¼pt/150ml double cream
1 rounded teaspoon vanilla sugar (or use icing sugar and a few drops of vanilla essence)

Method, briefly:

1 Make a custard in the usual way with the custard powder, sugar and milk. Pour into a basin and leave to go quite cold.

2 Liquidize (skin and all) at maximum speed until smooth and creamy, then spoon into a mixing bowl.

3 Whip the cream with the vanilla sugar until it holds light peaks – about the same consistency as the liquidized custard – then fold into the custard, blending them completely.

■ Covered, it will keep perfectly in the refrigerator for several days.

■ To enrich or make less rich, step up or reduce slightly the quantity of cream.

WHITE SAUCE, SWEET

See *white sauce*, page 176, and make the following adjustments:

1 Omit pepper.

2 Add 1 dessertspoon of granulated sugar to ½pt/250ml sauce just before dishing.

3 Add the flavouring of your choice. Essences are volatile, evaporating easily if a sauce re-boils, so they too should be added at the last minute. Shredded or grated chocolate can be dissolved in the milk.

18
Breads, continental breads and scones

GENERAL INFORMATION

Bread, rolls and scones you make yourself are totally different from anything you can buy, once you've learnt the ropes.

■ Two essential skills are knowing how to knead effectively and knowing the correct consistency of a dough, particularly a bread and an oven-scone dough. Bread isn't time-consuming – it's just that the minutes you do spend on it are spread out over a long period. If you have a home to look after, it shouldn't be too difficult to fit this kind of baking into your daily routine now and then, though it's bound to be more complicated for anyone who has to keep one eye on the clock: a mother continually ferrying children to and from school, for instance.

■ Most homemade bread keeps better and longer than bought, and if you have a freezer, it's almost as easy to make up a large amount of flour as a small. Apart from crusty loaves, which tend to part company with their crust, most breads freeze excellently. So do oven scones, if while still frozen you can pop them into a slow oven (page 313) to thaw quickly.

BREAD

Bread is almost a miracle: given just a morsel of yeast, a bag of flour with some salt and water changes into golden crusty loaves.

Ingredients

Strong flour (see page 97) is best for white bread. Although you can make it with plain household flour, only strong flour

will produce the perfect loaf with a crisp crust, a fine texture and a good structure. A dough made with strong flour will absorb slightly more liquid than one made with plain because the former contains more gluten. Such a dough also requires rather longer kneading to reach the same condition.

Yeast See page 130.

Vitamin C (ascorbic acid) tablets One of these to up to 3lb/1.5kg flour, crushed and stirred in with the liquid, strengthens the flour protein (gluten) and gives greater gas retention properties, thus speeding up the raising of a dough.

■ Some of the easy-blend yeasts now include ascorbic acid among their ingredients so, if using one of these, look on the packet before adding more.

Salt Besides giving flavour, it plays an important part in a bread dough: too little makes a dough sticky and more difficult to manipulate; too much inhibits the growth of the yeast and delays fermentation – so a dough then takes longer to rise. Use 2 level teaspoons of salt per 1lb/500g flour.

Fat Not a basic ingredient of bread but if even just a very small quantity is used, bread has a better flavour, a lighter texture and will keep fresh longer. Depending on the kind of bread you are making, the fat called for may be lard (I like to use a soft one because it is easily rubbed in), butter or margarine, or even a mixture of lard and butter or margarine. (A white cooking fat gives inferior results to lard.)

■ Unless using a dried, easy-blend yeast (see page 131), there is usually no need to rub the fat in: just cut it up into smallish pieces in the flour with a knife and it gets blended into the dough during kneading.

■ A higher proportion of fat to flour is used to make a bun dough: buns are soft, quite a different end result from bread.

The liquid Generally lukewarm. When using water, the ideal mixture is two-thirds cold, one-third boiling which gives a temperature warm enough for yeast to grow, but not hot enough to kill it. If leaving a dough to rise overnight, use cold liquid and put the dough in a cold place to continue its rising next day (when put in a warm place). (Depending upon how cold the dough is, it may take longer than you expect to warm up and rise.)

■ Milk, or a mixture of milk and water are used to make a milk bread or bap type of dough respectively. Milk gives bread a soft, golden crust – shiny too if you glaze it with egg yolk – and a soft crumb, whereas bread made with water has a crisp crust and a less nice texture. An excess of either liquid can give a poor crumb structure (close and heavy) and, to white bread, a grey colour.

■ In a rich dough containing eggs, these take the place of some of the liquid as, sometimes, may melted fat.

■ It is best to take your courage in both hands and add the liquid in one fell swoop to the flour. If you make the dough a bit too wet, it's easy to add a little extra flour, but if you hold back some of the liquid and make a tight (stiff) dough, you cannot then add more liquid, because the outer surfaces of the dough simply become a paste.

■ The consistency of the dough may be the making or marring of bread, because if too tight, it can't expand during fermentation and will make a close-textured, heavy loaf. The dough should be soft without being sticky, leaving the bowl and your fingers clean by the time kneading is finished.

■ A few tips about breadmaking:

1 I find the kitchen sink a good working height for kneading dough in its mixing bowl. Much depends on one's height.

2 The dough must be properly kneaded, whether by hand or with a dough hook, for bread to be a good texture. Kneading strengthens the dough, and spreads the yeast evenly through it: carry on until it looks smooth and slightly shiny, and feels firm and elastic. Allow 10 minutes for this, even if you're good at kneading. The more a dough is kneaded, the better the loaf. (By machine, 3 minutes is usually enough, but follow the manufacturer's directions.)

3 Dough rises perfectly in its bowl if enclosed in a huge polythene bag, to keep it soft and moist. These are ideal greenhouse conditions for fermentation, and much more effective than the old damp tea-towel idea. If you haven't got a bag large enough to enclose the bowl, put the dough straight into a smaller bag – oiled and loosely tied, to allow room for it to rise. (If the bag isn't oiled, the dough will stick to it, or if the dough isn't covered, to exlude air, a crusty skin will form on top.)

4 Make the first rising fit in with you, whether you're cooking, doing housework or want to sleep. It's immaterial how much the dough rises at this stage, providing the bowl is big enough, because the next stage is 'knocking back' – unless you're using the quick method, with just one rising. When fully risen a dough should, however, be at least doubled in size, swollen and shapeless in appearance and springy to the touch.

5 A warm dough will rise perfectly in a warm kitchen, but should you want to speed things up:

a Slightly increase the proportion of yeast to flour, e.g. use 1½oz/40g yeast to 3lb/1.5kg instead of 1oz/25g.

b Stand the polythene-covered bowl in 2–3in/5–8cm of water as hot as your hand can bear – say in your washing-up bowl. (Avoid raising dough in a metal bowl because the heat of the water would penetrate it and kill the yeast.)

6 Unless a risen dough is sticky, which it shouldn't be, avoid using any extra flour on the table when kneading it: it changes

a dough's character, making it difficult to manipulate. This second kneading, known as 'knocking back', is to give the bread a good even texture, and to knock out any air bubbles which would burst and leave holes in the baked bread.

7 If you brush bread tins with melted lard or a white cooking fat, which are *pure* fats, the bread won't stick to the tins. Using one of these, unless you're making bread for a competition – when a judge with an eagle eye might spot traces of grease on the corners of a loaf (acquired from an almost imperceptible accumulation of fat down the corners of the tin) – there is in fact then no need after every baking even to wash the tins. (Oil is less good because it tends to leave a sticky film on the tins.)

■ If the tins and/or baking sheets are warmed – never actually hot of course – proving will be quicker.

8 To prevent a proving dough, in bread tins, sticking to the polythene bag in which they're enclosed, brush the top of each loaf with melted lard or cooking fat when you put the dough into the tins.

The oven This must be very hot, at least initially, to kill the yeast and so stop the bread rising. I like to cook mine at gas 8, 450°F/230°C all the time, but Allinson advise turning the oven to its highest setting then, when heated, put in the loaves and turn it down immediately to the above temperatures. Put bread near the top, to start with anyway (unless a fan-assisted oven), but make sure to leave room for the bread to rise.

■ I also like to cover my loaves lightly after the first 10 – 15 minutes with a strip of foil, to prevent over-browning.

■ If feasible, give bread the oven to itself. If you have to adapt the heat to suit other foods or work out a jigsaw to fit them in, bread is seldom so successful.

■ To make especially crusty loaves, create steam by putting a roasting tin of boiling water on the floor of the oven. (The reason *why* the crust is so different from the crumb is because the moisture is dried out of the surfaces of the dough by the heat.)

■ Cool bread on a wire cake tray. If left in its tins, the crust will be tough and the crumb soggy, caused by trapped steam.

BREAD, BROWN

Made with 100 per cent stoneground wholemeal or wholewheat flour it is, healthwise, the best of all breads, see page 97. Though many people use brown flour entirely, the bread isn't quite as solid when a little of it is replaced with some white flour; say one-sixth or one-eighth of the total. With a little lard rubbed in, it's lighter still.

■ See also *bread*, page 307.

BREAD, GARLIC

Gives a meal character, whether a plate of homely soup, a light lunch, a buffet supper or a barbecue.

■ I prefer to use a Vienna loaf or milk twist, because the inside stays soft, while the outside goes beautifully crisp, without becoming as crusty as a French stick.
■ When cutting the loaf diagonally into thick slices, beware of cutting through the bottom crust, because this holds the loaf together after you've buttered both sides of each slice, and pressed the loaf back into shape again.
■ You'll need 1 clove of crushed garlic mixed with about 3oz/75g butter, the butter being easier to spread if first creamed with a dessertspoon of hot water.
■ Bake the foil-wrapped loaf for 15–20 minutes in a hot oven, gas 7, 425°F/220°C. If not served hot, preferably in a folded napkin to *keep* it hot, garlic bread is as unpleasant as it is indigestible.

BREAD, MILK

Is just a rich form of white bread. Where ordinary bread is made with water and very little fat (if any), milk bread is made with milk and quite a lot of fat. In addition, some recipes call for egg and the

Ingredients	Brief comments
1lb/450g strong white flour	
1 rounded teaspoon salt	mix together
1 level teaspoon granulated sugar	
2 oz/50g butter or margarine	rub into above dry ingredients
½oz/15g fresh, ¼oz/7g active (drum) dried, or 1 sachet dried easy-blend, yeast	see *yeast*, page 130
1 vitamin C tablet	see page 307, especially if using easy-blend yeast
about 9 fl oz/275ml tepid milk	enough to make a soft but not sticky dough
egg glaze	see page 66 if necessary
poppy or sesame seed	to decorate

making of a slightly sticky dough which, because it's too soft to knead, has to be beaten.

■ I use the quantities in the table above to make 16 – 24 dinner rolls, 2 milk twists or 1 large loaf:

■ A milk bread dough containing fruit, egg and extra sugar requires a little extra yeast because these slow down fermentation: use up to half as much again. (The greater proportion of these ingredients, the slower the fermentation.)

■ See also *bread*, page 307.

Baps These are made with a similar dough, but use 50/50 milk and water instead of all milk. The quantities above will make 12.

Milk twists Made with a milk bread dough. Providing you can plait – and, of course, make a good dough – a milk twist is plain sailing, despite looking complicated. Here's the method, from the stage when the dough has risen and been knocked back:

1 Form the dough into a huge sausage, then roll it out flat, smooth side uppermost, with a rolling pin, see fig. 1.

2 Cut *almost* from end to end into three equal strips, see fig. 2.

3 Open out the strips (fig. 3), plait them fairly tightly and press the ends together where they meet, see fig. 4. Lay bread on a greased baking sheet.

4 Cover with a clean tea-towel, prove (put to rise) and when about doubled in size, glaze with egg and sprinkle top lightly with poppy seed, to decorate.

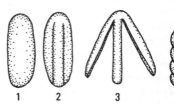

1   2   3   4

5 Bake near the top of a preheated hot oven, gas 7, 425°F/220°C for 10 minutes to kill the yeast, then reduce heat to gas 5, 375°F/190°C until golden all over and hollow-sounding when tapped underneath – about 25 – 30 minutes altogether. If getting too brown, cover bread with foil for the last few minutes.

6 Cool on a wire cake tray.

Rolls, bridge Also made with a milk bread dough, these are small elongated dinner rolls with a soft crust. ½lb/225g flour makes 16.

■ Some tips about their making:

1 Lay the cigar-shaped pieces of dough a finger's width apart from each other on a greased baking sheet. When risen, they'll join up into a strip.

2 When baked, instead of putting the rolls on a cake cooling tray, wrap and leave them in a slightly damp tea-towel for the first few minutes. The trapped steam makes them soft.

3 To fill quickly, leave them in a strip: make one operation each of splitting, buttering and filling, then separate them.

Rolls, dinner Homemade dinner rolls please almost everyone. See above for quantities.

■ The professionals shape dinner rolls two at a time in a matter of seconds, one under the lightly floured palm of each hand, on an unfloured board. This is a knack, needing a circular movement of each hand, not to mention just the right amount of pressure. It's worth asking someone who knows how, to show you.

■ For a perfect finish, sprinkle the glazed rolls lightly with poppy seed just before baking.

BREAD, WHITE

Quantities I like, to make 3 large loaves (or, of course, other loaves and/or bread buns) are:

Ingredients	Brief comments
1 bag/1.5kg strong white flour	use the whole bag, whether in metric or imperial weights
3 rounded teaspoons salt	
1 rounded teaspoon granulated sugar	mix together
good oz/30g lard	soft lard is the most easily rubbed in
1oz/25g fresh, ½oz/15g active (drum) dried, or 2 sachets dried, easy-blend yeast	see *yeast*, page 130
1 vitamin C tablet	see page 307
1¼pt+1 tablespoon/750ml tepid water	to make a firmish dough

TEA-BREADS

Made with plain flour and a raising agent, or with self-raising flour (never yeast), these are mostly quick and easy to make, good to eat, and freeze well. The fat is quickly incorporated because it is either rubbed in, or poured in melted. Bake these breads in loaf tins (page 47) rather than bread tins, which are deeper and less successful. They should be lined with greased greaseproof paper, otherwise the bread may stick – due to the sometimes high sugar content and sweet dried fruits.

■ Tea-breads are served sliced and are nicest generously buttered: excellent for picnics as well as for tea.
■ Varieties include soda bread, banana, date and walnut (*my* favourite), orange-nut, honey, malt.

BRIOCHE

One of the most delicious of all yeast doughs – light, soft and eye-catching when baked – it is used in lots of different ways: as a sweet, rich bread; to make various sweet or savoury dishes, including mouth-watering doughnuts.

■ These rolls, served often in France for breakfast (I, too, love to serve them then), are made from a dough rich with eggs and butter: almost a cross between cake and bread. Made into bread, it is baked in a fluted brioche mould (page 33), in smaller ones for rolls. Eaten warm or cold, the fat and eggs in it keep it fresh and moist longer than ordinary bread, although small ones dry out more quickly so must be served fresh.

A few tips:

1 If you like eating and enjoy making brioches, it's worth investing in the proper tins. If without, use a loaf tin rather than a deeper bread tin; use deep bun tins for individual rolls.

2 If making double quantities of this dough, be sure to double up on the yeast as well: the extra fat and eggs delay fermentation.

3 Bowl and fingers should all be clean when kneading is completed – no hint of stickiness.

4 Brioches freeze well: thaw at room temperature, then heat for 10 minutes in a slowish oven just before serving – preferably warm.

BUNWASH

A syrupy glaze brushed over certain buns and breads after baking. Sometimes two coats are needed, to give a good glaze.

■ It's very simple: dissolve 2oz/50g granulated sugar in 4 tablespoons of water (or sometimes 2 milk and 2 water) and simmer for 2 minutes.

■ Be sure to have both the glaze and whatever you're coating very hot, to give a really shiny finish.

CROISSANT

Comes from the French word for crescent. Croissants are said to have originated in Budapest in 1686. In besieging the city, the Turks had dug underground passages in an attempt to reach the centre of the town. Budapest bakers working during the night heard the noise, raised the alarm, and the Turks were repulsed. As a reward, the bakers were granted the privilege of making a special pastry in the form of a crescent; the emblem of the Ottoman flag.

■ Croissants need butter, for its flavour, and strong flour for its extra gluten. Only these will make the real thing – the traditional thin layers of characteristically flavoured pastry that won't collapse in the oven. They aren't worth making otherwise.

■ Croissants are a combination of a pastry and a yeast dough. This explains why the dough is kept cool during the early stages, is relaxed and chilled between rollings, but is finally left to rise at room temperature. If, however, proved in too warm a place, such as you might choose for a bread dough, the butter will melt.

■ It is generally quicker and easier in the long run to roll the pastry to a given-sized square or rectangle, than to roll it at random, and then cut it vaguely into squares: well-shaped croissants start as well-shaped triangles, but you *may* need to elongate the base of each slightly, to make a good crescent.

■ A hot oven is essential, to kill the yeast, and to prevent the butter melting and running out before the starch grains in the flour can burst and absorb it.

Canned croissants What could be easier? Better than most bought, all you have to do is open out the pastry, then roll, glaze, bake and eat the croissants!

DANISH PASTRIES

Aren't exactly a slimming cure but are worth every minute of the time they take to make. Serve them for elevenses, a buffet lunch, a teenage buffet supper, or with coffee as a light lunch.

■ A cross between a yeast mixture and puff pastry, everything must be kept cold because of the high proportion of butter. In fact once you're past the first stage, the dough is treated as puff pastry.

■ The dough is soft, like a scone dough, but is rolled and relaxed as pastry, keeping it square at the corners, and avoiding rolling and sealing it at the ends.

■ After making the dough into various shapes, and enriching them with almond paste etc., treat again as a yeast mixture and leave to rise at room temperature until puffy. If in *too* warm a place though, the butter will melt and spoil their texture.

■ Like yeast mixtures and any rich pastry, they need a preheated hot oven, gas 7, 425°F/220°C. Bake for about 10–15 minutes until golden and crisp, yet at the same time soft!

GRIDDLE CAKE

The Scottish name for a drop scone. See page 314.

OATCAKES

More tricky to make than bread or scones because oatmeal and water, unlike flour and water, don't form a paste and make an elastic dough. This is because oats, unlike wheat, contain no gluten.

■ Here are a few tips:

1 *The ingredients*
a Oatmeal Fine oatmeal cooks more quickly than medium or coarse, so is the most suitable when making oatcakes on a girdle. The coarser grains are fine for oven-baked oatcakes which have both top and bottom heat simultaneously.
b Salt 1 level teaspoon per 8oz/225g oatmeal – as important to oatcakes as to porridge.
c Fat Bacon fat, lard or dripping are traditional because in the past these were the fats always available. One can also make oatcakes with butter, margarine or white cooking fat. To make thin oatcakes, the fat is added melted and hot, with very hot water, to help the oatmeal swell and bind and make the dough pliable enough to roll out thinly. To make thick oatcakes, the fat can equally well be rubbed in.
d Bicarbonate of soda has an advantage over baking powder: it improves the brown colour of the oatcakes.
2 You need a softish dough because if too dry, it will crumble and be difficult to roll out: to make rolling easy, have plenty of oatmeal on your board and sprinkle more on top of the dough while kneading it, or if it sticks to the rolling pin. (You can do with oatcakes things you *can't* do when rolling pastry.)
3 Quick kneading and handling are essential when using hot melted fat and hot water because once the dough cools it is difficult to manipulate and more easily falls apart.
4 For cooking in the traditional way, on one side only on a greased girdle, the dough must be rolled very thinly. If too thick, the oatcakes won't cook properly, neither will they curl up at the corners. In cottage style, the second side was toasted in front of the fire but you can equally well finish them off in the oven.

ROLLS, ETC., REHEATED

Rolls, baps, buns, scones, tea-cakes, etc. can be reheated and made almost as good as fresh ones, direct from freezer to oven: put them on a baking sheet in a slow oven, gas 2, 300°F/150°C for about 10 minutes if preheated, otherwise nearer 20 minutes. Cool on a wire cake tray.

SANDWICHES

These earned their name from the fourth Earl of Sandwich. The story goes that he would gamble for days on end, without even stopping for a meal. In order not to interrupt play, he had his meat served to him between two pieces of bread.

■ Generously buttered sandwiches, made preferably with thinly sliced, crustless new bread, have many advantages over meanly buttered: quite apart from their flavour, they will keep soft longer, won't absorb moisture from the filling, and will dry out less if you freeze them. If you have many to make, it's easier to spread the butter – *and* it goes further – if you first beat a little hot water with it. Allow 1 dessertspoon of water to 4oz/100g butter.
■ Savoury sandwiches are usually made of brown bread and are served on a plain doyley, to distinguish them from sweet which are mostly made of white bread and are served on a fancy doyley.
■ Frozen sandwiches, wrapped first in heavy-duty foil and then in a polythene bag, will keep best if you put a crust or

slice of plain bread at the end of each pile.

SCONES, DROP

Always popular but, alas, seldom well made. They should be light as a feather, generously buttered and only hours old. The fresher the better.

■ If it's because you haven't got a good recipe that you don't make them (or perhaps aren't very successful when you do) here's a lovely one, to make about 12 scones.

3oz/75g plain flour
1 level teaspoon cream of tartar
½ level teaspoon bicarbonate of soda
good pinch of salt
1 level tablespoon granulated sugar
1 large egg
about 3 tablespoons (60 ml) milk

Method

1 Sieve the flour, cream of tartar, bicarbonate of soda and salt into a basin. Add sugar.
2 Mix to a thick batter with the lightly mixed egg and the milk, see below under *hows and whys*, 1.
3 Cook spoonfuls of the mixture until golden on both sides on a well greased hot girdle over moderate heat, turning them over with a pallet knife when biggish bubbles begin to form over the surface.
4 Put the scones straight from the girdle into the folds of a clean tea-towel on a wire cake tray. Leave there to cool.

The hows and whys

1 The correct consistency of the batter is essential. It should be thick enough for a trail dropped from the spoon gradually to disappear. If too thin, the scones won't rise properly; if too thick, there'll be an uncooked layer in the centre.

■ If you leave the batter for a while before cooking the scones, it will thicken. In that event, add a little extra milk before you do cook them, to correct the consistency.

2 I usually start heating the girdle when collecting the ingredients, then it's about the right heat when I'm ready for it. If it's too hot, the scones will be hard and too dark a brown. If too cool, they'll be leathery.

■ When in doubt, cook one scone to test.

3 It's better not to cook too many scones at a time. Even if you've got the knack of turning them – the pallet knife flat underneath, and a quick flick of your wrist – one's aim isn't always perfect. The fuller the girdle, the more difficult to turn each without spoiling another.
4 Cooling drop scones in a cloth is essential to their texture. This traps the steam, keeping them soft and springy.
5 Drop scones don't freeze well: their light texture doesn't recover.

SCONES, GIRDLE

These can be made from the same mixture as oven scones, but with a slightly stiffer dough. As they cook with only bottom heat, roll them to only half the thickness. If too thick, they'll burn outside before being cooked inside. Use a preheated girdle over lowish heat.

SCONES, OVEN

While oven scones aren't difficult to make, it's not often one meets the best because so many people seem to slip up over one or more of these things:

1 *By using the wrong flour* Self-raising flour makes heavy, poor scones because it doesn't contain enough raising agent. It's much better to use plain flour with cream of tartar and bicarbonate of soda. Do sieve the dry ingredients too, to trap air and to break up any tiny lumps of bicarbonate, which can't unite with the acid.
2 *The consistency of the dough* A scone dough is soft and moist, without being sticky – wetter than shortcrust pastry for instance.
3 *The thickness of the scones* They

should be *thick* – ½in/1.25cm. You should only get about 12 2in/5cm scones from ½lb/225g flour.

4 *The oven*, which needs to be pre-heated and very hot, gas 8, 450°F/230°C, to raise the scones fast, and to cook them until golden.

■ The cutter is a detail: a fluted one is normally used for sweet scones; plain for savoury, to avoid confusion. Dip it in flour and cut the scones without twisting it, to make them a perfect shape.

■ Just in case you aren't happy with your own recipe, these quantities make good scones:

½lb/225g plain flour
1 level teaspoon salt
1 level teaspoon cream of tartar
½ level teaspoon bicarbonate of soda
2 level tablespoons granulated sugar
2oz/50g margarine (lard gives no flavour and quite a different texture)
5–5½ tbsps/100–110ml milk
egg, to glaze (for perfection)

■ You can vary this mixture in all sorts of ways, like this:

Cheese scones Lovely hot. Omit the sugar and, after rubbing the fat into the flour, mix in 2oz/50g finely grated cheese. Use water instead of milk – and rather more of it. (As cheese is made from milk, these scones are heavy if you use milk also to mix them.)

Fruit scones Add 1–2oz/25–50g currants and/or sultanas with the sugar.

Ginger scones Heavenly fried, and served hot. Sieve 2 level teaspoons ground ginger with the dry ingredients. Roll the dough thin (¼in, or just over 0.5cm) and fry over lowish heat in hot lard for a few minutes on each side. Split, butter, sprinkle with caster sugar and eat at once.

Spice scones Sieve 2 level teaspoons of ground mixed spice with the dry ingredients, and add 1–2oz/25–50g sultanas with the sugar.

Syrup scones Use 1 level teaspoon of bicarbonate of soda instead of ½ level teaspoon, and add 1 dessertspoon of warmed golden syrup to the milk. (These are good hot as well as cold.)

Wholemeal scones Lovely for breakfast with butter, marmalade and clotted cream – and not out of the question for anyone with a freezer. Use three-quarters brown flour, a quarter white, and omit the sugar.

19
Cakes

GENERAL INFORMATION

An accurate oven temperature (see *oven thermostats*, page 19) and the right choice of ingredients probably affect cakes as much as, if not more than, most other things. For consistently perfect results, one also needs to weigh rather than guess because whether a cake is light or heavy, depends upon the right balance of dry and liquid ingredients, as well as upon skill in making.

■ To know more about the chief ingredients, see chapter 3, but here briefly are the main points.

Ingredients
Eggs which are new-laid and at room temperature make the lightest, biggest and best cakes, because the fresher they are, the more air they will trap when beaten, creamed or whisked (see also pages 142 and 143).

Butter, because of its lovely flavour, is the ideal fat for most cakes, those made with it usually keeping fresh longer as well. If I could always afford it, then I would generally use butter. Butter is difficult to cream properly if too cold so, for creamed mixtures, it pays to think ahead and ensure it is soft – but not oily. If soft enough, one can even use butter as a soft margarine to make an all-in-one mixture, see page 318.

Margarine creams well (see page 107), particularly the soft brands with which it takes only two or three minutes to make an all-in-one mixture – from start to oven. See also *all-in-one mixtures*, page 318.

White flour is always sieved, to entangle air, however fine the flour. Sieving also ensures that dry ingredients are completely blended, and that there are no lumps in anything. Generally speaking, plain household flour is much better than self-raising. It can be used for almost anything and everything, with a given amount of any raising agent; or with none, when air is the raising agent. Self-raising flour on the other hand has a stable quantity of one type of raising agent, whether a recipe calls for it, or not.

Sugar is more important than some may realize. Caster is best for creamed mixtures because, being so fine, it blends perfectly with butter. Granulated is good for rubbed-in mixtures, or when sugar is to be melted, when its coarser crystals don't matter.

Salt figures in many recipes. Without it, many cakes would be entirely flavourless. It also makes the gluten in the flour more elastic, so helping a mixture to rise well. (I usually use 1 rounded teaspoon to 1lb/500g flour.)

■ A *plain* or *rich* cake is determined by the proportion of fat and sugar to flour, not by a high or low proportion of dried fruit, etc. A plain cake has half, or less than half, fat to flour; while a rich cake has half, or more than half fat to flour. It's because plain cakes contain less fat that they go dry more quickly, and don't keep as well as rich.

■ *Sponge cake* (e.g. Swiss roll) belongs to a separate group because, technically, it contains no fat, see page 325 (not to be confused with a Victoria sandwich cake page 324).

■ The way in which the fat and sugar are incorporated with the flour usually distinguishes the type of cake: the fat is generally rubbed into the flour for plain cakes, or creamed with the sugar for rich. *Melted fat and sugar* are added to the flour for the gingerbread family.

Preparation It's usually wisest to prepare the cake tin, arrange the oven shelves as needed and turn the oven on before you start a cake. A pre-heated oven is generally essential because some raising agents begin to act as soon as moisture is added. In addition, air, beaten into, say, a sponge mixture, will be lost if the cake isn't cooked immediately. Once in a hot oven, the trapped air will expand and the egg will coagulate and hold the air.

■ As a general rule, small cakes are cooked at the top (or hottest part) of a hot oven, large cakes lower down, in a cooler oven. Some cakes, particularly fruit cakes, are cooked in falling heat, the oven temperature gradually lowered.

■ The choice of tin will often affect results. For instance, a cake cooked in a shallow tin such as a sandwich or moule à manqué tin, usually has a better texture than the same mixture in a deep tin, because the heat penetrates the mixture faster.

■ To be sure a cake won't stick to its tin, I like best to brush it with a pure fat such as melted lard or white cooking fat before dusting it out with flour. If you use butter or margarine, the salt in these tends to make a baked cake stick. For cakes requiring long cooking or with a high fat and/or sugar content, the tin ought to be lined, see *Lining a cake tin*, page 69.

When cooked Most cakes will shrink slightly from the sides of the tin when cooked. In addition, creamed mixtures will spring back if you press the top lightly with your finger tips. The centre is always the last place to set.

■ A cake tends to stick, and sometimes even to break, if you turn it out of the tin as soon as it's cooked. Given 2 or 3

minutes – or up to 5 minutes for a rich cake – to contract and firm up, there isn't the same risk. See also *fruit cakes*.

■ Certain cakes, such as shortbread, flapjacks and those with a high proportion of fruit like a wedding or Christmas cake, are not cooled on a cake cooling tray as this spoils such textures: most other cakes, however, must be, because trapped steam makes them heavy.

■ To turn a cake out of a loose-bottomed tin without having a burning-hot bracelet round your wrist, use something like a storage jar or a large can of fruit: stand it on a surface you can't damage, rest the cake tin on top and slide the tin off.

Flavourings and colourings These require careful use. If you can add a flavouring essence with a liquid, it blends more evenly than if added by itself.

■ As colourings last for years, it's worth buying the best. Coloured cakes such as Battenburg or Neapolitan tend to lighten rather than darken when baked, but for most purposes, use colourings sparingly. See also page 97.

Creamed mixtures These may curdle if the butter and sugar aren't beaten together until light and fluffy, if the eggs are very cold when added to the creamed fat and sugar, or if they're added too fast. Curdling is due to the fat, cooled by the cold egg liquid, separating out from the sugar and eggs – and, of course, a curdled mixture tends to make a heavy cake because it doesn't hold as much air. You can sometimes put it right by beating in a tablespoon of the sieved flour, which will absorb the excessive moisture in the eggs or fat. Another way to restore the creamy consistency may be to warm the bowl in warm water. Ideally, the eggs should be about the same temperature as the creamed fat and sugar, so if you *do* have to take them direct from the refrigerator or from a cold larder, whisk them for a minute or two in a warmed basin, standing it in a bowl of fairly hot water.

■ Although electric mixer instructions may tell you to add an egg whole, it still pays to whisk it first in order to trap more air.

■ Fold the flour and other dry ingredients into creamed mixtures with a metal rather than a wooden spoon, to make a beautifully light cake. See *folding*, page 62.

■ Make a shallow hollow in the middle of the mixture to prevent a large cake 'peaking' there. If, despite this, a cake does rise to a peak, it's generally because the oven was a bit too hot, or because you had the cake too high up in it. Creamed mixtures are cooked at a slightly lower temperature than rubbed-in mixtures.

All-in-one mixtures This modern version of a creamed mixture brings cake-making within the scope of all of us, even if you detest cooking! All ingredients should if possible be at room temperature – except a sunflower margarine, as this type is particularly soft and may oil (especially with an electric mixer) unless chilled. Here, in case you would like it, is the recipe; or you might like to use the weight of the eggs in fat, sugar and flour plus the other ingredients as given:

> 4oz/100g self-raising flour
> 1 level teaspoon baking powder
> ½ level teaspoon salt
> 4oz/100g soft margarine
> 4oz/100g sugar, preferably caster – but one can also use granulated or soft brown for some cakes
> 2 eggs
> flavouring, e.g. finely grated rind of ½–1 lemon or orange; 1 tablespoon coffee essence; 3 level tablespoons cocoa powder made into a soft paste with 2½–3 tablespoons boiling water and allowed to go cold

Method

1 Sift together the flour, baking powder and salt. (You need baking powder as well as self-raising flour to get a good rise.) Beat all the ingredients together for a minute or two in a mixing bowl until light, fluffy and completely blended.

2 Turn into a prepared cake tin (or 2 tins to make a sandwich cake), and bake in a slow/moderate oven, gas 3, 325°F/165°C, for approximately 30–35 minutes.

■ For a pudding, turn into a greased basin and steam for 1¾–2 hours, or until firm; only 1–1¼ hours for half quantities.

Serving and storing cakes

1 If you want to ice a cake which has risen too much in the middle, level it off, turn upside down and ice the bottom.

2 Small cakes such as Genoese fancies, cherry tartlets or butterfly cakes look more professional when served in white or coloured paper cake cases, and even the simplest cake looks more attractive on a fancy doyley, on a plate large enough to frame it.

3 Store cakes in separate airtight containers or, if nothing else, on a plate covered by a mixing bowl. At all costs avoid mixing cake and biscuits: the biscuits will absorb moisture from the cake and will be soft almost before you can say Jack Robinson.

4 Many cakes, but not all, store well in a freezer. As water in an icing is readily absorbed into the cake, especially if the cake isn't first glazed (see page 329), it is nearly always better, because of this and for appearance, to ice cakes after freezing. Biscuit-based cakes go soft.

BATTENBURG CAKE

Simply a variation of Genoese pastry surrounded by almond paste. It needs a special tin, with a divider, so that the coloured half of the mixture can't spread into, and mix with the other, uncoloured half.

BRANDY SNAPS

So called because, for the real thing, the cream is flavoured with brandy.

■ The ingredients need precise weighing because, if the mixture is the tiniest bit too stiff, it doesn't spread properly when baked; or if too soft, the snaps are so thin that they break easily when shaped. The recipe I like uses 1oz/25g each of butter, sugar and flour, 2oz/50g golden syrup, ½ level teaspoon ground ginger and a pinch of cream of tartar. (The cream of tartar makes the brandy snaps set harder, and keeps them crisp longer.)

■ It's better not to try and bake more than four at a time, on a well-greased baking sheet. They cool so quickly when cooked that it's difficult to manipulate more before they harden, almost in a matter of seconds.

■ If without cream cornet moulds, make pipe-shaped snaps instead, wrapping them round the greased handle of a thick wooden spoon. Lard is the best fat to grease cornets or spoon.

■ Put brandy snaps in an airtight container the moment they cool, unless you intend to fill and eat them right away. They soon go soft in the atmosphere, and should be eaten the same day unless sealed in a small tin.

■ Brandy snaps are only tip-top when crisp enough to earn their name, and to contrast with the soft cream inside, so fill at the last minute. It's easiest to pipe in the cream – ¼pt/150ml for 12 snaps, as above.

BUTTERFLY CAKES

One of the simplest examples of either a creamed or an all-in-one mixture, (see pages 317 and 318). When the weight of an egg is used in butter, sugar and flour with raising agent, you don't need any extra liquid. Using these proportions, cakes are lighter and stay fresh longer than when made with a larger quantity of flour, and milk in addition.

■ These little cakes, like queen cakes, are moister and have a soft outside when baked in paper cake cases – and much nicer I think than when baked direct in the bun tins, whether non-stick or otherwise.

■ To be feathery-light, cook them at the top (or hottest part) of a hot oven, gas 6, 400°F/205°C until golden and firm to the touch.

■ You can make all kinds of butterflies for a children's party, using the halved crest of each cake as the two wings, and with differently flavoured and coloured butter icings and decorations. See *butter icing*, page 329.

CHERRY CAKE

If the cherries are weighed down with syrup they can't *help* sinking: wash them in hot water, dry in a cloth, chop and then toss lightly in about a tablespoonful of the sieved, weighed flour.

COCONUT BUNS

Just a variety of rock cake, using desiccated coconut instead of the dried fruit and mixed peel. Allow 1½oz/40g of coconut to ½lb/225g flour.

COFFEE KISSES

The variety of rock cake (page 324) I like best – although it might be difficult to spot this dull base. Omit the dried fruit and mixed peel, replace the tablespoonful of milk with 3 dessertspoons of coffee essence, and roll the mixture into about 30 large marbles instead of piling it up in 12 heaps. Bake for 10–15 minutes in a moderate oven (cooler than for rock buns) until firm, light golden and a good brown colour underneath. Put together in pairs with coffee butter icing and top with coffee glacé icing.

ÉCLAIRS

Not as difficult and time-consuming to make as they may appear, the homemade variety kills any future appetite for bought éclairs. The important thing is to make good choux, see page 139.

■ Using a ½in/1.25cm plain pipe, be sure to press out with a pallet knife any pockets of air which may be trapped in the mixture in the piping bag, otherwise it's difficult to pipe the éclairs without the chain occasionally breaking.

■ Allow the choux to cool completely

before actually baking the éclairs, because they'll rise better if the mixture is cold.

■ If the choux is properly made and baked, the éclairs will be hollow. To make sure they're dried out inside, it pays to make a tiny slit in the side of each with the sharp point of a vegetable knife, after about 20 minutes cooking. If even after this the inside is still soggy, scoop it out carefully with the handle of a teaspoon, or it will spoil the éclair's texture.

■ It's usually quickest and neatest to *pipe* in the whipped cream, especially if you have many to fill. They're also easier to ice neatly if you tilt them lengthwise. Held like this over the icing basin, the chocolate glacé icing forms a straight strip down the middle, without dripping down the sides.

FLAPJACKS

One of the same group of cakes as gingerbread, where the fat is incorporated by melting it. The principal difference between them is that gingerbread is made with flour, flapjacks with porridge oats.

■Brown sugar gives flapjacks more flavour and a richer, darker colour than granulated, and butter or margarine give more flavour than lard or cooking fat.

■ Flapjacks aren't difficult to make as long as you just *warm* the fat, sugar and syrup. If overheated, the mixture becomes toffee-like.

■ Although these are not true flapjacks – because it's not traditional to replace half of the porridge oats with cornflakes – this recipe (making 16) is the best I've ever come across:

3oz/75g butter or margarine
3oz/75g soft brown sugar
2oz/50g golden syrup
2oz/50g porridge oats
2oz/50g cornflakes, fresh and crisp
good pinch of salt
1oz/25g chopped walnuts

Method

1 Melt the butter over low heat, stir in and dissolve the sugar and syrup, then mix in the porridge oats, cornflakes, salt and nuts (aside from the heat).

2 Spread evenly in a greased Yorkshire pudding tin (page 47) and bake at the top of a preheated slow/moderate oven, gas 3, 325°F/165°C for about 15–20 minutes or until a rich golden colour.

3 Cut into squares or fingers while very hot and leave in the tin to cool.

4 Divide up when cold and store at once in an airtight tin.

FRUIT CAKES

Fruit cakes with a high proportion of fat and sugar brown and burn more readily than plain mixtures. This explains why it pays to use a good quality tin and, when necessary, to line it with two or even three layers of greaseproof paper to come 2in/5cm above the top (see page 69). I'm afraid you can't skimp on your care either, because you can't turn a perfectly shaped cake out of a badly lined tin.

Wedding cake The original bride's cake was made from aromatic ingredients, crowned with an icing made from sweet sugar and bitter almonds, symbolizing the sweetness and pain in every marriage. When making a three-tier cake, if it's easier to make all the mixture at once, you can, if necessary, keep the two smaller uncooked cakes in a cold larder overnight, baking them the following day.

Fruit cakes in general Here are some tips about a few of the ingredients:

1 Use plain flour, with raising agent if required, for cakes with a high egg content. Self-raising flour contains too much raising agent, giving a cake a dry, crumbly texture. As the proportion of egg increases, the amount of raising agent decreases, so that in a very rich mixture such as a wedding cake, there may be no raising agent whatever.

2 Soft brown sugar is often used in a

fruit cake. Creamed with butter, it blends just as smoothly and well as caster sugar, and in addition gives a cake more flavour and a richer, darker colour.

3 Bicarbonate of soda used with vinegar may be the raising agent for a simple fruit cake. The bicarbonate helps to brown the cake, vinegar combining with it in the same way as does cream of tartar in scones, etc.

4 Ground almonds figure in many recipes. They help to keep a cake moist as well as giving flavour.

5 Brandy also makes a cake moist and gives flavour. In addition, it helps a cake to keep better and longer than it otherwise would.

■ To bake a Christmas or wedding cake containing a lot of dried fruit and requiring long cooking, protect it with newspaper: it's a bad conductor of heat and so reduces the penetration of heat to the cake. It also prevents a thick crust forming on the sides and bottom of a cake:

1 Tie several layers of newspaper round the outside of the tin.

2 Stand the cake on a thick pad of newspaper (or on a piece of thick card) on a baking sheet.

3 Rest a square of foil or thin card on top of the cake, to protect and keep the top soft as well.

4 Rich fruit cakes are usually baked in the coolest part of the oven, see page 317.

To test when cooked Fruit cakes are some of the most difficult to test because, with a paper-lined tin, it isn't easy to judge when a cake starts to shrink from the sides. The safest method is to stick a fine metal skewer down between the cake and the tin, to warm the skewer, then stick it into the centre of the cake. If the skewer comes out quite clean, the cake is cooked. If not, cook the cake for a further 10–15 minutes, then test again.

■ *To cool* a cake with a high proportion of fruit, leave it in its tin. This keeps the cake moist and helps to keep the crust soft – quite a different result from cooling the same cake on a wire cooling tray.

(The paper, which helps to keep a cake moist, should be left on until you want to ice or eat the cake.)

■ *To store*, wrap completely in foil and, if not too large for any of your tins, put in an airtight container as well.

■ See also *creamed mixtures*, page 317, and *royal icing*, page 334.

GÂTEAU

French for cake. Implies quite a different kind of cake in this country from such essentially British ones as say, gingerbread, cherry, madeira or fruit cake. Gâteaux here, and large gâteaux on the Continent, are usually huge featherweight sponges with soft rich fillings and delectable icings, *or* equally irresistible works of art with a sweet-pastry base. (See *Genoese pastry* (below), *French flan pastry* (page 137) and *crème au beurre fillings* (page 330).) These gâteaux are classics, bearing classic names such as gâteau moka aux amandes, caravelle, alcazar, St Honoré, usually according to their flavouring, filling and particular form of decoration.

■ A very large moule à manqué tin (page 47) is ideal for a sponge-based gâteau. Such a shape is easy to decorate artistically and will cut into a number of large servings, whether for a buffet lunch or supper, a dinner party, or for tea.

GENOESE PASTRY

The basic cake of the French cuisine. It is simply sponge cake – which technically is fatless – with butter added. Butter helps a sponge to keep better, giving it a moister and slightly closer texture which will crumble less when cut. This explains why Genoese is used in preference to a fatless sponge for gâteaux, petits fours and innumerable small fancy cakes collectively known as Genoese fancies.

■ One's choice of cake tin will depend on what one wants the Genoese for: a greased, lined Swiss roll tin for Genoese fancies, for instance, or something like a moule à manqué (greased, and the bottom lined) for a decorated cake or gâteau.

GENOESE COMMUNE

'Common' Genoese makes an excellent gâteau, and is also the sponge used for Genoese fancies and petits fours. It has a firmer texture than the richer Genoese Fine, so for these small cakes is easier to manipulate. Here is the recipe:

4oz/100g plain flour
pinch of salt
2oz/50g butter
4 large eggs, preferably new-laid
4oz/100g caster sugar

Method

1 Prepare tin: grease and line a Swiss roll tin, or grease and line the bottom of a moule à manqué (or other suitable) tin. Brush with melted lard and dust out with flour.

2 Sieve the flour and salt twice, then return them to strainer, ready to sieve a third time.

3 Melt the butter over minimum heat and set aside to cool.

4 Beat the eggs and sugar 'to the ribbon' (page 78) in a mixing bowl over very hot but not boiling water.

5 Beat for a further 2 or 3 minutes aside from the heat, to cool mixture.

6 Sift the flour all over the top of mixture, then very gently pour the cooled butter over this 'carpet' of flour. Using a tablespoon, fold and cut in the flour and butter together as quickly as possible, ensuring there are no pockets of flour either in the bowl of the spoon or at the bottom of the mixing bowl.

7 Pour at once into prepared tin, continuing to fold even while pouring, and quickly spread the mixture flat.

8 Bake a flat Genoese (in Swiss roll tin) at or near the top, or a moule à manqué tin in the middle of a preheated moderate/hot oven, gas 5, 375°F/190°C until golden and cooked. For cooking times, see tips, 6, below.

9 Turn out, remove paper and cool on a wire tray.

■ Some tips, in case you want them.

1 *The ingredients*
   a The *flour* should be slightly warmed to make a light sponge. If cold, it will chill the eggs which will release some of the air just beaten in. (As air is the only raising agent in a Genoese, everything you do is directed towards incorporating and retaining as much of it as possible.)
   b *Butter*, essential for flavour and to help the cake keep well, should be approximately the same temperature as the egg mixture to which it is added. If you heat rather than just melt it, it will oil and separate, then won't blend properly with the other ingredients. The proportions of butter to flour may range between half and equal quantities, as in Genoese Fine. The more butter there is, the more skill required to incorporate it.
   c *Caster sugar* is essential for a smooth even texture. Granulated doesn't dissolve so readily and gives the cake a speckly surface.

2 The water in the pan mustn't be deep enough to touch the bottom of the mixing bowl. If it does, or if it's actually boiling over heat when you beat the eggs over it, they'll cook and coagulate before you can beat air into them. The eggs need gentle, indirect heat if to become light and fluffy. I find it safest and easiest to take the pan of boiling water to the sink, and beat there.

3 If you fail to spread the mixture flat in the tin, it will bake unevenly, the shallow part being overcooked before the deeper is cooked. In addition, it will spoil the shape of a gâteau, or would vary the thickness of small cakes cut from it. Some cakes find their own level: this doesn't.

4 To cut cold Genoese with a (sharp) cutter, it's better – unlike other pastry – to twist the cutter slightly to right and left as you cut. A straight cut makes the edges ragged, crumbly and difficult to coat and decorate.

5 *The oven* should be quite ready: pre-heated, with shelf in correct place, then there's no serious loss of heat when you put the cake in.

6 *Approximate cooking times:*

3-egg mixture in a Swiss roll tin, about 12 – 15 minutes at top of oven

3-egg mixture in an 8in/20cm *top* diameter moule à manqué tin, about 30 – 40 minutes, in middle of oven

4-egg mixture in a Swiss roll tin, about 15 – 20 minutes at top of oven

4-egg mixture in a 9in/23cm *top* diameter moule à manqué tin, about 30–40 minutes in middle of oven.

7 *Flavourings* such as lemon juice aren't used because a liquid makes the mixture heavy. Dried fruit, glacé cherries, etc. are never used either because the mixture is too light to support them – they'd sink. You'll find, in fact, that flavourings such as chocolate, orange, lemon or coffee are usually added in the form of icings and fillings.

GINGERBREAD

One of the most popular kinds of melted fat mixtures – when the melted fat, sugar and syrup are added in liquid form to the sieved flour and other ingredients.

Some of the ingredients

Plain flour is essential because the raising agent in self-raising flour would conflict with bicarbonate of soda, which is necessary for a gingerbread's dark colour (see page 87).

Golden syrup and black treacle mixed are a good combination for flavour and colour. Black treacle by itself tends to give rather a strong bitter taste, while golden syrup alone makes an anaemic cake. It's always better to weigh the syrup. If gingerbread is doughy or sunken in the middle, you probably used too much.

Moist brown or Demerara sugar make a richer, better-flavoured, darker-coloured cake than white sugar.

A pure fat like lard, or good white cooking fat makes a better gingerbread than a fat which contains water, like butter or margarine. Some people (not I) prefer good clarified dripping.

A few tips:

1 Line the tin, otherwise with so much sugar and syrup the cake will stick to it.

2 Just melt and warm the fat, sugar and syrup. If over-heated, the mixture may be slightly toffee-like.

3 If you take ages to blend the syrupy liquid with the flour, the cake will have a tough shiny crust. A sharp-edged table-spoon is quicker for this job than a thick-edged wooden spoon.

4 Avoid the natural temptation to beat this mixture like a batter. Beating frees the gluten in the flour, and this gluten – being a sticky substance – prevents the mixture from rising properly, making the cake close in texture and shiny on top.

5 Gingerbreads – plain, rich, with fruit, nuts or spices – need a slow-to-moderate oven. In a hot oven, with such a high percentage of sugar and syrup, these would burn easily.

6 A gingerbread *should* be 24 hours old before you cut it. When first cold, the outside is crisp and rather hard – the way I love it, I must admit. During storage, this crispness disappears, the cake becoming soft and slightly moist.

7 Gingerbread deep freezes perfectly.

MADEIRA CAKE

So called because, in the nineteenth century, it was often served with a glass of madeira, being a suitably plain version of a 'rich' cake.

■ Citron peel (slightly different from lemon peel, see page 276) is correct, if available, to decorate the top, otherwise you may have to use orange or lemon. If not thinly sliced, free of sugar and put on top of the cake after the mixture has 'set', the peel will sink.

■ It is characteristic of madeira cake to rise and crack in the centre.

PETITS FOURS

Little oven cakes, *four* being French for an oven. This is why, strictly speaking, things like glacé or marzipan fruits and stuffed dates aren't actually petits fours, although they often appear in an assortment. Petits fours are, therefore, correctly, only of two groups: rich and dry. The former are mainly tiny filled and/or iced cakes, usually based on choux, Genoese or French flan pastry; the latter tiny biscuit-type cakes such as tuiles, macaroons or shortbreads.

■ However you make them and whatever their shape, they should all be to a similar scale, fitting into the same-sized paper sweet cases. They are the perfect ending to a sophisticated dinner.

■ See also *Genoese pastry*, page 321.

ROCK CAKES

So called because of their rock-like appearance when you put them in the oven, not because of their texture when cooked! Much depends on the quantity of milk used, too much making them solid.

■ As rock cakes are the simplest example of a rubbed-in mixture and, therefore – with varying minor alterations – the foundation of many other small cakes, you may like to have the recipe spelt out.

8oz/200g plain flour	or self-
1 level teaspoon baking powder	raising flour

1 level teaspoon salt
4oz/100g butter or margarine
3oz/75g granulated sugar
1oz/25g mixed peel
2oz/50g currants, sultanas or seedless raisins
1 large egg
1 tablespoon milk

Method

1 Sieve flour, baking powder and salt into a mixing bowl, then rub in the fat.
2 Add and mix in the sugar, finely chopped mixed peel and dried fruit.
3 Using a fork, mix to a stiff dough with the mixed egg and milk, using your hand if necessary to bind the mixture together.
4 Divide the mixture into 12 equal-sized lumps and pile on a greased baking sheet in rocky heaps, roughening the top of each with a fork.
5 Bake for about 10–14 minutes at or near the top (or hottest part) of a very hot oven, gas 8, 450°F/230°C until golden and firm. Cool on a wire tray.

■ Though unconventional, a sprinkling of Demerara sugar over the uncooked rock cakes makes them deliciously crunchy.

SANDWICH CAKE, VICTORIA

A cake dedicated to Queen Victoria, this isn't easy to make perfectly, probably because people don't cream the butter and sugar enough, aren't careful enough with the eggs (see *creamed mixtures*), or use too hot an oven. You may find the top of a slowish oven, gas 3, 325°F/165°C, gives more even rising and a larger, lighter cake.

■ The way to make this cake in a jiffy is of course with an all-in-one mixture (page 318) but, made with margarine instead of butter, it won't remain moist and fresh so long and nor will it have quite such a good flavour.
■ Traditionally, the filling is raspberry jam and the top is sprinkled with *caster* sugar. (In practice, we often add other flavourings and use other fillings, and I myself prefer it sprinkled with icing sugar.)

SHORTBREAD

Not worth bothering to make unless you use butter, no other fat giving this lovely cake its characteristic flavour. Caster sugar is also necessary because granulated tends to caramelize and make a speckled cake.

■ Rice flour or ground rice helps to prevent shortbread rising, as does pricking it all over with a fork before baking.

■ With such a high proportion of sugar, shortbread needs a greased baking sheet – and it's difficult to make a good one without a flan ring. Uncontrolled, it tends to spread and go thin at the edges, which may get over-baked if not burnt by the time the middle is cooked.

■ To be crisp and biscuity, shortbread needs a slow oven, gas 2, 300°F/150°C, until light golden in colour. It is cooled on the baking sheet, acquiring an uncharacteristic cake-like texture if you transfer it to a wire tray.

■ Have you ever added chopped walnuts to shortbread? As long as you like walnuts, you'll like this.

SPONGE CAKE

Technically, a fatless sponge, used of course to make various cold sweets as well as Swiss roll, sponge cakes, fingers and drops. With butter added, it becomes Genoese pastry.

■ Traditionally, sponge cake has a sugary crust: simply dredge the prepared cake tin with equal quantities of caster sugar and rice flour sieved together.

■ If your recipe gives a tablespoonful of hot water to a 3-egg sponge, this is thought to make a light cake.

■ See also *Genoese pastry*, page 321.

SWISS ROLL

Often made with butter, though a true sponge is made without. If, however, you aren't going to eat it all the first day, butter helps it to keep moister for longer. See *Genoese pastry*, page 321.

■ Without butter, you need a hotter oven for a shorter time than for Genoese – gas 7, 425°F/220°C, for about 7 or 8 minutes, or until golden and softly firm.

■ Waste no time once the sponge is cooked, otherwise you won't be able to roll it up. You'll find it easier to roll if you turn it upside-down on to a sheet of

sugared paper laid on top of a hot, wet, squeezed-out tea-towel: slip off the paper quickly and carefully, cutting off the cake's edges with a sharp knife before spreading the sponge with jam and rolling it up. If you're slow, the edges will go crisp as they cool, making the sponge crack when you roll it.

■ With the end tucked underneath, leave the hot tightly-rolled sponge in paper on the cake cooling tray for a minute or two, to set slightly and prevent it unrolling, then unwrap it and leave to cool.

Swiss roll, chocolate Better not attempted before mastering a plain roll. It needs butter because, if fatless, it is difficult to roll and unroll without splitting.

■ As butter icing obviously can't be spread on the hot sponge, the sponge must be pliable enough to unroll and fill when cold: one way to do this is to roll it rather loosely the first time, leaving it in the paper like a plain Swiss roll for a minute or two. Now unroll and roll it up again (without the paper), doing this once or twice more, as it cools.

■ If you like nuts, fold in 1oz/25g of chopped walnuts after the flour; or if you like Arctic roll, spread the sponge with ice cream instead of butter icing, wrapping it first in foil then in polythene, to freeze. Thaw at least 10–15 minutes before required.

Chocolate log Simply a chocolate Swiss roll piped lengthwise with butter icing or chocolate crème au beurre. A tablespoonful of sherry perks up the icing and it's easier to pipe if you start at the bottom of one side, not on the top.

TARTLETS

Cherry and other fruit tartlets should be made with flan or French flan pastry because both of these stay crisp and short, unlike shortcrust which is toughened by liquid from the fruit.

■ The fruit syrup makes a bright, clear and tasteless glaze when thickened with arrowroot – unlike cornflour, which has its own rather distinctive flavour, and makes a cloudy glaze.

Jam tartlets End up about the same size as the bun tins if you use a fluted cutter one size larger, to allow for the pastry shrinking slightly.

■ Each needs very little jam, otherwise it boils up over the edges when they're baked. Be mean with it.

TUILES

French for tiles, these biscuity cakes are shaped over a rolling pin like curved tiles. Serve them at teatime, with morning coffee, or better still as contrasting texture with a soft cold sweet like zabaglione, syllabub, fool, or apple snow.

■ I wouldn't try to put more than four at a time on a well greased baking sheet because, like brandy snaps, you have to catch them at the right moment for shaping, otherwise they quickly cool and go brittle. Watch them like a hawk when nearly cooked: one moment they're perfect, the next, overdone. They should be just brown round the edges, still darkstraw-coloured in the middle. Incidentally, if you spread them too thick on the baking sheet, you won't be able to shape them.

■ Lift each carefully but quickly on a pallet knife, and shape them one by one over a rolling pin, pressing the tile round it with a cloth, rather than with your hand,

to shape it. Pop them at once into an airtight tin when cold because they must be crisp. (It's usually for their texture that they're served.)

■ Shape tiny tuiles for petits fours over the handle of a wooden spoon.

VANILLA SLICES

An enjoyable way to grow fat. The way I like them best is spread with royal icing before you bake them. This means rolling the pastry very thin, otherwise the icing will burn before the pastry is cooked.

■ A small packet of thawed frozen puff pastry (7½oz/200g) will make about a dozen. Here's what to do:

1 Cut the very thinly rolled pastry into equal-sized rectangles.
2 Spread each almost to the edges with a quickly made, thick royal icing – sieved icing sugar, softened with egg white. (If too thin, it will run off and seal the edges, preventing the pastry from rising perfectly.)
3 Bake about 7–12 minutes on a wetted baking sheet in a hot oven, gas 7, 425°F/220°C, or until the pastry is golden and the icing caramelized.
4 Cool. Split, remove any doughy layer, spread lower half with apricot or raspberry jam, and whipped cream or crème chantilly. Put halves together again.

■ To serve as a dessert, cut into only 6 pieces – for 3–4 people.

Cake icings and fillings

GENERAL INFORMATION

Fillings and icings can transform the plainest cake. What, for instance, is simpler than a Genoese sponge, yet what more elaborate than the rich gâteau it can become? Time-consuming? Yes, but for anyone with a freezer and a mixer, it's seldom much extra work to step up the quantities and prepare enough fillings and trimmings for three or four cakes while you're about it.

■ With one or two Genoese or sandwich cakes in the freezer as well, even producing quite a sophisticated gâteau becomes more a matter of assembly than of labour. It just doesn't make sense – to my mind – to toil so much for one filling when you can equally well make and freeze more.

■ A few tips may be of help:

1 Try to make fillings and icings harmonize or contrast with the flavour and texture of the cake.

2 Cakes made in a moule à manqué tin are easy to ice professionally. The icing will flow smoothly and gradually down the outward sloping sides, instead of dropping down as over the edge of a precipice, leaving gaps.

3 If a cake is over-baked or a bad shape, doctor it:

a Where too brown, rub carefully with a very fine grater.

b If 'peaked', level the top and turn the cake upside-down to ice.

c If one side is deeper than the other, be generous with a filling and reassemble the cake so that it's flat: the thick part of the top over the thin part

of the bottom.

4 Before splitting a cake to fill, cut a tiny vertical wedge somewhere up the side, then it's easy to reassemble as it was.

5 A turntable helps one to give wedding or Christmas cakes a professional finish.

6 It's usually easier, except with fondant, to ice a cake on an inverted large plate than on a cake tray.

7 Sieve icing sugar, however fine. The tiniest lumps make an icing look rough, and the most microscopic will obstruct an icing tube. The longest way round is the shortest way home.

8 If you can be bothered, brush a sandwich or sponge cake over with apricot glaze (below), before covering with glacé or fondant icing.

9 Use colourings sparingly. They tend to darken when icing sets, and it's easy to add an extra drop but quite a performance to tone down a colour. You won't go far wrong if you dip the point of a hat pin or fine skewer into the bottle of colouring, then shake the drop off into the icing. See also page 97.

10 Keep any icing you aren't using straight away covered with a piece of damp cloth. Once exposed to air, the surface soons dries out, then when you stir it, lumps get into the icing.

11 Prick any air bubbles with a hat pin as soon as they form.

■ See also *paper icing bags*, page 11, and *icing tubes*, page 48.

ALMOND PASTE (MARZIPAN)

Can be made with yolks, whites, or whole

egg, depending on what you want it for. Yolk for instance is ideal for marzipan on a Christmas or wedding cake to be coated with royal icing, giving a lovely flavour and a rich golden colour. Egg white gives no flavour but a sharper, clearer colour than yolk if you're making coloured marzipan. It's a matter of primary colours, as with paints.

■ A few hints may be of help:

1 A *mixture* of caster and icing sugar is essential to give almond paste its correct texture and to make it easy to manipulate. For icing a cake, it should be firm enough to roll and handle, but not so dry that it will crack.
2 In uncooked almond paste, be sure to use the full amount of sugar, to preserve the raw egg.
3 Almond or ratafia essence helps to bring out the full flavour of the ground almonds.
4 Orange flower water gives fragrance.
5 If you over-work marzipan, the ground almonds will release too much oil, making the mixture sticky and difficult to roll. A little extra sugar may correct it.
6 Use caster sugar on the pastry board and rolling pin: flour spoils marzipan.
7 Keep the marzipan covered with foil, polythene or an upturned basin if working with only some of it. Uncovered, it soon dries out.
8 To colour almond paste is sometimes easier said than done. The tricky part is to blend the colour perfectly with the paste so that it will neither look streaky from under-working, nor be oily from over-working. Here's one way to do it:
  a Add as many – or as few – drops of colouring to the paste as you think necessary.
  b Roll the paste into a long sausage, knot the ends together, then squash it a little.
  c Roll again into a sausage, knot and squash. Continue in this way until the colour is completely blended.
9 If not covering almond paste with royal icing, give it a professional finish by brushing with gum arabic solution (see page 333).
10 Brush a fruit cake over with egg white or apricot glaze before covering with almond paste, to control any loose crumbs and to make the icing stick to the cake.

AMERICAN FROSTED ICING

Can be used on almost any type of cake from a light sponge to a Christmas cake. Firm and crisp outside, it is soft underneath, and bland enough to team up with almost any flavour of cake – splendid for a child's birthday.

■ Some tips:

1 Prepare cake decorations in advance, ready to place without delay.
2 A thermometer saves guesswork: if the syrup doesn't reach a high enough temperature, the icing won't set. If overheated it will set too hard.
3 Timing is important. Aim to have the egg whites whisked very stiffly just as the syrup reaches 238–40°F/115–16°C, then there's no delay in using it.
4 Pour the syrup from a *height* on to the whisked egg whites (whisking as you do so), to cool the syrup as it falls. If you hold the pan too close, the boiling syrup will cook and coagulate the whites, which will go lumpy instead of meringue-like.
5 Whisking takes several minutes, until the icing is a light spreading consistency. You can tell when it's ready to use because it changes its texture and appearance from a shiny soft texture to a dull very light one, not unlike cotton wool. If you don't whisk it enough, you'll find yourself *pouring* it over the cake, or if you whisk it too long, the icing will harden before you can coat the cake.
6 Use quick bold strokes to spread the frosting before it sets. If coating a Christmas cake, swirl it in peaks.
7 Allow to cool and set before eating, otherwise it won't have its characteristic texture.

Brown sugar frosting Similar to American frosted icing, but use Demerara instead of granulated sugar, and boil the syrup slightly higher, to 248°F/120°C.

■ Frosting and icing are words used interchangeably in America.

APRICOT GLAZE

Useful to brush over sponge cakes of all kinds before coating with glacé or fondant icing. You can also use it on a Christmas cake to make almond paste stick, or to seal the inside of a baked pastry case before putting in a damp filling which would otherwise spoil the pastry.

■ Brushed over cakes, it prevents any cake crumbs finding their way into the icing, helps icing to run smoothly over a cake, and prevents icing from going dull – because the cake doesn't absorb moisture from the icing so readily.

■ So often wanted and not always to be found, I think I should give the details. This quantity will coat one 8in/20cm cake:

    1 rounded tablespoon apricot jam
    2 teaspoons water or lemon juice
    2 rounded teaspoons granulated sugar

Method

1 Stir all together in a tiny pan over minimum heat until the sugar is dissolved. (Using a larger pan, evaporation is too rapid.)

2 Sieve and return to pan.

3 When required, bring to the boil and simmer for 3–5 minutes over moderate heat, or until the glaze hangs in heavy drops from the spoon.

4 Use while hot, to brush on evenly, but be sure to let it cool and set on a cake before icing it, otherwise it will melt the icing.

BUTTER CREAM FILLINGS

See *crème au beurre*, below.

BUTTER ICING

Has the best flavour when made with saltless butter. Use as little as half butter to sugar, or as much as equal quantities of each, depending on how rich you like or want it, but of course if you don't use icing sugar, the icing won't have its characteristic smooth texture.

■ If you beat the butter until soft and light before adding the icing sugar, a spoonful at a time, the sugar is less likely to fly everywhere. The bonus of creaming them until your arm aches, if you've no electric mixer, is the larger amount of icing – because of all the air beaten in – and a light fluffy mixture which will spread or pipe easily.

■ The colour generally indicates the flavour of a butter icing, and certain decorations tend to team up with that flavour.

Colour of icing	Usual flavour	Sort of decoration
pink	vanilla	glacé cherries
white	vanilla, or almond and/or ratafia essence	glacé cherries or almonds
green	almond and/or ratafia essence, or peppermint	almonds or chocolate
orange	orange juice and finely grated rind	angelica, mimosa or chocolate vermicelli, etc.
pale yellow	lemon juice and finely grated rind	mimosa, angelica, etc.
coffee	coffee essence	nuts – browned almonds or walnuts, etc.
chocolate	melted chocolate, or cocoa and vanilla essence	nuts or chocolate of some kind

COFFEE ICING

Best and most easily made with coffee essence. Allow about 1 teaspoon of Camp coffee and 2–3 teaspoons warm water to 4oz/100g sieved icing sugar.

CRÈME AU BEURRE

An icing, a filling, or both, which you can vary with all kinds of flavourings to make the sort of sponge gâteau one dreams about. Rich and ruthless for the figure, these butter creams are really neither very extravagant nor too difficult to make and usually emerge from a freezer as well as they go in, as long as you don't add nuts, which go soft. Use crème au beurre also to decorate Genoese fancies, petits fours or butterfly cakes, to fill meringues, to fill and ice a sandwich cake, or to ice a chocolate log etc. There's no end to the ways you can use them, and they are icings which, by and large, pipe or spread superbly because of their smooth, almost mayonnaise-like texture.

■ Two variations are made with egg yolks, another with egg whites, or there's a different, less good version made with crème anglaise. Their basic ingredients are butter, sugar, eggs and a flavouring.
Butter Saltless is best, for its flavour. Have it at room temperature, otherwise you may find it is difficult to blend but very ready to curdle. (Salted butter can be used.)
Icing sugar Gives this filling its characteristic smooth texture, but granulated is used when making the version with sugar dissolved in water.
Eggs Should be new-laid if to whisk well, otherwise you can't trap enough air to make the icing fluffy and light.
Flavouring Rather depends on the type of crème au beurre because some will accept more liquid than others. When using lemon or orange, zest is better than rind because it contains no bitter pith, won't spoil the smooth texture of the icing, and won't block an icing tube so easily.

■ If a butter cream is too soft to use when first made, chill it in a cold larder until of spreading or piping consistency.
■ These are my three favourite kinds:

Crème au beurre ménagère (household butter cream) Richer and, I think, not so light or quite so good as the other two, but it is child's play to make if you have a mixer. It's so easy in fact, I will jot down the recipe: beat together at moderate speed for about 5 minutes or until smooth and light 6oz/150g cut-up soft butter, 3oz/75g sieved icing sugar and 2 egg yolks. Then gradually beat in your chosen flavouring, e.g.:
2 tablespoons Grand Marnier or other orange liqueur (*my* favourite)
2 tablespoons rum or kirsch
2 teaspoons coffee essence
1½ tablespoons lemon juice and zest of ½ lemon
2oz/50g melted plain dessert chocolate (stir this all in at once, before it sets).

Crème au beurre à la meringue Most easily made with an electric hand-whisk. Be careful not to rest the basin over a pan of water which is either boiling or too deep, otherwise the heat will cook and coagulate the whites before you can whisk air into them.

■ If you don't whisk the meringue long enough, until it stands in peaks, or if you don't then whisk it aside from the heat until it's cold, it won't thicken properly when you beat in the butter bit by bit.
■ Flavour it with zest of orange or lemon, melted chocolate, coffee essence or browned nuts.

Crème au beurre mousseline A truly heavenly filling but not easy to make without a thermometer because the syrup has to be boiled exactly to 216–218°F/102–103°C.

■ Hold the pan high above the well-beaten yolks as you slowly pour and whisk the hot syrup on to them, because if it's too hot when it lands on them, the yolks will cook and coagulate before you can beat air into them. Another pitfall is that if you don't whisk the mixture thick enough at this stage – to the ribbon – you'll end up with something more like a liquid than a mousse.

■ Many recipes tell you to add butter to the mousse, but it's much less likely to curdle if you do it the other way round and add the mousse, spoonful by spoonful, to the soft, well-beaten butter.

■ You can use all sorts of flavourings with mousseline, usually adding the one of your choice to the made mousse. These are the quantities I use:

2½oz/65g caster sugar
3 tablespoons water
2 large egg yolks
5oz/generous 125g butter

flavouring of choice, e.g.:
 zest of 1 lemon or orange and about 1 tablespoon juice, to taste
 zest of 1 orange and about 2 tablespoons Grand Marnier, or to taste
 rum, kirsch or cassis, to taste
 2oz/50g melted plain dessert chocolate
 2–4oz/50–100g praline, pounded
 2–4oz/50–100g browned almonds or hazelnuts
 about 2 tablespoons sieved fresh strawberries or raspberries

■ Remember one can't pipe with nuts in the mixture!

CRÈME PATISSIÈRE

Also known as *pastry cream* or *confectioner's custard*. As its name suggests, a good filling for something like a flan, a fruit vol-au-vent or éclairs. It's useful because you can flavour it in various ways, it will refrigerate several days, or deep freeze perfectly. It also makes a creamy pouring custard if liquidized.

■ Be sure to pour the milk gradually on to the well-beaten yolks, sugar and flour, so that the yolks are gently warmed rather than suddenly cooked.

■ The starch in the flour, cornflour, potato flour or whatever you use, pre-

vents the custard from curdling when boiled, as it must be, to cook the starch.

■ If you want to use pastry cream cold, dot the top with a little softened butter to stop a skin forming – caused by evaporation from the surface. Alternatively, cover with a disc of foil, or stir the custard frequently as it cools.

■ Add a spoonful or two of cream when the custard is cold, if you can spare it. It's worth it, to give richness, flavour and a silky-smooth texture.

CRÈME ST HONORÉ

Although used also in tarts, cream puffs and as a dessert cream, this was first made as a custard cream filling for Gâteau St Honoré which commemorates a one-time Bishop of Amiens, considered to be the patron saint of pastrycooks and bakers.

■ You'll need a recipe, but it is just an elaborate version of crème patissière, with stiffly whisked egg whites added to the cooked mixture. This won't thin out and collapse as you might fear because the egg whites coagulate with the heat, then holding their firm texture like cooked meringue.

■ If you can't spare as many egg whites as this recipe calls for, use fewer. (If nothing else, a smaller number will make crème patissière go further.) Flavour crème St Honoré with a liqueur, orange zest, chocolate, praline or whatever your recipe calls for. If serving it cold, it should be well chilled.

FONDANT ICING

The perfect icing for a light sponge, for example gâteaux, petits fours or Genoese Fancies. The icing cuts easily because it remains soft – important when the cake underneath is feathery-light. Before icing a sponge, for best results, first brush the top with apricot glaze (page 329).

■ A few tips:

1 Make more icing than you need,

allowing 1lb/450g sugar for the average-sized cake. Stored in a plastic bowl with lid, any surplus icing will keep perfectly for future use on small cakes. Made at least a day or two before you need it, the icing will mature and improve.

2 If you're lucky enough to have a marble slab, this – well dampened – is the ideal thing on which to make fondant: it is better than anything else because it cools the syrup quickly, is steady as a rock to work on, and makes manipulation of the syrup easy. Using a wetted mixing bowl is more time-consuming because the syrup takes longer both to cool and to work.

3 Make the syrup in the usual way (see page 343), boiling it to 238–240°F / 115–116°C, then plunge the bottom of the pan into cold water to halt cooking. Liquid glucose or cream of tartar is used as a deterrent to the crystallization of the sugar.

4 When the syrup stops bubbling, pour it in a steady stream on to your marble slab, butcher's tray or whatever, leaving any final scrapings in the pan as these are liable to crystallize.

5 The syrup must be at the right temperature when you start working it. If too hot, the fondant will be rough and sugary. If too cold, you won't be able to manipulate it.

6 The aim is to make the syrup opaque and firm: on a flat surface, work it from the sides to the centre with a pallet knife or wooden spatula. In a bowl, mix it intensively with a wooden spoon in a repeated figure-of-eight movement.

7 When the syrup has 'turned', knead it (press with your fingertips), small lumps at a time, until smooth, keeping the remainder covered with a damp cloth to prevent drying out. (If it goes hard, cover with a damp cloth, leave for half an hour and then knead.) When you've got it all soft, in one lump now, cover with a damp cloth or put in an airtight container until required.

8 Warming the icing ready for use can be tricky. If you over-heat it, it will be hard and will lose its gloss: if not made warm enough it won't set well. It's quicker but more risky to warm it over direct heat, slow but sure to melt it over hot (not boiling) water, taking it off the water at intervals to prevent it getting too hot. Resist the temptation to beat it, as this traps air which will make the icing full of bubbles.

9 The correct consistency is essential. If too thick, the icing will set on the sides of a cake before you can coat them properly. It should be thick enough to coat a wooden spoon smoothly, and when trailed back into the bowl, the trail should disappear quite quickly. Thin it down, if necessary, with warm stock syrup. (You *can* use warm water, but the icing won't be so smooth and glossy.)

10 Colour and flavour fondant as you like (see page 329 for combinations).

11 If you ice a cake, or small cakes, on a cake cooling tray over a large mixing bowl, you can save and re-use the drippings another time.

12 Pour fondant all at once over top of a cake, if necessary tilting or tapping the cake tray briskly to make the icing flow evenly down the sides.

GLACÉ ICING

Takes its name from the French *glacer*, in cookery meaning 'to ice' or 'glaze'. If you want glacé icing to stay glossy, first brush a sandwich cake with apricot glaze (page 329).

■ Some people mix their icing with stock syrup to make it smooth and glossy, while others mix a few drops of oil with the liquid. Whatever you use, if the liquid is warm, it will help to melt the icing sugar.

■ I like a sweet-sour icing, if I may call it that, on something simple like a sandwich or coconut cake – icing sugar mixed with lemon juice. Unlike water, this gives some flavour and bite, even if it doesn't stay glossy long.

■ As far as possible, colouring and flavourings should match (see page 329).

Chocolate glacé icing Better made with cake covering than with dessert chocolate because it's softer when set and doesn't go so dull (see page 92).

■ If because of its flavour you prefer to use dessert chocolate, I'd choose a recipe calling for a good-sized piece of butter. This not only helps to keep the icing soft but in addition makes it deliciously fudgy.
■ Should you like the flavour of peppermint, why not add a few drops of oil of peppermint to your icing?

GUM ARABIC

Bought in the form of crystals (see page 100), this is excellent amongst other things for glazing almond paste.

■ ½oz/15g crystals will be enough to glaze the coloured almond paste on a Christmas cake, or lots of sweets or cake decorations modelled in almond paste.
■ To use it:

1 Wash the crystals in a fine strainer, to prevent them making the solution dirty, then crush with a rolling pin to make dissolve more quickly.
2 Put the crystals in something like a glass mustard jar which is small and not too thick, then cover with 3–4 dessertspoons of very hot but not boiling water. Stand this in a basin of hot water and stir frequently, replacing the water in the basin as it cools.
3 In about an hour, or when the crystals form a sticky solution, strain it through butter muslin and use. (If making a larger quantity, use a double saucepan over minimum heat.)
4 Colour the solution now, if you like, before painting on the almond paste like varnish, preferably with a top-quality paint brush. (Use it colourless for coloured almond paste.)
5 Covered, in something like a chemist's tiny pill bottle, any surplus solution will keep for weeks.

Frost Looks attractive sprinkled over the top of a red Christmas cake for instance.

■ To make: using a paint brush, spread the gum arabic solution as a film over a shiny-surfaced dish, leaving it to dry gradually. When it looks 'crazed', scrape off with a pallet knife and store in a small sealed container until required. (If you spread the solution too thickly, it forms a plastic-like sheet, or if you use a rough-surfaced dish, it won't form a film.)

LEMON CURD FILLING

Delicious for a sandwich cake, sponge gâteau, flan, tartlets or meringues, especially if the lemon curd is home-made: simply stir 4 tablespoons of lemon curd into ¼pt/150ml softly-whipped cream.

MARBLING OR FEATHER ICING

An attractive but very economical way to decorate an iced cake or biscuits: make a little more icing than needed to coat the cake, then put the extra in a small basin. Colour this, and with a little icing sugar added, make it very slightly stiffer before putting in a paper icing bag with its tip cut off. Ice the cake in the usual way, and

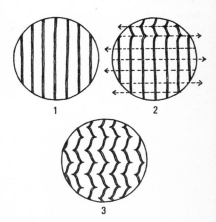

quickly, before the icing sets, pipe the coloured icing in straight lines across it, at regular intervals apart, see fig 1. Now run a hat pin or fine skewer *across* these lines at similar intervals, first in one direction, then the other. Where the lines cross each other, they'll be 'pulled', making a sort of zig-zag pattern, see figs. 2 and 3.

MARZIPAN

From the French *massepain*, a mixture thought to have been made originally by an order of nuns. See *almond paste*, page 327.

PASTRY CREAM

See *crème patissière*, page 331.

ROYAL ICING

Needs to be harder for a wedding cake than for a Christmas or birthday cake, both to support the weight of other tiers and to preserve the cake. A similar hard icing, made entirely with egg whites, is also the only one which can be used successfully for elaborate piping such as trellis-work.

■A few general tips may be helpful:

1 Avoid using an aluminium mixing bowl because it gives icing a greyish cast.

2 1 teaspoon of glycerine or pure honey per lb/450g of icing sugar, prevents the icing from becoming rock-hard.

3 Add a drop or two of blue colouring to give an illusion of whiteness. Alternatively, use a few drops of 'laundry blue', or a few grains scraped from it.

4 Beat a hard icing until it will stand up in straight peaks when you lift a wooden spoon sharply out of it.

5 It is quicker and less strenuous to use an electric mixer than to beat by hand, providing you don't let the icing get full of bubbles. To avoid these, beat the whites with just half the icing sugar at slow speed for only 5–7 minutes until light and fluffy, then stir in remaining

icing sugar by hand.

6 If too stiff, thin down royal icing with egg white, not with water.

7 Even while you're working with it, keep closely covered with a thick damp cloth any icing still in the basin – to prevent contact with air, which will make it set. Icing will in fact keep like this for weeks, as long as the cloth is kept damp. You can then use this icing as it is, or thin it down whenever you want to with more egg white. For example, any surplus from the first coating on a cake can be thinned down a week later as part of the second coating.

8 Using a hat pin, prick at once any air bubbles which form in the icing.

9 If possible, leave an iced cake to dry in a warm airy room. The faster it dries, the whiter it will be.

10 You can model royal icing like almond paste, providing it's stiff enough, to make things like Christmas roses, lilies of the valley or a bow of ribbon.

SUGAR, COLOURED

Not a real icing, of course, but a quick and colourful substitute, if you first brush the top of a cake with egg white, to make the sugar stick.

■ Use 2 or 3 drops of colouring per rounded tablespoon of sugar: put some caster sugar on a piece of waxed paper (say a piece from a cornflake box) and, with your fingertips, work the colouring evenly into it.

SUGAR, ICING

Can be sprinkled evenly over things like pastries or cakes from a tea strainer if you're without a sugar sifter.

■ To make an attractive pattern on the top of a cake with icing sugar, lay a doyley on it then dredge with sugar and lift doyley carefully off. The icing sugar will gradually dissolve, so don't prepare too soon.

21

Beverages

Beverages play a great part in our lives. Besides replacing water lost by the body in various ways, they are a central part of hospitality, warm us up when we are cold, refresh us when we are hot. Some help to rouse us in the morning, others soothe us to sleep, or keep us awake when we're tired, or even calm us down when suffering from shock. We cannot live without drink.

COCOA

In the tropical regions of America, the cocoa tree was cultivated even in prehistoric times. The Aztecs of Mexico and the Incas of Peru dried the beans in the sun, roasted them in pots, crushed and kneaded them into cakes. Using carved wooden beaters, the cakes were mixed together with water, vanilla and spices to make a cold drink. The beans were at one time even used as money, a hundred being enough to buy a slave.

■ Cortez, after conquering Mexico, brought back cocoa beans to Spain, and with them the secret of making a drink. Not until over a century later, however, in 1650, did the English learn to make it.
■ Cocoa and drinking chocolate are less stimulating but more nourishing than tea or coffee. In addition, from the health angle, they conceal the flavour of milk, even making it tempting as a hot drink or an iced chocolate milk shake to the child who doesn't want food or dislikes milk.
■ Because of the starch in it, some cookery books recommend quickly boiling cocoa after making, to give it more body and improve its flavour.

Rowntree Mackintosh, the experts, disagree with this, saying that as the amount of starch is comparatively low, it in fact makes virtually no difference to the drink's thickness, and spoils rather than improves the flavour of the milk.
■ See also *chocolate*, page 92.

COFFEE

Coffee drinking started for medicinal purposes (as it seemed to have enlivening properties) in the Middle East as long ago as 900 BC, and our word coffee derives from the Arabic *kaweh* – meaning strength and vigour. The brewing of coffee as a popular beverage is attributed to the Muslims who used it in an attempt to find a stimulating drink to replace alcohol which had been forbidden them since the Prophet proclaimed that only abstainers could enter Paradise. In the sixteenth century, camel trains carried coffee to many parts of the Near East and, in due course, about 1600, it found its way to Venice.

■ By 1637, the first coffee had arrived in England, via Holland, and coffee drinking soon became fashionable, with the first coffee house opening in Oxford in 1650. Coffee houses soon opened up in London, becoming centres of social, cultural and political activity. It was from one of these, in Tower Street, started by Edward Lloyd about 1688, that Lloyd's the underwriters originated. Another, the meeting place of stockbrokers, was the birthplace of the Stock Exchange.
■ Today, coffee is of enormous importance in world economy, with over

20,000,000 people employed in its growth and distribution. Next to oil, it is the second largest commodity of international trade.

■ Coffee beans are the kernels of the coffee cherry, the fruit of a large evergreen shrub growing in many tropical countries – it takes 2,000 beans to produce 1lb/450g of roasted coffee. It and tea both contain caffeine, a drug just strong enough to give a fillip, yet mild enough for us to be able to drink both or either daily, throughout our lives, without any ill effect. Coffee and tea in fact divide the world between them, national drinks possibly being linked with national characteristics – so strong are the effects of wine, which makes for drowsiness; coffee which wakens one up; tea which gives one a sense of well-being.

■ Making a really good cup of coffee calls for both knowledge and care. Even starting off with better quality coffee beans, it is said that, generally speaking, the British end up with a drink inferior to that of coffee-drinking countries. Here are a few tips:

1 Buy the best beans, the difference in price between these and the worst being hardly worth considering. The best come from high open hills in the colder regions of tropical countries, so if you don't know what's what, go to a specialist coffee shop, a first-class grocer or a reliable delicatessen. Also, if you shop where the quality is high, the beans should have been skilfully roasted – or you can roast your own.

2 Buy little and often: once ground, the aroma is so fugitive that 65 per cent is said to disappear in 24 hours, and within nine days has disappeared almost entirely. Store coffee in an airtight container, no bigger than necessary, for even whole roasted beans lose their strongest flavour in 2–3 weeks. (One authority states that, providing they are well sealed, 'they will keep reasonably for several months in the freezer'.)

3 Make coffee by a good method: some ways are excellent, some bad. Here are some examples:

The pressure principle, e.g. Espresso. This very strong and lovely black coffee is produced by heating water under pressure in a sealed chamber. The finely ground coffee itself forms the filter as, intensely heated, the water is quickly forced through it, extracting the 'heart' of the coffee. A darker-than-usual roast is required to give the characteristic slightly bitter taste.

By filtering Melitta or traditional French filter style, with a filter paper. This is the simplest method of all, making excellent coffee in a fraction of the time and cost (in electricity) of, for instance, a percolator. The coffee is clear, has a good flavour and can be made by the cup or jugful.

In a jug If without any efficient equipment – including a Cona glass coffee maker, for instance, the principal drawback of which is probably its fragility – use a *warmed* coffee pot or earthenware or china jug (not aluminium, which spoils both the flavour and colour of coffee). An expert's directions for this are:

a Measure the coffee (2 heaped tablespoons per pt/600ml water) into the warmed jug and stir in the (freshly run) boiling water. Set aside in a warm place, covered, for 5 minutes.

b Skim with a spoon, then leave another minute to develop further flavour.

c Strain, preferably through butter muslin, into cups or a warmed coffee pot, pouring gently. (Stir the coffee just before serving if a large quantity, as it tends to settle, the thin on top, thick on the bottom.)

■ A sophisticated version is the glass jug with a plunger which traps the coffee grounds.

■ Keep your coffee jug clean: a build-up makes coffee bitter.

In a percolator Generally speaking, percolators make poor, some of them even almost undrinkable, coffee. Coffee should be crystal clear: if the water actually boils, it will be cloudy, also the flavour is spoilt, which explains why percolator coffee can't be good because they can't perk *without* boiling. Only very occasionally have I drunk good coffee from a percolator.

4 Never reheat coffee: this ruins its flavour.

5 If adding milk, add it cold or warmed, never boiled. Boiling changes the flavour of milk, which in turn spoils the coffee. (Too much milk weakens the flavour of even the best coffee.) To heat milk skilfully, see page 108.

■ To make rich, smooth and heavenly coffee, I like best to serve cream, preferably Jersey or double.

Coffee essence See page 93.

Instant coffee According to the Nestlé Company, instant coffee came about from sheer necessity – a need to preserve excess coffee from over-productive years in a less bulky form. The idea had been around since the nineteenth century, but it wasn't until 1938 that Nestlé were able to sell it commercially. Instant coffee now has 90 per cent of the British market.

■ The difference between instant and coffee grounds is that the manufacturer has percolated the coffee and removed the grounds, then dried (to preserve) it. I find what happens so enthralling as to be worth spelling out in a little more detail:

1 The green beans arrive from various parts of the world.
2 An expert blends different beans into a mix acceptable to the consumer.
3 The beans are roasted to the rich brown colour with which we are all familiar: a high roast for a strong flavour; a lighter roast for a softer, milder flavour. They are then ground to a specific size under very carefully controlled conditions.
4 The coffee is made in vast percolators, after which the bulk of it is concentrated by evaporating off some of the water under vacuum.
5 It is now either sprayed, or freeze-dried:
Spraying is done in very fine jets through a stream of hot air to evaporate out the rest of the water so that each drop forms a little particle of instant coffee powder by the time it reaches the base of a tower three floors down.
Freeze-drying is done by freezing percolated coffee brew in a giant stainless steel container, then reducing the air pressure inside until the brew evaporates to leave just granules of coffee.

■ Either way, this extraction of water preserves the coffee, just as it preserves many foods out of which the water is taken. So, when we pour boiling water on to the coffee powder or granules to make a cup of coffee, we are, in fact, simply replacing the water evaporated off earlier.
■ For use in cooking, see page 93.

Spiced iced coffee Cool, creamy and delicious, this is how to make it:

1 Make 2pt/1 litre double or treble strength coffee and flavour with the pared rind of half an orange. (Soak it in the very hot coffee, stirring this occasionally as it cools.)
2 Strain and chill.
3 Stir, pour into long glasses, add a ball of vanilla ice cream and top with whipped cream and a hint of grated nutmeg.
4 Serve with a cinnamon stick, to stir.

Gaelic coffee If you have never had this, it's a drink to remember:

1 Warm a stemmed whisky goblet and pour in one measure of Irish whiskey. Add three cubes of sugar.
2 Fill the goblet with strong black coffee to within 1in/2½cm of the brim, stirring to dissolve the sugar.
3 Top up to the brim with double cream poured carefully over the back of a teaspoon, so that it floats on top of the coffee. Don't stir it! The best flavour comes with drinking the coffee and whiskey through the cream.

Highland coffee Similar to Gaelic, but uses Scotch whisky.

Coffee napoleon Use brandy instead of whisky.

Coffee balalaika Use vodka instead of whisky.

LEMONADE

This recipe is too good to omit. Serve it chilled, with chilled water and cubes of ice, preferably with a tiny mint leaf set in some of them. It also freezes well: in a polythene, not a glass bottle. (In the refrigerator it will keep about a week.)

To make approximately 2½pt/1.4 litres concentrated juice:

1lb 2oz/500g granulated sugar
1 large juicy orange
½ large juicy lemon
1¾pt/1 litre water
¾ – 1oz/20 – 25g citric acid (page 93), to taste, the larger amount if you like it sharp

Method

1 Put the sugar in a mixing bowl, and zest (page 85) the wiped orange and lemon over it.

2 Boil the water and pour over the sugar and zest, stirring to dissolve. Cool at least a minute or two – if to avoid losing the vitamin C from the fruit juices.

3 Stir in the squeezed fruits' juice, pulp and pips, also the citric acid, and leave to go quite cold (overnight if in a cold place), stirring a few times meanwhile.

4 Strain, pressing the zest, etc. with the back of a wooden spoon to extract all possible flavour.

5 Bottle and refrigerate.

6 Dilute to taste.

TEA

Tscha, Ch'a, Tcha – Chinese names for tea from which our word 'char' derives.

■ Introduced to the Western world

Blend	Origin	Characteristics
Earl Grey A blend of fine Oriental teas with flavouring.	A secret blend of Indian and Chinese teas with flavouring, passed to Earl Grey by a Chinese Mandarin over 125 years ago.	Delicately scented producing a pale clear liquor.
Darjeeling A blend of Darjeeling and other fine teas.	Darjeeling teas are grown in the Himalayan foothills of India.	Muscatel flavour.
Lapsang souchong A blend of lapsang souchong and other fine teas.	A blend from the Province of Fukien, in China.	Large leaf, pale liquor, slightly smoky flavour and aroma.
Keemun A blend of Keemun and other fine teas.	The tea of Old Imperial China.	Produces a light liquor – delicately flavoured – free of tannin.
Assam A blend of Assam and other fine teas.	Grown in the Assam region of Northern India.	Produces a full coloured liquor – the traditional British cup of tea at its best.

barely three centuries ago by the Dutch – who had learnt the habit of tea-drinking from the Chinese – tea is thought to have had a practical origin: the Chinese for centuries had had to boil their drinking water, so to mask its unpleasant taste, they started flavouring it with herbs. Extraordinary it is that this one particular leaf, also found to have strong medicinal qualities, should have completely overshadowed all others, to become one of the two daily beverages of the majority of mankind.

■ When first brought to England, tea was so heavily taxed that only the rich could afford it, so when Twinings started serving it in their first coffee house in 1706, it was more as a sideline and a gimmick than anything else. Not until the duty was removed in 1784 did the British people really begin to drink tea, so that by the early 1900s the 'cuppa' was part of life and a panacea in any time of stress.

■ When tea was at its most costly, tea-caddies – the word derives from the Malayan word *kati*, a measure of weight – were designed to store it under lock and key. Caddies were often divided into two sections, one for green tea and one for black, and the tea was considered so precious that the châtelaine herself kept the key. She also made the tea and so it was that afternoon tea parties became the fashion.

■ What most of us classify as Indian tea includes tea from India, Africa, Indonesia, Malaya, etc., whose teas are grown from Assam seed. China teas

How to serve	When to serve		Special dishes
	As a drink		
Hot with a drop of milk, or a slice of fresh lemon. Sugar optional.	As afternoon tea.		Good with shortbread and dainty sandwiches.
Hot, with milk or lemon and sugar to your liking. Iced, just with a slice of fresh lemon.	Mid-morning break. In summer.		Excellent after a curry.
Hot – without milk or sugar.	During the day, when you've time to enjoy the special flavour.		At its best with Chinese or Japanese food – drunk throughout the meal and with spicy foods.
Iced – with a slice of fresh lemon.	In summer, in the garden.		For any special occasion.
Hot – with a dash of milk but no sugar.	Afternoon tea.		Accompanying Chinese food.
Hot, with milk and sugar.	Early morning, and for breakfast.		Family tea.

By courtesy of Twinings of London

include keemuns and lapsang souchongs and other various exotic teas which are grown from China seed. Ceylon and Darjeeling teas were grown originally with China seed. Indian teas contain more tannin than China. Green teas, unfermented teas from China, contain none.

■ Tea varies not only from country to country, soil to soil and plantation to plantation, but also literally from one day to another on the same plantation, according to the rain. In low lying districts, plucking takes place about once every seven days – sometimes every 4 days – so any week's picking may be different from either the previous or the next. Yet we always expect to buy the same tea under a particular label! It is because a tea-taster will know precisely which leaves will blend with which, in never ending different combinations and in precisely the right proportions, that we can do so. The speed at which he tests scores of teas a day, his acute palate, his memory and infinite knowledge about tea together enable us to buy any specified tea with consistent qualities.

■ Just as you'd choose a wine for its flavour, bouquet, colour, the food with which it is to be served, the time of day, or your preferences, so it should be with tea. There are different teas for all occasions: a delicately flavoured tea, so lovely and cooling on a hot summer's day, isn't the one to make you sit up at breakfast; a stimulating strong Indian tea which *is* just right for breakfast, is certainly not the one to go to sleep on. I find the different characteristics of tea so absorbing that you also may enjoy knowing what Britain's oldest tea merchant says about some kinds you'll know well.

■ Considering that we make tea countless times a week for years and years on end, you'd think we'd all be specialists. Many people are, of course, but one doesn't have to be a connoisseur to know that a great many aren't! Here's hoping that the experts will forgive me for passing on a specialist's tips for the benefit of those less well-informed.

Tea Will keep fresh for 18 months – 2 years if in an airtight container and kept dry. It goes without saying that a good cup of tea starts with good quality tea. Use the quantity you like – one teaspoon per person and one for the pot may be too little for some, or too much for others. Why not try blending your own, say one part Earl Grey and three parts Darjeeling, to have the flavour and aroma of the former, with the stimulation and darker colour of the latter?

The teapot Should be as clean inside as out, otherwise a layer builds up, making all teas taste bitter: wash it thoroughly, don't just rinse it.

■ A china teapot makes the best tea. It scores, too, over silver or stainless steel because you can tell at a glance if the inside is clean. China takes more warming than metal though, which perhaps explains why people who forget to warm it well first, think china teapots make poor tea.

■ Aluminium turns tea blue, and if an enamel pot is chipped, the iron will react on the tea.

Sugar Spoils the flavour of a good tea – but gives extra energy if that's what you need. A leading authority once said, 'It would be almost as rational to add cream and sugar to wine as to fine and delicately flavoured China tea'.

Milk Should be poured into the cup first if to blend properly with the tea. Though this may not be the way you like it, it's said to be the correct way to drink tea with milk. Done the other way round, the milk is scalded, rather than more gradually heated by the tea.

A tea-cosy Brings out the worst in tea, extracting its tannin, the bitterness of which spoils any flavour. It is better to serve weaker, cooler tea, and perhaps relegate your cosy to keeping boiled eggs warm at breakfast.

Brewing

1 Discard any stale water in the kettle,

as well as any thought of using water from the hot tap – or for that matter any other kind of water which isn't drawn freshly from a well-run cold tap. Otherwise the tea will be flat.

2 Warm the teapot. Using a cold pot, the value of the boiling water, essential to draw the flavour out of the tea, is lost.

3 Put the teapot beside the kettle, to pour the water on to the tea the instant it boils. If you walk across the kitchen to the teapot, the water will lose its oxygen – and once again will make flat tea.

4 Stir tea, put on lid and infuse just long enough to extract the flavour: small leaf teas, due to their strength and pungency, need only about 2 – 3 minutes. Large leaf teas need 5 – 6 minutes. If infused longer, the tannin is also extracted. If a big teapotful, stir again just before serving because tea tends to settle, the thin on top, thick on bottom.

Tea bags Account for an ever-growing proportion (70 per cent as I write) of the total tea market and are a recognized alternative to loose tea. If you have a complex about them, have you contemplated the advantages?

1 Many of the best kinds of tea, even China, now come in tea bags, so with a Jack Sprat situation in your family, you can each have the tea of your choice.

2 They're a saving both of fuel and time. You need only enough boiling water to fill the cup/cups.

3 The tea infuses in seconds because it is so fine – ideal for that quick cuppa, especially in the early morning, either in the kitchen or at the bedside.

4 Depending on how many cups you drink, tea bags may be more economical than loose tea for the one or two-person household.

5 No teapot to wash up, no leaves to dispose of.

Iced tea Made like ordinary tea, but use four times the usual amount of tea leaves. When infused, strain the tea into an equal quantity of cold water. Pour cold tea on to ice cubes in large glasses, adding a little fresh lemon juice, sugar, or a leaf of mint if you like. See *Darjeeling* and *lapsang souchong*, page 338.

22

Miscellaneous

BISCUITS

A quick way to open any paper-wrapped packet of biscuits is to cut the packet in half with a sharp knife.

THE CHEESEBOARD

Seems an afterthought in many homes and restaurants because so little thought may be given to it. This is quite different in France, where cheese is served before the sweet and is an integral part of a meal. Fresh crusty French bread, crisp biscuits, butter and celery hearts when in season should all help to make the cheese course as tempting as any other.

■ If you can manage to serve three or four different types of cheese, then your selection will be more inspired. This is the sort of variety to think about:
One well-flavoured hard or semi-hard, e.g. Mycella, Stilton, Gorgonzola, Roquefort, Caerphilly, Canadian or a mature Cheddar, Lancashire, Leicester, Wensleydale, Cheshire.
One soft, e.g. Brie, Camembert, Dolcelatte, Pont l'Évêque, Bel Paese.
One reasonably mild in flavour, e.g. Gruyère, Jarlsberg, ordinary English Cheddar, Edam, Gouda, Double Gloucester.
One more unusual, e.g. Rambol, Gourmandise (two of my favourites), Roulé, peppered Brie, Esrom, Tôme au Raisin (another favourite), Caboc, a goat's cheese or a smoked or garlic cheese.
■ Serve the cheese on fresh vine leaves if you're lucky enough to have any, keeping the whole boardful covered and moist with Cling-film until the moment of serving.

■ It's usually better to buy cheese in smallish quantities and eat while perfect, especially some of the softer varieties like Brie. Such a cheese, at the peak of perfection, may be over-ripe and indigestible two days later.
■ See also *cheese*, page 91.

CREAM, MOCK

Just bearable, I think, for soups, sauces and pouring. Even then, I find it such a poor substitute for real cream that there's nothing to gain by giving you directions for its making. I'd rather keep some UHT cream in my refrigerator than make mock.

CROUSTADES

Cases made of pastry, hollowed-out bread rolls, or fried or baked bread filled with some tasty preparation such as duxelles, a creamy vegetable mixture, or the sort of filling you'd use for a vol-au-vent.

■ The quickest and easiest to make from bread, simply involve dipping large rounds of fairly thinly sliced bread on both sides in melted butter, pressing them into bun tins, and baking in a moderate oven for 20–25 minutes until crisp and golden. They're delicious, either for a homely or a sophisticated meal.

GARLIC POWDER

Make or buy it. It's an excellent way to preserve garlic should you have a surplus, or like to have some 'instant' at hand for an omelette, a stew or anything else.

■ The one snag about making it is its pungency. Do it while alone in the house, and with wide-open windows! Slice the peeled garlic cloves fairly thinly, then dry them out, first one side and then the other, in a slow oven until crisp but barely coloured. Pound in a mortar or with the end of a rolling pin, then sieve and store in an airtight jar or bottle.

MEAT GLAZE

Used to glaze meats such as galantine, slipper of tongue or brawn, to flavour soups and sauces, or you can use it in place of stock. It is made from best meat, veal or poultry stock, reduced to a syrupy consistency and becomes a stiff jelly when cold. (Poor stock will evaporate without going syrupy.) Any salt added becomes concentrated as well, of course, so it's important to undersalt the stock when making it.

■ The reducing is a long though trouble-free process, perhaps taking 3 or 4 hours, so it's not worth bothering with a small quantity. 5 pts/2.5–3 litres stock makes only ½–¾pt/250–375ml meat glaze. This is how to make it:

1 Boil the strained fat-free stock slowly in an uncovered pan until reduced to about 1½pt/750ml – exact quantities are immaterial.
2 Strain through butter muslin or a very fine sieve into a small saucepan, and now boil again to reduce it until syrupy enough to coat a wooden spoon lightly. (If you fail to strain and transfer the stock to a clean pan, the sediment will burn more easily in the final stages, when it needs watching carefully anyway.)
3 Strain and freeze any surplus to your needs as ice cubes, or refrigerate it in a covered jar. If the top develops a few spots of mould when refrigerated, it's said not to be harmful and is easily washed off under warm water (but I never feel too enthusiastic about this):

after washing it, simmer in a saucepan over low heat with a spoonful of water until again reduced to a thick syrup.

NUTS, DEVILLED

Salted nuts, with cayenne added to the salt.

NUTS, SALTED

Almonds and cashews are ten times better home-fried than bought. (Our word 'cashew' comes from the Portuguese *caju*.)

1 Fry the blanched nuts in preheated oil over low heat, the oil well-covering the bottom of the frying pan. Turn nuts constantly, to make sure they brown evenly. If cooked too fast, they'll burn before being crisp through.
2 Drain thoroughly, first in the draining spoon used to stir them, and then on absorbent kitchen paper, to avoid greasiness.
3 While still hot, toss in table salt. When quite cold, store in an airtight container, one just large enough to hold them.

POPPADOMS

Can be bought in tins or packets ready to cook. To be crisp and delicious, don't fry them before you must.

1 In a deep frying pan, heat oil about 1in/2½cm deep to about 340°F/170°C (use a deep-fat pan if preferred).
2 Cook poppadoms one at a time until crisp, turning them over with tongs when fully spread out, and curled. Drain on absorbent kitchen paper.
3 Stand them up against each other on a baking sheet – like a child's house of cards – and dry off for several minutes in a slow oven (otherwise they'll be greasy).
4 Serve in a basket or on a plain doyley on a very large plate.

SYRUP

Made with a metal spoon, because a

wooden one may pass on the flavour of other strong foods for which it has been used.

■ Many *old* recipes call for loaf sugar. At one time this was the purest form of sugar, and therefore less likely to crystallize than granulated or caster. Nowadays icing, caster, granulated and cube (replacing loaf) are all absolutely pure – and granulated is cheapest.

■ It's unwise to use a non-stick pan to make a syrup. Some non-stick surfaces are damaged by the grittiness of the sugar, and the syrup will be adulterated.

■ The main thing to remember about a syrup is that the sugar *must* be dissolved before the water boils, because a syrup with a high proportion of sugar will crystallize if stirred after. In fact, there is often so little liquid that the sugar is being melted and not dissolved. Stir it over low heat as much as you like, therefore, to dissolve it, then get rid of the spoon. Simply bring the syrup to the boil now and leave it alone.

■ A thermometer (but see page 44) is invaluable for a strong syrup which has to be boiled to a high temperature for specific purposes. Liquid glucose or cream of tartar is sometimes stirred into such a syrup as soon as the sugar is dissolved, acting as a deterrent to the crystallization of the sugar. Now cover the pan for a few moments so that the trapped steam can wash down any crystals which may have formed on its sides. If crystals form again later, brush down the pan sides with a pastry brush dipped in boiling water, but don't, whatever you do, agitate the pan to try and dissolve them because that just makes things worse.

■ If a syrup has to be boiled to say 240°F/116°C, it's safer to stop at 238°F/115°C, because the heat of the pan will still cause the temperature to rise. If, on the other hand, you leave it to reach the exact temperature called for, plunge the bottom of the pan momentarily into cold water, to halt cooking.

Sugar boiling A syrup must sometimes be boiled to a specific temperature, par-

ticularly in the making of confectionery. As the temperature increases above boiling, water is driven off and the syrup gradually thickens. (As soon as small bubbles appear very close together, the evaporation of any water is complete. At this precise moment, the sugar starts to cook and one needs an eagle eye to halt cooking at the degree called for because the interval separating any two stages passes rapidly: even more so as the temperature gets high. See also above.)

■ Before reaching the degree called *caramel*, the sugar passes through various stages designated by different terms. If you have a thermometer, use it. If not, there are ways of testing, but these are more complicated, more troublesome and less accurate. The six different stages (for the specialist, there are also intermediate ones) are called small thread, large thread, small ball, large ball, small crack, hard crack. Higher still than hard crack the sugar becomes caramel: 356F/180°C for a light caramel colour (suitable to use as a flavouring); 370–380°F/188–193°C for a darkish brown caramel (when needed for colouring). Beyond this point, a caramel rapidly goes black and bitter – unusable.

■ If without a thermometer, the experts would use their fingers, but most amateurs are too scared, so here are ways of testing:
Small (or short) thread – 215°F/102.5°C. Syrup dropped from a spoon spins a thread about 3in/7.5cm long.
Large (or long) thread – 219°F/104°C. Syrup dropped from a spoon spins a longer thread.
Small (or soft) ball – 238–240°F/115–116°C. Put some cold (not iced) water in a cup and drop a little of the boiling syrup into it off a teaspoon. Gathered up in the fingers, the syrup should form into a soft ball that will hold its shape until pressure is removed.
Large (or hard) ball – 248–252°F/120–122°C. Test as small ball above, but the ball should be more resistant – though not rigid.

Small (or light or soft) crack –
264°F/129°C. Test as small ball above,
but there should be a slight cracking
sound when one knocks the cooled syrup
against the side of the cup.

Hard crack – 289°F/143°C. Test as small
ball above, but there should be a definite
cracking sound when one knocks the
cooled syrup against the side of the cup.

■ Once a syrup has reached hard crack, it
will within seconds become caramel. See
also crème caramel, page 288, **1** and **2**.

Syrup for stewed fruit Is boiled 'in an
uncovered pan, usually for 5–7 minutes.
As the water evaporates, the syrup
becomes more concentrated, so sweetens
without being too watery.

SYRUP, STOCK

The sweetest of sweet syrups, with
various uses. You may just as well make a
quantity at a time because it keeps well in
the refrigerator, especially with a spoonful of liquid glucose added to it to prevent
the sugar graining. 2lb/900g sugar to 1pt/
600ml water make getting on for double
the original quantity of water.

■ Make it like a strong syrup, above,
boiling it to 215–220°F/102–104°C, then
cool it slightly and strain. If without a
thermometer, boil the syrup fairly rapidly
for 3–5 minutes, according to depth.

■ Use full strength or diluted, according
to need or recipe, e.g. to make a lighter
syrup for fruit salad or for fondant icing;
to make glacé icing (it prevents cracking);
to make water ices (sorbets); to make
certain sauces accompanying ice creams;
to syrup-freeze fruits, or simply to stew
fruit.

TOASTS

Anchovy toast Good if you like anchovies! Fry sliced bread in butter (or toast it
if too rich), spread with anchovy butter
(page 169) and top with anchovy fillets.

Cinnamon toast Tasty at teatime, so if
you make a quantity of the mixture at a
time, it's there when you want it. Sieve
together 3 parts caster sugar with 1 of
ground cinnamon. Sift generously over
hot-buttered toast. Alternatively, use
cinnamon sugar (page 126).

French toast Bread soaked in seasoned,
mixed-up egg – with a little milk to make
the egg go further if you like – then lightly
fried on both sides in hot fat. Some
people like it best served with bacon for
breakfast, others like it under a poached
egg or fried sardines, etc.

Melba toast Toast split through the
middle and toasted on the inside, made
originally for Dame Nellie Melba, the
famous Australian singer.

1 To keep the toast flat, toast the bread
until dry but not coloured on each side
before toasting either side golden.

2 While very hot, cut off the crusts, lay
your hand flat on top, split the toast and
pop it back under the grill to brown the
bready side.

3 Serve very fresh on a plain doyley on
a plate (with plenty of butter pats), to
accompany things with a soft texture like
pâté, soup, fish, etc. (Rich with butter
and spread with marmalade, it's delicious
even for breakfast.)

Bibliography

Simone Beck, Louisette Bertholle and Julia Child, *Mastering the Art of French Cooking*, Penguin, 1966.

Mrs Beeton, *Poultry and Game*, Ward Lock, 1974.

Michael Brander (editor), *International Encyclopaedia of Shooting*, Pelham Books, 1972.

A. G. Cameron, *Food and Its Functions*, Edward Arnold, 1968.

The Chamberlains, *Flavour of France: French Recipes*, Hamish Hamilton, 1960.

Julia Child, *From Julia Child's Kitchen*, Jonathan Cape, 1978.

A. O. Cooke, *A Book of Dovecotes*, Foulis, 1920.

Elizabeth David, *French Provincial Cooking*, Penguin, 1970; *Italian Food*, Penguin, 1970.

Len Deighton, *Où est le Garlic?*, Penguin, 1965; *Action Cook Book*, Jonathan Cape, 1965.

Muriel Downes, *Cake Making in Pictures*, Odhams, 1957.

Good Housekeeping, *Home Freezer Cook Book*, Ebury Press, 1972.

Lilli Gore, *Game Cooking*, Penguin, 1976.

Jane Grigson, *Jane Grigson's Fruit Book*, Michael Joseph, 1982; *Jane Grigson's Vegetable Book*, Michael Joseph, 1978

Dorothy Hartley, *Food in England*, Macdonald, 1975.

E. M. Hildreth, *Elementary Science of Food*, Mills and Boon, 1975.

Janet Horsley, *Bean Cuisine*, Prism Press, 1982.

Helen Jerome, *The Fine Art of Cooking*, Pitman, 1968; *Concerning Cake Making*, Pitman, 1966.

Kenwood Manufacturing Co. Ltd., *The Kenwood Recipe Book*, n.d.

Aileen King, *Better Cookery*, Mills and Boon, n.d.; *Dictionary of Cooking Terms*, Forbes Publications, 1976.

Lifespan Community Collective Ltd, *Full of Beans*, 1982.

Helen McCully, *Nobody Ever Tells You These Things*, Angus & Robertson, 1968.

Jill McWilliam, *Book of Freezing*, Woodhead-Faulkner, 1974.

Prosper Montagné, *Larousse Gastronomique*, Hamlyn, 1965.

National Federation of W.I., *Poultry and Game*, 1960.

Irma S. Rombauer and Marion Rombauer Becker, *The Joy of Cooking*, Dent, 1963.

Dora Seton, *Essentials of Modern Cookery*, Evans Brothers, 1963; *Advanced Cooking*, Evans Brothers, 1963.

André L. Simon, *A Concise Encyclopaedia of Gastronomy*, Rainbird MacLean, 1956.

André Simon & Robin Howe, *A Dictionary of Gastronomy*, Nelson, 1970.

Michael Smith, *The Best of British Cookware*, Macmillan, 1975.

Constance Spry & Rosemary Hume, *The Constance Spry Cookery Book*, Pan Books, 1972.

Katie Stewart, *The Times Cook Book*, Pan Books, 1974; *Katie Stewart's Cookbook*, Gollancz, 1983; *Katie Stewart Cooks*, Hamlyn 1971; also many articles in *The Times*.

Kathleen Thomas, *The Sporting Wife*, Farmer's Weekly, 1962.

Florence White, *Good Things in Eng-

land, Futura, 1974.
Anne Willan, *The Observer French Cookery School*, Macdonald, 1980.
Various authors, *Masterclass*, Jill Norman and Hobhouse, 1982.

OTHER SOURCES OF INFORMATION

Alcan Polyfoil Limited
Associated Health Foods Limited
Bejam News
Berry Bros. & Rudd (olive oils)
Brannan Thermometers
British Egg Information Service
Cadbury Typhoo Food Advisory Service
Cannon Industries Limited
Carnation Foods Limited
CPC (United Kingdom) Limited, Brown & Polson Division (corn oil)
The Electricity Council

Elizabeth David (catalogue)
Davis Gelatine Limited
Meat Promotion Executive
David Mellor (catalogue)
Metal Box Limited
The Nestlé Company Limited
Pasta Information Service
Paterson Jenks PLC (Camp coffee)
Felix Pavia & Son Limited (pasta products)
Princes Foods Limited
Quaker Oats Limited
RHM Foods (Atora suet and dried yeast)
Rowntree Mackintosh Limited
Southern Gas
Suttons Seeds
Tate & Lyle Refineries Limited
R. Twining & Company Limited
Van den Berghs (fats)
The Young Group of Companies

Index